# Child Development

# Development

## Karen Caplovitz Barrett
Associate Professor, Department of Human
Development and Family Studies
Colorado State University

## Kenneth D. Kallio
Associate Professor of Psychology
State University of New York, Geneseo

## Ruth Moffatt McBride
Assistant Director, Early Childhood Laboratories
Colorado State University

## Concetta M. Moore
Director, Gable Way Schools
Willingboro, New Jersey

## Mary Ann Wilson
Director and Associate Professor,
Early Childhood Programs
Sullivan County Community College
State University of New York

## GLENCOE

Macmillan / McGraw-Hill

New York, New York
Columbus, Ohio
Mission Hills, California
Peoria, Illinois

Send all inquiries to
GLENCOE DIVISION
Macmillan/McGraw-Hill
936 Eastwind Drive
Westerville, OH 43081

ISBN 0-02-801359-X (Student Edition)
ISBN 0-02-801361-1 (Instructor's Annotated Edition)

Printed in the United States of America

1 2 3 4 5 6 7 8 9 10   RRD-W   99 98 97 96 95 94 93 92 91

Library of Congress Cataloging-in-Publication Data

Child development / Karen Caplovitz Barrett ... [et al.].
      p.      cm.
   Includes biographical references and index.
   ISBN 0-02-801359-X
   1. Child development.   2. Child care.   3. Early childhood
education.   I. Barrett. Karen Caplovitz.
HQ767.9.C442   1993
649$^1$.1--dc20

                                                          93-27325
                                                          CIP

Co-developed by
Glencoe Division of Macmillan/McGraw-Hill
and Visual Education Corporation
Princeton, NJ

# Consultants and Reviewers

## Consultants

### Rosanne Dlugosz
Program Coordinator, Early Childhood Development
Scottsdale Community College

### Mary Zuzich
Project Director, Open Horizons
Tempe, Arizona
Visiting Faculty, Early Childhood Development
Scottsdale Community College

## Reviewers

### Barbara S. Beymer
Home Network Specialist
Child Care Resource and Referral Agency
Columbus, Ohio

### Mary W. Evans
Family Counselor
Columbus, Ohio

### Janet L. Garnon
Family-to-Family Project Coordinator
Owner-Administrator, Creative Alternative Child Care Programs
Hilliard, Ohio

### Rebecca A. Sheridan
Regional Resource Development Specialist
Columbus, Ohio

### Karen P. Shively
Former Special Education Teacher
Acton Elementary
Acton, California

### Nettamae Shively
Director/Teacher
La Canada Presbyterian Church Infant Care Center
La Canada, California

# Credits and Acknowledgments

Archives of the History of American Psychology, University of Akron: 28, 37, 42

Jim Ballard, Chicago, IL: 50, 128, 268, 338, 414

Julie Bidwell: 83 *bottom left*, 345

Esbin-Anderson Photography: 340, 436

Stephen Feld: 283

Innervisions: 186

Ken Lax: 115

Mary E. Messenger: 136, 195, 208, 260, 274, 438

Monkmeyer Press:
Lew Merrim: 301

Cliff Moore: 52, 119, 154, 169, 206, 250, 270, 311, 396

Photo Network:
Steve Agricola: 434

Photo Researchers, Inc. :
C. Edelmann/La Villette: 64, 343, 425

PhotoEdit:
Bill Aron: 121
Vic Bider: 89
Robert Brenner: 8, 72, 81, 87, 91, 157, 161, 162, 187, 193, 200, 212, 230, 232, 251, 304, 394, 401
Paul Conklin: 19, 108, 310, 371
Mary Kate Denny: 118, 172, 180, 215, 263, 299, 331, 374, 391, 404, 405
Amy Etra: 147
Myrleen Ferguson: 33, 34, 57, 160, 229, 248, 272, 295, 344, 362, 392, 398, 406, 407
Tony Freeman: 7 *top left*, 21, 80, 85, 95, 96, 130, 165, 192, 196, 207, 214, 224, 228, 234, 236, 276 *top left*, 276 *top right*, 278 *bottom right*, 293, 316, 351, 354, 356, 373, 382, 431

PhotoEdit: (continued)
Freeman/Grishaber: 9
Robert W. Ginn: 375
Jeff Greenberg: 111, 393
Richard Hutchings: 2, 98, 107, 110, 164, 298, 365, 367
Stephen McBrady: 138
Michael Newman: 83 *top right*, 104, 133, 178, 246, 278 *top left*, 319, 321, 322, 333, 357, 368, 416
Alan Oddie: 15, 210, 239
Tom Prettyman: 219, 227
Elena Rooraid: 285, 420
Rhoda Sidney: 65
Marlene Wallace: 141, 144
David Young-Wolff: 12, 16, 26, 38, 73, 78, 117, 123, 185, 254, 255, 257, 290, 306, 320, 327, 379, 380, 388, 409, 418, 426
Anna Zuckerman: 7 *top right*
Elizabeth Zuckerman: 4, 238

Picture Group:
Chas Cancellare: 70

Subjects and Predicates:
Janet Brown McCracken: 93, 422

Terry Wild Studio: 113, 171, 189, 202, 261, 325, 332

Zephyr Pictures:
Steven Whalen: 347

Chapter 8, Figure 8.1:
*Journal of Genetic Psychology, 37,* 514–527, 1930. Reprinted with permission of the Helen Dwight Reid Educational Foundation. Published by Heldref Publications, 1319 Eighteenth St., N.W., Washington, D.C. 20036-1802. Copyright © 1930.

# Preface

A knowledge of child development is essential for anyone who plans to work with children. Knowing what children can do and understand at different stages of development helps early childhood professionals provide skilled care and plan activities that are suited to each child's stage of development.

This book focuses on aspects of child development that are particularly relevant to people who will be professionally involved with children and their parents. Although it includes comprehensive coverage of the physical, intellectual, and emotional and social development of children at various ages, its orientation is distinctly practical. The book divides child development into four broad stages based on age:

- Infancy—children from birth to 1 year
- Toddlerhood—children from 1 to 3 years
- The preschool years—children from 3 to 5 years
- The school years—primary focus on children from 6 to 8 years plus coverage of children from 9 to 12 years and a brief overview of adolescents

## Content

The book begins with an overview of child development that sets the stage for the rest of the book. This first part includes a chapter on various methods of studying child development and a chapter on leading theories of child development.

Part 2 provides important background information for people working in early childhood education. It contains chapters on heredity and pregnancy, the family, and major issues in the child care profession, including multiculturalism, children with special needs, and health and safety.

The next four parts are devoted to a detailed examination of the physical, intellectual, and emotional and social development of infants, toddlers, preschoolers, and children in the school years. In these chapters, too, child development is viewed from the perspective of the child care professional, with particular emphasis on the abilities, needs, and special concerns of children at different stages of development.

The final part of the book consists of a step-by-step guide to planning a career and obtaining a job in the field of early childhood education. Throughout, the text uses either female or male examples in order to avoid awkward he/she and him/her constructions.

## Chapter Structure

Each chapter in the book begins with learning objectives and a list of the main headings in the chapter. These can be used as a preview of the material to be learned. Within the chapter, important terms are highlighted in *italics*; they are defined again in the Glossary at the back of the book. Author and publication date of each source are cited in the text (Erikson, 1972); full bibliographic information is provided in the References at the back of the book.

All the chapters in the book except the final one on careers contain sections entitled Implications and Applications. These show how the theory and information presented in the chapters relate to the classroom or child care setting. They underline the book's practical approach.

## Special Features

The practical approach is reinforced in a series of special features on topics of immediate concern to early childhood professionals.

"Focus on Cultural Diversity" covers a range of topics designed to illustrate differences in customs and values among various groups of people. The theme of multiculturalism runs through the text portion of the chapters as well, with topics such as curriculum, play, and classroom management discussed from a multicultural perspective.

"Focus on Communicating" presents discussions of both ordinary everyday problems and extremely sensitive topics. The feature illustrates one way—not necessarily the best—that a caregiver might communicate with parents or children. It invites students to consider other ways of handling the communication.

"Focus on Decision Making" challenges students to decide what they would do as child care professionals in a particular situation.

"Focus on Child Care Issues" presents different points of view on important topics in early childhood education and encourages students to evaluate these views and form their own opinions.

## End of Chapter Materials

Each chapter ends with a comprehensive chapter review. This includes a summary of important points covered and a list of chapter vocabulary terms. It also includes Acquiring Knowledge, a section that can be used to review chapter content, and Thinking Critically, a section that raises questions child care professionals need to consider. The Observations and Applications section proposes various situations in which students can practice observational skills and apply their knowledge of child development. The chapter review concludes with Suggestions for Further Reading for students.

## Supplementary Materials

The *Instructor's Annotated Edition* is a useful teaching support tool. The Instructor's Manual includes an overview of the program called Teaching Child Development. It also contains resources for Early Childhood Education and Teaching Strategies for each chapter in the text. Within the text pages, there are teaching, informational, and answer annotations.

The *Study Guide* provides students with a means of checking their mastery of the material covered in the text. Pretests review the content, concepts, and vocabulary of each chapter. Case Studies provide students with an opportunity to use their knowledge of child development to analyze a situation and propose a course of action.

The *Observation Guide* is a workbook that directs students in the field and encourages them to observe firsthand the kind of behavior and interactions they are studying in the text.

The computerized *Testbank* provides a variety of questions that can be used to build customized tests for students. The software leaves room for instructors to add their own questions.

# Contents

## Part 1
## Overview of Child Development 2

# Part 2:
# Background to Child
# Development 50

# Part 3:
# Infants                                                                    128

# Part 4:
# Toddlers                                                 200

## Chapter 10:
## Intellectual Development                                                    224

## Chapter 11:
## Emotional and Social Development                                            246

# Part 5:
# Preschoolers                                          268

## Chapter 12:
## Physical Development                                 270

# Part 6:
# The School Years 338

## Part 7:
## Careers in Early Childhood Education                          414

# Child Development

# PART 1

# Overview of Child Development

### CHAPTER 1
### Studying Child Development
Chapter 1 discusses different approaches to the study of the way children change—from conception through adolescence. It also describes different methods of studying these developments.

### CHAPTER 2
### Theories of Child Development
Chapter 2 explains leading theories on the way the mind and personality of a child develop, and discusses the insights that each theory provides into how children learn and why they behave as they do.

# 1

# Studying Child Development

## OBJECTIVES
Studying this chapter will enable
you to

- Explain what child development
  means and how it is studied.
- Discuss different approaches to
  studying child development.
- Describe the methods that
  psychologists use to gather
  information about child
  development.
- Explain why child care
  professionals need to study child
  development.

SOME YEARS AGO, Swiss researcher Jean Piaget was conducting a study of intelligence in children. His work led him to believe that children and adults think in different ways. In one particular experiment, he wanted to find out whether children between the ages of three and five are capable (as adults are) of seeing a situation from another person's point of view.

To explore this question, Piaget set up a model of a mountain range on a square table. The range consisted of three mountains—a large one, a small one, and a medium-sized one. The children who participated in the experiment were allowed to see the whole range. They were then seated on one side of the table, where they could see only the large mountain and part of the medium-sized one. Piaget asked each child to indicate what view of the mountains could be seen by another child seated on the other side of the table or to the right. From those positions, a person would actually be able to see all three mountains.

Piaget found that most children of this age believed that someone on the other side of the table would see the same mountains that they could see. This experiment led Piaget to conclude that preschoolers are "egocentric" thinkers; that is, they see things only from their own perspective and are incapable of seeing another's viewpoint (Piaget & Inhelder, 1956).

Many researchers today believe that Piaget's experiment was too complicated. They contend that he set up a situation that was unfamiliar to the children. In fact, when later researchers devised experiments in which familiar objects were used—asking children to analyze the viewpoint of dolls, for example—most preschool children showed that they were capable of seeing another person's point of view (Hughes & Donaldson, 1983). Modern child development experts have concluded that preschool children are indeed egocentric, but most of them are capable of perceiving the viewpoint of others at least to some extent.

Researchers use studies such as Piaget's three-mountain experiment to answer countless questions about how children grow, change, and learn over time. These studies can take various forms—from simply observing how children act and interact to setting up elaborate experiments designed to test specific theories. As you will learn in later chapters, Jean Piaget made an enormous contribution to the study of child development. His theories have shaped many of the ideas and practices of early childhood education. However, the three-mountain experiment illustrates some of the pitfalls that researchers must be aware of in studying children.

Young children can be difficult research subjects. They think differently from adults, and they have not yet developed the language skills to demonstrate their understanding of a problem or experiment. In addition, some aspects of development are not easy to test. Despite these difficulties, researchers have now gathered a great deal of information about how children progress in their physical, emotional, and intellectual development. This book examines and discusses much of that knowledge.

## What Is Child Development?

*Child development* is the study of how children change over time from infancy to adolescence. It tries to understand and describe how, when, why, and in what order these changes occur. Researchers define developmental changes as transformations that are universal, regular, and orderly, with one change building upon another. Infants all over the world learn to walk at about the same age and in much the same sequence. First, they learn to roll over and crawl. Next, they learn to pull themselves upright and to take a step while holding on to a person or an object. Finally, they learn to balance and walk without holding on to anything. Each of these actions is a developmental stage that can be predicted, observed, measured, and recorded. Researchers can determine an average age at which each stage occurs and then measure the progress of individuals against that average. Research studies of various aspects of child development can help adults understand children and care for them more effectively.

### Areas of Development

Most textbooks divide child development into three areas or domains: physical, intellectual, and emotional and social development. *Physical development* encompasses all the changes that take place in the body including growth, muscle development, the development of the senses, and the development of motor skills. *Intellectual development* (also called cognitive development) refers to the development of mental processes such as imagination, memory, learning, and perception. *Emotional development* is the evolution of emotions, personality, identity, moral judgment, and social skills. It is sometimes also called psychosocial development because it combines psychological and social development.

Early childhood specialists generally identify each step of development and categorize it as physical, intellectual, or emotional. For example, learning to walk is a milestone in physical development because it involves the development of muscle tone, muscular control, and balance. Learning language falls into the intellectual domain because it is an accomplishment involving the development of memorization, classification, and other mental skills. Expressing emotions, feeling shame, and making friends are ex-

Infants all over the world learn to walk at about the same age and in the same sequence.

amples of emotional and social development because they involve the way people feel about themselves and their ability to form relationships with others.

This book has been organized into the three areas of physical, intellectual, and emotional development because this is a clear and logical way to present the many strands of child development. Keep in mind, however, that as children grow, dramatic changes occur in all three areas simultaneously and that changes in one area affect each of the others as well. If, for example, an infant is abused or neglected, his physical growth can be slowed, his intellectual development may be delayed, and he may be emotionally traumatized.

## Quantitative and Qualitative Change

Developmental changes are both *quantitative*, changes in amount, and *qualitative*, changes in kind. Quantitative changes, such as increases in a child's height, weight, and age, can be readily observed and measured. These kinds of changes are referred to as growth and may affect several areas of development. Qualitative changes are changes in the kinds of skills a child demonstrates. In the area of language development, a six-month-old cannot talk, but a two-year-old can. In the area of emotional development, a three-year-old may have real fears about "monsters" under the bed. A ten-year-old knows there are no

such things as monsters but may fear the rejection of a friend. These qualitative changes are distinct differences in abilities and understanding within an area of development.

As children develop, they progress from mastering simple skills to more complex ones. For instance, when children first learn to talk, they usually speak in one-word sentences and have a limited vocabulary of a few dozen words. As their knowledge of language increases, they progress to speaking in complete sentences and their vocabulary expands to several thousand words. This progression represents both a quantitative change in the size of their vocabulary and a qualitative change in their understanding of language. Quantitative and qualitative changes take place simultaneously and strongly affect each other. A child cannot learn to run, jump, and climb (qualitative change) until she has also developed the muscular strength and control (quantitative change) to perform those skills.

## Individual Variation

Although developmental changes are universal in the sense that they occur in all children, they are subject to wide individual variations. Each child is an individual born with a distinct personality and set of inherited traits. In addition, each child grows up in a unique environment and is affected in different ways by the adults and other children around him or her.

Each child is a unique individual with a distinct personality and way of looking at the world.

The experience of an only child is quite different from that of a child who grows up with two or three siblings. One toddler may be quiet, shy, and content to observe others at play. Another is outgoing and self-confident and finds it easy to make friends. A child who attends a preschool and has been taken to zoos, parks, and museums is more knowledgeable about the world than another child of the same age who has never been away from home. It is these kinds of variations and differences that make the study of child development so interesting.

### The Goals of Child Development Study

The study of child development is carried out on several different levels. At the most basic level, researchers seek simply to describe changes in the growth and behavior of children. They might choose to record the first words that children utter, such as *mama* and *bye-bye*. At the next level, child development experts try to explain how and why changes in growth and behavior have taken place. How does a

child learn that the word *dog* is the name for a four-legged creature that says "woof"? Piaget and other researchers have devised elaborate theories that attempt to explain many aspects of a child's development. Some of the leading theories of intellectual and personality development are examined in Chapter 2 of this text; others are discussed in later chapters.

Once a developmental change has been observed, described, and explained, researchers can use that information to predict normal behavior. *Normal* behavior is behavior that a majority of children exhibit at any given age. It is usually expressed as a range of behavior, or norms. The average age at which infants start to walk is about one year, but children who begin to walk at 9 months and those who begin at 13 months still fall within the normal range. On the other hand, a child who does not begin to walk until she is two years old may be considered to be outside the normal range.

Finally, when psychologists can explain and predict behavior, they can try to modify it. Researchers have found, for example, that they can accelerate intellectual development to some degree by teaching or training children to comprehend certain concepts at an earlier than normal age. Asked to sort a pile of objects, most preschool children would classify them according to one characteristic, such as color, shape, or size. Yet researchers have been able to train children of this age to sort objects according to two characteristics at the same time (Denney, 1972). For example, instead of sorting objects into piles of red shapes and blue shapes, children can be taught to sort the objects into red squares, blue squares, red circles, blue circles, and so on.

Psychologists have found that the ability to modify the behavior of children is limited by their growth and development. No one can teach a four-month-old baby to walk or a one-year-old to read because their body and brain have not yet developed sufficiently to master those skills. Nevertheless, early childhood professionals routinely use their knowledge of child development to modify children's intellectual and social behavior in a variety of age-appropriate and beneficial ways. For example, preschoolers can be taught to resolve conflicts with their playmates verbally instead of physically.

## Different Approaches to the Study of Child Development

Like all human beings, children are complex creatures. They demonstrate many different kinds of behaviors and changes as they grow and develop from infancy to adolescence. Researchers have a number of different ways of organizing the information they gather in studying children. These various approaches can be useful in clarifying and explaining key issues of child development.

### Nature Versus Nurture

One way to look at child development is to try to determine the role of heredity and environment in specific developmental changes. Developmentalists and educators have long been engaged in a lively debate, popularly known as the *nature versus nurture* controversy, over the relative influence of heredity and the environment. Some traits of an individual, such as hair color, gender, and any inherited defects, are clearly determined by heredity.

Other characteristics, such as a person's height and intelligence, are largely determined by heredity but are susceptible to environmental influences as well. People are born with certain personality traits and potential talents or aptitudes. One person may become a talented musician, while another may have an aptitude for engineering. On the other hand, the important people in a child's environment—parents, caregivers, and teachers—have an enormous influence on the child's ability to develop inborn talents. If the child is never exposed to musical instruments or mathematical concepts, such inborn abilities may never be recognized or developed.

Environment plays a predominant role in many areas. For example, a child who lives in the United States and whose parents speak English will learn to speak English rather than Japanese or Swahili because English is the only language she ever hears. Nature versus nurture issues are discussed in more detail in Chapter 3 and other chapters throughout this book.

Another important element in the interplay between heredity and environment is maturation. *Maturation* refers to the appearance of a genetically determined physical trait or pattern of behavior over time. Children cannot learn to talk until their vocal cords mature so that they can control sounds. Further, they cannot learn to talk until their brain matures to the point that they can associate certain

*Adults can have a great impact on a child's ability to develop inborn talents.*

sounds with specific meanings and can remember those associations. Yet while maturation is a function of inheritance, it can be affected to some degree by environment. A poor diet, for example, may delay the onset of puberty but will not prevent it from occurring.

### The Topical Approach

Another way of examining child development issues is to use the *topical approach*, that is, to explore each major topic of child development separately. Major topics include language development, motor development, emotional development, the development of self-concept and gender identity, the development of social skills, and so on. Researchers who study self-concept, for example, might examine all the changes and developments involving self-concept from the moment of birth until the end of adolescence. They would trace self-concept from its emergence in infancy to its blossoming in toddlerhood and its steady development in the preschool years. Then they would examine the effect of school, puberty, and sexual maturity on self-concept in middle and late childhood.

The topical approach enables researchers to focus on the continuity of a particular trait or skill over a long period of time to see how it changes or endures as the child matures. One drawback of the topical approach is that its researchers may focus too narrowly on one strand of development and fail to consider how it relates to other developmental changes.

### The Ecological Approach

Just as biologists study the ecology of a forest to determine the impact of various aspects of the environment on the growth of trees, an early childhood specialist may examine how different environmental elements affect a child's growth and development. Researchers who take the *ecological approach* study the interactions between children and all of the many people, places, and processes that make up their environment. These include not only parents and siblings but also teachers, doctors, neighborhoods, classrooms, school boards, child protection laws, cultural attitudes, and so on.

Psychologist Urie Bronfenbrenner (1979), who developed the ecological systems theory, believes that children are influenced by four concentric systems, or rings, of environmental factors, ranging from the most influential to the most remote (see Figure 1.1).

- The innermost ring, the "microsystem," includes all of the factors that have the deepest and most immediate impact on a child's development and daily life, such as family, school, religion, health services, and peers.
- The next ring, the "mesosystem," is where members of the microsystem interact with one another, parent-teacher, pastor-family, playmate-playmate, and so on.
- The third ring is the "exosystem," where community institutions such as neighbors, the news media, and social agencies interact with the child.
- The fourth ring, called the "macrosystem," is where all of the other elements of the child's environment, such as cultural traditions and attitudes, politics, economics, laws, regulations, rules, customs, and values, come into play.

The ecological approach is particularly useful for studying complex social issues that affect children, such as public education, the welfare system, or rural poverty. It enables researchers to get a more complete overview of a child's development and to observe the child in his or her normal environment rather than in a laboratory. On the other hand, ecological research can be a very time-consuming method of study, and it does not always allow the researcher to disentangle the many separate threads of environmental factors that affect a child or group of children.

### The Ages and Stages Approach

Many early childhood specialists prefer to organize the study of child development into distinct *ages and stages*. This approach focuses on one age at a time and examines the physical, intellectual, and emotional changes that occur during this period of development. It takes the view that children do not develop in a smooth, even progression over time but in uneven patterns. It also assumes that qualitative changes occur abruptly at different ages and that these changes can be identified. For example, between the ages of 10 and 14 months, infants make the transition from crawling or pulling themselves

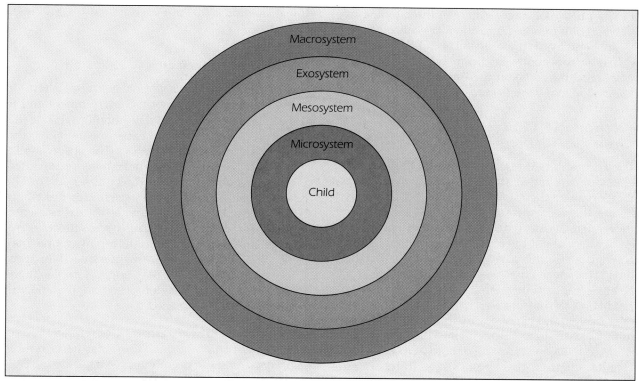

**FIGURE 1.1  Ecological Systems Theory.**   According to Urie Bronfenbrenner's ecological systems theory, child development is influenced by four concentric rings, or systems, of environmental factors.

up on furniture to walking on their own. The ages and stages approach enables psychologists to account for *critical periods*, periods of sensitivity at which children are most responsive to developmental change. It is thought that disruption during these critical periods can affect a lifetime of development. Many researchers believe, for instance, that the preschool years are a critical period for developing certain social skills.

While the ages and stages approach provides a general description of the changes that take place over time as children grow and mature, it should be kept in mind that the development of each child is unique. No child will conform completely to the ages and stages being described. Each child will demonstrate many individual differences or variations from the norm. One child will begin talking earlier than the average. Another will make friends easily; a third will have a gift for mathematics. This

book has been organized according to ages and stages because such a format presents information in a way that may be most useful to child care providers.

The text looks first at the prenatal months, the period from conception to birth, during which the fetus is developing into a full-term baby. Then it examines physical, intellectual, and social/emotional development during each of the following ages and stages:

- Birth to one year, the period during which children develop from the total helplessness of newborns to the age when they just begin to walk and say their first words
- The toddler stage, from age one to age three, when children learn the fundamentals of spoken language and begin to become autonomous individuals

- The preschool stage, from age three to age five, when children begin to interact with other children and learn fundamental social skills
- The early school years, from age six to age eight, when children begin their formal schooling and develop many intellectual skills

## Methods of Studying Child Development

The approach that researchers adopt to study child development refers simply to the way in which they organize the information they have gathered. Before they can formulate an approach, however, they must decide what methods they will use to gather data about the behavior of children. All psychologists use the *scientific method* to gather their data. This means that they formulate a question to be answered and develop a *hypothesis*, a reasonable prediction of the answer to that question. Next, they design and carry out methods of testing their hypothesis by gathering their data. Finally, they draw conclusions from the data to help answer the original question or hypothesis. Researchers publish their results so that others can replicate and build on their work.

Using the scientific method, researchers gather data in a variety of ways. In child development research, there are two basic approaches: the observa-tional method and the experimental method. (See Table 1.1.)

### Observational Research

The *observational method* enables researchers to study children in their normal environment and to describe behavior in everyday situations. While this method is less formal than experimentation, it also adheres to the scientific method. The observational method makes use of such techniques as interviews, questionnaires, and direct observation. The observational method is very useful for describing behavior, but it is not as useful as the experimental method for determining cause and effect. A researcher observing children on a playground may notice that boys are more aggressive than girls. While such observation may suggest explanations for the aggressive behavior, observation alone will not determine what caused it.

**Naturalistic Observation.**   Observational research takes many forms. The most basic type is *naturalistic observation*, observing a group of children in a normal setting such as a child care center, a playground, or a classroom. The main advantage of naturalistic observation is that the subjects usually do not know they are being observed and therefore will not "perform" or act in an unnatural

The main advantage of naturalistic observation is that subjects can be studied in a normal setting where they act naturally.

**TABLE 1.1**
**Methods of Studying Child Development**

| Type of Study | Characteristics | Advantages | Disadvantages |
|---|---|---|---|
| **Observational Research** | | | |
| Naturalistic Observation | Observation of a group of people in a normal setting | Allows researchers to study natural behavior | Observers may be biased |
| Clinical Observation | In-depth study of individual subjects | Provides detailed view of one person's behavior and abilities | Results cannot be generalized beyond the individual studied |
| Correlational Study | Observational study that measures the relationship between two variables | Indicates how two variables are related | Cause and effect cannot be determined |
| Cross-Cultural Study | Study that compares individuals from different cultures | Helps to identify changes or factors that apply universally | Conditions under which study is carried out may be difficult |
| **Experimental Research** | | | |
| Experiment | Controlled study used to investigate one variable | Enables researchers to test more easily for cause and effect | Subjects may act unnaturally, experiment may not test correct variable, results cannot always be applied outside the laboratory |
| **Research Examining Changes Over Time** | | | |
| Cross-Sectional Study | Study that examines a single variable in a large group of people of different ages | Allows researchers to obtain results relatively quickly | Changes in individual subjects over time cannot be charted |
| Longitudinal Study | Study that examines how change occurs in the same group of subjects over a long period of time | Yields a great deal of information | Research is costly, time-consuming, and difficult to do; subjects tend to drop out over time |
| Cohort Study | Research project that focuses on a specific age group | Enables researchers to examine variables in large group | Results may not generalize to people outside the group |

manner for the observer. Like all other forms of research, naturalistic observation requires meticulous record keeping. Observers maintain logs or diaries in which they note the kind and frequency of the behavior being observed as well as the context in which it occurs.

For instance, researchers studying preschoolers' play might observe children at a child care center over several weeks or months. They would keep careful records describing each time that a child engaged in play, how long the play period lasted, what type of play it was, whether other children joined in the play, whether one child became the director or leader of the play, and so on. The researchers could then analyze their recorded observations to draw some conclusions about the way preschool children play. For example, the researchers might find that preschoolers generally spend about 30 percent of

## FOCUS ON  Decision Making in Child Care

### Keeping Up-to-Date

Every spring the Gateway Preschool holds conferences with parents whose children will be entering kindergarten the following fall. During her conference, Ms. Warren stated that her daughter, Danielle, would be attending a private Waldorf school. She commented that many of the Waldorf signs of school readiness were based on physical changes in the body and mental changes in fantasy play and memory. Ms. Warren asked how these signs of readiness compared to the indications of readiness that Donna, the preschool teacher, usually considered.

Donna told Ms. Warren that she thought Danielle was perfectly ready for a traditional kindergarten but that she was unfamiliar with the Waldorf school. She offered to learn more about the Waldorf philosophy and to schedule another conference in a few weeks to address Ms. Warren's concerns.

During those weeks, Donna called the Waldorf school and asked the director to send her information on the school's program and approach. She also discussed Ms. Warren's question with the director of the Gateway Preschool. He gave her an article in a professional journal that explained the European origins of the Waldorf philosophy and how these ideas were put into practice in the United States. When she had the second conference with Ms. Warren, Donna was able to answer her question about Danielle's readiness.

*Did Donna respond to Ms. Warren's question appropriately? What are some other ways that caregivers can learn about different educational philosophies and new approaches in their field? Why should caregivers be concerned about staying up-to-date?*

---

their time playing alone with small toys or building blocks; 40 percent in activities that develop large muscles, such as swinging and riding tricycles; and 30 percent playing with one or more other children. The researchers could then apply these findings to future situations and predict how preschoolers will behave. This kind of information can help child care professionals know what to expect and how to provide for preschoolers in the classroom.

**Clinical Observation.**   The *clinical method* or case study involves observational research that focuses on individual subjects. The researcher uses a combination of observation, in-depth interviews of the subject and other people who know the subject, and a variety of developmental assessment techniques that can predict the subject's behavior.

The case study approach might be used to determine whether a child is ready to enter school. The process would involve observing and interviewing the child and his or her family. It would probably include one of the developmental screening tests that indicate how well a child is likely to do in kindergarten. The psychologist or counselor would evaluate all the information to determine whether it seemed best for the child to start school, to wait another year, or to enroll in an early intervention program. Case studies are most useful in identifying individuals who deviate from the norm or who need some kind of care or treatment. However, researchers can only use the clinical method to gather information about the person being studied. This method is not useful for drawing conclusions about people in general.

**Correlational Studies.**   A *correlational study* is a kind of observational study that measures the relationship between two variable factors. A familiar correlational study is the one that measures the relationship between height and weight. There is a

How are Japanese preschoolers similar to American preschoolers? How are they different? Researchers use cross-cultural studies to answer such questions and identify developmental changes that are universal to all children.

correlation between these two variables because in most cases the taller a person is, the more he or she weighs.

Like other observational research, correlational studies can only describe a relationship between two variables. They cannot determine whether one factor causes the other or whether other unknown factors are responsible for the relationship. For example, children usually gain weight as they grow taller. However, some tall children weigh less than some short children, and weight gain may be the result of dietary changes or other environmental factors, not the growth process.

**Cross-Cultural Studies.**    *Cross-cultural studies* are studies that compare children of different backgrounds to determine how children are alike and how they differ from one culture to another. Some cross-cultural studies compare children in different parts of the world who are growing up in very different environments; others compare groups of children in different social classes within the same culture. Cross-cultural studies help psychologists pinpoint developmental changes that are universal to all humans. For example, several cross-cultural studies of language development have shown that children learn the grammar of their native language at about the same age regardless of what language is being learned (Slobin, 1971). Another cross-cultural study might compare the way parents of different socio-economic classes discipline their children.

### Experimental Research

The second major method of studying child development is the *experimental method*, a procedure in which researchers systematically control conditions to investigate one variable. In many experiments, researchers compare the performance of one group of children against another. The children in each group are chosen by *random selection*; that is, they are chosen purely by chance so that the makeup of each group

Experiments are generally considered the most reliable method for studying child development. They are usually carried out in laboratories, where researchers can control conditions in order to investigate one particular variable.

is approximately the same and is representative of the entire population. The children in one group, the *experimental group*, receive some kind of treatment or training, while the children in the other group, the *control group*, do not. Then researchers try to explain any differences in behavior between the two groups by the differences in treatment.

To see how the experimental method works, assume that researchers are trying to determine whether a series of children's television programs can teach three-year-old children the alphabet. The researchers hypothesize that children will learn the alphabet if they watch the programs. To test their hypothesis, they divide a large group of children into two smaller groups. They provide one group of children, the experimental group, with screenings of the children's programs; the other group, the control group, does not watch the alphabet programs. Neither group is to be exposed to any other method of learning the alphabet during the test period. If the first group learns the alphabet but the second group does not, the researchers can conclude that the programs are an effective tool for teaching three-year-old children the alphabet.

A major advantage of the experimental method is that it enables researchers to test directly for cause and effect. When experimenters are able to

control many other variables or possibilities, then they can conclude that the one variable being manipulated is the cause of the behavior. In the example above, if the experimenters make certain that neither group of children learns the alphabet in any other way, they can be reasonably sure that the children's programs were the cause of children in the experimental group learning the alphabet.

Although experiments are the most reliable method of studying child development, experimentation does have some disadvantages. First, when people know they are being tested or observed, they often behave differently than they would in normal circumstances. If the children in the alphabet experiment knew that they were taking part in a test, they might have paid more attention to the educational programs than they ordinarily would have. Second, an experiment that is not well designed may not really test the correct variable. As you read earlier, Piaget's mountain experiment was too complicated for the children he was testing, so his conclusion was misleading. Finally, experimental results cannot always be applied to the real world. For example, in the alphabet experiment, children in the test group may have sat quietly in front of the TV set and watched the children's programs attentively. In the real world, however, the children would have been running, playing, talking, and paying only momentary attention to the TV screen.

### Other Research Techniques

People who study child development are also concerned with a central question: how do children change over time? There are two different ways to explore this question. Many researchers employ *cross-sectional studies* to compare children of different ages. In a cross-sectional study, the researcher studies a single developmental change in a large group of children of different ages at the same time. A researcher studying memory development might study a group of subjects that includes infants, toddlers, and preschoolers. The researcher might find that infants can remember an event for a day or two, that toddlers can remember the event for several weeks, and that preschoolers can remember the event for months. These memory differences would then be assumed to be the result of developmental and age differences. Cross-sectional studies are an

## FOCUS ON  **Cultural Diversity**

### Establishing a Bias-Free Environment

The environment in a classroom alerts children to what the teacher thinks is important or unimportant, acceptable or unacceptable. In order for children to develop high self-esteem, a positive self-image, and respect for others, the classroom materials must reflect a genuine commitment to diversity.

Photos, drawings, and books should show people of many races and cultural backgrounds engaged in everyday activities. However, diversity goes beyond racial and cultural sensitivity. Teachers can also promote positive images of diversity by choosing classroom materials that illustrate the following:

- Children with disabilities
- The elderly as part of family groups or alone
- People in a wide variety of occupations, such as carpenters, musicians, doctors, receptionists, and educators
- People in nontraditional gender roles
- Nontraditional families, such as single-parent and blended families
- Children in economically diverse family settings

It is equally important to avoid classroom materials that promote stereotypes, such as pictures of Indians wearing feathers and war paint or women as nurses and men as doctors. Select books that use gender-free terms such as *fire fighter* or *police officer* whenever possible and use gender-free terms in conversation regularly. Most important of all is to incorporate positive images of diversity into the classroom naturally on a daily basis rather than limit discussions of differences to special holidays or other occasions.

---

effective research tool because they can be conducted relatively quickly. However, they can only show average differences among different age groups; they cannot chart changes in individual subjects over time.

The only way to examine how developmental change occurs in individuals over time is to employ longitudinal studies. In a *longitudinal study*, the researcher collects information about the same group of subjects over a long period of time. Several longitudinal studies of the federally funded Head Start preschool enrichment program have followed Head Start graduates throughout their school years and into adulthood. These studies show that graduates of Head Start and similar programs have derived a number of long-term benefits from their early educational experiences (Lazar & Darlington, 1982; Schweinhart & Weikart, 1993). Longitudinal studies can yield a wealth of developmental information, but they are costly, time-consuming, and difficult to do. Some researchers have spent their entire professional lives conducting longitudinal studies of specific groups of people. One particular difficulty of carrying out a longitudinal study is that the subjects tend to drop out over time for various reasons, making all the material that has been gathered about them useless.

A group study is a special kind of longitudinal study that focuses on one specific group of people or compares one group of people to another over time. For example, medical researchers have studied certain religious groups whose members do not use tobacco or alcohol and compared their health with that of a population that does use tobacco and alcohol.

A cohort study is a research project that focuses on a group of people who were born at the same time. In a cohort study, researchers assume that the experiences of one generation of people are different from those of another generation. For example, children who grew up in cities in the 1950s may have had very different experiences from children who are growing up in cities today. In a cohort study, researchers can use both cross-sectional and longitudinal techniques to gather data about specific generations.

## FOCUS ON   Communicating with Parents

### Recognizing Unspoken Concerns

Beverly tried to put herself in a positive frame of mind as she caught sight of Linda DeLucca waiting to talk to her. Linda had recently enrolled her three-year-old son, Anthony, in the suburban child care center where Beverly works. Each afternoon when Linda comes to pick up her son, she quizzes Beverly about Anthony's day at the center.

At first Beverly thought it was Linda's concern about her son's adjustment that prompted the grilling. After a while, though, Beverly realized that Linda was dwelling on the small, negative things that happened during the day and was criticizing her for the way she handled routine situations. In fact, Linda rarely had anything positive to say to Beverly.

BEVERLY:  Anthony, here's your mom.

LINDA:  Did he eat all his lunch today?

BEVERLY:  Everything except a little bit of his sandwich.

LINDA:  I always make him a nutritious lunch, and I want him to eat all of it. What about his snack? Did he eat his snack?

BEVERLY:  I think so.

LINDA:  You didn't notice? Yesterday he said he didn't like the snack.

BEVERLY:  We don't make the children eat their snacks if they don't want to.

LINDA:  Did he get to play with the big blocks today? Last week he wanted to play with the big blocks but didn't get to. I want to make sure he gets balanced stimulation while he's here.

BEVERLY:  Everyone gets a turn with all the toys. Kids this age have short memories. Sometimes they forget they've played with something.

LINDA:  Well, I hope you're keeping track so he gets a turn.

After Linda and Anthony left, Beverly asked the director why she thought Linda was so negative. The director pointed out that Linda might be feeling guilty about going back to work full-time and placing Anthony in child care. She also suggested that perhaps Linda might be having difficulty reconciling the demands of a high-pressure sales job with those of being a mother.

*How would you handle Linda's complaints and questions? Do you think the director's comments were appropriate? Did they address Beverly's concerns? How can you distinguish between genuine complaints and those that reflect unspoken concerns?*

### Publishing Research Results

One of the fundamental obligations of researchers in all scientific fields is to publish the results of their work so that other scientists can learn from them and use them to guide future research. The results of experiments and studies are customarily published in professional journals after they have been reviewed and approved by other experts in the field. To be accepted as a valid contribution to scientific inquiry, a researcher's work must be replicable. That is, another researcher testing a similar group of subjects under identical conditions must be able to arrive at virtually the same results.

As Piaget's mountain experiment shows, even a flawed study can provide the inspiration for other, better-designed studies to test the same developmental change. Throughout this book, you will find references to research that has been published in the field of child development. If you are interested, you can use these references to read the original research.

## Why Study Child Development?

Any adult who wants a career working with young children or plans to become a parent needs to understand how children grow and develop. A child's early years are crucial in forming that child's personality, attitudes, values, beliefs, and self-esteem for the remainder of his or her life. These years are often called the formative years in recognition of their importance in molding the person the child will become. Early childhood professionals are in a position of enormous power and influence over the children in their care. The actions they take and the words they say may make a deep and lasting impression on young minds. Adults need to know how to use their power and influence wisely to provide a safe, happy environment in which their charges can grow and thrive. Studying child development provides valuable insights, information, and guidelines for early childhood professionals in a number of areas.

### Understanding the Growth and Behavior of Children

Studying child development will help you understand what behavior to expect from children at each age or stage of development. Children think and behave differently from adults and their understanding is limited. Caregivers need to know that nine-month-olds cannot be trusted to avoid dangerous objects because they have not yet developed the understanding or judgment to protect themselves. Similarly, early childhood professionals need to understand that it is inappropriate to punish a two-year-old for telling stories since toddlers have not yet acquired the ability to distinguish between reality and fantasy.

**Identifying Potential Problems.** Children who vary significantly from the normal range of development may have mental or physical disorders that are interfering with their development. Early childhood professionals should be able to recognize signs of mental retardation, learning disorders, and physical disabilities in children. When these problems are identified early, children can be enrolled in special programs that may help them overcome their disabilities and develop to their fullest potential.

Teaching children to stand in line is one example of how caregivers can modify the behavior of children.

**Intervening to Modify Growth and Behavior.** Children can greatly benefit from adult assistance and guidance in developing physical, intellectual, and social skills. For example, a preschooler who is extremely shy and is having difficulty making friends may benefit from some adult intervention. Child care providers can help by playing with the child, reading books about other children who overcame their shyness, and showing the child how to behave around other children.

Developing a child's potential is the goal of teaching. Caregivers and teachers routinely modify children's behavior in many ways throughout each day. They teach children to wash their hands before meals, to form a line, to share their toys, to play games, and so on.

### Implementing Quality Child Care

As more families need two paychecks to make ends meet, more and more mothers are reentering the work force while their children are still very young. The need for preschool programs and child care for infants and toddlers continues to increase. Well-trained, knowledgeable early childhood

### Ethics of Studying Children

In order for researchers to understand different aspects of child development, they must study large numbers of children. The American Psychological Association and the National Commission for the Protection of Human Subjects of Biomedical and Behavioral Research both publish ethics guidelines for researchers who study humans. These guidelines attempt to balance the rights of the subjects with the need for information.

The High Plains Child Care Center has been asked to participate in a research project organized by the education department of a well-respected university. Researchers will ask children ages 18 months through five years to perform certain physical and intellectual tasks. Each child will be tested three times.

The board of the High Plains center is divided over the advisability of participating in this study, which would be conducted at the center during working hours. Here are the opposing views of two board members.

Mary Lou Berger:
"The researchers who have asked us to participate in this study are experienced professionals. Their study has been evaluated by an independent peer review committee made up of other professionals in the early childhood field. It meets all the appropriate guidelines. I see no reason why we should not ask our parents to allow their children to participate.

"Few risks are involved in this study. The testing takes place in a safe, pleasant, familiar environment. All the testers are experienced in working with children. The tasks the children will be asked to perform are presented as games. All results will be kept confidential.

"Professionals who are doing research on early childhood issues help all of us become more effective caregivers. As a board, I think we should permit this study to be conducted at our center and encourage parents to allow their children to take part in the study. Of course, each parent will decide for his or her child."

Valerie Diaz:
"We cannot assume that a study is good for the people who are being studied, even if what is learned eventually benefits society as a whole. There are several things that worry me about participating in this study.

"First, can we be sure the results will remain confidential? We have no control over what the researchers do with the data after they leave our center.

"Second, the tasks the children are to perform are presented as games, but they aren't games. Even if a child has fun doing the task, he is being deceived as to the purpose of his work. Do we want to deceive children?

"Third, some children will be asked to do things they are incapable of doing. They will fail. Will this harm their self-esteem? I think it wrong to expose a child to failure intentionally.

"Finally, studying children is complicated by the fact that they cannot determine whether it is in their best interests to participate in an experiment. Children must rely on their parents and concerned adults to protect them.

"I have read the university's research proposal. It is a technical document that few parents will really understand. Instead, parents will give their consent on the basis of our recommendation. If there are any potential negative consequences to these children, we would be abusing their parents' trust in us by recommending participation in this study."

*Which argument do you find more convincing? Are there any points made by the other side that you think are worth consideration? What issues would be most important to you when deciding whether to allow a child to participate in an experiment?*

The children in this developmentally appropriate preschool take part in activities and play with materials that are tailored to their age group.

professionals will be needed to provide high-quality care for these children. Caregivers must know how to provide developmentally appropriate learning opportunities for young children and infants. A *developmentally appropriate* program is one that is based on a knowledge of how children grow and change. It is tailored to the age level of the group and also meets the needs of individual children (Bredekamp, 1987).

Years ago, preschool teachers tried to model their schools on elementary school classrooms with desks and blackboards and teacher-directed lesson plans. In today's developmentally appropriate preschool or child care center, children are allowed to choose their own activities, to play with each other or by themselves, to build with blocks and other materials, to express themselves artistically and musically, to run and jump and climb, and to be boisterous and energetic. Such programs are based on the idea that children learn best through play.

Most states now require that child care providers have some training in early childhood development. The National Association for the Education of Young Children (NAEYC) has developed extensive guidelines for training early childhood professionals in developmentally appropriate teaching methods (National Association for the Education of Young Children, 1985, 1990). These guidelines recognize that young children are natural explorers and scientists who learn by interacting with their environment and each other. Teachers are trained to provide opportunities for learning and to guide and assist children in developing new skills.

### Answering Future Needs

The study of child development came into being as a separate area of research only in the 20th century. It will continue to be an important field of study long into the next century as psychologists, educators, and early childhood specialists continue to make new discoveries about how children grow and develop.

Child development research offers many insights that can be used to plan and implement new educational policies. For example, a greater understanding of how children learn mathematical concepts has already led to the introduction of new teaching methods and materials in the elementary school classroom. In addition, child development research can suggest new social policies that will help provide a better life for children. Some of the policies that have been influenced by child development research in recent years include enrichment programs for preschoolers, parenting classes for teenage mothers, nutrition programs for pregnant women, educational programs for children with disabilities, family leave policies, child abuse laws, subsidized child care, and after-school care for "latchkey" children.

On a personal level, studying child development will also continue to benefit child care providers throughout their careers in a variety of ways. It will help them become more effective and responsive caregivers because they can recognize when children are going through developmental phases and assist them in overcoming problems. A knowledge of child development also enables caregivers to help parents understand and cope with developmental issues.

Studying the development of children is an ongoing process. Child care professionals study children in classrooms, with other care providers, and sometimes in home settings in a continuing effort to understand the behavior and special characteristics of children. This knowledge will help them become more competent and compassionate caregivers and teachers of young children.

## CHAPTER 1   REVIEW

### SUMMARY

- Child development is the study of how children grow and change over time. It can be divided into three domains: physical development, intellectual development, and emotional and social development.

- Developmental changes can be quantitative or qualitative. All children experience developmental changes, but they each develop in their own unique way.

- The goals of child development study are to describe and explain developmental changes and to modify children's behavior when appropriate.

- Researchers organize the study of child development in different ways. The most common approaches are the nature versus nurture approach, the topical approach, the ecological approach, and the ages and stages approach.

- In the ages and stages approach, researchers study physical, intellectual, and emotional development at each stage of growth.

- The two basic methods of studying child development are the observational method and the experimental method.

- The observational method includes naturalistic observation, clinical observation, correlational studies, and cross-cultural studies.

- The experimental method is a procedure in which the researcher systematically controls conditions to study the effect of one variable.

- The two methods of studying developmental changes across time are the cross-sectional study and the longitudinal study.

- Any adult who plans to work with children needs to study child development. Studying child development helps child care professionals and parents understand the growth and behavior of children, identify potential problems, and modify growth and behavior where appropriate.
- Any adult who plans to become a parent needs to understand how children grow and develop. He or she needs to develop appropriate expectations and consequences for children based on child development research and developmentally appropriate practices.
- Child care professionals need to be trained in developmentally appropriate practices in order to provide the highest quality care and education to young children.
- Child development research will continue to point the way for the development of new educational programs as well as for the development of new public policies to benefit children.
- The study of child development is an ongoing process that will benefit child care providers by making them more effective and caring professionals.

## BUILDING VOCABULARY

Write a definition for each vocabulary term listed below.

ages and stages approach
child development
clinical method
control group
correlational study
critical period
cross-cultural study
cross-sectional study
developmentally appropriate
ecological approach
emotional development
experimental group
experimental method
hypothesis

intellectual development
longitudinal study
maturation
naturalistic observation
nature versus nurture
normal
observational method
physical development
qualitative
quantitative
random selection
scientific method
topical approach

## ACQUIRING KNOWLEDGE

1. Define child development.
2. What is emotional development? Give an example.
3. How are quantitative changes different from qualitative changes?
4. What do child development experts mean by the term *normal behavior*?
5. How are researchers and teachers limited in their ability to modify the behavior of children?
6. The nature versus nurture debate concerns the relative importance of what two factors?
7. Define maturation.
8. What is the major strength of the topical approach?

9. What aspect of a child's life does the ecological approach emphasize most?
10. Explain how the ages and stages approach organizes the study of child development.
11. What are critical periods?
12. Researchers who gather data using the scientific method first formulate a hypothesis and then test it. What is the next step?
13. What are the two basic methods of conducting child development research?
14. What is the main advantage of naturalistic observation?
15. Under what conditions is the clinical observation method most useful?
16. What is a correlational study?
17. Why do psychologists use cross-cultural studies?
18. Name one possible disadvantage of the experimental method.
19. How do cross-sectional studies explore the ways that children change over time?
20. How are longitudinal studies different from cross-sectional studies?
21. What is a cohort study?
22. Why are a child's early years called the formative years?
23. How can studying child development help caregivers understand what behavior to expect from children of different ages?
24. What are some characteristics of a developmentally appropriate child care program?
25. Give two examples of social policies or programs that have been influenced by child development study in recent years.

## THINKING CRITICALLY

1. Some people argue that using young children in scientific experiments is unethical because they are incapable of giving their consent to participate. What position would you take on this issue? What other ethical questions do you think researchers face when experimenting with young children?
2. Child care professionals study child development to understand how children develop physically, intellectually, and emotionally as they grow older. How do you think caregivers use this knowledge in everyday situations?
3. Scientific research is subjected to a vigorous review process before being published. Why do you think this is necessary? What could be the consequences of applying an incorrect theory to young children?
4. Child development is a rapidly growing field. Who benefits from increased knowledge in this area? In what different ways can theories about how children develop be used? How can the general public become better informed about child development?
5. Psychologists using the observational method carefully observe young children, record in detail what they see, and then draw conclusions. How do you think child care providers can apply this method to their job?

## OBSERVATIONS AND APPLICATIONS

1. Arrange with a local preschool, child care center, or family day care to observe a group of children of different ages. Choose one activity to observe—perhaps playing in a sandbox. Look for similarities and differences in behavior among the children. How do the boys and girls play? How do children of different ages play? What other similarities and differences did you notice?

2. Observe one infant for three ten-minute periods in one day. Note the infant's development in the physical, intellectual, and emotional/social domains. Can the baby crawl, sit up, hold a spoon, stack three blocks? What sounds does the infant make? Does the baby allow you to hold him or her? What other characteristics did you observe that fall into each category of development? Make sure to note the infant's exact age.

3. Working one at a time with a group of children from ages two and a half to four and a half, ask each child to perform a sorting task similar to the one mentioned in this chapter. Have each child sort a pile of objects by color, by shape, and/or by size. You might also ask each child to try to sort by two characteristics, such as color and shape. Are there noticeable developmental differences in the ability to perform this task? Can two-and-one-half-year-olds sort the objects? Can they perform the task if you tell them what to do? Do you have to show them what to do? What about four-year-olds? Can four-and-one-half-year-olds perform the two-step task? Can two-and-one-half-year-olds?

4. Suppose that you are a child care provider in a child care center. You observe that a certain two-year-old is not walking independently and has a vocabulary of only a few words. Should you be concerned about this child's development? Why or why not? What could you do?

## SUGGESTIONS FOR FURTHER READING

Almy, M., & Genishi, C. (1979). *Ways of studying children: An observational manual for early childhood teachers* (2nd ed.). New York: Teachers College Press.

Beaty, J. J. (1990). *Observing the development of the young child* (2nd ed.). Columbus, OH: Merrill.

Best, J. W., & Kahn, J. V. (1986). *Research in education* (5th ed.). Englewood Cliffs, NJ: Prentice-Hall.

Bredekamp, S. (1987). *Developmentally appropriate practice in early childhood programs serving children from birth through age eight*. Washington, DC: National Association for the Education of Young Children.

Bronfenbrenner, U. (1979). *The ecology of human development*. Cambridge, MA: Harvard University Press.

Colombo, J. (1982). The critical period concept: Research methodology and research issues. *Psychology Bulletin, 81*, 260–275.

Miller, K. (1985). *Ages and stages*. Mt. Rainer, MD: Gryphon House.

Swick, K. J., & Castle, K. (Eds.). (1985). *Acting on what we know: Developing effective programs for young children*. Little Rock, AR: Southern Association on Children Under Six.

# 2 Theories of Child Development

## OBJECTIVES

Studying this chapter will enable
you to

- List some leading theories of child
  development and explain why it is
  useful to understand them.
- Summarize the main ideas in
  psychoanalytic theory as they
  apply to young children.
- Describe some of the contributions
  that different types of behaviorist
  and learning theories can make to
  the preschool classroom.
- Discuss what cognitive theories
  have to say about the
  development and guidance of
  young children.

P ET RABBITS are a natural in a preschool
classroom, right? Not always. During her
two years working at the Early Start
Child Care Center, Clarissa had amused her
groups of three-year-olds by bringing in Fluffy,
her pet rabbit. She had grown to expect that
Fluffy days were her best days: the children
became very gentle and were very involved,
learning a lot about caring for and respecting
the needs of an animal. Fluffy also enjoyed the
attention.

This year was different, however. Althea was
a little girl who was always rather shy around
Clarissa, though she got on well with Clarissa's
coteacher, Joel. As soon as Althea saw Fluffy,
she began to scream and ran against the wall.
Even though Joel went and put his arm around
Althea, he couldn't console her. Joel had to take
Althea out of the classroom.

Fluffy, too, had been frightened, and Clarissa
found that several of the other children also

seemed nervous. It took a long time for the group to settle down. Clarissa and Joel were forced to move on to the next day's plans, and Fluffy had to sit quietly in his box, being ignored. It just wasn't Fluffy's day.

Clarissa was surprised and disappointed. In previous years, her three-year-olds had reacted warmly to Fluffy, and she had expected the response to be the same this time. But each class is made up of different individuals—and individuals don't always behave in predictable ways. Today Althea screamed, and many of the other children became nervous. Clarissa wondered why.

Theories of child development offer explanations of the way the mind develops and how personality is formed. A knowledge of some of these theories can provide useful insights into how children learn and why they behave as they do.

## Theories of Child Development: Explaining Patterns and Differences

A *theory* is a logical set of ideas designed to explain a group of observations in a particular field. Theories of child development attempt to explain both the common patterns of growth and the uniqueness of individuals. This chapter reviews some of the main theories, including the psychoanalytical theories of Sigmund Freud and Erik Erikson; ethological theories; the behaviorist and learning theories of B. F. Skinner and Albert Bandura; and cognitive theories, including information processing and Jean Piaget's theory of cognitive development.

None of these theories cover all aspects of development, and they sometimes disagree with one another. But each theory suggests an explanation for some important observations that scientists have made. One reason for the differences between the theories is that they focus on particular aspects of development. Some theories concentrate on describing and explaining behavior; others focus on intellectual or emotional growth. For this reason, it is not easy to compare the effectiveness of individual theories with each other. But each theory can be considered on the basis of how well it explains and predicts some aspects of human psychological development.

Sigmund Freud, one of the most influential of all psychological theorists, had a profound impact on the way people view early childhood.

Why should you study these theories of child development? One reason is that they help to make sense of experience and observations, including some observations that seem contradictory. By describing the process of development, theories can help to explain the behavior of groups of children at various age levels. The major theories are based on many hours of careful observation and have been developed by creative thinkers with long experience in the field of psychology.

Studying theories of child development is a useful way to increase your understanding of child behavior, even if the ideas presented cannot explain every aspect of behavior and development. Included in this chapter are some of the implications that these theories have for the early childhood professional. Other implications will be covered in later chapters that deal with aspects of development at specific ages.

## Psychoanalytic Theories

One of the most influential of all psychological theorists was Sigmund Freud, the founder of psychiatry.

## FOCUS ON   **Cultural Diversity**

### Growing up on a Kibbutz

Started in 1909 in what is now Israel, the kibbutz movement is based on the ideal of communal living. Members of the kibbutz own no personal property. They work for the kibbutz farm, which provides for all their needs. About 3 percent of Israel's Jewish population live in kibbutzim.

Until recently, all kibbutz children lived, ate, and slept in separate infants' or children's houses rather than with their families. They were supervised by caregivers. This arrangement enabled both parents to work in the fields, but it also reinforced the kibbutz ideals of group unity.

Kibbutz children spend almost all of their time with their peers. From infancy, their peer group provides them with social and emotional security. It is within this group, rather than with adults, that the strongest emotional bonds are formed.

Education is provided from an early age in kibbutz schools, where industry, consensus building, and communal ideals are emphasized. Studies show that children educated in kibbutzim do as well as or better than most Israeli children on achievement tests.

Since there is no private property within the kibbutz, there is considerably less temptation to drop out of school and take a job to earn money for material possessions. Without private property, there can be no economically disadvantaged children. Generally, there is little crime, drug use, or delinquency among kibbutz children and adolescents. These children seem to be socially and emotionally well adjusted.

The kibbutz system is constantly evolving. In many kibbutzim, the communal arrangement for raising children has been modified. Families now live together for a longer period of time than in the past, and they are allotted more individual living space. Nonetheless, kibbutz children generally identify more strongly with their own age groups than with their biological families.

---

Freud published his first important works in 1895 and 1900. Since then other psychologists have studied, refined, and modified his ideas. Erik Erikson, for example, advanced theories about personality development that have a great following among psychologists today. But Freud should be studied because he is now part of our culture and because many of his insights have become a part of the way we think about ourselves and other people.

### The Theories of Freud

One of Freud's key observations was that much of what goes on in the mind is *unconscious*, or outside our awareness. This idea was considered revolutionary at the time. Freud said that people may think they are acting rationally for a particular purpose, but in fact other motives—of which they may be unaware—are often behind their actions. Some of these motives may be very childish or primitive; others may have to do with childhood experiences.

People may not even remember the early experiences that affect their behavior (Freud, 1970).

Freud treated people with psychological problems by encouraging them to talk about themselves—this was also revolutionary in his time. His form of treatment was called *psychoanalysis*, meaning analysis of the mind. Although the patients that Freud treated were mostly adults, his ideas have a great deal to do with early childhood because he theorized that early childhood experiences have an enormous effect on people's lives later on. For this reason, much of psychoanalytic theory focuses on development in the early years.

**Freud's Theory of Stages.**   Freud viewed early childhood as centered on very primitive feelings of pleasure. He felt that the *libido*, the force that seeks the satisfaction of basic biological urges, drives much human activity. During the first year, Freud argued, the child drew its main feelings of pleasure from the mouth. This pleasure explained why babies not only sucked in order to feed but sucked on many other objects, from blankets to fingers. Later, at around the age of one year, the main pleasure center moved to the anus, where the child could concentrate on the feelings of bowel movements and the muscles needed to control them. This coincided with the time when parents sought to toilet train the child. Then, around three years old, the child became aware of pleasures in the genital area and began to feel attraction toward the opposite-sex parent.

Related to these ideas, Freud outlined three stages in early childhood development. He called them the *oral* (mouth) *stage*, the *anal stage*, and the *phallic stage* (named for the phallus, or male sex organ). Because of the age in which he lived, Freud's viewpoint was very male-oriented, and so he defined sexuality in terms of the male organ. Freud's ideas about the stages of personality development are summarized in Table 2.1.

According to Freud, these stages were important not only for the child's pleasure, but also for the development of *personality*. Personality refers to a person's basic approach to life—loving or suspicious, shy or aggressive, for instance. Freud believed that personality was virtually fixed by the time a child reached school age.

Freud described two other stages. These were the latency stage from about five years to puberty, during which children were less driven by their primitive desires, and the genital stage after puberty, in which the full flowering of sexuality occurred. Freud's theories were shocking to his contemporaries, many of whom disapproved of discussions about sex and had an idealized image of the innocence of children.

**Freud's Theory of Personality Structures.**
Freud's account of childhood sources of pleasure is only part of his theory. According to Freud, these primitive feelings were a part of the *id*, the set of basic instincts behind human behavior, including sexual urges and aggression. Freud described two other elements of the mind, the ego and the superego.

The *ego* is the rational part of the mind that enables a person to work out effective ways to satisfy the id. This is not always easy because the same action that satisfies an urge may also cause pain. For example, eating food that is too hot may satisfy hunger but burn the mouth. In Freud's theory, the function of the ego is to mediate between the demands of the id and the superego, and to reconcile both with reality.

The *superego* represents a person's ideas about morality and acceptable behavior. Children are encouraged by their parents and other caregivers to do some things and are punished for others that are considered bad behavior. Freud believed that the fear of punishment—especially punishment for attraction to the opposite-sex parent during the phallic stage—leads to development of the superego. The social values and rules that children learn from their parents become part of the superego. The superego issues orders about behavior, and the ego mediates between these orders and the urges of the id.

As mentioned earlier, Freud believed that much of what occurred in the mind was unconscious. So, although people may think they are being rational, they may also be driven by hidden motives from the id and the superego.

**Freud's Theory of Defense Mechanisms.**
Freud saw the mind as a place of conflicts, and much of his description is in terms of struggle. One of his most influential ideas is that of *defense mechanisms*. A defense mechanism is a process that occurs in the mind when the conflict becomes overwhelming and the ego cannot handle it rationally. Freud described many different defense mechanisms. He argued that they could be helpful to a person who is temporarily under great stress. However, defense mechanisms could also be inappropriate, and in some cases they could lead to lasting problems.

One of the most important, and potentially damaging, defense mechanisms identified by Freud was *repression*. A memory or an urge that is repressed is permanently blocked from conscious awareness, yet it can still influence behavior. Repression was a major reason for psychoanalysis. Freud maintained that if a person with problems could be led to become aware of repressed thoughts, those problems would be cured.

Another important defense mechanism is *regression*. It occurs when people who are conflicted and confused regress, or temporarily move back to an

**TABLE 2.1**
**Freud's Original Theories about Stages in Development**

| Approximate Age | Characteristics of Stage | Tasks: Possible Personality Effects |
|---|---|---|
| Birth to 1 year | *Oral Stage*—the child focuses on pleasurable sensations from the mouth | Weaning: if this doesn't take place satisfactorily, child may develop "oral personality," becoming clinging, demanding, and dependent throughout life |
| 1 year to 3 years | *Anal Stage*—the child finds pleasure in sensing and controlling bowel movements | Toilet training: if this doesn't take place satisfactorily, child may become either very messy and aggressive or very stingy, compulsive, and overorganized. Freud described these as "anal personalities" |
| 3 years to 5 years | *Phallic Stage*—the child discovers pleasure in sensations of the sex organs | Mastering attraction for opposite-sex parent and in process developing superego: if this doesn't take place satisfactorily, child may become selfish, bragging, even psychopathic—what Freud called a "phallic personality" |
| 5 years to puberty | *Latency Stage*—sensual pleasures are under control, child is able to learn about world | Personality is fully formed |
| From puberty on | *Genital Stage*—adult sexuality starts | Personality problems from earlier stages may emerge |

earlier stage of development. Thus, a Freudian might feel that a five-year-old who loses her toilet training in a stressful situation is exhibiting regression.

How might a Freudian psychoanalyst have explained Althea's fear? Irrational fears are called *phobias*. Freud argued that these were often caused when a negative emotion needed to be repressed; the emotion might be "displaced" and felt as fear of a safer object. In this case, the argument might go, Althea's attraction to her father has led to very negative feelings toward her mother. But because she depends on her mother so much, the feelings are not acceptable, so she begins instead to feel an irrational fear of pets. Althea's hesitant attitude toward Clarissa might have been seen by a Freudian as part of the same problem.

### Erikson's Theory

Freud's ideas have been extremely influential in the area of psychology. Many later thinkers have been inspired by his ideas and have extended them further, making some alterations to suit their own perspectives. One of the most important of these later psychoanalytic thinkers was Erik Erikson, who modified and extended Freud's stages of development.

Freud emphasized particular areas of the body where he believed feelings are focused during the separate stages of development; Erikson emphasized the issues children face as they interact with other people. During the first year (Freud's oral stage), a child depends entirely on others for all care and gratification. She needs food, of course, but also physical affection (hugs) and comfort (diaper changes, for example). Erikson theorized that at this age a child would learn how much she could trust others to provide for her needs. Trust would be, therefore, a major focus of the child's life and could affect her attitudes toward the world at that age and later on as well (Erikson, 1963).

**TABLE 2.2**
**Erikson's Stages of Psychosocial Development**

| Age | Characteristics of Stage | Emotional and Personality Outcomes |
| --- | --- | --- |
| Birth to 18 months | Total dependency of child on caregivers | Trust vs. mistrust: security and hope or tendency to mistrust |
| 18 months to 2 years | Child becoming able to control self and environment | Autonomy vs. shame: autonomy and effective willpower or tendency to shame and self-doubt |
| 2 years to 5 years | Child starts to take initiative, undertake projects | Initiative vs. guilt: sense of purpose or tendency toward feelings of guilt |
| Elementary years | Child explores environment thoroughly, produces products | Industry vs. inferiority: feelings of competency and skill or tendency to feel inferior or inadequate |
| Adolescence | Child searches for self-identity and role in adult life | Identity vs. role confusion: firm feelings of self or role confusion |
| Young adulthood | Person seeks to establish intimate relationships | Intimacy vs. isolation: closeness and commitment to others or tendency toward self-absorption and loneliness |
| Adulthood (35 to 45 years) | Person strives to reach social and professional acceptance | Generativity vs. stagnation: feelings of contribution to world and next generation or tendency toward stagnation, self-indulgence, and hanging on to the past |
| Maturity | Person strives to make sense of own life as meaningful | Ego integrity vs. despair: feelings of integrity and satisfaction or tendency toward hopelessness and fear of death |

Similarly, Freud's anal stage was, for Erikson, the period when the child begins to feel some ability to do things for himself. Not only can he control his bowel movements, but he can also walk, feed himself, and master other important tasks. If he feels successful, he will attain feelings of autonomy, the ability to fend for himself. If he fails, however, he will feel self-doubt and shame, particularly if his parents show disappointment and frustration. Most children have both successes and failures during each of Erikson's stages. What is important is which type of experience predominates.

In Erikson's third stage, the child starts to take initiatives, to make some decisions on her own. If she is able to carry through with some of these undertakings, she gains confidence in herself and her world. However, repeated discouragement or punishment will lead to feelings of guilt and loss of initia-

tive. Each of Erikson's stages builds on the preceding stage. A child who has gained a good measure of autonomy is more likely to take initiatives.

Erikson's eight psychosocial stages are presented in Table 2.2. The word *psychosocial* reflects the key role that the child's relationships to his caregivers and other important people play in his development. The five other stages in Erikson's theory explore aspects of the development of the older child, the adolescent, and the adult.

## Implications and Applications of Psychoanalytic Theories

Psychoanalytic theorists such as Freud and Erikson have had a major impact on many aspects of 20th-century life, not least on early child care practices. Freud's observation that psychological problems often derive from childhood experiences has led people to focus far more on how they care for and nurture their children. Erikson's idea that children grow up in stages influenced by physical development and personal relationships is also a key to current thinking about early child care. Other psychoanalytic observations—such as the power of unconscious thought, the existence of defense mechanisms, and the sexual nature of children—are also very much accepted today.

However, psychoanalytic theory has been criticized on a number of grounds. One is that it is based on personal impressions of patients and on their reports of childhood memories, which may be distorted. This makes it highly subjective: one must rely on the insights of the theorist rather than the logic of science. Furthermore, psychoanalytic theory is based on relatively few observations. When dealing with human behavior, however, a broad range of observations from a wide variety of situations is necessary to support a theory. Insights gained from studying clinical cases do not always apply to mentally healthy individuals. In addition, psychoanalytic theory is criticized as being largely unverifiable. It discusses personality structures of the mind (id, ego, superego) that cannot be observed. It also offers alternative ideas (the two opposite outcomes of the anal stage, for example) that make testing some aspects of the theory almost impossible (see Table 2.1).

Erikson's view of development as a psychosocial process seems more directly relevant to child care and education. His theory has important implications because of the key role others play in the child's personality growth. As children progress from one stage to the next, they depend on their caregivers for types of treatment that will encourage positive growth. Infants are very dependent and need care that is loving, responsive, and consistent. Toddlers will thrive if their caregivers help them do things for themselves, neither overprotecting them nor expecting too much. According to Erikson, excessive expectations that toddlers may fail to meet can promote feelings of shame in the children. Preschoolers need an environment in which they can exercise their own inventiveness. Caregivers should encourage freedom, though obviously with limits for safety. And elementary school students benefit from feelings of achievement and accom-

According to Erik Erikson, children in the second stage of psychosocial development must deal with conflicting impulses—the drive for autonomy and feelings of self-doubt. This two-year-old is demonstrating his desire for independence.

plishment. Sensitive teachers can help by providing praise and recognition.

## Ethological Theories

A very different approach to behavior comes from a group of researchers, known as ethologists, who focus on inborn tendencies. The study of *ethology* is the study of how behavior patterns promote survival in a natural environment. Early studies were inspired by the naturalist Charles Darwin. Darwin had suggested that his theory of evolution, or natural selection through the survival of the fittest, applied not only to physical characteristics like strength and stamina but also to behaviors. Ethologists believe that the concept of evolution can be useful for understanding behavior. They study individual behaviors and try to determine how the behaviors evolved.

The theory here is that certain behavior patterns are in fact inborn and genetic. They are passed on

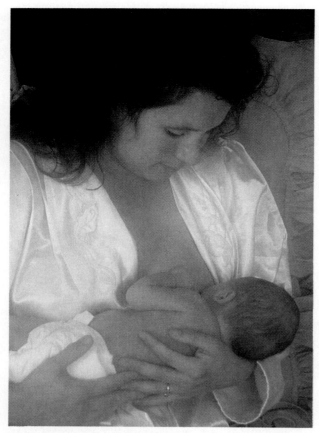

Breast-feeding comes naturally to babies. They are born with a rooting reflex that causes them to turn their head and suck when brushed softly on the cheek or held close to an adult's body.

from generation to generation because those who can produce the patterns are more likely to survive and have offspring.

Ethologists have found that many animals have a number of fixed action patterns. These are inborn behaviors that are performed in given situations. Courting behavior among birds such as peacocks, for example, follows a certain pattern. The rooting reflex in human babies (turning the head in response to a soft touch on the cheek and sucking) is another such example. Ethologists study such behaviors in context to look for the functions they serve. They are also interested in whether the behavior has some survival value. In these examples, courting is a prelude to mating and producing offspring, and rooting is the baby's way of finding food (Hinde, 1983).

Ethologists are also interested in behaviors that show clear patterns but that are adaptable to different situations. One example is an alarm response that is spread to the members of a group. This occurs when a flock of birds takes off suddenly if one member takes fright. The alarm response occurs among humans as well as animals. In the case of Clarissa's group of three-year-olds, other children became nervous because of Althea's alarm at Fluffy.

## Behaviorist and Social Learning Theories

Behaviorist learning theories represent yet another way of looking at personality development. The term *behaviorist* implies that the theories are based on observed behavior. Behaviorist researchers focus on *stimuli*, objects or actions, and *responses*, the way people react to the stimuli. Everything is observable and verifiable.

A consideration of reflexes in the newborn provides a clear illustration of the distinction between the Freudian and behaviorist approaches. Freud theorized that babies sucked on many things because it gave them physical pleasure. A behaviorist would instead study the stimulus (blanket or finger), how it was perceived (touch or sight), and record how the child behaved.

The behaviorist approach to psychology has yielded some important findings and insights. Because their research is based on observable behavior rather than on the inner working of the mind, behaviorists have often used animals as the subjects of their studies. This has allowed them to carry out precise laboratory studies that would have been far more difficult, if not impossible, with humans. But insights from these studies have often been shown to apply to people as well as animals.

### Behaviorist Studies and Theories

Behavioral psychologists have focused for the most part on how people and animals learn. In fact, an underlying assumption of behaviorist theories is that most human and animal behavior is learned. Any discussion of the behaviorist learning theory must start with *conditioning*, which is the learning process. There are two types of conditioning: classical conditioning and operant conditioning.

**Classical Conditioning.** Classical conditioning begins with a specific set of human behaviors—automatic reactions. These include reflexes such as the rooting reflex described earlier. They also include emotional responses. Classical conditioning can be used to explain irrational fears, such as Althea's fear of Fluffy. The explanation provided is very different from that provided by psychoanalytic theory.

The typical pattern in classical conditioning is as follows:

1. A particular stimulus automatically causes a response. For example, a puff of air directed at the eyeball causes the eyelid to blink.
2. A second stimulus occurs regularly at the same time as, or just before, the first stimulus. To continue the example, a buzzer may sound as the puff of air is sent toward the eye.
3. The second stimulus begins to cause the response, even before the air reaches the eye—and even if the puff of air never arrives. The buzzer causes the eye to blink, with or without the puff of air.

This pattern is illustrated in Figure 2.1.

How could this pattern have applied in the case of Althea? The thinking is as follows. Suppose that Althea's brother has a long-haired hamster or some other pet. Every time the hamster appears it moves around erratically, frightening Althea. Soon the sight of the hamster is enough to put her in a state. Now she sees Fluffy and feels the same fears, because his appearance is similar to the hamster's. Althea has generalized the hamster's appearance to Fluffy's appearance, even though Fluffy's behavior is totally different.

Classical conditioning has been studied extensively by psychologists. Their experiments have usually not dealt with emotional reactions but with physical reflexes, such as the eye-blink response. However, the same rules seem to work for emotional and physical reactions. From their investigations, psychologists have found the following patterns:

- If the second stimulus (conditioned stimulus) is presented a number of times without being followed by the first stimulus (unconditioned stimulus), then the learned response (conditioned

**GENERAL**

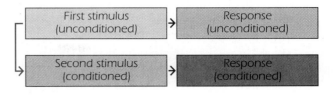

**EYE-BLINK EXPERIMENT**

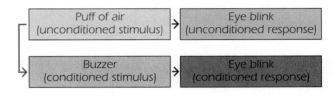

**ALTHEA**

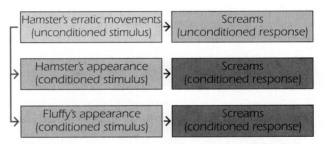

**FIGURE 2.1    The Pattern of Classical Conditioning.**
In classical conditioning, an automatic or unconditioned response to one stimulus is associated with another stimulus; in time, the second (conditioned) stimulus produces the response (conditioned) by itself.

response) will gradually stop occurring. Thus, if Althea can calm down and see that Fluffy's behavior is not threatening, she will stop being scared.
- If a similar stimulus to the conditioned stimulus is presented, the conditioned response will still usually occur. The appearance of a furry creature is a conditioned stimulus for Althea. Although Fluffy is not the same as her brother's pet, he looks similar enough to scare her. This transfer to a similar stimulus is called *generalization*.
- If Althea learned that Fluffy was not threatening, she might remain frightened of her brother's hamster but learn that Fluffy is different. Thus,

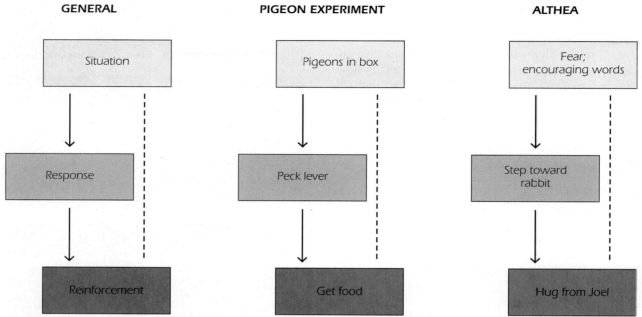

**FIGURE 2.2    The Pattern of Operant Conditioning.**    In operant conditioning, a situation in which a reinforcement is wanted (dotted line) can lead to learning the response that provides the reinforcement (arrows). In a similar situation the response is now more likely to occur. Sometimes the process begins on its own, with the response being produced by accident.

generalization would no longer occur; she would have learned to differentiate. This is called *discrimination*.

▪ If Althea learns that Fluffy is friendly but then doesn't see Fluffy till the following year, her fear may come back, though less strongly.

Such observations suggest that Althea will be cured of the fear if she discovers that Fluffy doesn't behave like her brother's pet. Either this will rid her entirely of her fear of small pets or it will teach her to discriminate, to realize that Fluffy is different. The only problem is, if Althea is so upset by Fluffy, she may never see that he is very well behaved.

**Operant Conditioning.**    Like classical conditioning, operant conditioning involves a specific type of learning. In this case, however, what is learned does not involve automatic responses. Instead, particular responses are learned because they provide a benefit. Some of the principles of operant conditioning could be used to help Althea see that Fluffy is not harmful.

The typical pattern for operant conditioning is as follows:

1. A particular situation is experienced. For example, Althea is feeling scared by Fluffy, but Joel is telling her to come and see how nice the rabbit is.
2. An action, or response to the situation, is tried. Althea takes a cautious step in the direction of the rabbit's box.
3. The action (or response) leads to a reward. Joel congratulates Althea on her bravery and gives her a big hug. The process of rewarding an action, making it more likely that the action will be repeated, is called *reinforcement*.
4. The response may be tried again. Althea takes another cautious step toward Fluffy.

This pattern is illustrated in Figure 2.2. Sometimes the process begins with a random behavior, perhaps even by accident. When this brings about a desired result, the behavior is reinforced.

A characteristic of operant conditioning is that it involves reinforcement. This is a very important principle and is of great importance in learning situations. The effects of reinforcement on behavior have been extensively studied.

One of the leading investigators of operant conditioning was the psychologist B. F. Skinner, an influential advocate of behaviorist learning theories. To find out more about learning behavior, Skinner studied animals. For one of his experiments, he developed a special box (Skinner box) that had buttons for pigeons to peck at. When a pigeon pecked at a button, a pellet of food would drop onto the floor. Using this simple reward, Skinner was able to investigate many different aspects of learning.

He discovered that many of the principles of classical conditioning applied to operant conditioning, too. For example, generalization (treating similar stimuli as the same) and discrimination (distinguishing between similar stimuli) occur in both types of conditioning. If a pigeon had been trained to peck at a red button, the pecking behavior would generalize to an orange button, too. But the pigeon could also be taught to discriminate between the two colors (Skinner, 1976).

Skinner and other behaviorists discovered a number of other principles related to operant conditioning. For example, positive rewards are not the only form of successful reinforcement—there are also negative reinforcers. *Negative reinforcement* occurs when a particular behavior leads not to something pleasant but to the removal of something unpleasant. This has the same effect as a reward; that is, it encourages the behavior that preceded it. For example, a child who has been grounded is permitted to go out and play after she apologizes; she will be more likely to apologize next time. But undesirable behaviors can also be reinforced in this way. For example, a child who is bored with practicing the piano may whine and make a general nuisance of himself until he is allowed to stop practicing. This negative reinforcement will make it more likely that the child will use the same tactics the next time he is bored with piano practice.

Negative reinforcers differ from *punishments*, because punishments tend to stop the behavior that preceded them instead of encouraging new behaviors. In operant conditioning experiments, punishments are often successful in controlling behavior, but they may also lead to unwanted effects. An animal that is punished may become nervous and re-

B. F. Skinner was a leading researcher of operant conditioning. He developed a number of experiments, including the famous Skinner box, to illustrate how animals learn through positive and negative reinforcement.

sentful, more likely to produce other undesirable behaviors. Also, punishment may cause generalization: an animal may learn to stop behaviors that are considered desirable. The same is true of children: a child who is punished too much may become rebellious or passive.

**Shaping.**  The conditioning procedure known as *shaping* begins with the reinforcement of behavior. Shaping is a way of encouraging complex patterns of behavior, patterns that are not likely to occur by chance. Shaping is used to train performing animals; it is also used in some cases to encourage behaviors in human beings who have difficulty learning by other methods. Severely retarded children, for example, have been taught to dress themselves and even to communicate by this method.

Shaping begins with dividing the behavior to be learned into steps. For example, saying the word *food* would be thought of as producing a sequence

A boy learns how to wash the car by imitating, or modeling, the actions of his father. According to social learning theory, children learn a great deal about adult behavior through modeling.

of sounds, beginning with *f*. To condition a child to say this word, a behavioral psychologist might initiate the following procedure. First, the psychologist would reward the child whenever she said *f*. Then the reinforcement would only occur if the child said *foo*. Next, she would be rewarded only for saying the whole word *food*. The final stage would be to require the child to say *food* when she wanted to eat.

Shaping can be a very useful strategy, but it requires slow and painstaking work. Babies may learn their first words in this way: *d, da, dada*. But older children learn words much faster. Similarly, most complex actions are mastered relatively quickly, by people and animals alike, without the long process of trial and error that is connected to rewards and punishments. Conditioning accounts for

very small steps. Can behaviorist theories be extended to explain the full range of human learning? Or are there other learning mechanisms besides conditioning?

### Social Learning Theory

Questions about behaviorist learning theories led psychologist Albert Bandura, and others, to propose a different explanation of the way people, and animals, learn behaviors. Bandura's ideas are a part of social learning theory. Social learning theory builds upon behaviorism by adding to the behaviorist principles of conditioning.

*Social learning* refers to learning from others by observing people in a social environment. Humans, and animals, too, learn a great deal by watching how others behave and learning from the experiences of others. In social learning, there is an observer who learns and there are *models*, the people or animals learned from. Psychologists have identified a number of different things that people and animals seem to learn through the observation of models:

How to act or perform certain tasks, including using language

What behaviors are desirable—because they earn rewards

What behaviors are undesirable—because they are punished

When particular behaviors are appropriate

When certain fears may not be appropriate (as Joel might try to demonstrate to Althea by holding and petting the rabbit)

By learning from models, children avoid the often frustrating and sometimes painful process of learning from their own experience, through rewards and punishments (Bandura, 1977).

Joel could take an approach based on social learning to help Althea conquer her fear of Fluffy. He might, for example, go and pick up the rabbit, obviously taking pleasure in holding and petting the animal. He might also talk to Althea, from a "safe" distance, about the pleasure he feels. Gradually, Althea might learn that Fluffy was not so fearsome and was actually fun to watch and pleasant to touch.

## FOCUS ON    Communicating with Parents

### The Importance of Play

Terri teaches a class of three-year-olds in a suburban preschool. She feels fortunate to have a group of interested and concerned parents who want their children to excel. But five weeks into the school year, one of the mothers, a successful career woman, raises questions about the "lack of curriculum."

MRS. REID:   You know, Terri, I've been meaning to ask you about a few things that seem to be missing from the classroom. I'd like to see some resources here to help the children begin to develop their reading skills. It's never too soon to start, you know.

TERRI [*surprised*]:   Really, Mrs. Reid. What kinds of materials were you thinking of?

MRS. REID:   Well, magnetic letters, flash cards—you know, basic materials to help them learn their letters. I've already started Jonathan with them at home. He almost knows how to spell his name!

TERRI:   In terms of readiness for reading, I think that we're already doing the most important things for this age group. As you know, twice a day we read aloud stories that the children enjoy. And we also have a wide selection of picture books that they can look at independently. I know Jonathan looks forward to story time every day. He's one of the first in the circle when I call the children.

MRS. REID:   But so much of the day seems to be spent just playing. Now that we're several weeks into the year, I'm sure the children are all well socialized and have gotten to know each other. Can't we devote a little time to *real* learning? I want Jonathan to be ready for kindergarten.

TERRI [*patiently*]:   For three-year-olds, playing *is* real learning, Mrs. Reid. At this age, it's the way they develop physical, social, and intellectual skills. So, it's the best way to lay the foundation for a successful start in elementary school. In fact, Piaget described how play is so important to children's learning and develop. . .

MRS. REID [*interrupting*]:   Well, the world is different now than it was in Piaget's day.

TERRI:   You're right about that, but I think that children are still very much the same. I'm convinced of the importance of play. And as for reading, there's no need to rush it. Most children are interested and ready to read between six and seven years old. Until then, I think that reading aloud and letting children look at books are the best ways of encouraging enthusiastic readers.

*What is your opinion of the way Terri handled this situation? What are some other ways that she could have responded to Mrs. Reid's concerns?*

### Implications and Applications of Behaviorist and Social Learning Theories

The behaviorist approach was the first that studied psychology in a scientific manner, using carefully designed experiments and precise, logical analysis. This approach has produced some interesting insights and also some important techniques. For example, the technique of classical conditioning is used to help people stop unwanted behaviors and to overcome irrational fears. Another behaviorist technique is shaping. Shaping enables psychologists to teach people or animals behaviors that would otherwise be almost impossible for them to learn.

A technique based on operant conditioning is *behavior modification*. This involves gradually changing a pattern of behavior and has been successful in treating conditions ranging from shyness to uncontrollable anger to smoking. These techniques are a

## Approaches to Discipline

Ms. Arceneaux is looking for a day-care center for her three-year-old daughter, Jodie. As a newly divorced parent, she needs to work full-time. Two centers near her home have immediate openings for her daughter. She visits each and asks about their discipline policies. This is what she is told.

Little People Child Care Center:

We believe childhood is a wonderful time of discovery. Children learn best by exploring, trying things for themselves, and watching other children at play. The more we tell them "no," the less they can discover for themselves. At our center there is no "right" way to play.

We have made the center child friendly and safe so that we need few rules. Of course, we never let children do things in which they will hurt themselves or others. If hitting or rough play starts, we separate the children. We explain that hitting is hurtful and guide them into a different activity. Generally, we try to intervene as little as possible and let the children work things out.

We encourage children to find their own activities and projects based on their interests. Then teachers enter in and contribute to the projects, praising the child's ideas and creativity.

We believe and teach that every child is different and special. Although we encourage certain daily activities, such as circle time, we do not insist that a child participate. Each morning at circle time we sing and children share their experiences. We try to make it a fun time and to bring all the children together.

Some children are so involved in their free play activities that they aren't ready to come to the circle. We let them continue to play on their own. We don't believe that anything is gained by making a child become part of a group. We try to be flexible and meet each child's needs.

First Steps Child Care Center:

We believe that children must learn socially acceptable behavior. We provide structure with rules that clearly state what is acceptable and what is not.

The rules keep children safe and teach them respect for the teacher, other children, and property. The children quickly learn to follow the rules even if they don't understand the reasons for them. We apply the rules fairly to every child without a lot of discussion or negotiation.

It is important for children to fit in with the group and learn from the start that they can't always do what they want. For example, at art time we expect all the children to do their art project. If a child won't participate, she must sit quietly with the rest and wait until everyone is finished. She isn't allowed to wander off and play with toys.

Of course, every child will test the rules. When this happens, we give the child a short time out. If the unacceptable behavior does not stop, we remove privileges, such as being allowed to play outside.

If the child continues to ignore the rules, she must visit the director's office, and we send a warning note to the parent. We inform parents of any discipline problems during the day when the child is picked up.

*At which day-care center would you feel most comfortable being a teacher or teacher's aide? Why? Were there any aspects of the other center's approach that you would consider using? In choosing an approach to discipline, would the age of the children—18 months, 3 years, or 5 years old—make a difference to you? If you were Ms. Arceneaux, what other questions would you ask?*

direct outgrowth of behaviorist theory. In addition, the social learning technique of modeling has also been very useful in dealing with fears. Modeling is one of the most important contributions of social learning theory to behaviorism.

Behaviorism has been subjected to considerable criticism in recent years. A major theme of this criticism is that behaviorist methods are mechanical, ignoring emotions and other human concerns. The therapies based on behaviorist theory are felt by some to disregard people's rights as individuals, to manipulate them too much. Psychoanalysts also say that therapy based on behavioral psychology is incomplete because it ignores the unconscious causes of behavioral symptoms, so the symptoms will reappear or emerge in other forms.

A second, sometimes related line of criticism is that behaviorism cannot fully explain learning, let alone human behavior. Furthermore, it does not take account of language, through which most people learn a great deal. Behaviorist theory does not show how listening to a sentence can change the way a child thinks and acts. Social learning theory, on the other hand, does incorporate thinking and feeling and points to imitation of models as an alternative learning mechanism.

Behaviorist principles are widely used in behavior management by parents, teachers, and therapists. Today, however, many psychologists are working with new ideas about people and the way their minds work. These ideas are based on theories of *cognition*, theories that investigate the way the mind and brain perform such processes as perceiving, thinking, remembering, understanding, problem solving, and making decisions.

## Cognitive Theories

Cognitive theorists agree with Freudian psychologists that what takes place in the mind should not be ignored. But there the agreement ends. Where Freud and his followers focused primarily on what people are thinking, cognitive theorists are interested in how people think.

Social learning theory, which began as an offshoot of behaviorism, has become an important strand in cognitive psychology. Social learning theorists emphasized the key role of mental activities. They pointed out that there is often a delay between

learning from a model and trying out the new behavior. For example, a child may see a friend rewarded for an action and not perform the same action until three or four days later. Or, she may witness the punishment of another child for a certain behavior and not have a chance to perform—or avoid—that behavior until the following week. Obviously, the child is remembering, and thinking about, what she has learned. Cognitive psychologists say that a theory about learning must take this mental activity into consideration.

Cognitive theories have developed from several other directions as well. One line of thinking, *cognitive development theory*, grew out of child development studies that focus on thought and intellect rather than on personality and problems. A second approach, the *information processing theories*, developed from a knowledge of the way computers—"electronic brains"—process data and information.

### Cognitive Development Theory

Jean Piaget was a Swiss researcher involved in testing the intelligence of children. In the course of his work, Piaget began to notice patterns in the mistakes that children made at various ages. He decided that this information could provide insight into the way that intelligence develops in children, and he started a lifelong study of children—his own and those in a child study institute of which he was director.

Piaget believed that there are real differences between the way a baby thinks and the way an adult thinks. These differences are partly the result of the physical development of the brain, which becomes more powerful as children grow older. But there is another aspect. According to Piaget, children are the main creators of their own thought processes and their own reality. Interacting with the environment, they develop ever more complex thinking strategies until they are able to understand their world (Piaget & Inhelder, 1969).

The idea of schemes plays a key role in Piaget's theory. *Schemes* are mental structures that allow a child to gain knowledge and act on his world. According to Piaget, the schemes of infants are patterns of action, such as sucking, grasping, eating, holding, and throwing. After the age of two a child's schemes may include objects as well as actions. A child forms schemes through exploration

Jean Piaget, a Swiss researcher, developed a comprehensive theory of cognitive development that explains how the thinking of children changes as they grow older.

and experience; using schemes, he learns to identify objects, predict events, plan actions, and pattern behavior.

Piaget contends that children learn when they encounter new objects or experiences that do not fit any of their existing schemes. Consider, for example, a newborn baby lying in a crib. She has been born with certain inborn reflexes, such as sucking and grasping. These actions form the first of the baby's schemes. Beyond these simple reflexes, her behavior consists of uncoordinated and unintentional movements, such as waving her hands and kicking her legs.

One day, while waving her hands, the baby accidentally brushes her hand across her mouth. Immediately, she begins to suck on her hand. Piaget would call this attempt to learn about a new object (her hand) by using an existing scheme (her sucking scheme) *assimilation*. He describes assimilation as a taking-in process, a way in which the child learns by taking in new objects and experiences using existing mental structures.

After sucking on her hand for a while, the child eventually learns that if she opens her mouth wider, she can put her hand in her mouth. Through her actions, the baby forms a new scheme, the putting-in-the-mouth scheme. According to Piaget, this attempt to learn about a new object (her hand) by forming a new scheme (the putting-in-the-mouth scheme) is called *accommodation*. While assimilation is a taking-in process, accommodation is an outgoing process. The infant learns by reaching out into her environment and changing her actions to accommodate a new object (Pulaski, 1971).

According to Piaget's theory, the infant in the example has now reached a state of equilibrium through both assimilation and accommodation. In other words, the baby has achieved a balance between a new object in her environment and the mental structures that she uses to organize her actions. Central to Piaget's theory is the idea that the infant herself was responsible for changing her actions to deal with an unfamiliar aspect of her world.

Piaget extended his study to the way young children use schemes. He wondered whether there was a difference between the general principles that babies use for developing and relating schemes and those used by older children. Piaget concluded that there was. He believed that the intellectual development of children involved more than adding new schemes, that there were also definite stages in the manner in which children process the schemes. These ideas led to his stage theory of intellectual development.

**Piaget's Theory of Stages.**   Piaget identified four main stages or periods in the development of thought (see Table 2.3). These periods do not occur at the same time for all children, because each child has different abilities and must deal with a different environment. Piaget even held that the fourth stage, formal operations, is not always needed and for that reason some people never move out of the third stage of concrete operations (Gruber & Voneche, 1977).

**TABLE 2.3**
**Piaget's Stages of Cognitive Development**

| Approximate Age | Characteristic of Stage or Period | Developmental Challenges |
|---|---|---|
| Birth to 2 years | *Sensorimotor Period*—schemes at first centered on the child's actions, though object schemes are developed later in the period | During period, child discovers independence of objects. Toward end, child finds that schemes can be used in symbolic play |
| 2 years to 7 years | *Preoperational Period*—schemes are applied more flexibly and can work through mental images, allowing great development of play and language | During period, child develops broad use of language, though this is egocentric and not fully logical. Toward end, child begins to understand conservation of volume and similar conservations—space and time |
| 7 years to 11 years | *Period of Concrete Operations*—schemes become logically related in keeping with the child's social environment and culture, allowing child to learn to function in adult world | During period, child expands knowledge of concrete world and improves logical skills. Toward end, child begins to perceive the methods of logic and other abstract ideas |
| 11 years to adulthood | *Period of Formal Operations*—schemes of abstract thought develop, permitting child to reason in a sophisticated way and explore hypotheses and other cultural systems | Child can begin to think about and refine full range of mental operations |

Piaget's first period, the *sensorimotor period*, covers the first two years of life. It begins with inborn reflexes and simple actions that help a baby meet its needs. Piaget believed that the first schemes children develop are, in fact, not schemes of objects but of actions they take. Experience of the inborn sucking reflex, for example, leads to a mental scheme of the features of that reflex. But the reflex leads to different experiences, depending on whether the child is sucking its mother's nipple, a security blanket, or its hand. This causes several different schemes to develop, Piaget believed, as the infant notices the different sensations of feeling and sucking on the different objects. These schemes are not schemes of different objects, however, but of different sucking experiences.

Later, as the child's life develops and its actions become more varied, this way of dividing up reality becomes inadequate and confusing. Objects become more important and their uses become more varied—the same blanket, for example, can be sucked, snuggled in, and pulled around. The child is forced to make a change—she separates object schemes from her old action schemes, perceiving that some of the features formerly assigned to her own motions are actually properties of objects outside herself. And, because she begins to see that the environment is separate from herself, she starts to form a self-concept, to think of herself as a person separate from the outside world.

Piaget believed that another important change leads to the next phase of intellectual development, the *preoperational period*. The child starts to play "pretend" games, using objects to represent other objects. A doll, for example, can "be" a baby in the child's game and the child can "be" a mother. In this phase of mental development, schemes can represent other schemes, and mental images can be used. For example, a four-year-old who wants to look out of a high window and sees a chair nearby might drag the chair over to the window and climb on it to look outside. Mental representation and play using imagination open up a whole new dimension for exploring reality.

This advance in thinking encourages the incredible development of language and mental ability that occurs between the ages of two and seven or eight. However, Piaget felt that there are still major differences between a child's thinking at this age and the mental functioning of an adult. Language, he believed, remains very personal to each child—they do not understand words in the same ways or grasp how different object schemes relate to each other. And children also lack an understanding about the underlying reality of the physical world—that the same objects can look very different under different circumstances.

When children have mastered these ideas, they have reached the third stage, the *period of concrete operations*. Children are now also able to develop complete classification systems of concrete objects, understanding that, for example, a Winesap is an apple, which is in turn a fruit, which is in turn part of a plant, which is in turn a living thing. Skill at classifying objects and words in this way makes it possible for children to think logically about real things. However, it is less easy for them to examine their logic: mastery of this skill takes them into the next period of development.

In the last period, the *period of formal operations*, children have developed the ability to think abstractly, to refine their thinking and create sophisticated arguments. Not only are they able to classify, but they can also talk about classification as a concept; not only do they think logically, but they can also discuss the principles of logic. This, for Piaget, is the final stage of intellectual development.

**Piaget's Theory of Equilibration.**     Piaget was also interested in how children move from one period to the next. As stated earlier, he did not believe this was solely a matter of physical development of the brain. He also thought that children actively work to enter the next stage in response to the demands of their expanding environment.

Piaget held that, during each period of development, children try to organize the new concepts they are forming to reflect the real world that they see. But the schemes will tend to be organized in the way that is characteristic of that period. The child attempts to assimilate the concepts, to fit them in with the current overall mode of thinking. For example, a child in the early sensorimotor period simply adds new action schemes to reflect new experiences. However, a point is reached when the system of action schemes clearly fails to encompass what the child is experiencing. It becomes increasingly necessary to revise the way of thinking so that schemes can represent objects as well as action. The process of accommodation allows the child to revise his system of thinking to handle new experiences. It permits a new balance or equilibrium between the child's thinking and the environment he seeks to master. Piaget felt that this process of *equilibration*, achieving a new equilibrium, drives mental development, both within each period and from one period to the next. In each case, the effort to assimilate new concepts meaningfully into the old system breaks down and has to be accommodated to achieve a new equilibrium.

Because Piaget viewed this search for equilibrium as an active process that was directed by the child, he perceived the teacher's role to be one of facilitating and helping. Children are not passive learners, unable to develop unless they are taught. Instead, they actively seek experiences that will allow them to master the environment. They seek to expand their awareness of the world, to challenge themselves and the systems of schemes that they are constructing.

## Information Processing Theories

A different view of mental activities emerged in connection with the development of the computer. The stimulus and response of classical conditioning can be compared to the input and output functions of a computer. In computers—and in the human mind—a number of other functions occur between the input and output. These include storage and processing, which can both be identified as parts of human thought as well.

**Memory.**     Storage in computers, of course, is often called memory, and memory is a vital element in the social and intellectual development of children. Psychoanalytic theory places great importance on the effect of unconscious memories from childhood. Most other psychological theories also include memory as a key component. Information processing theories incorporate ideas from different psychological thinkers and build them into a view of the brain as a highly complex computer.

## FOCUS ON · Decision Making in Child Care

### Integrating Children with Physical Handicaps

In August, John heard that four-year-old Kiesha would be joining the preschool class he taught. Kiesha has cerebral palsy, which affects her motor coordination and her ability to walk independently. She wears leg braces to stand and uses a walker or a wheelchair to move from place to place, depending on the distance. John was concerned about the best way to handle the situation. Did he have enough training to help Kiesha? Would she take too much of his time and energy away from the rest of the class? How would the other children react to her?

John started by getting all the information he could about cerebral palsy and about Kiesha. When he met Kiesha's parents, he asked about her strengths and her limitations and what tasks she needed special help with. He told them he would like to speak with her doctor and physical therapist to find out how he could help Kiesha move ahead in the right direction.

Working with his supervisor, John made sure that the school's facilities were appropriate for Kiesha. The school had already made some modifications to comply with the Americans with Disabilities Act. John found a few things that needed to be changed, such as raising the shelf in Kiesha's cubby.

To prepare the other members of the class, John told them about Kiesha and showed a film in which children with handicaps were part of the story. He used the film as a basis for a discussion about individual differences and similarities. When the children asked questions about Kiesha or the children in the film, he tried to respond with simple and direct answers.

John was pleased to discover that the children in his class were eager to meet Kiesha and to help her. But he tried to explain that they shouldn't do things for Kiesha that she could do for herself.

*If Kiesha were placed in your classroom, what would you do to ease her entry? Can you think of other ways to help her classmates be understanding and supportive? What do you think would happen if John did nothing to prepare for Kiesha's enrollment?*

---

A key finding is that there are actually different types of memory, a short-term *buffer* (to use the computer term) in which we hold schemes that are important for now and long-term storage for use later. The capabilities of the human mind's long-term memory have been found to be remarkable, but short-term memory is quite limited.

One reason why this is important is that people seem to use the short-term memory as a step in creating long-term memories. Suppose a teacher wants his class to learn some basic rules about school procedures. There are ways to present those rules that will make remembering them easier. If he reads a long list of rules, he can easily "overload" the students' short-term memory; research has shown that short-term memory can only handle about seven schemes at a time.

Instead, grouping the rules in a meaningful way—first the rules for coming in in the morning, then rules for going to the bathroom, then playground rules, and so on—makes them easier to remember. The same principle holds for almost anything that needs to be explained: ideas that are grouped in small chunks of related information—the process is actually called *chunking*—are far easier to understand and learn.

**Processing.** Information processing theories deal with other mental processes besides memory. They look at perception, decision making, problem solving, creativity, language, and other areas of psychology. As indicated, information theorists do not merely study the way computers work. They also consider how ideas and observations from psychology fit into a picture of the human mind as a computer. This type of work has produced valuable insights into how the human mind develops and works.

### Implications and Applications of Cognitive Theories

Cognitive theories are probably the most influential theories in psychology today. The careful observations and intricate analysis contained in Piaget's work have been extremely influential in developmental psychology, especially his exploration of different modes of thought at different ages. More recently, the information processing approach and computer simulations of human thinking are adding an extra dimension to cognitive theories.

Criticisms of cognitive theories come both from other cognitive theorists and from other theorists. Some have criticized cognitive theories for what they omit. For example, these theories hardly touch on emotional and personality development, or on how emotions color a child's ability to learn. Since computers do not have a social or emotional aspect, the information processing theory does not provide insights in those areas of development.

Piaget's theory has been criticized for underestimating the abilities of infants to learn about their environment (Harris, 1983). Some critics also claim that Piaget gave children overly complex tasks to complete in his experiments. According to more recent research, children given simpler tasks demonstrated abilities that Piaget claimed were impossible until older age levels (Gopnik & Meltzoff, 1987).

Nonetheless, Piaget has had a profound impact on developmental theory and research. Even those who do not agree with his views must refer to them in almost any article on cognition. In addition, most developmentalists think of babies as sensorimotor creatures and of young children as egocentric thinkers and must go to great lengths to demonstrate that the characteristics described by Piaget are not true.

Piaget's concepts are widely applied in education, particularly in preschool situations. His belief that children actually enjoy learning—when left to their own devices—is certainly relevant. Equally influential is the idea that curriculum must be developmentally appropriate, that is, that it must not require skills that are beyond the capacities of a particular age group.

## CHAPTER 2    REVIEW

### SUMMARY

- Theories of child development offer explanations of the way the mind develops and how personality is formed.
- To construct theories of development, researchers rely on careful observation of behavior, interviews, and their own experience.
- Freud believed that much of what goes on in the mind is unconscious, or outside our awareness, and that experiences of early childhood often have a profound influence on our behavior as adults.
- Freud described three stages of development in early childhood: the oral, anal, and phallic stages. According to Freud, the primitive feelings that were dominant in these stages are centered in a part of the mind called the id. The mind has two other parts: the ego (the rational part) and the superego (the part concerned with right and wrong).

- Freud believed that people use defense mechanisms, such as repression, as a way of coping with conflicts they cannot handle rationally.
- Erikson thought that children's physical and emotional needs influence their feelings for others. His psychosocial stages of early childhood each involve basic conflicts that need to be resolved before moving on to the next stage.
- Ethological theories start with the idea that babies are born with certain behavior patterns that help them survive.
- Behaviorist theories are based on observed behavior. As a group, behaviorists have focused primarily on how people learn and have explained learning and behavior in terms of conditioning.
- Classical conditioning involves a stimulus and an automatic response, and a second (or conditioned) stimulus leading to the same (or conditioned) response.
- Operant conditioning involves learning or changing behavior through the use of positive and negative reinforcements, or punishments.
- Social learning theory adds to behaviorist theory the idea of learning through observing models and learning from their experience.
- Cognitive theorists focus on how the mind works. Schemes (mental images of objects, actions, ideas) are a key feature of cognitive theories. Schemes take shape in the mind through experience and are used to identify objects, guide behavior, and plan actions.
- Piaget believed that children are the main creators of their own thought processes and their own reality. In an effort to understand their environment, children develop increasingly complex modes of thought through interaction with the world they live in. Piaget described four stages of cognitive development, beginning with the sensorimotor period.
- Advocates of information processing theories view the human mind in terms of computer functions such as input, memory, and output.

## BUILDING VOCABULARY

Write a definition for each vocabulary term listed below.

| | |
|---|---|
| accommodation | generalization |
| anal stage | id |
| assimilation | information processing theory |
| behaviorist | libido |
| behavior modification | model |
| chunking | negative reinforcement |
| classical conditioning | operant conditioning |
| cognition | oral stage |
| cognitive development theory | personality |
| conditioning | phallic stage |
| defense mechanism | phobia |
| discrimination | preoperational period |
| ego | psychoanalysis |
| equilibration | psychosocial |
| ethology | punishment |

regression
reinforcement
repression
response
scheme
sensorimotor period

shaping
social learning
stimulus
superego
theory
unconscious

## ACQUIRING KNOWLEDGE

1. What is a theory? Why are theories useful for understanding child development?
2. Why is it difficult to compare theories?
3. At what age does the oral stage occur, according to Freud's theory? Give an example of a behavior common to this stage.
4. What is the superego, and what is its function?
5. What is regression, and what type of situation causes it?
6. Name and describe the first of Erikson's stages of psychosocial development.
7. There are various differences between Freud's theory and Erikson's theory. Give an example of one.
8. What role does memory play in Freudian theory?
9. What is ethology?
10. How do ethologists explain fixed action patterns, such as the human rooting reflex?
11. How do behaviorists explain learning?
12. Explain the role of reinforcement in operant conditioning.
13. Give an example of how reinforcement might be used in a child care setting.
14. What is the difference between generalization and discrimination?
15. What is negative reinforcement? How can it be used to reinforce a behavior?
16. Why are behaviors divided into steps when they are taught through shaping?
17. Briefly describe Bandura's social learning theory.
18. Give an example of the kind of information that can be learned from models.
19. Give two criticisms of behaviorism.
20. What are schemes and how do they affect learning?
21. Explain the difference between assimilation and accommodation.
22. Cite two characteristics of Piaget's sensorimotor stage.
23. How does Piaget view the role of the teacher?
24. In what ways does the human mind function like a computer?
25. How is chunking used as an aid to memory?

## THINKING CRITICALLY

1. Human babies have an inborn rooting reflex, which causes them to turn their heads and suck in response to a soft touch on the cheek. How would a Freudian theorist and an ethologist explain this behavior?

Which viewpoint do you find more persuasive? Why?

2. Suppose two 18-month-old children arrive for their first day at a child care facility. One child hugs her parents, goes into the room, and begins to play, while the other child clings to her parents. Explain the behavior of the two children in terms of Erikson's theory of psychosocial development.

3. Describe a behaviorist approach to teaching a child to share toys with others. What techniques would a behaviorist employ?

4. According to social learning theory, children learn a great deal by observing models. Do you think the same type of learning might occur while watching television? Do you think the type of programming would affect what is learned? Explain your answers.

## OBSERVATIONS AND APPLICATIONS

1. Observe a child (age one to three) for at least an hour. What behaviors do you see that correspond to the oral, anal, or phallic stages described by Freud? Write a description of these behaviors. Discuss how the observed behaviors could be manifestations of a child's id, ego, and superego.

2. Arrange to spend a few hours at a child care center or a family day care. Observe the interaction between the caregiver and children. Pay special attention to the way caregivers react to disruptive behavior. Also note which behaviors result in praise and reward. How are the behaviors you observed evidence of operant conditioning?

3. Suppose that the community where you live is about to celebrate its 100th anniversary. You and your preschool class have been asked to present a dramatized version of local history and traditions. How could you use social learning and information processing theories to help the children learn their parts for this production?

## SUGGESTIONS FOR FURTHER READING

Blurton Jones, N. G. (1972). *Ethological studies of child behaviour*. Cambridge: Cambridge University Press.

Elkind, D. (1976). *Child development and education: A Piagetian perspective*. New York: Oxford University Press.

Flavell, J. (1985). *Cognitive development*. Englewood Cliffs, NJ: Prentice-Hall.

Forman, G. E., & Kuschner, D. S. (1983). *The child's construction of knowledge: Piaget for teaching children*. Washington, DC: National Association for the Education of Young Children.

Hinde, R. (1974). *The biological bases of human social behavior*. New York: McGraw-Hill.

Klahr, D. (1989). Information-processing approaches. In R. Vasta (Ed.), *Annals of child development*, vol. 6. Greenwich, CT: JAI Press.

Richmond, P. G. (1971). *An introduction to Piaget*. New York: Basic Books.

Salkind, N. (1985). *Theories of human development*. New York: Wiley.

Siegler, R. (1991). *Children's thinking*. Englewood Cliffs, NJ: Prentice-Hall.

Skinner, B. F. (1948). *Walden two*. New York: Macmillan.

# PART 2

# Background to Child Development

### CHAPTER 3
### Heredity, Pregnancy, and Birth
Chapter 3 explains how heredity and environment affect an individual's development from the moment of conception. The chapter describes prenatal development and birth and discusses steps that a pregnant woman can take to ensure the health and well-being of her child.

### CHAPTER 4
### Impact of Family
Chapter 4 examines how different types of families and different family members influence the way a child grows and learns. It discusses how child care professionals can help families cope with stress and change.

### CHAPTER 5
### Concerns for Early Childhood Professionals
Chapter 5 discusses ways that child care professionals can deal with cultural diversity, develop positive partnerships with parents, and create a safe, healthy, and nurturing environment for children.

# 3

# Heredity, Pregnancy, and Birth

## OBJECTIVES

Studying this chapter will enable
you to

- Explain the role of genetics in the
  development of individual traits.
- Discuss the effect of environment
  on a child's development.
- Summarize the causes and effects
  of developmental abnormalities.
- Identify the stages of fetal
  development and describe what
  occurs during each stage.
- Identify and describe various types
  of prenatal testing.
- Explain the influence that
  environmental factors can have on
  prenatal development.
- Describe the stages in the birth
  process and identify complications
  that may arise.
- Discuss the development of a
  child's individual traits in light of
  the "nature versus nurture"
  debate.

CARMELA had been working at the child care center for over a year. One day Ricky, a bright and talkative four-year-old, told Carmela a story about a little boy who saved his baby sister from a terrible dragon. At the end of the story, Ricky said, "When I get my baby sister, I'll take care of her and save her from dragons, too."

Ricky's father usually brought his son to the center, and Carmela wondered whether Ricky's mother was pregnant. She didn't have to wonder long. The next morning Ricky's mother brought him to the child care center, and Carmela noticed that she was indeed pregnant. Carmela congratulated her and asked when the baby was due. "In two months," Ricky's mother replied, and then she began to tell Carmela about how she had changed her life since she became pregnant. "I want a healthy baby," she said, "so I've stopped smoking, I eat right, and I don't drink anything alcoholic. I've heard about what cigarettes and alcohol can do to a fetus. I'm also taking classes in natural childbirth because I think that's best for the baby."

Carmela was impressed. "I think Ricky would like a sister," she said. "Yes, I know," his mother replied. "I've been seeing a doctor regularly and have had tests to make sure the baby is healthy. I also found out the baby's sex, but I won't tell Ricky yet. I want it to be a surprise." As she left the center, Ricky's mother smiled and whispered to Carmela, "Just between you and me, Ricky won't be disappointed."

## How Heredity Influences a Child's Life

Ricky's mother is doing what she can to ensure that her baby is healthy when it is born. She knows the importance of eating nutritious food, avoiding tobacco and alcohol, and seeing her doctor regularly. During the months she is pregnant, her decisions about such matters will have an important effect on her baby. These decisions will not, of course, change the baby's sex or the color of her eyes or hair. These characteristics have already been established.

This chapter focuses first on the factors that determine the traits and characteristics of each individual. It traces the development of the fetus during pregnancy and discusses various factors—both inherited and environmental—that can affect fetal development and a baby's health and growth after birth. The chapter also describes the birth process and possible complications.

### Genes and Heredity

Some brothers and sisters look so much alike that it is easy to tell they are siblings. Others may look so different that it is hard to believe that they are even related. The similarities and differences among siblings result from each child's *heredity*, the characteristics that the child receives from his or her parents and earlier ancestors. These characteristics are contained in *genes*, minuscule structures found in every living cell. Genes are made of molecules of a chemical called deoxyribonucleic acid or DNA. *DNA* acts as a code that carries instructions telling cells how to grow and function. Genes are grouped together

on threadlike bodies called *chromosomes*, which are also found in all cells. The genes on chromosomes determine most of a person's physical characteristics and biochemical properties.

Most cells in the human body contain 46 chromosomes. Some, however, contain only 23. These are the sex cells: the male's sperm and the female's egg. When these male and female sex cells unite, they produce a cell called a *zygote*, which has the full human complement of 46 chromosomes. This zygote, which eventually develops into an embryo and then a fetus, has thus received genes from its father's 23 chromosomes and from its mother's 23 chromosomes. The particular mix of genes it receives determines the characteristics the baby will inherit. In other words, the genes from both parents produce a kind of blueprint for traits and development throughout an individual's life.

The way that traits are expressed in an individual depends on the specific combinations of genes inherited. For example, Ricky's father has blue eyes and his mother has brown eyes. Why did Ricky end up with brown eyes rather than blue ones? The answer lies in the genes he inherited (see Figure 3.1). Some genes, such as the gene for brown eyes, are *dominant*, which means that they suppress the action of other, weaker genes. A weak gene, called a *recessive gene*, cannot produce a trait by itself. When two sets of genetic information combine, the dominant gene (brown eyes) will suppress the recessive gene (blue eyes) and determine the specific trait (eye color). Only if two recessive genes for the same trait are present and combine will the recessive gene determine the trait.

Ricky's father has two recessive genes for blue eyes; his mother has one gene for brown eyes and one for blue. Ricky inherited a recessive gene for blue eyes from his father and a dominant gene for brown eyes from his mother, making his eyes brown. If he had inherited a recessive gene from each parent, his eyes would have been blue.

Observable traits or characteristics, such as eye color, are known as an individual's *phenotype*. The individual's underlying genetic makeup is known as the *genotype*. Phenotypically, Ricky is brown eyed; genotypically, however, he has genes for both brown eyes and blue eyes. Phenotype and genotype are both quirks of fate based on which genes an in-

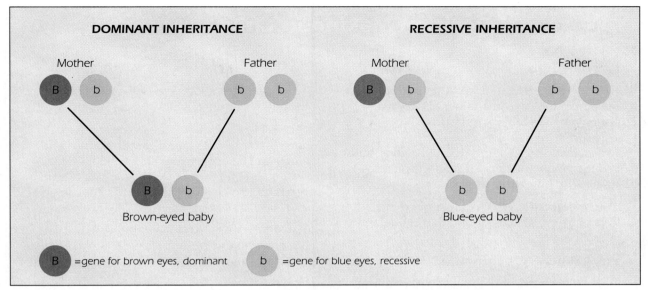

**FIGURE 3.1    Dominant and Recessive Genes.**   The baby of a brown-eyed mother (who has one gene for brown eyes and one gene for blue eyes) and a blue-eyed father can have either brown eyes or blue eyes. The baby's eye color will depend on whether the dominant gene for brown eyes or the recessive gene for blue eyes is passed on from the mother.

dividual inherits. The shuffling of genes in a sex cell can produce about eight million different combinations. Experts estimate that after an egg cell and sperm cell combine, about 70 trillion human genotypes are possible (Hetherington & Parke, 1979).

Genes are also an important factor in determining an individual's height, intelligence, and personality. In most cases, the genes a person inherits have a positive or neutral effect. Occasionally, however, inherited genes can cause birth defects or congenital disease. A number of prenatal tests have been developed to detect genetic problems, and scientists are now working on ways to alter genes and eliminate a number of potential problems.

### Heredity and Environment

Environmental factors also affect the development of an individual, both within the uterus and after birth. For example, when a substance such as alcohol passes through the umbilical cord, it can alter the prenatal environment. Such substances may interfere with the way the genes guide fetal development and result in birth defects. For this reason, it is important for a woman to make healthy decisions during pregnancy.

Many factors in the life of a child after birth can influence development. For example, a child who grows up in a nurturing family with stimulating experiences is likely to do better in school than a similar child who doesn't have these advantages. Researchers have studied twins to learn more about the roles of hereditary and environmental factors.

Since identical twins develop from the same fertilized egg, they share identical genes. Identical twins are nearly the same physically, of course. They also resemble each other psychologically. Studies such as the Minnesota Study of Twins Reared Apart, begun in 1979, document the strong influence that genes have on traits such as temperament, taste, and personality. The Minnesota study indicated that many identical siblings raised apart from infancy share numerous psychological characteristics (Bouchard, 1981). Research using twins has also underlined the importance of genetics in determining intelligence. One study compared the intelligence quotient (IQ) scores of identical twins and fraternal twins. The IQ scores of identical twins

## Prenatal Care

Emma is an aide at a rural child care center. At the end of the day, the mother of two-year-old Tommy arrives looking very tired.

EMMA: Hi! Here's Tommy. He had a great time sponge painting today. I'll send the pictures home with him when they're dry.

TOMMY'S MOTHER: What a day! I'm exhausted. This morning sickness is awful. It comes and goes all day.

EMMA: When is your baby due?

TOMMY'S MOTHER: I'm not exactly sure. I think I'm about three months along.

EMMA: Have you been to see the doctor?

TOMMY'S MOTHER: Not yet. I didn't have any trouble when I was pregnant with Tommy, so I thought I'd wait a while. Doctors are so expensive, and I don't have insurance.

EMMA: You know, the county has a free clinic for pregnant women. Some other mothers who have children here have gone to it. The doctor there is a woman, and they liked her a lot.

TOMMY'S MOTHER: Oh? Well, it's probably during the day when I'm at work.

EMMA: The clinic may have evening hours. But even if you have to take a couple hours off, it's worth it. The baby grows and develops a lot during the first three months. You want the baby to get off to a healthy start. The doctor can give you special vitamins so you'll stay healthy, too.

TOMMY'S MOTHER: At some of those clinics you have to wait forever, and then they treat you like you don't know anything about being pregnant.

EMMA: It's still a good idea to see a doctor right away and make sure everything is okay. I think we have a pamphlet about the clinic. I'll find it and give it to you tomorrow.

TOMMY'S MOTHER: Well, okay. Maybe I'll go if it's free.

*Were the reasons Emma gave for visiting the prenatal clinic early in pregnancy convincing? What other things might she have done or said to persuade Tommy's mother to go?*

were found to be much more similar than the scores of fraternal twins (Scarr & Kidd, 1983).

Other research on twins has shown that environment also plays a key role in development. Studies comparing the IQs of sets of identical twins have found a greater similarity in scores between twins who were reared together than those reared apart (Erlenmeyer-Kimling & Jarvik, 1963). In situations in which one identical twin is raised with extreme deprivation and the other with great enrichment, the effects of environment on the child are even more pronounced (Scarr & McCartney, 1983).

Studies of children in adoptive families shed further light on the influence of heredity and environment. In one long-term study, the Colorado Adoption Project (CAP), researchers concluded that heredity factors played an active role in the development of a child's environment, especially in the amount and kind of interaction with the adoptive parents (Plomin, DeFries, & Fulker, 1988). On the basis of these and other studies, many experts conclude that genes provide an innate potential for an individual's interaction with the environment. Genes influence the way an individual may develop, and they may limit certain kinds of development, but the environment in which traits emerge is also crucial.

While some traits, such as eye color, are clearly a function only of heredity, most traits are affected by both heredity and environment. Consider a person's height, for example. The potential height of an individual is determined by his genes. The ultimate height to which that person grows, however, is also affected by environment. A well-nourished, healthy individual is more likely to reach his potential maximum height than a poorly nourished, unhealthy one. The genes that enable an individual to grow to 6 feet will not be expressed if that person is deprived of adequate food during childhood. Height is an example of a *multifactorial characteristic*, one determined by the interaction of genetic predisposition and environmental conditions. Personality traits are also multifactorial. Although many individuals possess personality traits such as aggressiveness or friendliness, the way these traits are expressed is a factor of environment.

## Genetic Abnormalities

When sex cells unite to form a zygote, the random distribution of genes that occurs sometimes results in the transmission of genetic diseases or abnormalities to the developing fetus. In the United States, about 5 percent of the babies born each year have some genetically transmitted mental or physical abnormality, and about 20 percent of infant deaths result from these conditions.

### The Transmission of Genetic Abnormalities

Genetic diseases and abnormalities are transmitted in a variety of ways (see Table 3.1). One method is through a dominant gene. If one parent has a certain disorder, each child has a 50 percent chance of inheriting the dominant gene through which the disease is transmitted and getting the disease. This is the way Huntington's disease is passed on.

Genetic abnormalities can also be transmitted through recessive genes passed on by healthy parents. If only one parent has the recessive gene for the defect, he or she is considered a *carrier*. Each child has a 50 percent chance of becoming a carrier of the defect but will not contract the disease. If both parents have the abnormal recessive gene, each child has a 50 percent chance of being a carrier and a 25 percent chance of contracting the disorder. Cystic fibrosis and sickle cell anemia are transmitted through recessive genes.

Because they share identical genes, identical twins are the same physically. Studies have shown that they closely resemble each other psychologically as well.

Some genetic disorders are sex-linked, which means that they are transmitted by a recessive gene on the X chromosome. Females have two X chromosomes, while males have one X and one Y chromosome. A mother who carries a recessive abnormal gene on one of her X chromosomes has a 50 percent chance of passing the disorder on to her sons. This is because males have only one X chromosome, so they have no healthy gene to override the defective gene. Daughters may inherit a dominant healthy gene on their other X chromosome. While this means they are unlikely to have the disorder, they still have a 50 percent chance of being a carrier. Sex-linked disorders, such as color blindness and hemophilia, occur primarily in males.

Genetic abnormalities sometimes occur as a result of the interaction of genes with other genes. They may also result from the interaction of genes and environmental factors, such as alcohol or drug use. Cleft palate and spina bifida are examples of these multifactorial disorders.

Finally, genetic abnormalities may occur as a result of defective chromosomes or accidents affecting the transfer of chromosomes in the formation of eggs and sperm. For example, Down syndrome occurs when extra chromosomes are transmitted to offspring. The incidence of some chromosomal accidents increases with the age of the parents and can result in abnormalities in the developing organism.

**TABLE 3.1**
**Common Genetic Conditions and Diseases**

| Condition or Disease | Transmission and Incidence | Detection of Disorder Possible | Likely Outcome |
|---|---|---|---|
| *Cleft palate/cleft lip*<br><br>Two sides of upper lip or palate not joined | Multifactorial; drugs or injury during pregnancy; malnutrition; stress<br><br>1 in 700; varies with ethnicity | Prenatal—Sometimes<br><br>Carrier—No | Correctable with surgery |
| *Club foot*<br><br>Foot and ankle twisted | Multifactorial<br><br>1 in 300; more common in boys | Prenatal—Yes<br><br>Carrier—No | Correctable with surgery |
| *Cystic fibrosis*<br><br>Enzyme deficiency causes mucous obstruction | Recessive gene<br><br>1 in 2,000 live births among whites in U.S. | Prenatal—No<br><br>Carrier—No (1 in 25 white Americans is a carrier) | Few victims survive to adulthood |
| *Diabetes mellitus (juvenile form)*<br><br>Poor sugar metabolism due to deficiency of insulin | Recessive gene, polygenic; environmental factors may play a role<br><br>1 child in 2,500 | Prenatal—No<br><br>Carrier—No | Fatal if untreated; can be treated with insulin and diet |
| *Down syndrome*<br><br>Physical and mental retardation | Chromosomal abnormality: extra chromosome 21<br><br>1 in 600–700 births | Prenatal—Yes<br><br>Carrier—Possible in 5% of cases | Mental retardation; possible eye, ear, and heart problems |
| *Hemophilia ("bleeder's disease")*<br><br>Absence of blood clotting factor | X-linked gene; spontaneous mutation<br><br>1 in 10,000 live male births | Prenatal—No<br><br>Carrier—Yes | Possible crippling and death from internal bleeding; can be treated with blood transfusions |
| *Huntington's disease*<br><br>Deterioration of body, brain, and central nervous system in middle age | Dominant gene<br><br>Rare | Prenatal—Yes<br><br>Carrier—Yes | Fatal (possible treatment in near future) |
| *Klinefelter's syndrome*<br><br>Males fail to mature sexually at adolescence; sterility | Chromosomal abnormality; extra X chromosome (XXY)<br><br>1 in 1,000 white males in U.S. | Prenatal—Yes<br><br>Carrier—No | Emotional and social problems; treatable with testosterone |

**TABLE 3.1**
**Common Genetic Conditions and Diseases (continued)**

| Condition or Disease | Transmission and Incidence | Detection of Disorder Possible | Likely Outcome |
|---|---|---|---|
| *Muscular dystrophy (Duchenne's)* <br><br> Weakening and wasting away of muscles | X-linked gene, autosomal recessive, or multifactorial <br><br> 1 in 10,000 males under 20 years old | Prenatal—Yes <br><br> Carrier—Sometimes | Crippling; often fatal by age 20 |
| *Neural tube defects (anencephaly, spina bifida)* <br><br> Anencephaly: part of brain and skull missing; spina bifida: part of spine not closed over | Uncertain, possibly multifactorial; defect occurs in first weeks of pregnancy <br><br> Anencephaly: 1 in 1,000 live births; spina bifida: 3 in 1,000 live births | Prenatal—Yes <br><br> Carrier—No | Anencephaly: fatal; spina bifida: may survive with surgery, often have walking, bowel, and bladder control problems |
| *Phenylketonuria (PKU)* <br><br> Enzyme deficiency causes abnormal digestion of certain proteins | Recessive gene <br><br> 1 in 15,000 births (mostly whites) | Prenatal—Yes <br><br> Carrier—Sometimes | Mental retardation, hyperactivity; controllable with diet |
| *Sickle cell anemia* <br><br> Abnormal red blood cells | Recessive gene <br><br> 1 in 450 blacks in U.S. | Prenatal—Yes <br><br> Carrier—Yes (1 in 10 U.S. blacks is a carrier) | Possible heart or kidney failure; many survive to adulthood |
| *Tay-Sachs disease* <br><br> Lack of enzyme causes abnormal accumulation of waste material in nerve cells of brain | Recessive gene <br><br> 1 in 3,600 Ashkenazi Jews in U.S. | Prenatal—Yes <br><br> Carrier—Yes (1 in 30 U.S. Jews is a carrier) | Neurological degeneration; death by age 4 |

## Psychological Disorders

The relationship between genetic defects and physical abnormalities has been fairly well established. The link between genetic abnormalities and mental illness is less clear, but many experts believe that heredity plays a role in many psychological disorders. In the case of schizophrenia, it has been suggested that biological factors may predispose certain individuals to the disorder. However, stress and other environmental factors seem to trigger the disorder. Some psychological disorders do have a physical basis. Autism, for example, is now recognized as a biological disorder of the nervous system.

For a long time, it was thought that infantile autism was caused by cold, unresponsive parents. The symptoms of autism usually appear by the time a child is two and one-half years old and sometimes as early as four months old. An autistic infant may lie in his crib, oblivious and unresponding to other people. The older autistic child may not seek or want physical contact or affection, may not make eye contact with others, and may never learn to speak. Bizarre and obsessive behavior, such as having temper tantrums when the environment is slightly altered, repeating the same behavior over and over, or staring at objects for hours are also common symptoms. Autistic children are seen as living in a strange and impenetrable world of their own.

Autism is often found in conjunction with other conditions, such as epilepsy and mental retardation. Some studies suggest brain damage as a possible cause (Fein, Humes, Kaplan, Lucci, & Waterhouse, 1984). Research has shown that the brain of autistic children is not fully developed, and the failure to develop occurs during either the early prenatal period or the first two years after birth (Courchesne, Yeung-Courchesne, Press, Hesselink, & Jernigan, 1988). Considerable evidence supports the idea that heredity plays a significant role in autism (Cantwell & Baker, 1984). In studies of autism in twins, both twins were autistic in 96 percent of the cases involving identical twins; however, both twins were autistic in only 23 percent of the cases involving fraternal twins (Ritvo, Freeman, Mason-Brothers, & Ritvo, 1985).

Depression is another psychological disorder that may have a biological basis. It is considered the most serious of common psychiatric problems. Although everyone occasionally feels sad and depressed, some people suffer severe depression during which they cannot eat, sleep, or concentrate and during which they feel suicidal. Depressed people commonly feel a pervasive sense of hopelessness and withdraw from pleasurable activities. Such severe depression has even been documented in infants, making them unable to thrive (McDaniel, 1986).

Depression was long regarded as the overreaction of people to life's problems (Scarr & Kidd, 1983). Today, however, researchers believe that depression may have a biological basis and often be inherited. Laboratory studies have found that the use of certain chemical substances to elevate levels of acetylcholine, a chemical neurotransmitter in the brain that transmits messages between nerve cells, can cause bouts of depression. This evidence of a chemical link to depression has suggested to some experts that there may be a genetically varied response to the chemical stimulus. If this could be proved, it would show that depression, or a predisposition to it, is hereditary. Evidence to support this biological theory comes from studies showing that

depressed individuals and their depressed relatives have a greater sensitivity to acetylcholine than nondepressed individuals (Nadi, Nurnberger, & Gershon, 1984).

## Prenatal Development

The 266 days it takes for a human fetus to develop within its mother's uterus are in some ways more critical to future growth and development than the years after birth. This is a period of extraordinary growth and change. The initial fertilized egg is transformed into a fully formed baby, and any problems that develop during this time can have a profound effect on the future health and well-being of the individual.

The nine-month period of *gestation*, or development in the mother's uterus, is an unimaginably complicated, genetically directed process in which cells divide, assume different characteristics, and take on specialized functions. The sequence of development, which proceeds from the head downward and from the center of the body to the extremities, follows a fairly predictable timetable.

### The Stages of Prenatal Development

Prenatal development occurs in three basic stages, or periods: the germinal period, the embryonic period, and the fetal period. During each period, a number of very specific developmental events and changes take place (see Figure 3.2).

**The Germinal Stage (conception to 2 weeks).** The initial stage of prenatal development, the germinal stage, begins at conception, that is, when a sperm and egg unite to form a zygote. After conception, the zygote begins to divide and grow. Within three days, it has divided into 32 cells; a day later into 70 cells. By about the sixth day, this cell mass reaches the uterus and begins to attach itself to the uterine wall. As the cell mass continues to grow, it begins developing different layers. The outer layer, the ectoderm, will eventually develop into skin, nails, hair, teeth, sensory organs, and the nervous system. The digestive system, liver, pancreas, and respiratory system develop out of the innermost layer of cells called the

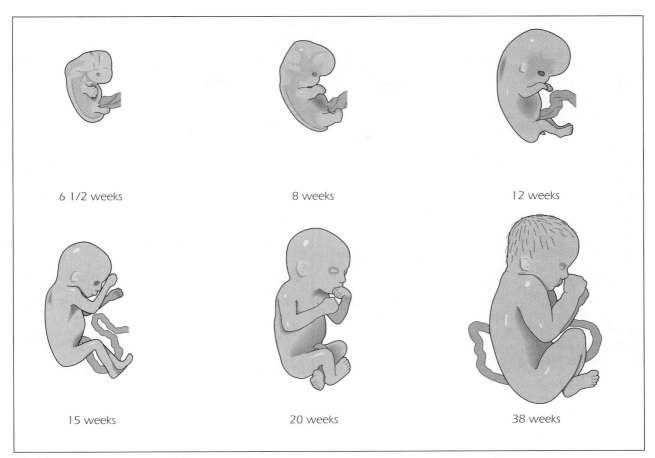

6 1/2 weeks

8 weeks

12 weeks

15 weeks

20 weeks

38 weeks

**FIGURE 3.2 Stages of Prenatal Development.**

endoderm. A middle layer of cells, the mesoderm, eventually develops into the muscles and the skeleton. The excretory, circulatory, and reproductive systems develop from the mesoderm as well. During the germinal stage, the cell mass also develops the placenta, umbilical cord, and amniotic sac that will, respectively, feed, anchor, and protect the growing embryo. By the end of two weeks, the cell mass is firmly attached to the wall of the uterus, and this marks the beginning of the next stage of development.

At the germinal stage of development, the danger of birth defects from environmental factors is not great. This is because substances that harm the prenatal environment will either affect all the cells and result in the death of the zygote or affect so few cells that the zygote can recover intact.

**The Embryonic Stage (3–8 weeks).** By the end of the first month, the growing organism, which is now called an *embryo*, is about one-half inch long. It has blood flowing through minuscule veins and arteries and a tiny heart that beats about 65 times per minute. The brain, kidneys, liver, and digestive tract are all beginning to develop. It is still too early to determine the gender of the embryo. By the eighth week, the embryo is about 1 inch long and weighs 1/13 ounce. The face is starting to develop, and buds of teeth and a tongue appear. The arms have hands and fingers, and knees, ankles, and toes are evident on the legs. During this stage, the sex organs develop, the stomach produces digestive juices, the liver makes blood cells, and the kidneys are functioning. The skin is also sensitive enough to react to touch.

**The Fetal Stage (9 weeks to birth).**   By the ninth week, the growing embryo has attained the status of a *fetus*. At about 12 weeks, the fetus is 3 inches long and weighs 1 ounce. It has fingernails, toenails, eyelids, vocal cords, lips, and a nose. The fetus can breathe and even urinate. Its ribs and backbone are formed primarily of cartilage, although the first bone cells appeared at about the eighth week. The fetus can move its legs, feet, thumbs, and head, and it has reflex behaviors if touched. As the fetus continues to develop, major body parts and organ systems grow and become more specialized as structures and functions are refined. The fetus becomes more active: kicking, stretching, even hiccuping. By the fifth month, a fetal heartbeat can be heard. The respiratory system, however, will not be developed fully enough to sustain life outside the mother until the seventh month. Babies born before the seventh month do not usually survive. During the eighth and ninth months, the brain develops significantly. The fetus also acquires a layer of fat during this time that will provide nourishment and protection in the first few days after birth.

**Critical Periods in Prenatal Development.** During certain periods of prenatal development, the embryo or fetus is particularly vulnerable. When something goes wrong during these periods, it can affect the development of a particular organ or system, leading to organ damage, malformation, and malfunction. Most birth defects—including heart defects, deafness, blindness, cleft palate, or missing limbs—occur during the first trimester (three-month period) of pregnancy (see Table 3.2). It is during this critical period that pregnant women need to pay particularly close attention to their health and nutrition in order to provide a safe and healthy prenatal environment. This means avoiding foods, drink, drugs, and other environmental hazards that may adversely affect the embryo or fetus. Unfortunately, pregnancy is not always apparent at this early stage, and a woman may not realize she is putting her child at risk. That is why a healthy lifestyle is important at all times and why a woman should seek professional medical care as soon as she suspects she is pregnant.

| TABLE 3.2 **Sensitive Periods in Prenatal Development** | | |
|---|---|---|
| **Body System** | **Highly Sensitive Period** | **Less Sensitive Period** |
| Central nervous system | 3 to 6 weeks | 6 to 38 weeks |
| Heart | 3½ to 6½ weeks | 6½ to 8 weeks |
| Arms | 4½ to 7 weeks | 7 to 8 weeks |
| Eyes | 4½ to 8½ weeks | 8½ to 38 weeks |
| Legs | 4½ to 8 weeks | 8 to 9 weeks |
| Teeth | 6¾ to 9 weeks | 9 to 16 weeks |
| Palate | 6¾ to 9¼ weeks | 9¼ to 16 weeks |
| External genitalia | 7½ to 9 weeks | 9 to 38 weeks |
| Ear | 3¼ to 9½ weeks | 9½ to 21 weeks |

### Prenatal Testing

The importance of prenatal care cannot be overemphasized. Prenatal care monitors the health of both mother and fetus and helps assure the birth of a healthy infant. For many women, prenatal care includes a number of tests during the early stages of pregnancy that can help diagnose potential problems, including genetic disorders.

One common type of prenatal testing is *ultrasound*, a noninvasive technique that uses high-frequency sound waves to detect structural disorders in a fetus, such as anencephaly, the absence of all or part of the brain. Ultrasound can also determine the presence of kidney disease and indicate the approximate age of the fetus. Another common prenatal test is amniocentesis, which is performed after the fifteenth week of pregnancy. In *amniocentesis*, a syringe is inserted through the mother's abdomen and some amniotic fluid is removed. This fluid contains "discarded" fetal cells, which can be analyzed for chromosomal abnormalities and other genetic problems and to determine the overall health of the fetus. Amniocentesis also confirms the gender of the fetus.

*Chorionic villi sampling* carries slightly more risk to the fetus than the other tests, but it can be performed earlier. It involves removing a sample of the placenta, which includes some embryonic tissue, and analyzing it for indications of genetic or developmental defects. The test can be performed in the eighth week of pregnancy, almost two months earlier than amniocentesis, which is used to detect similar problems. Other more specific tests are administered when conditions such as malformation of the fetus or a neural tube defect are suspected.

## Environmental Influences on Prenatal Development

Environmental factors arising outside the uterus can have a significant influence on the developing fetus (see Table 3.3). Anything that enters the body of a pregnant woman can affect the fetus. Some things, such as a healthful diet, will have a positive effect. Certain factors, however, can harm the fetal environment, resulting in abnormal development and birth defects. Some factors called *teratogens* include various drugs and chemical substances, disease, and radiation that pass through the placenta. Other factors such as poor nutrition, stress, and the age of the woman can also have a harmful effect on the embryo or fetus.

### Harmful Substances

Ricky's mother knew that she could control and eliminate some common substances that could have a negative effect on her unborn child. She stopped smoking because nicotine and other substances in tobacco are linked to spontaneous abortion and low birth weight babies. Studies show, for example, that a woman who smokes is twice as likely to deliver a low-weight baby as a nonsmoker (Sexton & Hebel, 1984). Ricky's mother also stopped drinking alcoholic beverages to protect her developing fetus from *fetal alcohol syndrome* (FAS). This condition, which occurs in about 50,000 newborns each year, results in infants who are addicted to alcohol, who grow slowly, and who have slow motor and

**TABLE 3.3**
**Environmental Influences on Prenatal Development**

| Environmental Factors | Possible Effects on Fetus |
| --- | --- |
| Accutane, Dilantin, tetracycline, Valium | Heart defects, mental retardation |
| AIDS | HIV infection causing vulnerability to disease; facial abnormalities |
| Alcohol | Fetal alcohol syndrome (FAS): slow motor development, facial and limb abnormalities, heart defects, mental retardation |
| DES (diethylstilbestrol) | Reproductive disorders; possible increased risk for certain cancers |
| Diabetes | Respiratory distress, low blood sugar (hypoglycemia) |
| Heroine, cocaine | Withdrawal symptoms; damage to genitourinary tract and circulatory, endocrine, and central nervous systems; behavioral problems |
| Poor nutrition | Impaired brain development, poorly developed bones and teeth, low birth weight, anemia, mental deficiency |
| Rubella | Blindness, deafness, mental retardation; effects especially severe if disease is contracted during first trimester |
| Tobacco | Low birth weight, retarded growth |
| Toxic chemicals (PCB) and radiation | Birth defects, mental deficiency |

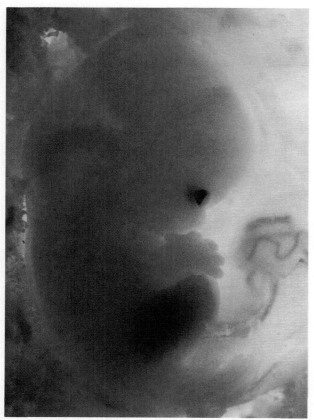

During the embryonic stage of prenatal development, the heart and kidneys begin to function, and hands, fingers, knees, and toes become evident.

intellectual development. Infants with FAS may also have a small head, abnormalities of the face and limbs, and heart defects. Studies have shown that mental retardation is one of the most serious consequences of FAS and that about 20 percent of all cases of mental retardation are caused by FAS (Abel, 1980; Hymes, 1990). Even drinking only one glass of beer or wine per day during pregnancy may have an effect on a developing fetus. Some experts believe that there is no "safe" level of alcohol consumption for pregnant women.

Use of heroin, cocaine, or other illegal drugs can cause great harm to a developing fetus. Babies born to addicted mothers are usually addicted themselves and may exhibit behavior indicative of drug withdrawal. Physiologically, these children may suffer damage to their genitourinary tract and circulatory system. Unfortunately, increasing numbers

of infants are being born to drug-addicted women. A 1991 study showed that between 13.5 and 18 percent of the infants born in the United States were exposed to one or more illicit drugs while in the uterus (Gomby & Shiorno, 1991). As such children grow older, they may continue to experience a variety of effects from the drugs, including damage to the genitourinary tract and circulatory, endocrine, and central nervous systems. These may result in behavioral problems such as impaired motor control, short attention span, lack of self-control, and aggression.

Tobacco, alcohol, and illegal drugs are not the only drugs that can harm a developing fetus. Some prescription drugs can be harmful as well. Drugs taken to control seizures (Dilantin, phenobarbital), to relieve emotional stress (Valium, Librium), to treat acne (Accutane), and to combat the common cold (tetracycline) can have a harmful effect on the fetus. Even the caffeine in coffee, tea, cola drinks, chocolate, and some over-the-counter medications can be harmful if used excessively. Because of the possible effects of such substances, it is important for a pregnant woman to tell her physician about any prescription and nonprescription drugs she takes. In many cases, reduced dosages during critical stages in prenatal development can reduce or eliminate the risk of harmful effects.

Another category of harmful substances includes toxic chemicals. These can be particularly insidious since they are often present in common household products, but people are rarely aware of them. Certain substances have been linked to the risk of birth defects and should be avoided completely. These include pesticides and herbicides, industrial chemicals, and household chemicals found in solvents, paint thinners, and furniture finishers. Another serious hazard is the chemical PCB, which, until recently, was used extensively by industry and often dumped into waterways. In some areas, certain types of fish are contaminated with PCBs or with heavy metals such as lead that can cause birth defects. These fish should not be eaten by pregnant women.

Radiation is another potential teratogen. Before having x-rays, a woman who is pregnant should make her condition known and make sure proper precautions are taken. Pregnant women should not work near radiation-producing equipment.

## Disease

A number of diseases can act as teratogens. If rubella (German measles) is contracted during the first trimester of pregnancy, it can cause serious birth defects such as blindness, deafness, and severe mental retardation. A blood test can reveal whether a pregnant woman is infected with rubella. Other teratogenic diseases include mumps, chicken pox, polio, syphilis, and diabetes. Infants of diabetic mothers have a higher than normal risk of dying shortly after birth. They are also more likely to be born with problems such as respiratory distress and low blood sugar (hypoglycemia). However, with special care and intensive monitoring during pregnancy, many infants of diabetic women are born without complications.

A pregnant woman who has acquired immunodeficiency syndrome (AIDS) or HIV, the virus that causes AIDS, may infect the fetus during the course of pregnancy or birth. In recent years, AIDS has affected tens of thousands of infants born to women with AIDS or HIV. As in adults, AIDS weakens the immune system, making the infants vulnerable to disease. Infants infected with HIV usually die within a year after the appearance of AIDS symptoms. However, some children infected with HIV at birth are now reaching their teens. It is estimated that about 10,000 children in the United States now have HIV ("Growing Up in the Shadows," 1993).

## Age

The greatest risk of stillbirths and infant deaths occurs with young teenage girls and women over the age of 35. Women in these age groups are also at greater risk than women in the optimum 20- to 30-year-old range of giving birth to children with birth defects, mental retardation, or low birth weight.

Between 1985 and 1990, the number of babies born to single teenage mothers increased by 16 percent (Center for the Study of Social Policy, 1993). Unfortunately, girls in their early teens are not yet fully mature and ready for childbearing. Moreover, they often have poor nutritional habits and thus may not provide proper nourishment for a developing fetus. At the other end of the spectrum are women who become pregnant after age 35. At this age, a woman's reproductive system is on the de-

Teenage girls run a higher risk of giving birth to babies with birth defects, mental retardation, and low birth weight.

cline. Sometimes this may result in chromosomal abnormalities that can cause birth defects, such as Down syndrome. For women of all ages, the incidence of miscarriage or birth defects is highest for the first pregnancy and after the fourth pregnancy.

## Poor Nutrition

Lack of proper nutrition at critical stages in prenatal development can have devastating effects on the embryo or fetus. For example, undernutrition during the first major period of brain growth (from the 10th to the 20th week of pregnancy) may result in impaired brain development leading to poor intellectual performance and physical development

(Werner, 1979). Children deprived of proper nourishment during such critical periods do not catch up with their peers, even if they are given nutritional supplements during childhood. If malnourishment occurs during less critical stages, providing a proper diet with nutritional supplements can help the child attain normal growth (Tanner, 1973). Deficiencies in the diets of pregnant women may lead to other problems in their infants, including poorly developed bones and teeth, low birth weight, anemia, and mental deficiency (Annis, 1978).

### Stress

Prolonged periods of anxiety, stress, or emotional upset are being studied for their possible effects on fetal development. Although the relationship is uncertain and research is, as yet, inconclusive, some researchers believe that a pregnant woman experiencing long-term severe stress may give birth to a "cranky" baby who continues to exhibit behavior problems throughout infancy.

### The Birth Process and Possible Complications

Not long ago, conventional wisdom held that infants do not develop the ability to smile until they are several weeks old. Upon emerging into the world, newborns wail and their facial expressions reveal "a mask of agony, of horror." The French obstetrician who described newborn infants, or *neonates*, this way and who was determined to change their initial experience of the world outside the womb was Frederick Leboyer. Leboyer reflected on the newborn's experience of the birth process and the causes of its "mask of agony." As he saw it, the fetus is pushed and squeezed out of the womb and its protective amniotic sac. It is thrust from a dark, floating environment of low stimulation into the brightly lighted, highly stimulating outside world. It moves from an environment with a constant, comfortable temperature into a much different one. It must breathe on its own and is no longer fed through the mother's placenta.

Reflecting on such an experience, Leboyer designed a birth environment that would reduce or eliminate as much trauma to the newborn as possible (Leboyer, 1975). In a Leboyer birthing room, the lights are dim, the room is warm and quiet, and the umbilical cord remains attached to the newborn until it has had time to adjust to its new environment. Immediately after birth, the infant is placed on its mother's stomach where it can hear her heartbeat and sense her body warmth. The baby is gently massaged to soothe it after its ordeal. Once the umbilical cord has been cut, the baby is placed in a warm bath.

Although the Leboyer method of childbirth is not widespread in the United States, the birthing environment has been modified in many places. In numerous hospitals and birthing centers, birthing rooms are furnished like bedrooms and the baby's father may be present to assist in the birth.

Today, women can choose between medicated and natural (or prepared) childbirth. During medicated delivery, the mother receives anesthetics or analgesics (painkillers) to make labor less painful. In natural childbirth, women learn relaxation techniques to make the birth process easier; painkillers may be taken as needed. In prenatal classes, such as Lamaze preparation, women learn to breathe, relax, and control the muscles that will aid in delivery. Men learn how to assist and encourage their partner.

The trend to prepared childbirth has received enthusiastic support in recent years. For one thing, research has found that drugs given during delivery may have the temporary effect of making the neonate sluggish and unresponsive (Sepkowski, 1985). In some cases, mothers may feel alienated from infants who don't respond immediately to affection or nursing. In addition, the use of anesthetics may lower the mother's blood pressure and reduce the amount of oxygen available to the fetus. This can cause significant harm. These factors have led many women to choose methods of childbirth that involve as few drugs as possible.

### The Stages of Birth

The birth process can be divided into three stages: dilation to delivery, birth, and the expulsion of the placenta. Each woman is unique, and the sequence and duration of each of these stages may vary with the individual.

**Dilation to Delivery.** Several days prior to labor, the pregnant woman's cervix begins to dilate, perhaps up to 3 centimeters (a little more than an inch). By the time of delivery, the cervix will be dilated enough, about 10 centimeters (4 inches), to allow the baby to be born. Actual labor begins with the breaking of the amniotic sac and the draining of its liquid out of the woman's body.

Lower back pain, indigestion, and abdominal cramps are also signs that labor has begun. A woman's first contractions are usually short, lasting only about 30 to 45 seconds. At first, the muscle movements occur about every 15 to 20 minutes. As labor progresses, however, contractions become more frequent and intense. Lower back pain may also intensify. Contractions build in frequency and intensity until the baby is ready to be delivered. The first stage usually lasts between 12 and 14 hours in first births and between 8 and 10 hours in subsequent births.

**Birth.** The second stage of labor begins when the woman's cervix has dilated to 10 centimeters and the head of the fetus pushes through the cervical opening into the vagina. Pain from contractions, which now occur about a minute apart and last for 60 seconds, may become severe. At this point, the woman must use her muscles to bear down and push the baby out of her body. Typically, the head appears first, and after further contractions and pushes, the rest of the infant's body emerges. This stage typically lasts from one to two hours.

**Expulsion of the Placenta.** During the final stage of the birth process, the placenta, or afterbirth, is ejected from the woman's body. The placenta is usually expelled within five to ten minutes after birth.

### Complications During the Birth Process

The birth process usually proceeds normally, with few complications. Sometimes, however, problems arise that can affect the health and well-being of the baby and the mother as well.

In certain instances, the flow of oxygen to the fetus can be dangerously reduced or cut off. This condition of oxygen deprivation is called anoxia. With too little oxygen reaching the cells, the brain and nervous system of the fetus can sustain significant damage, which may result in cerebral palsy,

**FOCUS ON Cultural Diversity**

### Cultural Attitudes Toward Circumcision

Circumcision is the cutting off of the foreskin that covers the head of the penis. It is an operation that is performed on many male infants a few days after birth.

There are many reasons why circumcisions are performed. In some cultures, people circumcise babies for religious reasons. For Jews, ritual circumcision on the eighth day after birth symbolizes a covenant with God. Followers of Islam also circumcise male children in religious celebrations.

Following World War II, male babies born in hospitals in the United States were routinely circumcised. It was believed that circumcision promotes better hygiene and prevents future health problems. This attitude is not shared by people living in Europe, parts of Asia, Australia, and even Canada, where the rate of circumcision has consistently been half that in the United States.

After a long study of the question, the American Academy of Pediatrics Task Force on Circumcision reported in 1975 that there is no absolute medical reason for circumcision. Since that time, more parents in the United States are choosing not to circumcise their sons. While about 65 percent of male newborns were circumcised in 1979, that number dropped to 59 percent in 1990 (National Center for Health Statistics).

### Children's Rights

Sarah, a child care provider, is attending a professional development workshop. One session featured a panel on children's rights. Sarah learned that there are two types of laws that specifically affect children. The first are laws that control adult behavior toward children, such as child abuse laws, child support laws, and compulsory schooling laws.

The second type of laws concern adult rights that are not extended to a minor. These include the right to medical treatment without parental consent, the right to marry without parental consent, and the rights of a minor to enter into contracts and to sue.

Two panelists had sharply differing views on what rights should be extended to children. This is what these panelists had to say.

Roger Goldberg:

"Children are part of the human family from birth. Some people argue that they are part of this family even before birth. Yet children often have their human rights violated simply because they do not have the physical and social skills necessary to insist that society respect their rights.

"In 1989, the United Nations General Assembly approved the Convention on Rights of the Child. This document outlines the economic, social, political, cultural, and civil rights of children. It sets standards for access to affordable health care from before birth. It guarantees a free primary education for all children and equal access to higher education.

"The convention prohibits discrimination against children on the basis of race, language, or religion. It also establishes the right of every child to an adequate standard of living.

"To guarantee these rights, the convention requires governments to establish antidiscrimination programs and to assist parents who cannot provide health care, education, and a reasonable standard of living for their children.

"At present, the United States has not signed the convention. I believe that it is vital to our children that we do so immediately. We must recognize the rights of children as basic to our society.

"Children should be permitted to sue to enforce their rights. They should have access to medical care, even without parental permission. Some people even advocate that the political rights of children include the right to vote. These are basic human rights and should not be dependent upon a person's age."

Emily Ramachandra:

"Adults are considered responsible for themselves. They are able to decide what is in their own best interest. Children are not physically, intellectually, or emotionally able to take responsibility for themselves and to safeguard their own interests. Because of this, the law must single out children for special attention. The law makes parents the primary guardians of their children's rights.

"All children should have adequate health care, education, and a reasonable standard of living. But whenever a parental obligation such as health care becomes a 'right' of the child, it infringes on a parent's freedom of choice.

"Of course, there are limits to a parent's freedom, which is why we have child abuse laws. However, the wholesale mandating of children's rights is not the way to improve children's lives. Instead, we need to recognize the parent-child relationship as a special kind of guardianship, legally different from other relationships.

"Children are not equipped to make all their own decisions. That is why there are arbitrary age limits for certain activities. A 10-year-old can't get a driver's license because most 10-year-olds don't have the judgment and skills necessary to drive safely. A 14-year-old cannot marry without parental consent because most 14-year-olds lack the judgment to determine whether they're ready for the legal and emotional commitments of matrimony.

"Children need to be protected, but not by giving them the same rights as adults. Society cannot afford to have children exercising their rights at the expense of their parent's or

guardian's rights. Children are different from adults and should be regarded as special under the law."

*Do you think children have a "right" to proper care? If so, who should determine whether the care they receive is adequate? Can you think of several situations where the needs of a child and the rights of his parents might conflict?*

---

epilepsy, mental retardation, and even death. Behavior problems in later life, such as hyperactivity or learning disabilities, may be linked to anoxia as well. Anoxia may occur if the umbilical cord is wrapped around the fetus's neck during birth or if the umbilical cord is pinched during delivery. Maternal fatigue during delivery may also contribute to fetal anoxia. The condition can arise during pregnancy if the mother smokes or is anemic.

Another possible complication of pregnancy is a breech birth. In normal births, the baby's head emerges from the woman's body first, followed by the rest of the body. In breech births, however, another part of the baby's body—usually the buttocks, feet, or even the umbilical cord—is positioned to emerge first from the cervix. Complications may arise if the infant is not repositioned. A pinched umbilical cord occurs more commonly in breech births than in normal births.

When a pregnancy involves potentially dangerous conditions, such as breech birth, anoxia, fetal distress, prolonged or obstructed labor, maternal diabetes, or genital herpes, doctors may decide to remove the baby surgically from the mother's uterus. This procedure is called a cesarean section, or C-section. In a C-section, the mother is first anesthetized and prepared for surgery. Then an incision is made in her abdomen, and the baby is lifted out of the uterus. If the baby is experiencing anoxia or other problems, he or she is rushed to a neonatal intensive care unit for immediate treatment.

There is some controversy in the United States today about the use of cesarean sections. The percentage of C-sections has risen from less than 5 percent of all births in 1965 to over 23 percent in 1990 (Taffel, Tlacek, & Kosary, 1992). Although the need for C-sections in specific life-threatening situations is undisputed, critics maintain that many cesarean sections are performed because doctors fear malpractice lawsuits, not because the procedure is medically necessary.

### Assessing the Health of the Newborn

After a baby is born, professionals examine the newborn to make sure he or she is healthy and to evaluate how the newborn has coped with the trauma of birth and the task of breathing on his or her own. They do this by using a device called the *Apgar scale.* An Apgar score is obtained by observing the newborn at 1 minute, 5 minutes, and sometimes 15 minutes after birth. Five categories are evaluated during this observation: appearance (skin color), pulse (heart rate), grimace (reaction to slight pain), activity (motor response and tone), and respiration (breathing adequacy). Each category is scored 0, 1, or 2. A total score of 7 or above usually indicates that the newborn is doing well. A score of between 5 and 7 indicates that the newborn may require some additional care. A score of 4 or below indicates a life-threatening situation requiring immediate medical attention.

## Premature and Low Birth Weight Babies

It is estimated that about 10 percent of babies born in the United States are born prematurely (between the 20th and 37th week of pregnancy) and that 7 percent have low birth weight (less than 5 pounds) (National Center for Health Statistics, 1990). Small birth size can be a result of premature delivery, retarded growth and development in the uterus, or both. Overall, premature babies ("preemies") and babies with low birth weight from other causes account for 85 percent of neonatal deaths. Premature babies are also at greater risk than full-term infants for developmental problems in later years. One study of babies 42 weeks old found that the "preemies" displayed greater stress on awaking than full-term babies and also showed some motor and neurological problems (Duffy, Als, & McAnulty, 1990).

Despite the problems associated with premature birth, more premature infants and low birth weight babies are now surviving and developing normally as a result of better methods of caring for them. For extremely premature infants (some weighing as little as a pound), neonatal intensive care units are designed to be as "womblike" as possible, with little stimulation, low lights, and little noise. For less severely premature infants, occasional tactile stimulation, such as gentle stroking and massaging, is used to improve their development. To help prevent the respiratory problems that are common in premature infants, drug therapy is used.

Numerous studies point to the benefits of providing counseling, medical, and other support services for the parents of premature and low birth weight babies ("Preemies' IQ," 1990). This support is designed to reassure the parents and help them cope with the stress of dealing with premature infants. As these infants get older, specially designed programs can be beneficial in helping them develop normally.

A number of different factors may contribute to the incidence of premature birth or low birth weight infants. The first is age: physically immature teenage girls are more likely than mature girls and women to have low birth weight babies. A woman's physical and medical condition may also be a factor; there is a high incidence of low birth weight babies among women who are extremely underweight, who have had another birth very recently, or who have anemia, chronic hypertension, or diabetes. Very premature labor is another factor. This is sometimes brought on by the mother smoking, drinking alcohol, abusing drugs, or being malnourished.

Malnourishment and poor prenatal care are, unfortunately, often found in women living in poverty. Thus, poor women with little access to medical care are most at risk for giving birth to low birth weight babies. Community and privately sponsored prenatal programs that provide education, nutritious food, and medical care can go a long way toward preventing the prevalence of low birth weight infants among such women.

*Advances in neonatal care have increased the chances for survival of premature and low birth weight babies. These infants need intensive medical care and often spend their first few months in the hospital.*

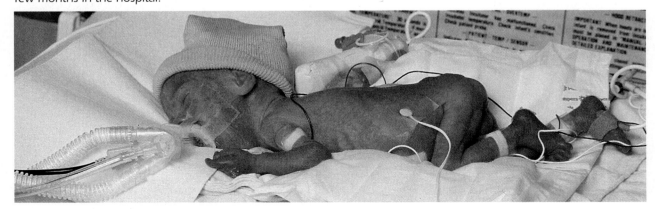

## FOCUS ON | **Communicating with Children**

### Where Babies Come From

It is share time at the Palm Grove Child Care Center. Luz, the caregiver, is sitting on the floor in a circle with six five-year-olds. The children have been asked to tell about something that has happened to them recently. Raymond, usually a quiet child, can hardly wait to speak.

RAYMOND [excited]: Guess what! I'm getting a brother.

ANOTHER CHILD: Where are you getting him?

RAYMOND: He's growing in my mom's stomach. When he gets big he'll come out.

ANOTHER BOY: How do you know its going to be a brother?

RAYMOND: 'Cause I told my mom I didn't want any girl babies at our house.

LUZ: Raymond, it's wonderful that your mother is pregnant. But you know the baby could be either a girl or boy. Your mom can't choose which one she wants. She won't know until the baby is born whether it's a girl or boy. Do you all want to talk about babies? [*The children nod.*] Well, every baby has a mother and father.

GIRL [*upset*]: That's not true. I don't have a daddy. I just have a mommy.

LUZ: Your family is the people you live with who take care of you. You live with your mother. Some children live with their aunt or their grandmother. Some children live with just their father. But to make a baby, you need a man and a woman.

RAYMOND: My dad said Mommy's stomach is going to get real big and fat and stick out.

LUZ: Babies grow in a special place in the mother called the uterus. Raymond is right; his mother's stomach is going to stick out because the baby is growing inside her. When the baby is a little bigger, Raymond will be able to put his hands on his mother's stomach and feel the baby kicking inside.

RAYMOND: Then it's going to kick its way out of the hole where she pees.

LUZ: Not exactly. When the baby has grown enough, your mother will use her muscles to push it out. She pushes it out of a special place called the vagina.

RAYMOND: Can I bring the baby in for share time?

LUZ: The baby has to grow inside your mother for a long time—for nine months. You'll be in kindergarten by the time the baby is born.

RAYMOND [*sounding sad*]: Oh! I don't want to wait that long to have a brother to play with.

*Do you think the information Luz gave the children about babies was appropriate for their age? How would you have responded to what Raymond shared with the class? What are some other questions children of this age might ask about pregnancy and birth? How would you answer those questions?*

### Implications and Applications

People who care for children must take the individual character traits of their young charges into account, as well as their individual physical and mental abilities and disabilities. Some of these children's traits may be genetically programmed; others are learned or environmentally based. Child care professionals can best serve the children in their care by understanding the origins of the children's diverse qualities and responding accordingly to their needs.

By providing ample opportunities for physical play, parents and caregivers can encourage children to develop and hone motor skills.

## Nature Versus Nurture

In the early part of this chapter, you read about the influence of heredity and environment. For decades, experts have been engaged in the debate over "nature versus nurture," arguing whether individual traits are determined by heredity or environment. In recent years, many developmental psychologists have begun to discard this either/or argument in favor of a more interactionist approach. Proponents of this approach regard an infant as genetically equipped with a variety of potentials that may or may not develop, depending on the opportunities offered by the environment. They believe that neither heredity nor environment has complete control over a child's development. Genes are the foundation of the child's innate potential, while the environment is the context in which this potential is or is not realized.

This view has significant implications for child care providers. Consider the studies of twins discussed earlier in the chapter. Researchers have found that identical twins separated at birth share a remarkable number of physical, intellectual, and emotional characteristics as adults but that different childhood environments lead to individual differences. The impact of the environment on the development of the child points to the critical role of the child care environment today as more children spend more time in day care and preschools. An enriching environment with attentive and caring child care professionals can contribute to maximizing a child's physical, intellectual, and social and emotional development.

## Physical Growth and Development

Physical growth refers to the increase in body size and changes in body proportions that occur as one grows older. Physical development, or maturation, involves a subtler reorganization of anatomy and physiology, such as changes in motor skills. The relationship between a child's physical growth and the environment is often rather obvious. For example, a child may have the genetic potential to grow to be 6 feet 4 inches tall, but if his environment does not provide enough healthful foods, his body will probably not attain that height. In less obvious ways, changes in physical development are also related to the environment. For example, the continuous refining of a child's motor skills may determine how the child interacts with the world and, thus, how well she learns, relates to others, and so on. By encouraging children to hone their motor skills through challenging and engaging activities, caregivers are providing an environment in which the individual's physical development can flourish. Allowing an infant plenty of exercise develops muscles that will help the child walk; depriving a child of exercise hinders the child's maturation in this area. In fact, long-term deprivation of any of an infant's needs—nutrition, affection, exercise, play—will very likely slow the process of maturation.

## Intelligence

The nature versus nurture controversy has probably been most hotly debated in relation to intelligence. Behavioral geneticists have conducted more studies of intelligence than of all other traits combined (Plomin, 1983). The results of these studies are often contradictory. Some conclude that heredity determines intelligence; others demonstrate the overriding influence of environment. The truth most likely lies somewhere in between: both heredity and environment play a role in the development of intelligence.

Twin and adoption studies, such as the ones mentioned earlier, are the most helpful in addressing this issue. The studies do not conclusively resolve the nature versus nurture debate, but they do provide evidence suggesting that an intellectually enriching environment may play a significant role in a child's intellectual development.

This information is important to child care professionals. Caregivers work with many children, and each has a different intellectual potential. Yet by providing a rich and stimulating environment, they can give each child the opportunity to develop his or her intelligence to its fullest.

## Personality

In the past, many people viewed a newborn baby as a *tabula rasa*, or blank slate, on which they could inscribe the temperament and personality traits they thought fitting and desirable. Today, however, personality is generally accepted to be a genetically based phenomenon that can be modified by environmental factors and experience. One study has shown that traits of temperament, such as acceptance of new people and situations, sensitivity to noise and bright light, and a tendency toward cheerfulness or unhappiness, are present in infants almost from birth (Thomas, Chess, & Birch, 1968). Research has also supported a genetic basis for personality traits ranging from shyness to nail biting, sleepwalking, and motion sickness (Kagan, Reznick, Clarke, Snidman, & Garcia-Coll, 1984). These findings may shed some light on ways in which caregivers can effectively deal with children who have different personalities. The message for caregivers seems to be that while a child's behavior and temperament can be modified somewhat, for the most part it is necessary to learn to work with the personalities of children as they exist.

## Enriching the Environment

Most research points to the conclusion that the inborn genetic tendencies of an infant are primarily potentials that can be enhanced by the opportunities afforded by an enriched environment. In addition to the basic physical requirements of good nutrition, plenty of rest, and adequate medical care, infants need the opportunity to develop motor skills and cognitive and language skills. And they need the more subtle enhancement of emotional support.

The nurturing, care, attention, and sense of security and worth an infant receives from his or her family are formative experiences that often lay the foundation of that individual's lifelong outlook on the world and relationships with others. The social and emotional development arising out of these initial experiences constitute what psychologist Erik Erikson describes as "basic trust versus basic mistrust"—attitudes that may affect the individual's entire life.

Unfortunately, infants born into families that are dysfunctional are usually severely deprived in

A stimulating and enriched learning environment can help reverse the effects of poverty-based deprivation early in life.

terms of their social and emotional needs. Poverty can also significantly limit many aspects of an infant's formative environment. Infants born to impoverished mothers may suffer from poor nutrition (both before and after birth), inadequate medical care, and lack of attention. The home may not be in good repair; moveover, if the family lives in an old building, there is a danger of peeling, lead-based paint, which can cause brain damage in young children. In addition, schools in low-income areas are far more likely to be underfunded and overcrowded, providing fewer educational challenges and opportunities for students. Being born into such an impoverished environment often re-

sults in impaired or less-than-optimum development of a child.

Child care professionals have the opportunity to help enrich the environment of all children. Child care programs that provide good nutrition, a stimulating learning atmosphere, and emotional support can enhance children's optimal development. A gifted and caring teacher or child care provider can also help reverse the effects of poverty-based deprivation and encourage children to reach their full potential. All children, no matter what their innate genetic inheritance, can and will thrive in an environment enriched by varied educational opportunities and the loving attention of caregivers.

# CHAPTER 3   REVIEW

## SUMMARY

- The basic units of inherited characteristics are called genes. Found in every living cell, these genes are grouped together on structures called chromosomes.
- The way traits are expressed in an individual depends on the specific combinations of genes inherited. Observable traits are known as phenotype, while underlying genetic makeup is called genotype.
- An individual's traits and characteristics are determined by both heredity and environment.
- Some individuals carry genes for disease or defects that may be passed on to their offspring. These genes may sometimes be affected by the prenatal environment. Abnormal genes—caused by genetic mutations or teratogens—may cause birth defects in an embryo or fetus.
- The human fetus develops in a woman's womb for about 38 weeks. This period of gestation includes three stages: germinal, embryonic, and fetal.
- Prenatal medical testing can often detect fetal malformations or disease.
- Environmental influences, such as chemicals and drugs, certain diseases, age, stress, and poor maternal nutrition, can have a serious effect on prenatal development.
- The three stages of the birth process are dilation to delivery, birth, and expulsion of the placenta. Complications during this process, such as anoxia or breech birth, can affect the health and well-being of the baby.
- Medical personnel assess the health of newborns using a device called the Apgar scale.

- Small birth size may be a result of premature delivery or retarded growth and development. Teenage mothers and women over 35 are more likely than other women to have low birth weight babies.

- Natural childbirth, which uses relaxation techniques to make the birth process easier, is generally healthy for both mother and child. However, in cases of anoxia, breech birth, and certain other conditions, a cesarean section may be required.

- Although heredity provides the potential for development, environment provides the context in which the genetic potential can be realized. A loving, stimulating environment can ensure the optimum development of a child and, in some cases, help overcome environmental deprivations.

## BUILDING VOCABULARY

Write a definition for each vocabulary term listed below.

amniocentesis
Apgar scale
carrier
chorionic villi sampling
chromosome
DNA
dominant gene
embryo
fetal alcohol syndrome
fetus
gene

genotype
gestation
heredity
multifactorial characteristic
neonate
phenotype
recessive gene
teratogen
ultrasound
zygote

## ACQUIRING KNOWLEDGE

1. Define heredity.
2. What is a zygote?
3. What is the difference between a dominant gene and a recessive gene?
4. Explain how phenotype differs from genotype.
5. Why are studies of identical twins important for determining whether certain characteristics result from heredity or environment?
6. Define and give an example of a multifactorial characteristic.
7. Describe one way that genetic diseases or abnormalities are transmitted from parents to children.
8. What is autism?
9. What are the three basic stages of prenatal development?
10. Why is the danger of birth defects not as great during the germinal stage as in the other stages of prenatal development?
11. During which period of pregnancy do most birth defects occur?
12. What is amniocentesis used for?
13. What is a teratogen? Give two examples.
14. Name three factors that can be harmful to a developing baby.
15. At what ages are women at greater risk for giving birth to babies with birth defects, mental retardation, and low birth weight?

16. Describe the possible effects of poor nutrition on a fetus.
17. Explain the Leboyer method of childbirth.
18. Why do many physicians advise women to take as few drugs as possible during delivery?
19. What is the afterbirth?
20. What conditions in pregnancy might lead a physician to perform a cesarean section?
21. What is the Apgar scale and how is it used?
22. Why is counseling important for the parents of a premature or low birth weight baby?
23. Why are poor women at risk for having low birth weight babies?
24. What is the nature versus nurture debate?
25. What is the most important aspect of an infant's environment?
26. Explain how poverty can influence an infant's development.

## THINKING CRITICALLY

1. It is now generally recognized that many individual traits are determined by a combination of heredity and environment. What implications do you think this recognition has for child care providers?
2. Teratogens are environmental factors, such as tobacco, alcohol, and toxic chemicals, that can significantly harm a developing fetus. How can information about teratogens be useful to child care professionals?
3. Studies have shown that poverty can significantly reduce the chances of a baby being born healthy. What do you think could be done to ensure that every child has a chance for a healthy start? What do you think the government's role should be? Explain.
4. It is often difficult to tell whether developmental problems in children are the result of heredity or environment. The issue is a sensitive one for parents because they may feel that they somehow caused a child's difficulties. What information do you think preschools should request about a child's background, especially with respect to developmental problems?
5. Significant advances in the care of premature babies has meant that more infants are surviving at lower birth weights. However, such intensive medical care is very expensive and often cannot prevent the severe problems that extremely premature babies will have throughout their lives. Who do you think should pay for this care? How do you think decisions should be made about whether or not to treat such babies?

## OBSERVATIONS AND APPLICATIONS

1. Tour a neonatal unit of a hospital. Tours are routinely given to expectant parents. Most hospitals should be willing to add you to a tour if you make arrangements in advance. Do labor, the birth process, and recovery all take place in one room or in different rooms? What does a labor room look like? Is the Leboyer method ever used at the hospital? Were babies in the nursery wrapped in traditional pink and blue? What is the hospital's

policy about babies rooming with their mother? How long is the average stay for a vaginal delivery? For a cesarean? If possible, also visit a local birthing center. What are the differences between having a baby at a birthing center and at the hospital? What provisions have been made at the birthing center for emergency situations that arise during childbirth?

2. Visit a child care center that accepts infants. What is the minimum age of infants accepted? What special provisions, if any, must be made for them? What is the infant-caregiver ratio? How often do caregivers pick up and hold the infants?

3. Suppose that a four-year-old boy named Brian attends the child care center where you are employed. Brian has an extremely short attention span. He even has trouble sitting still long enough to listen to a brief story. When his mother asks how he is doing, you tell her that you are trying to help Brian increase his attention span. His mother replies, "Oh, you won't have much luck. He takes after me. I'm the same way. It's a hereditary trait. My mother always reminds me that I couldn't sit still for even five minutes as a child." How would you respond?

4. Imagine that the mother of a child in your child care center confides to you that she thinks she may be pregnant. The woman has been on a diet for some months and has already lost 40 pounds. She tells you that until she finds out for sure that she is pregnant, she is going to stick to her diet, which involves drinking a diet milkshake for breakfast, eating a diet granola bar for lunch, and drinking another diet milkshake for dinner. What advice would you give this mother?

## SUGGESTIONS FOR FURTHER READING

Berezin, N. (1983). *The gentle birth book: A practical guide to Leboyer family-centered delivery*. New York: Pocket Books.

Farber, S. L. (1981). *Identical twins reared apart: A reanalysis*. New York: Basic Books.

Goldberg, S., & Devitto, B. (1983). *Born too soon. Preterm birth and early development*. San Francisco: Freeman.

Guttmacher, A. F. (1984). *Pregnancy, birth, and family* (rev. ed.). New York: Signet.

Jacob, F. (1976). *The logic of life: A history of heredity*. New York: Vintage Books.

Maurer, D., & Maurer, C. (1989). *The world of the newborn*. New York: Basic Books.

Nance, S. (1982). *Premature babies*. New York: Berkley.

Nightingale, E. O., & Goodman, M. (1990). *Before birth: Prenatal testing for genetic disease*. Cambridge, MA: Harvard University Press.

Nilsson, L., Sundberg, A., & Wirsen, C. (1981). *A child is born*. New York: Dell.

Smotherman, W. P., & Robinson, S. R. (1988). *Behavior of the fetus*. Caldwell, NJ: Telford Press.

Tannenhaus, N. (1988). *Preconceptions*. Chicago: Contemporary House.

# 4

# Impact of Family

## OBJECTIVES

Studying this chapter will enable
you to

- Describe different types of families
  and examine the effect of different
  family patterns and circumstances
  on child development.
- Identify different styles of
  parenting and explain how those
  styles influence children's behavior.
- Describe the specific roles of
  mothers, fathers, and siblings in
  the family structure.
- Discuss how child care
  professionals can help families
  cope with the stresses of parenting
  and deal with changes within the
  family.

B OBBY WATERS was always one of the most cheerful, cooperative, and outgoing children in June's preschool class. He was an even-tempered three-and-a-half-year-old who seemed largely unaffected by his parents' separation two months earlier. Then June began to notice a change in Bobby. He became aggressive, hitting other children and demanding their toys. He cried, had frequent temper tantrums, and at times seemed anxious and fearful.

June decided to discuss the situation with Mrs. Waters. Bobby's mother was concerned. She said that she had noticed similar changes in Bobby at home. He was uncooperative and angry. He did not want to visit his father, but neither did he want to leave his father at the end of their visits. He had also occasionally reverted to wetting the bed at night.

"Give him some time," June advised Mrs. Waters. "This kind of behavior is pretty normal after a separation. Young children often think they are losing one parent and are afraid of losing the other as well. They may also believe that they are responsible for the separation because they did something wrong or weren't lovable enough."

June stopped for a moment to glance around the room. "The only thing I can suggest is that you and your husband continue to maintain a warm, loving relationship with Bobby and try to reassure him that you will both always be there for him. Tell him that the separation is not his fault and that his father and you are happier apart. If there are no additional complications," she assured Mrs. Waters, "I think you will probably see Bobby return to his old self in a few months."

June was right. Within a few months Bobby seemed to have adjusted to the new family situation. His bed-wetting, aggressiveness, and anxieties gradually disappeared, and his easy-going personality reemerged.

Mrs. Waters told June about the signs of improvement in Bobby's attitude and behavior. Then she added, "It's difficult to know what to expect or what to do when you're suddenly on your own, like I was. I appreciate your helping me understand what was happening with Bobby."

## The Influence of the Family on Young Children

The family is by far the most important influence on children's lives. In most cases, parents, siblings, and other family members make up a child's first world and provide for the child's physical and emotional needs.

Family members interact with each other continually and in many complex ways. Moreover, their relationships change because a family is not a static entity but a dynamic group in which change can occur suddenly and frequently. Children are born and grow up; older siblings move out of the household; parents change jobs; parents separate or divorce; families move; grandparents retire and move away; family members die. Any of these changes may affect a child profoundly and sometimes in unpredictable ways. Such changes may cause stress and require major readjustments within the family.

This was the case in the Waters family. Brad and Jill Waters started out as a loving couple who joyfully welcomed Bobby into their midst. Eventually, the husband and wife decided to end their marriage and have Bobby live with his mother. Each family member had to make adjustments to the new situation and to modified relationships with other family members.

In any type of family there are many variables that shape the child's environment and affect the way the child develops. These factors include the parents' age, level of education, and economic status; the number of other people in the family and the child's position—youngest, oldest, in the middle—among siblings; the health of family members; and the family's ethnic background.

### The Family's Support System

A family's *support system* is any combination of family members, friends, and health and child care professionals that help the family function successfully. A key issue in child development is the kind of support system each family has. When a family is in crisis, family members usually turn to other family members or friends for emotional, financial, and practical support. For example, working parents may drop their baby off at Grandma's every day on their way to work. Or a young single mother may move back into her parents' home with her baby while she finishes school.

The family is a child's most important source of physical and emotional support. The way that family members interact is complex and constantly changing, and it can have a great influence on a child's development.

The family's support system may also include various community resources, such as schools and recreational organizations, social service agencies, and medical clinics. A good support system is especially important for single-parent families and for families in which both parents work outside the home.

## Family Trends

Families today are smaller than those of earlier generations. The *birthrate*, or ratio between births per year and the total population, peaked in 1957. In the years since then, the birthrate has gradually declined or remained stable (National Center for Health Statistics). The average American family now includes either one or two children.

Families today come in increasingly diverse forms. A child care professional is likely to work with children from two-parent, single-parent, blended, and multigenerational families and possibly from interracial and gay families as well. In many two-parent families, both the mother and father work outside the home. In the past, women with preschool-aged children tended to stay at home with the children. Now more than half of these women go to work. In addition, an increasing number of women are waiting until they are in their thirties before starting their families. Some may decide to work until they and their partner feel financially secure; others want to work long enough to establish a career. These women tend to return to the workplace after having their babies rather than stay at home.

American families are also highly mobile. Every year nearly one out of five American families moves across town or across the country (Bureau of the Census, 1990). Long-distance moves often separate people from extended families and friends and other support systems they have developed.

## Different Types of Families

Children are born into many different types of families (see Figure 4.1). The two-parent family is still the norm in the United States, but other types of family groupings have become more common in recent years. Today, one-fourth of American children live in single-parent homes. In some cases, the

Moving away from relatives and friends separates families from support systems they have developed over time.

mother never married; in others, the parents separated or divorced, or a parent died while the child was young.

An *extended family* is an arrangement that includes a parent (or parents), children, and one or more relatives (uncles, aunts, grandparents, cousins). When an extended family consists of two or more generations, it is called a multigenerational family. Today, almost a million children are being brought up by their grandparents because their parents are incapable or unwilling to care for them. Alcohol abuse, drug addiction, and teen pregnancy are some of the reasons for this situation.

## Two-Parent Families

According to the U.S. Census Bureau, most families in this country are still based on the traditional two-parent model. The 1990 census showed that 75 percent of American children under 18 years of age lived in a household with two parents.

In two-parent homes, both parents contribute to the social, emotional, and intellectual development of the child. In most cases, the parents provide primary support systems for each other. Together they develop a mutual system of beliefs, parenting styles, and practices that becomes the family culture. Their personalities, beliefs, goals, and desires

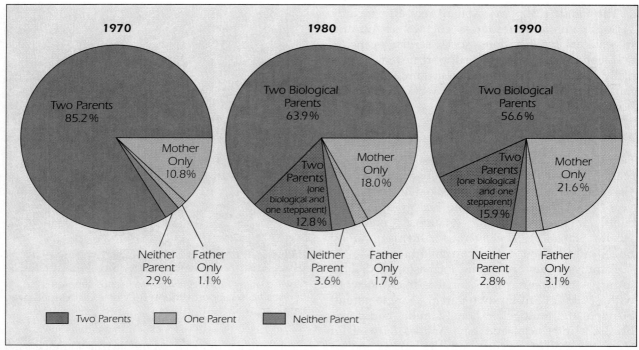

**FIGURE 4.1    Different Types of Families.**    Children under 18 living with two parents, with a single parent, with neither parent.

have an enormous impact on the way children respond to the world.

In today's two-parent family, both parents are likely to work outside the home. This reduces the amount of time they can spend with their children. On the other hand, it provides more financial resources to invest in the family. In homes where both parents work, the parents usually must make some kind of arrangement for the care of their children during the working day. This may involve a grandparent, a live-in or at-home child care provider, family day care, or some form of child care center or preschool.

**Single-Parent Families**

In more than 75 percent of single-parent homes, the parent is separated or divorced from his or her spouse or the spouse has died. The remaining 24 percent of single-parent homes are made up of mothers who never married. As in Bobby's family, the overwhelming majority of single-parent families are headed by mothers. In 1991, only 3.8 percent

of American families were headed by single fathers (Lewin, 1992).

Single-parent families are often under much more emotional and financial stress and have fewer resources than two-parent families. Bobby's mother had to return to work full-time after she and her husband separated. Each parent maintained a separate household. Although Bobby's father saw him on a regular basis, the father and son were spending far less time together than they had before the separation.

Every year about one million American children move from two-parent to one-parent households as a result of separation or divorce. Before the parents separate, they often go through a period of emotional conflict that can have a lasting effect on the children, causing more developmental problems than the actual separation. In one study, marital conflict resulted in an increase in behavioral problems and juvenile delinquency among the children in the families studied (Rutter, 1981). Some researchers believe that it may be more beneficial for children to grow up in a single-parent home than to grow up in a home where bitter, feuding parents "stay together for the sake of the children" (Block, Block, & Gjerde, 1986; Hetherington, Cox, & Cox, 1982).

Divorced parents often go through an extremely stressful period of emotional turmoil in which they feel inadequate, lonely, and anxious. The custodial parent must assume the roles of both father and mother in guiding and nurturing the children, often without the advice and support of the absent mate. In addition, one-parent families headed by women tend to be poorer than two-parent families or those headed by men. Most single mothers work full-time, but their average salary is less than $20,000 a year. All of these factors—working, trying to perform parental duties, and adjusting to a lower income—can lead to "role overload," causing enormous stress within the family.

A crucial factor in coping with the stresses of divorce or separation is the network of support that is available to the single-parent family. A single mother's father or brothers may be called upon to supply the male interaction that an absent father once provided. A single father's mother, sister, or other female

After a divorce, noncustodial parents must often make special arrangements to visit their children. Many noncustodial parents, such as this father, spend time with their children on weekends or holidays.

A majority of American children live in two-parent homes such as this one. In two-parent families, both parents foster the child's development and provide support for each other.

relatives often help fill the void of an absent mother. Child care professionals also play an important role in providing support for single-parent families. In Bobby's case, for example, June, his preschool teacher, noticed his unhappiness and discussed her concerns with Bobby's mother. She thus became a key element in the support system of the Waters' family.

### Blended Families

A child's life may also be altered by the addition of a new parent to the family. Many widowed and divorced parents remarry and combine their households. Children may acquire not only a new father or mother but new step-siblings as well. About

### Responsibility to the Custodial Parent

Yolanda and her aide at the Laurel Gardens Preschool knew that Sara's parents had recently gone through an unpleasant divorce. It had been a difficult time for all concerned, but it was over. They also knew that Sara's mother, Tracy, had gained custody of the child and that Tracy seemed determined to make a secure and happy home for her daughter.

One afternoon as Yolanda returned from a walk with the class, she was surprised to see Sara's father waiting for them outside the building. "I've come to pick up Sara," he said; "Tracy's sick." Taking his car keys out of his pocket, he moved closer to Sara.

Yolanda shifted uncomfortably. "Just a minute. Tracy didn't call to let us know you'd be coming." Sara's father replied, "She's feeling real bad. She probably forgot to call."

"Perhaps," said Yolanda, walking over to Sara and taking her firmly by the hand. "But just the same, I need to know that we have her permission. I'll just see if there's a message from her in the office."

Taking Sara with her, Yolanda walked quickly to the director's office. There was no message, but she explained the situation to the director. The director went out to speak with Sara's father, but his car was already pulling out of the driveway as she emerged from the building.

Yolanda had responded quickly to a possibly threatening situation. Fortunately, just a few weeks earlier, the director had reviewed the school's policy regarding noncustodial parents. She had advised the teachers that unless they were specifically told by the custodial parent to release the child to the noncustodial parent, the noncustodial parent could not take the child from the center under any circumstances.

*If you had been in Yolanda's position, what would you have done? Do you think she might have responded differently if the school had not had a clear policy regarding noncustodial parents?*

---

seven million American children now live in such blended families. Children in blended families have to adjust to the new parent and to relationships with step-grandparents and others in the new extended family. Children must also adjust to new siblings and to a new position in the family order. The oldest child in a single-parent family may now become a middle child in the blended family. Most step-siblings get along well when they live together, but if they are close in age, sibling rivalries may become very intense. Each child is apt to think that the stepparent gives favored treatment to his or her own children (Hetherington et al., 1982). Families headed by gay parents are also sometimes blended families. The children in these families may come from a parent's previous marriage.

Children in newly blended families may have to deal with moving to a new home and new school. Sometimes they have problems with a noncustodial parent who resents the intrusion of the new stepparent into the family relationship. All these changes require major adjustments. Some children develop the same sort of behavioral problems when faced with the remarriage of a parent as they did during the divorce.

An important issue in blended families is what role the stepparent will play in parenting the children. Disagreements over parenting can cause major conflicts between parents and between stepparent and child. Nevertheless, the effect of a remarriage on children is usually positive. The relationship between a child and stepparent seems to develop more smoothly if the two are of the same gender. Boys especially seem to benefit from the presence of a stepfather (Santrock, Warshak, & Elliott, 1982). Furthermore, children may derive an indirect benefit from a new stepparent who provides emotional

Multigenerational families are on the rise in the United States. While parents and grandparents may disagree on how children should be raised, the children often benefit from additional nurturers, role models, and mentors.

support to the parent, relieving the stress of single parenthood. This may enable the parent to be more attentive to the children. If both spouses work, the financial stress on the family is usually reduced. Unfortunately, the divorce rate for second marriages is high. Children who are forced to go through a second cycle of separation and change suffer considerable emotional stress.

### Other Types of Families

**Multigenerational Families.** The extended family that includes more than two generations living in the same household has become increasingly common. Multigenerational households, in which grandmothers, sisters, aunts, and cousins all participate in raising the children in the family, are the customary pattern in many cultures, especially in rural Africa and Asia. The pattern is often repeated when people from African and Asian cultures immigrate to the United States.

The multigenerational household may be a temporary arrangement caused by economic factors. For example, if a young couple with a toddler cannot afford a home of their own, they may move in with the husband's parents. The arrangement carries the potential for intergenerational conflict between parents and grandparents over such issues as feeding and discipline or the disruption caused by having a young child in the house. At the same time, however, grandparents can provide an invaluable support system to young parents, and the children benefit from additional nurturers, role models, and mentors.

**Teenage-Parent Families.** Families in which the parents are teenagers present a number of special problems. The parents are often immature and not equipped to support a family financially or emotionally. In most cases, the mother is the one who takes care of the child or children. She may not have finished high school and may have no means of supporting herself and her child. She is likely to rely on her parents for some financial support and possibly to share the parenting responsibilities. Teen mothers who do not marry or live with their own parents must often rely on welfare.

The number of teenage mothers is increasing in the United States. About 13 percent of all babies are born to teenage mothers and about two-thirds of these mothers are unmarried. What is particularly alarming is that the greatest increase is occurring among young teens 15 to 17 years of age (Children's Defense Fund, 1991).

**Interracial/Intercultural Families.**   Marriages in which the partners come from different races, ethnic groups, or cultural or religious backgrounds have become more common in recent years. Such marriages often present special challenges. In the case of an interracial marriage, the couple and their children not only must cope with the usual problems of adjustment that occur in every family but must also confront a number of broader issues. These may include racial prejudice, different and perhaps conflicting customs, and possibly divergent views of family roles. In addition, their children may feel that they are caught between two worlds and do not fully belong to either one.

**Adoptive and Foster Families.**   Infants who are adopted into a family usually follow exactly the same developmental course as children who are born into the family. However, children who enter a family at a later age must adjust to a new home, new parents, new caregivers, and sometimes new siblings. Many adopted children are troubled by feelings of having been abandoned by their birth parents and by intense curiosity about those parents. Interracial adoptions of black children and of Asian children by white parents are increasing. According to one study, children in interracial adoptions usually fare as well as those who are raised by their birth parents (McRoy & Zurcher, 1983).

Foster parents are couples recruited by social service agencies to be temporary caregivers to children until their parents can provide adequate homes or until adoptive families can be found for them. However, some children grow to adulthood in one or more foster homes, where they are cared for but never become permanent family members. Some foster children grow up to be troubled adults with strong feelings of abandonment and inadequacy. Nevertheless, many foster parents have exceptional parenting skills and are able to provide loving homes for their charges.

## Families in Special Situations

### Families Facing Illness or Death

Some children are born into families with members who are chronically ill or have permanent disabilities. In these families, the parents often have to struggle heroically to provide all their children with the attention, affection, and nurturing they need.

It is difficult for parents to avoid focusing all their attention and energy on the family member who is ill and to avoid making healthy children feel guilty for demanding a normal share of love and affection. Children who experience the death of a parent or sibling need a great deal of emotional support, and some need professional counseling. It sometimes takes years for the children to adjust. The period of adjustment is usually marked by behavioral and emotional problems.

### Dysfunctional and Homeless Families

A *dysfunctional family* is one that is overwhelmed by various problems, such as drug or alcohol abuse, that prevent the parents from being able to care for and nurture their children. Children may grow up in homes where spouse battering is common, or they may themselves be physically, emotionally, or sexually abused. In some cases, parents who are unable to cope with raising their children put them up for adoption so that they can be raised by another family, or the children may be placed in a temporary foster home.

In recent years, thousands of children have experienced the trauma of being homeless for some period of their lives. The family itself may not be dysfunctional, but the lack of a home base makes the possibility of a normal family life virtually impossible. Homeless children grow up in an environment that is socially and physically unhealthy, and their schooling is likely to be irregular or nonexistent (Children's Defense Fund, 1992).

## The Role of Parents and Siblings

The process of parenting begins before a baby is born and evolves gradually over time as the growing child and the parents interact with each other. Parents are responsible for providing for the child's basic physical needs, such as food, clothing, and shelter. Beyond this, parenting includes such tasks as teaching children about social interaction, good hygiene, and safety. The job of parenting also involves imparting ethical and religious beliefs and fostering attitudes about such matters as education, work, sexuality, and relationships with others. Brothers and sisters also play a crucial role in shaping the family environment and in teaching a child about getting along with others.

### Parenting Styles

The methods each parent uses to guide, educate, and discipline his or her child make up his or her parenting "style." Psychologist Diana Baumrind (1967) studied a group of preschool children and their parents in the 1960s and concluded that *parenting styles* can be divided into three main types: the authoritarian, the permissive, and the authoritative.

According to Baumrind, *authoritarian* parents emphasize obedience, respect for authority, and proper behavior. They tend to establish a set of rules and to punish their children, even physically, for misconduct and are quick to criticize them. Children in authoritarian households are not allowed to question their parents' decisions or encouraged to express their opinions and feelings.

In contrast, *permissive* parents set few rules and place few demands on their children. They tend to rely on reason and negotiation rather than punishment to control their children, and they typically tolerate a wide range of immature, destructive, and aggressive behavior. They avoid intervening in their children's play and other activities. In the extreme, permissive parents are inattentive or indifferent to their children and keep them at a distance.

The *authoritative* style of parenting strikes a balance between the other two styles. Although au-

*This child knows she has broken the rules. Authoritative parents give children the freedom to explore their world but also establish limits and boundaries.*

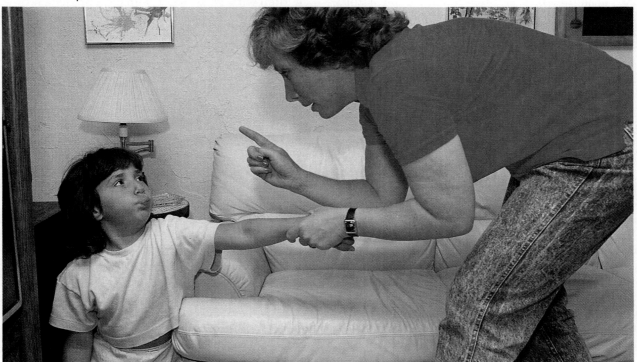

thoritative parents set rules, they discuss the rules with their children and do not expect rigid adherence to them. Authoritative parents expect much of their children, but they are warm, accepting, and willing to listen to the children's point of view and to make compromises. They establish limits and boundaries but also give children the freedom to explore and enlarge their world.

A simplified example will serve to illustrate the three parenting styles. Suppose a child requests a candy bar, knowing that her parents do not like her to eat candy. In all likelihood, an authoritarian parent would refuse the child's request without explanation; if the child picked up the candy, this parent might even slap her hand to make her put it back. A permissive parent, on the other hand, would probably buy the candy bar because the child is allowed to make her own choices or perhaps because that would be the easiest thing to do. An authoritative parent might compromise with the child. That is, the parent might agree to buy the candy bar if the child promised to save it until after dinner.

**Effects of Parenting Styles.**   The three styles of parenting have various effects on children. When Baumrind rated the children in her sample according to their degree of independence, self-control, achievement, cooperativeness, and contentment, she found some clear differences. The children of authoritarian parents were overly dependent and hostile, and they tended to be poor achievers. The children of permissive parents were also overly dependent, had little self-control, and were poor achievers. In contrast, the children of authoritative parents were friendly, cooperative, self-reliant, and high achievers (Baumrind, 1967).

Few parents consciously set out to adopt one parenting style rather than another. Most new parents have no training in parenting and little knowledge of how to go about the job of raising children. Many simply follow the same style their parents used or else adopt a style opposite to that one. A parent's temperament may strongly influence her or his parenting style. A fussy, meticulous, impatient individual would probably lean toward the authoritarian model, while an easy-going person who is not bothered by disorder would tend to be more permissive. The temperament and needs of each child also help determine what parenting style will be followed. No single style is appropriate for every child. The parents of a difficult, willful child may adopt an authoritarian style in order to exercise a reasonable amount of control over the child; the parents of a self-reliant, self-controlled child may find that they can be fairly permissive because the child exhibits few behavior problems.

No one style of parenting is necessarily right or wrong. In fact, most parents use a combination of styles. When parents do adopt a particular parenting style, the most important factor they should keep in mind is to use one that makes a good fit between the child's personality and abilities and their own expectations and demands. It is also important for parents to maintain a reasonable degree of consistency. If a parent punishes a child for violating a rule one day and then ignores similar rule breaking the next, the child will be confused and upset.

No matter which style parents adopt, they will be most effective if they develop a warm and accepting relationship with their children. Parents who are supportive and sensitive to their children's needs and point of view are likely to raise happy children with a positive self-image. Parents who are cold and rejecting are more likely to raise hostile, unhappy children with a poor self-image (Maccoby & Martin, 1983). Children's self-esteem is enhanced when their parents are actively involved with them and show them concern and affection. Increased self-esteem can lead to improved social skills.

**Parenting Styles and Socioeconomic Status.** According to some researchers, parenting styles are also influenced by socioeconomic status. Glen Elder (1962) found that the authoritarian style is more common in lower-income families. Another researcher, Jerome Kagan, found that working-class parents talk less to their children, issue prohibitions more often, and are less likely than other parents to explain punishments (Kagan, 1978). Elder has theorized that low-income parents have different expectations of their children than middle-class families do. They tend to value conformity, obedience, and order, while middle- and upper-class families place more value on independence, individuality, and curiosity.

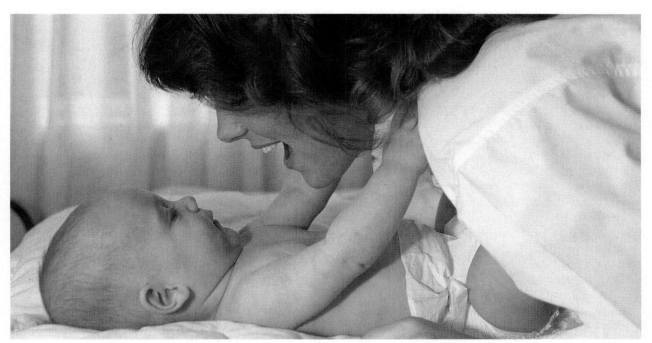

Babies thrive on positive interaction with their mothers. Researchers believe that a mother's love and encouragement are key elements in producing self-confident and capable children.

Researchers have also found that middle-class and upper-class families tend to place more emphasis on deferring work and continuing education. Middle- and upper-class children are encouraged to seek out opportunities for self-development and to value their intellectual abilities (Hess, 1970). One reason for this may be that their families have more financial resources to educate their children. Working-class families, on the other hand, tend to emphasize the value of work and the stability and respectability that work provides (Blau, 1972). Of course, there is a great deal of variation among families at all socioeconomic levels in their attitudes toward work and education. America's history as a nation of immigrants is founded on the belief that both education and hard work can enable anyone to advance in the world.

### The Role of the Mother

Infants come into the world with the beginnings of their own personality and their own special needs. The quality of a mother's parenting—how she reacts to her baby's personality and how well she fulfills the infant's needs—is an important factor in shaping the child's development. Some experts believe that a key element in producing competent children is positive interaction between the mother and child. *Positive interaction* involves the things the mother does to nurture, stimulate, educate, and encourage the child and the child's response to them.

Imagine a normal day at home with a mother and an 18-month-old toddler. The mother talks frequently to the toddler. One minute she may be praising him for using a cup successfully or admiring a pile of blocks he has built; the next minute she may be naming the parts of his body or various articles in the room. Throughout the day, she repeats the words and sounds the toddler says, asks him questions, plays simple games with him, asks him to show her colored blocks or pictures of dogs or cows, rocks him when he gets tired, and so on.

This mother and child are working hard at positive interaction. She is giving him affection, showing an interest in his accomplishments, and

## FOCUS ON  Child Care Issues

### Accessible Quality Child Care

Sandra and Wenona, both child care professionals, are listening to a debate between two candidates running for governor. One of the most controversial issues in this election is whether the state should guarantee child care for all children between six weeks and six years of age.

The candidates differ in what the government's role in providing child care should be. Here is what each candidate has to say.

T. Morris Brown:

"Many women today have to work. They simply don't have the option of staying home with children. It is the responsibility of the government to see that all parents have access to affordable, quality child care.

"If I am elected governor, I will work for a bill that will establish government-run child care centers with equal opportunity access for all people. No longer will child care be a privilege of those who can afford it. Instead, it will be a right of all working parents.

"To fund these centers I propose a special child care tax on all corporations in the state with more than five employees. Working heads of family will qualify for vouchers equal to the cost of sending their child to the government day-care center in their county.

"If families prefer, they may use these vouchers to send their children to family or private day-care centers that will be licensed and regulated by the state to assure quality.

"Many European countries, including France and Denmark, provide state-supported child care from infancy. We must not lag behind in providing this vital service."

Sally Hunter-Smith:

"I recognize the need for working parents to have access to quality child care. However, it is a mistake for the government to step in and provide that care. Parents who choose child care so that they can work should pay for this service. After all, parents who use child care are the ones who benefit economically by working.

"Families have the right to choose their life-style. By providing government funding for one particular life-style—that in which parents work and children are placed in alternative care—we eliminate choice and degrade and devalue the parenting skills and traditional family values of parents who choose to remain at home and care for their own children.

"It would be enormously expensive for the state to become involved in establishing centers and increasing the oversight of private and family day care. We already have seen how bogged down in expense, bureaucracy, and fraud the welfare system is. The same thing will happen if the state gets directly involved in providing child care.

"Raising taxes to establish child care centers will drive industry and jobs away from our state and hurt everyone. Instead, I support increasing the availability of day care by giving corporations a tax break for providing child care for their employees.

"I support government-guaranteed low-interest loans for people who wish to become educated as child care providers. I support limited child care credits to get welfare recipients back to work. But I do not support making the state directly responsible for providing child care to working parents."

*Do you think establishing state-run child care centers would make child care more widely available? Do you believe child care providers and family day-care homes should be licensed and regulated by the state? Can you think of some reasons why society should pay for child care rather than leaving the expense solely to the parents?*

encouraging him to talk and think. Such positive interaction not only promotes independence but provides support when needed. It helps the child form a positive self-image and also strengthens his self-confidence and motivation to learn.

It seems that older mothers are often more sensitive to their infants' needs. Among the growing number of women who are postponing childbearing until they are in their thirties, researchers have noted that they tend to be more relaxed and to enjoy the mothering experience more than younger women (Ragozin, Basham, Crnic, Greenberg, & Robinson, 1982).

**Mother-Child Attachment.** In addition to stimulating cognitive development, the interaction between mother and child results in the development of *attachment*, the emotional tie between one person and another. When Mary Ainsworth studied the strength and quality of attachment between toddlers and their mothers, she discovered distinct patterns of attachment (Ainsworth, 1973). Mothers who met the needs of their infants, who talked to them and provided appropriate stimulation, produced children with a *secure attachment*. Ainsworth observed that securely attached toddlers used their mother as a safe base from which to venture out and explore their surroundings. When they were disturbed, they returned to their mother for reassurance but soon ventured off again.

Ainsworth (1973) also observed what she calls *insecure attachment*. Some insecurely attached toddlers clung to their mother and refused to explore their surroundings. Others separated from their mother easily when she left the room and actively avoided her when she returned.

Some researchers believe that these differences in attachment are not only accurate indicators of the quality of mothering children receive but also provide some indication of how well the children will function later on. Ainsworth concluded that the quality of the attachment influences such traits as self-esteem, problem-solving abilities, and sociability and that secure attachment produces the most competent and self-reliant children.

**Working Mothers.**   As noted earlier, the stay-at-home mother is no longer the norm in the United States. According to the Bureau of Labor Statistics,

This is the way the day begins for many working mothers. Some mothers feel guilty about leaving their children in child care. Studies have shown, however, that quality programs may actually enhance the social skills of older children.

in 1990, almost 75 percent of women with children between the ages of 6 and 17 were in the work force; 58 percent of women with children under the age of 6 worked outside the home. For many employed mothers, working is a necessity to ease the financial pressures on the family. One-fourth of all working mothers are single parents who provide the primary income for the family. Even in two-parent homes, the mother often goes to work because a single wage earner cannot earn enough to provide a comfortable standard of living.

The attitude of each parent is an important factor in how well children adjust to their mother

## FOCUS ON   **Cultural Diversity**

### Cultural Differences in Development

Culture is a way of life shared by a group of people. Our society has many different cultures based on common beliefs, religion, race, ethnicity, economic status, gender, or sexual orientation. Most people belong to more than one culture.

Different cultures emphasize certain abilities and values over others. Some cultures place great value on education. Others emphasize hard work, physical labor, or athletic ability. Some cultures value interdependence among adults and children, while others stress independence.

The attitude that people have toward time varies from culture to culture. Some cultures, for example, do not place great importance on being prompt or sticking to a schedule. A child who comes from a family where there are no set mealtimes and no set bedtimes may have difficulty adjusting to a day-care setting where activities are scheduled for specific periods of time. The child may have problems shifting from one activity to the next.

Recognizing the differences between your values and those of the child's family will help you be more understanding and flexible, and you will be in a better position to help the child adjust to the day-care environment.

---

working. For many women, work is an important source of satisfaction and self-esteem. When a mother is happy in her work and has a husband who supports her decision, the children are likely to be better adjusted than when the mother resents having to work or when her husband disapproves of her working. Generally, mothers in middle- and upper-class families are more likely than those in working-class families to want to work and to be supported in this decision by their husbands; some working-class men believe that their wife's employment reflects on their own ability to support their family (Lamb, 1982; Scarr, 1984).

Many mothers experience a sense of guilt when they return to the work force. They fear that leaving their children, especially very young children, will be harmful to the children's development. However, most research does not support such fears (Hoffman, 1989; Rubenstein, Hower, & Boyle, 1981). Working mothers tend to spend as much time interacting with their children as do nonworking mothers. Moreover, the quality of attachment is apparently about equal between working and nonworking mothers and their children. When infants are well cared for during the day by someone other than their mother, they develop secure attachments to their mother and to their primary caregiver. All types of secure attachments work in the same way to motivate the children to explore and learn about their world.

Some researchers have found that children in child care situations are better adjusted socially and relate better to their peers than children who stay home with their mothers (Gold & Andres, 1978). It seems that sons of working mothers have more behavioral and psychological problems than the sons of nonworking mothers, but the differences are small. On the other hand, school-age daughters of working mothers tend to be more self-reliant and to have a more positive image of women than do school-age daughters of nonworking mothers. It has also been found that children of working mothers generally seem to have fewer stereotypes about gender roles. This may be because their parents express more egalitarian attitudes about role divisions and because fathers perform more traditionally female chores around the house (Huston, 1983).

Overall, children of working mothers are raised in a more structured environment and are encouraged to be more independent than children of stay-at-home mothers. The former are often required to share household chores and to assume more responsibility for caring for younger siblings. These responsibilities build self-confidence and self-esteem, which help them succeed in other areas of their lives (Bronfenbrenner & Crouter, 1982).

### The Role of the Father

Although the mother is usually the primary caregiver in the home, the father plays a very important role. In a two-parent family, the father is usually supportive of the mother, enabling her to function efficiently. Research has shown that fathers tend to interact less than mothers with their infants, and when fathers do interact, it is in a different style. According to studies of infant-parent interaction, fathers tend to be louder, more playful, and more stimulating than mothers, who are generally more soothing and calming (Parke & O'Leary, 1976). Babies seem to enjoy and benefit from both kinds of interactions. Interaction between father and child increases as the child becomes a toddler, particularly when the child is a boy (Clarke-Stewart, 1980; Lamb, 1981).

As children grow and develop, they feel better about themselves if they have a supportive father. In families where both parents work, the father is likely to perform more caregiving functions. In some homes, the father stays home with the children and becomes the primary caregiver while the mother works. In these cases, infants will readily form a secure attachment to their father as well as to their mother. Studies have shown that when fathers are highly involved with their children, children of both sexes tend to score higher on tests of cognitive skills and to be more independent and self-motivated (Radin, 1982; Sagi, 1982).

### Adjusting to the Loss of a Parent

The loss of a parent through divorce or separation can be traumatic for a child. The specific effects of growing up in a single-parent household vary widely according to the reason for one parent's absence, the family's financial circumstances, and the age, sex, and number of children in the family. Children of single-parent families often have more difficulty in school and are less happy at home than children of two-parent families. But a child who has a good relationship with one parent is likely to be better adjusted than a child who grows up in an unhappy two-parent family (Rutter, 1983).

Caregivers can help children weather the effects of a divorce by being extra supportive.

It appears that boys are more adversely affected by the absence of a father than girls are. Some studies indicate that boys raised by their mother may be more aggressive, unruly, and anxious than boys raised in two-parent homes (Huston, 1983; Levy-Shiff, 1982). Studies also show that boys under the age of six who are separated from their father are more likely to have problems in gender-role development and may take on fewer masculine characteristics than boys in two-parent families (Biller, 1981; Hetherington, 1979). Both boys and girls adjust better to their parents' separation if they live with the parent of the same gender (Santrock et al., 1982).

The effect of divorce on children's intellectual development varies among children in different cultural and socioeconomic groups. In Hispanic and Asian-American families, where the father is traditionally a dominant family member, the absence of the father seems to have a negative impact on the intellectual performance of the children. Among working-class families, the intellectual development of children also tends to be adversely affected by the absence of the father (Radin, 1981). For children of middle- and upper-class white families, on the other hand, the father's absence appears to have a much smaller impact.

The negative impact of a divorce or separation on children generally decreases over time. It is greatest during the first year or two after the event. Problem behavior seems to decline after two years, and girls appear to recover faster than boys (Hetherington et al., 1982). However, during adolescence, children of divorced parents may develop behavior problems as they discover their own sexuality and may be unsure about how to relate to the opposite sex. When the parents maintain an amicable relationship and continue to work as a parental team, the family functions better and recovers more quickly from the effects of divorce. It appears that frequent, regular visits by the noncustodial parent help children adjust better to divorce.

Children whose parents divorce may have to adjust to several other significant changes in their lives in addition to family separation. They may have to move to another home and school, for example. Their mother may take a full-time job and be less available to them. The family's living standard may go down because financial resources are stretched to accommodate the new living arrangements or because one parent does not provide sufficient child support.

## The Role of Siblings

Children within the same family can differ markedly in their behavior and self-image just by virtue of their position within the family. Parents tend to be more anxious and more demanding with their firstborn child. As a result, firstborns are often high achievers and may be more responsible and conscientious than their younger siblings. Later-born children, on the other hand, tend to be lower achievers, more accommodating, more sociable, and more realistic about themselves.

When people think about the role that brothers and sisters play in each other's lives, they tend to think first of *sibling rivalry*, the pattern of vying for parental attention and of aggressive behavior toward siblings. One survey showed that more than 80 percent of children between the ages of 3 and 17 behave aggressively toward their siblings, usually slapping and shoving but also kicking, punching, and biting. The survey also indicated that such behavior is more common in families where all the children are boys (Straus, Gelles, & Steinmetz, 1980).

However common sibling rivalry may be, it is just one of many complex sibling interactions. Although older siblings often act in an aggressive, competitive, and hostile way toward their younger brothers and sisters, they may also show nurturance, helpfulness, tolerance, protection, and cooperation. Younger siblings, on the other hand, usually spend a good deal of time imitating their older brothers and sisters.

A younger sibling is more likely to model the behavior of an older brother or sister when the two are of the same gender (Abramovitch, Peplar, & Corter, 1982). In a one-parent home, for example, an older brother sometimes provides the model that helps a younger boy establish appropriate masculine gender roles. Furthermore, because younger siblings are smaller and weaker, they learn how to accommodate and negotiate with their older siblings (Bryant, 1982). These behaviors help younger siblings develop social skills that carry over into their relationships with others.

A firstborn or older sibling is naturally jealous when his or her place in the household is threatened by the birth of a new baby. Commonly, toddlers and preschoolers react to the birth of a new brother or sister by regressing to more infantile behavior, such as clinging, crying, and bed-wetting. Parents can do much to foster positive relationships among siblings by preparing the firstborn for the birth of a younger brother or sister. An older child's resentment of a new infant can be greatly reduced if parents are careful to pay frequent, undivided attention to the older child and refrain from comparing one child unfavorably to the other. Involving the older child in making some decisions about the younger one's care can help foster a sense of nurturing and responsibility in the older sibling. In many cultures, older sons and daughters are routinely required to care for younger siblings from a very early age. This practice encourages interdependence and closeness among siblings that can last a lifetime (Whiting & Whiting, 1975).

Sibling relations are often marked by displays of aggression. Yet siblings are also likely to be nurturing and protective toward their brothers and sisters.

As the trend toward smaller families continues, many couples are having only one child. Only children tend to do as well or better than children with siblings (Falbo & Polit, 1986). Only children are very similar to firstborns. Their parents expect more from them, and as a result, they tend to become high achievers. As only children, they benefit from receiving all of the attention and affection that parents would divide among siblings in larger families. Moreover, since parents usually involve only children in play groups and preschools, these children experience the same socializing influences that siblings exert on one another (Falbo, 1984).

## Implications and Applications

The great increase in the number of single parents and working mothers has led more families to rely heavily on child care professionals. Many parents look not only for day-to-day care but also for insights and advice about the growth and development of their children. Professional caregivers become im-

portant partners in children's rearing. They must be ready to provide specific suggestions for training and counseling. An ability to communicate clearly and empathetically with parents about their children's behavior and feelings is a great asset.

In many cases, child care providers and parents exchange information at the end of each day. Just as June talked to Mrs. Waters about changes in Bobby's behavior, a child care professional may provide information about a child's behavior during the day, about his relationships with other children and adults, and about current activities. Did the child miss a nap, eat a late snack, have a toileting accident, draw a picture, throw a temper tantrum? All of this information is important for parents to know.

However, communication is a two-way process, and early childhood professionals also need to be good listeners. Although parents may talk freely about their children, they may be less forthcoming in discussing situations at home that affect the children's behavior. If a child's parents are expecting

Communication is an important element in the relationship between parents and other caregivers. Child care professionals should cultivate good listening skills and ask about any changes that may affect a child's needs or behavior.

another child, going through a divorce, or experiencing a period of unemployment, the child is going to feel the effects of the situation and may need special attention. The caregiver can often elicit relevant information by listening, asking questions, and offering support.

Child care professionals need to be very sensitive to the changes taking place in each child's life and must help the child adjust to those developments. The birth of a sibling may provoke regressive behavior in one preschooler, and the recent separation of another child's parents may cause that child to become anxious and fearful. Child care providers must recognize such changes in the children in their care and identify the underlying reasons for those changes.

Caregivers also need to be aware that children come from different backgrounds and that their parents have different needs and expectations. All parents want their children to be clean, safe,

healthy, and well fed. For a single working mother or father, the most important concern beyond these basics may be that good child care is always available during the working hours even when the children are sick. Affluent parents may not need or desire full-time child care. However, they may demand high-quality, part-time preschool programs to help their children develop their social and cognitive skills.

Child care is a necessity for millions of working parents. Typically, parents seeking child care look first to their own extended families, next to home-based or *family day care*—where individuals care for their own and a small number of other children in their home—and then to child care centers and preschools. According to one survey, about 27 percent of child care is provided by relatives, 20 percent by family day-care providers, and 38 percent by child care centers (Children's Defense Fund, 1992). In the United States, the demand for day care greatly

**Communicating with Children**

### Talking to Five-Year-Olds About Being Homeless

Sharon teaches at a child care center in a city where homelessness is a growing problem. Yesterday she found out that a five-year-old boy is going to join her class next week. The boy, Damian, lives with his mother in a nearby motel. Sharon feels that she should prepare the children in her class for Damian's situation, and she raises the matter during circle time.

SHARON: Today, I'd like to talk about what it's like to be homeless. Do you know what that word means?

TRACY: It means you don't have anywhere to live.

WILL: You have to sleep on the sidewalk in a box.

SHARON: Sometimes, but for lots of families it may just mean that they don't have a house or an apartment to live in like you do. In our city, many homeless people live in shelters or in motels. Some families just stay there for a while until they can get their own place to live. Why do you think some people are homeless?

STEVIE:  Maybe their house burns down.

TRACY: Maybe their daddy lost his job so they don't have money for rent and they get kicked out by a mean landlord.

WILL: Maybe their house was so old it just fell down—boom!

SHARON: That's right. Those are all reasons why a family might not have a house or apartment to live in anymore. What do you think your life would be like if your family were homeless?

TRACY: You wouldn't have a yard to play in.

WILL: You probably couldn't have a dog or a cat. And where would you keep your toys and things?

SHANNA: There'd be no place to have your friends over to play.

STEVIE: Yeah, and your parents might be mad all the time, too.

SHARON: Life would be difficult if you were homeless, wouldn't it? What could you do if you had a homeless friend? How could you make your friend's life more fun?

SHANNA: I'd invite her over to my house to play. I'd give her my second-favorite doll.

CATHY: I could make some cookies with my mom.

STEVIE: He could play baseball with me and my brother.

SHARON: Those are all great ideas. You'd sure make your friend feel better. It would still be hard not to have a home, but with good friends like you, it would be a little easier. Can you think of anything else?

TRACY: I wouldn't let anyone make fun of my friend just because she's homeless.

SHARON: That's one of the best ideas of all, Tracy. It could really hurt people's feelings to make fun of them because they're homeless. They need all the help they can get until their families have their own home again. Right? *[The children nod in agreement.]*

*Do you think Sharon was right to talk to the children about homelessness or should she have waited to see how things developed when Damian joined the class? How would you have handled the situation?*

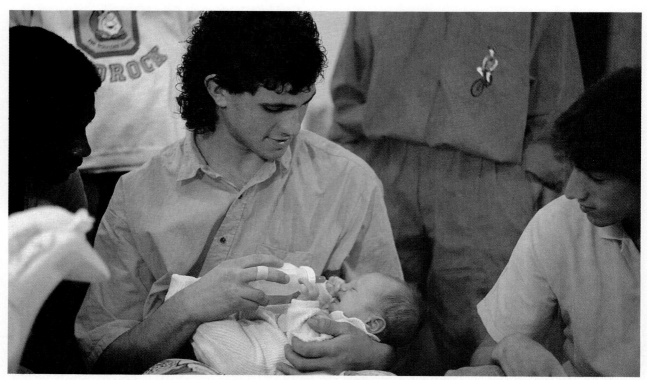

Good parenting is not based exclusively on instinct. Parenting classes can give people the knowledge and skills to deal more effectively with important issues in their child's development.

exceeds the supply. In recent years, many new family day and child care centers have opened to respond to the growing need for infant day care and for after-school care for students in the lower elementary grades. In addition, a growing number of companies now provide child care at the workplace for their employees.

The child care provider is an important part of the parents' support system. The best kind of child care program functions as an extension of the family and is geared to respond to the family's needs. The ratio of caregivers to children is kept small so that the children can receive the same kind of individual attention and stimulation they would receive at home.

### Forming a Partnership

Just as there is a certain "fit" between parent and child, there is a certain fit between the child care program and the family. The degree to which the two do not quite match is called *discontinuity*. Because no family and program match perfectly, there will always be some discontinuity. For example, it is not unusual for parents and preschool teachers to differ in their goals for children. In some cases, parents are more demanding and believe that their children should be able to master developmental skills at an earlier age than teachers believe is possible. Some parents place considerable value on social skills such as politeness and conformity. Teachers are likely to be more flexible and less demanding and to place more emphasis on independence.

Child care providers and parents can also differ in styles of discipline. Parents need to be informed of the philosophy and rules of conduct of the child care establishment. Children from rigidly authoritarian or extremely permissive families may experience some stress in adjusting to the authoritative style used by most child care professionals.

A certain amount of discontinuity is not harmful to children. In fact, children's intellectual and social skills may be enhanced when the children are exposed to other children and adults from different cultures, ethnic groups, and socioeconomic backgrounds. Children may also learn to be more adaptive in adjusting to differing expectations from family and child care providers. On the other hand, discontinuity may be harmful to minority children if they are placed in an environment in which the dominant culture is emphasized and their own is disparaged, however unconsciously and unintentionally.

### Helping Parents

Today's child care professional looks for ways to help busy, working parents become more competent in dealing with their children. For example, one child care provider might offer a teenage parent advice on parenting skills. Another might try to persuade immigrant parents to attend English-language classes.

Early childhood educators are finding that they must look for ways to help parents become more effective first teachers of their young children. Some child care programs focus on the parent's role in early childhood education. The federally funded Head Start preschool program, for example, works closely with parents to develop at-home teaching skills. Head Start began in 1965 as a comprehensive program providing health, education, and social services to children in low-income households and their families. The program refers families to government agencies for help with medical and dental care, mental health and substance abuse problems, and homelessness and other social problems that interfere with the functioning of the family.

Child care professionals need to be aware of community-based programs that are available to help parents of all socioeconomic groups develop better parenting skills. Some schools, hospitals, and social service agencies have established parenting centers where parents can take courses to become more effective parents. A number of high schools offer parenting classes to introduce students to the subject. In some areas, parenting classes, parent support groups, and parent discussion groups have been formed to help parents deal with concerns and issues involved in raising a family. High-quality parent programs depend on a collaboration between the parents and the program's staff. Such a collaboration helps parents strike a balance between attending to their own needs and the needs of their children. These parenting programs offer another opportunity for early childhood educators to become part of the family's support system.

## CHAPTER 4 REVIEW

## SUMMARY

- The family is the first and most important influence on a child's life and development. The members of a family interact with each other in many complex ways. Families are dynamic entities that can change over time as the result of births, deaths, divorce, and remarriage.
- Many variables shape a child's family environment. These include the number of people in the family, the parents' ages and their level of education, and the family's ethnic background.
- A family's support system is any combination of family members, health and child care professionals, and community organizations such as schools and social service agencies that help the family function.

- Families are changing: They are getting smaller and more diverse; women are waiting until they are older to become mothers, and most mothers work; families are very mobile.

- Two-parent families are still the most common type, but today both parents are likely to work.

- Single-parent families often have fewer resources and suffer more stress than two-parent families.

- When divorced or widowed parents remarry and form blended families, children must adjust to many changes.

- The number of multigenerational families—those that include more than two generations in the same household—is increasing. The potential for intergenerational conflict may be offset by having a valuable addition to a family's support system.

- The number of teenage mothers in the United States is on the rise. Families in which parents are adolescents present special problems. The parents are often immature and unable to support a family.

- Intercultural and interracial families, families facing illness or death, dysfunctional families, and adoptive and foster families are subject to stresses above and beyond the normal stresses of family life.

- Parents adopt specific parenting styles to bring up their children. Styles range from the rigidly authoritarian to the excessively permissive. The children of parents who practice the middle-of-the-road authoritative style tend to be independent, self-reliant, and high achievers.

- Working-class parents often adopt an authoritarian style of parenting, while middle- and upper-class parents tend to prefer authoritative or permissive styles of parenting.

- When mothers interact in a positive manner with their infants, they develop securely attached, competent children. Securely attached children use their mother as a safe base from which to explore the world. Insecurely attached children either cling to their mother or avoid her.

- About 58 percent of women with children under the age of six work outside the home. The attitude of a working mother toward her work and the amount of time she spends with her children are important factors in the children's adjustment.

- Fathers play a different but equally important role in their children's development. The absence of fathers can adversely affect children, especially boys.

- Children are adversely affected by the loss of a parent through death or divorce, but most recover within two years.

- Siblings are rivals for their parents' attention and affection, but older siblings are also models and caregivers for younger brothers and sisters. Only children can thrive as well as children with siblings.

- The increase in the number of working mothers and single parents leads families to rely heavily on child care professionals for help and support. Caregivers must be sensitive to the changes occurring in the families of their charges as well as to racial, cultural, and socioeconomic differences among families.

- Child care options range from care by relatives to home-based or family day care to child care centers and preschools. High-quality child care can be beneficial to a child's development.
- Child care professionals are often part of a family's support system. They must look for ways to help parents become more competent. Communication between parents and other caregivers is essential to children's welfare.
- Discontinuity refers to the degree to which child care programs and parents fail to match up in terms of expectations and parenting styles. There is always some discontinuity between programs and parents.
- Child care providers can help parents become more effective teachers of young children. Various programs are available to help parents.

## BUILDING VOCABULARY

Write a definition for each vocabulary term listed below.

| | |
|---|---|
| attachment | insecure attachment |
| authoritarian | parenting style |
| authoritative | permissive |
| birthrate | positive interaction |
| discontinuity | secure attachment |
| dysfunctional family | sibling rivalry |
| extended family | support system |
| family day care | |

## ACQUIRING KNOWLEDGE

1. How does the modern family differ from families of earlier generations?
2. Name two variables in a child's family environment that can affect the child's development.
3. What constitutes a family's support system?
4. What is an extended family? A multigenerational family?
5. The number of children being reared by their grandparents has increased in recent years. Give a reason for this increase.
6. What is the most common type of family in the United States?
7. List two of the advantages of a two-parent home.
8. What causes the "role overload" that many single parents experience?
9. Are boys and girls equally affected by the absence of a father?
10. List two of the changes to which a child of recently divorced parents may have to adjust.
11. Describe a problem that children in blended families may have to face.
12. Why do teenage parents often have difficulty in coping with the responsibilities of parenthood?
13. Give an example of a problem some interracial families face.

14. What is a dysfunctional family?
15. What does parenting involve?
16. Describe the three parenting styles.
17. What is positive interaction?
18. How is a child's adjustment to his mother working affected by parental attitudes?
19. How does a father's interaction with a child usually differ from a mother's?
20. What is sibling rivalry?
21. How is a firstborn likely to react to a new baby in the family?
22. Why are child care professionals an important part of a family's support system?
23. Explain discontinuity between parents and a child care program and give an example.
24. Describe the effects of discontinuity.
25. Name three family issues to which child care providers need to be sensitive.
26. How can child care professionals help parents become more competent and deal with child-rearing issues?

## THINKING CRITICALLY

1. Many TV sitcoms are based on families. Do you think children get false or idealized views of family life from these programs? Do you think these programs discuss real family issues of the nineties? Discuss several TV programs as they relate to your own concept of family.
2. In recent years, increases in crime and violence, unemployment, drug and alcohol addiction, lower test scores, and school dropouts have all been blamed on the breakdown of the family. Do you agree or disagree with this? Give reasons for your answer.
3. The majority of mothers now work outside the home, and women have made significant gains in the workplace. Do you think that the role of the woman as full-time homemaker/caregiver has been devalued in our society? Explain.
4. The demand for day care greatly exceeds the supply. What, if anything, do you think government should do to help families find affordable child care? Defend your answer and, if necessary, provide alternative ideas for dealing with this problem.
5. Child care providers often learn a great deal about the personal problems of the families of the children they care for. How involved do you think they should get with a family's problems?

## OBSERVATIONS AND APPLICATIONS

1. Visit a child care center and select two or three children to observe for several hours. What can you guess about the family background of each child? Note in particular the way each child interacts with caregivers and see whether you can guess what parenting style—permissive, au-

thoritarian, authoritative—is used in the child's home. What elements of each child's behavior led you to your conclusions?

2. Attend a meeting of an organization, such as Parents Without Partners, in which single parents meet for mutual support and recreation. On the basis of what you see and hear at the meeting, draw up a list of the major concerns of these single parents. Pay particular attention to any discussion of child care providers and child care facilities. What points were made about child care?

3. The arrival of a new baby can have profound effects on other children in the family. Suppose that a four-year-old boy in your child care center tells you he hates his new sister and would like to hurt her. What would you say to him? How could you help him adjust? What would you say to his parents?

4. One little girl in your child care class is very hard to control. If given a little freedom to do her own work or play, she quickly becomes aggressive and bossy. She seems unable to control her behavior. When you discuss this with the child's mother, the mother is surprised. She tells you that at home both parents are very strict with their daughter and she is not allowed to misbehave. What conclusions can you draw about the child's behavior? What measures might you take to change the situation?

## SUGGESTIONS FOR FURTHER READING

Brazelton, T. B. (1989). *Families: Crisis and caring*. Reading, MA: Addison-Wesley.

Brazelton, T. B., & Cramer, B. (1990). *The earliest relationships: Parents, infants, and the drama of early attachment*. New York: Delacorte.

Diamond, S. (1985). *Helping children of divorce: A handbook for parents and teachers*. New York: Schocken.

Edelman, M. W. (1986). *Families in peril: An agenda for social change*. Cambridge, MA: Harvard University Press.

Galinsky, E. (1986). How do child care and maternal employment affect children? *Child Care Information Exchange, 48,* 19–23.

Grollman, E., & Sweder, G. (Eds.). (1986). *The working parent dilemma*. Boston: Beacon Press.

Hochschild, A., & Machung, A. (1989). *The second shift: Working parents and the revolution at home*. New York: Viking.

Honig, A. S. (1986). Stress and coping in children. *Young Children, 41*(4), 50–63; *41*(5), 47–59.

McNamee, A. S. (1982). Helping children cope with divorce. A. S. McNamee (Ed.), *Children and stress: Helping children cope*. Washington, DC: Association for Childhood Educational International.

Powell, D. R. (1986). Parent education and support programs. *Young Children, 41,* 47–53.

Powell, D. R. (1989). *Families and early childhood programs*. Washington, DC: National Association for the Education of Young Children.

Scarr, S. (1985). *Mother care/other care*. New York: Warner Books.

# 5 Concerns for Early Childhood Professionals

## OBJECTIVES

Studying this chapter will enable you to

- Explain why it is important for early childhood professionals to understand the cultural background, type of family, and special needs of the children in their care.
- List steps child care professionals can take to develop good working partnerships with parents.
- Describe the principal features of a safe and healthy environment for young children.
- Discuss what early childhood professionals can do to create an environment that promotes the mental, physical, and cultural well-being of all children and their families.

IN THE THREE YEARS that Anna had been working at Sunshine Preschool, she had never had a child quite like Charles. The three-year-old spoke little and did not respond to Anna's efforts to engage him in conversation. When Anna tried to build up Charles's self-esteem by praising his work in front of the other children, he grew confused and even more withdrawn. In fact, he began to resist doing any independent work at all. Anna knew that Charles was a Native American, but she needed to find out more about his background to understand his behavior.

Anna spoke to Charles's father. She learned that the family had only recently moved to the city from a Navaho reservation. He explained how different their new life was from that on the reservation. And he felt it was important for the family to continue to follow their traditional customs at home and to maintain close ties with other members of their extended family.

Learning something about Charles's background and reading about Navaho culture helped shed some light on the child's feelings and behavior. Among other things, Anna discovered that the Navaho, like most Native Americans, generally value group effort far more than individual achievement. She stopped trying to give Charles an opportunity to shine on his own and worked instead to integrate him in group activities.

Anna's experience with Charles is not unique or even unusual. Early childhood professionals across the United States report that the children they serve come from increasingly diverse backgrounds. The children represent a wide variety of cultures and have many different types of families and support systems. Many children also have special needs. Dealing with *diversity*, that is, with people of different races, religions, and ethnic backgrounds, is one of the key concerns of early childhood educators today.

## Dealing with Diversity

Statistics support what many Americans see around them: the "face" of our nation is visibly changing. The 1990 census revealed that African Americans make up more than 12 percent of the nation's population, while Hispanics constitute 9 percent. Asians and Native Americans make up 2.9 percent and 0.8 percent, respectively. Of particular significance is the fact that these "minority" segments of the population are growing much more rapidly than the white population. Population projections for the next century indicate that this trend will continue.

### Diverse Cultural Backgrounds

What do all these numbers mean in terms of the nation's children? More than a quarter of the people of this country are members of groups commonly referred to as minorities. Those attending child care, preschools, and grade schools reflect this ethnic and racial diversity, and they bring with them a wide variety of customs, attitudes, behavior styles, values, language, and religious beliefs. To best promote the

development and learning of these children, child care professionals need to be aware of and have some knowledge of the values, expectations, and goals of people from various cultural backgrounds. Cultural awareness promotes better understanding and communication between caregivers and children, between caregivers and parents, and among the children themselves.

Child care providers can become more culturally aware by observing parents and children closely and by doing some homework on unfamiliar cultures. Knowing how people of other cultures feel about personal space, smiling, eye contact, touch, and time concepts are vital pieces of information in learning to communicate across cultures (Gonzales-Mena, 1993). Many Native Americans, for example, view time "as flowing and relative; things are done as the need arises rather than by the clock or according to some future-oriented master plan" (Little Soldier, 1992, p. 20). Thus, a caregiver may find that a Native American child has difficulty adjusting to an imposed schedule of daily activities.

For early childhood professionals, a knowledge of the child-rearing practices of different peoples is an important part of cultural awareness. In one study, researchers compared three- to four-month-old infants in middle-class homes in Japan and the United States. They found that American mothers talked to and stimulated their babies a great deal, while Japanese mothers spent more time lulling and soothing their babies. The study concluded that children of this age are already learning to behave in particular ways because of the styles of nurturing in their cultures (Caudill & Frost, 1974). Caregivers need to be aware and respectful of these differences.

Culture can influence the learning style of children as well. Native American children, such as Charles, grow up in extended families and are raised to be group oriented. This leads them to "value group membership and harmony over individual achievement in the classroom" (Little Soldier, 1992). Many black children are also raised in an extended family environment, and they tend to be very people oriented. Interpersonal interaction appears to be an important part of the learning process of black children (Hale-Benson, 1986). In Vietnamese families, listening is emphasized more

Children attending child care programs reflect the nation's ethnic and racial diversity. Caregivers can promote the development of all children by being aware of different cultures.

than speaking. For this reason, the children may be reluctant to speak out in class (West, 1983).

### Diversity Among Families

Another factor that influences the behavior and learning style of children is the type of family to which the child belongs. In Chapter 4 you learned about the increasing diversification of the American family. The chapter discussed the challenges faced by single-parent families and the stresses experienced by the many children living in blended families with stepparents and step-siblings. It also touched on the special concerns of teenage-parent families and of children from dysfunctional families. Child care professionals need to be aware of and sensitive to the special problems and concerns of children and parents from all types of families.

Children of parents who are divorcing or children of single parents may show signs of stress and problems in school. For example, they may be aggressive toward their peers, withdrawn, or disrup-

tive in class. These children and those with interracial parents, adoptive parents, foster parents, and same-sex parents may need extra help in asserting their identity in a family structure still generally considered "nontraditional." It is important to note, however, that there is no longer a "traditional" family structure in our changing society.

Child care professionals should recognize that "problem" behavior may be a child's way of responding to stress and try to help the child cope with the causes of the stress. Learning about the children and their families is the first step toward understanding each child. Providing a loving environment is also critical. Good communication with parents will help them become more aware of how their family environment both supports and influences their child.

### Children with Special Needs

To many people, the phrase "children with special needs" brings to mind images of children with dis-

Mainstreaming encourages children with disabilities to develop social skills. It also helps avoid the labeling of children as "special" or "different."

abilities, such as motor problems, visual impairment, chronic illness, or mental retardation. But these are only some of the children who need some sort of special education or special services. Among the other groups of children who should be included in this special needs category are those who are gifted and talented, those who have been abused or neglected, and those from families that are homeless.

**Children with Disabilities.**    A recent survey by the National Center for Health Statistics found that one in every five children under age 18 has a developmental, emotional, behavioral, or learning problem (Children's Defense Fund, 1991). In the past, children with mental and physical disabilities were denied access to most child care settings, preschools, and public schools. Child care and school facilities were not designed to accommodate children with disabilities, and the lack of adequate facilities was frequently cited as the reason for not accepting these students. As a result, parents were forced to place their children in special schools that isolated them from the general population. Often these special schools were expensive and far away, putting an additional burden on the parents and the children with special needs.

To remedy this situation, Congress passed Public Law 94-142, or the Education for All Handicapped Children Act of 1975. This law guarantees a free and appropriate public education for all children with disabilities between the ages of 3 and 18. The law also requires that children with disabilities be placed in the "least restrictive environment." By *least restrictive environment*, the government means the least specialized classroom in which a child will benefit most. The goal of the legislation is to see that as many children with disabilities as possible are educated in regular classrooms while getting the special services they need. The law also requires that an *individualized educational plan* (IEP) be written for each child, describing the program that has been designed to meet the child's specific needs. An important provision in this law concerns the right of parents to make decisions about their child's school placement and program. The law created a team with the parents as full partners in determining what is best for each child.

In 1986, Congress passed Public Law 99-457, which established an Early Intervention Program for children under the age of two who are developmentally delayed. This law specifies that states must provide programs for infants and toddlers with disabilities to qualify for federal funds under the Education for Handicapped Children Act.

In 1990, Congress passed the Americans with Disabilities Act. This law defines a *disability* as a "physical or mental impairment that substantially limits one or more major life activities." It outlaws discrimination against people with physical or mental impairments. To prevent discrimination, the law requires all public facilities to ensure access for people regardless of disability. As a result, child care centers and family child care homes cannot deny access to individuals because of a disability. These establishments must take "readily achievable" steps to modify their facilities and practices to accommodate a child with a disability.

Integrating children with special needs into regular classrooms is called *mainstreaming*. In this process, children with disabilities take part in regular classes for all or part of the day. This integration can help those with disabilities develop social skills and learn how to get along in a group of people who are not disabled. In addition, mainstreaming can help those without disabilities understand that people with disabilities are more like them than different from them. Integration can also help a child avoid the harmful effects of being labeled "special" or "different." Labeling encourages a child with a disability to think of himself only in terms of that disability, thus lowering his self-esteem and making him feel inferior. However, learning in a mainstreamed classroom does not just happen. It requires planning, understanding, and hard work by the teachers, parents, and children involved (Allen, 1992).

The term *disability* includes *learning disability*, a disorder in the basic process of understanding or the use of language or numerical concepts. Children with learning disabilities may have problems listening, speaking, reading, or writing. They may also have difficulty with math. Some of these children are hyperactive, impulsive, and easily distracted from work or play. Others may persevere with an activity well past the point of appropriateness. Many children with learning disabilities are poor listeners; some have poor motor coordination.

Early intervention is important for children with disabilities. Special programs of supplementary training and assistance are designed to help children and their parents have a positive educational experience. Head Start, an early intervention program for children of low-income families, requires that at least 10 percent of its enrollment be available to children with disabilities.

Child care providers need to work with parents and special education professionals to create goals and objectives that address each child's strengths and needs. Caregivers must be sensitive to the needs of parents and involve them in decision making and program development. Parents of children with disabilities often have complex concerns. Their children may require more physical care and emotional support than able-bodied children, adding stress to their daily lives. The future is a cause of great concern to these parents because they are often unsure how well their children will get along in society as they grow older. At the same time, many of these parents may feel some guilt for having a child with a disability. Adjustment to and acceptance of a child with special needs within the family is a changing

---

## FOCUS ON Cultural Diversity

### Diverse Life-Styles, Basic Similarities

Holly teaches a class of four-year-olds at Orange Park Preschool. This year the school's theme is Cultures Around the World. Holly wants to emphasize how people around the world are similar, even when they dress differently or speak different languages. Here are some ideas she shares with the children:

- All over the world people share basic similarities. They all need food and shelter. They all live in families. They all enjoy music and games.
- The kind of houses people build depends on the climate where they live. People in hot countries build houses designed to stay cool. People in cold climates live in houses that are easier to heat.
- People eat different foods depending on which foods are most abundant and least expensive in their country. For example, rice grows well in Japan, so it is a basic food for the Japanese. Corn grows well in Mexico, so many Mexican foods are made with ground corn.
- In the United States, we usually think of a family as one or two adults living with one or more children. In parts of Africa, a family includes dozens of people—grandparents, aunts, uncles, cousins, parents, and children—all living in the same village. Although these families are of different sizes, both types have members who care about and help each other.

Showing children similarities among people rather than emphasizing their differences creates enrichment and inclusiveness from diversity.

Caregivers can help gifted children develop their special abilities by providing them with a stimulating and enriched learning environment.

process. By communicating and interacting with parents, early childhood professionals can have a significant impact on the success and self-esteem of both the parents and the children.

Early childhood professionals also need to know how to handle the curiosity and questions of other children in an honest, sensitive, and accurate way. Louise Derman-Sparks suggests finding out how the child's parents are explaining the specific disability to the child and to others. She also recommends helping children who have disabilities find the words to answer questions themselves. They should know that "they have the right to choose to answer another child's question, say they don't want to answer, or say they would rather the child ask the teacher" (Derman-Sparks, 1989, p. 42).

Finally, child care professionals need to create an environment that is safe and accessible for children with disabilities. This may mean installing wheelchair ramps and widening doorways or rearranging tables and shelves so that these children will have a suitable work space and easy access to materials and toys.

Children with visual or hearing impairments may need to be seated closer to materials or to the adult presenting a lesson or activity. Children with speech and language impairments may need extra time to respond to questions or requests. The child care professional, working with parents, other teachers, and various specialists, needs to develop a plan to address each child's needs.

**Gifted Children.**     Estimates of the number of schoolchildren in this country who are gifted range from 2 to 5 percent. *Gifted children* are those who have shown the potential for outstanding achievement in intellectual, artistic, or other creative areas. Only about half of these children receive any special enrichment classes or activities to develop their capabilities (Horowitz & O'Brien, 1986). Unfortunately, gifted children who are left to their own devices without any encouragement may become bored with school, disruptive, or withdrawn.

Some gifted children may seem easy to identify. We know that a child of three who can read sentences and write words might be considered gifted because these are skills most children do not acquire until much later. Other types of giftedness are not as easy to measure, and few tests exist to identify them.

Child care professionals need to be aware of certain signs in order to identify gifted children and provide encouragement and a stimulating environment. Besides doing things earlier than most other children, gifted children usually demonstrate above-average curiosity about the world around them. They also have better than average language skills and good memory skills. They are able to concentrate for long periods and are independent at an early age.

Caregivers of gifted children need to provide them with opportunities for using, enhancing, and advancing their special talents. However, caregivers also need to be aware that a child who is gifted in one area may need help in other areas. A child who is very advanced verbally, for example, may have difficulties in physical coordination.

**Homeless Children.**     Estimates of the homeless population of the United States are hard to verify. Many of the people who are homeless do not live in shelters or government-sponsored camps. Instead, their cars are often their homes. In 1990, the government counted more than 200,000 homeless people, but many experts believe this figure was too low. They claim that the homeless population is closer to one to three million. Whatever the actual figure, experts agree that homelessness is a serious and growing problem in many parts of the country.

People who are homeless are actually a diverse group. Besides the "tramps" and alcoholics that one may envision when the word *homeless* is mentioned, the term may also include people with skills who have lost their job and have no source of income. Many of these people have children; some are single women who have been abused or abandoned or are simply divorced and have no means to pay for a home. Estimates of the number of homeless children range from 68,000 to 500,000 (Children's Defense Fund, 1991).

Homelessness and its causes take an enormous toll on young children. Researchers who have studied young children who are homeless find that they have higher levels of problem behavior than other children their age who are not homeless. Children who are homeless also tend to have one or more developmental delays and frequently suffer from severe depression, anxiety, and learning difficulties (Bassuk & Rosenberg, 1987). Separation problems, signs of emotional disturbance, and nutritional deficiencies are also common.

How can a child care provider address the special needs of children who are homeless? According to McCormick and Holden (1992, p. 64), "Homeless children often have no place to play, so providing rich play opportunities is of utmost importance. Play helps children cope with stress and form friendships, two of the children's big needs." These children also need activities that will help build their self-esteem, provide outlets for their feelings, and enhance their social skills.

Child care professionals also need to be sensitive to the problems and stresses homelessness places on parents. For example, seemingly simple tasks such as bathing a child or arranging transportation to day care may require enormous effort on the part of parents. Patience, flexibility, and sensitivity will foster better relations with parents and help them regard the child care setting as a source of support.

Early childhood professionals have a unique opportunity to help eliminate bias in young children. As a first step, caregivers must become aware of the bias in themselves.

## Confronting Bias in Yourself and Others

Diversity in early childhood education can enrich the experience of caregivers and children alike. To profit from the diverse cultural and racial backgrounds in a group, however, child care professionals first need to be aware of bias, in themselves, in the children they care for, and in the children's parents. As defined by Louise Derman-Sparks (1989), *bias* is any attitude, belief, or feeling that results in, and helps to justify, unfair treatment of an individual because of his or her identity.

For example, researchers have found that teachers tend to treat girls differently from boys and to treat children with disabilities differently from able children. Teachers are more likely to help three-year-old girls put on their jacket than boys of the same age and to help children with disabilities (whether boys or girls) with their clothing. This attitude about the relative competence of children is the first step toward a syndrome of "learned helplessness" (Froschl & Sprung, 1983).

A caregiver's bias may be expressed in expectations about what a child is capable of doing. Such expectations may be communicated through body language and verbal expression without the caregiver being aware of the fact. The child is likely to respond by acting in ways that confirm these expectations. For example, a teacher who expects a

## Mainstreaming Students with Disabilities

Sonya is a six-year-old who was born deaf. She lives with her parents and two brothers, all of whom can hear. She and her family have learned basic sign language. Sonya is not able to speak, but testing shows that her cognitive, motor, and other nonverbal communication skills are within normal expectations for her age.

Sonya's school district is offering her the option of attending the local school with a sign language interpreter or attending a special school for the deaf 30 miles from her home. In either case the cost of services would be paid for by the school district.

Sonya's parents seek the advice of two educational psychologists who are experienced in working with children with disabilities. This is what they are told.

Dr. Evan Morgan:

"Children who have handicaps need to learn skills that help them function in society. By placing Sonya in a regular public school class with her own sign language interpreter, she will have the opportunity to practice getting along in the hearing world. She may learn skills like lip reading that she might not learn in an environment where everyone signs. Ultimately, this could give her more independence in a hearing world.

"Instead of knowing only other children who are deaf, Sonya will meet hearing children through a wide range of school and neighborhood activities. She will have the opportunity to participate in the typical school-related activities of any elementary school. Of course, some children may be unkind to her because of her disability, but with proper preparation of the class, this kind of thoughtless behavior can be minimized.

"Sonya's teacher won't have specific training in teaching children who are deaf, but she will be assisted by a special education consultant provided by the school. It may be difficult to learn certain concepts because of the language delays associated with an interpreter, so additional special help may be needed."

Dr. Alice Chang:

"Children need to be comfortable in their environment in order to learn. In a school for the hearing impaired, Sonya will be surrounded by children who share her disability. Since children and teachers all communicate in sign language, Sonya will have an easier time making friends as well as making her wants, needs, ideas, and opinions known to others. In addition, she will be exposed to role models who are deaf and learn more about deaf culture. Special experiences or equipment may be made available to her in the special school that she might not otherwise get.

"Besides feeling comfortable with her environment, Sonya will have teachers who have specific training in methods for educating children who are deaf. They will use specialized approaches for teaching subjects such as reading that are traditionally difficult for children with hearing impairments.

"At such a school, Sonya will have access to intensive speech therapy to help her learn to speak. Of course, as Sonya becomes immersed in deaf culture her family may lag behind her in their own sign language communication skills.

"Although Sonya won't attend school with children who live nearby, she can meet neighborhood friends through weekend, vacation, and other out-of-school activities."

*What other questions would you ask if you were Sonya's parents? What else would you do before you made your decision? If you were a teacher at the local elementary school, what would you do to prepare for having Sonya in your classroom?*

Hispanic child to have trouble learning to read English may create doubt in the child's mind about her ability to master the skill. Experts believe that this phenomenon, called *self-fulfilling prophecy,* is a particular concern for teachers and caregivers when they belong to a class or race that is different from that of children they care for.

Because child care providers may have biased attitudes of which they are unaware, it is important for them to examine their behavior critically. Experts in the anti-bias field suggest that caregivers videotape themselves with the children or have others observe them so that any biased behaviors or attitudes can be identified and changed. Caregivers should look for differences in the way they respond both verbally and nonverbally to girls, boys, children with disabilities, and children of color. They should examine their responses to children's questions about skin color or other physical differences.

Child care professionals also need to help children deal with bias in themselves. Exposing children to others who are different from them is not enough to prevent prejudicial behavior. Caregivers must set limits and intervene immediately when biased behaviors or responses surface. When teachers intervene, they must respond both to the discriminator and to the target of the discriminatory behavior. The first child must be helped to determine the real reason for the conflict or discomfort; then the second child needs comfort and support. In some cases, a teacher may need to work on a long-term plan to help the children overcome any prejudices.

Many child development experts believe that the nation's diversity offers those working with children a unique opportunity to eradicate bias in young children. "Young children are very open to developing anti-bias attitudes and behaviors if adults actively counteract the negative impact of sexism, racism, and handicappism" (Derman-Sparks, 1989, p. 31).

*Parents can provide caregivers with insight about the development of their child and feedback on the effectiveness of programs and activities.*

on the effectiveness of various school programs and activities. They can provide perspective. Together, teachers and parents can help smooth the gap between a child's school and home environments.

### Developing a Partnership

Building partnerships with parents takes time and effort on the part of the caregiver. Some parents may be reluctant to involve themselves at all in their child's preschool or child care experience. They may have the attitude that the "teacher knows best" or that the child care professional will not take their ideas seriously. Caregivers should anticipate

## Working with Parents

Although child care providers may consider working with children to be their main job, parents are an important part of the picture, too. Parents can provide caregivers with invaluable information and insight about the development, experiences, and problems of their child. They can provide feedback that parents will respond in different ways to efforts to involve them. In most cases, however, the willingness of parents to become involved is a reflection of cultural and social factors, as well as personal resources. Parents who are not involved in their child's school program may actually be very concerned about their child. A wide variety of parent involvement activities will help encourage the participation of diverse groups of parents.

A partnership with parents implies closely cooperating with each other as equals. Child care professionals can make parents feel like partners by making an effort from the very beginning to get to know each family and home environment. Being sensitive to a family's special problems and concerns will help build trust. It is important for caregivers to be aware of family circumstances—such as divorce, parents who don't speak English, unemployment, or alcoholism—that could affect the child's behavior or welfare. If, for example, a child's parents have a limited understanding of English, finding a translator to be present at parent conferences is a necessary first step in building a working relationship. Moreover, whenever possible, information that is sent home should be written in English and in the parents' native language.

Child care professionals should make every effort to make parents feel as comfortable as possible. Parents should know they are welcome to observe or participate in the child care setting at any time.

## FOCUS ON  Communicating with Parents

### Discussing a Discipline Problem

Jordan is an energetic three-year-old who has been at Brookfield Day Care for only four weeks. He enjoys the group activities, but at free play he becomes impatient if other children do not do what he wants. Sometimes, like today, his impatience leads to physical roughness. Elaine, the head teacher, has a chat with Jordan's mother when she comes to pick him up.

ELAINE: Jordan certainly loves to sing. He already knows all the words to the new song we learned this week. And at circle time he told us all about visiting his grandma.

JORDAN'S MOM: I think Jordan's getting along really well. I was worried that he'd have a hard time getting used to being here all day.

ELAINE: I think he's doing fine. But sometimes he gets a little rough with the other children. He's so energetic and has so many ideas. He always wants the other children to play the games he thinks up. Today, I had to give him a time out because he hit another boy who wouldn't play X-Men with him.

JORDAN'S MOM: Oh, sometimes he gets very physical when he's frustrated. I'm sure he didn't mean to hurt anyone.

ELAINE: I'm sure he didn't, but he has to learn not to hit. He gets so involved that he forgets that not everyone wants to play his way.

JORDAN'S MOM: He's like that at home with his sister, too. He gets upset if she won't let him be the boss.

ELAINE: Well, we have to help him remember he can't use his fists when things don't go his way. Maybe we could do some of the same things at school and at home so that he gets the message. Is now a good time to talk about this in my office, or shall we make an appointment soon?

*Why do you think Elaine brought up Jordan's love of singing first? Do you think Elaine explained her concern to Jordan's mother in a reasonable way? Would you have done it differently? Do you think Elaine should do anything differently in the way she handles Jordan's roughness now that she knows he acts the same way at home?*

They should also know that caregivers are willing and available to talk with them—by telephone or in person—whenever a concern arises. Parent group meetings can be organized to give parents a chance to discuss their feelings about day care or preschool and can also provide caregivers with an opportunity for presenting programs on parenting skills.

Fathers need to be encouraged to get involved in their child's day-care or preschool experience. Scheduling parent conferences for a time when both parents can come makes it clear to the father that his input is important, too. The participation of both mothers and fathers can be increased by weaving parents' careers or talents into the curriculum and inviting them to share their skills and knowledge with the children. Parents can be invited to share a story, a talent, or an enjoyable activity. Asking a parent to participate in a specific activity is often the most effective way of increasing his or her involvement and addressing diversity in the curriculum.

Opportunities for communication with parents occur on a daily basis when parents drop off and pick up their children. By taking a few moments to chat whenever possible, caregivers can gain information that may help a child's day go more smoothly, and parents can learn about their child's day-care activities. Caregivers should schedule parent conferences at least twice during the year to provide parents with a more detailed picture of their child's progress and experiences. At these meetings, parents should be encouraged to ask questions or express any concerns they may have about their child or the program. Having children take their projects and artwork home is another way of letting parents know what is going on in the classroom. For the parents of infants and toddlers, a daily information sheet on eating, sleeping, and any health concerns is crucial.

## Resolving Conflicts

Conflicts with parents are inevitable. As human beings, child care professionals make mistakes. It is important to admit errors and to keep parents informed of attempts to deal with previous concerns. Regular, open communication builds trust, which helps maintain positive relationships when conflicts arise.

*Parents who are under stress sometimes take their frustrations out on caregivers.*

Some conflicts may stem from differences in attitude or personality. Some actually have nothing to do with the caregiver. In these instances, a caregiver may simply be an outlet for a parent's frustration. For example, Jimmy's mother exploded when June, the preschool teacher, showed her the broken zipper on Jimmy's winter jacket. Jimmy's mother wasn't really angry at June but at the fact that she would have to find the time or the money to get the jacket fixed. The zipper problem may simply have been one more aggravation at the end of a very frustrating day. As a professional, the caregiver has a responsibility to remain calm and open in difficult interactions with parents and to keep the matter confidential.

It is hard to listen while feeling attacked. Yet it is critical for a parent to know that he has been heard. Restating a parent's words gives him the opportunity to explain further. It also enables the caregiver to get a better idea of what the parent wants. Then the caregiver can state another view and the reasons for it, paving the way for a dialogue instead of a shouting match.

Some conflicts with parents have deeper causes than aggravation or impatience. People from different cultures may have different expectations and attitudes about child care. For example, many Hispanic children are spoon-fed and bottle dependent far beyond the age of most other children. While the child care provider may find this practice backward and try to promote independence in the children, the behavior is a reflection of cultural values, in this case a belief in the importance of interdependence (Gonzales-Mena, 1993). The key here is to work with parents toward mutual understanding and a resolution that is acceptable to all.

Child care professionals can sometimes play a role in resolving parent-child conflicts by providing support and suggestions. They can recommend reading material on a particular issue or organize discussion groups for parents to talk about mutual concerns. Inviting parents to observe or participate in the child care setting is another way for parents to learn more about their child's behavior. It is important to remember that good parenting is a skill and that skill building takes time. For issues that seem to be beyond the scope of the caregiver, a community resource list or a list of local children's services should be readily available. This list should be available in both English and Spanish and include a wide variety of organizations.

## Safety and Health

Accidents are the leading cause of death in children between the ages of 1 and 11 years. In fact, children under 6 sustain more injuries than people of any other age group. In child care settings, most injuries are the result of a fall. Accidents involving a mechanical device or object are also common.

Three factors contribute to the likelihood of an accident: the child's activity level, the safety level of the play space, and the level of supervision. While accidents most frequently occur in outdoor play areas, accidents can and do happen anywhere. Child care providers must look carefully at all areas where children can possibly be to make sure the environment is safe.

### Arranging the Environment

What is a safe environment for children? A safe environment is one that has been examined thoroughly and from which all potential hazards have been removed. Some experts suggest that after the basic fire and electrical safety measures and sanitary protections have been put in place, caregivers should crawl around the space on hands and knees. This will give them a view of the facility from the child's

perspective and may reveal some additional hazards that need to be removed or shielded from the children.

To prevent the risk of fire, smoke alarms must be installed in all areas of the center or preschool and checked regularly. Fire extinguishers need to be within easy reach of all rooms. Space heaters, woodstoves, fireplaces, and hot plates are not recommended. Electrical circuits should not be overloaded, and all wiring and plugs must be checked to make sure they are in good condition. Matches and lighters must always be placed out of the reach of children. Only flame-retardant materials should be used in the facility. Trash, especially newspapers, should be stored in covered containers and disposed of regularly. Child care professionals must also draw up fire evacuation plans and practice them with the children.

Electrical safety includes covering all electrical outlets with caps or outlet covers and making sure that all power tools, appliances, and electrical cords are out of the reach of children. Caregivers must unplug appliances when not in use and keep the floors near appliances dry.

Caregivers must also be alert to other potential hazards in indoor spaces. Any window that a child might be able to reach needs to be secured. Stairways must have safety gates. High chairs should be placed where children cannot reach things that might hurt them. Drapery cords should be tied up out of children's reach, and rugs should have a nonslip backing. Unstable furniture or furniture with sharp edges must be removed. All cribs and baby furniture need to meet Consumer Product Commission safety standards. Other measures to take for ensuring a safe environment include placing cleaning solutions and medicines in a locked cabinet out of reach of children, setting tap water at 120 degrees or lower to avoid accidental burns, and removing any poisonous plants from play areas. Using a microwave oven to heat baby bottles is not recommended because the formula is heated unevenly.

According to the National Academy of Early Childhood Programs, each child requires a minimum of 35 square feet of usable floor space. In choosing equipment for a room, it is essential to make sure furniture and toys are sturdy, child sized, and easy to clean and repair. Toys should not have

Band-Aids are an essential item in the child care setting. Children under age six have more accidents than any other age group.

small parts that could become loose and be swallowed. Indoor climbing equipment should have mats underneath to reduce the impact of a fall; carpeting alone is not enough to prevent injury.

Keeping play areas and equipment clean is part of providing a safe and healthy environment. Floors need to be cleaned daily, as should toys and play equipment, especially in settings where children are still putting objects in their mouth. In bathrooms and kitchens, the use of dispenser soap and paper towels will help prevent the spread of germs. Diaper changing areas and food preparation areas should be cleaned after each use. Frequent hand washing is important for caregivers and children alike.

All adults should be instructed in the proper handling of blood and body fluid spills. When coming into contact with blood, vomitus, mucus, urine, and feces, *universal precautions* should be the rule. This means that blood and body fluids should be handled as if infected with a communicable disease—whether they are or not. Contact, cleanup, and disposal procedures should include the regular use of latex gloves and disinfectant. Hands should be washed thoroughly with soap after diaper changing and contact with mouthed toys and soiled tissues.

Outdoor play areas need to be child friendly and safe, too. The outdoor play space should be enclosed or fenced. Climbing equipment must have a safety surface beneath it—such as sand, pea gravel, wood chips, or shredded tires—to absorb the impact of falls. All outdoor equipment should meet Consumer Product Safety Commission standards and be properly installed. Play equipment should be adequately spaced so that children on one piece of equipment will not get in the way of children on another piece. The placement of outdoor equipment is also important. It should be situated so that it is easy for caregivers to see and supervise the children.

Outdoor playground equipment should have a safety surface, such as sand or wood chips, beneath it to absorb the impact of falls.

### Supervising Children

Supervising children on the playground involves more than watching them carefully. It also means knowing what children of a particular age are able to do and making sure that they are using equipment that is appropriate for them. Children under three years of age, for example, should only use swings that support them completely and do not go very high.

To provide the safest possible environment, child care facilities need trained, competent adults to supervise the children, as well as a sufficient number of supervisors. The National Association for the Education of Young Children has established recommended ratios of caregivers to children for each age group. For infants, the recommended ratio is one caregiver for every 3 children. For toddler groups, there should be one caregiver for every 6 children, and the group should be limited to 12 children.

"Adults must constantly and closely supervise and attend every child younger than the age of 3. They must be close enough to touch infants when awake, catch a climbing toddler before she hits the ground, be aware of every move of a 2-year-old, and be close enough to offer another toy when 2-year-olds have difficulty sharing" (Bredekamp, 1987, p. 12). Four- to five-year-olds should be in groups of no more than 20 children with a minimum of two adults. Five- to eight-year-old groups should not exceed 25 children with at least two adults supervising (Bredekamp, 1987).

Another aspect of supervising children involves dealing with emergency situations. Child care providers must know what to do in case of accident, sudden illness, and fire. Most states require that every child care center or preschool have at least one person on duty at all times who has current certification in first-aid and cardiopulmonary resuscitation (CPR) techniques. A chart illustrating basic first-aid techniques and a poison control telephone number or hot line should be posted in every room. In addition, procedures to be followed in case of fire or medical emergency need to be defined and practiced.

Child care establishments must have phone numbers where parents can be reached in an emergency. They should also have a health history for each child, including the record of a required annual physical exam with updated immunizations, information about allergies and medications, and the names and phone numbers of family doctors, dentists, or other health professionals and specialists. Parents must be aware of the center's policy regarding sick children, and child care providers need to be familiar with the symptoms of common illnesses.

### Teaching Children

One of a caregiver's most important responsibilities is to educate children about health and safety. Caregivers can do this in many ways, but one way to start is by setting a good example. Making the environment safe and clean and preparing nutritious meals and snacks help children learn good habits. Children should be encouraged to develop good

Caregivers can teach children about good nutrition through everyday activities such as preparing a healthy lunch or snack.

hygiene habits, such as washing their hands before eating and after going to the bathroom.

In addition to these everyday routines, the curriculum and activities should teach the children about nutrition, hygiene, and safety. Children can participate in setting up rules for safe behavior in indoor and outdoor areas. Simple signs, posters, and illustrations can help remind children of health and safety rules.

Demonstrations of proper dental care and toothbrushing techniques can be useful. It is important that each child have an individual, labeled toothbrush, that the toothpaste be distributed by a sanitary method, and that disposable cups be used. Two-year-olds are capable of understanding that certain foods and behaviors are good for teeth while others are not (Comer, 1987).

Early table foods for infants may include such items as yogurt, mashed fruit and vegetables, and well-cooked freshly ground meat (Pipes, 1989). Toddlers' diets can have more variety and can include finger foods, such as graham crackers, soft cheese cubes, or bananas. Foods such as whole grapes, popcorn, hard candies, and nuts should be avoided, however, because young children can choke on them. A balanced diet for older children should include foods from all the food groups. Nutritional guides for the recommended serving quantities for each age group are widely available. (See Appendix F; also, U.S. Department of Agriculture, 1992, *Nutrition Guidance for the Child Nutrition Programs*.)

One way of educating children about proper nutrition is by involving them in food selection and preparation. Preschool children can help take out the equipment and ingredients needed to make certain dishes. Preschoolers can also help spoon the ingredients into measuring cups, pour them into bowls, and stir them. There are many simple snack recipes that young children can prepare themselves. Activities that involve food preparation offer an opportunity to talk with children about good nutrition.

### Protecting Children

Child care professionals have the additional responsibility of protecting children. While a care-

**FOCUS ON** **Decision Making in Child Care**

### Reporting Abuse

Josie stood in the doorway of the ABC Child Care Center greeting the children as they arrived and having a few words with parents. Her eyes narrowed as she saw Jimmy and his mother approaching. As usual, Jimmy was downcast and subdued. His mother was telling him that he was to go to his father's house that evening. "And you behave yourself when you're there, Jimmy. Your father can't stand you at the best of times." Reaching the doorway and seeing Josie, Jimmy's mother had some final words before she left: "Well, here's Jimmy for the day—and you're welcome to him."

As Jimmy walked slowly into the center, Josie made her decision: she would speak to the director of the center and request that Jimmy's mother be reported to the authorities for emotional abuse of her child. This was certainly not the first time she had heard Jimmy's mother put him down; in fact, Josie could not remember ever having heard a good word about Jimmy from his mother. In the past couple of weeks, she had also noticed that Jimmy was avoiding other children and spending more and more time sitting alone in a corner.

A child does not have to suffer bruises to be abused. Emotional abuse of children leaves no physical evidence, but it can be equally damaging. Because it is hard to prove, however, child care workers may be reluctant to report cases of suspected emotional abuse. At a teachers' meeting the previous week, everyone had decided to write down evidence of damaging comments by Jimmy's mother as well as descriptions of Jimmy's behavior. They had several days' worth of documentation now. Josie believed that she had a moral obligation to report her concerns. She was also aware that her state required child care providers to report suspected cases of child abuse.

*If you had been in Josie's position what would you have done? Would you have spoken to Jimmy's mother? Ignored the situation hoping it would right itself? Reported Jimmy's mother to the authorities? What about Jimmy's father?*

giver does everything possible to protect the children from hazards, illness, and poor nutrition in the child care setting, she also needs to help protect them from abuse or neglect. It is estimated that at least a million children are abused each year and that between 2,000 and 5,000 die each year as a direct result of child abuse (Kendrick, Kaufmann, & Messenger, 1991).

The National Committee for Prevention of Child Abuse (NCPCA) defines *child abuse* as a "nonaccidental injury or pattern of injuries to a child for which there is no 'reasonable' explanation." Child abuse can take the form of nonaccidental injuries, neglect, sexual molestation, or emotional abuse. The incidence of abuse and neglect is probably higher than the figures of reported cases suggest. Although the number of such reports in child care settings is quite low, it is clear that even one incident is too much.

What makes an adult abuse a child? Some abusers have been found to be isolated and under stress and to feel a deep sense of failure. Many were abused themselves. Some do not know how to control their emotions or are under the influence of alcohol or other drugs that impair their ability to control their emotions. In many cases, the cause of child abuse can be traced to personal problems, such as unemployment, or to social factors, such as the lack of a supportive family or community. In addition, the idea that violence is a way to deal with problems may be a contributing factor (Kendrick et al., 1991).

**Signs of Abuse.** Because child care professionals spend so much time with children and are trained to observe each child's appearance, behavior, and development, they are in a very good position to notice a possible case of abuse or neglect. Among the indicators of physical abuse are repeated or unexplained injuries—such as burns, fractures, bruises, bites, eye or head injuries, and clustered injuries—beyond the usual bumps and bruises of active children (Kendrick et al., 1991). Children who have been physically abused may display an unusual fear of adults or become withdrawn, disruptive, anxious, or uncommunicative. They may show signs that they have been given alcoholic beverages or drugs. Such signs include breath that smells of alcohol or dilated pupils.

Children who have been sexually abused may have difficulty walking or sitting. They may complain of pain in the genital or anal area, or these areas may be bruised. Sexually abused children may be unwilling to have their clothes changed or to be helped with toileting. They may exhibit sudden and extreme changes in behavior or show unusual interest or knowledge of sexual matters. Some children may tell a caregiver about the sexual abuse or act out such experiences in dramatic play with dolls or other children.

*Emotional abuse* is the use of words or actions that make the child feel rejected, ignored, or terrorized. Signs of emotional abuse include low self-esteem, general unhappiness, and a fear of adults. Emotionally abused children often react without emotion to unpleasant statements and actions. Adults who belittle or degrade children may be abusing them emotionally.

Physical or emotional neglect involves a lack of physical, emotional, intellectual, or social support from parents or other primary caregivers. Children who are suffering from neglect usually lack supervision, adequate clothing, good hygiene, medical or dental care, nutrition, and shelter and are frequently absent from the child care setting. However, in identifying neglect, it is important that caregivers be sensitive to different cultural values, different child-rearing practices, and homelessness as possible explanations for a child's condition. Some children may be inadequately clothed because their parents cannot afford to buy them proper clothing.

Child care professionals have a responsibility to report cases of suspected child abuse or neglect to the appropriate authorities.

"Neglect is not necessarily related to poverty; it reflects a breakdown in household management, as well as a breakdown of concern for and caretaking of the child" (Kendrick et al., 1991, p. 193).

**Helping Abused Children.** It is the responsibility of child care professionals to report any case of suspected child abuse or child neglect to the appropriate authorities. In some states, there are penalties for failing to do so. Caregivers should also advise the parents of any such action unless they believe that this will endanger a child further and possibly cause the parents to flee with the child. Apparently, many parents are grateful when their abusive behavior is reported, especially if bringing the behavior out in the open results in supportive services.

**Working with Parents and Children.** Child care providers can use their influence and knowledge to prevent potentially abusive situations from growing worse. As role models and authority figures, they should share their knowledge of child development and child-rearing techniques with parents. As a link with community services, they should let parents know about agencies that can provide them with support services such as counseling, temporary shelter, drug treatment, or food stamps. The timely intervention of a caregiver could save a child from harm and might help keep a family together.

Child care professionals also need to let children know they are in their corner. As role models, caregivers must show appropriate kinds of physical contact with the children and treat each child with respect. As children's advocates, child care providers should educate youngsters about their right to say no and teach them the difference between "good" and "bad" touching. Perhaps most important, caregivers should help children learn how to tell a trusted adult about experiences that are upsetting to them.

## Implications and Applications

Transforming an awareness of diversity into action is the challenge facing child care professionals. How should they deal with diversity and make it a positive, enriching element in the child care setting? Child care providers must first screen the classroom environment. This means thoroughly reviewing the toys, books, and other materials used by the children to eliminate anything that reinforces racial, ethnic, gender, or differently abled stereotypes.

The setting should reflect the multicultural backgrounds of the children, the community, and the nation. Books and toys need to show diversity in gender roles, in racial and cultural backgrounds, and in family life-styles and incomes. Louise Derman-Sparks suggests displaying pictures of all the children, their families, and the staff, as well as pictures of a broad spectrum of people at work and play. She also recommends finding out at the beginning of the year the terms each family uses to identify their ethnic group, what and how each family teaches their children about their culture, and how the family celebrates various occasions. Child care providers can then use this information to develop

activities that allow the children to explore cultural diversity through frequent, concrete, hands-on experiences. Instead of teaching children to ignore differences, Derman-Sparks recommends helping children celebrate them. Children also need to understand that despite cultural or ethnic differences, people everywhere have similar characteristics (Derman-Sparks, 1989).

In child care settings where participant diversity is limited, caregivers can implement a "sister schools" program (Koeppel, 1992). Such a program usually involves two centers or schools in which the children are from different racial, ethnic, economic, or geographic backgrounds. Through an exchange of photographs, art, and language-experience stories, the children learn about people who have different ideas and different ways of doing things.

It is crucial to involve parents in implementing a multicultural program. Parents can offer suggestions and make invaluable contributions to the program, and they are a necessary ingredient in enlarging their children's horizons. Involving parents also helps avoid confrontation by giving them a chance to express their reservations and ask questions (Ramsey & Derman-Sparks, 1992).

Applying the multicultural approach to infant care is somewhat different. In this case, the equipment, material, and activities used are less relevant because the focus is on interaction with people. Nevertheless, child care providers should survey the premises and remove any inappropriate materials. What is most relevant is the understanding the baby's parents and the caregiver reach about the way the caregiver feeds, diapers, holds, and interacts with the baby (Gonzales-Mena, 1993). Making parents a part of the planning process—whether in curriculum planning or in tending to a child's basic needs—will enhance relationships with parents as well as promote multicultural understanding.

For children with special needs, caregivers must develop goals and activities that are appropriate to their developmental and behavioral abilities. Caregivers should recognize that some children need more time than others to complete a task, that some children need their work divided into smaller tasks, and that many children need to practice what they are learning. However, children with special needs also have strengths. The early childhood professional must help identify these talents and capitalize on them in everyday activities.

The job of the child care professional is to provide care for families, not just children. In many ways, caregivers are like members of the extended family, providing support for children and parents alike. Involving the family is the best way to create continuity between the child's home and the school or child care center. One way to do this is by having children make family albums and by encouraging parents to observe and participate whenever possible. Regular communication through formal and informal contact is essential. Allowing children to bring from home a favorite toy or book that is labeled with the child's name may also help bridge the gap between home and the child care establishment.

What parents want above all from their child care arrangement is a safe, healthy, nurturing environment. Child care professionals have a responsibility to keep their facilities clean, free of hazards, secure, and child friendly. They should also make a point of sharing information with families to help keep children safe and healthy at home. A daily health check with the parent present can be included in the everyday greeting procedure. Daily health checks provide a brief but regular opportunity for discussion about each child's health and well-being. Caregivers can invite guest speakers to talk with parents at parent meetings on topics such as nutrition, fire safety, or teaching street smarts. They can also send children home with information on these topics. Some centers have lending libraries that parents are welcome to use.

The child care setting should reflect the multicultural background of the children and portray different cultures in a positive way.

When problems arise with children or their families that are beyond the scope or training of child care professionals, it is important to know what community resources are available. For example, a child who appears to be having visual problems can be referred to the appropriate agency for a vision screening. A parent who suddenly needs a place to live can be referred to agencies that provide emergency shelter. Community service directories, resource/referral agency listings, and even the Yellow Pages of the phone book list many services for children and families. Child care professionals should contact various community agencies to learn more about the services offered and their costs and consider inviting officials of various social service agencies to parent meetings to explain what they do and how they can help.

## CHAPTER 5    REVIEW

### SUMMARY

- The increasing diversity of the population of the United States means that child care professionals will be caring for children from a greater variety of racial, ethnic, and religious backgrounds. Caregivers need to learn about the cultural backgrounds of the children in their care.

- Child care providers can become culturally aware by observing parents and children closely and by reading about other cultures and their child-rearing practices.

- Caregivers must be sensitive to the problems, needs, and concerns of different types of families. A child's behavior in the care setting will reflect his home situation and his relationship with his parents.

- By law, child care establishments may not deny admission to children with disabilities. "Readily achievable" steps must be taken to adapt the physical environment of the care setting to meet the needs of children with disabilities.

- Children with special needs include children with disabilities, gifted children, children who are homeless, and children who have been abused or neglected. Caregivers should learn to recognize signs that a child may have special needs.

- Those caring for children with special needs should work out individualized programs with goals and objectives for each child in cooperation with the child's family and other professionals.

- For diversity to be an element that enriches lives rather than something that contributes to divisiveness, caregivers must take a good look at bias—in themselves as well as in the children they care for and their families.

- A good working partnership with parents benefits all concerned. Caregivers must work to foster this relationship by getting to know the families, making them feel comfortable, providing them with opportunities to talk with caregivers and other parents, and maintaining good communication.

- The primary responsibility of child care professionals is to create a safe and healthy environment for children, that is, one in which all hazards and potential hazards have been removed.

- Caregivers must know what to do in emergencies and have complete health information about each child.

- Child care professionals need to provide a healthy, balanced diet for children. Knowledge of good nutrition and age-appropriate foods is important.

- Child care professionals must create and maintain a healthy and clean environment for children through rigorous hygiene procedures. Caregivers must model healthy practices themselves and follow measures to prevent the spread of contagious diseases.

- Child care professionals are the most likely people in a child's world to notice possible cases of abuse and neglect. Knowing the signs of child abuse and neglect and what to do to help a child and his family is critical.

- Child care professionals must create a bias-free multicultural learning environment. Involving parents is an important part of the process.

- Some problems are beyond the scope and training of child care providers. In such situations, the caregiver should be able to refer parents and children to resources and services in the community that can give them the help they need.

## BUILDING VOCABULARY

Write a definition for each vocabulary term listed below.

bias
child abuse
disability
diversity
emotional abuse
gifted children

individualized education plan (IEP)
learning disability
least restrictive environment
mainstreaming
self-fulfilling prophecy
universal precautions

## ACQUIRING KNOWLEDGE

1. Why is dealing with diversity a key concern of child care professionals today?
2. Why is it important for caregivers to be aware of a child's cultural background?
3. What steps could a child care provider take to become more culturally aware?
4. Name three factors that could influence a child's learning style and behavior.
5. Give two examples of children with special needs.
6. What does the term *least restrictive environment* mean?
7. What is the purpose of mainstreaming?
8. What is a learning disability?
9. Many children with learning disabilities enter child care undiagnosed. What are three characteristics that may indicate that a child has a learning disability?
10. How can caregivers help children with disabilities?
11. List two characteristics of young children that may be indications of giftedness.
12. How does homelessness affect young children?
13. What are the special needs of homeless children?
14. Define and give an example of bias.
15. What can child care professionals do to help children deal with bias in themselves?
16. What type of relationship should caregivers try to develop with parents?
17. What are some methods of resolving conflicts that may arise between child care professionals and parents?
18. Name three factors that could contribute to the likelihood of a child having an accident.
19. How should the child care environment be arranged to avoid the risk of fire?
20. What electrical and sanitary precautions should be taken to ensure a safe indoor environment for children?
21. How can outdoor play equipment be arranged to avoid accidents?
22. What are the recommended ratios of caregivers to infants and to toddlers?
23. What kind of food is appropriate for toddlers?

24. What are some signs of physical abuse of children?
25. What can child care professionals do to create an environment that presents diversity in a positive way?
26. What do parents want most in a child care environment?

## THINKING CRITICALLY

1. In many cases, the values of immigrant and minority groups are at odds with those of mainstream American culture. Children are often caught in the middle. What do you think early childhood professionals can do to help children from these backgrounds reconcile the divergent cultures without abandoning their own heritage?
2. In the past 20 years, Congress has passed a series of laws banning discrimination against people with mental and physical disabilities. How have these laws affected the lives of children with disabilities? How have they affected early childhood professionals? Do you think the results have generally been positive? Explain your answer.
3. Some experts claim that there may be as many as 500,000 children in this country who are homeless. How do you think child care providers can make the child care experience an enriching rather than humiliating one for these children?
4. Studies have shown that by the time children reach middle school, girls are less likely than boys to speak out or raise their hand in response to a question. What reasons can you think of for this behavior? Do you think child care professionals should try to change it?
5. Children may have to face a variety of difficulties, from family problems to abuse. What do you think the proper role of the child care professional is in dealing with the problems of the children they care for?

## OBSERVATIONS AND APPLICATIONS

1. Arrange to attend a program at a child care center or family day-care facility in which parents are invited to participate. This program could be a parent conference or orientation. Observe the interaction of parents and caregivers. What types of activities are planned to involve parents in this program? What other preparations have been made so that parents (and children) will feel welcome?
2. Arrange to spend an hour as children are arriving at a child care center for the day. Observe the way parents and caregivers greet and interact. Find out whether there is a routine children must follow when they arrive. (For example, are they required to hang up their coats and use toys in the play area until all the children have arrived?) During this time, observe the way caregivers respond to boys, girls, and children with special needs. What is your overall opinion of the way the caregivers at this center greet children and parents?
3. An individualized education plan (IEP) describes the program designed for a child with special needs. Interview a caregiver to learn who is responsible for completing IEPs at her school or center and what type of information is requested on the forms. Find out what types of activities or

materials are recommended for a child with learning disabilities. On the basis of what you have learned about IEPs, do you think they serve a useful purpose? How might they be improved?

4. A gifted four-year-old has recently joined your class. Ever since he arrived, the other children have bullied him, and he seems unable to stick up for himself. What can you do about the situation? Do you think you ought to take steps to prevent the bullying, or should you let the boy fight his own battles? What would you say to the boy's parents? Would you discuss the situation with other parents?

## SUGGESTIONS FOR FURTHER READING

Bosque, E., & Watson, S. (1988). *Safe and sound: How to prevent and treat most common childhood emergencies.* New York: St. Martin's Press.

Derman-Sparks, L. (1989). *Anti-bias curriculum: Tools for empowering young children.* Washington, DC: National Association for the Education of Young Children.

Endres, J., & Rockwell, R. E. (1990). *Food, nutrition, and the young child.* Columbus, OH: Merrill.

Fallen, N. H., & Umansky, W. (Eds.). (1984). *Young children with special needs.* Columbus, OH: Merrill.

Froschl, M., Colon, L., Rubin, E., & Sprung, B. (1984). *Including all of us: An early childhood curriculum about disability.* New York: Equity Concepts.

Gaumer, N., et al. (1992). *Day care for all children: Integrating children with special needs into community child care settings.* Springfield: Illinois Department of Children and Family Services.

Hale, J. (1991). The transmission of cultural values to young African American children. *Young children, 46*(6).

Kendall, F. (1983). *Diversity in the classroom: A multicultural approach to the education of young children.* New York: Teachers College Press.

Kendrick, A. S., Kaufman, R., & Messenger, K. P. (Eds.). (1991). *Healthy young children: A manual for programs.* Washington, DC: National Association for the Education of Young Children.

Kitano, M. K. (1982). Young gifted children: Strategies for preschool teachers. *Young children, 37*(4).

Meisels, S. (1985). *Developmental screening in early childhood; A guide.* Washington, DC: National Association for the Education of Young Children.

Neugebauer, B. (Ed.). (1992). *Alike and different: Exploring our humanity with young children.* Washington, DC: National Association for the Education of Young Children.

Peterson, N. L. (1987). *Early intervention for handicapped and at-risk children.* Denver: Love.

Ramsey, P. G. (1986). *Teaching and learning in a diverse world: Multicultural education for young children.* New York: Teachers College Press.

Ramsey, P. G., Vold, E. B., & Williams, L. R. (1989). *Multicultural education: A source book.* New York: Garland.

Wolfe, J. (1989). The gifted preschooler: Developmentally different, but still 3 or 4 years old. *Young Children, 44*(3).

# PART 3

# Infants

### CHAPTER 6
### Physical Development
Chapter 6 describes how infants grow and change and how they develop motor skills during the first year. The chapter also discusses the effects of heredity and environment on physical development during infancy.

### CHAPTER 7
### Intellectual Development
Chapter 7 explains how infants develop cognitive skills such as language and memory. The chapter summarizes Piaget's theory on sensorimotor learning during the first two years of life.

### CHAPTER 8
### Emotional and Social Development
Chapter 8 describes how leading theories define and explain infant emotion. It also discusses milestones in the social and emotional development of infants.

# 6 Physical Development

## OBJECTIVES
Studying this chapter will enable
you to

- Describe how an infant's body,
  nervous system, and sensory
  system grow and develop during
  the first year.
- Explain how an infant acquires
  movement patterns and skills.
- Discuss how heredity and the
  environment affect an infant's
  physical development.
- Identify ways in which child care
  professionals can promote the
  physical development of infants
  and work with parents to provide
  infants with a safe and stimulating
  learning environment.

CHARLENE heard crying and looked at her watch. She knew it was Zachary. The six-month-old was up from his morning nap and ready for a bottle. Charlene peered over the side of the crib and the crying ceased, although his face was still damp and flushed. As she lifted Zachary, he reached forward with one hand to grasp the bottle she had placed on the table next to his crib. She spoke softly to him while she settled him comfortably in a seat. Then she watched as he shook the bottle and moved it from hand to hand a few times before holding it to his mouth to drink.

Charlene looked around the infant room of the Sunnyside Children's Center. The other six-month-old, Julia, was awake, too, but she was lying quietly in her crib, staring at a mobile that was gently circling above her. As Charlene approached her, Julia shifted her gaze, raised her head, and made a gurgling noise. Charlene said, "Are you thirsty, too, Julia?" and Julia moved her arms and legs excitedly. Charlene lifted her up and gave her a bottle, and soon Julia was busy drinking, too.

## Principles of Physical Development

When do infants begin to sit up? When do their teeth come in? What can infants see? All these questions relate to the physical development of the infant. An infant's physical development involves more than changes in the size and shape of his body; it also includes changes in his brain and nervous system, changes in his sensory system, and the development of motor skills.

Not all infants develop at the same rate. At the age of six months, Zachary was able to reach forward and grasp a bottle. Julia, on the other hand, was not at the stage where she could control her movements. Her movements were more reflexive. Both were perfectly normal.

This chapter describes the physical growth and development of infants during the first year. It also discusses the influence of heredity and environment on physical development and considers how caregivers can contribute to an infant's health and developing motor skills.

## Sequence of Development

While no two infants are exactly alike in their growth and development, certain principles govern the sequence of their physical development. All humans grow in a *cephalocaudal*, or head-to-foot, direction. That is, the upper body parts develop before the lower body parts. Thus, at birth, the head is the most fully developed part of the body, making up one-fourth of the newborn's total body length. The legs are the least developed part. As the infant grows, the head continues to grow but at a much slower pace than the rest of the body. In a one-year-old baby, the head is one-fifth of total length; in an adult, the head is one-eighth of total length. In a newborn, the legs account for one-fourth of body length; in an adult, they account for half of the body length.

Physical development is also *proximodistal*, going from the center outward. Thus, at birth, the head and trunk are more fully developed than the arms and legs, the arms and legs are more fully devel-

oped than the hands and feet, and the hands and feet are more fully developed than the fingers and toes. The same principle applies to muscle development. As the infant grows, the muscles of the head and trunk will mature first. Proximodistal muscle development means that an infant learns to hold her head up before she sits up, to sit up before she crawls, and to crawl before she stands.

## Rate of Development

Children follow a certain sequence in their physical development, but they do not grow or develop at a constant rate. For example, in the first five to six months of life, infants gain weight rapidly, often doubling their birth weight. After this, their weight gain eases slightly, so that by their first birthday, they weigh about three times their birth weight. Weight gain slows even more in the years that follow. Most children put on weight or grow taller in sudden, short periods of time.

Infants also develop at individual rates. Some infants crawl at 5 months, while others do not begin crawling until they are 12 months old. Although a small number of babies are born with teeth, some do not get their first teeth until they are more than one year old. There is no absolute timetable for the developmental changes and growth an infant experiences. Instead, there is a range of time during which most infants reach certain milestones. For example, most infants can be expected to pull themselves up on furniture when they are between 6 and 12 months of age and to stand alone when they are between 9 and 16 months old.

This variation in the rate of growth and development is largely hereditary. However, environment and culture do play a role. The infant of crawling age who is allowed to explore a room freely is likely to crawl sooner than one confined to a playpen. Studies have shown that infant care patterns can be responsible for variations in development (Belsky, 1988).

Because infants grow at varying rates, parents often compare their infants with other infants of the same age. Child care professionals need to reassure parents that differences in the rate of development are normal. Parents should be reminded that there is a range of ages for growth and development rather than an average age. This is often referred to as the "range of normalcy." Concern is appropriate when an infant's development deviates greatly from the normal developmental ranges in a number of categories.

## Critical Periods

There are specific times during development when all children must have appropriate experiences if they are to develop in a normal way. These times are referred to as critical periods. For example, if infants are undernourished in the critical period just after birth, their central nervous system will be permanently impaired (Galler, Ramsey, & Solimano, 1984, 1985). The same effect does not occur in children who are undernourished at a later period.

Much of the research regarding critical periods has been done with animals. One study showed that when young cats were fitted with goggles that blinded them to horizontal lines, they were unable to see horizontal lines when they matured (Hirsch & Spinelli, 1970). When the same procedure was tried with adult cats, their vision was unaffected. This led the researchers to conclude that crucial cells relating to vision develop early in life. If these cells are not properly programmed during the critical period, then vision will be permanently affected.

## Growth and Development of the Body

Children grow more rapidly in their first year of life than at any other time. At birth, the average infant weighs 7½ pounds and is 20 inches long. At one year of age, the average baby will weigh about 22 pounds and will be about 30 inches long.

As mentioned earlier, the head makes up about one-fourth of a newborn's total length. As the infant grows, her body shape changes. The trunk and arms and then the legs and feet start to catch up with the head. By the time she is a year old, the head comprises one-fifth of the infant's total length.

In the first few months, much of the weight an infant gains is fat. The fat is a source of insulation and can provide nourishment should some problem, such as teething or a cold, force an infant to reduce his intake of food. At about nine months, bone and muscle make up a greater part of weight gain.

The rate of growth and development in infants is closely linked to good nutrition. Nutritional defi-

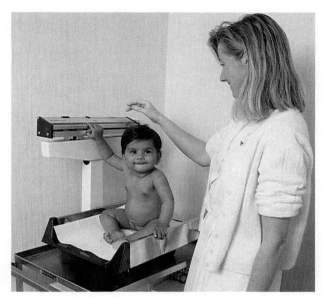

*Most pediatricians advise that infants be brought in for a checkup four times during the first year.*

ciencies in early infancy can cause irreversible damage. Providing infants with the nutrients they need is one of the most important jobs of parents and caregivers.

Infants between the ages of birth and four months can meet their nutritional needs on a diet of breast milk or formula. Breast milk is considered to be the best food for infants because it contains substances that make it easier for the infant to digest. Infants are also less likely to be allergic to it. However, pediatricians recommend that breast-fed infants receive supplements of vitamin D, iron, and fluoride. Commercial formulas contain a mixture of nutrients similar to breast milk but lack the infection-fighting factors of breast milk. Only the version that is fortified with iron should be used.

Formulas are sold in three forms—as powder, concentrated liquid, and ready-to-use liquid. Caregivers who use powdered and concentrated formula must take care in diluting and preparing them. Cleanliness is important to avoid contamination with bacteria that cause illness.

The time to introduce solid foods depends on the infant's individual needs and the advice of the pediatrician. Infants who are ready for solids will start to demand more milk and seem unsatisfied after being fed. Solid foods should be introduced one at a time and fed to the child for a week before other

**TABLE 6.1**
**Infant Immunization Schedule**

| Age | Hepatitis B | Diphtheria, Tetanus, Pertussis (DTP) | Haemophilus Influenza (HIB) | Polio |
|---|---|---|---|---|
| Birth | ✓ | | | |
| 1–2 months | ✓ | | | |
| 2 months | | ✓ | ✓ | ✓ |
| 4 months | | ✓ | ✓ | ✓ |
| 6 months | | ✓ | ✓ | |
| 6–18 months | ✓ | | | |
| 12–15 months | | | ✓ | |

Adapted from the recommendations of the American Academy of Pediatrics, 1992.

foods are introduced in order to check for allergic reactions. In most cases, infant rice cereal is the first solid food offered to babies. As infants come to rely on solids for their nutritional needs, providing a balanced diet of foods from all the food groups becomes essential.

Well-baby checks and immunizations are also crucial to infant growth and development. *Well-baby checks* are periodic visits with a physician during the first two years of life to monitor growth, development, and behavior. The first visit usually occurs within the first two weeks after birth. Usually, pediatricians want to see the baby three more times during the first year. In addition to measuring height, weight, and head circumference, the pediatrician checks the infant's hips, feet, eyes, and ears.

*Immunizations* protect infants from infectious diseases and are vital to their growth and development. The American Academy of Pediatrics recommends immunizing infants against hepatitis B; diphtheria, tetanus, and pertussis (DTP); Haemophilus influenza (HIB); and polio in the first year of life (American Academy of Pediatrics, 1992). (See Table 6.1.)

### Bones and Teeth

A newborn's bones are very soft. As the infant grows, the bones go through two processes: calcification and ossification. *Calcification* is the process by which the bones harden through the deposit of calcium salts in the body tissues. *Ossification* is the process by which the bones grow; it involves the conversion of the cartilage or membrane at the bone ends into bone. Thus, as infants grow, their bones become strong enough and large enough to support them in a sitting and then a standing position.

The skull bones of infants are separated by *fontanelles*, which are commonly referred to as soft spots. Fontanelles are intervals where the bones of the skull have not yet fused together. They close up when children are between 9 and 18 months of age.

When infants are about four to eight months of age, teeth begin to move through the bone of the jaws and the gums into the mouth. The first teeth to come in are the two lower front teeth. They are followed by the two upper front teeth. Then the upper side teeth arrive, followed by the lower side teeth. Most infants have six to eight teeth by the time they are one year old.

Although these teeth, called *primary teeth* or milk teeth, are not permanent, it is important to keep them clean and free of foods that cause decay. Decayed teeth can make chewing difficult and may inhibit speech and communication. Tooth decay is caused by bacteria that live on sugars and starches that come in contact with the teeth. The bacteria produce an acid that eats away at the enamel of the teeth and creates holes. Infants can develop a decay problem called baby bottle mouth, or nursing bottle caries, if they are allowed to fall asleep with a bottle. Formula or juice will pool in the mouth as they sleep and coat the teeth with decay-producing sugars. It is therefore not advisable to give infants a bottle when putting them to sleep. Parents and other caregivers can also promote dental health by wiping the teeth and gums with a gauze pad after meals and not giving infants sweet snacks between meals.

Thumb sucking is a common habit among infants and young children. Thumb sucking by young infants is usually an indication that they have not satisfied their sucking need with the bottle or breast. Later, infants suck their thumb as a way of comforting themselves. Thumb sucking in infancy can displace the primary teeth, but if stopped by age four or five it has no effect on the permanent teeth, which do not begin coming in until about age six.

## Muscles

The motor skills that allow infants to explore their world depend to a large extent on muscle growth and development. Infants cannot hold their head up until the neck and shoulder muscles are sufficiently strong. Infants cannot sit up by themselves without strong stomach and back muscles.

All the muscle cells a human will ever have are present at birth. As the infant grows, the muscles become longer and thicker. Muscle growth and development follow cephalocaudal and proximodistal patterns. For example, the muscles that Zachary and Julia use to suck and those used to move their eyes developed before the muscles they will use in walking. Likewise, both infants gained control of their whole arms before they could control their hands and fingers.

Another principle that governs muscle development is *differentiation*, or the progression of development from the general to the specific. This means that infants make generalized movements before they can make specific movements. They use their large muscles before they use their fine or small muscles. (The large muscles of the body enable humans to make big movements, while the small muscles permit more precise movements.) Infants make whole-body movements before they can use specific muscles for a task.

This developmental process was observed by Charlotte Buhler in 1929. She studied the reactions of infants at various ages when their mouth and nose were covered by an observer's hand. Newborns responded with the whole body: arms and legs went about in random motions and the body twisted. Several weeks later, the infants used their arms more prominently and directed their arms toward the center of their body, increasing the likelihood that they would bat away the hand. By six months of age, the infants could push the hand away with a precise swipe (Buhler, 1930).

## Effects of Heredity and Environment

Almost every description of infant development contains a statement advising the reader that growth and development will vary from infant to infant. While there are average times when an infant will reach certain developmental milestones, there is a wide range of normal or typical development. Why are there such broad differences among infants? Growth and development are influenced by heredity and the environment.

As you learned in Chapter 3, heredity lays the foundation for the course that growth and development will take. For example, body type, whether it be tall, short, stocky, or thin, is determined by the genes. Heredity is responsible for a number of other differences among infants. Male infants tend to be heavier and longer than female infants. The bones of black children harden earlier than those of white children, and their permanent teeth come in sooner (American Academy of Pediatrics, 1973). Researchers have also found that identical twins are more likely than fraternal twins to reach developmental milestones, such as sitting up and walking, at the same time (Wilson & Harpring, 1972). Thus, heredity plays a significant role in determining when an infant will reach certain developmental milestones.

However, environmental factors such as nutrition and living conditions can also affect height and weight. In one study, researchers found that children raised in impoverished and neglectful conditions during the first year of life showed delayed physical growth and skeletal development. Their height and weight were far below those expected for their age (Barbero & Shaheen, 1967).

Heredity plays an important role in determining the rate of a child's development. These identical twins are likely to reach developmental milestones, such as walking, at the same time.

The emotional environment plays a key role in development, too. During the 1930s, René Spitz conducted a study of infants raised in a foundling home who were given adequate care but little attention and affection. The study showed that these infants were below average in height and weight and were highly susceptible to disease. Moreover, only two of the children between the ages of 1½ and 2½ could walk, say several words, and feed themselves. Spitz concluded that a lack of "mothering" had caused the infants to be physically, emotionally, and intellectually impaired. He called this condition "failure to thrive" (Spitz, 1965).

More recent research confirms that lack of emotional interaction with caregivers is an important factor in an infant's "failure to thrive." This lack of interaction occurs in extreme cases of abuse or neglect. But it can also occur when parents are unable for some reason to adjust to the stresses of parenting or when emotional problems or substance abuse render parents unable to meet their child's emotional needs (Whaley and Wong, 1991).

In an effort to promote growth and development, caregivers need to give infants attention and affection. They should provide infants with an environment where they can practice their motor skills and safely explore the world around them and use a wide variety of toys and infant equipment that promote development. Appropriate toys provide visual stimulation and they give older infants an opportunity to explore colors and textures and to practice newly acquired skills. For example, noisemakers, balls of different textures, and squeeze toys stimulate infants and help develop the sensory system. Other appropriate infant toys include large plastic beads and keys, nesting toys, wooden blocks, and beanbags.

Recently, both the American Medical Association and the American Academy of Pediatrics have come out against the use of walkers by infants. Infants in walkers are prone to injuries, such as falling down stairs, falling into swimming pools, or pulling pots off stoves. Many doctors also feel that the walkers do not help infants learn to walk because in a walker they use different leg muscles. Child care professionals need to examine infant equipment and toys carefully to make sure they promote development and do so safely.

## Brain and Nervous System

The key to infant growth and development lies in the nervous system. Without healthy growth and development of the brain, the spinal cord, and nerves, an infant will not thrive and may not survive. During an infant's first year, the brain almost triples in weight, indicating that enormous gains in development are taking place. The growth of the brain makes the corresponding growth in motor and intellectual activities possible.

The parts of the brain develop at different rates. At birth, the brain stem and midbrain, or *subcortex*, are the most highly developed parts. They regulate basic biological functions such as breathing and digestion. The cerebral *cortex*, or outer layer of the brain, is responsible for thinking and problem solving. It is not well developed at birth. As the infant matures, the nerve cells, or neurons, that transmit messages from the cerebral cortex to the rest of the body, become encased in *myelin*, a fatty insulating substance that helps messages travel faster and

**TABLE 6.2**
**Primitive Reflexes in Infancy**

| Reflex | Description | Duration |
|---|---|---|
| Rooting | When a newborn's cheek is stroked, the newborn turns his head and opens his mouth to search for the object. | Disappears at about fourth month. |
| Sucking | When a nipple or finger is inserted into the infant's mouth, rhythmic sucking occurs. | Changes into voluntary sucking by second month. |
| Palmar Grasp | When pressure is applied to an infant's palms, the fingers curl in a strong enough grasp to support the infant's own weight. | Weakens after third month and disappears by one year. |
| Moro | A loud noise or jolt causes infants to extend their arms and then bring them back toward the body in a grasping action. Also called the startle reflex. | Disappears at about fifth month. |
| Babinski | When the side of an infant's foot is stroked from the heel toward the toes, the toes fan out and the foot twists inward. | Disappears at about ninth month. |
| Tonic Neck | Infants placed on their back tend to turn their head to one side and extend the arm and leg on that side while flexing the limbs on the other side, resembling a fencing position. | Disappears at about fourth month. |
| Stepping | Infants who are held above a surface will make stepping movements like walking. | Disappears at about third month. |
| Righting | Newborns who are held upright try to keep their head up and eyes open. Also called the china doll reflex. | Disappears at about third month. |
| Swimming | Newborns who are placed in water make swimming motions. | Disappears within first few months. |

more efficiently. The myelination process enables a child to think and act more effectively.

## Reflex Behavior

Because the myelination process takes time, newborns need some mechanism to protect them in their new environment and to help them adapt. *Reflexes*, or automatic, involuntary responses to external stimulation, ensure the infant's survival. (See Table 6.2.) Most of these reflexes are controlled by the subcortex.

*Primitive reflexes* are reflexes controlled by the subcortex that gradually disappear during the infant's first year. The Moro, or startle reflex, is an ex-

ample of a primitive reflex. This reflex is triggered by a loud noise or sudden jolt. The infant responds by throwing the arms outward and then returning to an embracelike position. The Moro reflex disappears by the fifth or sixth month of life. Primitive reflexes change or disappear as the growth of the brain shifts from the subcortex to the cortex.

Some primitive reflexes, such as the sucking reflex, promote survival. A newborn will automatically suck when an object is placed in his mouth, helping him obtain food. Other reflexes seem to have lost their usefulness as humans evolved. The grasping reflex, for example, helps infant monkeys hold on to their mothers' hair. However, the primi-

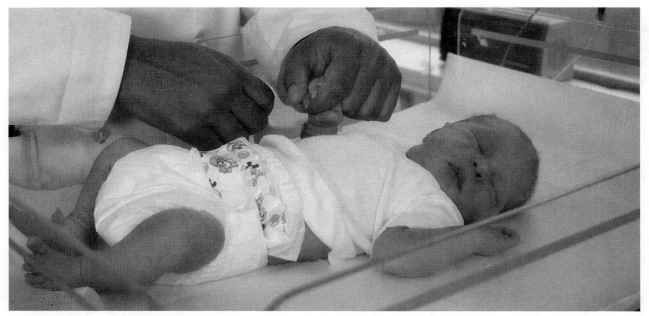

*This newborn boy exhibits a primitive grasping reflex when pressure is applied to his palm.*

tive reflexes do provide important developmental signposts. When and if these reflexes appear and when and if they disappear give an indication of whether an infant is developing normally. Although pediatricians test these reflexes during well-baby checkups, caregivers should be familiar with them. A caregiver who notices an inappropriate reflexive behavior can encourage parents to talk with their doctor before the next scheduled checkup.

A second group of reflexes are known as *protective reflexes*. These reflexes are essential to basic survival and grow stronger with age. Breathing, sucking, blinking, gagging, yawning, coughing, and shivering are some of the protective reflexes. Because these reflexes persist, they are of less interest to developmentalists.

### Influence of Environment on Brain Development

As noted earlier, undernourishment can cause brain damage. Without sensory stimulation and the freedom to move, certain areas of the brain may never develop. The disabilities that result may be permanent. The brain therefore has the capacity to be shaped by experience. This capacity is technically referred to as *plasticity*. The brain is most malleable during infancy, when it is growing rapidly.

Although an unstimulating environment can limit brain growth and function, an enriched environment can enhance it. Rats and other animals raised in cages with various stimulating apparatuses were found to have heavier brains with thicker cortical layers than similar animals raised in basic cages (Rosenzweig, 1984). Studies such as these have led some parents and educators to believe that the learning process can be accelerated and that with the right kind of environment, we can create "superbabies." Organizations such as the Better Baby Institute in Philadelphia offer classes that teach parents how to teach their infants to walk and swim. Classes also teach parents how to get their toddlers to read poetry, speak foreign languages, and play musical instruments.

Many developmentalists and early childhood educators are uneasy with programs like these. They feel that such programs place undue stress and pressure on young children to perform and also put infants at risk for injury. David Elkind (1987) describes infant enhancement programs as the "miseducation of young children." He believes these programs establish expectations for infants that are developmentally inappropriate and potentially harmful. Swimming, for example, puts infants at risk for middle ear infections, for asphyxiation from swallowing water, and for diarrhea from urine in the water.

Other developmentalists point out that accelerating the development of infants does not guarantee that they will maintain their head start in the future. The implication for child care professionals is clear. Too much stimulation can be as harmful as too little. Infants need an environment that is sufficiently stimulating to grow and develop.

## Sensory System

All five senses—sight, hearing, taste, smell, and touch—are present at birth. They are the newborn's major source of information about the outside world. The senses are part of the sensory system. They take in information such as light or sound or smell, which is transformed into nerve impulses and sent to the brain.

While all the senses are present at birth, some are more developed than others. As infants grow, the sensory system matures. Significant maturation seems to occur at about two months and eight months of age.

### Sight

From the moment infants are born, they can discern light and dark. The pupillary reflex begins to operate immediately, narrowing the pupils in bright light and causing them to widen in dim light. Within a few hours of birth, many infants can coordinate the movement of both eyes so that they can focus on a nearby object. This process is known as *convergence*. Infants begin to develop visual coordination at a very early age.

By two or three days after birth, newborns can follow a slowly moving object with their eyes, but their action is not smooth or accurate. By eight weeks of age, most infants can perform this action, called *tracking*, smoothly. Infants can follow more rapidly moving objects by four months of age. In early infancy, babies are also capable of *visual fixation*, which means they can look at an object with sustained attention. Infants also respond to different colors at an early age (Bornstein, 1984, 1985).

At birth, infants possess limited *visual acuity*, or the ability to see in fine detail. While researchers have not conclusively determined the reason for this, they believe the answer lies in the transmission process from the eye to the brain (Banks & Salapatek, 1983). If you want to show something to a newborn, you should hold it within about 8 to 12 inches of the face. This is approximately the distance between an infant's face and an adult's face during a feeding. Over the next few months, visual acuity improves, and by four months of age, infants can focus their eyes on more distant objects and see clearly. Six-month-old Julia, introduced at the beginning of this chapter, uses all of these visual skills to gaze at the mobile circling above her.

### Hearing

Children are born with the ability to receive and process sounds. However, infants are much less sensitive to sound than adults are. Researchers have found that noises must be 10 to 20 decibels louder for infants to hear them than for adults (Schulman-Galambos & Galambos, 1979). Sensitivity to sound slowly improves with age, taking approximately 12 to 13 years to equal that of an adult.

Newborns can track the direction from which sounds come, and they are sensitive to the frequency and duration of sounds. Studies have shown that babies a few days old can distinguish the sound of their mother's voice from that of a stranger (DeCasper & Fifer, 1980).

By about six months of age, infants can recognize small differences in loudness and in pitch (Aslin, Pisoni, & Jusczyk, 1983). Research also indicates that infants can hear higher frequencies than adults, which may explain why infants respond to high-pitched baby talk.

### Taste and Smell

Although newborns respond to differences in taste, their sense of taste appears to be poorly developed at birth. They show a definite dislike for bitter flavors and a preference for those that are sweet. However, when given a choice between a nipple delivering milk and a nipple delivering a weak sugar solution, infants tend to choose the milk (Nowlis & Kessen, 1976). Other research shows that the ability of infants to notice differences in flavors

### Eating and Sleeping on a Schedule or on Demand?

The Middletown Family Resource Center offers parenting classes, speakers, and seminars for new parents and caregivers of young children. Recently, a psychologist spoke to the group about quality care during the first years of life. He explained that babies can thrive both physically and emotionally in a variety of child-care situations.

The psychologist pointed out that attitudes about appropriate eating, sleeping, or toileting behaviors are acquired from one's cultural environment. Although these attitudes may be strongly held, there is no "best" approach to these issues so long as babies receive loving and attentive care.

His comments sparked a strong reaction from two women in the audience, both with eight-month-old babies. Each mother felt sure that the approach to caregiving used in her family was best for her child.

Annette:

"My son, Nicholas, is eight months old. I have been working ever since he was born to get him to eat and sleep at regular times. I don't think it's healthy to give a baby a bottle or the breast every time he cries. A child who is fed on demand ends up snacking all day. That doesn't mean I let Nicholas cry and fuss. I hold him and rock him, but I don't automatically offer him food.

"When babies are fed at regular intervals, they get used to eating only a few times a day. This regular schedule helps them sleep better at night. They don't wake up and expect to be fed so often.

"It's okay to adjust a baby's sleep habits, too. Why shouldn't Nicholas be awake in the day and asleep at night just like the other members of the family? I always put Nicholas down for a nap at a regular time and awaken him after he has slept a certain length of time. Now he has an eating and sleeping pattern that fits with the routine of the rest of the family.

"Being on a schedule lets me plan better. I know when Nicholas will be hungry and when he'll be tired. I don't wait until he's overtired or overly hungry to respond to his needs.

"When Nicholas was a newborn and wasn't on a schedule, I was exhausted. Now that his eating and sleeping are more regular, I'm more rested and that makes me a better parent."

Mary:

"I think young children, like my daughter Amanda, should eat when they are hungry and sleep when they are tired. It isn't natural to make Amanda conform to a schedule that suits the adult world. As the adult, it's better for me to adjust my activities to her needs.

"Babies are born knowing when they are hungry. They also know when they are full, and stop eating. Putting a child on a schedule and encouraging her to eat only at certain times destroys the natural control that balances eating and hunger.

"I think many eating and weight-control problems in older children begin because caregivers feed children when they think they should eat, not when they really are hungry. It also doesn't make any sense to me to withhold food from a hungry baby just because it isn't time by your schedule for her to eat.

"I feel the same way about sleeping. When Amanda is tired she falls asleep. Making her take a nap every day at one o'clock, even if she isn't tired, turns nap time into an area of conflict. She'll develop the habit of resisting sleep, and soon every nap time and every bedtime will become a fight."

*Can you think of activities other than eating and sleeping where expectations and child care practices vary mainly for cultural reasons? Do you think both babies are receiving quality care? Why or why not?*

is influenced by how well fed they are. Those who have had an inadequate diet take longer to notice differences in the flavors of food.

Whether infants can distinguish among bitter, sour, and salty substances is not clear. Although infants are born with the taste buds to detect these flavors, their nervous system may not have developed fully enough to interpret signals from these receptors.

Newborns have strong reactions to odors, especially unpleasant ones such as the smell of ammonia or vinegar. Their breathing rate and activity level increase when there is an unpleasant odor in the air. The more concentrated the odor, the more infants respond. Infants show less of a response to odors that adults find highly agreeable. As infants grow, they seem to use their sense of smell more, sniffing new foods to gain information about them.

### Touch

The sense of touch first appears between 7½ and 14 weeks of gestation (Hooker, 1952). It continues to mature during the prenatal period, and by the time of birth, certain parts of the body are quite sensitive. The area around the mouth, the nose, the cheeks, the skin of the forehead, and the soles of the feet respond strongly to touch. In fact, many of the primitive reflexes discussed earlier are triggered by touch. In the past, it was generally believed that newborns did not feel pain during procedures such as drawing blood. Recent research, however, indicates that infants are sensitive to temperature, pressure, and pain as early as one day after birth (Anand & Hickey, 1987). They become more sensitive to pain and pressure as they mature.

Touch is critical to healthy development. Infants begin their tactile explorations of the world by way of the mouth. As their motor skills improve, however, infants make greater use of their hands. Researchers who have observed infants between 6 and 12 months of age have noted that they use their senses to learn about objects in the following ways: they alternate mouthing and looking at objects, they hold an object in one hand and finger it with the other, they use one or both hands to rotate objects, and they move objects back and forth between the hands (Ruff, 1984).

Infants can tell the difference between sweet and bitter flavors and show a distinct preference for foods that are sweet.

### Influence of the Environment

Stimulation of the senses in infancy is vital to healthy growth and development. Sensory deprivation experiments with animals have shown that sensory deprivation can cause permanent impairment. What is the right amount of stimulation? This varies with each child. Caregivers need to discuss with parents what they have observed regarding their infant's sensory preferences and attempt to create an appropriately stimulating environment. Caregivers should also be sensitive to any cultural traditions associated with sensory stimulation. It is important for caregivers to find out about the cultural practices and beliefs of the families they work with.

**FOCUS ON** ◢ **Cultural Diversity**

### Breast-Feeding—How Long?

Breast-feeding is a healthful, economical way to feed a baby. Breast milk contains all the nutrients an infant needs to thrive. Certain antibodies are passed from mother to child in breast milk. This gives infants an increased resistance to some diseases. Breast-feeding also eliminates the introduction of foods, which when given too early in development, may cause allergic reactions in infants.

Although there are advantages to breast-feeding, the nutritional needs of babies can also be met in other ways. The decision to start breast-feeding and when to stop breast-feeding varies widely in different cultures.

In industrialized countries such as the United States, Australia, and France, many women stop breast-feeding after a few months, when they return to work. In these countries, even mothers who remain at home full-time often wean their children after about one year.

In other countries, children are nursed from two to four years. In Zimbabwe, for example, it is common for mothers to feed their children only breast milk for the first year. After that they add solid foods while continuing to nurse for two to three more years.

The decision on how long to breast-feed is often based on cultural factors rather than the nutritional needs of the baby.

---

In general, a stimulating environment is one in which infants can experience a variety of sights, sounds, smells, and textures. Quiet times are also important to avoid overstimulation and to help infants appreciate the differences in various kinds of sensory stimuli.

Toys should be touchable and mouthable. They should present a variety of shapes, sizes, and colors, and some should make noises. Objects should be visually interesting so that infants are motivated to reach for them and ultimately move toward them. While toys and other objects play a major role in stimulating infants' senses, the human voice, face, and touch are even more important. Caregivers must not only structure the sensory environment, but they must also be key players in it.

### Motor Development

Motor development is the process of acquiring movement patterns and skills. Many of the same principles that govern physical development also affect motor development. Motor development follows cephalocaudal and proximodistal sequences.

Infants first learn to lift their head, then their shoulders, and then their trunk, acquiring the motor skills necessary to be able to sit up. Development from the center out can be observed in the way an infant's arm movements develop. Infants can control the whole arm before they are able to control their hands and fingers.

Motor development also proceeds from the simple to the complex, according to the principle of differentiation. For example, when newborns see an object dangling above them, they will wave their arms and feet at it in an attempt to reach it. By three months of age, infants can hit the object but cannot grasp it because they cannot effectively control the opening and closing of their hands. At six months, most infants can grab and hold on to the object. (See Figure 6.1.)

The midbrain controls motor development at first. This explains why many of the movements newborns make are reflexive. In infants of four months and older, the cortex has matured to the point where it begins to control most movements. As the cortex continues to develop, more of the infant's movements are deliberate rather than reflexive.

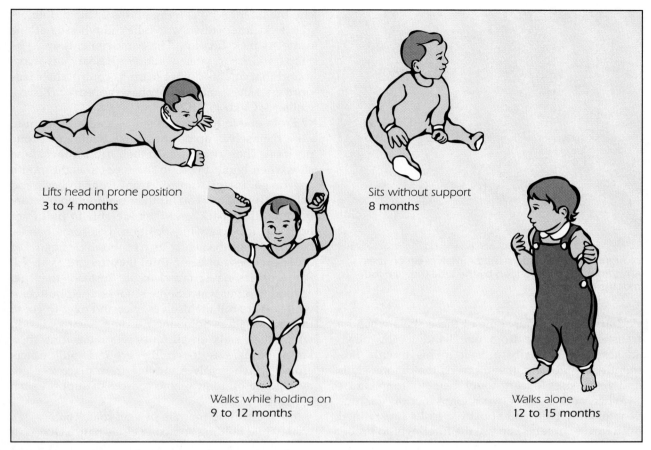

**FIGURE 6.1    Stages of Motor Development in Infants.**

## Sequence of Motor Development

An important area of development during the first year of life involves gaining control of the hands. Newborns cannot use their hands in any purposeful way. They are born with a grasping reflex, which prompts them to firmly grasp objects that come in contact with their hands. Their grip is so strong that some babies can hang by their hands for as long as one minute. However, while newborns can grasp in response to a stimulus, they cannot reach out and grab things that they see.

By the time an infant is three or four months old, the grasping reflex begins to disappear and voluntary grasping begins. The grasping motion at this age looks as if the infant had a mitten on. Infants draw objects into their palm using all the fingers together. Although infants can now pick up things, the grasping reflex makes it impossible for them to let go. For this reason, it is not a good idea to give young infants a rattle to play with. Unable to let go, they may accidentally hurt themselves with the rattle.

By about six months of age, infants can voluntarily let go of what they are holding. At about this time, they also begin using what is known as a "pincer grasp," or the thumb and forefinger to pick up things. For example, infants can use this grasp to pick up an object as small as a staple from the carpet. Caregivers and parents should look over the carpet carefully to make sure that no dangerous objects are embedded there. Infants often try to put the objects they pick up into their mouth. When this happens, the protective gag reflex helps prevent suffocation.

At this age, infants can also manipulate objects with greater ability, making use of many motions.

Most infants are able to raise themselves up on their arms from a prone position by the time they are four months old.

Zachary is trying out some of these skills when he transfers his bottle from one hand to the other, shakes it, and finally puts it in his mouth. Six-month-olds are hard at work using their motor skills and their senses to learn about their environment.

When infants are between eight months and one year of age, their manipulative skills are refined even further. Infants can use the forefinger to probe, poke, and hook. They can carry out different activities with each hand. And they can perform more complicated tasks, such as stacking objects, taking one object out of another, taking covers off objects, and even getting a spoon to their mouth.

The other important area of motor development during the infant's first year is *locomotion*, or the ability to change position and move from place to place. Any movements newborns make with their arms and legs are random and largely reflexive. For example, when newborns are held upright and their feet touch a flat surface, they will move their legs up and down as if they were walking. This reflex, called the stepping reflex, disappears within two months of birth. The same response, however, will emerge again in older infants in readiness for walking.

Infants between one and six months of age start making repetitive, rhythmic leg movements. These leg movements—for instance, kicking like a frog—are not reflexes. Instead, something happens to ex-cite the infant who is lying on his back, and he begins to kick repetitively, as Julia did when Charlene came to pick her up. These movements may be preparation for later walking. Researchers have found that infants do not learn to control their legs until after these movements have appeared (Rovee-Collier & Gekoski, 1979).

From one to four months of age, infants learn to raise themselves up on their arms while in a prone position. They also can turn their head from side to side when lying down. In the four- to eight-month age range, infants can roll from front to back and back to front. They can lift their head when they are lying on their back, and they are able to pull their body up to a crawling position. For some babies, crawling begins as early as five months of age. For others, it does not begin until they are one year old. Some babies never crawl at all. Instead, they get around in other ways. Some scoot on their buttocks, while others roll themselves over and over to get to their destination. Some infants do a "bear walk," in which they walk on all fours without letting their knees or elbows touch the ground. Still others cruise, which involves moving from place to place by holding on to available sources of support such as furniture.

By about nine months of age, many babies can walk while holding someone else's hand. Unassist-ed walking begins at one year on average. Walking marks the end of infancy and the beginning of toddlerhood.

Motor skills are acquired by all healthy children in roughly the same order. (See Table 6.3.) However, there can be wide disparities among infants in the ages at which these skills develop. Parents may express concern that their infant has not acquired a particular skill by the time the "average" infant is expected to do so; they may worry that their infant is "delayed." It is important to remind parents that the age range of normal development is wide.

## Importance of Motor Development

Motor development does not simply happen. Infants must practice their motor skills over and over again and perfect them before they are ready for the next skill. During their waking hours, infants should be in an environment where they are free to move. Putting infants in seats or swings that confine them

**TABLE 6.3**

**Milestones of Motor Development: Birth to Age One**

| Age | Milestone |
|---|---|
| Birth | Grasping reflex<br>Stepping reflex |
| 3 to 4 months | Hits but cannot grasp dangling objects<br>Grasps objects but cannot let go<br>Lifts head and moves head from side to side while in a prone position |
| 5 months | Rolls over<br>Pulls body into crawling position<br>May begin to crawl |
| 6 months | Grasps and releases objects voluntarily<br>Uses pincer grasp |
| 8 months | Begins to use hands to perform more complex tasks<br>Sits without support |
| 9 to 12 months | Uses forefinger to poke, probe, hook<br>Transfers objects from hand to hand<br>Walks while holding on |
| 12 to 15 months | Walks unassisted |

will restrict their movements and limit their ability to practice their skills.

Infants should not be put into positions they cannot get into by themselves. For example, instead of putting an infant who has never stood in a standing position, put her on the floor near a sturdy piece of furniture that has a toy on it and let her learn to pull herself up. In this way, caregivers can facilitate development while allowing infants to develop a sense of accomplishment.

It is not necessary to protect infants from all physical stress. Some stress will stimulate growth and strengthen the body. For example, if a baby has rolled over into what appears to be an uncomfortable position, let him try to change his position on his own. If he becomes frustrated and distressed, then you can help him.

Motor development enables children to explore the world and develop cognitive concepts. It promotes self-awareness as infants discover their capabilities, and it can help children develop a positive sense of self. The ability to move gives infants who have not yet learned to speak a way to express themselves, and it allows them to interact with others. Motor development also contributes to infants' general health and physical well-being by helping them develop muscle strength and physical endurance.

### Influence of Heredity and Environment

Motor development is affected by a number of factors, including heredity, status at birth, and birth order. A child's nutrition and family environment also influence the rate of development.

Hereditary factors such as size, body proportions, and rate of maturation play a role in infants' readiness to acquire motor skills. For example, infants who are very long and those who are muscular and small-boned tend to walk sooner than other infants. African American children develop motor skills sooner than white children during the first year. On some motor tasks, white and African American infants are ahead of Hispanic infants (Solomons, 1978).

Birth status, or an infant's condition at birth as determined by certain observable characteristics, is an important factor in motor development. As discussed in Chapter 3, the Apgar scale is used to rate a newborn's heart rate, breathing, muscle tone, skin color, and reflexes. Newborns who experience respiratory problems suffer delays in motor development, as do low birth weight and premature infants.

Environmental factors such as nutrition also affect motor development. The bones and muscles of undernourished or malnourished infants do not develop at normal rates, and this delays the acquisition of motor skills. In addition, undernourishment and malnourishment can damage the central nervous system, affecting infants' coordination and ability to control their movements.

Overweight infants may also suffer developmental delays. Their extra weight may affect their moti-

## FOCUS ON     Communicating with Parents

### Health Concerns—Head Lice

Michelle is a child care provider at the Pomona Playschool. During the morning, she noticed two-year-old Wendy scratching her head almost continuously. Michelle took Wendy aside at free play and checked her scalp. She found nits, the eggs of head lice.

She reported this to the school's director, who called Wendy's mother and asked her to pick up her child. Wendy's mother was angry at the idea of having to leave work when her daughter wasn't even "sick." She did not appear for two hours.

MICHELLE:  Wendy is waiting for you in the director's office. She's worried that you took so long to come for her.

WENDY'S MOTHER [annoyed]: This is ridiculous. Wendy isn't sick. Couldn't this have waited till I picked her up tonight? Anyway, how could Wendy have lice? We're not dirty people, and I wash her hair every other day.

MICHELLE:  We know Wendy is clean, but regular shampoo doesn't kill lice. Head lice are very contagious, and once you get them, they're hard to get rid of.

WENDY'S MOTHER:  Maybe she got them here.

MICHELLE:  That's possible, but I don't think so. We checked all the other children in her group, and she is the only one with lice. But just in case, we're going to put the dress-up clothes away and remind the kids not to wear each other's hats. We have to be careful.

WENDY'S MOTHER:  So how do I get rid of them?

MICHELLE:  You have to use a special shampoo that you get at the pharmacy. You can call your pediatrician if you have any questions. You'll also have to check everyone else that lives in your house. Then, after you use the shampoo, you have to pick the nits out of Wendy's hair. She can't come back until she is nit-free. You also have to wash all her bedding and clothes in hot water so she won't get reinfected.

WENDY'S MOTHER [getting angrier]:  That's a lot of work. Why do I have to pick the nits out of her hair if the shampoo kills them?

MICHELLE:  Our policy is that a child must be nit-free to return. That's the only way we can be sure she won't infect someone else.

WENDY'S MOTHER:  Well, I think that's ridiculous. You're making such a big deal out of it.

MICHELLE:  I'm not making a big deal out of anything. I'm telling you our policy.

WENDY'S MOTHER:  I'm going to talk to the director.

*Wendy's mother was already angry when she arrived at the school. What could Michelle have done to help reduce that anger? Are there other ways Michelle could have given Wendy's mother the information about how to treat head lice? How would you have handled the situation? What do you think would have happened if Michelle had not taken action when she discovered Wendy's lice?*

---

vation to practice certain motor skills. However, parents and other caregivers should not reduce the fat and calories in an infant's diet in an effort to avoid obesity. It is generally advised that infants who are old enough be given whole milk, not milk with a reduced fat content. Infants are growing rapidly and need sufficient calories to maintain their growth. They also need fat, which is a major component of myelin, the tissue that surrounds the nerves as they mature. Thus, fat is needed in an infant's diet for healthy neurological functioning (Eichorn, 1979). The best way to avoid infant overweight

Overweight babies may suffer developmental delays and show a lack of motivation to practice certain motor skills.

is to pay attention to infants' cues. When they are full, infants will turn away from the bottle or nipple and move their body in an effort to get away from the food.

Firstborn children tend to develop motor skills at an earlier age than their younger siblings. The difference in development may be attributable to the degree of parental attention and involvement. Parents often attach great importance to a first child, and their expectations for the child may be higher than for later-born children.

The environment can also affect infant rates of development. It promotes motor development by providing infants with opportunities to explore and practice. In this way, infants can learn and test their capabilities.

## Implications and Applications

Child care providers should familiarize themselves with the broad ranges for normal infant development and with the developmental milestones of in-fancy. They will then be aware of any possible developmental problem.

What are some warning signs of developmental problems? If an infant fails to notice and pick up small objects when she is at the age where infants are refining their grasping skills, she may have a vision problem. If an infant does not respond to vocalizations by six weeks of age, if she does not turn her head in response to a soft and familiar sound by six to nine months of age, or if she does not understand simple directions by one year of age, she may have a hearing impairment. Similarly, one-year-olds who do not wave goodbye, play games like peek-a-boo and pattycake, or respond to their name when called may have developmental problems. Infants who sleep excessively are also cause for concern.

In the area of language and speech, normal infants usually start babbling at around six months of age and will say one or two words by the time they are one year old. An infant who does not display these behaviors may have a developmental problem.

Suspected developmental problems should be verified through screening and assessment tests.

## FOCUS ON  Decision Making in Child Care

### Sudden Injury on the Playground

Helene and her aide were on playground duty watching a group of infants and toddlers. While Helene was trying to settle a dispute in the sandbox, 12-month-old Andrew climbed up to the top of the toddler slide. Before Helene or the aide could get to him, he stood up on the top step, lost his balance, and fell to the ground.

Helene rushed toward him. Andrew was crying hard. The other children pressed around. Pushing her way through the children, Helene asked, "Andrew, are you hurt? Where does it hurt?"

Helene didn't see any blood or obvious injuries, but Andrew continued to cry hard. Some of the children tried to tell Helene that Andrew had hit his head when he fell.

Leaving the aide in charge on the playground, Helene scooped Andrew up and carried him inside to the director's office. Andrew continued wailing. The director and Helene were unable to calm him. All he did was cry.

The director called the paramedics to take Andrew to the emergency room. Helene accompanied him. The director also called Andrew's mother and asked her to go to the hospital.

The director was not happy about the way Helene handled the accident. At her next staff meeting she reviewed the procedure for dealing with sudden injuries, especially falls. She also stressed the importance of supervision in preventing accidents.

*Why do you think the director was unhappy with what Helene did? What would you have done if you had been the caregiver in charge on the playground? What is the most important rule to remember if you suspect a child may have a head or neck or back injury?*

Note: The point of this feature is to make caregivers aware that moving a child who has a potential neck, back, or head injury, or broken bone, is not appropriate. Much as Helene wanted to comfort Andrew and get him away from the other children on the playground, she could have aggravated his injuries by picking him up and carrying him inside.

---

One of the most widely used screening tests for children under the age of three is the *Denver Developmental Screening Test*. This test assesses development according to milestones of motor development, social development, and language development. It will not provide a precise evaluation or diagnosis, but it will indicate the presence of a problem. Child care professionals can sometimes help by referring parents to appropriate local agencies.

Child care providers can promote growth and development by making sure that the care setting is safe and clean. Because the immune system of young children is not fully developed, they are especially susceptible to disease. Diarrheal diseases cause dehydration and in severe cases can cause in-fants to lose so much weight that their growth and development are affected. Cytomegalovirus (CMV) affects newborns and can cause hearing loss and impair motor and intellectual development. Diarrheal diseases are frequently transmitted through oral-fecal contact, while CMV is found in the urine and saliva of children. To prevent the spread of such potentially harmful diseases, caregivers should clean and disinfect toys and shared surfaces such as tables and doorknobs on a daily basis. Diapering areas should be disinfected after each use. The hands of caregivers and children alike need to be constantly and carefully washed. According to some experts, hand washing is the best way to keep infectious diseases from spreading (Kendall & Moukaddem, 1992).

It is also important for caregivers to stay abreast of the latest infant health research and to share this information with parents. For example, a recent study found that newborns whose mothers expose them to cigarette smoke are twice as likely as infants of nonsmoking mothers to die of sudden infant death syndrome (SIDS) (Schoendorf, 1992). A 1992 report by the American Academy of Pediatrics warns that infants who sleep on their stomach are at increased risk for SIDS and recommends that infants be put to sleep on their back or side (American Academy of Pediatrics Task Force on Infant Positioning and SIDS). Caregivers can keep parents up-to-date through daily conversations or by sending a newsletter home periodically.

A healthy environment provides for an infant's nutritional needs. Caregivers should adjust themselves to the infant's eating and sleeping schedule and should respect the food preferences and eating style of each infant. Mealtime should always be a sociable and happy time, and foods with nutritional value should be served.

The National Association for the Education of Young Children recommends that an appropriate program for infants incorporate play, active exploration, and movement, providing "a broad array of stimulating experiences within a reliable framework of routines and protection from excessive stress" (NAEYC, 1989, p. 3). Relationships with people are an essential element of any program. Specifically, the NAEYC recommends placing mirrors where infants can observe themselves, making the environment colorful and cheerful with pictures at infants' eye level, changing play areas periodically so that infants can view the world from different perspectives, providing infants with plenty of room to move, and playing music for their listening, movement, and singing pleasure. Many child development experts also recommend that caregivers add movement education to their infant curriculum in an effort to provide infants with a rich movement experience.

Toys should be safe and too large for infants to swallow. They should range from the simple to the complex. Infants particularly enjoy toys that respond to their movements such as balls, bells, large snap beads, music boxes, and squeeze toys.

Equipment should also be chosen with safety in mind. Infants who are learning to roll and crawl should spend their waking time on a soft blanket on the floor. Those who are learning to stand need sturdy furniture with no sharp corners to hold on to. Low climbing structures and steps that are well padded will also promote motor development. (See Table 6.4.)

What kinds of activities are appropriate for encouraging the development of infants? For newborns, being carried in different positions, rocking, and swinging teach them about movement and stimulate the senses. Older infants enjoy crawling after objects such as rolling balls. Infants enjoy grasping and releasing objects, which can be turned into a motor skill activity by giving the infant

| **TABLE 6.4** **Safety Checklist for Infants** | |
|---|---|
| **Toys** | √ Too large to swallow |
| | √ No loose parts to swallow |
| | √ Unbreakable |
| | √ Smooth and rounded edges |
| | √ Nontoxic finishes |
| **Environment** | √ Cribs and baby furniture meet consumer protection safety standards |
| | √ Crib mattress firm and fits tightly into crib frame |
| | √ Play area covered by soft blanket |
| | √ Climbing steps well padded |
| | √ Furniture sturdy with no sharp corners |
| | √ Safety gates installed on doorways and stairways |
| | √ Hazardous materials locked up and out of reach |
| **Feeding** | √ No raw fruits and vegetables except ripe bananas |
| | √ No citrus fruits, egg whites, shellfish, chocolate |
| | √ No honey |
| | √ Test temperature of foods before feeding; do not heat liquids in microwave |
| | √ Give whole milk when infants are old enough, not skim or 2% milk |

sponge balls, blocks, or jar lids to drop into a large can. The pincer grasp can be developed by putting some dry cereal on a table or tray. Moving infants while singing songs or reciting rhymes encourages them to imitate movements and learn words at the same time. To promote hand-eye coordination, infants can be shown how to play catch with inflat-able beach balls. Caregivers and parents should carefully supervise infants during all activities.

The joy that infants experience when they reach developmental milestones can be shared by care-givers. What it takes is the desire and determination to provide young children with a safe, healthy, stimulating, and loving environment.

## CHAPTER 6   REVIEW

### SUMMARY

- Human growth and development proceed in a cephalocaudal, or head-to-foot, and proximodistal, or center outward, sequence.

- Infants do not grow or develop at a constant rate. Growth is rapid during the first five to six months of life and then eases slightly.

- Infants develop at individual rates. There are broad ranges of time during which normal infants are expected to reach certain milestones.

- Variations in the rates of growth and development are influenced by heredity and environmental factors. Environmental factors include nutrition, affection and attention, culture, and stimulation.

- During their first year of life, most infants triple their birth weight and gain 10 inches in length. Because of this rapid growth rate, it is important that infants receive good nutrition, periodic well-baby checkups, and immunizations.

- During the first year, an infant's bones harden and grow. Teeth begin to appear at between four and eight months of age. Good dental care is important to the child's health and speech development.

- Muscle development follows cephalocaudal and proximodistal patterns. Muscle movement develops from the general to the specific. Infants make whole-body movements before they are able to use specific muscles for a task.

- The parts of the brain develop at different rates. The brain stem and the subcortex, which regulates basic biological functions, are the most highly developed at birth. Most infant behavior during the first few months of life is reflexive. Some of these reflexes promote survival. Reflexes are useful in gauging whether an infant is developing normally.

- All of the senses are present at birth, although some are more developed than others. Stimulation of the senses is vital to healthy growth and development. The "right" amount of stimulation varies with each child.

- Motor development also follows cephalocaudal and proximodistal sequences and proceeds from the simple to the complex. The midbrain controls motor development at first. After four months of age, the cortex begins to control most movements.

- Motor skills are acquired by all healthy children in roughly the same order. However, there are wide differences among infants in terms of the ages at which these skills develop.
- Caregivers should be able to recognize when an infant is experiencing developmental problems and should advise the parents. Developmental problems can be verified through screening and assessment tests.
- Growth and development can best be promoted in an environment that is safe and clean and that provides for an infant's nutritional needs. Caregivers should encourage play, movement, and exploration through activities and equipment that stimulate the mind and the body.

## BUILDING VOCABULARY

Write a definition for each vocabulary term listed below.

calcification
cephalocaudal
convergence
cortex
Denver Developmental Screening
    Test
differentiation
fontanelle
immunization
locomotion
myelin
ossification

plasticity
primary teeth
primitive reflex
protective reflex
proximodistal
reflex
subcortex
tracking
visual acuity
visual fixation
well-baby check

## ACQUIRING KNOWLEDGE

1. What is cephalocaudal growth?
2. What is proximodistal growth?
3. Describe the rate of growth during an infant's first year. Is it constant? Is it slow or rapid compared with that of older children?
4. Do all children normally learn skills, such as crawling or walking, at the same age? Explain your answer.
5. What are "critical periods"?
6. What should infants be fed during the first few months of life?
7. How do caregivers know when to begin giving an infant solid food?
8. What are well-baby checks?
9. Why are immunizations important during infancy?
10. What is the difference between calcification and ossification?
11. What can caregivers do to prevent tooth decay in infants?
12. What is differentiation?
13. Most reflexes are controlled by the subcortex. What is the subcortex?
14. Describe two primitive reflexes found in infants.
15. How does an infant's sight change during the first few months of life?
16. How does an infant's hearing differ from that of an adult?
17. Where does the proximodistal development of an infant's arm movements begin?

18. Why is it that at about four months of age, infants can pick up objects but find it difficult to put them down?
19. Within what age range do most infants begin to roll over? What stage of motor development usually comes next?
20. How does nutrition affect physical development?
21. What signals tell adults that an infant has had enough food during a feeding?
22. Describe two warning signs of developmental problems that might appear in a child's behavior.
23. What is the Denver Developmental Screening Test?
24. What are two methods of preventing the spread of disease in a child care setting?
25. Describe an appropriate play activity for each of the following: newborns, infants learning to sit or crawl, infants learning to walk.

## THINKING CRITICALLY

1. At birth, the average child weighs 7½ pounds and is 20 inches long. What hereditary and environmental factors affect how much a child will weigh and how tall she will be when she is 12 months old?
2. In your opinion, is it helpful or harmful to compare the abilities of children of the same age? Why? How can child care professionals advise concerned parents about differences that exist between children?
3. Some educators feel that it is possible to speed up the learning process and, for example, teach infants to swim. Give your opinion about such programs. Do you think there are advantages to learning advanced skills at an early age?
4. Describe how a six-month-old might use his senses to investigate a new plastic squeak toy. What could a caregiver do to encourage the child's process of discovery?
5. Newborns have a reflex that causes them to firmly grasp objects that touch their hands. However, they cannot yet reach out and grab an object. By age one, most children can stack some crackers on a tray and pick them up to eat them. Describe the changes an infant goes through to get to the latter stage of manual skills.

## OBSERVATIONS AND APPLICATIONS

1. Spend time at a child care facility that accepts infants and observe how feeding is handled. What are the facility's routines and policies concerning the feeding of infants? Are babies awakened at certain times to be fed or fed when they wake up on their own? Do caregivers ever hold the infants during feeding? Are infants put in infant seats to be fed? At what age are high chairs used? Are several babies fed at the same time? Are cookies served? Are sweetened drinks served? Do any mothers leave expressed breast milk in bottles for their babies? Do child care providers wash their hands before feeding the babies?
2. Arrange to observe four infants that range in age from one to nine months. Take along a checklist of behaviors that you want to look for so

that you can compare the development of the babies. Observe each infant individually, noting his or her exact age. If you put your finger in the baby's hand, does her hand curl around yours? Does she put your finger in her mouth and suck on it? Make note of the presence or absence of other reflexes. Note each baby's ability to control his or her hand movements. Does the baby seem to have a preference for using one hand over the other? Does the baby use the pincer grasp? Note developmental milestones such as sitting, crawling, and standing.

3. A child care center that accepts infants as well as older children must have appropriate toys for each age group. However, some toys that are appropriate for a three-year-old may be dangerous to an infant. If you were running a child care facility, what steps would you take to ensure the safe use of toys by all age groups? What other safety guidelines should child care providers keep in mind when evaluating toys?

4. A parent with a three-month-old baby is trying to evaluate various child care facilities and asks your advice. He wants to make sure that his baby will be well cared for, of course, but he also wants her to receive appropriate physical and intellectual stimulation. What advice would you give him?

## SUGGESTIONS FOR FURTHER READING

Adebonojo, F., & Sherman, W. (1985). *How baby grows: A parent's guide to nutrition*. New York: Arbor House.

Bower, T. G. R. (1982). *Development in infancy* (2nd ed.). San Francisco: Freeman.

Dittmann, L. L. (1984). *The infants we care for* (rev. ed.). Washington, DC: National Association for the Education of Young Children.

Endres, J. B., & Rockwell, R. E. (1990). *Food, nutrition, and the young child* (3rd ed.). New York: Merrill/Macmillan.

Gallahue, D. L. (1982). *Understanding motor development in children*. New York: Wiley.

Kendrick, A. S., Kaufmann, R., & Messenger, K. P. (1991). *Healthy young children: A manual for programs*. Washington, DC: National Association for the Education of Young Children.

Leach, P. (1983). *Babyhood* (2nd ed.). New York: Knopf.

National Association for the Education of Young Children. (1989). *Developmentally appropriate practices in early childhood programs serving infants*. Washington, DC: Author.

Segal, M. (1985). *Your child at play: Birth to one year*. New York: Newmarket.

Slater, A. M., & Bremner, J. G. (Eds.). (1989). *Infant development*. Hillsdale, NJ: Erlbaum.

White, B. L. (1990). *The first three years of life* (new rev. ed.). New York: Prentice Hall Press.

## OBJECTIVES

Studying this chapter will enable
you to

- Explain how the development of
  physical and sensory capacities
  enables infants to develop
  intellectually.
- Summarize how infants learn
  through their senses and how
  they develop language and
  memory skills.
- Name and describe the six stages
  in Piaget's theory of sensorimotor
  intelligence.
- Discuss what caregivers can do to
  enhance the learning experiences
  of infants.

A
S MARIA prepared supper in the
family kitchen, Casey, her 12-month-
old daughter, played happily nearby.
Casey loved to open drawers and cabinets and
dump out their contents. To keep her daughter
out of mischief, Maria had stocked one cabinet
with a variety of plastic, metal, and wooden
dishes and utensils that were safe to play with.
Casey crawled over to "her" cabinet, pulled the
door open, and peered in expectantly.

First, Casey found a plastic measuring cup.
She banged it on the floor and then brought it
up to her mouth and tried to bite it. After
sucking thoughtfully on the cup for a few
minutes, she tossed it aside. Next, Casey took
out a wooden spoon and a saucepan.
Grasping the spoon, she struck the pan with it.
She seemed to listen intently to the sound the
spoon made. She hit the pan again, then hit
the cupboard door with the spoon and listened
again. Next, Casey struck the plastic cup and

the floor with the spoon, paying attention to the sounds produced by the different objects.

As Casey played, her mother spoke to her from time to time encouraging her. "Hey, Casey. Hit the pan again. Listen to the sound it makes!" When Casey became bored with hitting things with the spoon, Maria took the measuring cup and put it underneath the overturned saucepan. Her daughter watched. "Where's the cup, Casey?" Maria asked. Casey immediately lifted the pan to reveal the cup. Then she put the cup under the pan herself. When she lifted the pan and found the cup again, she smiled proudly.

## Interrelationship of Development Processes

Infants go through an amazing transformation in the first year of life, changing almost miraculously from totally helpless newborns into competent little explorers. In the first few weeks of life, infants cannot even turn themselves over and their powers of communication are limited to crying. But 12 months later, they have become energetic crawlers or toddlers who enthusiastically explore every inch of their environment.

All infants have an inherent, spontaneous desire to learn about themselves and their world. They are active, self-motivated participants in their own education, and they begin to interact with their environment almost from the moment of birth. As their sensory and physical abilities develop, their world expands, enabling them to take in more and more information. Their senses, motor control, nervous system, and brain all mature in a coordinated fashion. Just a few weeks after birth, babies begin to lift their head to look around. They stare at interesting objects and people and learn in time to distinguish their parents' faces and voices from those of others. Over the next few months, they learn to roll over, reach for and pick up an interesting object, crawl, pull themselves up on furniture, and eventually walk.

This chapter focuses on the intellectual, or cognitive, development that takes place during the first year. It describes how the ability of infants to observe, to remember information, and to recognize cause and effect grows by leaps and bounds during this period. It also examines the remarkable progress infants make in communication—learning to understand and eventually to speak the language those around them are speaking. These intellectual changes do not occur in isolation, however. Many depend on specific advances in the infant's physical development, and they are most likely to occur in a warm, supportive atmosphere in which the infant feels secure. Casey could not explore her environment and investigate the shapes, textures, tastes, and sounds of objects until she could move around independently and manipulate objects with her hands. And if her emotional needs were not met and her natural curiosity had been discouraged, she would be less likely to venture off in pursuit of new and exciting adventures. For Casey and other infants, physical, social and emotional, and cognitive development is a continuous and interrelated process, one that begins before birth and continues throughout childhood.

## Development of Specific Cognitive Capacities

As infants mature, their ability to gather information through their senses expands. They see colors, hear sounds, taste flavors, feel textures, smell odors. They begin to distinguish among and categorize these sensations very soon after birth. Mother's milk tastes different from cow's milk. Dad's voice sounds different from all the other voices the baby hears. The ceiling over the infant's crib is always the same color and that color is different from the color of the walls. This perceiving, distinguishing, and categorizing is the very beginning of cognition. As you will recall from Chapter 2, cognition is the process of acquiring knowledge and the process of thinking.

### Perceptual Development

Exactly how do newborns perceive the external world? Do they see, hear, smell, taste, and touch differently from adults? Because young infants cannot talk, they are unable to tell researchers what they are perceiving. One investigator, Robert Fantz, devised a method of measuring infants' perceptions in the 1960s. He discovered that babies will look at an unfamiliar object longer than they will look at a familiar one. When an object becomes familiar, the babies get bored and look away (Fantz, 1964). This process, called *habituation*, can also be measured by monitoring changes in an infant's heart rate or the rate at which he sucks on a pacifier. Heart rate speeds up and sucking slows or temporarily stops when infants become interested in a new stimulus. Fantz realized that he could use the habituation phenomenon to test an infant's vision by showing him an object that was only slightly different from a familiar one. If the baby looked at the new object longer, it meant that the infant discerned the new object as different. But if he looked at the new object for the same length of time as he had observed the familiar object, then it meant that the infant could not distinguish between the two objects and saw them as the same.

Infants like to look at mobiles and other objects that have bright color patterns and moving parts.

**Vision.** A great deal of research has been done on infants' visual perception through use of the habituation technique. At birth, an infant's vision is blurry because the brain is not yet mature enough to process visual information. Fantz and others discovered that until infants are about two months old, all objects appear blurry to them regardless of the distance. However, vision steadily improves until by six months of age, they can see almost as well as adults.

Fantz found that newborns have a preference for looking at patterns with bright colors, with strong contrast between light and shadow, or moving parts. He also learned that they like to look at human faces, which have a great deal of contrast (Fantz, 1963, 1965). Five-month-old babies can distinguish between individual faces, and six-month-olds can distinguish between different facial expressions on the same face (Maurer & Barrera, 1981; Olson & Sherman, 1983). Some researchers have concluded that infants have a predisposition to look at the faces of their caregivers, establishing the first means of communication between newborns and adults.

How do infants perceive the shape and size of objects? Do they believe that an object is getting bigger as it comes toward them or that it has changed its shape when it is viewed from another angle? Work by several psychologists shows that babies begin to perceive shapes as constant in form and size at about three months of age (Banks &

Salapatek, 1983; Caron, Caron, & Carlson, 1978). Babies as young as two months seem to have some depth perception, and it is certainly well developed by the age of six or seven months, when infants begin crawling (Campos, Hiatt, Ramsey, Henderson, & Svedja, 1978; Gibson & Walk, 1960).

**Hearing.** Infants can hear in their mother's uterus, and their hearing is already well developed at birth. However, the hearing of newborns is not as sensitive as that of adults, and therefore sounds must be significantly louder before newborns can hear them. Newborns react to a sound by turning their head toward it. This is called the *orienting response*. They also react to different sounds with distinctly different responses. A loud, sudden sound will cause them to stiffen their body and cry in distress. As the sound becomes louder, the infants' heart rate and agitation increase. On the other hand, low-pitched, rhythmic sounds, such as a heartbeat or soft music, have a soothing effect on infants. According to some studies, newborns who hear a heartbeat cry less than newborns who do not. Since infants have listened to their mother's heartbeats for two months or so before they are born, it is reasonable to expect that they would continue to be comforted by the sound after birth as well.

Infants seem to prefer the human voice over other sounds, and they are very good at distinguishing between different speech sounds. They can distinguish their mother's voice within two or three days after birth. By the age of two months, infants can distinguish between other voices and between different tones of voice spoken by the same person. Researchers have found that the ability of one-month-olds to discriminate between speech sounds is fine enough for them to be able to distinguish between *p* and *b* sounds. As they get older, this ability to distinguish individual speech sounds becomes even more finely tuned (Eimas, Siqueland, & Jusczyk, 1971). This early ability to discriminate between speech sounds is important for later language development and indicates that infants begin the process of language acquisition very soon after birth.

**Smell.**   Newborn babies are able to discriminate between different odors, and they react to various smells in much the same way as adults. Researchers can tell by infants' facial expressions and body movements whether they like or dislike an odor when a sample is held beneath their nose. In one experiment, the infants reacted positively to odors such as lavender and banana but negatively to strong odors such as fish (Steiner, 1979). In another experiment, five-day-old infants were able to distinguish between the odor of their own mother's breast milk and that of other nursing mothers (Macfarlane, 1977).

**Taste.**   The sense of taste is closely related to the sense of smell. Studies show that very young infants can distinguish between a sweet taste and water or other tastes, but it is not clear when they learn to differentiate among salty, bitter, and sour tastes. Their preference for sweet-tasting substances may be related to the fact that their first food, breast milk or formula, has a sweet taste. Pleasurable tastes reinforce eating, one of the infant's earliest activities.

The sense of taste is an important one for infants because it helps them perceive much of their world. As babies grow and develop, virtually everything they can grasp goes into their mouth. Just as Casey sucked on the plastic measuring cup, infants acquire substantial information by sucking and biting objects. By putting an object into their mouth, infants can discover whether or not the object can be eaten, whether it has a pleasant or unpleasant taste, whether it is hot or cold, whether it is soft or hard, and whether it is smooth or rough or fuzzy.

**Touch.**   The sense of touch is also well developed before birth. Newborns are sensitive to heat, cold, pain, and pressure just as adults are. The sense of touch promotes learning in two ways. First, many of the pleasurable things that are done to an infant in the course of caregiving—caressing, washing, cuddling, carrying, patting, stroking, rocking—are communicated to her through the sense of touch. These generate feelings of comfort and safety. Second, the baby's sense of touch is the source for a great deal of information. As with sucking and tasting, infants can learn from their sense of touch whether objects are soft or hard, rough or smooth, sharp or rounded, heavy or light, and so on. The sense of touch begins to develop with the grasping reflex of newborns. As the ability to grasp improves, infants learn to reach for, hold, transfer, bat, shake, throw, and drop objects, demonstrating their growing ability to influence their world.

### Learning and Memory

Several different forms of learning and memory in infancy have been studied. In the preceding section, you learned about the phenomenon of habituation, in which an infant will stare at a new object longer than at a familiar one. Psychologists know that infants have the capacity for habituation virtually from the moment they are born. Even infants as young as three days old have shown that they can recognize certain sights, sounds, odors, and tastes, such as the sound of their mother's voice or the taste or odor of her milk. Clearly, habituation has to be a function of memory because an object or stimulus cannot become familiar to an infant unless he or she recognizes it from one exposure to it to the next (Slatter, Morison, & Rose, 1984).

How long very young infants remember what they have learned is an important question because the process of learning involves storing information in the memory permanently or for long periods of time. Researchers have found that infants less than a month old are less likely than older infants to retain information for more than 24 hours (Rosenblith & Sims-Knight, 1985). Psychologist Carolyn Rovee-Collier taught babies aged two to four months to kick their legs to make a mobile move. The infants remembered to kick to move the mobile for up to eight days. After two weeks, the babies no longer

## FOCUS ON  Cultural Diversity

### Parents Who Don't Speak English

Abby takes care of infants at the Parkside Child Care Center in a small town in Southern California. Over the past six months, a number of Mexican families have moved to town and have enrolled their children at the center. On the whole, the Mexican babies are adjusting very well. However, Abby and the other teachers are having communication problems with many of the parents because they don't speak English.

Abby brought up this problem at a staff meeting, and it led to a wide-ranging discussion. Abby was asked to write a memorandum summarizing the ideas suggested at the meeting. Her memo included the following recommendations for easing the communication gap between the Spanish-speaking parents and the mostly English-speaking staff.

- When parents first bring their children to the center, a translator should be present to introduce the parents and child to the teacher. Parents will then have an opportunity to ask questions and relay special information about their children to caregivers.
- A brochure outlining the policies and practices of the center will be prepared in

Spanish. It will also provide information on safety and health care.

- The staff will welcome non-English-speaking parents warmly with smiles and eye contact. The parents may not be able to understand what the teacher is saying, but the effort to make them feel welcome should reassure them and make them feel that their children will be well cared for. Parents will also be encouraged to spend time at the center whenever they can, so that they will become familiar with the routines and feel more comfortable at the center.
- Caregivers will make an effort to speak slowly and clearly and to use simple phrases when talking to parents.
- A weekly Spanish class will be set up to teach caregivers some basic phrases that will help them communicate with parents about their children's health and development.
- Teachers will encourage parents to learn English by making them aware of community resources, such as classes in English as a Second Language offered at the local high school.

remembered how to kick to activate the mobile, but when they were shown the mobile the day before testing, they once again remembered to kick (Rovee-Collier, 1987). This suggests that the memory was not actually lost; seeing the mobile the day before may have helped the infants retrieve the memory.

Rovee-Collier's studies have demonstrated that babies can learn and remember complicated information. She trained them on mobiles of different shapes and colors and even used different mobiles on different days. The babies showed by their kicking responses in later sessions that they recognized and remembered these differences. These experiments indicate that even very young infants can organize information, recognize the relationship of

cause and effect, and remember how to reproduce an effect.

Habituation is the first and most primitive form of learning. Infants also learn by classical and operant conditioning, observation and imitation, and trial and error. Even when babies learn something as basic as sucking their thumb, they may use several of these learning methods. First they observe their hands and fingers and experiment with moving their arms and hands. Once they learn which motions bring their hands to their mouth, they repeat the motions. Finally, they operantly condition themselves to suck their thumb by performing an action (sucking) that produces a reward (pleasure), reinforcing their desire to do it again.

Infants gather a great deal of information as they explore their world. As their long-term memory improves, they are able to store and organize this information.

According to one study, newborns only a few days old appear to imitate the facial expressions of adults by sticking their tongue out or opening their mouth (Meltzoff & Moore, 1983). Other researchers believe that early imitation of facial expressions may just be a reflexive action that soon disappears. According to Piaget's research, infants are not able to learn new behaviors through observation until about eight months of age. In any event, starting a few weeks after birth, babies do begin to learn to use facial expressions and gestures such as smiling, gazing, looking away, reaching, and flinching in response to their feelings.

As infants get older, their long-term memory capacity improves significantly, and they acquire an impressive store of information that they can use to explore their world. They have also demonstrated the ability to organize the information they have learned into useful categories. For example, one researcher found that seven-month-olds who are habituated to pictures of different male faces and then shown female faces are able to categorize faces into male and female (Fagan, 1979).

By the age of eight months, babies are developing an idea of the independent existence of objects and learning that they can make things happen. These new abilities motivate them to discover cause and effect. They delight in dropping things from their high chair to watch them fall. They see that water always runs downward if they tip over a cup. They discover that a rattle always makes the same noise if they shake it but that another rattle makes a different noise. They find that dirt doesn't taste good but cookies do. Through these kinds of experiences, they gradually acquire a vast store of knowledge about themselves and their world.

By the time they are eight or nine months old, babies begin to apply the idea of independent existence to people as well as objects. They clearly remember individual people, particularly their parents and siblings, and they recall that those people continue to exist even when they are out of sight. At this age, many infants become wary or frightened of strangers. Infants also exhibit separation anxiety, such as crying when a parent leaves them. This behavior indicates that infants have formed a strong attachment to their primary caregivers.

## Learning to Communicate

One of the most amazing things about children is that they are able, within the first three or four years of life, to master what may be the most difficult and complicated intellectual task of all—learning to understand and speak a language. Infants speak their first words at around 12 months of age, but the process of learning to speak and understand language begins almost from the moment of birth.

Many people use the terms *communication* and *language* interchangeably, but they are not exactly the same. *Communication* includes everything one person does—gesturing, body posture, crying, staring—to convey a message to another. Language is just one form of communication, but for humans it is the most important and complex form. *Language* is a system of symbols organized by the rules of grammar. These rules are an essential part of speaking, writing, listening, and reading.

As with other cognitive abilities, the learning of language involves innate or inborn abilities as well as physical development and environmental and social influences. Various theories of how children learn language skills are discussed in Chapter 10. Many psychologists believe that children inherit a mechanism or biological program for learning, and some believe that there is a specific mechanism for learning language. In addition, language development is greatly affected by the child's experiences with his environment and with other people.

Communication between infants and their caregivers begins almost immediately after birth. Mother and child look into each other's eyes. The mother caresses the child's skin, places her finger in the child's palm, and holds the child securely, conveying feelings of safety, warmth, and love. The newborn cries when he feels discomfort, and the mother reacts by searching for the reason for the discomfort—hunger, cold, soiled diapers, stomach upset—so that she can alleviate it. Thus, children and their caregivers embark on a natural, ongoing, almost unconscious reciprocal process of communication in which each responds to the behavior of the other.

Newborns arrive in the world with the ability to hear the human voice and to make vocal sounds of their own in response. Infants only three weeks old can respond to adult voices with vocalizations and body movements indicating pleasure. By three to four months of age, they anticipate some events such as feedings by stretching out their arms, smiling, and cooing.

Adults, including parents, grandparents, and older siblings, usually respond automatically to infants in what psychologists call *motherese*. This is not baby talk but rather a slow, high-pitched, repetitive form of speech. Motherese involves using short words and sentences, repeating words frequently, and asking questions, just as Casey's mother did while she watched her daughter play in the kitchen.

Researchers disagree on whether motherese helps children learn language skills. One researcher concluded that motherese helps children learn new words and sentence structure and helps them put ideas into words (Snow, 1972). Others, however, believe that motherese has no effect on language acquisition. It may not be very important exactly how adults talk to infants but rather how much attention and encouragement they provide.

*Many adults talk to infants in motherese, a slow, high-pitched, repetitive form of speech.*

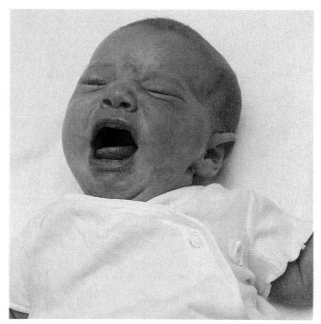

Crying is the primary way that infants respond to their feelings and needs.

### Steps in Language Development

Children raised in different cultures and environments all learn to speak the language that is spoken around them. Language skills begin to develop at birth and continue to improve, so that by the end of infancy most children use some words. The process is a gradual one, but it can be broken into three stages that describe the major features of language development in infancy.

**From Birth to Three Months.**   As you learned earlier, babies can orient to sounds from birth, and they show a preference for the human voice over the other sounds they hear. They not only listen to sounds and voices, but they respond by making sounds of their own. The first sound that newborns make is crying. Crying is the primary way that newborns respond to their feelings and needs. They also begin cooing, an expression of pleasure or contentment, in response to an adult's voice, a toy, or other pleasant stimulus.

**From Three to Nine Months.**  Infants between the ages of three and nine months begin to develop a number of nonverbal signals to communicate with their caregivers. Psychologist Peter Wolff analyzed the cries of infants and concluded that babies vary their cries in pitch and intensity when they feel three basic emotions—hunger, anger, and pain (Wolff, 1973). By the time they are three months old, infants have added gurgling and vowel sounds to their repertoire, and they start to respond to their caregivers' vocalizations with vocalizations of their own. When they are six months old, infants begin to babble, or repeat combinations of consonants and vowels, such as *ba* and *ga*.

Throughout this period, their tongue and vocal cords are growing and maturing, which enables them to make more and more complex sounds. Six-month-old infants may accidently repeat or imitate a sound made by an adult, but they don't begin to imitate the sounds of adults on purpose until they are about nine months old. Psychologists call this period of language development *prelinguistic speech* because the infant is using sounds to communicate without using words.

At this stage, infants are not only learning to vocalize, but they are also learning to communicate with adults through a wide variety of gestures and actions. These include clapping, laughing, bouncing up and down, pointing, reaching, stiffening their body, and so on. For example, an infant who wants to get down off her mother's lap will stiffen her body and lunge forward, pushing her heels against her mother and struggling to pull her arms out of her mother's grasp. Mom can't help but get the message that baby wants to be put down.

**From 9 to 15 Months.**   Babies normally say their first word by the age of one year, but some may be two or three months ahead of or behind schedule. The first word is usually *mama* or *dada* because these are easy sounds for infants to make. By this time, infants know the names of many objects and actions and can typically comprehend more words than they can produce. They recognize familiar words such as their own name, *no*, *cup*, and *cookie*. They also understand that *chair* is the object you sit on and *sit* is what you do in the chair. Now that words have become the symbols for things and actions, the process of communication really begins to develop. For example, when an adult tells a 15-month-old to sit in the chair, he or she knows what is being said and can carry out the instruction.

**TABLE 7.1**
**Piaget's Substages of Sensorimotor Development**

| Substage | Age | Characteristics |
|---|---|---|
| 1. Reflexive stage | Birth to 1 month | Newborn is not aware of difference between environment and self<br>Newborn makes reflexive actions—sucking, crying, rooting, and grasping<br>As reflexive actions are repeated, infant begins to gain information and experience about environment |
| 2. First acquired adaptations stage | 1 to 4 months | Infant begins to make more use of senses and to organize experiences<br>Beginning of hand-eye coordination, enabling infant to take action on own instead of relying on reflexes<br>Primary circular reaction—infant gets pleasurable reaction that causes him to repeat an action, such as sucking on his fingers |
| 3. Make interesting things last stage | 4 to 8 months | Infant learns to differentiate between self and environment—becomes interested in objects and people<br>Secondary circular reaction—infant performs action and gets a response, causing repetition of action<br>Beginning of understanding of object permanence—infant can find partially hidden object |
| 4. Coordination of secondary schemes stage | 8 to 12 months | Infant learns to combine and coordinate two or more previously learned behaviors to reach goal, such as grasping object and putting it in mouth<br>Understanding of object permanence improves; infant searches for fully hidden object |
| 5. Tertiary circular reaction stage | 12 to 18 months | "Little scientist" stage—infant tries out new behaviors with objects to see what will happen<br>Infant usually walking at this stage; will climb and use vastly improved motor skills, senses, and cognitive abilities to explore world and process information |
| 6. Invention of new means through mental combination stage | 18 months to 2 years | Beginning of symbolic thought<br>Beginning of "deferred imitation," when child imitates a behavior observed at some time in the past<br>Full grasp of object permanence |

## Piaget's Stages of Cognitive Development

In Chapter 2 you learned about Jean Piaget's theory of the stages of cognitive development. As you will recall, Piaget believed that there are four main stages or periods in the development of thought as children grow from infancy to adulthood: the sensorimotor stage, the preoperational stage, the period of concrete operations, and the period of formal operations (Piaget, 1952). This chapter takes a closer look at the first stage, the sensorimotor stage, which Piaget defined as the period from birth to age two. See Table 7.1 for the substages of this period.

### Piaget's Sensorimotor Stage

"Sensorimotor stage" is an apt description of the first two years of a child's life. During this period, the senses and muscles begin to mature, gradually enabling the helpless infant to become mobile and to interact with his environment. As the senses and muscles mature, the infant's brain and nervous system also develop, making it possible for him to progress from purely reflexive actions to the beginnings of symbolic thought. These three sequences of sensory, muscular, and cognitive maturation and development are intertwined and dependent on each other. Piaget divided the sensorimotor stage into six substages.

**Substage 1.**   The first substage, the *reflexive stage*, begins at birth and lasts for about a month. During this phase, infants are not aware of the difference between themselves and their environment. Newborns can only make simple movements. When you put something to their lips, they will suck on it. When you place a finger in the center of their palm, they will grasp it. And when you hold newborns above a hard surface with their feet touching, they will flex and extend their legs in stepping movements.

These actions are reflexes, automatic inborn reactions to a stimulus. They are the only schemes that newborns can form for interacting with their environment. As they repeat each reflex over and over, they begin to gain information and experience about their environment. Take the rooting reflex, for example. In Chapter 6 you learned that when an object touches an infant's cheek, she turns her head toward it to suck—whether it is her mother's breast, a finger, or some other object. As the infant sucks on different objects, she accumulates different sucking experiences. Her mother's breast is soft, but her father's finger is hard. She has to suck forcefully to extract milk from her mother's breast, but she doesn't suck hard on her father's finger because she soon learns that she gets no nourishment from it.

**Substage 2.**   The second substage is called the *first acquired adaptations stage*, and it extends from one to four months. Infants expand on the reflexes from substage 1 to develop schemes centered about the body. They suck on their hands, grab their feet, or play with their voice.

Infants begin to make more use of their senses during this period. They stare at their hands for several minutes at a time, they track or follow movements with their eyes, and they turn their head to try to locate a noise. It is also during this phase that *hand-eye coordination* begins to develop, which enables infants to take actions on their own instead of

During the sensorimotor stage, infants become experts at investigating and manipulating objects with their fingers and mouth.

having to rely solely on reflexive action. In substage 1, infants suck on their fingers when the fingers accidentally come in contact with their mouth; in substage 2, they learn to move their fingers to their mouth when they want to suck on them.

When babies suck on their fingers, they are experiencing what Piaget called a *primary circular reaction*. This means that the baby's actions cause an interesting or pleasurable reaction that prompts him to repeat the action. He sucks his fingers and feels pleasure so he sucks his fingers again. When the infant repeats this process again and again, it becomes a habit. Piaget called this sequence "primary" because it stems from the baby's own actions.

**Substage 3.**   At between four and eight months of age, infants go through the substage Piaget called the "make interesting things last" stage. In this phase, infants learn to differentiate between themselves and their environment, and they learn to recognize and manipulate more and more objects. Infants in this phase perform *secondary circular reactions*. They perform an action and it gets a response, which prompts them to repeat the action. A baby may discover by accident that a cup makes a noise when he bangs it against his high chair tray. He will then beat the cup against the tray intentionally to make the noise again and again. This is what Piaget meant by making interesting things last.

Piaget called this process a secondary rather than a primary reaction because it is an object or person who triggers the reaction rather than the infant's own body. During this stage, adults contribute to a baby's cognitive development by their reactions. Smiling, touching, and talking to babies when they perform an action causes them to perform the action again.

Infants also begin to learn about cause and effect in substage 3. They learn to perform actions to achieve goals. For example, a baby who wants to investigate a new toy might pick it up, bring it to her mouth, and try to chew on it.

**Substage 4.**   The fourth substage, the *coordination of secondary schemes stage*, lasts from about 8 to 12 months of age. It is given this name because infants are learning to combine and coordinate two or more previously learned behaviors to reach a goal. They develop a sense of purpose about their actions. For example, in substage 3, Casey learned how to grasp objects and how to make objects move toward her by pulling at them. Now she can combine her grasping and pulling skills to achieve a purpose, opening the cupboard door.

Substage 4 is also the period when infants make significant advances in the development of *object permanence*, the understanding that objects, such as the dishes and utensils in the cupboard, continue to exist when they are out of sight. Countless studies have demonstrated that object permanence develops in a very specific sequence. When Casey was two months old, she showed no interest in an object after it had been hidden from her. As far as she was concerned, if it was out of sight, it was out of mind. At between four and eight months (substage 3), she began to develop the rudiments of object permanence. She did search for partially hidden objects, and she momentarily gazed after things she had dropped. Since she was eight months old, Casey has been steadily developing a much clearer understanding of object permanence. Now at a year, Casey knows that the measuring cup she has been playing with exists whether she can see it or not, and she instantly retrieves it from under the pan. Casey's understanding of object permanence will continue

Once infants learn to apply the concept of object permanence, they love to play the game of peekaboo.

to grow. By the time she is in substage 6, Casey will have a mature understanding of the concept.

Determining precisely when a child has acquired object permanence is difficult. Some psychologists feel that infants who have the concept may still make errors when searching for hidden objects. They may have established a pattern of searching for an object in some other location, or they may not have the motor skills to lift a cup or cloth to find the object. However, it is clear that the development of object permanence is a major intellectual milestone for infants because it enables them to separate their environment from themselves. The infants begin to realize that they are only a part of the world and that people and things exist apart from themselves. Once they develop the concept of object permanence, they begin to show a preference for specific objects, such as a favorite stuffed animal or blanket, over others. In addition, once infants are able to apply the concept of object permanence to people, they love to play the game of peekaboo. It is also during substage 4 that infants develop the capacity to anticipate events. If they are placed in a high chair, they know they are going to be fed; if they are dressed in a hat and coat, they know they are going outdoors.

**Substages 5 and 6.**    Substage 5, from 12 to 18 months, is the *tertiary circular reaction stage*. Piaget called this the "little scientist" phase because instead of just repeating already learned behaviors, infants begin to try out new behaviors with objects in order to see what will happen. Tertiary circular reaction means the infant will manipulate the same objects in several different ways or different objects in the same way to observe the results. When Casey struck her wooden spoon against the pan, cupboard door, floor, and plastic cup to hear the different sounds they made, she was engaging in a tertiary circular reaction. Each new sound motivated her to experiment further by striking a new object. In this substage, novelty becomes its own reward. Each new and different result seems to provide the motivation to try yet another experiment and seek a new result. By this stage, infants are usually walking and have the freedom to explore a much wider world. Now they can learn by trial and error how to manipulate objects to achieve their goals.

Substage 6, called the invention of new means through mental combination stage, lasts from 18 months to two years of age and marks the beginning of symbolic thought. This substage is discussed in detail in Chapter 10.

### Critics of Piaget

Piaget's theories have long set the standard for discussing the cognitive development of infants. His substages lay out a clear, logical progression of the development of thinking in humans, from the primitive unconscious reflexes of the newborn to the symbolic thought of adults. Nevertheless, Piaget is not without numerous critics and qualifiers.

Even researchers who agree with Piaget's overall scheme of intellectual development do not all accept his model in every detail. Many feel that he underestimated the abilities of infants in a number of important areas. Studies have shown, for example, that infants in substage 4, and possibly younger, have a better developed sense of object permanence than Piaget proposed (Baillargeon & De Vos, 1991). Some researchers have even concluded that infants as young as six months begin to develop mental concepts. Their conclusions contrast with Piaget's view that infants are limited to sensorimotor schemes (Mandler, 1988).

Other researchers feel that Piaget greatly overemphasized motor development at the expense of the sensory aspect of cognitive development. A growing body of research indicates that very young infants are learning much more from watching and listening than they are able to show because their motor skills are not yet sufficiently developed (Bower & Wishart, 1979; Gibson, 1979, 1982).

In general, parents and caregivers must keep in mind that Piaget's stages are not separate and distinct intervals. Infants do not leap fully proficient from one stage to the next. Rather, they progress from stage to stage in a gradual, almost imperceptible, continuous manner.

## Individual Difference in Cognitive Development

Cognitive development is the growth in mental abilities that enables people to understand and respond to their environment. Infancy is a period of very rapid cognitive development. However, infants do not all develop at the same rate. Caregivers who are familiar with the normal sequence and pace of growth may notice when an infant is developing faster or slower than usual.

### Cognitive Development and Intelligence

Measuring the intelligence of infants is difficult because they cannot yet talk. Various standardized tests are used to measure motor control, language development, and adaptive and social behavior. The Brazelton Neonatal Behavioral Assessment Scale, for example, measures characteristics in newborns such as sensory and social responsiveness, alertness and habituation, motor movement and muscle tone, and response to stress. The Bayley scales of infant development are used to assess developmental progress from birth through about age two. These tests provide a reliable measurement of an infant's current abilities, but they do not usually predict how the infant will perform on intelligence tests given in later childhood (McCall, Eichorn, & Hogarty, 1977). For example, on the Bayley tests, scores of near normal and above normal do not relate to later intelligence test performance. Only very low scores predict later performance (very low scoring infants are likely to have developmental

## FOCUS ON Communicating with Parents

### Normal Range of Language Development

Kim provides child care in her home. One of the toddlers she cares for is 15-month-old Rosalba. Rosalba is a cheerful, healthy child who is constantly in motion. One Monday afternoon when Rosalba's mother comes to pick her daughter up, Kim notices that she seems worried.

ROSALBA'S MOTHER: We went to visit my sister this weekend. Her baby, Eduardo, is two weeks younger than Rosalba. Eduardo is already talking. He calls his brother's name, asks for milk, and says a lot of other words, too. My sister wondered why Rosalba hasn't started talking yet.

KIM: Well, children start talking at different times. I don't think you need to worry. Toddlers can't learn everything at once. Right now Rosalba uses so much energy exploring that she doesn't have any left over for learning to talk.

ROSALBA'S MOTHER: My sister thought maybe there was something wrong with her. She thinks that maybe we should have her hearing checked.

KIM: I'm almost sure her hearing is okay. When I say it's time for juice, she runs to the table, climbs up in her chair, and waits for me to get her cup. She understands a lot even though she doesn't say anything.

ROSALBA'S MOTHER: I've noticed she makes a lot of sounds, but they aren't words. My husband thinks she gets mixed up because we speak Spanish to her at home and she hears English here. He's afraid it isn't good for her and she won't learn either language.

KIM: Kids can learn two languages at once, but sometimes it takes them a little longer. If you're really worried, you can talk to her doctor, but I think she's perfectly okay.

ROSALBA'S MOTHER: I just wish she would start talking like Eduardo. Of course, he's with his mother all day and she only speaks Spanish to him. Maybe that's why he's talking and Rosalba isn't.

*Do you think Kim took the mother's concerns seriously? Do you agree or disagree with what Kim told her? Under what circumstances would you advise a parent to seek professional advice if their child was not speaking?*

---

problems later). Some researchers believe that infant tests fail to predict later scores because they measure different forms of intellectual development. While infant tests focus primarily on sensorimotor skills, tests for older children measure verbal or mathematical skills.

One area in which researchers can better predict later intelligence is the area of memory. This is often tested by measuring an infant's visual recognition memory. Infants who show an ability to remember and recognize something they have seen before tend to have IQ scores later in life that are higher than

children who did not show this ability as infants (Lipsitt, 1986; Rose, Feldman, & Wallace, 1992). Infant intelligence tests are also helpful in identifying infants with abnormalities or disabilities and for exploring differences in child rearing.

### Inheritance and Environment

Various studies of twins have shown that genetic factors play a significant role in intelligence (see Chapter 3). The relationship between genetics and intelligence is less noticeable in infants and becomes

**TABLE 7.2**
**Milestones of Intellectual Development**

| Age | Milestones |
|---|---|
| *Birth to 1 Month*<br>Sensorimotor | Reflexes—rooting, walking motions, sucking, blinking, grasping; startles to loud noise<br>Prefers bright colors, high contrast, faces |
| Memory | Habituates to some sounds, sights, tastes; first sign of memory |
| Communication | Orients to sounds<br>Prefers human voice<br>Cries in response to distress |
| *1 to 4 Months*<br>Sensorimotor | Brings hands to mouth, sucks thumb<br>Kicks, bats at objects with arms<br>Observes fingers and hands, tracks objects with eyes<br>Beginning of hand-eye coordination |
| Memory | Remembers for more than 24 hours<br>Recognizes mother's face and voice |
| Communication | Can imitate some facial expressions<br>Orients to voices<br>Begins to vocalize; adds smiling, cooing, gurgling |
| *4 to 8 Months*<br>Sensorimotor | Can transfer objects from hand to hand<br>Explores objects by biting, sucking, chewing |
| Memory | Distinguishes objects by size, shape, color, hardness, and number of objects<br>Beginning of object permanence—looks for dropped objects, searches for partially hidden objects<br>Distinguishes mother's face from stranger's, distinguishes mother's and father's voices from stranger's<br>Remembers learned behaviors for up to 8 days |
| Communication | Listens intently to human voice<br>Makes different sounds to express emotions<br>Begins babbling, primarily vowel sounds |
| *8 to 12 Months*<br>Sensorimotor | Places small objects inside larger ones<br>Learns to combine behaviors to achieve a goal<br>Understands that objects exist even when out of sight |
| Memory | Distinguishes familiar people from strangers—separation anxiety develops<br>Can recognize objects by touch<br>Long-term memory well developed |
| Communication | Has developed different gestures to communicate; can answer question with nod of head<br>Recognizes several words for objects or actions<br>Babbling continues, consonant sounds added, will repeat adult's sounds<br>Says first word at about 12 months |

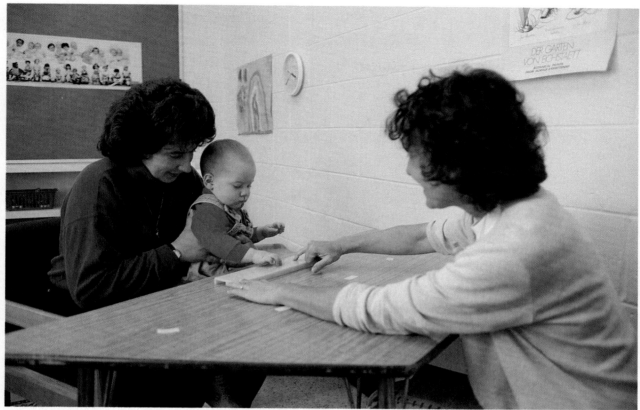

*Standardized tests such as the Bayley scales of infant development are able to provide an accurate assessment of a baby's skills. But these tests cannot reliably predict future performance or intelligence.*

more apparent with age (Scarr & McCartney, 1983; Wilson, 1983). The cognitive development of children is also affected by a child's temperament and personality. Children are born with individual personalities. These inborn characteristics begin to appear soon after birth and remain stable over time as a child grows and matures. Some infants are fussy and impatient, while others are easygoing. Some want to move all the time, while others are content to spend more time observing. Some infants are friendly and outgoing toward strangers; others are shy and anxious. These personality differences affect how each child acquires and processes information. A child's temperament can also determine the way other people respond to her. In this way, the child's genetic makeup has an effect on her environment.

Environment also plays a key role in an infant's intellectual development; it provides material for early sensory impressions. A child's environment consists of his physical surroundings, the people around him, and his interactions with them. Adults serve as mediators, shaping the infant's world and experiences and starring as featured actors.

The amount and kind of care that infants receive from their adult caregivers has a significant impact on their intellectual development. Research has shown that an inadequate environment during infancy can have drastic consequences for development (Dennis, 1973). Imagine a baby who is left to lie in a crib all day with nothing to look at and without adult attention. His caregivers rarely speak to him, and they often fail to respond to his needs. That child is going to languish, and his intellectual

### Intelligence Testing for Young Children

Mr. and Mrs. Brandon live in Atlanta. Their son, Nathan, starts kindergarten next year. The Brandons plan to send him to a private school. They have discovered that some private schools require intelligence testing as part of the admission process.

Mrs. Brandon thinks that testing a four-year-old is unreasonable. Mr. Brandon believes testing will provide some useful information. Here is what each has to say.

Mrs. Brandon:

"Nathan is an active, verbal child with normal social skills, but he does not feel at ease in new situations. How can anyone expect him to take a test with a psychologist he has never met before and have it mean anything?

"Young children are not good test takers. They don't understand what is expected of them. There are too many things outside the test that influence the final results, like whether the child got a good night's sleep or feels comfortable around the test giver. Dr. Sue Bredekamp, director of professional development for the National Association for the Education of Young Children, says that the only valid measures of young children are taken by people who know them well (Segal, 1990).

"There are other reasons not to test preschoolers. Scores change depending on how the test giver interprets a child's verbal answers. Two psychologists can look at the same responses and arrive at scores that can vary by as much as ten points.

"IQ tests can last an hour or more. The testing doesn't stop until the child answers a certain percentage of questions incorrectly. This is stressful. It's too much to expect a preschooler to stay focused and interested for that long. I don't think Nathan should be labeled at such an early age, especially when there's no guarantee the tests are accurate."

Mr. Brandon:

"Nathan isn't the first four-year-old to take an IQ test. Different versions of these tests have been used for three generations, so test givers have a lot of experience interpreting the results, even the results of young children's tests. Psychologists who specialize in testing preschoolers are trained to make them feel comfortable. They say that many young children enjoy the experience and don't see it as a test at all. It's usually the parents who get upset.

"Intelligence tests measure reasoning and memory skills and give a good indication of a child's potential. Many child development experts believe that on standardized intelligence tests, children pretty well reveal where they're headed educationally by age three.

"By having an early indication of Nathan's abilities, we can select a school where he'll be comfortable. I don't want to push him into a school he can't handle academically. On the other hand, I don't want to hold him back either.

"I agree with Dr. Burton White, who has spent years studying preschool children. He says that testing young children during early years is of fundamental importance if we are going to give each child the best possible chance of making the most of whatever he or she brings into the world (White, 1985).

"Nathan is a well-adjusted little boy. If we don't make a big deal out of the testing, he won't get upset. All I'm asking is that we have some objective idea about his abilities before we select a school for him."

*Which parent do you agree with more? Are there arguments the other parent presents that you think are valid? In what other ways can parents, teachers, and schools evaluate a child without using IQ test scores?*

development will suffer. In all likelihood, it will be more limited and delayed than that of a child whose caregivers interact with him constantly and provide an abundance of attention, stimulation, and care.

Although research has not established exactly what makes up an ideal learning environment for infants, it is clear that attention needs to be paid to the infants' physical and emotional needs and intellectual stimulation. The first and most important job of parents and other caregivers is to provide for infants' basic physical needs and to establish a safe, secure environment in which the infants can begin to develop. This means not only keeping them warm, dry, and well fed but also responding warmly to them.

Emotional support and intellectual stimulation can be provided by offering an infant a variety of backgrounds and experiences in a warm, nurturing atmosphere. Talking softly and soothingly to the infant, singing and reading to her, playing with her, maintaining eye contact, and carrying her around so she can get to know her environment and the other people in it are ways of accomplishing this goal.

Physical surroundings, too, are an important element in an infant's environment. Rooms with bright colors, objects of different shapes and textures, mobiles, toys, pictures, and music will stimulate an infant's senses and offer opportunities for acquiring information. Casey's cupboard, for example, was well stocked with objects of different sizes, shapes, textures, and colors for her to examine and manipulate. As she played, her mother talked to her, naming objects, repeating her name, and praising her achievements. Casey was being given the opportunity to gain a great deal of visual, verbal, and sensory information from her surroundings and from one of the principal caregivers in her life.

Physical surroundings and the way children are treated vary from culture to culture, and infants' experiences will vary accordingly. For example, in some cultures babies are carried around most of the time. This can affect the way that babies first learn to communicate. Because of the constant physical closeness with the caregiver, the infants can send signals with their body. They have less incentive to communicate verbally than babies who spend most of their time physically separated from the caregiver.

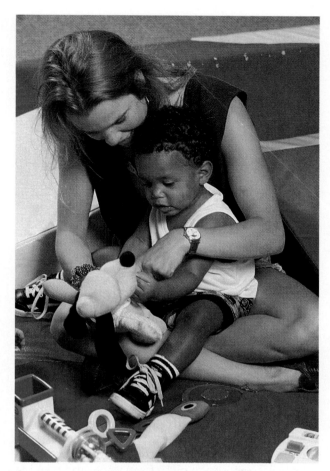

Caregivers can foster the intellectual development of infants by providing them with sensory stimulation and ample opportunities to explore and learn about their environment.

For adults, one of life's greatest pleasures is watching infants develop from helpless newborns to competent and eager toddlers. It is important for caregivers to remember that while the sequence and time schedules of cognitive development are generally alike for all children, each child is an individual. No infant will adhere exactly to any schedule or chart. Some children will be faster in some areas of development and slower in others. One infant may skip crawling, while another may begin speaking in sentences instead of single words. Early childhood educators can help parents understand and appreciate these differences.

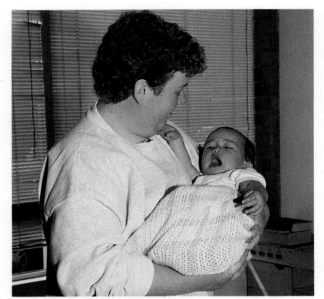

Holding, patting, and stroking are all forms of physical contact that a caregiver can use to give an infant a sense of warmth and security.

## Implications and Applications

What newborns and very young infants need most of all to promote cognitive development is interaction with their caregivers. With the continuing growth of infant day care, child care professionals will be called upon to fill in for parents and provide stimulation and interaction during the workday. Caregivers should respond to the infant's needs quickly, warmly, and patiently. This helps build the foundation of security and trust that will later give the infant confidence to explore his or her world.

Even the youngest infants need an abundance of sensory stimulation such as movement, bright colors, and pleasant sounds. At this age, infants' toys should include mobiles, balls, and small toys to grasp. Caregivers should change the babies' positions and view frequently and make sure they have opportunities to kick their legs, wave their arms, and learn to roll over. Infants also need plenty of skin contact with caregivers. Stroking, patting, touching, and holding are all important means of conveying feelings of warmth and security to infants. In their early months, infants sleep a great deal, so it is important to provide a suitable place for them to rest.

Most importantly, infants need to hear human voices and language. This means talking to them at every opportunity—while changing their diapers and clothes, feeding them, rocking or carrying them. Repeat their names often, as well as the names of objects and actions. Sing to infants, read them books in an enthusiastic voice, and play music and recorded stories for them.

Caregivers should always keep in mind that infants learn about their world by interacting with it. After the first few months, they need a wide variety of safe, interesting objects to suck, grasp, open, close, bang, throw, push, and pull. Infants will learn from nesting and stacking toys, pull toys, cardboard books that they can open and close, and action toys, such as jack-in-the-boxes that they can manipulate to produce an effect. Often the best toys are simple household objects such as unbreakable cups, dishes, and spoons. Toys and other objects should be large and easy to manipulate.

Older infants learn a great many small skills and experiences that they will later build on to learn to perform more complicated tasks. For example, a one-year-old may only be able to grasp a crayon awkwardly. Later he will use the fine motor skills he is already developing to learn to draw and write. The infant who is busy putting things together and taking them apart today may become tomorrow's architect, engineer, or builder.

Once infants can crawl, they need a safe, attractive environment to explore. Caregivers should try to anticipate the infants' needs and provide opportunities, activities, and toys that will help them develop their cognitive abilities. Casey's mother wisely stocked a low cupboard with safe, varied objects for her daughter to examine and manipulate. As Casey played, Maria remained close by and frequently talked to Casey and interacted with her.

Keep in mind that caregivers are always any infant's most interesting and stimulating toy. Infants love to play simple games such as peekaboo and hide-and-seek. When Maria played hide the cup with Casey, she was reinforcing the infant's grasp of object permanence. By remaining close by, Maria also gave Casey the opportunity to "return to base" when she felt the need.

You may recall from Chapter 4 that infants who have developed secure attachments to their caregivers use the adults as safe bases from which to

## FOCUS ON  Decision Making in Child Care

### Parents Who Are Late

For the third time in two weeks, Katherine was late picking up her daughter Sara at the All Day Child Center. Carlos, the caregiver, looked at his watch anxiously, while an aide who was waiting with him tried to comfort three-year-old Sara. The child seemed upset and asked where all the other children had gone. As they waited, Carlos could feel his anger growing.

Finally, 40 minutes after closing time, Katherine rushed in. She apologized for being late, explaining that the store where she worked had been too busy for her to leave. Carlos told Katherine that her lateness was a problem and that having a store full of customers was not an excuse. Trying hard to keep his temper in check, Carlos reminded her that he had things to do after work and that staying late caused problems in his life. He also pointed out that Sara became upset when her mother didn't arrive on time.

Katherine looked at Carlos and sighed. She told Carlos that her job was important and that she couldn't just get up and leave anytime she felt like it. She said that she didn't think being a few minutes late now and then would be such a big deal. Carlos decided it was better not to say anything else. That evening, he thought about what had happened and wondered what he should do.

The next morning Carlos told the center's director what had happened. She agreed that lateness was a problem and asked Carlos for his ideas. Carlos suggested that the center establish a policy on lateness. Parents who arrived after closing time without calling would be charged a small fee. He also suggested that children of parents who were always late be dropped from the center. The director agreed to discuss these ideas with the board and the other caregivers.

Carlos's proposal was accepted and the policy on lateness was incorporated in the parent's handbook. The director also wrote a letter notifying the parents of the center's new policy. Carlos gave the letter to each parent, thanking the parents who were rarely late. With Katherine and other parents who frequently arrived after closing time, Carlos made a special effort to explain the reason for the new rules. Carlos hoped that the new policy would solve the problem and that he wouldn't risk losing his temper with another late parent.

*Do you think Carlos handled the situation with Katherine well? How effective do you think the new policy will be? What other strategies can caregivers use to discourage lateness?*

venture out and explore. They know that if they are frightened or alarmed, they can quickly return to their caregiver. This secure attachment gives toddlers the self-confidence to interact with their environment and thus continue to learn from it.

Virtually from birth, infants are hard at work developing their sensory and motor abilities and acquiring the knowledge and skills that they will need later. They are, in effect, learning to learn. Caregivers need to be aware that infants develop mentally and physically in a relatively set sequence and pattern. It is important that they understand that the newborn's stare, the four-month-old's obsession with putting everything into his mouth, and the ten-month-old's babbling are all integral, necessary parts of that pattern. The child care professional's primary job is to provide infants with stimulation, interaction, and a warm and safe environment so that these budding athletes, explorers, linguists, and scientists can get on with their work. Caregivers can also play a role in helping families learn about environments and behaviors that will promote and enhance their children's intellectual development.

## SUMMARY

- Infants go through tremendous changes in their first year, progressing from virtually helpless newborns to mobile 12-month-olds with well-developed senses, an ability to remember individuals and objects, and rapidly expanding communication skills.

- The vision of newborn babies is limited, but within a few months they can see clearly at a distance. The senses of hearing, smell, taste, and touch are nearly as well developed in newborns as in adults.

- Infants use their senses to gather information about their environment; as their intellectual capacities expand, they learn to compare, organize, and classify this information.

- Memory is essential to learning. The ability to remember information seems to be present at birth. The ability to remember over long periods of time develops rapidly in young infants.

- Infants spend their first year listening to human speech and learning how to communicate in a variety of ways. Language skills begin to develop at birth. By the end of their first year, infants begin to speak their first words.

- Infants learn language in a universal sequence. First they cry, then they gurgle and babble. They say their first words when they are between 9 and 15 months old. All through this sequence, they learn to associate words with the objects or actions that they name.

- Piaget divided the first two years of a child's development, the sensori-motor period, into six substages. These phases describe the infant's growing intellectual competence; he called them the reflexive stage, the first acquired adaptations stage, the make interesting things last stage, the co-ordination of secondary schemes stage, the tertiary circular reactions stage, and the invention of new means through mental combination stage.

- An important milestone in Piaget's developmental sequence occurs in substage 4, when infants develop the concept of object permanence. This means that objects and people continue to exist for the infant even when they are out of her sight.

- Piaget's critics say that he overestimated the age at which infants develop certain abilities and that he placed too much emphasis on motor rather than sensory development.

- Intellectual, or cognitive, development, refers to the process of acquiring, comprehending, and using information; it is affected by a wide variety of environmental and hereditary factors.

- To develop normally, infants need warm, accepting interaction with their caregivers, a stimulating and safe environment, plenty of skin contact, objects and toys that enable them to learn about their world, and the sound of human voices.

## BUILDING VOCABULARY

Write a definition for each vocabulary term listed below.

communication
coordination of secondary schemes
    stage
first acquired adaptations stage
habituation
hand-eye coordination
language
motherese

object permanence
orienting response
prelinguistic speech
primary circular reaction
reflexive stage
secondary circular reaction
tertiary circular reaction stage

## ACQUIRING KNOWLEDGE

1.  How does an infant's vision change in the first four months of life?
2.  How do researchers measure habituation?
3.  Which type of objects do infants tend to look at longer—familiar or unfamiliar ones?
4.  How do infants respond to visual contrast?
5.  How do newborns react to sudden loud noises?
6.  Can infants perceive different odors? How might they react to a strong fish odor, for example?
7.  What kind of tastes do infants prefer?
8.  Give an example of how an infant might use the sense of touch to acquire information.
9.  What role does memory play in habituation?
10. Give an example of something an infant might learn through imitation.
11. How does the ability to organize information help infants distinguish male faces from female faces?
12. Give an example of something an infant might do with a cup to experiment with cause and effect.
13. How does the concept of object permanence change the way infants think about their parents when the parents are out of sight?
14. How do communication and language differ?
15. Give an example of how a mother communicates with her newborn.
16. Describe motherese and explain how adults use it.
17. What sounds do newborns make when they feel pleasure or pain?
18. What role does babbling play in language acquisition?
19. At what stage do infants begin to say their first words?
20. Give an example of a secondary circular reaction. How does it differ from a primary circular reaction?
21. What is one criticism of Piaget's description of sensorimotor development in infants?
22. What types of skills do infant intelligence tests measure?
23. What elements make up an infant's environment?
24. What role does listening to a caregiver's voice play in an infant's development?
25. How do bright colors affect infants?

## THINKING CRITICALLY

1. Suppose that a mother is leaning over the crib of her three-month-old son, who is looking up at her. What can the infant perceive about his mother through his senses?
2. Do you think caregivers should speak to infants in motherese? In your opinion, what are the advantages or disadvantages of using motherese?
3. Describe the cognitive processes that take place when a newborn wakes up hungry, cries, and is eventually fed. What does the newborn learn from the experience?
4. In what ways are infants "little scientists"? Give examples of how infants gather information and conduct experiments to learn about the world.
5. It has been shown that infant intelligence test results generally do not predict a child's performance on intelligence tests later in life. Do you think there are any benefits to be gained by testing the intelligence of infants? Are there arguments against testing infants? Explain.

## OBSERVATIONS AND APPLICATIONS

1. Observe an infant between the ages of three months and one year, making note of his or her language development. Write down the vowel sounds the baby makes and note the combinations of consonants and vowels. Does the baby say any words? Does he or she consistently make the same sound when shown a ball, for example, even if that sound is not the word *ball*? When does the baby make sounds? In response to a caregiver? When interacting with other children? When lying alone in the crib? In response to his or her name? What else do you observe about this infant's language development?
2. Observe three infants who range in age from three months to one year, making note of differences in the way they play with toys. What kinds of toys does each infant enjoy? What differences do you observe in the way each child interacts with the same toy? What does a three-month-old do with a small stuffed animal? What does a six-month-old do with the same toy? Try to identify the substage of cognitive development each infant has reached.
3. Compare the ability of a one-year-old to use language with his or her ability to understand it. First, observe the language development of a one-year-old as outlined in number 1 above. Then, ask the child to perform some simple tasks. "Bring me the ball." "Where is your nose?" "Do you want some juice?" Were you able to confirm that infants understand more than they can say?
4. To learn more about the development of the concept of object permanence, try the following experiment with four infants ranging in age from 2 months to 18 months. One at a time, show each infant an object. Then, cover it with a cloth (or hide it behind your back, under the table, etc.). Does the infant try to find the object? Describe each infant's behavior. Do the children you observed follow the sequence of development outlined by Piaget?

**5.** Mr. and Mrs. Chandler are first-time parents. They are overwhelmed by all the products available to buy for infants. They have a limited budget, however. They want to buy items that will be of the most value to their infant son Richard. What types of toys would you suggest they purchase? What else can they use as toys that would not cost them extra money but would provide stimulation for their son?

## SUGGESTIONS FOR FURTHER READING

Anisfeld, M. (1984). *Language development from birth to three.* Hillsdale, NJ: Erlbaum.

Bredekamp, S. (Ed.). (1987). *Developmentally appropriate practice in early childhood programs serving children from birth through age 8.* Washington, DC: National Association for the Education of Young Children.

Bruner, J. S. (1983). *Child's talk.* New York: Norton.

Caruso, D. (1988). Play and learning in infancy: Research and implications. *Young Children, 43*(6), 63–70.

Fenichel, E. S., & Eggbeer, L. (1990). *Preparing practitioners to work with infants, toddlers, and their families: Issues and recommendations for the professions.* Arlington, VA: ZERO TO THREE/National Center for Clinical Infant Programs.

Flavell, J. H., Miller, P. H., & Miller, S. A. (1993). *Cognitive Development* (3rd Ed.). Englewood Cliffs, NJ: Prentice-Hall.

Forman, G. E., & Kushner, D. S. (1983). *The child's construction of knowledge: Piaget for teaching children.* Washington, DC: National Association for the Education of Young Children.

Goldman, J., Stein, C. E., & Guerry, S. (1983). *Psychological methods of child assessment.* New York: Bruner/Mazel.

Gunzenhauser, N. (Ed.). (1987). *Infant stimulation.* Somerville, NJ: Johnson & Johnson.

Honig, A. S. (1984, Winter). Why talk to babies? *Beginnings,* pp. 3–6.

Lamb, M. E., & Bornstein, M. H. (1987). *Development in infancy.* New York: Random House.

McCall, R. B. (1979). *Infants: A psychological guide to normal development.* Cambridge, MA: Harvard University Press.

Melkman, R. (1988). *The construction of objectivity: A new look at the first months of life.* New York: Karger.

Rosenblith, J. F. (1992). *In the beginning: Development from conception to age two.* Newbury Park, CA: Sage.

Smolak, L. (1986). *Infancy.* Englewood Cliffs, NJ: Prentice-Hall.

Snow, C. W. (1989). *Infant Development.* Englewood Cliffs, NJ: Prentice-Hall.

White, B. L. (1988). *Educating the infant and toddler.* Lexington, MA: Lexington Books.

# Emotional and Social Development

## OBJECTIVES

Studying this chapter will enable
you to

- Identify and describe four theories
  of emotional development.
- Describe important milestones in
  the emotional development of
  infants.
- Identify and describe two theories
  of temperament.
- Explain the concepts of bonding,
  engrossment, and attachment,
  and describe some of the findings
  regarding each concept.
- Discuss the important features of
  Bowlby's attachment theory.
- Describe Ainsworth's strange
  situation procedure and how it is
  used to classify infants' patterns of
  attachment.

D AVID has been an easygoing child
since birth. His parents like to go out
from time to time and when they do,
they leave him with a warm and experienced
babysitter. In the past, David has accepted this
sitter cheerfully and has been easy to care for.
Now David is seven months old, and his
parents are getting ready to go out. When the
babysitter arrives, David doesn't show much of
a reaction. When the sitter reaches over and
picks him up, however, David begins to
whimper and then to wail. David's parents are
surprised by their son's reaction. David and this
sitter have always gotten along splendidly
before. They wonder why he is behaving this
way. Could their son be ill?

This story illustrates a baby's emotional reaction to a social encounter. Babies seem to experience a variety of emotions in such situations, including love or attachment to a special caregiver, distress at separation from this person, and distress or fear at the approach of strangers. Even during infancy, children are remarkably "tuned in" to other people, and social and emotional development go hand in hand. This chapter focuses first on the emotional development of infants and then takes a look at their social development. You will hear more about David's reaction to his babysitter in connection with various points being made.

## Emotional Development in Infancy

Experts disagree on when infants begin to have real emotions. Some believe that reactions such as crying when hungry or smiling at adults should be considered simple reflexes rather than true emotions such as those experienced by older children and adults. More recently, however, experts have found evidence that infants express a variety of emotions.

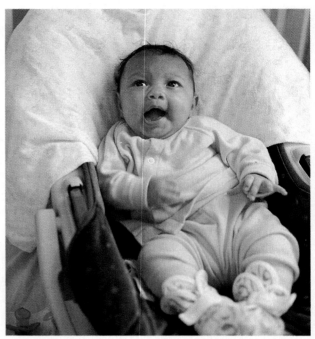

*Some experts believe that babies express real emotions early in infancy. Others believe that reactions such as smiling and crying are simply reflexes.*

### What Is Emotion?

Before discussing the development of emotions, it is important to define what emotion is. Different theorists and researchers have very different definitions of emotion, and these variations have important implications for our understanding of the development of emotion.

**Emotion as Feeling.**    Most people think of emotion as feeling, and historically this definition has been a major focus of theories of emotion. Theorists interested in adults' emotions typically focus on feeling, and they rely on people's reports about their own feelings when studying emotion. Although it is possible that feeling is central to emotion during infancy, feeling cannot really be studied during this period. Babies cannot report on how they feel. For this reason, if researchers want to study emotion, they must go beyond feeling in defining emotion.

**Emotion as Facial Expression.**    Some theorists think that during infancy, facial expressions

indicate emotion. Researcher Carroll Izard, for example, believes that, while feeling is important during infancy, facial movements directly indicate what is being felt. Izard's differential emotions theory, which is quite clear in making this point, is discussed in more detail later in the chapter. There is also evidence that, across a wide variety of cultures, adults judge the same facial movements to communicate the same emotions (Ekman, 1973; Izard, 1971). This finding leads theorists like Izard to think that the relationship between facial pattern and feeling is based on biology rather than cultural teaching. This makes Izard comfortable in concluding that those same facial movements indicate the same emotions during infancy. Some pros and cons of this view are considered later in the chapter.

**Emotion as Interaction with the Environment.**    Other theorists believe that emotions cannot be reduced to feelings, facial patterns, or any other single measure. Instead, they suggest that emotions are two-directional processes relating a person (and other animals) to the environment

## FOCUS ON    Cultural Diversity

### Holding the Baby?

In this country, many child care workers encourage infants to explore their environment by putting them on the floor and letting them play with toys and other objects. This allows the children to explore and learn about their own environment through movement and manipulation.

Traditions among many Mexicans are different, however. Rather than putting their babies on the floor, they like to hold them all the time; this keeps them out of harm's way and also provides close human contact. If the mother can't hold the baby for some reason, she hands the child to a companion, perhaps one of her older daughters.

This cultural difference could cause real problems. The difficulty would not be with the child—children are very adaptable and usually learn the ways of a new environment quite easily. But the parents might feel their child was being neglected and endangered.

Based on Gonzalez-Mena, 1992.

---

(Barrett & Campos, 1987). When people interact with the external environment (or the internal environment in their head), certain things that occur are significant to them. These significant events have important implications for how well people can get along in that environment, and they also elicit emotion. A theory that relies on this definition of emotion, the functionalist theory, is discussed later in the chapter.

**Implications.** It is evident that different theorists have very different ideas about how to define emotion, and these definitions determine what, if anything, seems sensible to study during infancy. Those who focus on feeling may conclude that true emotion is not possible during infancy (or, at least, in early infancy) because babies do not have the thinking abilities that would enable them to feel emotion. These theorists might conclude that David could not really be experiencing sadness or fear because this would be impossible in a baby. At the least, they might say that it is impossible to know whether David is actually experiencing emotion since at age seven months, he cannot yet speak. Those who focus on facial expression, on the other hand, would conclude that David is experiencing emotion because according to their definition, the expressions on his face reveal his emotions. Finally, theorists who believe that emotion involves signifi-

cant interactions with the environment would also conclude that David is experiencing emotion, and they might study facial, vocal, and other behavior to determine the nature of the emotional reaction. Even if David's facial expression did not seem to fit a particular emotion, adults might be able to guess what emotion he is probably experiencing. The next question to consider is how emotion, defined in these various ways, develops.

### How Do Emotions Develop?

There are many different theories about how emotions develop. In most theories, infants are believed to have fewer emotions at birth than they have later. Some theories view emotions as entities or systems that become possible only at certain ages. Other theories distinguish between real emotions and precursors or forerunners of true emotions. Still other theories maintain that particular versions of emotions become possible as a child gets older.

**The Differentiation Approach.** According to the differentiation approach theory, babies are born with very general emotional states that break down into more specific types of emotions as children mature. The classic version of this approach is that of Bridges, who claimed that babies are born with only the ability to have a general state of excitement. As

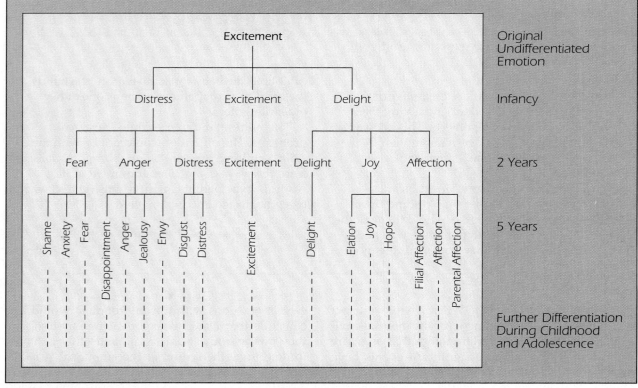

**FIGURE 8.1**    **Bridges' View of When Various Emotions Become Possible.**    According to K. M. Bridges, newborns only have a general emotional state of excitement. This general state is differentiated into more specific emotions as infants get older.

they grow older, infants become able to experience the positive and negative emotions of delight and distress; delight gradually becomes differentiated, or broken down, into more specific positive states, and distress becomes differentiated into more specific negative states (Bridges, 1930). Figure 8.1 summarizes Bridges' view of when various emotions become possible.

The concept of differentiation is very common in the field of child development, and it is easy to understand. Moreover, recent research on facial patterns and emotion suggests that virtually all types of negative facial patterns—those associated with anger, distress, and sadness, for example—are displayed in virtually all situations that elicit negative emotion in infants (Camras, Malatesta, & Izard, 1991). This observation is consistent with the possibility that during infancy, emotions are only differentiated into generalized positive and negative states.

Unfortunately, Bridges did not explain exactly what it is that indicates whether or not emotions are present. Moreover, recent research has demonstrated that negative emotion is possible in newborn infants, and such findings are contrary to Bridges' model (Gunnar, Fisch, Korsvik, & Donhowe, 1981; Porter, Porges, & Marshall, 1988). Despite these shortcomings, the general idea that emotions differentiate is still widely accepted by many experts.

**The Brain Maturation Approach.**    Carroll Izard's differential emotions theory is an example of a brain maturation approach (Izard & Malatesta, 1987). According to this theory, babies are born with a limited number of emotions, and additional emotions only become possible when the brain and nervous system mature. Izard contends that there is an innate, or inborn, correspondence between facial patterns and feelings. Thus, a particular neural process (that is, one involving the brain and nervous system) leads to a particular facial pattern and its corresponding feeling. Although feeling is considered important in this approach, thought is not crucial to emotion, and the approach considers emotion both possible and measurable during infancy.

The brain maturation approach has both advantages and disadvantages. One of its advantages is that feeling is a central feature of the approach, which views emotion as both possible and measurable in infants. These notions are consistent with the view of emotion that many lay people hold. The approach is also consistent with a large number of studies indicating that particular sets of facial muscle movements communicate the same emotion across a wide variety of cultures.

The brain maturation approach also has several drawbacks. First, it assumes that the meaning of facial patterns is known. However, knowledge of the meaning of facial patterns is based primarily on studies of the emotional meaning of "peak" facial patterns (patterns with all movements present) in adults. The assumption is that if infants show the same facial patterns, they are experiencing the same emotions identified by adults. This may not be true, however. Babies often display these facial patterns when the emotions they are thought to express do not make sense. For example, researchers have found instances in which babies consistently displayed the facial pattern associated with surprise in the same familiar, recurring context, such as being placed under a light. Yet surprise is typically associated in adults with new, unexpected events, not similar, recurring ones.

A second disadvantage of this approach is that some of its propositions are not testable. It is impossible, for example, to know whether facial patterns are associated with feeling states in young infants. A third drawback is that there is only limited evidence linking specific neural programs to particular emotions.

### The Cognitive Prerequisite Approach.

According to the cognitive prerequisite approach to emotional development, babies are born with a limited number of states and behaviors that are precursors to true emotions. True emotions require certain cognitive abilities that are not possible at birth. Once these cognitive abilities develop, the emotions requiring them emerge. For example, according to one cognitive prerequisite theory, rage requires a person to have an intensely desired goal that he believes he has a reasonable expectation of attaining and that he is actively pursuing. A newborn would be incapable of knowing whether or not she has a reasonable expectation of achieving a goal. Thus, she would only experience distress, not rage, in similar contexts (Case, Hayward, Lewis, & Hurst, 1988). Various researchers have proposed other versions of this approach that have been very influential (Case et al., 1988; Lewis, Sullivan, Stanger, & Weiss, 1989; Sroufe, 1984).

The primary advantage of the cognitive prerequisite approach is that it is logical and allows one to predict when emotions should be possible during child development. The prediction is based on a knowledge of the stages in development when the cognitive prerequisites become possible. The most significant disadvantage of this approach is that it is not really possible to prove or disprove it. For example, if a researcher observes something that looks like anger before anger is supposed to be possible, a proponent of this approach can characterize the "angry" response as a precursor state such as distress.

### The Functionalist Approach.

The fourth theory of emotional development is the functionalist approach. According to this approach, emotions occur when a person's interactions with the environment bring her or him into a particular significant relationship with that environment (Barrett & Campos, 1987). For example, anger is likely to appear when a child senses that she is not getting what she is after but is still struggling to attain it. Imagine a baby in a high chair who is struggling to reach an interesting toy just beyond her grasp. The baby reaches and reaches for the toy, but she cannot get it. Soon she begins to fuss with frustration and then screams angrily. The baby may not understand what the goal is, what will bring about the goal, or what is preventing the goal from being realized. She may simply sense that she is not getting what she wants, despite all attempts to do so.

As a result of such interactions, behaviors that affect the person-environment relationship are triggered. In the case of anger, for example, behaviors that could overcome barriers, such as hitting or

## FOCUS ON   Communicating with Parents

### Getting Fathers Involved with Infant Care

Only a few fathers drop off or pick up their infants at the Bright Start Child Care Center. Roberta, the center's director, realizes that fathers often feel uncomfortable with their role as parents of infants. She knows that many have no male role models for parenting because they grew up in families where child care was the responsibility of the mother.

Roberta wants Bright Start to be a welcoming place for fathers. She starts by making sure that there are many pictures around the center of fathers caring for babies. She holds staff meetings that stress the importance of the father as a caregiver. She encourages her staff to find positive ways to communicate with the fathers who do come to the center. Still, she knows that the center is only reaching a small number of fathers. So Roberta applies for and receives a small grant from a local foundation for a trial program to address the special needs of new fathers. Here is a copy of the letter she sends to the fathers of infants in the center's program.

Dear Infant Program Dad,

As a father, you are one of the most important people in your baby's life. You work hard to give your child food, clothing, and a warm, safe home. But in today's world, your baby needs more from you than physical care. Your baby needs your emotional support and involvement in providing a loving, caring, and happy environment.

Fatherhood isn't something you get to practice for. The responsibility is scary. The demands of an infant can be frustrating and exhausting. Unlike mothers, few fathers have role models to guide them. Yet being a father can be the most rewarding thing you will ever do. At Bright Start Child Care Center, we value our fathers as part of the caregiving team. We want them to have the knowledge and skills to give their babies the best start they can.

To help fathers and babies get off to a great start together, we are offering a series of six free workshops called Fantastic Fathers. The workshops are for you and your baby. They will be held on Saturday mornings from 9 to 11. Each session features a professional speaker who is a father himself. There will also be time for you to play with your baby and socialize with other fathers.

These workshops cover more than preparing bottles and changing diapers. Here are some of the topics that will be discussed:

- Playtime with your baby
- When your child is sick
- Coping with grandparents
- Help, my wife is a mom now

We hope that you will join us for these workshops and become a Fantastic Father.

*How do you think the fathers will respond to Roberta's letter? What are some other topics of interest to fathers that might be covered in the workshops? Can you think of other ways a child care center can get fathers more involved in the care of their infants?*

screaming, are launched. The behaviors exhibited will vary with the person and situation; the important feature of the behaviors is their function.

Emotions are viewed as members of "families" of related emotions, but in these families certain emotions may appear earlier than others. For exam-ple, fear of heights and fear of forming an intimate relationship are two members of the "fear" family of emotions. While fear of forming an intimate rela-tionship is unlikely during infancy, fear of heights is highly likely. Emotional development involves adding particular emotions to the families of emotions as a result of socialization, cognitive development, and personal experience.

As with the other theories of emotional development, the functionalist approach also has advantages and disadvantages. Its main advantage is that it bases judgments about the onset of particular emotions on studies of people interacting with the environment rather than on beliefs and logic. Moreover, it does not rely on a single measure of emotion, which may or may not be a clear-cut indicator of emotion. On the other hand, emotion is more difficult to study in this approach because there is no single measure that is considered a clear indicator of emotion. Some critics also argue that the functionalist approach puts too little emphasis on feeling.

## Milestones in Emotional Development

As children mature, certain emotional responses change in fairly predictable ways. During infancy, there are a number of these milestones in emotional development. In some cases, theorists disagree as to whether the responses indicate the true emotion or not. This section outlines some important milestones in the development of smiling and laughter, fear, and anger, distress, and pain.

### Smiling and Laughter

Smiles begin very early in the developmental process, and laughter follows a short time later. These emotional responses are particularly rewarding to parents and other caregivers. They also set in motion a cycle of trust and affection that creates a strong bond between child and parent.

**Birth to One Month.**  During the period between birth and one month, babies sometimes smile during *rapid eye movement (REM)* states, the stage of sleep during which dreams occur. Contrary to popular belief, these smiles are not due to "gas pains." Furthermore, most research suggests that the smiles of newborn babies are not brought on by the people around them or by external events. As a result, smiles during this period are known as endogenous smiles, which means that they are reflexes triggered

Smiling and laughter are emotional responses that create strong bonds of trust and affection between parent and child.

by the baby's central nervous system (Emde, Gaensbauer, & Harmon, 1976).

**One to Three or Four Months.** Beginning at around one or two months of age, babies begin to smile in response to events around them. Such smiles are called exogenous smiles because they are triggered by something outside the baby. Exogenous smiles are also known as social smiles because they are often elicited by some type of social interaction. One of the best ways of getting a baby to smile during this phase is to put your face in front of the baby's face (and as the baby gets older, to move your head up and down, make faces, and talk). Social smiles cause caregivers to feel, for the first time, that babies are smiling at them. Research has shown that infants also respond to nonvisual stimuli. Blind children, for example, smile in response to human voices (Fraiberg, 1977).

**Three to Four Months and Older.** Beginning at about three or four months of age, babies smile selectively—smiling more at the primary caregiver than at other people. This usually makes the mother or other primary caregiver feel special, helping her form a relationship with the baby. At about this age, babies also begin to laugh (Emde et al., 1976).

### Fear

It is easier to study the development of smiling and laughter, which are specific behaviors, than to study emotions such as fear. The determination of when fear develops depends on what behaviors or responses are considered to be evidence of fear. For example, the facial pattern associated with fear is not seen very often in infants in laboratory settings, even when stimuli assumed to provoke fear (such as the approach of a stranger or an apparent cliff) are presented. Yet fear facial patterns are sometimes exhibited by babies as young as ten weeks of age in situations that are less obvious sources of fear (Camras et al., 1991). Thus, if the fear facial pattern defines fear, fear is possible quite early in infancy. However, it occurs only rarely and under conditions that might not be expected to create fear. On the other hand, if such things as avoidant behaviors, heart rate increases, crying, or sober (serious) facial patterns (in appropriate contexts) are considered

evidence of fear, then babies display fear during most of infancy. Moreover, if the fear facial pattern is not assumed always to indicate fear, then its appearance in unexpected contexts is not troublesome.

**Stranger Wariness.** At as early as four months of age, infants may show mild wariness of strangers, as indicated by sober facial patterns or looking away when a stranger approaches. By about six or eight months, many infants show this wary reaction, and some will show more obvious distress at the approach of a stranger, particularly if the stranger is tall or male and tries to pick the child up or to control the interaction (Horner, 1980; Lewis & Brooks, 1974; Sroufe, 1977). David's reaction to his babysitter would thus be considered quite typical for his age group. By about 18 months, stranger distress usually becomes less intense. This may be due in part to changes in how strangers treat toddlers. Most people give older babies and toddlers more control over the interaction (Mangelsdorf, 1992).

**The Visual Cliff.** Named for a structure used to test babies' perception and fear of heights, the visual cliff consists of a tall table with a clear, plexiglass surface. Directly under the plexiglass on half of the table is a checkerboard-patterned surface that appears solid. Beneath the other half of the table, the checkerboard pattern is on the floor. If an infant is

*The visual cliff structure is used by researchers to test infant perception and fear of heights.*

placed on the centerboard that divides the two halves, she perceives one side as a solid surface and the other as a huge drop-off (a visual cliff), even though the surface over both areas is actually solid. At around seven or eight months of age, infants' heart rate increases when they see the visual cliff, and they avoid crossing it even when their mother encourages them to do so. Wariness of the apparent drop-off becomes more likely once the children have crawling experience (Campos, Bertenthal, & Kermoian, 1992). If the visual cliff is changed so that the apparent drop-off is only about a foot, 12-month-olds avoid crossing it when their mother's face communicates fear or anger but cross it when their mother's face communicates joy or interest (Sorce, Emde, Campos, & Klinnert, 1985).

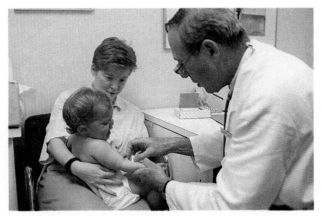

*As infants get older, they more often show an angry facial pattern in response to painful situations, such as being vaccinated.*

### Anger, Distress, and Pain

Often, when babies cry, their face displays an angry facial pattern. This facial pattern is identical to the one associated with discomfort and pain except that the eyes are open but squinting in the angry pattern and closed in the pain pattern. Since the facial patterns are so similar and most research on anger relies on facial pattern, these emotions will be discussed together.

**Birth to Two Months.**   Until recently, scientists thought that newborns could not experience pain. Mainly for this reason, doctors usually did not use anesthetics during painful procedures like circumcision. (Another reason was the difficulty in determining dosage and administering anesthesia at this early age.) Now, however, there is strong evidence that medical procedures such as circumcision, vaccinations, and blood tests provoke distress in newborns. When newborns undergo procedures, they react with the distress/pain facial pattern, as well as hormonal, heart rate, and crying responses (Gunnar et al., 1981; Izard, Hembree, & Huebner, 1987).

Newborns also display the distress/pain facial pattern in situations that would be expected to provoke anger rather than pain (for example, gentle arm restraint). And they often display the anger facial pattern in response to painful procedures such as vaccinations (Izard et al., 1987; Stenberg & Campos, 1990). Taken together, these findings suggest that newborns respond negatively to stimuli ex-

pected to cause anger and/or pain. Whether any of these negative responses should be considered anger depends on the perspective. According to Carroll Izard and other advocates of the brain maturation approach, anger is present when the anger facial pattern is shown and pain is present when the pain pattern is shown. According to the functionalist approach, situations in which the infant displays either facial pattern in response to a nonpainful obstacle, such as a gentle arm restraint, would be considered anger, especially if the infant tries to overcome the obstacle. To proponents of the cognitive prerequisite approach, the newborns' responses would not be considered true anger.

**Two Months and Older.**   As infants grow, they increasingly display the angry facial pattern in response to both painful and nonpainful negative situations. By about eight months of age, they begin looking at people who might help relieve their distress, while displaying distress responses (Izard et al., 1987; Stenberg & Campos, 1990).

### Infant Temperament

Developmental trends such as those discussed above are concerned with behaviors and emotions all babies are expected to exhibit. Nevertheless, individual infants differ from each other in many ways. Among the most notable differences is *temperament*, characteristic emotions, moods, and ways

### Separation Anxiety

Cynthia has been taking her 18-month-old daughter, Ari, to family day care for six months. During the past week, Ari has been crying and clinging to her mother when she leaves. Since Ari rarely objected to her mother's leaving before, Cynthia is worried that something has happened to make Ari dislike day care. This morning when Odette, the caregiver, reaches for Ari, the familiar cycle of crying and clinging begins again.

ODETTE:  Come on, Ari. Your mom has to go to work.

CYNTHIA:  I don't know why she's started doing this. She never used to cry when I left. Are you sure nothing has happened to upset her?

ODETTE:  I can't think of anything that has changed here. I don't think she's really unhappy. Once you leave, she settles down and has a great time playing with the other kids. She never even mentions you until it is almost time for you to pick her up. I think she's just going through a stage.

ARI [*sobbing and clinging*]:  Mommy no go! No go!

ODETTE:  Do you have a toy she likes that you can leave here today? I know she always has her blanket, but maybe a special toy would help. [*Cynthia hands Odette a small rag doll.*]

ODETTE [*to Ari*]:  Look, your dolly is going to stay with you today. You can push her in the carriage. Steven and Marianne are here already. You and dolly can play with them. [*Ari looks briefly at the doll, then starts crying again. Firmly, her mother pries Ari's hands off her leg and begins to leave.*]

CYNTHIA:  Ari, I have to go to work. You know that. I go to work every day, and then I come back and get you. [*To Odette*] Are you sure she's okay after I go?

ODETTE:  Believe me, five minutes after you leave, she's busy playing. If you want, call me when you get to work to see how she is.

CYNTHIA:  Okay, I'll do that. [*Firmly to Ari*] I'm going to work now. Odette will take care of you. I'll be back to get you after work, and then we'll stop at Aunt Sara's house for supper.

As Cynthia leaves, Odette tries to pick up Ari to comfort her, but the child pushes her away and continues crying. Once Ari is convinced her mother isn't coming back, she lets Odette wipe her tears; then she picks up her doll and puts it in the doll carriage.

*What would you have said to Cynthia about Ari's sudden separation anxiety? Can you think of anything else Odette could have done or said to help Ari accept her mother's departure? What are some reasons that young children develop separation anxiety?*

of interacting with people, objects, and events in the environment. Most theorists agree that temperament characteristics are primarily biologically based and are relatively stable over time. Temperament is viewed as the seed out of which later personality grows. A baby's temperament is central to his social development as well. This is because his temperament greatly affects the way others react to him and the kinds of experiences he will have with the environment.

### Thomas and Chess: Theory and Findings

A study by Alexander Thomas and Stella Chess, published in 1977, set off a surge of excitement about temperament. In their New York longitudinal study (NYLS), the researchers found that certain temperament characteristics are relatively stable from infancy onward and that some of these characteristics are predictors of mental health problems in later childhood. They came to believe that a major influence on childhood behavior problems is how well the child's temperament fits into his or her environment.

**Temperament Characteristics.** According to the initial findings of the NYLS study, infants differ along nine temperament characteristics (Thomas & Chess, 1977):

- *Threshold of responsiveness*, the amount of stimulation needed to make an infant react
- *Activity level*, the tendency to be either more or less active
- *Rhythmicity*, the predictability or unpredictability of functions such as sleeping, eating, and defecating
- *Distractibility*, the tendency for other stimuli to alter the direction of ongoing behavior
- *Attention span*, the length of time an infant pursues a particular activity
- *Quality of mood*, the relative frequency of positive versus negative behavior
- *Adaptability*, the ability to adjust to changes
- *Intensity of reactions*, the energy level of both positive and negative responses
- *Approach/withdrawal*, the tendency to approach rather than withdraw in response to new stimuli

**Easy, Difficult, and Slow-to-Warm-Up Children.** On the basis of specific groupings of these nine characteristics, Thomas and Chess classified children into three general categories of personality traits: easy, difficult, and slow-to-warm-up. They cautioned, however, that not all children can be classified into one of these types. "Easy" children are rhythmic; high in approach; positive in mood, with mild to moderate intensity of mood; and quick in adaptability. "Difficult" children are arrhythmic, or unpredictable; high in withdrawal; negative in mood, with high intensity of mood; and slow in adaptability. "Slow-to-warm-up" children are slow to adapt to changes; withdraw initially from new stimuli, showing mild to moderate intensity of such withdrawal responses; and eventually adapt to new

Temperamentally "difficult" children are unpredictable and slow to adapt to changes in their environment.

situations. Studies have found that difficult children are at increased risk for developing behavior disorders. But, according to Thomas and Chess, this is affected by how well a child fits into her environment. For example, in cases where parents value the strong will of a difficult child, the child should be at lower risk for behavior disorders.

One of the most significant aspects of the NYLS study is that the temperament characteristics identified were derived from extensive observations of children over time. These characteristics are noticeable by both parents and clinicians. One criticism of the study's findings is that some of the characteristics identified—rhythmicity, for example—are more relevant to infancy than to older ages. As a result, it is difficult to ascertain the stability of such dimensions because they are hard to measure at older ages. Another criticism is that Thomas and Chess's classifications of easy, difficult, and slow-to-warm-up are not really characteristics of children but a person's perceptions of children. For example, one person may find a certain child "difficult," whereas another person might find that same child "easy." Yet these classifications are treated as if they were children's inborn traits rather than aspects of children's relationships to their environment.

## Buss and Plomin: Theory and Findings

Another view of temperament has been proposed by researchers Buss and Plomin. According to Buss and Plomin, in order for personal characteristics to be considered temperament, they must meet two requirements. First, such characteristics must be heritable, or capable of being inherited. While learned traits may be part of personality, they are not temperament. Second, temperament characteristics must be observable in the first year of life. After that age, these characteristics are likely to be greatly influenced by socialization (Buss & Plomin, 1975).

**Temperament Traits.**    Three traits meet Buss and Plomin's criteria:

- *Emotionality*, the tendency to display negative mood
- *Activity level*, the tendency to be either more or less active
- *Sociability*, the tendency to approach and enjoy interactions with others

These are the only traits that Buss and Plomin consider temperament. A major advantage of Buss and Plomin's view of temperament is that it is well defined; moreover, the kinds of findings that will support or refute the theory are also well defined. If a trait is not present in infancy or is not heritable, then it is not temperament. Critics, however, say that Buss and Plomin's criteria are unreasonable. Why must temperament be observable during infancy? Even if temperament is completely biologically based, children might need to mature enough to display a particular trait. Or they might not be exposed to the kinds of situations that would elicit the trait, whereas older children might. Furthermore, parents begin teaching children how to act from birth; thus, even measuring temperament during infancy does not rule out the possibility that the traits are learned rather than inherited.

**David and Temperament.**    One point on which both theories of temperament can agree is that David's reaction to the babysitter could have been affected by temperament. Perhaps a child who was higher on Thomas and Chess's "approach" scale or on Buss and Plomin's "sociability" rating would have had a more positive reaction to the babysitter. Moreover, a child who was lower on "approach" and "sociability" might have reacted even more negatively to the babysitter or might have reacted negatively at a younger age. This example really illustrates how one particular behavior pattern—reaction to strangers—is affected by many things. In David's case, his temperament and stage of emotional development probably both affected his reaction to the babysitter. As you shall soon see, David's relationship with his parents may have affected it as well.

## Parent-Infant Relationships

Probably the most important area of social development during infancy is the blossoming relationship between parent and child. Some studies have focused on how the parent comes to love the baby; others have focused on how the baby comes to love the parent. This section deals with these early parent-child relationships.

### Bonding and Engrossment

The term *bonding* usually refers to the loving and accepting attitude that a mother takes toward her baby. Animal research has shown that the first minutes after birth are crucial in causing a mother to accept her offspring. For example, if a nanny goat is separated from her newborn kid soon after birth, she will reject that kid when it is brought to her later. Such research suggests, then, that there is a critical period, right after birth, during which bonding must occur. Animal studies also suggest that this bonding process is affected by hormonal changes connected with childbirth.

In noting these findings, researchers wondered whether similar processes occur in humans, and early studies suggested that they do. More recent studies have shown that although contact between mother and baby immediately after birth may help the mother form a relationship with her child, such contact is not necessary in order for a mother to bond with her infant. Mothers can and do form healthy, positive bonds with their babies even when they do not have contact with them immediately after birth. This is very important because it is

## FOCUS ON  Child Care Issues

### Effects of Full-Time Day Care

When her daughter, Caitlin, was born, Sally Burns took a six-month maternity leave from her job as office manager in an insurance company. Sally enjoys her work and feels she is contributing to the family by working.

Before her daughter's birth, she was sure she would return to work. Now Caitlin is four months old, and Sally is not sure what she should do. She worries about the effect of full-day child care on her daughter's development.

Recently Sally shared her concerns with two friends. Their responses were quite different.

Debbie Amwell:

"I loved my job, and I made good money, but after Mark was born I decided to stay home. A parent is a child's best caregiver. No one, no matter how well trained and professional, will give Mark the love and care that I will.

"I want my son to get the best possible start in life. To me, that means spending lots of time with him, giving him one-on-one attention. We talk, we play, we read books. When he cries, I'm there to pick him up. He doesn't have to wait his turn for attention.

"I can give Mark enrichment and stimulation he would never get in a child care center. We go to a parent-child exercise class and to the library, and to visit my friends and their children.

"Small children need security. In child care centers, caregivers come and go. They can't provide the consistency of care that a parent can.

"Consistency is also important in setting limits and teaching values. I'm willing to take tough stands because I know I'll have to deal with the consequences as Mark grows up.

"We're making financial sacrifices so that I can stay home. But Bob and I feel that there's no substitute for the love and attention a parent gives a child all day, every day."

Janet Komuro:

"I put my daughter, Lauren, in full-time child care at the age of four months. I know that good caregivers can provide a nurturing, stimulating environment, even for infants. For me, the issue was not whether Lauren should have full-time care but how to locate quality care.

"I wanted to continue working, but that wasn't the only reason I put Lauren in child care. I wanted her to learn early how to get along with other people. In the three years she has been in child care, Lauren has learned a lot about sharing and taking turns. She copes well with new situations and is more flexible than children who spend all day with one parent in the home. I think these early group experiences have helped her develop important social skills.

"The child care professionals at Lauren's center all have special training in working with children. Lauren benefits from that experience and from the genuine interest the caregivers have in helping children grow and develop.

"Besides, there are plenty of opportunities for enrichment at her center. The rooms are well equipped, and they have a marvelous playground. Lauren gets to play with developmentally appropriate toys I could never afford to buy her, and she has art and music every day.

"I often think child care is more of a problem for parents than for the child. Some parents can't stand the idea of giving up control over part of their child's day. Lauren is thriving in full-time care and growing into a bright, outgoing little girl, while I'm contributing to the financial well-being of our family."

*What do you think are the positive effects of full-time child care? What do you think are some negative effects? How do you think a parent's values affect his or her views on the desirability of full-time care?*

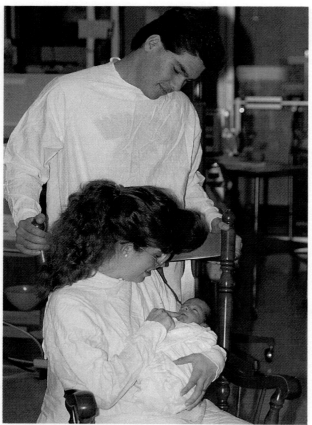

The process of forming a relationship between parents and child begins right after birth.

sometimes impossible for a mother to have contact with her child immediately after birth. Parents who adopt their children, for example, are not present at the time of birth. Some mothers, such as those having emergency Caesarean sections, are not awake when their babies are born. It is reassuring to such mothers to know that they can have just as special a relationship with their babies as mothers who were present and alert at the time of birth.

While bonding occurs between mother and baby, the father is also a part of a baby's early relationships. The term *engrossment* refers to a father's feelings of extreme happiness, excitement, and interest in his baby following the baby's birth. Until fairly recently, fathers were almost never present at birth, and their positive feelings for their newborns were not acknowledged. However, it is now clear that fathers often feel very excited about and close to their newborns, and such feelings are most likely in fathers who are involved in labor and delivery and are exposed to their babies from the beginning.

### Bowlby's Theory of Attachment

While bonding and engrossment are strong emotional ties emanating from the parents to the child, attachment refers to a strong relationship directed from the infant to the parents or other caregivers. During the 1950s and 1960s, John Bowlby did important research on attachment. The theory of attachment he formulated reflects strong influences of psychoanalytic and ethological (animal behavioral) theories. Like the psychoanalytic theories of Sigmund Freud and Erik Erikson, Bowlby's theory emphasizes that a baby's attachment to a special "mother-figure" is crucial to personality formation.

Following ethological thinking, Bowlby highlights how attachment helps human babies adapt to their environment. According to Bowlby, a baby's attachment to a caregiver helps him stay close to the caregiver, enabling the helpless infant to adapt to the surrounding environment. This function of promoting closeness, or proximity, is served by many infant behaviors, most of which have counterparts in mothers' behavior. For example, infants cry, cling, and suck from birth, and these behaviors all promote proximity by causing the caregiver to move closer or remain close to the baby. Later, babies smile, crawl, walk, and use other behaviors to seek proximity to the caregiver. Eventually, they empathize with their caregiver and seek psychological closeness with the caregiver and others (Bowlby, 1969).

**Phases of Attachment.**    According to Bowlby, infants go through four phases in the development of attachment. During phase 1, extending from birth to one or two months, babies do not discriminate between the mother-figure and anyone else. They do, however, produce behaviors, such as crying and clinging, that help an attachment form. In contrast to Bowlby's belief, current research suggests that infants of this age can discriminate between their mother and others by means of hearing and smell (Cernoch & Porter, 1985; DeCasper & Fifer, 1980). They cannot visually discriminate their mother from other people, however.

Bowlby calls phase 2, from one or two months to six or seven months, the discriminating phase or the phase of "attachment in the making." During this period, babies can distinguish the attachment figure from others by sight, and they are comforted more easily by that person than by others. The attachment relationship still is not considered to be enduring and permanent, however. If the mother-figure is lost due to separation or death, the infant can become attached to another with relative ease.

During phase 3, from six or seven months to two or three years, babies' attachments become specific and long lasting. By this time babies have formed a stable attachment to one or more people, and they will mourn the loss of that person or those people if such a loss should occur. Also at this age, babies turn to a special attachment figure (usually the mother in our culture) when in stress or ill, and they may show distress when that person goes away even briefly or interacts with a stranger. David's reaction to the babysitter therefore would be considered a normal part of phase 3 and shows that David considers his mother to be special.

During phase 4, two to three years and older, the attachment relationship becomes two-directional—what Bowlby calls a goal-corrected partnership. Now toddlers begin to consider their parents' needs and intentions rather than just their own needs when seeking closeness. Moreover, toddlers may now comfort parents as well as seek comfort from them. Parents often enjoy their children's new ability to understand (at least occasionally) that parents may be busy and cannot play.

### Ainsworth's Strange Situation and Security of Attachment

Bowlby's theory describes the normative development of attachment, the phases through which all babies are believed to pass. Mary Ainsworth and her colleagues have expanded upon this theory by focusing on the differences between infants in the quality of their attachments. One of the research tools they used was a procedure called the strange situation, the purpose of which is to measure differences in the security that home-reared American infants derive from their parents' presence (Ainsworth & Wittig, 1969). The procedure includes a series of episodes that involve the approach of a stranger

Between the ages of 6 and 36 months, infants form a stable attachment to one person and will turn to that special attachment figure when in stress.

and the departure of an attachment figure. Typically, 12- to 18-month-olds participate in these studies. At this age level, stranger and separation distress are expected to occur, creating mild stress. Attachment theorists believe that it is important to create mild stress because infants are more likely to display attachment behavior when under stress. The behavior of infants in the strange situation, particularly during their reunion with the attachment figure after she or he has left and returned, has been used to classify different patterns of attachment in infants.

**Patterns of Attachment.**   Four patterns of infant attachment have been identified as a result of the strange situation studies. This section examines how various babies in strange situations act when their mother returns following a brief separation. It also focuses on the characteristics of each pattern of attachment.

Anna hardly notices when her mother leaves the room, and she continues to play. When her mother returns, Anna barely even looks up from her toys. She does not cry in her mother's absence or try to be picked up when her mother returns. Anna's behavior is typical of a pattern of attachment called *avoidant attachment*. This pattern is generally considered to represent an insecure form of attachment. Avoidantly attached infants usually do not show distress when their attachment figure leaves the room or during this person's absence, and they show indifference or active avoidance when the attachment figure returns. About 20 to 25 percent of typical home-reared infants fall into this group.

Benjy, on the other hand, protests when his mother starts to leave and cries intermittently while she is gone. When she returns, he cries briefly, crawls over to her as quickly as he can, and gestures to be picked up. Once Benjy's mother picks him up, he quickly moves from tears to smiles. Babies who exhibit this pattern of attachment, known as *secure attachment*, are eager to be reunited with their attachment figure, even following a brief absence. They may or may not show distress when the attachment figure leaves and while she or he is gone. When the attachment figure returns, these babies go up to her or him and may try to get picked up. If they are picked up, they try to stay in the attachment figure's arms. Such babies do not avoid or try to resist the attachment figure when he or she returns. While these babies may get somewhat upset when their attachment figure leaves, they are comforted fairly easily by the attachment figure when she or he returns. In other words, these babies do all of the things you would want your baby to do to show that you are special. About 60 to 65 percent of typical infants who are reared in a home fall into this group.

Chris seems a bit distressed even before his mother leaves, and when she does leave, he screams and wails at the top of his lungs. When his mother returns, he cries even louder, gestures to be picked up, and continues to scream while in her arms, pounding on her shoulder. This pattern of behavior, known as *resistant or ambivalent attachment*, is considered an insecure form of attachment. Babies with this pattern usually become quite dis-

tressed by the attachment figure's absence. They do not avoid the attachment figure when she or he returns, and they do go over to try to get picked up; however, they also resist the attachment figure and are extremely hard to console, even after this person returns. Approximately 10 to 15 percent of typical infants who are reared in a home fall into this group.

Although Denise does not seem overly upset before her mother leaves, her face briefly shows a look of terror when her mother actually departs. Then Denise's eyes take on a dull, unfocused look, and she begins rocking back and forth on the floor, staring off into space. When her mother returns, Denise starts to approach her, but then turns away, collapsing on the floor with her legs curled up. When her mother starts to pick her up, Denise pushes her away and scratches her mother's face. She then looks over at her mother and smiles feebly, after which she turns away and begins to rock again. This pattern of behavior, known as *disorganized attachment*, is considered an insecure form of attachment and is the most worrisome pattern of all. Babies who exhibit this pattern seem to fall apart when the caregiver leaves, and they show disorganized behavior upon reunion with the attachment figure. These children may go to the attachment figure and try to get picked up and may even try to stay in this person's arms after being picked up. However, then they may squirm to get down and avoid and resist the attachment figure. Such children often look dazed or depressed, and they may rock back and forth aimlessly, lie on the floor in the fetal position, or display other signs of disturbance following the attachment figure's return. About 5 to 10 percent of typical home-reared infants fall into this group.

These classifications of 12- to 18-month-olds in strange situations are predictors of many behaviors during the preschool years and beyond, including sociability, joy in problem solving, aggressiveness, and hyperactivity. Most studies simply contrast securely attached babies, such as Benjy, with all other types of babies, who are viewed as insecurely attached. And in most cases, these securely attached babies perform in a more desirable fashion at the time of follow-up than do all others (Arend, Gove, & Sroufe, 1979; Bates, Maslin, & Frankel, 1985; Park & Waters, 1989).

## Implications and Applications

Findings on emotional and social development have important implications for early childhood education. One of these involves the issue of separation anxiety and how it can affect child care. It is important to consider, for example, what the best age is for beginning day care. If babies begin day care during the first three or four months of life, they usually will not show separation distress when their parent leaves them. Does this mean that this is the best age to begin day care? Research suggests that if infants do begin day care during their first three or four months, parents need to spend enough time with their babies to become sensitive to their needs, and they need to respond sensitively to their babies when they are with them.

It is considered normal for older babies to become distressed when their mother leaves them, and most infants in day care do show such reactions at first. How many days or weeks of separation distress should be considered normal and acceptable? How does such daily distress affect a baby? How can caregivers minimize separation distress? Much more research is needed to answer these questions conclusively.

A second important issue concerns the fear of heights. Babies do not seem to be fearful of heights until they are about seven months of age. Yet they typically can roll over before that age. It is therefore very important that caregivers do not leave babies unattended, even briefly, on high objects such as changing tables. It is amazing how quickly babies can squirm or roll off such places, and their lack of fear makes them unmindful of the danger. Even older babies will need to see the drop-off to become afraid, so safeguards must be taken with all ages.

Research reveals that at least some temperament differences among infants are based on biological tendencies. As a result, infant caregivers need to acknowledge these differences and try to adapt their practices to better fit each child's individual needs. For example, a very active baby will be very frustrated by attempts to keep her in a high chair. In this case, the caregiver should provide for activities that the child can engage in on the floor, where there is more freedom to move around.

One of the most controversial applications of research on social development during infancy in-

Infants with disorganized attachment often display signs of disturbance, such as staring into space or rocking back and forth aimlessly.

volves the effects of infant day care on attachment. The issue is controversial in part because researchers, like others, are emotionally committed to a particular perspective. Some people believe that mothers should stay home with their children and that children are likely to suffer if they do not. Others believe that babies can be satisfactorily nurtured by other caregivers and in other settings.

Research findings on this issue are far from clearcut. There is a slightly increased likelihood of an insecure pattern of attachment in children who begin full-time day care during the first year of life. Some studies not involving attachment show that children who begin full-time day care before 12 months of age are somewhat more aggressive during toddlerhood than children who did not attend day care full-time before that age. Some researchers believe that these two sets of findings, taken together, are cause for concern (Belsky, 1988).

High-quality child care programs try to promote the development of social skills, even among toddlers.

Others are much less concerned about the effects of full-time day care, pointing out a general trend toward aggressiveness from the toddler to the preschool years. They also find that children who attend high-quality infant day care tend to be more socially skilled when dealing with their peers (Clarke-Stewart, 1988; Ramey & Campbell, 1979; Ramey et al., 1982). This issue requires additional research.

Another issue raised by attachment research is whether the strange situation procedure is a reasonable measure of attachment for children in day care. You will recall that this procedure attempts to create mild stress by separating babies from their attachment figure and having a stranger approach them. The separation from the attachment figure lasts three minutes at most. The stranger is typically a friendly adult female. Consider this situation from the perspective of a baby who has been in day care for many months. Such a baby is separated from parents for eight or nine hours every day and is exposed to a variety of strangers, often friendly females. Would the strange situation create as much distress in this infant as in a baby taken care of by his mother at home?

Some support for the idea that babies in day care are not less securely attached than other infants comes from recent studies. However, because these studies are based on mothers' reports of their babies' behavior, the issue is not resolved. It is possible that mothers whose babies are in day care want to think of their children as well adjusted, and they report behaviors accordingly.

Research on attachment has other important implications for infant day care. The pioneering work of Bowlby (1969) and Spitz (1965), as well as more current research, reveals the importance of nurturance and sensitivity to the developing baby. This research also suggests that babies become attached to a particular person who is there when they need him or her. The implications of this research are clear. Infant day-care providers need to be nurturing, sensitive individuals, and turnover in care providers needs to be minimized. Unfortunately, staff turnover is a significant problem. Day-care providers are not paid well, and they often turn to other employment to earn more money. Yet babies need a special person on whom they can depend. The problem of meeting the needs of both infants and day-care providers is not easy to resolve.

## SUMMARY

- Emotional and social development are closely connected during infancy.

- Theorists disagree on which emotions babies have at different ages. It seems clear, however, that even young babies display negative emotion, and particular patterns of distress and of smiling can be observed at certain ages.

- There are four basic theories about how emotions develop: the differentiation approach, the brain maturation approach, the cognitive prerequisite approach, and the functionalist approach.

- Although there are different theories of infant temperament, most theorists agree that temperament involves relatively stable differences among babies that are at least partially unlearned.

- Researchers Thomas and Chess have described nine temperament characteristics: (1) threshold of responsiveness, (2) activity level, (3) rhythmicity, (4) distractibility, (5) attention span, (6) quality of mood, (7) adaptability, (8) intensity of responding, and (9) approach/withdrawal.

- Buss and Plomin have described three temperament traits: (1) emotionality, (2) activity, and (3) sociability.

- Bowlby's theory of attachment recognizes four phases of infant-parent attachment. During phase 1, infants cannot discriminate between the caregiver's appearance and others' appearance. During phase 2, infants begin to form attachments, but they are not stable. During phase 3, infants form a lasting relationship with a special person. During phase 4, infants become more aware of the attachment figure's needs.

- Four patterns of attachment have been described by Ainsworth and her colleagues: (1) avoidant attachment, (2) secure attachment, (3) resistant or ambivalent attachment, and (4) disorganized attachment.

- Caregivers must consider separation anxiety, temperament, and attachment in order to respond to and meet the needs of infants.

- Research on infant attachment suggests that caregivers need to be sensitive, nurturing, and dependable individuals.

## BUILDING VOCABULARY

Write a definition for each vocabulary term listed below.

| | |
|---|---|
| activity level | engrossment |
| adaptability | intensity of reactions |
| approach/withdrawal | quality of mood |
| attention span | rapid eye movement (REM) |
| avoidant attachment | resistant or ambivalent attachment |
| bonding | rhythmicity |
| disorganized attachment | temperament |
| distractibility | threshold of responsiveness |

## ACQUIRING KNOWLEDGE

1. Cite three definitions of emotion.
2. Why is the concept of feeling difficult to study during the period of infancy?
3. Why do some theorists believe that the relationship between facial pattern and feeling is based on biology rather than learning?
4. Describe the differentiation approach to emotional development.
5. What is the brain maturation approach to emotional development?
6. What is the basic idea behind the cognitive prerequisite approach to emotional development?
7. Explain the functionalist approach to emotional development.
8. What are endogenous smiles, and at what age do they first occur?
9. What milestone in the development of smiling and laughter occurs between one and four months of age?
10. At what age do infants first begin to laugh?
11. Why is it easier to study the development of smiling and laughter than fear in infants?
12. Name several avoidant behaviors that may be considered evidence of fear in infants.
13. Describe the changes in stranger wariness that occur between the ages of 4 months and 18 months.
14. What is the visual cliff, and what is its purpose?
15. How does the facial pattern for anger compare to that for distress or pain?
16. What evidence is there to suggest that infants between birth and two months of age can experience pain and distress?
17. What role does temperament play in personality development and social development?
18. What general conclusions about temperament were made as a result of the New York longitudinal study (NYLS) by Thomas and Chess?
19. Name the nine temperament characteristics established by the NYLS study.
20. What three general categories of personality traits are based on Thomas and Chess's nine characteristics of temperament?
21. What three personality traits fit Buss and Plomin's definition of temperament?
22. What are bonding and engrossment?
23. What is the basic premise of Bowlby's theory of attachment?
24. What four patterns of attachment have been identified as a result of Ainsworth's strange situation studies? Briefly define each.

## THINKING CRITICALLY

1. Some infants smile more than others. What effects might this have on the parent-child relationship and on later social development?
2. All four theories of emotional development reflect a clear connection to intellectual development. There does not seem to be a clear connection to physical development, however. Which theory of emotional development seems most dependent on physical development? Explain.

3. According to Thomas and Chess, temperament characteristics are relatively stable from infancy onward. What does this suggest about the source of these characteristics? Do you find this idea plausible? Why or why not?

4. In some cases today, fathers are assuming the role of primary caregiver for their children, even very young infants. What does the research on attachment suggest about a father's ability to fulfill this role?

## OBSERVATIONS AND APPLICATIONS

1. Observe an infant of about six months of age and make note of his or her facial expressions. Does the baby smile in response to a caregiver? Does he or she smile when no one is in view? What other facial expressions do you observe? Anger? Pain? Curiosity? Surprise? Joy?

2. Observe at an infant child care center at the beginning of the day and again at the end. Make note of the infants' reactions to being dropped off and picked up. Note how parents and caregivers react to infants who cry when their parents leave. Note the ages of the infants who cry when left. How long do they continue to cry? Are there any infants who cry because it is time to leave the center? How old are those children?

3. The parents of a 12-month-old girl with a slow-to-warm-up personality ask your advice. Their daughter clings to them in new situations and is reluctant to try anything new—whether it is new food or a new play situation. The mother has taken a year off but plans to return to work next month. She is concerned that her daughter will not adjust well to being left in a child care setting. What advice can you give the parents to help ease the transition?

## SUGGESTIONS FOR FURTHER READING

Brazelton, T. B. (1981). *On becoming a family: The growth of attachment.* New York: Delacorte/Seymour Lawrence.

Brazelton, T. B., & Yogman, M. W. (Eds.). (1986). *Affective development in infancy.* Norwood, NJ: Ablex.

Fraiberg, S. H. (1959). *The magic years.* New York: Scribner's.

Greenspan, S., & Greenspan, N. T. (1985). *First feelings: Milestones in the emotional development of your baby and child.* New York: Penguin Books.

Honig, A. S. (1993). Mental health for babies. *Young children, 48*(3).

Kaplan, L. J. (1978). *Oneness and separateness: From infant to individual.* New York: Simon & Schuster.

Klaus, M., & Kennell, J. H. (1982). *Parent-infant bonding* (2nd ed.). St. Louis: Mosby.

Lewis, M., & Worobey, J. (Eds.). (1989). *Infant stress and coping.* San Francisco: Jossey-Bass.

National Association for the Education of Young Children (1989). *Developmentally appropriate practice in early childhood programs serving infants.* Washington, D.C.: Author.

Stern, D. (1985). *The first relationship* (4th ed.). Cambridge, MA: Harvard University Press.

# PART 4

# Toddlers

### CHAPTER 9
### Physical Development
Chapter 9 describes the physical growth of toddlers and discusses how physical development relates to cognitive and social and emotional development.

### CHAPTER 10
### Intellectual Development
Chapter 10 summarizes Piaget's ideas on the cognitive development of toddlers and also describes various theories on how toddlers form concepts and acquire language skills.

### CHAPTER 11
### Emotional and Social Development
Chapter 11 discusses some theoretical approaches to the emotional development of toddlers and describes the emergence of self-awareness, awareness of others, and prosocial behavior during this period.

# Physical Development

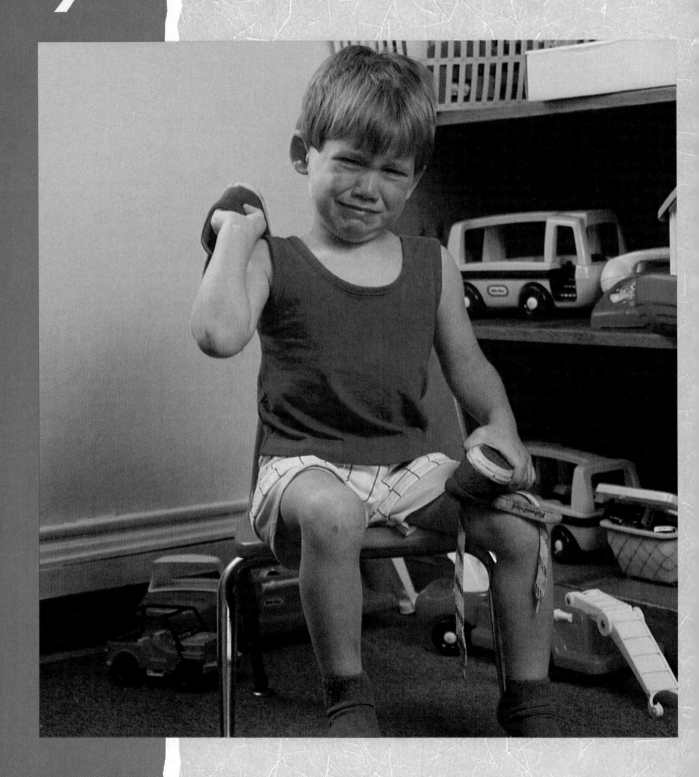

## CHAPTER OUTLINE

## OBJECTIVES

Studying this chapter will enable you to:

- Describe the physical changes children experience during the toddler years.
- Explain how the physical development of toddlers affects their mobility and motor skills.
- Describe how toddlers' physical development is related to their intellectual, social, and emotional development.
- Identify important developmental milestones of the toddler years.
- List ways in which child care professionals can promote the physical development of toddlers.

CHRISTOPHER, a two-year-old, was busy scribbling with crayons on a large sheet of paper when Linda came over to help him put on his shoes for outdoor play time. "No!" shouted Christopher as he pulled his feet away, "Let me!" Linda knew that Christopher probably would not be able to get the shoes on his feet by himself. But instead of engaging in a battle of wills, Linda decided to let Christopher do what he could for himself while she helped some of the other children.

A few moments later, Linda heard crying and turned to see Christopher running toward her with his shoes in his hands. He ran right into her lap, clung to her, and cried. Linda gave him a hug and some words of comfort, telling him that putting on shoes takes lots of practice. Then she put his shoes on and tied them and watched him run outside as if nothing had ever happened.

The toddler years can be as trying and frustrating for caregivers and parents as they are for toddlers themselves. But they can also be a time of great joy for everyone concerned. Between the ages of one and three, which are the toddler years, children evolve physically, intellectually, emotionally, and socially. They grow from infants who are completely dependent on others to meet their needs into individuals who are capable of doing many things for themselves.

## From Dependence Toward Independence

The two developmental processes that promote the movement toward independence are unassisted walking and rapid language development. Toddlers are able to go where they wish—barring adult intervention—and to express many feelings and desires.

Toddlers go through numerous changes between one and three years of age. In the period between 12 and 18 months, they are whirlwinds of activity. They walk for the sake of walking, paying little attention to where they are going. By the age of three, they have become more goal oriented and capable of recognizing mistakes. Young toddlers begin with the limited abilities of an infant. By the end of toddlerhood, they have developed the more sophisticated skills of a young child. Of course, the rate at which they develop varies from toddler to toddler as a result of environmental and hereditary differences.

As they become more capable of doing things for themselves, they gain some *autonomy* (the ability to fend for oneself). It is during this period that toddlers confront what Erikson described as the second crisis of ego development: autonomy versus shame and doubt. As you may recall from Chapter 2, Erikson believed that if toddlers are allowed to learn to do things for themselves, such as walking or dressing and feeding themselves, they gain a feeling of autonomy. If they are not allowed to do so, feelings of shame and self-doubt will haunt their sense of themselves, and they will have trouble with the next phase of development.

The physical changes of the toddler years can be a source of tension for both caregivers and children. Once children learn to walk, they get into every-

thing. Caregivers have to keep an eye on toddlers whenever they are free to roam about. Some conflicts can be avoided by channeling toddler energy in creative ways. One study found that the creativity required in responding to toddlers takes an enormous amount of physical and mental energy (Holden & West, 1989). This may be why some parents feel their toddlers go through a "terrible twos" stage. Not all toddlers go through this stage, but there are some who seem to personify the "terrible twos." Caregivers should keep in mind that these toddlers are not trying deliberately to be difficult; they are simply asserting their developing sense of independence.

During the toddler years, young children first become aware that they are separate beings with power over themselves. Thus, Christopher was trying to assert his independence and desire to do things for himself when he insisted that he put his shoes on. Toddlers also begin testing the power of those around them. Because toddlers are not yet fully reasonable, their self-assertiveness can be stressful for caregivers.

Toddlers, too, experience great internal tension. They are torn between the security their intimate relationships have given them and the need to independently explore the world around them. "A healthy toddler's inner world is filled with conflicting feelings—independence and dependence, pride and shame, confidence and doubt, self-awareness and confusion, fear and omnipotence, hostility and intense love, anger and tenderness, initiative and passivity" (Bredekamp, 1987, p. 24). This was evident in Christopher's desire to put his shoes on himself. He had not yet mastered this skill, and his inability to put on his shoes caused frustration and anger. He ran to someone who could comfort him. Caring adults can make the toddler's journey through this phase of his life less stressful.

## Interrelation of Areas of Development

Toddlers are growing and developing in many ways. Not only are their bodies changing, but their senses are also becoming more refined. Greater coordination and control of their muscles allow toddlers to explore, master skills, and move around

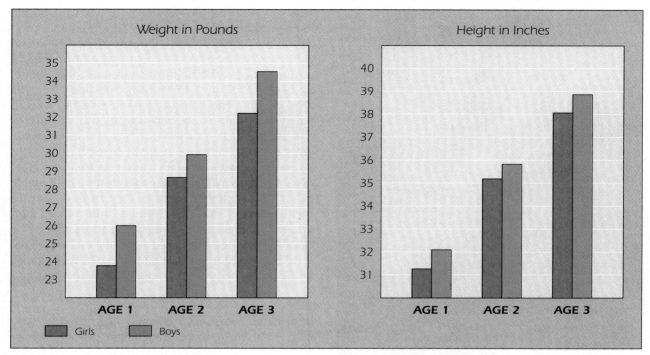

**FIGURE 9.1**   Height and Weight Charts for Boys and Girls Ages One to Three Years.

more easily. As you will see, the physical changes toddlers experience are closely linked to their intellectual, emotional, and social development.

### Growth and Development of the Body

While infancy is characterized by rapid growth, the toddler years are a time of fairly steady, even growth. Most toddlers gain about 10 pounds and grow about 8 inches between their first and third birthdays. The average one-year-old girl weighs 24 pounds and is 31.3 inches tall. By her third birthday, she weighs almost 33 pounds and is over 38 inches tall (see Figure 9.1). The corresponding figures for the average boy are slightly higher.

Although the rate of growth slows after infancy, girls continue to grow at a faster rate than boys. Girls reach about half of their adult height by 18 months and boys by two years. Hereditary factors are the cause of other differences between boys and girls. Boys are taller and more muscular than girls. They also have greater forearm strength and lose their "baby fat" sooner than girls.

Heredity and the environment both play significant roles in the growth rate of toddlers. For example, researchers have found a variety of factors—both hereditary and environmental—that influence height. A preschooler will be taller than average if he is male, is the firstborn in a small family, lives in an urban area, has African or northern European ancestors, has a mother who is a nonsmoker, and is well nourished (Meredith, 1978; Vaughan, 1983).

Physically, toddlers look different from infants. Cephalocaudal and proximodistal patterns of growth create changes in their body proportions. The torso, legs, and arms lengthen and make up a larger proportion of the body. By the time toddlers are two years of age, the head is no longer the dominant feature it was in infancy, now making up approximately one-fifth of total body length.

Although most toddlers still have a protruding belly, they are beginning to lose the chubby look of infancy. This slimmer look is related to the type of weight toddlers put on. A toddler's weight gain is mostly in the form of bone, muscle, and tissue, not fat. The toddler's slimmer physique has develop-

The three-year-old boy has a leaner, slimmer physique than the one-year-old on his right. His body proportions are more like those of an adult.

**Teeth.**    During the toddler years, teeth continue to emerge from the gums. A healthy diet and good dental hygiene will foster the growth and health of these teeth. Caregivers can begin promoting the importance of proper toothbrushing and dental care. At between 12 and 15 months, toddlers get their first molars. The second molars usually come in when the toddlers are between 20 and 24 months old. By the time toddlers are two and a half years old, most have a complete set of 20 teeth.

The eruption of molars can cause toddlers great discomfort, which is often manifested in irritable behavior. Toddlers find that they cannot comfort themselves by sucking because this makes their gums hurt even more. The pain of teething may be eased by giving toddlers something cold to bite on. Putting a toddler's drinks in a cup rather than a bottle will keep additional pressure off the gums.

**Brain and Nervous System.**    The rapid increase in cortical connections that began during infancy continues until the second birthday. This, combined with increasing myelination and the growth and formation of new brain cells, contributes to the brain's rapid growth. By age two, the brain reaches about 80 percent of its eventual adult weight. After this, the brain continues to grow but at a slower rate.

Although the brain develops rapidly in the first two years of life, the various parts develop at different rates. For example, the growth of certain motor areas of the cortex slows down between the ages of 6 and 15 months. Children have acquired control of their arms and hands, but gaining control of their legs takes more time. This explains why it is not uncommon to find some 15-month-olds who are still not walking.

By age two, the primary motor and sensory areas of the cortex are quite advanced. In addition, the areas of the cortex that form mental connections between the sensory and motor areas continue to develop. These *cortical association areas* are necessary for the performance of higher cognitive functions such as reasoning. As cortical association areas develop, patterns of behavior become more complex. Toddlers begin to coordinate their movements with information from the environment. For example, when an older toddler walks into a dark room, she will reach up to turn on the light switch.

mental significance because it is suited for the motor skills associated with this age, principally walking, running, and climbing.

As toddlers become more active, their weight gains decline. At the same time, eating habits begin to change. Many toddlers become picky eaters. Most child-rearing experts agree that nagging or threatening a child into eating does not work and makes mealtime a negative experience. Mealtime can be made enjoyable by letting toddlers eat what they want, in any combination they want, and by the method they want (Leach, 1989). This advice assumes that toddlers are being offered foods that are part of a balanced diet. Providing a wide variety of nutritious foods is important and encourages toddlers to develop healthy eating habits at an early age. Toddlers should also be allowed to decide when they have had enough to eat.

During the toddler years, there is also growth of short-term memory, but scientists have yet to unravel the physical basis of memory and its development. Memory is probably the result of a complex chain of chemical changes and reactions that involve many substances.

**Sensory System.**  The toddler's sensory system continues the maturation process begun in infancy. As vision improves, toddlers between the ages of 12 and 24 months spend significant amounts of time simply staring to gain information. Despite their sharper vision, toddlers remain farsighted; that is, they can see distant objects well but things that are close may be blurry. This is due to the fact that the fovea, the part of the eye where vision is sharpest, has not completely developed. Caregivers should keep this fact in mind and avoid activities that might strain toddlers' eyes.

With a maturing sensory system, toddlers particularly enjoy using their senses to explore the world. Sensory exploration is also a learning experience. Toddlers can learn a great deal, for example, by being asked to listen attentively to the sounds of nature or the sounds of the city when they are outdoors. They also benefit from an environment that gives them a variety of active, hands-on sensory experiences, such as comparing the way water and sand feel.

One classic study showed how important sensory stimulation and affection are to human development (Skeels, 1942, 1966). The researcher took a group of toddlers from an orphanage where they received little stimulation and affection and placed them in an institute for retarded women. In this new environment, each toddler was cared for and loved by one of the women. Before the transfer, all the toddlers had been identified as being developmentally delayed. A year and a half after the transfer, all were judged to be near normal. Their IQ had increased, and they were energetic and playful. The researcher then measured the IQ of the toddlers who remained behind in the orphanage and found that their IQ had declined. Studies such as this one have led developmentalists to conclude that intervention in the form of stimulation and affection, even as late as age two or three, can influence and change the course of development.

Learning to walk requires coordination, balance, and a great deal of practice. Young toddlers usually walk with an unsteady gait and fall often.

### Motor Development and Activity

During the toddler years, children's coordination in both gross and fine motor skills improves. *Gross motor skills* are skills that involve the large muscles of the body, while *fine motor skills* involve the smaller muscles of the body. Gross motor skills include walking, climbing, jumping, and throwing. Grasping, scribbling, and manipulating objects are examples of fine motor skills. Toddlers spend significant amounts of time practicing both types of motor skills and expanding upon them.

Walking is one of the first milestones of toddler motor development. In fact, the word *toddler* refers to the physical gait children exhibit during the early part of this period of development—they toddle. Their feet point outward and are spread wide apart for balance and stability as toddlers propel themselves forward in small steps. In spite of their efforts to remain balanced and steady, new walkers frequently fall and trip. Falling seems to have little

Children become adept at grasping and picking up small objects with their hands during the toddler years.

effect on toddlers, however; they get up and try over and over again with unwavering determination. Because they are not particularly stable on their feet, toddlers need an environment that is safe.

Practice and maturation enable toddlers to refine their walking style. By age two, children generally walk with their feet closer together and their knees less flexed. Their toes are pointed more in the direction they are headed. These changes make their walking much smoother. By the time toddlers are three, walking is second nature to them, and they no longer pay much attention to it.

As toddlers acquire greater control of their legs and feet, they begin to run, climb, and jump. Many begin running and climbing stairs at about two years of age. When toddlers first climb stairs, they bring both feet up on a step before going up the

next step. By about age three, toddlers start to climb stairs as adults do, using one foot per step. Descending stairs is a bit more difficult. Most children are not able to climb down stairs by themselves until the age of two and a half, and they use two feet per step until they are about four.

Many children gain control over their bladder and sphincter muscles when they are toddlers. During infancy, these muscles operate reflexively, opening when the bowel and bladder are full. At about two years of age, the bladder and sphincter muscles mature to the point where a child can control them.

In terms of fine motor skills, the toddler years are the time when children refine their hand and finger movements. The pincer grasp enables them to use their hands and fingers with more precision. The more they practice picking objects up with their

## Talking with Parents About HIV-Positive Children

Cheryl is the director of a large urban child care center. She knows that 2 percent of reported AIDS cases are children and that sooner or later an HIV-positive child will enroll in her center. Cheryl realizes that the issue of HIV-positive children is an emotionally explosive one. She has followed the legal battles between parents of HIV-positive children who want their children integrated into public schools and the parents of uninfected children who want HIV-positive children kept isolated.

To discuss the center's response to the potential problems of enrolling an HIV-positive child, Cheryl has organized an open meeting with parents.

CHERYL:  As you know, an increasing number of children are being born carrying HIV, the virus that causes AIDS. We feel that our center should be prepared to respond to the possibility that an HIV-positive child will be enrolled.

PARENT:  Are you saying there are kids with AIDS here? I don't want my daughter playing with any kids with AIDS. We're talking about a fatal disease, not something like mumps or chicken pox.

CHERYL:  So far as I know, there are no HIV-positive children at the center now. But many parents of HIV-positive children conceal their children's medical condition as long as possible for fear that the children will be shunned and excluded.

PARENT:  Would you tell us if a child like this enrolled?

CHERYL:  I would review the circumstances of each case individually. There are antidiscrimination laws that regulate what information is made public.

PARENT:  You mean our kids could be mixed in with these HIV-positive kids and we'd never even know it?

CHERYL:  It's possible that none of us would know. Let me review what we know about HIV. First, there has never been a documented case of transmission of the virus in a child care setting. Second, the virus cannot be transmitted by contact with vomit, urine, stool, tears, or saliva. Playing with an infected child's toy or hugging the child won't transmit the virus. The only known way that the virus can be transmitted is through contact with the blood or certain other body fluids of an infected person.

PARENT:  What about a child who bites? Wouldn't that transmit the virus?

CHERYL:  Transmission through a child biting is extremely unlikely. The American Academy of Pediatrics emphasizes that the virus is not highly contagious among children—it is highly contagious through adult sexual contact—and takes the position that HIV-infected children should be admitted freely to all activities at child care centers.

PARENT:  Should we screen children for HIV when they enroll?

CHERYL:  No, I think that would be an invasion of privacy.

*Do you think the approach Cheryl took in preparing the parents was a wise one? What are some other aspects of the issue that she might have to deal with? What are the possible advantages and disadvantages of a caregiver knowing a child is HIV-positive?*

hands, the smoother their movements become. By the end of the toddler years, children pick up objects with minimal attention and effort.

Toddlers use their newfound or refined motor skills to learn about the world. Between the ages of one and two, they spend much of their time engaged in exploratory activities. They focus their attention on small objects that they can manipulate with their hands or put in their mouth. They try out a pattern of standard actions to investigate objects, striking objects against different surfaces, throwing them, and dropping them (White, 1990).

After the age of two, mastery activities also become important. Mastery activities are simple skill-building interactions with various objects. The toddler's interest goes beyond an object itself to what can be done with it. Opening and closing doors, putting objects through openings in a container, or putting objects together and taking them apart are commonly observed mastery activities. It has been estimated that exploratory and mastery activities combined take up about 20 percent of a toddler's waking hours (White, 1990).

Exploratory and mastery activities require toddlers to use both their perceptual and motor skills. Toddlers smell, touch, taste, and listen to the sounds made by the objects they pick up. As they begin to use objects for mastery activities, toddlers put hand-eye coordination to work. This is the ability to connect hand movements with an object. Using a spoon to feed yourself, for example, requires hand-eye coordination. It is important to note that the areas of the brain associated with hand-eye coordination are not fully myelinated until children are four years of age. This helps explain why 24-month-old Christopher found putting on his shoes such a frustrating task.

The exploratory and mastery activities that engage toddlers are made possible to a great extent by their increased mobility. The ability to move allows toddlers to choose their surroundings and activities. For example, a toddler may spot some blocks across a room and walk over to explore them or to pile them up. That toddlers seem to be constantly moving, exploring, and practicing has been confirmed by researchers. They have found that the activity level of two- and three-year-old children is higher than it is at any other period of life (Eaton, 1983).

As many an exhausted caregiver will testify, toddlers are constantly on the move. The activity level of two- and three-year-olds is higher than at any other period of life.

## Developmental Interrelationships

As noted earlier, toddlers' physical development is closely related to their intellectual, emotional, and social development. Researchers have found that children who cannot master gross motor skills such as running, hopping, and jumping often have learning problems as well. Children who cannot master holding a pencil or crayon will have difficulty learning to write. Mastering motor skills gives toddlers confidence.

Toilet training provides a useful illustration of the interrelationship of these areas of development. *Toilet training* (or toilet learning) is the process through which children learn to control their bladder and bowel movements and to use the toilet successfully. Caregivers can play an important role in this process by providing toddlers with positive and consistent support. Toilet training should occur in an atmosphere of enthusiasm and cooperation; shaming or punishing a child for wetting his pants should never be allowed (Bredekamp, 1987).

Before toddlers can learn to use the toilet, they must be physically mature enough to control the bowel and bladder muscles. However, physical maturation alone is not enough. Toddlers must also want to learn this new skill and be cognitively mature enough to understand and follow instructions and to remember them. This is why many child-rearing experts recommend waiting to begin toilet training until a toddler is about two. As with other motor skills, toilet training requires practice on the part of the toddler and positive reinforcement on the part of the caregiver.

## Hallmarks of Development

The physical skills that toddlers acquire follow a sequential developmental pattern. For example, toddlers walk before they run and scribble before they begin to draw deliberately. Many of the skills toddlers learn are related to taking care of themselves or being able to do things for themselves.

The toddler years can be divided into time periods during which specific and significant developmental skills are acquired (see Table 9.1). The acquisition of these skills is an indicator of normal growth and development. It is important to keep in mind, however, that these time periods are approximate. Individual and cultural differences can account for variations in timing. There is also a degree of overlap between time periods for some of these milestones. For example, while the average age for walking backward is 14.6 months, the normal range for accomplishing this gross motor skill is from 11 to 20 months.

Caregivers should be familiar with the normal range of ages at which children acquire developmental skills so that they can identify potential problems. For example, most toddlers begin walking when they are between 12 and 18 months old. If a child is well beyond 20 months and is not yet walking, this should be viewed as a warning signal that something may be wrong. Further assessment of the child may be necessary to determine whether she or he is developmentally delayed or whether some type of intervention is required.

### From 12 to 18 Months

Walking is the most significant developmental milestone of the period from 12 to 18 months of age. Before toddlers can walk, however, they must de-

**TABLE 9.1**

**Milestones of Motor Development: Ages One to Three Years**

| Age | Milestones |
| --- | --- |
| 12 to 18 months | Toddles sideways, holding support with both hands <br> "Cruises" using one hand for support <br> Stands alone <br> Takes several steps to reach support <br> Walks unassisted <br> Walks backward |
| | Masters pincer grasp <br> Holds marker in fist and scribbles <br> Builds tower three to four blocks high <br> Turns book pages <br> Feeds self using hands <br> Drinks from cup |
| 18 months to 2 years | Walks steadily <br> Attempts to run <br> Starts to climb stairs and jump <br> Bends over to pick up object without falling |
| | Dumps items from container and puts them back <br> Threads beads on string <br> Draws circle |
| 2 to 3 years | Runs <br> Jumps with both feet together <br> Climbs steps with one foot over other <br> Rides tricycle <br> Achieves daytime toilet control |
| | Picks up tiny items <br> Holds marker in hand <br> Pours liquid from one container to another <br> Tries to dress and undress self |

velop sufficient strength and balance. Children acquire several skills in the months before their first birthday that prepare them for walking. At 8 months, most infants will be able to sit up straight without using their hands for support. Reaching this milestone frees the hands so that infants can

Most children begin to show a preference for using one hand over the other by the time they are 18 months old.

As their manipulative skills and their hand-eye coordination improve, toddlers become very eager to do things for themselves, particularly in the area of personal care. For example, by 15 months of age, most toddlers can use their hands to feed themselves and can drink from a cup.

During this period, toddlers show a preference for using one hand rather than the other. Handedness is not a conscious decision by the toddler. It is determined by the brain. As the brain develops, one side of it becomes dominant. If the left side of the brain becomes dominant, the toddler will be right-handed. If the right side of the brain dominates, the toddler will be left-handed. It is important to let toddlers show, through their developing manual skills, which hand they prefer. Children should never be pressured to change their hand preference. The part of the brain that controls handedness also controls spoken and written language. Interfering with hand preference can cause language difficulties later on (Leach, 1989). Once a preference is shown, caregivers should encourage the child to use the preferred hand.

### From 18 Months to Two Years

By 18 months of age, toddlers are steady walkers. Once their walking is more assured, toddlers make their first attempts at running. Early running is not "true" running because young toddlers have difficulty maintaining their balance and cannot start or stop quickly. What adults consider to be running appears in the next period of development.

At about 21 months of age, toddlers become interested in climbing stairs. As noted earlier, toddlers first climb stairs by bringing both feet to a step before going on to the next one. This is also the time when toddlers start jumping, usually from a low step. They first jump with one foot in a sort of exaggerated stepping motion and usually land on the heel.

By the time toddlers are 21 to 24 months old, their balance has improved to the point where they are able to bend over to pick something up without falling over. And they will pick up just about anything they see.

Toddlers in this age range are capable of many new gross and fine motor skills. They can dump items from a container and put them back. They can

reach out to pull themselves up while holding on to furniture. Most infants can pull themselves up to a standing position by the time they are 10 to 12 months old. Within about four weeks of this accomplishment, infants will start toddling along sideways while holding on to a support with both hands. As they practice and gain confidence, they begin to "cruise" along with only one hand on the support. By 13 to 15 months, toddlers can stand by themselves and take several steps to reach a support. Walking backward is one of the last gross motor skills developed during this period. It is important to note that not all toddlers go through every one of these steps before they start walking. Often a step in this progression is skipped altogether.

While toddlers are learning to walk, they are also becoming more adept at using their hands. By the age of one, children will have mastered the pincer grasp. Within the next few months, they will be able to hold a marker and make scribbles. However, their grip is not like an adult's grip. Toddlers hold markers or crayons with the thumb on one side and fingers on the other. By the age of 18 months, toddlers can carry blocks and make a tower three to four blocks high. They can also turn the pages of a book, though not necessarily one at a time.

## FOCUS ON ❯ Decision Making in Child Care

### Helping the Child of Alcoholic Parents

Aaron, a three-year-old at the Springfield Community Child Center, has been wearing the same dirty clothes several days in a row. Often he arrives late and begs for a snack when he gets to the center, saying he has not had breakfast.

Aaron is reserved in his play with other children, usually preferring to watch rather than actively participate. Twice recently, Deborah, his caregiver, has seen him in the housekeeping center pretending to pour a drink and be drunk.

From these observations, Deborah suspects that Aaron is living with an alcoholic. Although she sees no signs of physical abuse, Deborah has read that the National Council on Alcoholism estimates that 60 percent of alcoholic families experience domestic violence. She is concerned about Aaron's well-being at home.

Deborah tries to develop more open communication with Aaron's mother, but she rarely responds to Deborah's conversation. Aaron's father has left the family, and the center has no way of reaching him.

Following the center's professional guidelines, Deborah shares her concerns with the director. They both want to help Aaron but know that intervention might be seen by Aaron's mother as an invasion of privacy, which could aggravate the situation. Together Deborah and the director decide what steps to take.

Deborah continues to observe Aaron. She keeps a log of the days he arrives unkempt and hungry and stays alert to any signs of physical abuse and behavioral changes. And she keeps trying to develop a friendly relationship with Aaron's mother.

Meanwhile, Deborah contacts the county social service agency to review child neglect laws and to determine when social service agencies can intervene in a family problem. She also finds out what assistance is available for adult alcoholics and their children.

The director calls the child's pediatrician to discuss her concerns. The doctor says that he has never seen signs of physical abuse.

After a month, the situation is neither better nor worse. Some days Aaron arrives clean, fed, and on time. Other days he is hungry and dirty. Aaron's mother remains distant and uncommunicative. Regretfully, the director decides there is not enough evidence of neglect to request outside intervention.

*Do you think Deborah handled this situation correctly? Is there anything else she might have done to help Aaron? What might have happened if she had confronted Aaron's mother directly rather than taking her observations to the director?*

---

also thread beads on a string. By the end of this period of development, many toddlers are able to draw a circle.

Self-help skills improve during this time period. As far as dressing is concerned, toddlers can do a few things by themselves, but for the most part, they require the assistance of an adult. By the time they are two, many toddlers can remove their shoes (if they are untied) and their socks. Although some two-year-olds can put their shoes on, they will not always be on the right feet. Toddlers can help in pushing down their pants, although putting their

pants on is too difficult for them. At this age, most children will still put two feet into one pant leg. If an adult helps them get their feet into the legs of pants, some toddlers will be able to pull the pants up.

### From Two to Three Years

Toddlers between the ages of two and three love large muscle activities. They are becoming better runners and better jumpers. They can now jump with both feet together, and when they jump, their arms are in a winglike position behind them. Tod-

*Riding a tricycle is an activity that encourages toddlers to practice their gross motor skills and sense of balance.*

dlers are also ready to descend stairs without help. By the time they are three, most toddlers begin to climb stairs as adults do, with one foot over the other. Many children of this age can ride tricycles.

This is also the time when most toddlers achieve daytime bowel and bladder control, although bowel control usually comes first. About 90 percent of girls and 75 percent of boys can control their bowels by the time they are two and a half. Bladder control soon follows (Spock, 1985).

During this period of development, small muscle skills are refined further. Toddlers pick up tiny items and their drawing becomes more deliberate. By age two and a half, some toddlers can hold a pencil in their hand rather than in their fist. They can also pour liquids from one container to another, although spills are common.

As their abilities and skills increase, toddlers want to do more things for themselves. By the age of three, many children begin to try dressing and undressing themselves, although most cannot master this task until the age of four or five.

## Implications and Applications

Toddlerhood is an exciting stage of development. At this time, children are beginning to do things by themselves, and they delight in learning and practicing new skills. Toddlers are naturally curious and eager to explore and examine every inch of their environment. With their developing abilities to walk, run, jump, and climb and with their high activity level, toddlers pose a challenge to caregivers. However, caring for toddlers can also be a highly rewarding experience. Child care professionals can play an important role in helping toddlers leave behind the dependency of infancy and start to become independent young children capable of expressing themselves.

First and foremost, caregivers must make sure that the environment is healthy and free of hazards. At the same time, they must structure the setting so that toddlers have ample opportunities to move about, to explore, and to practice their new skills. Activities and toys should be selected with the needs of the toddler in mind. Caregivers must also remember that each child develops at his or her own pace. This means giving each toddler the freedom to walk or not walk, to run or not run, to use the toilet or not use the toilet. The most important thing to keep in mind is that all young children will acquire these skills in time.

### Nutrition and Health

With so much to see and do, toddlers need adequate rest and a balanced diet to keep their energy level high. During this period, napping patterns change. Most one-year-olds need two naps a day, one in the morning and one in the afternoon. At about 15 to 18 months of age, toddlers begin to give up the morning nap. By age two, the average child sleeps 10 to 12 hours each night and has a 1- to 2-hour nap each day, usually in the afternoon. As toddlers approach their third birthday, they may give up napping altogether.

Most toddlers who no longer nap still need to rest or have a period of quiet playtime after lunch. Caregivers should watch toddlers for signs of being overtired. Although children do not necessarily slow down their activity level when they are tired, they may begin to find some activities more difficult (Leach, 1989).

Toddlers need lots of energy to grow and learn. Meals and snacks should be nutritious and prepared in such a way that toddlers can easily feed themselves.

A nutritious diet gives toddlers the fuel they need to maintain their busy pace. Experts recommend that toddlers have two to three small servings of protein a day, two to three servings of milk and milk products, six servings of breads and cereals, two to four servings of fruit, and three to five servings of vegetables (U.S. Department of Agriculture, 1992; see more detailed recommendations in Appendix F). Because growth slows down during the toddler years, children now need fewer calories per pound and their appetite decreases. It is important that the foods they eat have nutritional value. Because sweets and salty snacks can spoil the small appetite of toddlers, such foods should be limited so that toddlers will eat foods that contain the vitamins, minerals, and proteins they need.

It is not unusual for toddlers' appetite and food preferences to be erratic. Toddlers may eat everything you give them one day and almost nothing the next. They may go through a phase where they eat only one food and refuse all others. Furthermore, they may eat foods at times that seem strange to adults, such as having soup for breakfast. Child-rearing experts advise caregivers not to be alarmed by this behavior. Toddlers will not let themselves starve. Moreover, they will choose a balanced diet as long as they are offered a wide variety of nutritious foods (Leach, 1989).

Toddlers should be given foods that they can feed to themselves and chew with their teeth. However, it is important to cut their food into tiny pieces to prevent choking and to peel fruits and vegetables that have thick skin. Among foods to avoid because they are known to cause choking are hot dogs, raw carrots, popcorn, peanuts, grapes, and fruits with pits. Young children should not be given any food to eat while they are toddling about because of the increased choking risk this presents. Regardless of what they are eating, children should always be closely supervised when they are eating.

To keep the child care setting as healthy as possible, it is important for toddlers to be immunized against infectious diseases. The American Academy of Pediatrics recommends that children be immu-

**FOCUS ON** **Child Care Issues**

### School Readiness

In 1992, the National Governors' Association established the first national education goals. The governors took the position that "by the year 2000, all children in America will start school ready to learn." However, before early childhood educators can determine how to reach this goal, they need to agree on what "ready to learn" means. When 500 kindergarten teachers were asked to complete the sentence "Readiness is . . . ," dozens of substantially different answers were received. Here are two very different—yet professionally respected—views about "readiness."

Children Should Be Ready for School:

Readiness for school means that a child is emotionally, socially, physically, and academically prepared to learn the materials in the school curriculum. Children need certain cognitive and language skills before they are ready for formal education. These include recognizing colors, counting, and prereading skills such as letter recognition.

Academic readiness is only one part of school readiness. Even academically bright preschoolers may not be socially and emotionally ready to learn. For success in kindergarten, children need enough developmental maturity to exercise self-control, follow directions, and build peer relationships.

Each child develops at his or her own pace. There is no fixed chronological age when a child is ready for formal instruction. However, there is a direct relationship between development and learning. A child who enters kindergarten without both cognitive and social readiness starts school in a position of weakness and is less likely to experience success. It is much better to let such a child spend another year in a less demanding, more developmentally appropriate setting. When she begins school a

year later, she will be much better prepared for formal education.

One way to assess school readiness is by using screening tests such as the Gesell School Readiness Test. These tests can provide some indication of readiness, but they should be used in conjunction with evaluations of the preschool teacher and parent.

Schools Should Be Ready for Children:

Children are ever-ready learners. They grow into the intellectual and social life around them. A stimulating environment promotes learning and development.

Rather than waiting for children to possess certain skills, such as letter recognition, we should ensure that all children are placed in public school learning situations upon reaching a specific age. Schools should be ready to meet the needs of all children and accept them wherever they are in their development.

Readiness tests are notoriously unreliable. Children are not good test takers, and their willingness to cooperate with the test giver fluctuates widely. Some research indicates that up to 50 percent of children are misdiagnosed as unready by the Gesell test. In personal evaluations, standards of readiness are so variable that a child may be deemed ready by one teacher but not by another.

Minority children and children from low-income families are overrepresented in the group of students who are kept out of school after they are chronologically eligible. This increases the social inequality between these children and the "ready" group. Keeping children out of school because they lack certain skills only puts them at a greater disadvantage. Moreover, research indicates that many children who are kept out of school an extra year

---

**FOCUS ON**    *Child Care Issues (continued)*

perceive themselves as failures and have a poor attitude toward future schooling.

School entry standards must be unbiased so that all children, regardless of income, race, language, or gender, have equal access to school services. Chronological age is the only clear and unbiased entry requirement we have available. Rather than preselecting children who should enter kindergarten, we need to accept all

children and provide them with a flexible, developmentally appropriate education within the school system.

*Which position do you agree with more? Are there arguments made by the other side that you feel are valid? As a child care professional, how can you help parents make a decision about the proper time for their child to begin formal schooling?*

---

nized against Haemophilus influenza at 12 to 15 months and against measles, mumps, and rubella (MMR) at 15 months (American Academy of Pediatrics, 1992). At 18 months, they should be given diphtheria, pertussis, and tetanus (DTP) immunization and trivalent oral polio vaccine (TOPV). Child care providers should advise parents of these recommended immunizations, make sure immunizations are current, and keep records for each child.

A healthy child care setting is a clean setting. To control the spread of infectious diseases, child care providers must clean and disinfect the areas where children play and the toys they play with on a daily basis. Diapering areas should be cleaned and disinfected, and caregivers should wash their hands after each change and before handling food. As toddlers learn to use the toilet and feed themselves, they should also learn to wash their hands after going to the toilet and before eating.

### A Safe and Suitable Environment

Toddlers need an environment that is safe, uncluttered, well equipped, and roomy. Because toddlers want to go everywhere and touch everything, it is critical that the child care setting be child-proofed. Floor areas should be carpeted or covered with mats. Toy storage areas need to be well anchored so that they do not tip over. Sharp corners should be covered with foam rubber. Drawers and cabinets that contain hazardous items should have child-proof locks on them. Careful adult supervision is essential at all times.

The toys that toddlers play with should be thoroughly examined for potential hazards. Toys that are small or have tiny parts, such as marbles or small puzzle pieces, pose a choking risk to toddlers. Toys that have sharp edges or are small and heavy enough to be thrown should not be allowed in the child care setting. Metal toy soldiers, for instance, are small enough to be thrown by a toddler but heavy enough to cause injury. Toys should be reexamined periodically to make sure they are in good working order and have not lost any parts that could harm a child.

In choosing equipment, child care providers should consider the gross and fine motor skills that toddlers are learning and make sure the equipment will safely promote the development of these skills. For example, some care settings may not have stairs on which toddlers can practice climbing skills. Caregivers can compensate by providing toddlers with sturdy, free-standing steps that can be placed against a wall. A slide that has steps to climb will also work. If toddlers are going to practice jumping, they need to have soft landing spots such as mattresses or outdoor play areas covered with sawdust.

It is important for toddlers to have opportunities for active, large muscle play both indoors and outdoors. In addition to ramps and steps, toddlers need a play area that is separate from that of older children. Toddlers also need equipment geared to their size and skills, such as small climbing equipment, swings, and low slides (Bredekamp, 1987). Sunscreen and hats should be used to protect toddlers from the sun when they are playing outdoors.

## Cultural Differences in Toilet Training Expectations

The same words take on different meanings for different adults, depending on their experiences and culture. To most child care providers in the United States, toilet training (or toilet learning) means that a child recognizes the need to use the toilet, gets herself there, removes her clothing, cleans herself, flushes the toilet, and washes her hands. These activities require an independence and maturity that is not generally found in children under three years of age.

In other cultures, however, toilet training means that the child no longer wears a diaper. Toilet training in this sense may begin near the end of the first year; its success is based on the interdependence of the caregiver and the child. The caregiver recognizes signs that the child needs to use the toilet and takes her there. The caregiver also performs other functions for the child such as cleaning, flushing, and hand washing. Because the child is encouraged to use the toilet at set intervals, she develops a regular schedule. Using this system makes it possible for children as young as one year to be out of diapers.

Problems sometimes arise when caregivers and parents have different views on what toilet training means. Talking about each other's expectations can be helpful. Although both sets of expectations cannot always be accommodated in a day-care setting, respecting parents' ideas rather than labeling them wrong or ignorant helps bridge the gap between home and day care.

## Activities

As young children make their way through the toddler years, their skills and interests expand and mature. Child care professionals need to provide different toys and activities for children who are at different levels of development and who have different abilities and interests. For example, teaching a two-year-old how to tie a shoe will be an exercise in frustration for the child because her hand muscles are not mature enough to master the skill. Most four-year-olds, however, will find this activity challenging. It is important that activities be challenging but not frustrating. By giving toddlers the opportunity to learn and master new skills through challenging activities, caregivers can help them develop self-esteem and a positive self-image.

What kinds of activities do toddlers enjoy? They love activities that involve using their senses, such as water play, sand play, finger painting, and tasting different flavors.

They are enthusiastic about large-motor activities such as follow the leader or throwing and catching balls or balloons. Toddlers also enjoy moving to music. Circle activities that incorporate songs, movement, and following directions help toddlers practice their motor and listening skills.

Toddlers also love to paint, draw, and manipulate clay. Caregivers should let toddlers explore and manipulate these materials in the way they choose without expecting toddlers to produce a recognizable product. Art projects give toddlers the opportunity to learn to use their senses. They also give toddlers the opportunity to scribble. Researchers have found that scribbling by toddlers is as significant a development as babbling by infants (Gardner, 1980). While babbling is an early step in mastering speech, scribbling is a prewriting skill. Providing toddlers with crayons, markers, paints, and paper will allow them to practice this important skill and, at the same time, give them an opportunity to express themselves through art.

As independent as toddlers try to be, they do need and benefit from the attention of adults. Adults should therefore be available for more than encouragement or comfort. They need to involve themselves in toddlers' play. When adults play with toddlers, toddlers can learn how to use their imagination by, for example, having a "tea party." Toddlers can also learn new skills by modeling what adults are doing. If a caregiver shows a group of toddlers how to pour water and encourages them as they practice doing this, the group will learn pouring skills sooner than toddlers who have no help. In addition, adults can help toddlers stay interested in an activity for a longer period of time. In this way, adult participation promotes learning.

Caregivers should be aware that toddlers are egocentric and are only beginning to have the capability to share toys and materials. Generosity is learned very gradually, and it is normal for a two-year-old to refuse to share at times (Spock, 1985). The implication for the child care setting is to have multiples of many toys. If a tug-of-war breaks out over a particular toy, caregivers can provide the children with identical or similar toys and avoid a crisis. Children do not truly play with, as opposed to alongside, other children until they are about three. It is then that they become more able to share.

Finally, toddlers need to be allowed to proceed at their own pace. Muscular coordination relies on the development of the brain and nervous system. If these systems mature at a slower rate than average, a child may not, for example, begin walking until she is 18 months old. Expecting her to walk simply because she has reached her first birthday and because many children walk at that age is unfair. Setting goals for toddlers will only frustrate and demoralize them. The best that a caregiver can do is to help and encourage toddlers as they develop.

This is probably most evident in the area of toilet training. Some toddlers have learned to use the toilet by the time they are one year old, while others do not use the toilet until they are five. Some toddlers learn to use the toilet in a matter of days; others take months. Child-rearing experts stress that the age at which a child learns to use the toilet and how long this takes are not what counts. What counts is how the child experiences it.

To make toilet training a positive experience, most experts recommend that caregivers wait until toddlers have given indications that they are physically and emotionally ready. Initiating toilet training before a child is ready to learn is likely to be stressful and unsuccessful (Leach, 1989).

Caregivers should choose play equipment that safely promotes the development of gross and fine motor skills.

One of the first signs that a toddler is ready to begin toilet training is a dry diaper after a reasonably long period of time, such as a nap. Caregivers can begin leaving the diaper off if toddlers continue to stay dry. They should also encourage or periodically ask toddlers to use the toilet because toddlers can easily be distracted. Caregivers should realize that there will be accidents. They should be prepared for accidents with extra changes of clothes, and they should always be sympathetic. Most toddlers stay dry all night by the time they are three. Boys and high-strung children tend to take a little longer (Spock, 1985). Caregivers should be aware that although bed-wetting may have environmental causes such as stress, it also appears to run in families (Fergusson, Horwood, & Shannon, 1986).

A toddler's physical development, whether it is learning to walk, use a spoon, take off shoes, or go to the toilet, cannot be forced or rushed. Each child develops in an individual way. Caregivers who remember this will promote the well-being, happiness, and growth of the children in their care.

## SUMMARY

- During the toddler years, young children develop physically so that they are no longer completely dependent upon adults to meet their needs. They become capable of doing many things for themselves.
- The two developmental processes that enable toddlers to become more independent are unassisted walking and rapid language development.
- The rate at which toddlers develop is influenced by both heredity and the environment.
- The toddler years are a time of tension as toddlers vacillate between their need for the security of intimate relationships and their need for independent exploration, which will ultimately lead to autonomy.
- Toddlers do not grow as rapidly as infants. Their body proportions change as the body lengthens, and they lose baby fat. The slimmer physique makes it easier for toddlers to acquire the motor skills of this age group.
- During the toddler years, children get their first and second molars. By the age of two and a half, they have a full set of teeth.
- The development of cortical association areas in the brain enables toddlers to coordinate their motor activities with information they receive from the environment. Their behavior patterns become more complex.
- The maturing sensory system of toddlers enables them to explore and learn about the world through their senses.
- During the toddler years, children's gross and fine motor skills become increasingly coordinated. Walking, running, climbing, and jumping are the major gross motor skills that toddlers acquire. They use their motor skills to explore and manipulate their environment.
- Toilet training is an example of the interrelationship of physical development and intellectual, emotional, and social development. Toddlers cannot learn to use the toilet until they can physically control their bowel and bladder muscles, understand and follow instructions, and want to use the toilet.
- The physical development of toddlers follows a sequential pattern. The toddler years can be divided into time periods during which specific and significant developmental skills are acquired. These skills are indicators of normal growth and development.
- The major hallmarks of physical development for children between 8 and 18 months of age include walking, climbing, and the refinement of the pincer grasp to pick up small objects. Toddlers also show a preference for one hand during this period.
- Toddlers between 18 months and two years of age learn to climb stairs and begin to take an interest in dressing themselves. When they are between two and three years old, toddlers become good runners and jumpers and learn to control their bowels and bladder.

- Toddlers need adequate rest and a healthy diet to maintain their high activity level. During the toddler years, many children give up their morning nap, and by the end of this period, some give up napping altogether. However, toddlers still need a quiet time. Although many toddlers have an erratic appetite, they will choose a balanced diet if offered a wide variety of nutritious foods.
- To promote a healthy environment, caregivers should examine toys for potential hazards, toddlers should receive all necessary immunizations, and caregivers should keep the setting safe and clean.
- Toddlers need an environment that is safe, uncluttered, well-equipped, and roomy. The child care setting should be child-proofed. Toys and activities should accommodate children who are at different levels of development and who have different abilities and interests. Child care providers need to take an active role in toddler activities.
- Toddlers must be allowed to proceed at their own pace.

## BUILDING VOCABULARY

Write a definition for each vocabulary term listed below.

autonomy
cortical association areas
fine motor skills

gross motor skills
toilet training

## ACQUIRING KNOWLEDGE

1. What are the two main developmental advances that promote the toddler's movement toward independence?
2. Define autonomy.
3. According to Erikson's theory, what conflicting feelings do toddlers experience as a result of the second crisis in ego development?
4. Briefly describe how children's physical changes during the toddler years can be a source of tension for caregivers.
5. In terms of physical appearance, how are toddlers different from infants?
6. What often happens to a child's appetite during the toddler years?
7. How can mealtime be made more enjoyable for toddlers?
8. Why do children gain control of their arms and hands before gaining control of their legs?
9. What are cortical association areas?
10. As the cortical association areas of toddlers develop, how does their behavior change?
11. Describe the visual limitations of toddlers.
12. What is the difference between gross motor skills and fine motor skills?
13. Describe the origin of the word *toddler*.
14. Why is it particularly important that a toddler's environment be safe and free from potentially damaging objects?

15. What gross motor skills do toddlers begin practicing as they gain greater control of their legs and feet?
16. What are mastery activities? Give an example.
17. Why do children younger than four find activities involving hand-eye coordination frustrating?
18. Name two skills that children usually acquire as preparation for walking.
19. How should caregivers respond when they notice a child beginning to prefer using one hand rather than the other?
20. List three gross or fine motor skills that toddlers usually acquire between the ages of two and three.
21. How do napping patterns usually change during the toddler years?
22. When serving meals and snacks to toddlers, what can caregivers do to reduce the risk of choking?
23. What types of toys should caregivers avoid giving to toddlers?
24. What skill is encouraged by giving toddlers plenty of opportunities to scribble?
25. How do toddlers benefit when adults get involved in their play?
26. How can caregivers avoid fights between toddlers over particular toys?

## THINKING CRITICALLY

1. According to Erik Erikson, if toddlers are not encouraged to do things by themselves, they will be haunted by shame and doubt and have trouble reaching the next stage of development. Discuss the implications of Erikson's ideas for caregivers working with toddlers. How do you think his ideas could be used in a practical way by child care professionals?
2. Experts stress the importance of helping children learn how to use the toilet only when they are physically and emotionally ready. Discuss what you think would happen if caregivers and parents disagreed over a particular child's readiness for toilet training. Do you think such readiness can be determined objectively, or is it a matter of opinion?
3. Many child development professionals believe that toddlers should be allowed to develop new skills and abilities at their own pace. Discuss how caregivers can promote individual development in a group setting.
4. Whether a toddler finds an activity challenging or frustrating depends on his or her particular level of development. How do you think caregivers can learn about a toddler's capabilities?
5. Why do you think it is important for caregivers to understand the physical changes that children go through as they develop?

## OBSERVATIONS AND APPLICATIONS

1. Observe a group of two-year-olds in a preschool or child care setting. First, observe their behavior during an indoor free play period. Make note of toys and activities they choose. What are the most common choices? Do the children play together or engage mainly in individual activities? What is the role of the caregiver in indoor play? Next, observe the same group during an outdoor play period. Again, make note of play choices

and the type of play. What is the role of the caregiver outdoors? Explain how the behavior of the children is similar to or different from what you expected. Is the role of the caregiver different during indoor and outdoor play?

2. Compare the gross and fine motor skill development of an 18-month-old and a three-year-old. For gross motor development, notice how these children play with balls and playground equipment. Can they climb up the steps of a slide without help? Can they climb down stairs? Can they jump? For fine motor development, note how much the two children are able to help in dressing themselves. How do they handle crayons? Can they feed themselves with a utensil? Can they drink from a cup without spilling? Can they put differently shaped objects into matching holes? What other similarities and differences do you notice?

3. The parents of three-year-old Margaret ask your advice. For some time, Margaret has been a picky eater, but now she wants to eat macaroni and cheese and nothing else. Mealtime has become a series of battles between Margaret and her parents. Macaroni and cheese do not constitute a well-balanced diet, and Margaret's parents are concerned that if they give in to her, she will not be well nourished. What advice would you give these parents?

4. Toddlers are natural explorers. You are on the advisory board of a new child care center for infants and toddlers. On the basis of what you have learned in this chapter, draw up a set of guidelines that can be used to create a learning environment that is stimulating to the toddlers but safe as well. Mention specific types of activities that are appropriate and beneficial for children of this age.

## SUGGESTIONS FOR FURTHER READING

Ames, L., & Ilg, F. L. (1980). *Your two year old*. New York: Dell.

Anderson, R. D., Bale, J. F., Jr., Blackman, J. A., & Murphy, J. R. (1986). *Infections in children: A sourcebook for educators and child care providers*. Rockville, MD: Aspen.

Cratty, B. J. (1986). *Perceptual and motor development in infants and children* (3rd ed.). Englewood Cliffs, NJ: Prentice-Hall.

Highberger, R., & Boynton, M. (1983). Preventing illness in infant/toddler day care. *Young children, 38*(3), 3–8.

Kendrick, A. S., Kaufmann, R., & Messenger, K. P. (Eds.). (1991). *Healthy young children: A manual for programs*. Washington, DC: National Association for the Education of Young Children.

Leach, P. (1989). *Your baby and child: From birth to age five*. New York: Knopf.

National Association for the Education of Young Children (1990). *Developmentally appropriate practice in early childhood programs serving toddlers*. Washington, DC: Author.

Snow, C. W. (1989). *Infant development*. Englewood Cliffs, NJ: Prentice-Hall.

U.S. Department of Agriculture. (1992). *Nutrition guidance for the child nutrition programs*. Washington, DC: Author.

White, B. L. (1990). *The first three years of life* (new rev. ed.). New York: Prentice Hall Press.

## OBJECTIVES

Studying this chapter will enable
you to

- Summarize Piaget's ideas on the
  cognitive development of
  toddlers—from the end of
  sensorimotor learning to the use
  of symbolic thought for problem
  solving.
- Discuss different theories on how
  toddlers form concepts and
  develop scripts.
- Describe the development of
  language skills and the beginnings
  of literacy.
- Explain why play is important to
  the cognitive development of
  toddlers and discuss how parents
  and other caregivers can facilitate
  learning.

TWO-YEAR-OLD Jeremy was playing with a shape box on the living room floor. A variety of blocks of different shapes were scattered around him, and he was trying to put the blocks into matching holes in the box. Jeremy picked up an oblong-shaped block and looked at it and the box for a few seconds with an expression of intense concentration on his face. Then he reached out and tried to put the block into the box's oblong-shaped hole. But the block wouldn't fit through the hole because the long and short sides of the block and the hole didn't match. Jeremy then grasped the box firmly in one hand and rotated the block until it dropped into the hole. As the block slipped into the box, he smiled gleefully and clapped his hands.

After several minutes, Jeremy became bored with the shape box and picked up a book. He carried it over to his father, Steve. "Read book!" Jeremy told his father.

"Okay, Jeremy," Steve said as he placed the toddler on his lap and began reading the book out loud. As his father read, Jeremy listened attentively and stared at the pictures on each page. Occasionally, he pointed to a picture and proudly exclaimed, "Doggy!" or "Car!" when he recognized objects. Lifting his hands up to an imaginary wheel and moving them as if he were driving a car, he loudly intoned, "Vroom, vroom."

When Steve finished reading the book, Jeremy climbed down from his lap. Then he noticed Steve's shoes under the chair and tried to put them on his father's feet. "Put on!" Jeremy ordered while trying to push the shoes on Steve's feet.

Toddlerhood is an exciting time for both children and their caregivers. Children change from helpless infants into little people capable of walking, running, climbing, holding conversations, working out problems, and understanding a great deal of information. Toddlers are bold and tireless explorers, eagerly examining and testing every new object and event. They are becoming aware of themselves as separate individuals who can have an impact on the people and objects around them.

Jeremy has come a long way from infancy. He has mastered many skills, including the ability to think clearly about a problem and rehearse solutions mentally. He is capable of speaking in simple sentences, and he is working to learn other new language skills. In addition, he can pretend and imitate actions that he has seen in the past. Through his actions, it is clear that Jeremy understands that he is an individual separate from his father and that he can influence his environment. Such actions and behaviors are important milestones in the intellectual, or cognitive, development of toddlers.

## Advancing Cognitive Development

Infants learn about the world almost entirely by using their motor skills and senses to explore and make sense of their environment. An infant learns about a rattle, for example, by grasping it, shaking it, sucking on it, looking at it, and throwing it. As motor skills mature, infants are able to move around and try new behaviors, and their world expands as a result of this mobility. In addition, cognitive skills such as memory and categorization improve gradually but significantly throughout the first year.

Toddlerhood is generally considered to begin at about age one, when an infant starts walking, and to last until age three. Although walking is the event that signals the beginning of this period, the most significant cognitive development that occurs at this stage is the transition from sensorimotor learning to symbolic thought. Toddlers do not stop using their sensory and motor skills to gather information about the world, but they do begin using their cognitive abilities more. In putting the oblong block into the box, Jeremy not only used manual dexterity but also his ability to think about a solution to the problem.

This chapter focuses on the cognitive development that takes place between ages one and three and on the changes that occur during this period. It examines how toddlers learn new causal relationships, how mental images help them learn, and how they become more aware of themselves as individuals. It also takes a look at how toddlers' expanded thinking skills help them learn language. Interestingly, cognitive development proceeds at a similar pace in all countries and cultures. Studies have shown that cognitive skills such as pretending, observing, and imitating develop at about the same time in children in widely varying cultures (Yando, Seitz, & Zigler, 1978). Although the environments of the children are very different, the types of mental tasks they perform at certain ages are the same the world over.

## Piaget's Perspective on Cognitive Development

In Chapter 7, you learned about Jean Piaget's theories on the cognitive development of infants. He called the period from birth to age two the sensorimotor period because children in this age group learn about their environment through their senses and act on it with their body. Within the sensorimotor period, Piaget identified six substages that he believed characterize the growth of intelligence from birth to age two (Piaget, 1952). You learned about the first four substages—the reflexive stage, the first acquired adaptations stage, the secondary circular reaction stage, and the coordination of secondary

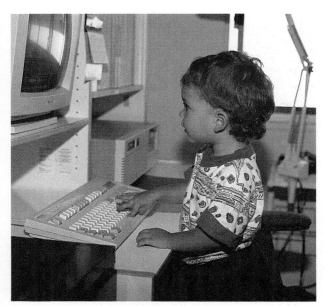

*Toddlers use their vastly improved motor skills and cognitive abilities to test and explore every inch of their environment.*

schemes stage—in Chapter 7. These all occur during infancy. Substages 5 and 6 characterize the toddler years.

**Becoming a Toddler.** Piaget's substage 5, the tertiary circular reaction stage, occurs between the ages of 12 and 18 months. It marks the transition from infancy to toddlerhood. During this stage, children become little explorers and scientists, tirelessly applying what they have learned to new situations. They put smaller objects into bigger ones, open and close boxes, and take lids off jars. They mash, smear, and tear their food; they drop and throw objects to watch their movements. They climb on furniture to get to out-of-reach objects. Toddlers in substage 5 are using their vastly improved motor skills, senses, and cognitive abilities to take in as much information as possible, often much to the exasperation of the adult caregivers who have to protect them and clean up after them.

As toddlers explore and test their environment, they learn about cause and effect and discover countless new causal relationships through trial and error. They learn, for example, that twisting a knob may open a door or turn on a television set. They learn that pushing on a toilet handle causes the toilet to flush and that pulling a cat's tail makes the cat yowl and scratch. Such discoveries change the way toddlers relate to their environment. The knowledge that an action may cause a certain effect encourages them to act in purposeful ways.

As you may recall from Chapter 2, Piaget noted that children use schemes to understand the world around them. The tertiary circular reactions phase is characterized by the use of a greater variety of schemes, which are an essential part of the toddler's ongoing explorations.

**The Beginning of Symbolic Thought.** Piaget viewed substage 6 of the sensorimotor period, the time from 18 months to two years, as the beginning of symbolic thought. He called this stage the "invention of new means through mental combinations" because it is the period during which children begin to think through the steps involved in solving problems. Jeremy, for example, paused and stared intently at the block and shape box before trying to fit the two together. He seemed to be forming mental images of what would happen when he placed the block over its corresponding hole. The images he formed were mental representations of his actions, and the symbolic thought process he employed enabled him to solve the problem.

A variety of other mental abilities become fully developed during this time as well. Toddlers understand the concept of object permanence and apply this idea to their world. They know that objects continue to exist out of their sight, and they can envision an object mentally and imagine it being moved from place to place. Along with an understanding of object permanence comes an understanding of the concept of time. Toddlers are beginning to anticipate events such as a trip to the zoo or a visit from Grandma. They can also anticipate the possible consequences of events. For example, a toddler may take extra care when holding a glass of milk because he can think ahead and imagine what would happen if he dropped the glass. As toddlers develop these mental abilities, they continue to experiment and apply their skills to new situations as they did in substage 5. In substage 6, toddlers are capable of solving simple problems through insight and reasoning alone. They no longer have to act out each step.

During substage 6, deferred imitation and symbolic play begin to appear. Both of these new skills are signs of the fundamental change to symbolic representation and thought. *Deferred imitation*, or delayed imitation, is the duplication of an action hours or days after it occurred. When Jeremy acted out driving a car, he was imitating his father driving the family car. He had to have been remembering and recalling the action of driving in order to be able to imitate it. Such imitation is a valuable cognitive skill because it enables children to acquire new information rapidly and efficiently.

*Symbolic play*, or pretending, is play that involves symbolic thought, such as assuming the role of another person or pretending that a block of wood is a truck. The ability to think symbolically enables toddlers to use familiar objects in new and creative ways. A shoe box may become a doll's bed, or an inverted pot may be used as a stool. Building blocks can be used to construct anything from a car to a skyscraper. As toddlers play and experiment with such objects, they also become very adept at sorting and classifying them according to color, size, function, and other categories.

Another significant aspect of substage 6 is the development of self-recognition. Children in this stage become aware of themselves as separate from their environment and from other people. They can recognize themselves in a mirror, and they begin to use the terms *I*, *me*, and *you*. In one study of self-recognition, researchers held a mirror up to children ranging in age from nine months to two years so that they could see their reflection. The researchers then daubed rouge on each child's nose and held up the mirror again. The two-year-olds immediately touched their nose, but the younger children did not. The experiment showed that only the older ones were aware that they were looking at themselves in the mirror (Lewis & Brooks-Gunn, 1979).

**The Preoperational Period.**   You may recall from Chapter 2 that Piaget classified the stages of cognitive development between birth and adulthood into four major periods—the sensorimotor period, the preoperational period, the period of concrete operations, and the period of formal operations—each with several substages. The substage just described marks the end of the sensorimotor

As toddlers develop self-awareness, they become able to recognize themselves in the mirror.

period and the beginning of the preoperational period. Piaget used the term *preoperational* to indicate his belief that while children at this stage can think symbolically, they are not yet capable of more complex logical, or operational, thinking.

During the preoperational period (ages two to six), children continue to acquire and expand the symbolic thinking skills they began to use at the end of the sensorimotor period. The increased ability to think symbolically plays a major role in the development of language, one of the most significant cognitive achievements of childhood. Language skills blossom and expand rapidly during this stage. The average two-year-old can speak about 50 words and understands about 300. By age three, normal toddlers are speaking in short, grammatically correct sentences and can already comprehend about 1,000 words.

Children in the preoperational stage are acute observers, especially of other people, and they imitate much of what they see. They will imitate many of the things they see their parents doing—cooking, talking on the phone, shaving, mowing the lawn—as well as many of their parents' mannerisms and behaviors. If a mother scolds her child, the child may soon be seen scolding a doll or stuffed animal. Because toddlers are such keen observers, they notice and talk about small details and discrepancies, such as a disfigured face, an abnormally overweight person, a car with a missing wheel.

During the preoperational period, toddlers engage more and more in symbolic play, using toys or other objects to represent something else. A large cardboard carton may become a spaceship or a fort, and a paper towel roll may become a periscope or a megaphone. In symbolic play, toys also become agents or actors in a child's fantasies. A toddler may act out scenes with a boy doll and a girl doll, for example, pretending to be first one doll and then the other and carrying out conversations with them. In acting out these scenes, the child may be using the dolls to represent his mother and father or himself and a friend. In symbolic play, the child is creating and directing the action. This ability to engage in pretend play is an important milestone in cognitive development because it signals the child's ability to hold two or more representations of an object (the cardboard carton as carton and as spaceship) in mind at the same time. This is Piaget's notion of *mental combination*.

Children in the preoperational stage are intensely curious and thoughtful, and they thrive on new experiences and new opportunities to learn about their world. If you watch a two-year-old trying to place different-sized rings on a cone, from the largest to the smallest, you can almost see the child thinking out the solution to the problem. She may pause for several seconds while staring at the rings and cone, her brow wrinkled in concentration, before suddenly reaching out and grasping the appropriate ring. As toddlers become older, their ability to carry out more complicated activities and solve more difficult problems increases. A two-year-old may pause and think before acting; a three-year-old can carry out activities and solve problems much more quickly.

Another characteristic of children in Piaget's preoperational period is egocentrism. Piaget believed that children in this stage are *egocentric thinkers*, fixed in their own perspective and incapable of understanding another person's point of view. A toddler who is talking on the phone to her grandfather will not understand why he cannot see the doll she is holding. While such egocentric thinking is typical of toddlers, recent research indicates that children of this age are also capable of appreciating the viewpoint and feelings of others (Borke, 1983). If a

Symbolic play, in which children use a toy or other object to represent something else, is an important milestone in cognitive development.

toddler sees another child crying, for example, he may ask why the child is crying and may try to comfort the child.

### Developing Concepts and Representations

One of the intriguing questions about the cognitive development of toddlers is how they mentally organize the great amount of information they acquire. How, for example, do they form *concepts*, mental representations for groups of related objects and events? To study this process, researchers have devised and tested various theories about how children learn to conceptualize. Most researchers look first at how young children classify and sort objects and events as their knowledge and experiences expand to include new information. Recent research has provided other theories about the way toddlers develop concepts. These theories often make a distinction between object concepts and event concepts.

**Object Concepts.**    The question of how children form categories for objects in their environment is somewhat controversial. The most widely accepted view is that of Eleanor Rosch, who argues

Researcher Katherine Nelson believes that young children use scripts of routine events, such as going to the store or getting dressed, to understand new situations.

that children first categorize objects at what she calls the basic level. Children then build upon basic-level concepts by making more general and more specific distinctions (Rosch, Mervis, Gray, Johnson, & Boyes-Braem, 1976). For example, a child may learn the word *dog* before the word *animal* or *collie*.

This view has been challenged by Jean Mandler. Mandler and her colleagues theorize that children establish *global concepts* first and then learn to make finer and finer distinctions within categories as their knowledge and understanding increase (Mandler, Bauer, & McDonough, 1991). Global categories are somewhat broader than basic-level categories. An 18-month-old, for example, may not be able to distinguish between four-legged animals, such as dogs, cats, and horses. However, he can distinguish dogs from other broad groups of animals such as birds or fish. At age three, the same child can readily recognize differences among dogs, cats, horses, and other four-legged animals because he has learned more about these animals and can thus make finer distinctions.

Mandler has also theorized that toddlers classify objects not only by appearance and other perceptual clues but by other more abstract characteristics,

such as function or movement, as well. Thus children recognize dissimilar-looking objects such as a pot and a can opener as objects that are used in the kitchen. Similarly, they recognize that dogs and people are alive because they move but that a statue of a dog or a person is not alive because it doesn't move (Mandler et al., 1991).

**Scripts.**    Another theory about the conceptual development of young children focuses on the formation of event concepts. Researcher Katherine Nelson has theorized that young children construct certain basic *scripts*, or mental representations of routine events, as they learn more about their environment. Eating a meal, getting dressed, taking a bath, and going shopping are all examples of scripts that toddlers acquire as their experiences broaden. Nelson believes that children begin constructing such scripts before the age of three and that they use these scripts to learn about new situations by substituting different actions into an already scripted event. For example, when a child goes to a restaurant for the first time, he may recognize that certain actions are just like the script for eating at home. He sits down, gets food, and eats the food. Other actions, however, are new. There is a menu that lists a variety of new things to eat and drink, a waiter or waitress who serves the food, and a bill for the meal that his parents pay. On the basis of this new experience and its new actions, the child constructs a new script based on his eating-at-home script, and in this way he learns about and understands eating in a restaurant.

Nelson believes that parents and other caregivers help children develop scripts by describing and labeling new events. For example, parents are likely to describe a visit to the dentist before taking their child there for the first time. Doing this allows the child to construct a script for the event and to have some idea of what to expect. By helping to shape the script, the parents also set up expectations that will affect how the child perceives and understands the event when it occurs (Nelson, 1986).

**Memory and Pretend Play.**    The ability to categorize objects and events and construct scripts of routine experiences are only two of the mental representational skills that toddlers are developing. The ability to engage in deferred imitation and pre-

## FOCUS ON  Cultural Diversity

### Helping Children Who Don't Speak English

Non-English-speaking children placed in a child care center often feel lost and disoriented. Cut off from their natural means of communication, they fear that they will be unable to make even simple needs understood.

Without a common language, it is difficult to explain the center's routine. Children in this situation may become anxious because they don't know what is expected of them. Parents of these children, many of whom speak little English, also have increased concerns about leaving their child in a center.

As a child care provider, there are things you can do to help orient non-English-speaking children and make them more comfortable.

- Try to look directly at the child and speak slowly and distinctly.
- Use whole body communication and gestures to clarify what you are saying. Likewise, be receptive to gestures and nonverbal cues used by the child.

- Learn a few basic phrases such as "Do you need to go to the bathroom?" and "Are you thirsty?" in the child's native language.
- Do your best to help the child feel a part of the group.
- Ask the child to share things from his or her home.
- If possible, pair the child with another who speaks his language and also speaks English.
- Invite the parent to stay for part of a day and watch the class. Some activities such as free play and circle time are easier to explain when observed. Beware of using words such as *cubbies*, which have specific meaning to you but not to the parent.
- Introduce the parent to other parents to encourage play dates between English-speaking and non-English-speaking children.

tend play is also growing because of the greater memory and attention span of children of this age. Toddlers can play with one toy or work at a task for longer periods of time without losing interest because they are able to remember the goal they set for themselves at the onset of the activity.

By the time toddlers are three, their memory is well enough developed to enable them to recognize and recall an impressive amount of information. In one experiment, two- and three-year-olds were asked to recall and reconstruct a display of toys. Most of the children could remember where at least six of the eight toys belonged (Cohen, Perlmutter, & Myers, 1977). At this age, children are already memorizing nursery rhymes, commercial jingles, and "Sesame Street" songs with ease and remarkable accuracy.

Bolstered by their increased memory and attention span, toddlers typically engage in a great deal of pretend play, in which they take on a variety of roles. These representational skills—memory, pre-

tense, and the ability to recognize the difference between the image and reality of objects and people—are essential for the acquisition of language.

### Interplay of Cognitive Development and Communication

The development of language is one of the most dramatic changes that occurs in the toddler years. The ability to communicate has important implications for cognitive development. Learning to speak a language involves two separate cognitive tasks: learning to comprehend the meaning of spoken language and learning to speak the language. Both of these tasks begin in infancy. From birth, children start listening to the human voice, and in a matter of months, they understand the meaning of words such as *mama*, *bye-bye*, *bottle*, and *no*. They also start vocalizing and babbling in early infancy, pronouncing their first intelligible word at about the age of one year.

As their language development progresses, children are able to ask questions and communicate their needs and desires.

Once children begin to speak, they acquire language with astonishing speed. By the age of three, they are talking in sentences and already comprehend the meaning of many of the everyday words they will use throughout their lives. They understand and correctly use the basic structure of their native language and correctly apply most of its grammatical rules, no matter how complex the language. If they are read to frequently, most three-year-olds will also begin to understand that the symbols on a printed page stand for spoken words and have meaning. As their language skills expand, children are able to communicate with others—to ask and answer questions, to understand and follow directions, and to request new information about their environment. Their success in communicating encourages language development as well as learning.

### How Language Is Acquired

The acquisition of language by toddlers and young children is truly an amazing achievement. Although many questions remain unanswered, psychologists have proposed a variety of theories to explain how children are able to learn their native language and how language and thought are related.

As you have already read, Piaget and other cognitive theorists have suggested that children must possess certain cognitive skills before they can learn a language. These skills include the ability to think symbolically, to form mental images, and to categorize objects and events. The concept of object permanence also plays a role in language acquisition.

**Behavioral Theorists.** According to B. F. Skinner and other behavioral theorists, language is simply verbal behavior that has been reinforced. Children use words and sentence structure correctly because they are repeatedly rewarded by their parents and others around them for doing so. Gradually, this process of shaping and conditioning transforms children's speech from unintelligible babbling to the language of adults. While behaviorists do describe some of the tasks involved in learning language, their theories cannot explain all the complex aspects of language acquisition. Children's speech is not, in fact, continually reinforced by adults, and children acquire many basic principles of structure and syntax with little or no reinforcement.

Social learning theorists add the concept of imitation to the process of language acquisition. Children hear their parents and others around them speak, and they model their own attempts at speaking on these examples. Parents, for example, normally engage in a great deal of naming behavior with infants and toddlers. This allows children to learn to imitate the sounds their parents make.

**Nativists.** Another school of thought, the *nativist theory* of language acquisition, holds the view that language acquisition is so complex and difficult a task that children must be born with a biological mechanism or propensity for learning language. The linguist Noam Chomsky calls this mechanism the "language acquisition device." He reasons that language must be a function of biology since children all over the world learn language at the same time and in the same sequence, even though they belong to different cultures and learn different languages (Chomsky, 1968). Some nativists believe that children are predisposed to learn language during a specific "sensitive period" between the ages of 18 months and puberty. During this period, children can be expected to learn language in a normal manner. Outside this sensitive period, learning a lan-

## FOCUS ON    **Communicating with Parents**

### Supporting Self-Help Skills

Mrs. Marcus has arrived to pick up her three-year-old daughter, Vicky, from family day care. She waits patiently while Vicky gets ready to leave. Beth, who is in charge of the day care, sees them off.

BETH:  Before you go, Vicky, you need to pick up those blocks you were playing with and put them in the box.

VICKY:  All right. [*Vicky picks up some of the blocks and dumps them in a box in the corner, then returns to her mother.*]

BETH [*ignoring the remaining blocks*]:  Oops, you don't have your shoes on. Vicky, where are your shoes? Can you find your shoes? [*Vicky's shoes are clearly visible in the corner of the playroom, but Mrs. Marcus and Beth do not point to them. Vicky eventually finds her shoes and brings them back to her mother.*]

BETH [*turning to Mrs. Marcus*]:  I try to encourage the children to do things for themselves. I know it takes longer to get ready this way, but in the long run it's good for them—and for us.

MRS. MARCUS [*tying the shoes*]:  I try to let Vicky help where she can. In the morning, I usually

end up dressing her because I'd never get to work otherwise. At least after work, I'm not in such a rush. Vicky, get your coat, dear. [*Vicky goes off to get her coat.*]

BETH:  It's important for parents to make an effort to get their children to do things for themselves. I know some parents who are still dressing their five-year-olds. They say it's faster and simpler that way. I know it's hard for them to watch their children fumble, but the kids are always so proud when they learn a new skill like zipping a coat. [*Vicky has wandered back, dragging her coat.*]

BETH:  Vicky, let's show your mom how fast you can put your coat on. I'll count and you see if you can get it on before I get to five. Ready! Set! Go! [*Vicky gets one arm in the coat and gives up. Beth helps while counting.*] Well, we did it together. Bye; see you tomorrow.

*Do you think the things Beth and Mrs. Marcus expect Vicky to do for herself are appropriate for her age? Were the ways Beth avoided a power struggle over putting away all the blocks and putting on the coat good strategies? How would you have handled the situation?*

guage is more difficult. One famous case that seems to support this theory is that of Genie, a victim of severe child abuse who was kept in isolation and who never heard spoken language until she was 13 years old. Although Genie subsequently learned to speak a primitive form of English, she was never able to use language as fluently as children who learn it as toddlers (Curtiss, 1977). Another observation that seems to support this idea is that children who learn a second language during this sensitive period can achieve fluency fairly easily. As children grow older, it becomes more difficult for them to attain fluency in a second language (John-

son & Newport, 1989; Labov, 1970; Lenneberg, 1967).

**Vygotsky.**    Russian psychologist Lev Vygotsky offered an interesting view on the interaction between thought and language. Vygotsky theorized that cognition and language skills develop separately in infants but that they merge when children are about two years old. From then on, words and thoughts interact and reinforce each other, and the nature of the child's development changes dramatically as a result. Vygotsky observed that small children often talk out loud to themselves while carrying out a task or trying to solve a problem. This overt speech, he believed, helps children integrate their thoughts with their actions. Children's overt speech changes to inner speech as their mastery of the task improves. As their language skills expand, children gain more control over their own behavior (Vygotsky, 1962).

The debate over the relationship of cognition and language continues. Does language depend on cognitive development? Is cognitive development affected by language? While there is still much to be learned, it is clear that cognitive development and language acquisition are interrelated, and both are absolutely necessary for the healthy development of normal children.

### Acquiring Meaning in Language

During the past ten years, a great deal of research has focused on how children learn *semantics*, the meanings of words. Researchers know that from about the age of 18 months, children learn an average of nine new words a day. How do they learn the meaning of so many words so quickly? And how can children distinguish among the different possible meanings for words and assign a particular meaning to a particular word? How, for example, does a toddler know that the word *car* means the vehicle itself and not the road the car is driving on, the person driving the car, or the car's tires?

One researcher, Ellen Markman, believes that children's ideas about the meaning of a new word are constrained in some way so that they screen out most of its possible meanings. One constraint children use is to assume that words refer to whole objects rather than parts of objects. Thus, if an adult points to an object and uses the word *car*, the child assumes the whole object is called car. Markman and others refer to the process of matching words to meanings as *mapping*. By using various constraints to map new words, children eliminate other possible meanings and are able to learn a great number of new words very rapidly. To map words to meanings, children must already be proficient in the cognitive skills of categorization and concept formation (Markman & Hutchinson, 1984).

While toddlers are refining their language skills, they often make errors in word usage. One error involves applying a word to an object outside the

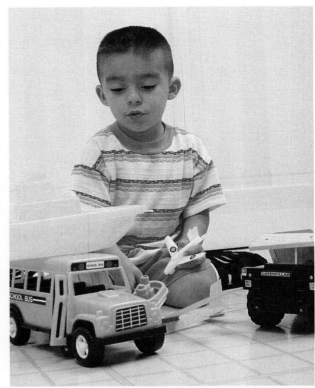

Toddlers often engage in overextension. For example, a child might use the word <u>car</u> to refer to all the vehicles he is playing with—whether they are trucks, buses, or airplanes.

group of objects to which it usually refers. This is called *overextension*. A child may, for example, use the word *car* to refer to other kinds of vehicles, such as trucks, airplanes, and boats. Some psychologists believe that overextension occurs when children understand what an object is but cannot come up with a word for it. To compensate, they produce a word for a similar object or category of objects in an attempt to indicate their understanding. For example, a horse may not be exactly like a dog, but it is a similar kind of four-legged creature; until a child can say the word *horse*, she uses the word *dog* to convey her understanding of four-legged animals. Other theories suggest that overextension is not a language error but rather a reflection of a defect in a child's early conceptual categories. Some children engage in *underextension*, using a word for an object in some circumstances but not in others. In underextension, a child may call her pet a *cat* but will not apply the word to other people's cats or cats at the zoo. Underextension is most commonly used during the slow period of vocabulary growth from ages 12 to 18 months. Overextension is most common at around 18 months of age and becomes less frequent as the child grows older.

## Acquiring Structure in Language

In addition to trying to determine how children learn the meaning of words, researchers are also interested in how children acquire *grammar*, the rules for forming words and sentences. When toddlers first begin to talk, at about one year old, they typically use one word at a time to express their needs or desires. These single-word phrases, called *holophrases*, are usually labels for objects, such as *ball*, or words for actions, such as *more*. They are used to convey a whole sentence worth of meaning. Children may also use holophrases to communicate more than one meaning. They may, for example, use the word *doll* to mean "Look at the doll" or "Give me the doll."

At around 18 months, toddlers begin to use two-word "sentences," such as "Want more" or "Where mama?" or "Cookie gone." Most toddlers start out with a handful of two-word sentence combinations and then gradually add more until they are using several hundred. Such two-word combinations are often called *telegraphic speech* because they employ the fewest words possible to communicate meaning. As children acquire more grammatical rules, they begin to add other elements of speech, such as prepositions and articles, and to communicate more complex meanings and ideas (Brown, 1973).

When toddlers use telegraphic speech, it is clear that they are acquiring the fundamentals of grammar. Even in simple two-word sentences, they put the words in the correct order, saying, "[The] cookie [is] gone" instead of "Gone [is the] cookie." As children add more words to their sentences—"I want more milk," for example—they continue to keep the words in the correct order. This shows that they understand the basic grammatical relationships between words and can express these relationships in their speech. This phenomenon exists not only among children learning English but also among children learning different languages all over the world (Slobin, 1971).

One way to observe how toddlers learn grammar is to look at how they form verbs. In English, chil-

dren must learn the general rule that the past tense of regular verbs is formed by adding *-ed*. They must also learn that the rule does not apply to irregular verbs. Although young children often start out using irregular verb forms correctly, this changes once they learn the *-ed* rule for regular verbs. Then they are likely to apply it to irregular verbs, using *swimmed* for *swam* and *sitted* for *sat*. This tendency to overapply a grammatical rule is called *overregularization*. Toddlers do the same thing with irregular

**TABLE 10.1**
**Milestones of Language Development**

| Age | Milestones |
|---|---|
| 5 to 6 months | Begins to babble or vocalize sounds that echo language of parents and others<br>Uses crying, gestures, and body language to communicate feelings and needs |
| 12 months | Speaks first intelligible word<br>Employs wide variety of sounds, gestures, and nonverbal cues to communicate |
| 12 to 18 months | Uses single words to communicate wants and needs<br>Overgeneralizes the meaning of words to include various items in same category |
| 15 to 24 months | Understands simple questions<br>Has speaking vocabulary of about 50 words<br>Begins using two-word sentences<br>Learns about nine new words a day |
| 24 to 36 months | Has speaking vocabulary of about 200 words<br>Understands about 1,000 words<br>Uses pronouns, prepositions |
| 36 months and older | Begins speaking in longer, grammatically correct sentences<br>Asks questions that reflect understanding of syntax and grammar |

plurals, adding -s to the singular form of a noun, such as *mouse*. Researchers have found that overregularization is less common than was once believed; in any case, the phenomenon tends to disappear as children become more proficient at using spoken language. The foregoing examples do show, however, that even very young children attempt to apply grammatical rules and to formulate mental strategies for making language make sense (Marcus, Pinker, Ullman, Hollander, Rosen, & Xu, 1992).

## The Beginnings of Literacy

Most people think that children don't begin the task of learning how to read until they enter school. But like other cognitive and language skills, the process of learning to read and write begins in the first years of life. The first step in developing literacy occurs when children become aware that printed or written words have meaning, that they stand for objects, actions, and events. At age two, Jeremy is already familiar with books and has some understanding of their function. He recognizes that pictures of dogs and cars are representations of real objects, and he knows that his father is "reading" to him by looking at "symbols" on each page and translating them into words. After a particular book has been read to Jeremy several times, he usually remembers some passages, which he recites along with the reading.

During the toddler years, parents and caregivers begin to familiarize children with the alphabet and the relation of letters to sounds (*D* is for dog) by using alphabet books, rhyming songs, "Sesame Street" scenarios, and other learning aids. Children at this age also learn about printed words from television and advertising. A three-year-old may recognize the Coca-Cola logo and understand that Coca-Cola is a type of soft drink simply because he has observed the logo so often on television or on the side of soda cans (Goodman, 1980).

Children who have frequent encounters with printed words soon come to associate these symbols with meaningful objects in their lives. This visual recognition is enhanced as parents read to their children and use pictures in books to point out and name objects. As toddlers are learning to associate symbols with words—the basis of reading—they are also beginning to learn how to write by scrib-

Caregivers can use books, songs, and toys such as magnetic letters to begin familiarizing toddlers with the alphabet.

bling with crayons. By age three, these scribbles become simple pictures of familiar objects, and still later they become letters of the alphabet. This sequence is similar for children the world over (Kagan, 1981). Such activities help prepare children for literacy long before they enter a classroom.

Another important factor in the development of literacy is the interaction of meaningful experiences with both spoken and written language. Such experiences may include caregivers and children "reading" together, drawing or "writing" together, and other shared activities. Positive experiences of this kind not only facilitate literacy but also encourage cognitive development.

## Implications and Applications

Cognitive development does not occur in isolation. As children's mental abilities develop, so do their bodies, their motor skills, their emotions and sense of self, and their ability to socialize with others. All these developmental processes are interrelated, each influencing and facilitating the growth and development of the others.

The expanding physical, intellectual, and emotional and social capacities of toddlers present par-

## FOCUS ON  Decision Making in Child Care

### Referral of a Child to Special Services

Mira, a caregiver at a suburban day-care center, works with three- and four-year-olds. Over the past few weeks, she has been paying particular attention to a pleasant, well-behaved four-year-old named Peter.

Peter has difficulty expressing himself in sentences or repeating a story in sequence. He tries hard but often cannot focus on the task at hand and follow directions. Physically, Peter is clumsy and less coordinated than most other children his age.

Mira can think of a number of reasons for Peter's apparent developmental delays, including mild mental retardation and an auditory processing problem. Following the guidelines of her center, Mira begins to document the difficulties Peter is having.

Mira also discusses her concerns about Peter with her supervisor, and she shows him her notes. She is eager to refer the child to the county special education early intervention program. However, her supervisor points out that although the center may make a referral, no evaluations can be done without the consent of Peter's parents. He says that the first step is to schedule a conference with the parents.

Meanwhile, Mira collects information on the process of evaluating a child's needs for special services: how the evaluations are performed, the professionals to be consulted, the parents' rights, and the obligations of the county to provide a free education in the least restrictive setting for children with special needs.

At the conference, Mira explains the situation to Peter's parents and gives them specific examples from her observation notes. The supervisor then explains that the parents must give their permission for an evaluation. He tells them that the evaluating team will consist of a psychologist, a specialist in learning disabilities, a speech and language specialist, a social worker, and possibly a physician. He reviews the parents' rights to seek an independent evaluation, to have the purpose of all testing explained to them, and to review the results.

Peter's parents are upset. They argue that all children develop at different rates. Gradually, however, they admit that they have noticed that Peter is a bit behind other four-year-olds, and they agree to support an evaluation.

*Do you think Mira's concerns and actions were appropriate? How much evidence does a caregiver need before approaching parents about a suspected disability? Suppose that Peter's parents had not agreed to the evaluation; do you think Mira and the supervisor should have pursued the matter?*

---

ents and caregivers with a new set of challenges. The nine-month-old infant who was content to sit on the kitchen floor babbling and banging on a pot with a spoon has turned into an energetic three-year-old running around the house or child care center, jumping on furniture, asking an endless stream of questions, learning rhyming songs, playing with friends, and making it clear that she has an opinion about what she is going to wear or what she is going to eat for lunch. Caregivers must respond to a greater range of activities and situations, providing support and guidance while allowing

toddlers to fully develop their emerging skills and abilities.

Along with a growing self-awareness, children between one and three years of age often become very uncooperative and difficult (recall "the terrible twos," discussed in Chapter 9). They seem to say no constantly, and they stubbornly resist suggestions or attempts to persuade or direct them. Although these can be trying times for parents and caregivers, toddlers are simply experimenting with the newfound realization that they are independent beings who can act on the rest of their world. When Jeremy

*Play provides children with opportunities to think symbolically, to socialize with others, and to be creative.*

told his father to read to him and put on his shoes, he was exercising and enjoying his ability to direct and influence his environment.

The emergence of language helps caregivers respond to the challenges of these years. Toddlers can communicate their needs and desires through words instead of physical action, and caregivers can respond appropriately. The ability to communicate also brings one of the great pleasures of the toddler years. Caregivers can now have real conversations with children, answering their questions and telling them about the world. Such conversations provide caregivers with countless opportunities to stimulate the children's cognitive development.

### Toddler's Play

Play is the work of toddlers. According to psychologist Catherine Garvey, *play* is a spontaneous, pleasurable, and voluntary activity that has no practical objective or goal. In other words, play is an activity that children engage in because they want to, not an activity that adults make children perform so that they will learn something. While play may not be

goal oriented, it provides many real benefits. It gives children the opportunity to explore their environment, manipulate objects, and practice new motor skills. Garvey notes that play often involves four steps: exploration, manipulation, practice, and repetition (Garvey, 1977).

Play also provides opportunities for children to think symbolically and form mental representations, as when they engage in pretend or symbolic play. The child who uses a cardboard box for a house or a broomstick for a horse is one whose mind is soaring far beyond the confines of the playroom. Furthermore, play is an important opportunity for socialization. It helps children learn how to interact with others—they begin to learn about sharing and taking turns. When toddlers play together, they talk to one another, and this gives them a chance to practice both their language and social skills.

Another important aspect of play is that it is creative. It stimulates the imagination. Playing with blocks, crayons, paints, and other materials allows children to use their imagination to create works that are theirs alone. Many toys and games help

Appropriate toys for toddlers include large markers and crayons, shape boxes, blocks, dolls, toy tools, and dress-up clothes.

children build on their experiences, solve problems, use symbols, classify objects, construct scripts, and perform other tasks that stimulate cognitive development. A child playing with a shape box, for example, is learning about the size, shape, and color of various objects. A toddler who is playing with an assortment of toy vehicles may be learning their names, their characteristics, and how to categorize them. Parents and caregivers can facilitate such learning experiences by playing along and following the child's lead. Playing along with a child provides an opportunity for the caregiver and child to interact in a meaningful and pleasurable way.

Caregivers must, of course, see that toddlers' playthings are safe and appropriate. For example, toys for children of this age should be large and easy to handle, with no small parts that could be swallowed or lost. Assortments of large crayons, markers, finger paints, and paper are basic equipment for toddler play. Other appropriate toys include shape boxes and similar toys designed to promote cognitive development, as well as plastic and wooden blocks, toy cars and trucks, playhouses, dolls and stuffed animals, and toy versions of appliances, tools, and household equipment. Toddlers especially love to collect things and push things. Among their favorite toys are baby carriages and toy shopping carts that can be filled with dolls, stuffed animals, and other objects and pushed around. Since pretend play is an important activity at this age, a closet or trunk full of hats, shoes, and clothes is useful for dress-up play. Similarly, out-

door play areas and equipment should be safe yet challenging to the toddler and provide the opportunity for exploration (see Chapter 9).

### Providing a Safe and Supportive Environment

Because caregivers play a crucial role in the cognitive development of toddlers, they need to provide a safe and stimulating environment in which toddlers can develop their new capabilities. In addition to providing play areas stocked with appropriate toys and books, caregivers can also introduce children to new environments—through outings to a park, a playground, or a fire station—that stimulate and educate.

The feelings of toddlers are often subject to sudden, wide swings. Providing emotional support is another important responsibility of caregivers. Although dealing with a stubborn, single-minded, unhappy child can be difficult, caregivers must strive to be warm, accepting, patient, and ready to provide assistance and comfort when needed. They should also be ready to convey sincere approval and praise whenever a child has mastered a new skill. Providing emotional support to toddlers and praising them for their accomplishments help build the self-esteem and self-confidence they need to keep on exploring and learning.

### The Role of Adults in Language Development

Children expand their language skills by hearing the people around them speak and then trying to speak themselves. On a typical day, caregivers engage in hundreds of verbal exchanges with toddlers, naming objects, repeating sentences, asking and answering questions, and giving directions. Each of these exchanges is a language lesson for the toddler. Imagine, for example, a conversation between a caregiver and a toddler looking at a picture book of farm animals. "What's that?" the child asks, pointing to an animal. "That's a cow. Cows go, 'Moo,' and give us milk," the caregiver answers. "That?" the child asks about another animal. "That's a horse. People can ride on horses," the caregiver responds. These questions and answers can go on and on. Such exchanges provide a wealth of new information for

### Children at Risk

Some children have specific physical or mental conditions that place them at risk of not reaching their full potential. Other children may be "at risk" because of social or economic circumstances in their lives.

Educators and government agencies often disagree about the best way to help children who are at risk. Some advocate expanded programs for children with special needs and early intervention programs; others emphasize broad social reforms that would address the underlying causes of such special needs. Little agreement exists on the most effective way to fund and implement these programs.

During a meeting of a task force charged with making recommendations about at-risk children to a state department of education, two experts presented their different views on the appropriateness and effectiveness of early intervention programs.

Alice Rosen:

"We need to expand our early intervention programs for children who are at risk. Comprehensive early intervention is the most effective way to help these children. This has been demonstrated by numerous studies. For example, a group of four-year-old children who were born prematurely to low-income families were provided with comprehensive early intervention services; these children scored 15 points higher on IQ tests than a control group of four-year-olds who received no specialized services. It was also found that HIV-positive children showed significant improvement in cognitive, motor, and communication skills after one year of intensive early intervention services.

"The idea of early intervention is not new. The Head Start program is based on the idea that some children need special, intensive assistance to reach their maximum potential. However, early intervention must address more than issues of school readiness to be effective. It needs to focus on how children can be made socially and emotionally competent to cope with the risk factors in their lives.

"As many as one-third of all children in this country may be at risk. The Children's Defense Fund estimates that for every dollar spent on improving preschool education, we will reduce by at least $3 the cost of special education services, crime prevention and punishment, and welfare support funds. As a society, we have a legal and moral obligation to help children who are at risk in the most effective way possible. This means expanding comprehensive early intervention services so that such children become physically and emotionally healthy and are able to fulfill their potential."

John Hsu:

"Studies have shown that if a teacher is given a class of children with average abilities and told that they are exceptionally able students, the quality of the students' work rises. The children fulfill the expectations of the teacher, who unconsciously demands more from children she believes to be above average.

"Early intervention programs for at-risk children are in danger of leading to a similar self-fulfilling prophecy. Because these students are labeled at a very early age as being likely to fail, they often do fail.

"The indicators we use to identify children who are at risk are broad and have more to do with the children's economic and cultural backgrounds than with the children themselves. We will be placing children in programs mainly because of who their parents are and how they live.

"Another problem with early intervention programs is that they tend to be 'one size fits all.' This means that a child who is at risk because of exposure to lead may be treated the same way as a child who is at risk because his mother is on crack.

"What we need are programs that address children's specific needs, based on the type and severity of the factors that cause them to be at risk. I believe that children who are at risk would be better served if we expanded the programs we already have to help children with disabilities.

"Finally, many states allow prereferral intervention for children who are at risk. This means that children go into intervention programs before they receive a professional evaluation of their needs. The practice of prereferral intervention runs the risk of inappropriate labeling of children on the basis of superficial factors such as race or economic status. I believe that we do more harm than good by labeling these children through special early intervention programs."

*Overall, do you think that early intervention programs are helpful or harmful or a combination of both? Why? How do you think these programs should be funded? Who should decide which children are considered to be at risk?*

children and encourage them to ask more questions so that they can gather additional information.

These kinds of exchanges also help children develop scripts and form and refine cognitive categories so that they can better understand what they have learned. Lev Vygotsky called this process of building on a child's experiences to provide new information *scaffolding*. He believed that children need scaffolding from parents and other adults in order to learn (Vygotsky, 1978).

Most experts agree that no formal teaching needs to take place during the toddler years. Paraphernalia such as workbooks and flash cards are not needed or desirable. Toddlers learn much more efficiently simply by having the opportunity to converse with adults and older children and by having adult examples to imitate. Parents and other caregivers need to be sensitive to toddlers' abilities and limitations. In responding to questions, it's best to use short, simple sentences and avoid overloading the child with information. Caregivers should also take care not to correct a toddler's language errors directly. If a child says, "I sitted in the chair," it is helpful for an adult to respond by rephrasing the words correctly: "Yes, you sat in the chair." Such positive restatements provide children with the correct information they need without criticizing them or making them feel that they have failed in some way.

Because reading is an important language activity of the toddler years, caregivers should get in the habit of reading to toddlers every day. The children should be allowed to participate in the reading and to interrupt to look at the pictures, ask questions, or repeat phrases. They should have a wide variety of books to choose from, and they should be allowed to decide what story they want to hear. Caregivers can make group story times more lively by incorporating puppets, games, songs, and other activities. This may also help keep children's interest longer at an age when their attention span is still fairly short. These early reading experiences play an important role in helping children develop literacy competence.

Although children acquire cognitive and language skills in a relatively set sequence and according to a fairly set timetable, individual children can vary enormously in the rate at which they learn particular skills. Caregivers should keep this fact in mind when providing opportunities for cognitive and language development. Caregivers must also remember that children are developing physically, emotionally, and socially at the same time. No one area should be overemphasized at the expense of the others. By providing toddlers with a variety of opportunities and experiences, parents and other caregivers are giving toddlers the freedom to grow in all these areas.

## SUMMARY

- Toddlerhood, the period from ages one to three, marks the transition from sensorimotor learning to other kinds of thinking. The cognitive skills of toddlers enable them to think through solutions to problems and learn to understand and use language.

- Piaget called the period from 12 to 18 months substage 5, the tertiary circular reaction stage. During this stage, toddlers begin to apply what they have already learned to new situations. They use objects in new ways. They begin to understand causal relationships and make greater use of schemes.

- In substage 6, from 18 months to two years, children begin to use symbolic thought to solve problems. They have a greater understanding of object permanence and of concepts of time. Deferred imitation, symbolic play, and mental combination appear during this substage.

- According to Piaget, substage 6 marks the end of the sensorimotor period. At about the age of two, children enter the preoperational stage. Their cognitive abilities expand, and they learn how to use language.

- According to Nelson, children develop concepts by categorizing information and constructing mental scripts. Their improved memory enables them to retain information over longer periods. They engage in pretend play and are able to distinguish between an object and the symbol for it.

- There are various theories about the relationship between cognitive development and language acquisition. Piaget believed that children must learn to think symbolically before they can acquire language. Nativists assert that the ability to learn language is inborn; according to Vygotsky, language and cognition develop separately and later merge.

- Children may learn the meanings of words by mapping and categorization. They seem to understand that language follows certain rules, and they look for and follow the rules as they learn how to form words and sentences.

- The first step in developing literacy occurs when children become aware that printed or written words have meaning and that they represent objects, actions, or events.

- Adults play several important roles in helping toddlers develop cognition and language skills. They provide a safe and stimulating environment, emotional support, and opportunities for play.

- Play is very important for cognitive development because it gives children the opportunity to explore their environment, develop social skills, be creative, and think symbolically.

- Verbal exchanges between children and adults are important in language acquisition, providing critical information about language and concepts. Reading to children is an important activity for helping them develop literacy competence.

## BUILDING VOCABULARY

Write a definition for each vocabulary term listed below.

concept
deferred imitation
egocentric thinker
global concept
grammar
holophrase
mapping
mental combination
nativist theory

overextension
overregularization
play
scaffolding
script
semantics
symbolic play
telegraphic speech
underextension

## ACQUIRING KNOWLEDGE

1. How does the role of sensorimotor learning change from infancy to toddlerhood?
2. How does the pace of toddlers' cognitive development compare across cultures?
3. At what age do most children go through Piaget's tertiary circular reaction phase?
4. Name two cognitive abilities that develop during Piaget's substage 6, between 18 months and two years.
5. What is deferred imitation and what enables a child to perform it?
6. Give two examples of a toddler's symbolic play.
7. How does Piaget refer to a child's ability to hold two or more representations of an object in mind at the same time?
8. In what way is a toddler's thinking egocentric?
9. How do toddlers use global concepts to help them learn about new objects?
10. Give an example of a characteristic that toddlers use to classify objects.
11. What purpose do scripts serve for young children?
12. Give an example of a toddler's play behavior that depends upon the use of memory.
13. What are the two cognitive tasks involved in learning a language?
14. At what age do children usually speak their first words?
15. Name one cognitive skill that a child must possess in order to learn a language.
16. What is the "sensitive period" of language acquisition and how does it affect the child's ability to learn language?
17. How does mapping help a child learn the meaning of a new word?
18. What common error in word usage is a child making when she uses the word *apple* to refer to other fruits, such as oranges, peaches, and pears?
19. How do holophrases differ from other single words?
20. In what sense is a child's early speech "telegraphic?"

21. What common error in word formation results in a child saying "runned" rather than "ran" or "gooses" rather than "geese"?
22. Describe an activity that prepares toddlers for literacy before they begin to read.
23. According to Catherine Garvey, what are the four steps involved in play?
24. Give an example of a toy that would help a child develop the skill of classifying objects.
25. Toddlers need to have self-confidence to explore and to learn. What can caregivers do to help build toddlers' self-confidence?
26. Give an example of a toy or game that would help a child construct scripts.
27. Name two typical caregiver-toddler verbal exchanges that help the toddler learn to speak.

## THINKING CRITICALLY

1. Describe the ways in which a toddler might play with a set of wooden blocks and the cognitive skills that could be developed through each type of play.
2. In your opinion, what are the advantages or disadvantages of trying to teach toddlers the alphabet as soon as they begin to speak? Do you think this would have an effect on the children's future literacy? Would you recommend such a practice? Why or why not?
3. How might a caregiver use mealtime as an opportunity to facilitate a toddler's cognitive development? What learning activities could be incorporated and which cognitive skills would they reinforce?
4. Give examples of what a child might say at various stages of toddlerhood to indicate that he has dropped his teddy bear and would like someone to pick it up. Include in your examples a holophrase, an example of telegraphic speech, a complete sentence, and an example of either overextension or overregularization.
5. Choose one of the following groups of theorists and give their explanation of the process by which a toddler learns to say "bye-bye": cognitive theorists, behavioral theorists, social learning theorists, nativists, and followers of Vygotsky.

## OBSERVATIONS AND APPLICATIONS

1. Observe a group of three-year-olds playing dress-up, house, superhero, or some other activity involving symbolic play. Describe aspects of their play that are imitative of behavior they have probably observed either firsthand or on television. Do the children include any activities that are not dependent on behavior they have observed? Describe any interesting uses of objects. For example, caregivers who ban toy guns often find children constructing them out of any number of objects. Make note of the verbal interactions among the children. Note how an activity begins. Does one child suggest an activity and others join in? Does the activity change as the children play? If so, in what ways?

2. Observe the verbal interactions between a two-year-old and an adult. Describe the child's use of language. Note examples of when the adult uses language to inform, to expand the child's verbal expressions, and simply to converse. Does the adult use simple sentences? How does the adult respond when the child makes a language "error"? Describe the child's errors. What happens when the adult does not understand what the child is trying to communicate? Does the child respond to the adult as well as initiate verbal interactions?

3. The father of 18-month-old Jorge tells you he thinks he should spend more time reading to his son. However, Jorge has a short attention span and does not like to sit still for very long. He asks your advice. What would you suggest that Jorge's father do to encourage the literacy development of his son?

4. Tasha is a two-year-old girl. Tasha's mother does not want to push her to read before she is ready, but she does want to help her daughter develop language and cognitive skills. What can Tasha's mother do to help her daughter develop these skills besides read and talk to her?

## SUGGESTIONS FOR FURTHER READING

Brown, R. (1973). *A first language: The early stages*. Cambridge, MA: Harvard University Press.

Butler, D. (1982). *Babies need books: How to share the joy of reading with your child*. New York: Penguin Books.

Curtiss, S. (1977). *Genie: A psycholinguistic study of a modern-day "wild child."* New York: Academic Press.

Fenichel, E. S., & Eggbeer, L. (1990). *Preparing practitioners to work with infants, toddlers, and their families: Issues and recommendations for the professions*. Arlington, VA: ZERO TO THREE/National Center for Clinical Infant Programs.

Forman, G. E., & Kuschner, D. S. (1983). *The child's construction of knowledge: Piaget for teaching children*. Washington, DC: National Association for the Education of Young Children.

Garvey, C. (1984). *Children's talk*. Cambridge, MA: Harvard University Press.

Gottfried, A. W. (Ed.). (1984). *Home environment and early cognitive development*. New York: Academic Press.

Johnson, J. E., Christie, J. F., & Yawkey, T. D. (1987). *Play and early childhood development*. Glenview, IL: Scott, Foresman.

Kimmell, M. M., & Segal, E. (1988). *For reading out loud! A guide to sharing books with children*. New York: Delacorte.

Oppenheim, J. F. (1987). *Buy me, buy me! The Bank Street guide to choosing toys for children*. New York: Pantheon.

White, B. L. (1990). *The first three years of life* (new rev. ed.). New York: Prentice Hall Press.

## OBJECTIVES

Studying this chapter will enable
you to

- Describe the theories of Erikson
  and Mahler in relation to the social
  and emotional development of
  toddlers.
- Discuss the development of a
  sense of self in toddlers.
- Describe how awareness of others
  changes during the toddler years.
- Discuss the emergence of
  prosocial behavior in toddlers.
- Explain the concept of social
  referencing and discuss its role in
  the emotional development of
  toddlers.

TABATHA, a 24-month-old, is playing with a puzzle. Whenever she gets a piece to fit, she smiles broadly, throws her arms up into the air, and claps. Her mother, who is sitting nearby, looks over from time to time and smiles. Tabatha continues working on the puzzle until there are a few pieces left that she cannot put in place. She makes one more attempt at fitting the pieces in and then becomes completely frustrated. She starts to push the whole puzzle off the table. Tabatha's mother sees what she is doing and sternly tells the toddler to stop. Tabatha reacts by smiling sheepishly. She then looks away from her mother and nervously fingers her lips.

This sequence of events would never occur with a young infant. An infant does not have a good sense of right and wrong or of appropriate behavior. But during the toddler years, some important changes take place. Children of this age become increasingly aware of other people's points of view and of the things that they should and should not do. At the same time, their interactions with others grow more complex.

Toddlers are trying to set out on their own, to do things by themselves. Yet their abilities are still quite limited, so they must often turn to others for help. Toddlers are no longer babies, but they have not reached the level of autonomy of preschoolers. This chapter focuses on toddlers' emotional development and the social development that goes along with it.

## Theories of Social Personality Development

Infants are very dependent on others. Between the ages of one and three, however, children become increasingly independent individuals. The toddler struggles with his need for nurturance, support, and guidance from his parents, on the one hand, and his desire to do things by himself, on the other. This theme is echoed in the most prominent theories of social/personality development during toddlerhood, including those of Erik Erikson and Margaret Mahler.

### Erikson's Theory

Erik Erikson's theory has been one of the most influential psychoanalytic theories of development. Erikson studied with Sigmund Freud's daughter, Anna, and was very much influenced by the work of both theorists. However, he went well beyond their theories, moving the study of children from the Freuds' emphasis on thought and analysis to an emphasis on observable behavior. Rather than focusing on elaborate events theoretically occurring inside children's minds, Erikson places the child squarely within the social environment. He believes that throughout life each individual is continually struggling with important, two-sided issues. An individual's personality is formed through the resolution of those struggles.

*Toddlers seem to feel a real sense of accomplishment when they succeed in doing things on their own.*

According to Erikson, during the first year of life infants struggle to develop a sense of trust, that is, a sense that they can rely on others to take care of them and support their development. At times, infants have feelings of mistrust. When they are hungry and cry, for example, it may take a while before someone feeds them. Sometimes, even when a caregiver is present, they may experience pain or discomfort, such as when getting an inoculation. The desirable environment for an infant is one in which trust predominates. When she needs food, food is provided quickly. When she is with a parent, there is usually no pain. These positive experiences help the typical infant develop a sense that the world is good and that she can trust others to be there for her.

Once children have a basic sense of trust in others, they are able to develop the confidence to try things on their own. If they do not develop this basic trust, however, they will be more restricted in their behavior, feeling too strong a need to cling to their parents to get support when they need it. Children who have not developed a basic sense of trust will not be able to move fully into the toddler stage, with its central theme of autonomy.

During the second year of life, as toddlers become more sure of themselves, they begin to move

## Toys That Affirm Diversity

Children need positive images of themselves to grow up emotionally healthy. Many images children have of themselves develop through play. Providing toys that reflect a variety of ethnic groups expands children's visions of themselves and others and builds self-esteem.

Ethnically accurate action figures and dolls come in a variety of skin tones, and their facial features and hair are sculpted to reflect their racial identity. Often the dress of these figures reflects their cultural heritage. Their presence in a child care setting conveys positive messages of self-worth.

Even in child care settings with little racial diversity, it is important to provide dolls and action figures that represent a variety of ethnicities. In the United States, 37 percent of children under age ten are children of color. Today's children will live and work with many people different from themselves. Affirming the worth of all people through play helps establish a basis for understanding and accepting diversity.

outward into the world, trying things on their own and exploring their environment. Such exploration invariably leads toddlers to do things that others find undesirable. For example, when Tabatha started to push the puzzle off the table, her mother told her to stop. Toddlers are often corrected, told no, and punished in some way for doing things that adults or others find undesirable. This creates in toddlers a feeling of shame for the "bad" things they have done and doubt in their ability to do things. These feelings of shame and doubt come into conflict with their developing sense of autonomy.

This conflict is evident when toddlers are learning to use the toilet. Like Freud, Erikson believes that toilet training is an important experience for toddlers. As they learn to control their bodily functions, toddlers struggle with the conflict between a desire for autonomy and the sense of shame they feel when they defecate or urinate in "the wrong place." Toddlers often display negative reactions when they have "accidents" and positive reactions when they have used the toilet successfully. They seem to feel a sense of accomplishment when they go to the bathroom properly. When toddlers wet their pants, however, they may cower and cry and appear to be ashamed.

Erikson goes well beyond the toilet-training situation in his discussion of autonomy versus shame

during the toddler years. For him, toddlerhood is a time when children are trying to do a great many things, and they struggle with feelings of shame and doubt when they don't succeed. A toddler who is trying to build a tower of blocks is likely to become distressed when the tower falls down. A toddler who is trying to express himself in words may become upset when others cannot understand him (Erikson, 1963). Recent research has supported Erikson's belief that toddlers are concerned with doing things "right." Before reviewing that research however, it will be useful to consider another important theory of social/personality development.

### Mahler's Theory

Margaret Mahler is another psychoanalytic thinker who has focused attention on infancy and toddlerhood. Her theory of social/personality development has been very influential among clinical psychologists, especially those working with children. Like Erikson, Mahler emphasizes the child's interactions with the social world. Mahler, however, presents a more detailed portrait of development during toddlerhood, highlighting the growth of the child's sense of self and other. Mahler sees the toddler as struggling with dependence on and attachment to her mother and a desire to explore the world and other people at the same time. For example, the typical toddler entering child care for the first time is torn between an interest in the new toys and children and a longing to be with her mother.

According to Mahler, the personality development of infants is built on both their relationship with their mother and their ability to become individual beings separate from their mother. She says that between the ages of about five months and two or three years, children gradually develop a separate sense of self and other—a process Mahler calls *separation-individuation*. She emphasizes the ability to be separate from the mother psychologically as well as physically. Mahler goes on to describe four subphases of separation-individuation from the mother: differentiation, practicing, rapprochement, and object constancy (Mahler, 1968).

**Differentiation.**    According to Mahler, infants learn to distinguish their mother from others and then to prefer her to others from about the age of five to ten months. (As you may recall from Chapter 8, some research suggests that infants can distinguish their mother from others at an even earlier age.) Starting sometime within the first few months, an infant is comforted more easily by his mother than by others, he smiles more readily at his mother than at others, and he shows a preference for her in a number of other ways.

**Practicing.**    Beginning at about 10 to 12 months of age, with the onset of skillful crawling or walking, toddlers enter the practicing subphase, which lasts until about 16 to 18 months of age. During this phase, children's crawling or walking takes them away from their mother, and this helps teach them about their mother's separateness. They learn to say, "Mama," and to think of their mother when she is gone. Children in this stage explore in their mother's presence, checking back with her periodically.

**Rapprochement.**    During the rapprochement phase, which begins at around 15 months of age and continues to about 22 months, toddlers become more concerned about their mother's absence and also the presence of strangers. Toddlers seem to be torn between their desire for autonomy and their desire to be reunited with their mother. At this stage, they begin to understand that their needs and the

According to Mahler, children between 10 and 18 months of age begin to "practice" their independence by playing alone but checking back with their mother periodically.

needs of their mother may sometimes conflict. They want their mother to love them, and this motivates them to try to do what they are supposed to do.

**Object Constancy.**    Starting at about two years of age and continuing to about three, toddlers become able to think about their mother as someone whom they feel strongly about. They form a mental image of their mother and attach these strong feelings to that image. Children at this stage can separate from their mother more easily by keeping an image of her in their mind. The ability to maintain this image is called *object constancy*.

### Common Threads

There are several common threads in the theories of Mahler and Erikson. Both theories suggest that although toddlers are striving for autonomy, they are still quite dependent on others. Both also view the toddler years as a time when children are beginning to learn right from wrong and are trying to behave appropriately. However, the two theories focus on different areas. Mahler emphasizes the role of the mother and the role of the child's understanding of self and other. Erikson, on the other hand, highlights the child's feelings of shame and doubt.

Bowlby and other theorists believe that a child comes to know herself from the way others treat her. If parents are loving toward the child, the child will see herself as lovable.

Mahler's ideas bear a certain similarity to those of John Bowlby (see Chapter 8 for a discussion of his theory of attachment). Both theorists believe that infants show a strong preference for a special person (usually the mother) by the end of the first half-year of life. Moreover, Bowlby's final attachment phase and Mahler's rapprochement stage both deal with the child's learning that the mother/attachment figure has needs that may differ from those of the child. (Bowlby's final stage occurs at around 24 to 36 months of age, somewhat later than Mahler's rapprochement period.)

## Increasing Awareness of Self and Other

Many current researchers and theorists agree with Mahler that the toddler years are a period of tremendous development in the understanding of self and of the notion of other. While an infant may see and react to "the baby" in the mirror, a toddler begins to recognize that she is the baby in the mirror. An infant cries because she is hungry, but a toddler begins to talk about why she or other people are crying. Whereas an infant is happy when she gets something she wants and frustrated when she does not, a toddler is starting to recognize that she can get some things but not all things, and she knows when to persist and when to give up.

Some theorists assume that the development of self and the awareness of other occur simultaneously. They hold that the child learns that he is both separate from his mother and different and thus develops senses of self and other (Mahler, 1968). Other theorists believe that the understanding of self develops before the understanding of other. There are elements of truth in both points of view.

### Theories of Self and Other

How people come to know themselves is an issue that has intrigued philosophers and social scientists for centuries. According to theorists such as James Mark Baldwin (1897), Charles Horton Cooley (1902), and George Herbert Mead (1925), interactions with other people are crucial to the development of a

### Talking to a Jealous Parent

Beverly provides family day care in her home for four children. Christine Wilson, a four-year-old, arrives every day at around 7:00 A.M. and is the first child to leave when her mother, a single parent, picks her up at about 5:00 P.M.

Lately, Christine has fussed about going home when her mother comes for her. Her mother is both embarrassed and annoyed that Christine is not eager to go home. Although she thinks Beverly is an excellent caregiver, Ms. Wilson worries because Christine spends so much time in child care. Today is no exception.

MS. WILSON:  Hi, Chris. How's my girl? Are you ready to go?

CHRISTINE:  No. I'm playing. I want to stay.

MS. WILSON [*annoyed*]:  Chris, you don't mean that. It's time to go home. I've missed you all day. You'll see your friends tomorrow.

BEVERLY [*enthusiastically*]:  Christine had so much fun today. We had a picnic on the floor at snack time with all the stuffed animals.

CHRISTINE [*turning away from her mother and continuing to play*]:  Why do I have to go? We're playing puzzles.

MS. WILSON [*angrily*]:  Christine, it's time to go home.

MS. WILSON [*to Beverly*]:  I don't know what's gotten into her. You'd think she never had any fun at home.

BEVERLY:  She tells me all about the things you do at home. Today she told me that you're going to visit her cousin this weekend. Right now she's just having trouble making a transition. A lot of kids find it hard to stop playing and leave, especially when their friends are still here.

MS. WILSON [*tensely*]:  She could seem a little happier to see me. I rush from work and get here as soon as I can.

BEVERLY:  You're the most important person in her life. Remember the day your car broke down and you were late? When Willie's mom came to get him and you weren't here yet, Christine started fussing and worrying. Every two seconds she asked me when you were coming.

MS. WILSON:  I wish I could find a job with a shorter commute so she didn't have to be here so long. Come on Chris, it's time to go home with Mommy.

*Many times parents do not state clearly what is bothering them. What were Ms. Wilson's unspoken concerns? Did Beverly recognize these concerns and respond to them? Could Beverly have said or done something different to ease the situation?*

sense of self. Cooley used a colorful metaphor—the *looking-glass self*—to capture the importance of the other in the development of a sense of self. According to this way of thinking, individuals mirror what other people think about them as expressed through these other peoples' reactions, talk, body language, and so on. For example, if people treat a child as though she is extremely intelligent and tell her she is extremely intelligent, then the child is likely to form an image of herself as extremely intelligent. If people react to a toddler as capable or lov-ing (or both), then the child should come to view herself as capable or loving. The child's interactions with others do not merely teach her that she is separate from them; they also teach her what her separate self is like.

Bowlby acknowledges these two roles of the other in his concept of "working models." He believes that an infant uses her experiences with attachment figures to build mental models of the other and the self simultaneously. The model of the other is based on how the other treats her. For example, if the attachment figure always seems to be there when needed, the infant comes to view the attachment figure as good and helpful. The attachment figure's actions also communicate something important to the infant about herself. If the parent loves the child, the child sees herself as lovable.

In most theories of development of the self, the other is extremely important. But until quite recently, there was very little research on the development of an understanding of self during toddlerhood and almost no research on the development of an understanding of other. Many researchers and theorists in past decades assumed that infants and toddlers were much too young to have developed a concept of self and certainly had no concept of other.

One reason for this assumption was the influence of Piaget. His theory of development states that even four- and five-year-old children are unable to distinguish their point of view from that of another. According to Piaget, the infant learns about the world by acting upon it. At first, she only knows her own actions and does not understand that objects and other people are separate from her own behavior; the infant is thus said to be egocentric. At about 6 months of age, the infant begins to distinguish objects from her own actions, but it is only at 12 months that the child truly distinguishes those objects from her own actions and at 18 to 24 months that she can think about objects (Piaget, 1952, 1954). Even so, the child's thinking is still egocentric; she knows only her own point of view and her own experiences. The infant knows the world in terms of her own actions but does not realize that those actions are hers; the toddler or preschooler doesn't really understand her own perspective because she cannot see that it is a particular perspective different from that of others.

Piaget's description of the development of self and other suggests that toddlers should be able to talk about and think about the world as they see it. But they are too young to realize that their view is different from that of others. In any event, they would not really know who they are or who others are. Research suggests otherwise. There is evidence indicating that certain aspects of the understanding of other precede certain aspects of the understanding of self and vice versa (Pipp, Fischer, & Jennings, 1987).

## Awareness of Self

The development of a sense of self involves a growing awareness on several fronts. In becoming more aware of themselves, toddlers also become more aware of such things as their feelings, their physical features, their abilities, their independence, and certain recognized standards of behavior.

**Awareness of Own Feelings.** Toddlers begin to talk about their own feelings almost as soon as they begin putting words together. By about 20 months of age, toddlers are able to talk about pain, distress, disgust, affection, and even moral conformity, using such words as *hurt*, *cry*, *yucky*, *love*, and *bad*. By 28 months, they have developed a remarkably rich vocabulary of words to describe how they feel (Bretherton, Fritz, Zahn-Waxler, & Ridgeway, 1986). This emerging vocabulary can be an enormous help to the parents and teachers of toddlers in that it allows toddlers to communicate their needs. Moreover, it also suggests that they are learning quite a bit about themselves and how they feel.

**Visual Recognition.** During the toddler years, children begin to know what they, as individuals, look like. From sometime during their second year, toddlers can visually recognize their own facial features and can identify themselves in pictures and in mirrors (Lewis & Brooks-Gunn, 1979; Pipp et al., 1987). Although young infants enjoy looking in mirrors, they do not seem to realize that they are looking at themselves. They do, however, begin to see that when they move, "the baby in the mirror" also moves (Lewis & Brooks-Gunn, 1979). Parents often place infants in front of mirrors and tell them who it is they see, but children do not learn that they are "the baby in the mirror" until the toddler years.

In research studies, children's ability to recognize themselves, their *self-recognition*, is typically measured by having mothers unobtrusively put rouge on their children's nose and then place the children in front of a mirror. If the toddlers rub their nose while looking in the mirror, it is assumed that they know that their nose is not usually red and that they are looking at themselves in the mirror. Toddlers who recognize themselves are more likely to show self-conscious or embarrassed behavior

By the age of two, most toddlers are able to recognize their own facial features in a mirror.

when asked to perform in front of others or when they see themselves in the mirror (Lewis, Sullivan, Stanger, & Weiss, 1989). Some psychologists draw a connection between toddlers' ability to recognize themselves in a mirror and their ability to become embarrassed, ashamed, and guilty, as well as their ability to feel empathy for others (Lewis et al., 1989).

**Awareness of Abilities.**    Throughout the second and third years of life and beyond, toddlers become increasingly aware of their own abilities. Infants have some sense that they are not always able to get what they want (such as making a toy work), but they do not seem to be able to anticipate that a particular task is too difficult for them.

During the toddler years, children become increasingly aware of which tasks they can and can-

not accomplish. By 12 or 15 months of age, they persevere longer at tasks that they have a reasonable chance of accomplishing than at more difficult ones. At 24 months, toddlers have a greater awareness of self. They are even less likely to persevere in tasks that are too difficult for them, and they are less likely to smile during those extremely difficult tasks. By about 36 months, toddlers also persist less at tasks that are too easy (Barrett, Morgan, & Maslin-Cole, 1993).

**Wanting to "Do It Themselves."**    Although toddlers are increasingly aware of their abilities and less likely to persist at tasks that are too difficult for them, they often are unwilling to accept help from others. Toddlers often want to do things themselves, even when they are unable to achieve their goal. This desire to accomplish things on their own is viewed as an important feature of mastery and achievement motivation (Geppert & Kuster, 1983). Toddlers who try things on their own become more oriented toward independent mastery instead of allowing others to solve a problem for them. They also get a better sense of what tasks they can and cannot achieve by themselves, and this knowledge serves as motivation. Toddlers (as well as their parents and teachers) may become extremely frustrated when they insist on doing tasks that are too difficult by themselves. Eventually, however, a proper balance is reached between their desire for autonomy and the recognition of a need for help. As toddlers develop a better sense of what they can do, they often allow others to help when it is truly necessary.

**Awareness of Standards for Behavior.** During the toddler years, children begin to recognize *standards of behavior*, the things that they should and should not do. For example, they will begin to describe themselves—or others—as "good" when they adhere to a rule or "bad" when they break a rule. This sense of standards is important to the development of the self because only after such standards are learned can toddlers learn to regulate their own behavior. Most researchers and theorists consider this *self-regulation* an important aspect of the self.

The process of learning standards of behavior begins quite early. By the end of their first year, children will change their behavior in response to a negative adult reaction. Research has shown, for example, that infants will stop approaching a strange-looking toy or a ledge if their parents appear frightened (see Klinnert, Campos, Sorce, Emde, & Svejda, 1983). At this age, infants almost never follow a rule spontaneously (Barrett, MacPhee, & Sullivan, 1992). Rather, they respond to the reactions of others around them.

During the second and third years of life, toddlers learn even more about what they should and should not do. They learn to comply with the requests of others and to regulate their own behavior. By the time they are 17 months old, most children spontaneously follow some social rules, such as sharing. Parents provide cues by reacting more positively when a rule is followed than when it is broken (Barrett, 1993). By about this same age, children may even stop themselves before they do something "wrong." For example, as they reach for an

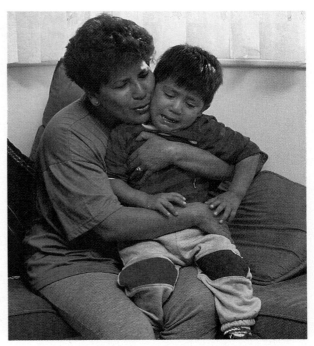

Toddlers may become frustrated when they insist on doing difficult tasks by themselves.

electrical outlet, they may shake their head, signifying no (Kopp, 1982).

Parents play a major role in shaping their children's standards of behavior. They correct toddlers' behavior frequently—on the average of once every five or six minutes (Lytton, 1976; Power & Chapieski, 1986). And they react with positive emotion when children do something right (Barrett, 1993; Stipek, Recchia, & McClintic, 1992). If parents allow toddlers some ability to control what they do but also give clear rules and explanations regarding what they are not allowed to do, the children are more likely to comply with the rules and less likely to defy them (Crockenberg & Litman, 1990; Maccoby & Martin, 1983).

## Awareness of Others

By the end of the toddler years, children know quite a bit about themselves and how they should act. But what about their awareness of others? Until fairly recently, it was assumed that toddlers, and

## FOCUS ON       Decision Making in Child Care

### Toddlers Who Bite

Mark is a caregiver for a group of toddlers at a large urban child care center. Several times in the past two weeks, Ramon, a 20-month-old in Mark's group, had bitten another child.

Mark spoke sharply to Ramon and isolated him after each biting incident, but this was not effective in ending the biting. Parents of the other children were extremely concerned and asked that Ramon be removed from the group if he continued to bite.

After talking to other caregivers and reading about the causes of biting, Mark realized that Ramon's biting occurred only during afternoon free play, when he was tired and frustrated. Mark developed a plan to reduce or eliminate the situations in which Ramon was most likely to bite.

First Mark made sure that when free play began Ramon was settled into an activity with a toy he enjoyed. As Ramon moved around the room, Mark watched him closely. When Ramon seemed to become overly excited or frustrated, Mark stepped in and redirected him to a quieter activity.

If Ramon and another child were in conflict over a particular toy, Mark quickly moved to Ramon's side and told him to use words to tell the other child how he felt. Although Ramon's "words" were often screams, Mark praised him for using his voice to express himself. When conflict over a toy occurred, Mark found it easier to redirect both children to other activities rather than try to work out equitable sharing, a concept that the toddlers did not understand.

Keeping track of Ramon was difficult and took away from the time Mark needed to spend with other children. Since the center uses high school volunteers several times a week, Mark requested that one of them be assigned to his free play period to assist in monitoring Ramon.

Several times Mark and the volunteer intervened just as Ramon was about to bite. When this happened, they spoke sharply to him, emphasizing that biting hurt and was not allowed behavior, and then separated him briefly from the other children.

Ramon continued to try to bite during free play. The amount of individual attention needed to keep him from biting seriously interfered with supervision of the rest of the group. Finally, Mark recommended that Ramon be transferred to a different, smaller group of slightly older toddlers. He hoped that the group's smaller size, different group dynamics, and the older children's behavior would discourage Ramon's biting habit.

*Did Mark handle this situation effectively? Are there other solutions he might have tried before transferring Ramon?*

even preschoolers, are unable to understand another person's point of view. According to Piaget, young children are not capable of seeing something from another person's spatial perspective. He used the three-mountain experiment, discussed in Chapter 1, to demonstrate his theory. In the past decade or so, however, research has shown that even toddlers have some understanding of other points of view. In fact, they must have some awareness of others' feelings because they label those feelings and even attempt to comfort hurt loved ones.

**Awareness of Others' Feelings.**     By the time toddlers are about 18 or 20 months old, many begin to talk about the feelings of other people. By about 30 months, most of them use at least some words with emotional implications to describe other people. They may talk about others as being happy, having fun, liking or loving, being good, being sad, being bad, being scared, being mad, and so on. Toddlers not only label other people's feelings, but they can also talk about the reasons for those feelings. For example, a child may say that his mother is angry because he did something naughty or happy because he hugged her (Bretherton et al., 1986).

Toddlers also respond to other people's feelings. When someone is unhappy, a toddler may try to comfort the individual (Zahn-Waxler, Radke-Yarrow, & King, 1979; Zahn-Waxler, Radke-Yarrow, Wagner, & Chapman, 1992). The toddler's attempt to respond often involves offering things that would comfort the toddler rather than the person who is unhappy. The toddler may, for example, offer her favorite teddy bear or recruit her mother to help. Nevertheless, the fact that toddlers try to comfort others suggests that they have some understanding that others need comfort.

**Visual Recognition of Others.** The growing awareness of others during the toddler years extends to visual recognition. Toddlers can recognize and point out their mother's and father's facial features. In fact, they are able to recognize their parents' facial features even earlier than they can recognize their own, and they become increasingly aware of their parents' physical characteristics throughout toddlerhood (Pipp et al., 1987). Recognition of one's own facial features is often considered the hallmark of toddlers' understanding of self during this period.

### Awareness of Gender Differences

One important aspect of self and other is gender. By about two or three years of age, toddlers can say who is male and who is female. To some extent, they can even distinguish objects that males and females would be most likely to use. They can say, for example, that a man is more likely to use a hammer and a woman is more likely to use a broom. At this stage, their distinction between male and female is based mainly on physical characteristics, such as the length of a person's hair or the clothes the person wears. Moreover, toddlers do not realize that gender is stable, that someone who is female today will always be female (Huston, 1983; Kohlberg, 1966). A three-year-old girl may say that she wants to grow up to be a daddy or even that she wants to grow up to be her daddy.

Young toddlers are not yet highly gender-role stereotyped in their behavior. Although they show some preference for traditionally considered gender-

Most three-year-olds show a clear preference for what are traditionally considered gender-appropriate toys.

appropriate toys, male toddlers may happily play with dolls, and female toddlers may enjoy playing with trucks. Quite often, however, toddlers are not given the opportunity to play with "inappropriate" toys. Some parents may not even consider buying a doll for their son or a punching bag for their daughter. In addition, children at this age are exposed to both obvious and subtle messages from advertisements, adults, and other children telling them which toys are good for boys and which are good for girls. By three years of age, most children clearly prefer toys and activities that have traditionally been considered appropriate for their particular gender.

### Interaction with Peers

All the material reviewed so far shows that despite their young age, toddlers are remarkably aware of both their own and other people's behavior. It is not surprising, then, that toddlers enjoy playing with other toddlers. Recent evidence suggests that even

## Gender Stereotyping

Marta and Diane are to be coteachers for a class of three-year-olds at the Green Willow Nursery School. The school serves children from a fairly conservative, white, middle-class neighborhood. Before the school year begins, Marta and Diane meet to prepare their classroom. It soon becomes apparent that they have different views on how actively they should oppose gender-stereotyping behavior in their classroom.

Diane:

"I want to make some collages that show women and men doing nontraditional work. I want to emphasize that gender equality is important in our classroom. Both girls and boys need to know that they can do any work they choose, regardless of their gender.

"It's never too early to expose children to the concept of gender equality. Many prejudices are formed during the preschool years. Because children are exposed to so much gender stereotyping in the media and in society, we need to work vigorously to counteract these stereotyped attitudes.

"Let's go through all these books in the library corner and get rid of the ones that are old-fashioned and out of date—the ones that show mothers staying home and fathers going off to work. There's no place in our classroom for books that promote the idea that girls should be cautious caregivers and boys should be the assertive leaders. I know that some of these books have won awards in the past, but their attitudes are now out of date and harmful.

"I also want to buy some male dolls for the boys to play with. We need to teach the boys that they can be caregivers, too. In fact, I think we should insist that mixed-gender groups play together in our housekeeping center. I also want to discourage the boys from playing the traditional "going off to work" father role. We need to actively encourage these children to experiment with nontraditional role-playing.

"I plan to assign children to play centers so that boys and girls get equal time playing with dolls and large blocks. I also want to encourage the girls to participate in physical play outside and to let them know that it's all right if they get dirty. As teachers, we need to be an active force in counteracting the negative gender stereotyping that occurs in our society."

Marta:

"These children are very young. The roles they're familiar with are those they see in their own families. In this community, gender roles tend to be traditional. Insisting that children in our class act differently will confuse them.

"It's true that many of the books in the library corner show traditional activities for mothers and fathers, but most of our children come from this type of background. It's comforting for them to see reflections of their home life in books and stories. Besides, if we eliminate this material, what will we replace it with? Our budget for new books is limited. Some of these older books are good, familiar stories. I don't think the classroom environment will be improved by getting rid of them.

"I also believe that insisting that children play in mixed groups is the wrong way to promote equality. Children should choose their friends on the basis of a number of factors, not just gender. Of course, we don't want to encourage "No girls (or boys) allowed" behavior, but each group needs to learn to form bonds and interact with those of their own gender. The nature of peer group bonds is different for girls and for boys.

"Children should choose where they want to play and the materials they play with. Different children enjoy different activities. I think we

**FOCUS ON** **Child Care Issues (continued)**

should have a variety of play materials available for every child, but as teachers we should remain neutral in how and when children use that material. I think three-year-olds are too young to really understand the meaning of gender stereotyping."

*What do you think the role of the teacher should be in promoting specific attitudes on social issues such as*

*gender equality? Does it matter if these attitudes are not shared by the community the teacher serves? What are some compromises Diane and Marta might make on the issue of gender stereotyping in their classroom?*

---

infants are interested in and responsive to one another. However, the amount of interaction among peers increases dramatically during toddlerhood, especially among children who are familiar with each other.

During the toddler years, a number of particular patterns of peer interaction seem to emerge. For example, toddlers express increased positive emotion while interacting with their peers. They seem to have more fun when playing with peers than when playing alone. Toddlers also engage in more *complementary and reciprocal rituals* with peers; that is, they play together in ways that cannot be accomplished with only one person, such as rolling and catching a ball. They seem to learn the rules of simple play activities and follow these rules in playing with one another. Toddlers also begin forming preferences for particular children within peer groups. Those who are involved in regular play groups grow to like some children more than others, and they seek out these preferred children.

As toddlers become familiar with their peers, these peers begin to function as attachment figures, helping to provide comfort and prevent distress. When toddlers are placed in new or slightly stressful situations, they adjust more easily if they are with other children whom they know. For example, if a toddler were taken to a gymnastics class for the first time and left there by his mother with only unfamiliar children in the class, he might become distressed. However, if the child were taken to a class in which he knew other children, he might not be upset at all. Familiar peers can thus help reassure children.

By age three or four, well-acquainted children engage in increasing amounts of cooperative behavior. For decades, researchers have observed that older preschoolers play with each other in more complex and social ways than toddlers do. Until recently, it was assumed that toddlers only play by themselves (*solitary play*), watch others play (*onlooker behavior*), or play the same activity as other children without really interacting (*parallel play*). Truly social play, in which children actively interact with one another, was believed to be too difficult for children between the ages of one and three (Parten, 1932). In the most social type of play, *cooperative play*, children work together toward a joint goal. For example, they may devise roles for one another as part of a particular scenario they are acting out. This type of play is very complex, but recent research indicates that children who are familiar with one another may engage in such cooperative play by about three years of age. Older toddlers who are in full-time child care are more likely to display this type of cooperation than children who are only in part-time day care (Field, Masi, Goldstein, Perry, & Parl, 1988).

A final pattern of interaction that emerges during the third year is increased flexibility in friendships (Hartup, 1983). As toddlers grow older, they seem better able to adjust to the behavior of a variety of other children and to play happily with many different peers. However, at this age, friendships typically are not very stable; a child may consider another his best friend simply because the other child gave him a cookie that day. Even so, some preferences in peer relations do exist at this time.

Toddlers often engage in prosocial behavior such as hugging or patting in response to the distress of another person.

## Prosocial Behavior

Toddlers have a growing understanding of the fact that others have needs and feelings and a growing knowledge of social standards such as sharing. They are also developing relationships with peers. These factors probably contribute to the increased tendency of children at this age to engage in *prosocial behavior*, behavior that is aimed at helping others (Eisenberg & Fabes, 1991). Some researchers distinguish *altruism* from other forms of prosocial behavior, defining it as prosocial behavior that does not involve a benefit to the helper. Other researchers, however, find this definition difficult to use. Here prosocial behavior will be defined as behavior that is aimed at helping others.

There has been little research on prosocial behavior during toddlerhood; the research that does exist indicates that toddlers do try to help others. In one recent study, about half of the 13- to 15-month-olds who were studied made at least one prosocial response to another person's distress. Typically, these young toddlers hugged or patted the distressed person. By 18 to 20 months of age, the toddlers responded to the distress of others with a wide variety of prosocial behaviors: by physically or verbally comforting the hurt individual, giving advice, helping (directly or by summoning an adult), sharing, distracting, or defending and protecting the person. By 23 to 25 months, all but one of the children in the study engaged in some prosocial behavior in response to others' distress (Zahn-Waxler et al., 1993).

The same study showed that the number of prosocial behaviors increased from 13 to 25 months of age. As toddlers grew older, they were more likely to show empathic concern for distressed people. However, they were also more likely to become upset themselves and/or to act aggressively when it was their fault that another person was upset. In other words, if an older toddler hit a younger child and made the child cry, the older toddler might cry himself but continue to behave aggressively toward the victim.

The study also provided some evidence that self-recognition is related to prosocial behavior. At 23 to 25 months of age, children who were better at recognizing themselves in the mirror were more likely to engage in prosocial behavior in response to someone else's distress. This was not the case with the children at the other ages.

## Emotional Development

It is somewhat artificial to discuss emotional development separately from social development because the two go hand in hand during the toddler period. Much of the research on emotional development during this period focuses on emotions that are believed to involve self-consciousness, some awareness of behavior standards, and some awareness of one's abilities. Other research concerns the communication of emotion, which can help the toddler learn how to behave. Both areas of research point toward the increased sensitivity and emotional expressiveness of toddlers, as well as the close relationship between emotional and social development.

### Social Referencing

People communicate emotion in a variety of ways, including facial expression, tone of voice, and body language. During the toddler years, children begin to "read" these cues to help them deal with situations. This practice of using the reactions of another person to guide one's own behavior is known as *social referencing*.

Research on social referencing has shown that by about one year of age, children look to others for information about novel events and use others' emotional signals to guide their reactions to those events (Klinnert et al., 1983). For example, if a young child sees a strange-looking toy robot coming toward her and her mother smiles and says, "What a nice robot," with a positive tone of voice, the child may approach the toy. However, if the mother looks apprehensive and says, "Don't touch the robot. It may hurt you," then the baby will be much more reluctant to approach the toy. In most studies, a parent or other adult's facial expression of fear was enough to make a child reluctant to approach, and a smile was enough to increase the child's willingness to approach.

For both infants and toddlers, social referencing is an important way of learning about the world without directly experiencing the consequences of their actions. It is also an important way of learning how to react emotionally to various types of situations.

## Social Emotions

Social referencing and other ways of communicating emotion may help toddlers learn so-called social emotions, such as shame or embarrassment, guilt, and pride. By observing the emotional cues of others, toddlers may learn which situations are "good" and which are "bad" and whether they should approach or avoid certain situations. Children may feel bad when they do things that they are not supposed to do and good when they do the "right" thing. The feelings of shame or embarrassment, guilt, and pride are closely related to a sense of "doing right" or "doing wrong." According to both theory and research, toddlers are capable of feeling and expressing shame or embarrassment and pride (Barrett, Zahn-Waxler, and Cole, 1993; Lewis et al., 1989; Stipek et al., 1992). The idea that toddlers experience guilt is more controversial, but there is some evidence that guiltlike behavior is possible in toddlers (Barrett et al., in press).

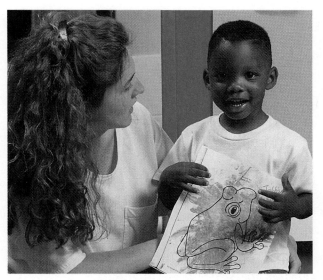

According to cognitive prerequisite approaches, children cannot have social emotions such as pride until they have developed an understanding of self.

## Theories of the Development of Social Emotions

There are a number of theories about the development of social emotions. One approach suggests that these emotions are related to certain cognitive abilities, most notably an understanding of self, an understanding of standards for behavior, and/or an understanding that one exerts choice over behavior (Buss, 1980; Kagan, 1980; Lewis et al., 1989). According to such cognitive prerequisite approaches, children cannot have social emotions until they develop the requisite cognitive abilities. One group of researchers, for example, contends that embarrassment requires the development of a sense of self, as measured by the rouge-on-the-nose mirror test described earlier. They believe that shame and guilt also require this sense of self, as well as an understanding of standards of behavior (Lewis et al., 1989).

Functionalist theory emphasizes the role of socialization in the development of social emotions. It highlights the importance of communicating emotion and the interaction between parents and children. Although the proponents of this approach acknowledge that cognitive development may influence the development of such emotions, they do not believe that cognitive development alone can bring about the development of emotions. For a child to respond with shame or guilt when he does something that he should not do, he must care about following the rules of his parents and other socializing agents. Simply knowing the rules and knowing that he has gone against them is not enough to make him feel guilty or ashamed.

In the view of psychoanalytic theorists, guilt is not possible until about age five or six, that is, when the child's Oedipus complex is resolved and the superego begins regulating ideas about morality and acceptable behavior. Although shame is possible in toddlerhood, guilt is not expected until later. Recent research, however, provides evidence that children experience embarrassment by about age two and a half and shame, pride, and possibly guilt at the end of their third year (Barrett et al., 1993; Lewis et al., 1989; Stipek et al., 1992).

## Implications and Applications

Much of the recent research on development that takes place in toddlerhood has important implications for child care professionals. For instance, there has been a reevaluation of the ability of toddlers to understand what they should and should not do. Many people assume that physical punishment or removal of the child from a situation are the only types of discipline possible at this age. Research suggests otherwise. When caregivers talk about the direct consequences of negative behaviors, toddlers generally understand. For example, if a toddler hits another child, the caregiver can point out that the victim is crying and that hitting hurts people. This technique of telling children about the consequences of their behavior for others is called *induction*.

Similarly, toddlers are able to understand simple descriptions of rules, or standards for behavior. In the preceding example, the caregiver could first point out the consequences of hitting another person and then note, "We never hit people." Research suggests that this approach is very effective (Zahn-Waxler et al., 1979).

Another finding that has implications for child care professionals is that toddlers are able to develop some prosocial behaviors. For this reason, caregivers should support children's attempts to help others and also model prosocial solutions to problems in order to encourage prosocial skills.

**TABLE 11.1**

**Milestones of Social and Emotional Development**

| Age | Milestones |
| --- | --- |
| 12 months | Social referencing<br>Practicing subphase (Mahler)<br>Child distinguishes objects from own actions (Piaget) |
| 15 to 18 months | Stage of autonomy versus shame (Erikson)<br>Self-recognition in mirror<br>Beginning of prosocial behavior<br>Rapprochement subphase (Mahler)<br>Beginning of true thought (Piaget)<br>Persistence at solvable tasks<br>Desire to do things independently<br>Awareness of standards of behavior<br>Embarrassment |
| 20 months | Beginning awareness of feelings of self and other |
| 24 months | Beginning of sense of gender and gender roles<br>Beginning of guiltlike behavior, pridelike behavior, and shamelike behavior<br>Stage of initiative versus guilt (Erikson) |
| 36 months | Preference for traditional gender-appropriate activities<br>Cooperative play among well-acquainted children |

Yet another implication of the research on toddlers' social development is that toddlers should be expected to want to do, or even insist on doing, things by themselves even when they are not quite capable. Whenever possible, it is useful to involve toddlers in activities where they can succeed by themselves and then to compliment them for their success. This might involve making sure that toddlers have foods they can eat by themselves and toys they can operate by themselves. It is important not to make the tasks too easy, though, because tod-

*If adults explain the consequences of negative behavior, toddlers can understand.*

dlers are starting to recognize and understand their capabilities.

Toddlers' desire for autonomy also has implications for child care professionals. If toddlers are given a direct order (such as, "Donnie, pick up the toys!"), a power struggle between child and adult is likely to follow. If they are asked whether they want to or will do something ("Donnie, would you like to pick up your toys now?"), the answer is often no. To help toddlers maintain a sense of autonomy, it is best if you can lead them to want to do the required task ("Donnie, let's see if you can put all the toys in the basket. I bet you can!"). Toddlers will usually comply happily under these circumstances.

Child care providers can apply the newfound ability of toddlers to think about themselves and others in creating different types of play activities. One enjoyable activity could involve puppets with expressions of various emotions. Toddlers and caregivers could use the puppets to act out scenarios about different emotions and to talk about the words for those emotions. Puppets representing various ethnic groups could be used to help chil-

dren understand that there are important similarities among cultures and peoples.

Many important changes in social and emotional development occur during the toddler years. Toddlers become much more aware of their gender, their looks, their feelings, their abilities, and their actions. They become much more independent, wanting to do things for themselves even though they may not be capable of accomplishing their goals. They show emotional responses, such as shame, pride, embarrassment, and possibly guilt, which many believe are connected to these new understandings of self as well as to a greater understanding of authority. Indeed, toddlers become more aware not only of themselves but also of others. They become increasingly aware of others' feelings, appearance, and gender, and they begin to really interact with peers. In short, toddlers are becoming more active participants in a social world. No longer just receiving nurturance and support from others, they are learning about others, caring about them, and helping them. Toddlers have thus come a long way during their first three years.

## SUMMARY

- Children become increasingly independent during the toddler years.
- According to Erikson, personality is formed through the resolution of two-sided issues throughout life; during the toddler years, this struggle is between a desire for autonomy and feelings of shame.
- Mahler believes that the personality development of infants and toddlers involves a process of separation-individuation, in which the child gradually develops a separate sense of self and other.
- Mahler identifies four subphases of separation-individuation: differentiation, practicing, rapprochement, and object constancy.
- Mahler's theory is similar in some ways to Bowlby's theory of attachment, but Bowlby places more emphasis on real behavior.
- Most research supports the idea that the toddler years are a period of tremendous development in the child's understanding of self and other.
- According to Cooley, individuals develop a sense of self by mirroring what other people think about them.
- Bowlby believes that the child builds a mental model of himself and the other on the basis of experiences with attachment figures.
- Until recent years, little research was done on the development of an understanding of self and other because people assumed that infants and toddlers were too young to have developed these concepts. One of the reasons for this assumption was the influence of Jean Piaget.
- Piaget believed that the thinking of infants and toddlers is too egocentric for them to perceive the viewpoints of others; thus they would not really know who they are or who others are. Later research, however, suggests otherwise.
- The development of a sense of self involves a growing awareness on several fronts: an awareness of one's own feelings, visual recognition of oneself, an awareness of one's own abilities, a desire to do things for oneself, and an awareness of standards for behavior.
- The development of a sense of other during the toddler years involves an increasing awareness of the feelings of others, a visual recognition of others, and an awareness of gender differences.
- During the toddler years, children enjoy interacting with their peers. Peer interaction at this time follows a number of particular patterns, including increased emotion during interaction, complementary and reciprocal rituals with peers, increased cooperative behavior, and increased flexibility in friendships.
- Toddlers' growing understanding of others contributes to the development of prosocial behavior, behavior aimed at helping others.
- During the toddler years, children begin to "read" cues from other people to help them deal with emotional situations, a process known as social referencing.

- Social referencing and other forms of communication help children learn so-called social emotions, such as shame or embarrassment, guilt, and pride. This helps them develop a sense of right and wrong.
- Three types of theories explain the development of social emotions: cognitive prerequisite theories suggest that certain emotions cannot develop until the child reaches a certain level of cognitive development; functionalist theory emphasizes the role of socialization and interaction between individuals; psychoanalytic theory contends that certain social emotions are not possible until a child's Oedipus complex is resolved.
- Caregivers must consider toddlers' ability to understand standards of behavior, their prosocial behaviors, and their desire for autonomy when dealing with them and their interactions with other children.

## BUILDING VOCABULARY

Write a definition for each vocabulary term listed below.

altruism
complementary and reciprocal
   rituals
cooperative play
induction
looking-glass self
object constancy
onlooker behavior

parallel play
prosocial behavior
self-recognition
self-regulation
separation-individuation
social referencing
solitary play
standards of behavior

## ACQUIRING KNOWLEDGE

1. According to Erikson, under what circumstances will infants develop a sense of trust?
2. Why does Erikson believe that toilet training is an important experience for toddlers?
3. What conflicting feelings does Mahler believe children face during the toddler years?
4. What is separation-individuation?
5. What do infants learn during Mahler's differentiation subphase?
6. Describe the main concerns of toddlers in Mahler's rapprochement subphase.
7. How does acquiring object constancy help two-year-olds separate from their mother more easily?
8. How are the theories of Erikson and Mahler similar?
9. Describe Piaget's view of self-awareness in children under four.
10. How does the emerging ability of toddlers to talk about their own feelings help parents and caregivers?
11. How do toddlers benefit from their desire to do things on their own?

12. How do children learn about standards of behavior during infancy?
13. How do parents shape their children's standards of behavior during the toddler years?
14. How might a toddler respond when someone around him is unhappy?
15. What is the significance of a toddler's ability to recognize herself in the mirror?
16. How does the gender-role behavior of toddlers change as they get older?
17. What are complementary and reciprocal rituals?
18. Define cooperative play and give an example.
19. How does peer interaction change as toddlers grow older?
20. Name two prosocial behaviors.
21. What is social referencing?
22. According to functionalist theory, what factors have the greatest influence on the development of social emotions in children?
23. Define induction.
24. How can caregivers support the desire of toddlers to do things for themselves?
25. What types of activities can caregivers use to teach toddlers about emotions?

## THINKING CRITICALLY

1. According to Erikson, Mahler, and Bowlby, a toddler's parents play a crucial role in helping him develop a sense of independence. How do you think caregivers can best support parents during this important stage of development?
2. If you were opening a child care center, what rules would you establish concerning acceptable social behaviors? Which behaviors would you be careful to promote? Which would you try to discourage? How do you think caregivers can promote some behaviors and discourage others?
3. Some psychologists note that toddlers who can recognize themselves in the mirror are more apt to feel embarrassment, shame, and guilt. Why do you think this is so? How do you think self-recognition and self-awareness are related?
4. Using induction as an example, explain how research in child development can challenge commonly held assumptions about disciplining or teaching children.
5. If you were a child care provider, how would you react if the father of a two-year-old boy in your care complained about his son being allowed to play with dolls?

## OBSERVATIONS AND APPLICATIONS

1. Observe what happens in a child care setting when one toddler is upset. What do other toddlers do? Do they try to comfort the child who is upset? Do they try to find out the cause of the problem? Do they try to get an adult to help the child who is upset? Note what caused the child to become upset and what succeeded in soothing him or her.

2. Observe how a caregiver handles the conflicts and emotional upsets of toddlers. What does the caregiver do when one child grabs a toy from another? When one child hits another? How does the caregiver respond when a child tries to do something and cannot? When a child is crying? Note different ways that the children respond to the caregiver.

3. The father of three-year-old Jeffrey picks him up every day at the center where you work. You notice that he constantly criticizes Jeffrey. When Jeffrey shows him a piece of artwork, his father says, "I think you could have done a neater job." When Jeffrey shows him a book he picked to take home, his father says, "That book is too long for me to read to you." He also criticizes Jeffrey because by the end of the day, his clothes are usually dirty. Describe the impact this constant criticism might have on Jeffrey's emotional development.

4. In your class at the child care center, there is a two-year-old girl named Paula who cries every time her parents leave her in the morning. Paula asks for help during every activity and needs a lot of encouragement to do things independently. How would Erikson interpret Paula's behavior? How would Mahler? What can you as a caregiver do to encourage Paula to become more independent?

## SUGGESTIONS FOR FURTHER READING

Brazelton, T. B. (1984). *To listen to a child*. Reading, MA: Addison-Wesley.

Curry, N. E., & Johnson, C. N. (1990). *Beyond self-esteem: Developing a genuine sense of human value*. Washington, DC: National Association for the Education of Young Children.

Eckerman, C. O., & Stein, M. R. (1982). The toddler's emerging interactive skills. In K. H. Rubin & H. S. Ross (Eds.), *Peer relations and social skills in childhood*. New York: Springer-Verlag.

Fraiberg, S. H. (1959). *The magic years*. New York: Scribner's.

Greenberg, P. (1991). *Character development: Encouraging self-esteem and self-discipline in infants, toddlers, and two-year-olds*. Washington, DC: National Association for the Education of Young Children.

Leipzig, J. (1992). Helping whole children grow: Nonsexist child rearing for infants and toddlers. In B. Neugebauer (Ed.), *Alike and different: Exploring our humanity with young children*. Washington, DC: National Association for the Education of Young Children.

Marion, M. (1991). *Guidance of young children*. Columbus, OH: Merrill.

National Association for the Education of Young Children (1986). *Helping children learn self-control*. Washington, DC: Author.

Schrank, R. (1984). *Toddlers learn by doing: Toddler activities and activity log for parents and teachers*. Atlanta, GA: Humanics.

# PART 5

# Preschoolers

## OBJECTIVES
Studying this chapter will enable
you to

- Describe the ways in which the
  body grows and develops during
  the preschool years.
- Identify gross and fine motor skills
  that are acquired during the
  preschool years.
- Explain the relationship between
  the developing sensory system of
  preschool children and their motor
  activity.
- Discuss how the health of
  preschool children is affected by
  their developing respiratory and
  digestive systems.
- List ways in which early childhood
  professionals can promote the
  physical development of
  preschoolers.

S USAN stood outside Eastside Montessori, waiting for her daughter Emma to finish preschool. While she was waiting, Susan started to think about how much her three-and-a-half-year-old had changed in the six months she had been in preschool. Emma was becoming very independent. She now liked to go to her dresser in the morning and pull out the clothes she wanted to wear. She often tried to dress herself, although in most cases she needed some help from her mother to finish the job. When Emma came downstairs for breakfast, she raised the window shades by pulling on the cords. Then she would climb into her chair and pour her juice while Susan made breakfast. These developments pleased Susan. She was proud of Emma's newfound abilities and accomplishments. And she was delighted with Emma's independence, for this allowed Susan to devote more of her energies to doing things with rather than for her daughter.

## Growth and Development of the Body

Preschoolers are markedly different from toddlers in appearance and physical abilities. Although growth and development level off during the preschool years, the body changes that occur during this period enable preschool children to acquire many new skills and to become more independent. The preschool age covers the years from three to five.

### Height, Weight, Proportions

The physical appearance of preschoolers is different from that of toddlers because their body proportions are changing. These changes follow cephalocaudal and proximodistal growth patterns. Between three and five years of age, the trunk, arms, and legs lengthen, giving preschoolers a much leaner appearance. During this period of development, the legs grow faster than the rest of the body. At two years, the legs represent 34 percent of total body length. By the age of five, the legs are 44 percent of body length. (In adults, the legs make up 50 percent of body length.) In addition, the chest circumference of preschoolers increases, and the stomach flattens. The head, although still relatively large in proportion to the rest of the body, now makes up about one-sixth of total body length. Because of all these changes in body proportions, a preschooler's shape is beginning to resemble that of an adult.

There are some differences in the growth patterns of males and females. These have been documented by *anthropometry*, the study of human body measurements. Males tend to be slightly taller and heavier than females during the preschool years; females are physically more mature in terms of skeletal and muscular development (Tanner, 1970). (See Figure 12.1.)

There are also differences in growth patterns among ethnic groups. For example, children of European heritage are generally taller than their Asian counterparts and generally shorter than children of African descent. Differences in genetic background and nutrition among ethnic groups are the most important factors accounting for these variations in height (Meredith, 1978). Ethnic differences are also evident when body proportions are compared. Children of African descent tend to develop longer arms and legs and narrower hips than the children of other ethnic groups. In comparison, children of Asian descent often develop shorter arms and legs and broader hips (Eveleth & Tanner, 1976).

While growth rates vary from child to child, the average preschooler grows about 3 inches and gains about 4½ pounds each year. In North America, the average five-year-old is 43 inches tall and weighs approximately 40 pounds.

Preschoolers and toddlers have different body proportions. Preschoolers have longer legs and arms and a flatter stomach than toddlers.

### Musculoskeletal System

During the preschool years, bones become denser, joints grow less flexible, and ligaments and muscles become more firmly attached. As the preschool child ages, the proportion of cartilage in the skeletal system decreases because it is hardening into bone.

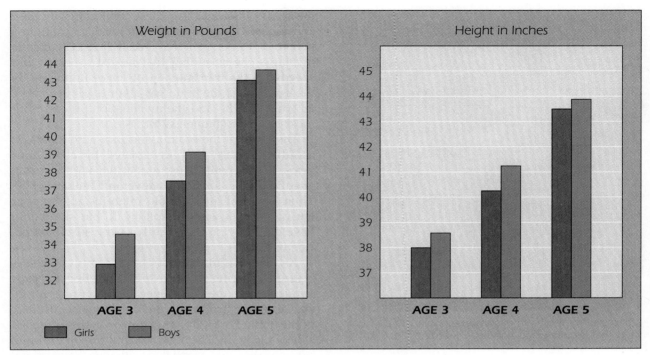

**FIGURE 12.1    Height and Weight Charts for Boys and Girls Ages Three to Five.**

This process, called ossification, can be measured by taking x-rays of a person's hand or foot. The degree of ossification of the small bones indicates the person's *skeletal age*. Examining a child's skeletal age is one way of diagnosing a growth problem. Doctors usually take x-rays when a child's height, weight, or head circumference is considerably different from the norm. The child's x-rays are compared with those of a child of the same age of average skeletal maturity. A significant variation from the average skeletal age may indicate a growth problem.

Growth problems can be the result of genetic disorders, physical problems, or environmental factors. Dwarfism, for example, is a genetic disorder in which the legs and trunk are disproportionately short at birth and grow more slowly than other parts of the body. Disorders such as kidney disease, infections such as hookworm or dysentery, or prolonged malnutrition can affect a child's growth. Children whose growth has been stunted for these reasons can usually reach their normal

height if these problems are corrected in time (Lowrey, 1978).

There are some differences in the musculoskeletal development of preschool boys and girls. While the bones of girls ossify more rapidly than those of boys, boys are more muscular and have greater forearm strength than girls (Tanner, 1978). Girls are slower than boys to lose their "baby fat," and they maintain higher levels of body fat throughout childhood. In spite of these differences, the musculoskeletal development of boys and girls is very similar at this age.

Changes in muscle and fat have much to do with the preschooler's transformation from a chubby toddler to a slender child. Fat decreases rapidly from the age of nine months to two and a half years, then more slowly from two and a half to five and a half years. Meanwhile, muscle tissues grow at a decelerating rate during infancy and childhood.

Most children have a full set of 20 baby teeth by the time they are two and a half. They will keep these teeth until about age six, when their perma-

Maturation of the brain allows preschoolers to perform tasks that require good hand-eye coordination.

nent teeth begin to come in. Girls generally lose their primary teeth earlier than boys.

It is important to keep this first set of teeth clean and healthy. The primary teeth help the jaw grow properly and provide space for the permanent teeth to come in. Early childhood educators can promote good dental health by encouraging children to brush their teeth after meals, by serving low-sugar snacks and fresh fruit instead of candy and gum, and by teaching children about the harmful effects of sugar on their teeth.

Many preschoolers still suck their thumb. Thumb-sucking is not harmful as long as children stop before their permanent teeth come in (Herrmann & Roberts, 1987). Preschoolers who suck their thumb do so more out of habit than emotional need. If a child is having difficulty breaking this habit, one of the most effective methods is the use of a dental appliance that makes sucking difficult.

## Brain and Nervous System

From the end of infancy, a child's brain has a full complement of nerve cells, or neurons, but the connections between the neurons are limited. Between the ages of three and five, these connections increase and become more complex as a result of continued myelination. As you may recall from Chapter 6, myelin is the sheathing that insulates nerves and speeds up the transmission of nerve impulses. By the age of five, the brain has attained 90 percent of its adult weight, and the myelination process is almost complete (Tanner, 1978).

The areas of the brain associated with hand-eye coordination are fully myelinated by about four years of age, while those associated with focusing attention take longer to develop (Tanner, 1978). Thus, a typical five-year-old might be able to pour her own drink without spilling it, but she would have difficulty pouring neatly over a sustained period of time.

As the brain matures, it also becomes more specialized. Specific abilities are controlled by each hemisphere of the brain. Speech and writing, for instance, are controlled by the dominant hemisphere of the brain. For right-handed people, this is the left side of the brain. The nondominant side of the brain contains the areas associated with visual and spatial orientation, artistic appreciation, and creative thought. Most preschool-age children show a marked preference for one hand rather than the other.

The two hemispheres of the brain need to be able to communicate with each other if a person is to function normally and fully. Without communication between the two hemispheres, a person might, for instance, see a fire raging out of control but be unable to call for help. A thick band of nerve fibers called the corpus callosum links the two hemispheres and facilitates communication. (See Figure 12.2.) Significant myelination of the corpus callosum occurs between the ages of two and eight (Yakovlev & Lecours, 1967). Thus, during this period, the two hemispheres of the brain become progressively more integrated. This means that children can perform more complex motor and intellectual tasks. The integration of the two hemispheres of the brain does not always proceed normally, however. One possible problem in this area becomes evident when a child draws on one side of a piece of paper with one hand and then switches hands to draw on the other side. Children who draw or write in this way should be referred to a physician for further assessment.

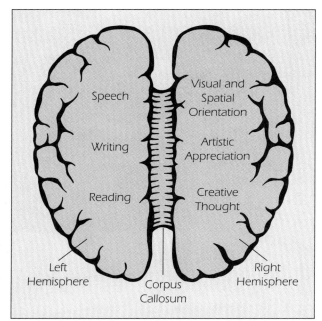

**FIGURE 12.2    Right and Left Hemispheres of the Brain.**   Each hemisphere of the brain controls specific abilities. As the corpus callosum develops, the right and left hemispheres are able to communicate more effectively. This explains why children can perform increasingly complex motor and intellectual tasks as they get older.

improvements in locomotion, and gains in strength. (See Table 12.1). Between the ages of three and four, children are normally expected to develop such gross motor skills as hopping with both feet, pedaling a tricycle, and throwing a ball underhanded. The skills of four- to five-year-olds are likely to include the ability to bounce and catch a ball, run in even strides, ascend and descend stairs smoothly with a foot-alternating pattern, and jump and hop.

How are preschool children able to acquire these increasingly complex motor behaviors? Stronger muscles, greater lung power, and a more highly developed cortex enable them to coordinate their thoughts and feelings with their actions. Children also become more aware of their own body during the preschool years, and this awareness contributes to motor development and the ability to control different parts of the body.

Preschool children have a harder time mastering fine motor skills because motor development follows the same proximodistal pattern that physical development does. In other words, children gain control over gross motor movements, such as waving, before being able to use their hands for fine motor tasks, such as drawing. Between three and four, most preschool children are able to cut

Throughout childhood there are small spurts in brain growth. A small spurt takes place at about two years of age, followed by a larger spurt between the ages of three and five. By the time a child is six, brain growth has significantly slowed (Fischer & Pipp, 1984).

## Motor Development and Activity

The physical changes that preschoolers experience enable them to acquire and refine many motor skills. Using their motor skills, preschoolers not only build strength and develop coordination, but they also learn about themselves and their abilities, and they develop self-confidence.

### Motor Development

The motor development of preschoolers can be seen in age-related patterns of increasing coordination,

| TABLE 12.1 | |
| --- | --- |
| **Milestones of Motor Development, Ages Three to Five** | |
| **Age** | **Milestones** |
| 3 to 4 years | Hops with both feet |
| | Pedals a tricycle |
| | Throws a ball underhanded |
| | Cuts paper |
| | Works a puzzle of several pieces |
| | Draws simple shapes |
| 4 to 5 years | Bounces and catches a ball |
| | Runs in even strides |
| | Ascends and descends stairs smoothly and with a foot-alternating pattern |
| | Jumps and hops |
| | Pours liquids from various containers |
| | Dresses self fairly well |
| | Prints letters and numbers |

By age five, preschoolers have refined their motor skills and have begun to enjoy testing their sense of balance and motion.

paper, work a puzzle of several pieces, and draw simple shapes. By the age of five, the typical preschool child can dress himself or herself fairly well, pour from various containers, and print letters and numbers.

While these fine motor skills are impressive, they require a great amount of effort on the part of the children. Some preschool children still have short, fat fingers, which make these skills difficult. They may also lack the muscular control to perform these skills because their nervous system is not yet completely myelinated. To avoid frustrating the children, classrooms and play spaces should have utensils and toys that preschoolers can handle easily and that are appropriate for their age.

### Posture

Posture is the way in which the body is balanced at all times. Good posture is achieved through good muscle tone and skeletal development and general physical and mental health. Children express their personality, attitude, and sense of well-being through their posture. Poor posture can be a sign of a health problem. When caregivers see a child whose body is sagging or slumping, they should be aware that something may be wrong.

### Activity Level

As you may recall from Chapter 9, young children are in their most active period between the ages of two and three. During the preschool years, the activity level of young children drops significantly. Preschoolers are less likely than toddlers to be seriously injured in an accident because of this decrease in activity level, but they are still at risk for accidents and should be supervised closely.

Close supervision is especially important for preschool boys. In general, boys are more active and take more risks than girls. As a result, boys tend to have more accidents (Solomons, Larkin, Snider, & Paredes-Rojas, 1982). Activity level also varies from child to child. Some children are highly active and tend to be less cautious and obedient and more competitive than others.

In addition, researchers have found cultural differences in activity level. In some studies, African American children were found to have higher activity levels than other children (Morgan, 1976). Caregivers need to consider many elements of a child's background before concluding that the child may be hyperactive. Classifying an active African American child as hyperactive—without proper testing and observation—can lead to inappropriate courses of action.

## Sensory System

Many of the motor activities that preschool children engage in are linked to their sensory system and the information, or perceptions, their sense organs relay to them. For instance, a preschooler will see blocks and build a tower with them or will feel clay and begin to roll it, knead it, or shape it. When Susan's daughter Emma eats, she likes to blow bubbles in her milk and lick the peanut butter off her toast before she eats the bread. Because children learn about their environment through sensory experiences, caregivers should encourage preschoolers to use their senses to explore and manipulate.

Preschoolers also enjoy activities that allow them to explore senses other than the primary ones of touch, taste, sound, smell, and sight. They take great pleasure in testing their sense of balance and motion. Emma loves to walk on top of a low wall near her house and use the playground equipment at preschool.

The pleasure that preschoolers derive from sensorimotor experiences should be taken into account in determining appropriate and engaging activities. Drawing, cutting, and water pouring are examples of activities in which children use their senses and motor skills at the same time.

The sense of sight continues to improve during the preschool years, but children do not reach visual maturity until the age of six. The eye muscles have not yet developed to the point where preschoolers can scan a line of fine print. Most preschoolers are still farsighted as well.

Between the ages of three and five, children develop the ability to distinguish between perceptions (perceptual differentiation) and the ability to integrate different kinds of perceptions (intersensory integration). These skills help children organize their experiences.

Some researchers have approached the subject of the development of perception through children's art. Rhoda Kellogg studied the drawings of children to explore the influence of culture. What she found was a striking similarity in the drawings of children of the same age from a variety of national and ethnic backgrounds. For instance, the early drawings of three-year-olds generally consist of shapes such as circles, squares, or triangles. The children then move on to a stage where they combine these shapes into more complex patterns. Drawing at this level is more abstract than representational. In other words, children at this age are drawing designs, not their interpretations of what they see (Kellogg, 1970). Kellogg's research also led her to conclude that early drawing reflects the maturation of the brain.

## Health

For young children to achieve optimal growth and development, it is important that they maintain good health. Good health involves preventing and treating illness. It also means ensuring that children eat nutritious meals and develop healthy eating habits.

### Respiratory System

Preschool children often seem to have perpetual colds. In fact, the average preschooler has seven to eight colds or other respiratory infections per year. As unpleasant as a respiratory infection is for both the children and their caregivers, it actually provides some benefit to children by immunizing them against the virus in the future. The antibodies that are produced in response to exposure to the infection protect young children from being reinfected by the virus.

Respiratory diseases can, however, be life threatening. They are the major cause of death among infants and small children. When a viral infection becomes serious enough to interfere with a child's daily routine or to cause her development to slow down, a physician should be consulted.

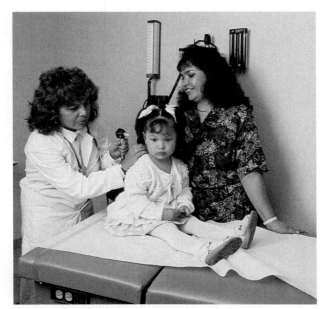

Visits to the doctor are common during the preschool years. The average preschooler has seven to eight colds or respiratory infections per year.

As children progress through the preschool years, their bouts with respiratory illnesses decline. Five-year-olds have fewer colds than they did when they were younger. They have already been exposed to many of the common viruses, and their immune system is more highly developed. In addition, children of this age have a longer and wider trachea, or windpipe, which means that their bouts with respiratory illnesses are less severe.

### Digestive System

A similar pattern of development characterizes the digestive system of preschoolers. Older preschoolers get stomachaches less frequently than younger preschoolers. As their digestive system matures, it functions more regularly and is less sensitive to food.

The stomach of a four- or five-year-old has less than half the capacity of an adult's stomach. However, a preschooler's calorie requirements are almost twice as great. What this means for caregivers is that preschool children do not eat big meals, but they do need to eat often. Caregivers should be sure to offer several snacks during the day.

**Appetite.**     Because preschoolers are growing at a slower rate than toddlers and infants, their calorie requirements per pound of body weight are lower. Caregivers will notice that the appetite of preschoolers begins to dwindle. At the same time, many of them become picky eaters. They use food as a means of exercising independence and control over their lives. Being able to choose the foods they want to eat enhances their sense of self.

Preschoolers are often reluctant to try new foods. When they do try something new, they are likely to take a small taste and then reject the food. A young child may need seven or eight exposures to a new food before accepting it. Preschoolers are also suspicious of casseroles and foods that are mixed together. They prefer their foods to be separate on the plate. They also like to know what they are eating. Most prefer simple, identifiable foods and foods that they can eat with their fingers.

Because preschoolers are so aware of the appearance of food, caregivers should make an effort to make food look appealing. Providing children with food that has variety in color, shape, and texture will increase the likelihood that the children will eat it. In addition, most young children prefer their food

It is not uncommon for preschoolers to refuse to eat particular foods. Many children of this age use food as a means of exercising independence and control over their lives.

## Decision Making in Child Care

### Getting Families Involved

Moana, a caregiver at the Fremont Family Resource Center, would like the families of the children in her care to become more involved with the center. She has found that family participation enriches the center, helps parents understand what their children are doing, and boosts children's self-esteem.

Moana is aware that many of the children at her center live with a single parent. These parents work long hours and have little opportunity to visit the center during the workday. She does not want involvement to become another burden in their already overloaded schedules.

Moana looks through a number of professional journals for ideas on increasing parent involvement. Among the suggestions she comes across are the following:

- Send home a classroom newsletter on a regular basis.
- Invite parents to a special share day for families.

- Ask parents to make something special (a pillow, a toy) for the center.
- Establish a lending library for parents, with books and magazines on parenting and other family issues.
- Ask children to bring in photographs of their family for a special family display.
- Plan a family picnic for each class at the center.

After considering the list of ideas, Moana decides to organize an early evening potluck picnic for the families of the children in her group. She also plans to set up a lending library for parents, with books and magazines in both English and Spanish.

*Why do you think Moana decided on those two particular activities? Which ones would you have chosen? Why? Can you suggest other activities that would involve parents in their children's life at the child care center?*

to be lukewarm. Foods that are too cold or too hot may be rejected or fiddled with until they reach the right temperature.

Preschoolers' appetites frequently fluctuate, usually in conjunction with periods of growth. During growth spurts, young children seem to eat everything in sight. However, when growth slows or when a child is ill, the appetite diminishes. It is not uncommon for a preschooler to eat almost nothing at a particular meal. Caregivers should not be alarmed if this happens; children will not starve themselves. If a child eats little at lunch, he will make up for it at snack time. What is important is to make sure that all the food he is offered is nutritious.

**Eating Habits.**　The preschool years are a critical time in terms of establishing eating patterns and

food preferences. Many of the preschooler's food and eating habits will be carried into adult life. Early childhood professionals can promote good eating habits by providing children with a variety of nutritious foods and by eating with the children and showing enjoyment. Showing enjoyment is important because young children closely observe adult behavior and mimic it. Preschoolers will sense any negative reactions adults have toward particular foods and imitate them.

Teaching young children about nutrition is an important part of shaping good eating habits. In a study of a nutrition education program for young children and their parents, the researcher found that the children's food knowledge increased significantly during the program. The children also tended to select a broader range of foods when eating. The re-

### Confronting Racism

At a professional workshop on confronting racism, caregivers broke into small groups to discuss their experiences with biased behavior. Here are two examples that preschool teachers in one group shared.

Sandra Case:
"In my class, an African American girl, Stacy, picked up a white doll and began to play with it. A white child, Danielle, came over and said, 'You can't play with that doll. You play with the black doll.'

"When I heard this, I went over to the girls and said, 'Stacy, in our class anyone may play with any toy. Danielle has no right to say you must only play with the black doll.' Then to Danielle I said, 'I didn't like what you said to Stacy. In our class the rule is that everyone plays with all the toys. Why did you tell Stacy she couldn't play with the white doll?'

"Danielle replied, 'My mom says black kids and white kids should play with their own kind. She says blacks are lazy bums on welfare.'

"What Danielle said made me very angry, but I tried to stay calm. I told her that in our class, everyone played together, and everyone shared all the toys. Then I told her that I didn't agree with her mother and that I would talk to her about our school rules and our different ideas.

"Later I called Danielle's mother. From our conversation it was clear that she did hold biased beliefs about blacks. I told her that in our school we did not permit words or behaviors that were biased and hurtful. She told me that I could make the rules at school but that she would make the rules in her home.

"I didn't think this was a very satisfactory conclusion, but it was clear that continuing our conversation would not change Danielle's mother's attitude.

"Since then, I've stepped up my effort to read stories at group time that show minorities in positive everyday life activities. I haven't heard Danielle using any more biased language at school, but I feel sure she is still exposed to biased beliefs at home."

Isabel Garcia:
"Our school serves a mixed population of whites, Hispanics, and African Americans. Three Hispanic boys were playing together on the playground and speaking Spanish. A white, English-speaking boy, Jon, repeatedly asked to join their game. They told him he couldn't play because he was a dummy who couldn't speak Spanish.

"I went over to the group and told them that they weren't being nice and that they had to let Jon play. They half-heartedly allowed him to join the group but continued speaking Spanish among themselves.

"The next day, the same thing happened. I didn't want to make a big deal out of this so I steered Jon into another activity.

"Then a group of Spanish-speaking girls began monopolizing the housekeeping center during free play and excluding a black girl who didn't speak Spanish. Within a week, the class was divided into play groups of English speakers and Spanish speakers.

"Finally, I made the rule that we would speak only English in the classroom. This made some of the Spanish-speaking parents very unhappy. Behind my back, they went to the director and complained. After that, the director withdrew the rule about speaking only English and moved some of the Spanish-speaking troublemakers out of my class. Since then, things have been much better."

After the small groups finished discussing personal experiences with racism, the speaker, an expert in developing anti-bias curricula, addressed the issue. Her main point was that to handle issues of biased behavior effectively you must do the following:

- Intervene immediately when biased behavior is observed.
- Support and comfort the target of the biased behavior or language.
- Determine the underlying reason for the conflict.
- Take positive action to prevent future episodes of bias if the underlying reason for the conflict is based on prejudice.

*Which caregiver do you think responded more appropriately to the biased behavior she witnessed? Taking the incident the other caregiver described, can you suggest how she might have responded more effectively? Can you think of other things these teachers could do to promote bias-free behavior in their classrooms?*

searcher concluded that teaching children about nutrition is worthwhile because children are capable of learning new information and attitudes about food (Church, 1979).

Another common food-related problem among preschool children is dawdling at meals. Preschoolers eat more slowly than adults, but they may also dawdle purposely. Dawdling can occur because children are full or because they would rather eat something else. Some children dawdle because it is a way of getting attention. Child care providers can prevent this problem by setting aside an appropriate period of time for meals and letting the children know when the meal's end is approaching. In most cases, this practice cuts down on dawdling.

**Nutrition.**    Because of the increase in the number of working parents, meal preparation habits have changed in the United States. Parents today are looking for convenience and speed when mealtime rolls around. Some find that convenience in microwave ovens and frozen meals; others take the family out to eat, often to fast-food restaurants. Early childhood professionals should discuss eating practices with parents and make sure parents know that many fast foods are high in calories, fat, and salt and low in vitamins A and C and calcium. It is important that the foods a child eats for other meals contain the vitamins and minerals that may be missing from fast-food meals.

Many caregivers and parents are also concerned about the possible effect of sugar and food additives on behavior, notably in the case of hyperactivity. Studies have failed to show a link between sugar and additives and hyperactivity, but there may be other harmful effects (Rapoport, 1986). Sugar causes tooth decay and can also depress the appetite. Children who eat a lot of sugary foods will not be hungry when a nutritious meal or snack is offered.

## Implications and Applications

Many factors influence the growth and development of preschool children. Nutrition plays an important role as do opportunities to develop and practice motor skills. Making the environment healthy, safe, and suitable to the needs of preschoolers should be a primary concern of caregivers.

### Growth

As noted earlier, children grow at different rates. In addition to genetic and gender factors, certain environmental factors also affect growth. In general, children of high socioeconomic levels tend to be larger because of better nutrition and medical care (Hamill, Johnston, & Lemeshow, 1972). Good nutrition contributes to growth, and poor nutrition inhibits it.

Hunger has become a serious problem in the United States. According to the Tufts University

## FOCUS ON  Cultural Diversity

### Food Customs

Every culture uses certain foods to celebrate and discourages or prohibits the use of other foods. Many ideas about which foods we should eat and which we should avoid have their roots in religious beliefs. Many Jews and Muslims do not eat pork products. Hindus prohibit the eating of beef, and Mormons do not drink caffeinated beverages.

Child care providers need to be sensitive to each child's food customs. To avoid problems over food, the caregiver can take the following steps:

- Become informed about the food customs of different groups. Remember that within any group there is a wide variation in the degree to which dietary rules are observed.
- When a child enters the school, inquire about any dietary restrictions. If there are restrictions, find out what kinds of food are prohibited and what foods are allowed. If your program cannot accommodate the dietary requirements, inform the parent before the child enrolls.
- Encourage children to talk about and share special foods that are important to their family's heritage.
- Develop and distribute to parents a set of guidelines for snacks that can be brought from home to share with the class. These guidelines should be based on both nutritional and cultural considerations.
- Emphasize similarities. Remind children that all families use food as part of their celebrations. Only the choice of food differs.

Center on Hunger, Poverty, and Nutrition, hunger has increased 50 percent since the mid-1980s. More than one in ten Americans is undernourished. Among low-income children, 90 percent are below the recommended dietary intake for iron, and more than 50 percent lack one or more essential vitamins (Cook & Brown, 1992). These kinds of deficiencies can affect skeletal development, energy level, and brain growth. For instance, iron deficiency anemia is the most common nutritional problem among preschoolers. It stems from a lack of quality meats and dark green vegetables, and its main symptom is chronic fatigue. Iron deficiency anemia affects 10 percent of all low-income preschoolers, with black and Hispanic children most severely affected (Children's Defense Fund, 1991). Deficiencies in vitamin A can cause vision impairments and night blindness. A diet lacking in vitamin C can lead to bleeding gums, swollen joints, and slowness in the healing of wounds.

While many inadequately nourished children are poor, undernourishment occurs among all socioeconomic groups. With more mothers working outside the home, families have less time for healthy meal planning and preparation. In addition, many parents are not able to be on hand to see what their children are eating. In families like these, there tends to be a greater use of processed foods instead of fresh foods.

Caregivers should be aware of the signs of poor nutrition so that corrective action can be taken. An undernourished child may display symptoms such as dry and flaking skin, bleeding gums, sluggishness, irritability, puffy arms and legs, cracks in the skin at the corners of the mouth, and decayed teeth (Marotz, Rush, & Cross, 1989). If a child's diet can be modified to include the necessary vitamins, minerals, and protein, then the child's normal growth pattern can resume and he will catch up physically with his peers. But if the undernourishment is chronic, or long term, it will have a permanent effect. An undernourished child will grow up to be smaller than he would have been with adequate nutrition (Alford & Bogle, 1982).

Severe malnutrition is unusual in the United States. It generally occurs only in cases of prolonged famine or during wartime. When children do not get the level of calories they need to maintain their body and grow, they become very sluggish and inactive, showing little interest in play or their environment. As their intake drops further, they stop growing. Malnutrition first affects the weight of the child, then the child's height, and finally brain circumference, where permanent damage can occur. However, the physical effects of limited periods of malnourishment can usually be overcome.

What can early childhood professionals do to promote the healthy growth and development of preschoolers? The first step is to provide the children in their care with nutritious meals and snacks. The second is to try to educate the children and their parents about good nutrition.

## Movement

Giving preschool children opportunities to move their body and use their motor skills is critical to their social, emotional, and intellectual development. Movement allows children to discover many things about themselves. They learn what their body can and cannot do, and this contributes to the image they form of their body. Children also gain a sense of mastery by testing their motor skills and doing things independently, and this contributes to their concept of self. In addition, young children use movement to express their feelings and emotions. They may stamp their feet and throw something in anger or literally jump for joy in happiness. Movement is a way of communicating. Finally, movement enables children to explore the environment, enhancing their intellectual capabilities. As one child care expert notes, "Because preschool children feel at one with their bodies they do not separate physical activities, thinking activities, and feeling activities as adults tend to do. Doing helps them think; thinking makes them do" (Leach, 1989, p. 424).

Movement occurs most frequently when young children are engaged in play. Activities such as finger painting, putting puzzles together, and playing tag exercise a child's fine and gross motor skills. For this reason, play is an important element in the development and mastery of physical skills.

Play brings children into contact with a variety of sensory stimulation, and this encourages them to practice their motor skills. Most preschoolers, for instance, love moving to music, playing with their food, and petting small animals. Play also provides an incentive for children to acquire new skills, such as using scissors, pouring water without spilling it, and dressing themselves.

Rough-and-tumble play is particularly important to the mastery of movement and motor skills. *Rough-and-tumble play* is active play such as running, jumping, chasing, and make-believe fighting in a nonhostile way. While rough-and-tumble play may look aggressive, it is only mimicking aggression. In fact, researchers have discovered that it contributes to the development of a child's social competence. Children who engage in this type of

Rough-and-tumble play provides children with physical exercise and contributes to the development of social competence.

## FOCUS ON   Communicating with Parents

### A Mysterious Illness

Five-year-old Alex lived in a lovely old Victorian house that his parents were busy restoring. Over the past few months Alex had been lethargic, complained of stomachaches, and seemed to have some coordination problems. A visit to the doctor hadn't turned up anything specific, but more tests were scheduled. His parents had mentioned the problem to Polly, Alex's teacher at Twin Cities Preschool. She, too, had noticed some changes in Alex, and she did some research. She decided to tell Alex's father about it.

POLLY:  Good morning, Gregg. How's Alex doing?

GREGG:  About the same. In fact, we were playing ball yesterday and his coordination difficulties seemed more noticeable.

POLLY:  You know, I've been reading a book about children's disabilities, and something I came across may be connected to Alex's problem.

GREGG [*a bit put off*]:  Really, Polly? But I don't think he has any kind of disability.

POLLY:  Well, it seems that certain disabilities can be caused by lead poisoning. And the early symptoms are a lot like Alex's.

GREGG:  Lead poisoning! Isn't that something that children get from eating flakes of paint in rundown tenements?

POLLY:  Yes, but it can also be caused by dust created by sanding walls covered with lead paint. I've been thinking about all that renovation you've been doing.

GREGG:  Yes, we've refinished just about every wall in the house, but . . .

POLLY:  Well, it may be a long shot, but just in case, I picked up this brochure from the clinic. They're offering a blood screening test, too.

GREGG:  Well, thanks. I'll read the brochure and ask Alex's doctor about it.

*Lead poisoning is the number one environmental problem facing young children. When Polly suspected it might be the cause of Alex's illness, she took an active role in gathering information and talking to his father. Do you think Polly's conduct was appropriate for a teacher? As it turned out, she was right about the lead poisoning. What if she had been wrong?*

play are more likely to take part in games that require cooperation and are less likely to be involved in aggressive play (Pellegrini & Perlmutter, 1988). Thus, rough-and-tumble play is not only a source of physical activity for children, but it also contributes to social development.

One of the first educators to put into practice the idea that play serves an important role in developing skills was Maria Montessori. In the early 1900s, Montessori, an Italian physician and educator, developed a system of education designed to help children realize their full potential. She believed that by focusing preschool education on the development of motor skills, the sensory system, and language education, young children would acquire many of the skills they would need as adults. Montessori emphasized the development of motor skills that teach children how to care for themselves and to deal with tasks of everyday life. In Montessori programs, children learn how to sweep, clean tables, and care for plants and animals. Studies comparing preschool programs have found that

Montessori schools prepare children well for formal learning (Miller & Bizzell, 1983).

### Gender Differences

While differences have been found in both the gross and fine motor skill abilities of young girls and boys, these differences usually do not become apparent until the first or second grade. It is unclear just how much gender differences should be attributed to physical differences and how much they should be attributed to the different activities in which children traditionally engage. Researchers have found that boys tend to be better at skills that involve arm strength, such as throwing and hitting a ball. They are also superior at jumping and going up and down ladders. On the other hand, girls excel at jumping jacks, balancing on one foot, hopping, and catching a ball. Girls also tend to have better fine motor skills (Cratty, 1979).

Some early childhood specialists argue that these differences are largely due to practice. Research has shown that boys of preschool age spend more time than girls playing outdoors and that they are frequently involved in running, climbing, and rough-and-tumble activities. Preschool girls tend to spend more time interacting socially, playing indoors, and listening to stories (Edwards & Whiting, 1980).

### Physical Environment

Much of preschool education consists of arranging the environment so that young children are free to develop their motor skills on their own and at their own pace. Preschoolers need space where they can run, jump, skip, and climb so that they can use their large muscles. They also need equipment, such as large balls, beanbags, and musical instruments, that requires the use of the muscles of the upper body. Young children need opportunities to develop small muscle skills through play activities such as puzzles, painting, cutting, and similar activities (Bredekamp, 1987). A well-rounded daily program should include activities that involve both large and small muscles. To promote freedom of movement, child care providers should encourage parents to dress their children in loose clothing.

If young children are provided with a suitable environment, they will learn to jump and climb and

Caregivers can help prevent accidents by carefully supervising children and making sure they know how to use play equipment safely.

hop on their own. The role of the early childhood professional should be to act as a guide or facilitator. Caregivers should prepare the environment so that the materials available to the children are stimulating and challenging. By observing the children closely, child care professionals can monitor their progress and present them with new challenges when they are ready.

Children of preschool age need to be physically active. Attempting to keep them still for long periods of time will probably fail and will do the children no good. Those who work with preschoolers must recognize their need to move and the importance movement has for their development.

The other major consideration in arranging the environment is to make sure that it is safe. Equipment and toys need to be inspected regularly. Children must be attentively supervised when they are playing outdoors because that is where many accidents occur. In addition, children should be taught how to use equipment safely. Even with careful planning, supervision, and education, however, accidents will happen. It is important that caregivers be trained in first aid and CPR for infants and children. Because accidents pose more of a health risk to preschoolers than disease, a safe environment is extremely important.

## SUMMARY

- Between the ages of three and five, young children begin to resemble adults, as their legs, trunk, and arms lengthen.

- While differences exist between preschool-age boys and girls in terms of height, weight, and musculoskeletal development, they tend to look more physically alike than different. Physical differences have also been noted among cultural groups.

- Caregivers can promote good dental health by encouraging children to brush their teeth after meals, by serving healthy snacks, and by teaching children about the harmful effects of sugar on the teeth.

- By the age of five, the child's brain is almost completely myelinated. The brain also becomes more specialized as it matures.

- During each of the preschool years, children become progressively more coordinated, their locomotion improves, and they become stronger. Fine motor skills lag behind gross motor skills because of the proximodistal pattern of motor development.

- Posture is the way in which the body is balanced. A child's posture is affected by his or her overall physical and mental health.

- Preschoolers are less physically active than toddlers. Differences in activity levels have been observed between boys and girls and among different cultural groups. Caregivers should consider a child's background before concluding that the child may be hyperactive.

- The sensory system of preschoolers is closely linked to their motor activities. The pleasure that preschoolers derive from sensorimotor activities should shape their preschool environment.

- Preschoolers commonly get many respiratory infections. These infections can provide benefits to the children by immunizing them against the virus in the future. Most children get fewer infections as they get older.

- Because preschoolers have a small stomach but a high activity level, they usually do not eat big meals, but they need to eat often.

- Eating habits change during the preschool years. Appetites fluctuate greatly, dwindling during periods when growth slows down and increasing during growth spurts. Preschoolers are also selective about the foods they eat, using food as a means to exercise independence and control over their lives.

- The preschool years are a critical time for establishing attitudes about food. Early childhood educators can promote healthy attitudes by providing children with a variety of foods and by eating with them and showing enjoyment. Teaching children about good nutrition is also important.

- Good nutrition plays an important role in preschoolers' growth and development. Skeletal growth, energy level, and brain growth are all affected by the amount and quality of food that is eaten. Undernourishment occurs in all socioeconomic groups.

- Movement is critical to the social, emotional, and intellectual development of preschoolers. Play is an important part of preschoolers' development. It teaches them many of the motor, social, and intellectual skills they will need as adults.
- Differences have been found in both the gross and fine motor skills of young girls and boys. How much of this difference is due to physical differences and how much is due to the types of activities they engage in is unclear.
- Preschoolers need an environment where they are free to develop their motor skills on their own and in safety. The role of the early childhood educator should be to act as a guide or facilitator.
- Children of preschool age need to be physically active. Caregivers must recognize preschoolers' need to move and the importance movement has for their development.

## BUILDING VOCABULARY

Write a definition for each vocabulary term listed below.

anthropometry                     skeletal age
rough-and-tumble play

## ACQUIRING KNOWLEDGE

1. Compare the body proportions of preschoolers and toddlers.
2. Why type of information does anthropometry provide?
3. How do the growth patterns of males and females differ?
4. How does the skeletal system change during ossification?
5. How can doctors tell whether a child's skeletal age is keeping pace with chronological age?
6. Name one condition or environmental factor that might affect a child's growth.
7. What happens to the quantity of body fat in a child's body during the preschool years?
8. Describe the differences between the musculoskeletal development of boys and girls.
9. Why is it important to keep a child's first set of teeth healthy?
10. What can caregivers do to promote dental health in preschool?
11. By age five, the myelination process in the brain is nearly complete. What effect does this have?
12. Name two gross motor skills that children develop between the ages of three and five.
13. Why do fine motor skills tend to develop later than gross motor skills?
14. What does poor posture indicate in a preschool child?

15. Why do preschool boys tend to have more accidents than preschool girls?
16. Give an example of a sensorimotor activity that preschool children might enjoy.
17. In what way do preschoolers benefit from catching frequent colds?
18. Compare the eating patterns of preschoolers and adults. Explain the reason for any differences.
19. Why do preschoolers sometimes become picky eaters?
20. How do sugar and sweet foods affect the health of preschool children?
21. Name two symptoms of malnutrition in preschool children.
22. How do preschool children use movement as a way of communicating?
23. How does rough-and-tumble play contribute to a child's development?
24. What differences have been found between the motor abilities of girls and boys?

## THINKING CRITICALLY

1. Caregivers are sometimes the first to suspect that a child may have a physical problem. For example, a caregiver may suspect that a particularly active child is hyperactive. What do you think is the caregiver's responsibility in such a situation?
2. Should preschool children who are ill with a cold attend school, or should they stay at home? What policy do you think would be best, and how would it affect the children, the school, and the families involved?
3. Suppose a healthy four-year-old gradually begins to eat less at mealtimes. At the same time, he asks for frequent snacks. He begins to refuse foods he once liked and is unwilling to try new foods. How would you interpret this behavior?
4. Explain how the following equipment promotes the physical development of preschoolers: an open, grassy area; a climbing frame; a box containing a variety of large balls; and finger paints.
5. What issues should caregivers be aware of in discussing a child's diet with parents? Do you think that educating parents about nutrition is part of the responsibility of child care providers?

## OBSERVATIONS AND APPLICATIONS

1. Observe children between the ages of three and five at a preschool or child care center while they draw self-portraits. Note which body parts are typically included and excluded from the self-portraits at each age. What basic differences are there in the self-portraits of a typical three-year-old and a typical five-year-old? Note individual differences within age groups as well.
2. Observe a class of four-year-olds, making note of differences and similarities in behavior of the genders. During instruction time, are children of one gender reminded more frequently to pay attention? Do children of both genders play together, in separate groups, or both? Are there differences in the games, toys, and activities chosen by children of each

gender? Are some activities more "gender neutral" than others? If so, which activities are they?

3. When Ms. Walker picks up her daughter Jessica from preschool, she asks your advice. Jessica is an active four-year-old. When it comes to playing outside, she plays nicely. However, when it is time to come inside, Jessica wants to play the same kinds of games she plays outside. Ms. Walker finds these activities to be inappropriate for indoor play. Prevented from running around the house or throwing balls, Jessica watches hour after hour of television. Ms. Walker finds this unacceptable as well. She would like Jessica to play indoors in ways that promote motor development but do not destroy her house. What suggestions would you give Ms. Walker?

4. Mr. Cox calls the preschool to tell you that Darren, who is in your class for three-year-olds, will not be coming to school today. He is home with a cold and fever. Mr. Cox mentions that he is concerned about Darren because he seems to get one cold after another. Mr. Cox asks whether you know of anything he can do to help keep his son healthy. What information should you give Mr. Cox about preschoolers and colds? What advice can you give him to help keep Darren healthy?

## SUGGESTIONS FOR FURTHER READING

Andress, B. (1991). From research to practice: Preschool children and their movement responses to music. *Young Children, 47*(1), 22–27.

Eddowes, E. A. (1989). Ideas! Safety in preschool playgrounds. *Dimensions, 17*(2), 15–18.

Frost, J. L., & Wortham, S. (1988). The evolution of American playgrounds. *Young Children, 43*(5), 19–28.

Greenman, J. (1988). *Caring spaces, learning places: Children's environments that work.* Redmond, WA: Exchange Press.

Kane, D. N. (1985). *Environmental hazards to young children.* Phoenix, AZ: Oryx.

Kendrick, A. S., Kaufman, R., & Messenger, K. P. (Eds.). (1988). *Healthy young children: A manual for programs.* Washington, DC: National Association for the Education of Young Children.

Kruger, H., & Kruger, J. (1989). *The preschool teacher's guide to movement education.* Baltimore, MD: Gerstung.

Moukaddem, V. (1990). Preventing infectious diseases in your child care setting. *Young Children, 45*(2), 28–29.

National Association for the Education of Young Children (1992). *Developmentally appropriate practice in early childhood programs serving young preschoolers.* Washington, DC: Author.

Poest, C. A., Williams, J. R., Witt, D. D., & Atwood, M. E. (1990). Challenge me to move: Large muscle development in young children. *Young Children, 45*(5), 4–10.

Roger, C. S., & Sawyers, J. K. (1988). *Play in the lives of children.* Washington, DC: National Association for the Education of Young Children.

U.S. Department of Agriculture (1992, April). *Nutrition guidelines for the child nutrition programs.* Washington, DC: Author.

## OBJECTIVES

Studying this chapter will enable
you to

- Describe Piaget's approach to
  understanding the cognitive
  development of preschoolers.
- Discuss recent research that
  supports and contradicts Piaget's
  views.
- Analyze the language
  development of preschoolers.
- Examine the role of parents and
  schools in enhancing intellectual
  development.

MOLLY, age five, and her friend Jason, age four, were playing with a toy kitchen set and dress-up clothes from a chest in the family day-care home.

"Let's play house," Molly said. "You can be the daddy and I'll be the mommy. Okay?"

"Okay," said Jason. "What do we do?"

"We'll pretend we're getting married," Molly replied. "Here's my wedding dress and here's your suit," she said, handing Jason an old jacket from the dress-up chest and selecting a white dress for herself.

"This will be our house," Molly said pointing to the couch. "Now you have to pretend you're going to work, and I'll make your breakfast."

Molly busied herself at the kitchen set getting out dishes and pots and pans. "Do you want eggs for breakfast," she asked Jason, using a tone of voice that indicated she was playing a role, "or do you want toast?"

"I think I'll have eggs," Jason said, also using a role-playing tone of voice.

"Hmm. What can we use for eggs?" Molly asked in her normal tone of voice. "We'll just pretend this plate has eggs on it."

"Here are your eggs, dear," she said, switching back to her role-playing voice and handing the plate to Jason.

"Thank you, dear," said Jason gravely while pretending to eat the eggs.

"Now you go to work," Molly told Jason.

"And what will you do?" Jason asked her.

"I'll cook dinner," said Molly, putting some toy pots and pans on her toy stove.

"Cook, cook, cook. Cook, cook, cook," she crooned as she shuffled the toy utensils.

Like other preschoolers, Molly engages in a great deal of pretend play, or symbolic play. She is able to move easily from being herself to playing a role. This ability to pretend is the result of her developing representational skills and expanding experiences. In addition, maturing language skills enable her to communicate easily with others.

When Molly was a baby, she learned primarily through her senses—watching, touching, tasting, smelling, and listening to people and objects. She learned a great deal about the world in this manner. She discovered that some things are hard, while others are soft. Some make noise, while others do not. As her motor skills developed, she learned how to manipulate objects, and she began to learn about cause and effect. She learned, for example, that if she dropped a ball, it bounced, but if she dropped a stuffed animal, it just fell down.

When Molly became a toddler, she could walk, say a few words, and understand the meanings of dozens of other words. She began to understand the world through symbols and representative images. When her stuffed dog, Spot, was out of sight, she could remember what it looked like. Sometimes, she could even remember where she had left it. Molly could also think through the steps involved in solving a problem, such as getting a cookie from the cookie jar on the kitchen counter, without having to act out all the steps involved.

Now, as a preschooler, Molly is undergoing a period of tremendous intellectual growth. She has made great strides in learning how to use language. She has progressed from using one- and two-word sentences to using complete sentences. Her vocabulary has expanded enormously; in addition to using nouns and verbs, she is using other kinds of words, such as prepositions and adjectives. Molly's other cognitive skills—memory, perception, classification, attention, and problem solving—are also improving markedly. She is tremendously curious, always asking questions, such as, "Why is the sky blue?" She is also better able to perceive the viewpoints and feelings of others.

Despite these cognitive advances, Molly's thinking skills are still somewhat limited. Her brain can take in and organize information, but adult thought processes are still beyond her. For example, she has not worked out mental strategies for remembering things that are important to her, and she becomes confused when appearance and reality do not coincide. She is approaching—but has not quite arrived at—the point where she can begin formal education. She can, however, benefit from guided instruction from adults, as well as from imitation and learning by doing.

This chapter focuses on the cognitive development of children of preschool age, from three to five years old. You will learn about Piaget's views on cognitive development during this period, as well as the views of his critics and of more recent researchers. You will see the ways in which memory, representation, mathematical skills, and language continue to develop during the preschool period. You will also learn about the standardized tests used to measure intelligence at this age. Finally, you will learn about ways in which caregivers and parents can enhance the language and cognitive skills of preschool-age children.

## Different Views of Intellectual Development in Preschoolers

As in other areas of study, researchers and experts in cognitive development hold a variety of views about how the intellect develops during the preschool years. The best-known view of development is that of Jean Piaget. Other researchers, however, have criticized Piaget's work and developed theories of their own.

### Piaget's Constructivist Approach

A central theme of Piaget's theory of cognitive development is the idea that children actively construct their knowledge or schemes themselves. Schemes, you will recall, are mental or sensorimotor structures that allow children to gain knowledge about their world. Piaget believed that as children interact with their environment, they construct more efficient mental strategies for processing information. Gradually, this process enables them to make sense of their world. Thus, according to the constructivist approach to cognitive development, every encounter that a child has with an object, an event, or another person is a learning experience. And every learning experience contributes to the further development of such cognitive skills as classification, memory, and language.

The constructivist approach to the acquisition of knowledge differs from two traditional views—rationalism and empiricism. Piaget did not believe that children are born with all the knowledge and skills they will need throughout life (the view of rationalists). Nor did he think that children are merely passive receivers of knowledge waiting to be taught (the view of empiricists). Rather, Piaget believed that new cognitive skills develop as new knowledge is acquired and as the child progresses to a further stage of development. In other words, development and learning build on each other in accordance with the child's experiences and physical maturation.

**The Preoperational Period.** As you may recall from Chapter 2, Piaget's stages of development include a preoperational period (ages 2 to 6) and a period of concrete operations (ages 7 to 12). Piaget defined preoperational cognitive development, in many respects, by what children cannot do rather than by what they can do.

According to Piaget, preschool-age children are more intuitive than logical and tend to base judgments on appearances. They are also limited in their thinking by *centration*, or centering, which means that they tend to focus on only one aspect of

Preschoolers have difficulty understanding conservation. They tend to think that the tall glass contains more water than the short one, even after seeing the same quantity of water poured into each glass.

a problem. For example, if a preschooler is asked to classify a pile of blocks, she will probably sort them by shape or color but not by both characteristics.

A dependence on appearances limits children's thinking in other ways as well. Piaget believed, for example, that preschool-age children are egocentric thinkers who are incapable of seeing things from another person's point of view. This is because their thinking is dominated by their own perceptions. Piaget also found that children of this age do not understand the principle of *conservation*, the idea that the same quantities can look very different under different circumstances. A famous experiment developed by Piaget illustrates this point. He poured an equal amount of water into two identical glasses, and the children agreed that the quantities were the same. He then observed the children's reactions as he poured the water from one of the glasses into a shorter, wider one. Preoperational children believed that the tall glass contained more water than the short one; children who had reached the period of concrete operations recognized that the quantity of water remained the same.

**Applying Piaget's Theories to Education.**
Piaget was not particularly interested in how his theories might be used by educators because he did not believe that basic cognitive skills should or can be taught in a formal way. Rather, he advocated that early childhood educators should provide a rich environment in which children can learn naturally. By providing opportunities for experimentation and hands-on exploration of objects and situations, educators would allow children to develop cognitive skills on their own. According to Piaget, the role of adults and older children is to provide information and support as children conduct their own experiments, think about the results, and learn about cause and effect relationships. Through this process, children gradually sharpen their perceptions and construct their own knowledge.

Early childhood educators have taken Piaget's assumptions and translated them into a set of prescriptions about how to influence preschool learning. These prescriptions center around the idea that children should be given opportunities for exploring materials and making discoveries on their own. Such opportunities may include a wide variety of educational toys and creative materials; activities such as story hours and games; trips to zoos, playgrounds, and museums; and special projects, such as growing plants or taking care of animals.

**Piaget's Critics.**    Critics of Piaget argue that he tended to underestimate the cognitive capabilities of young children. For example, his belief that preoperational children are egocentric thinkers is based on the three-mountain experiment described in Chapter 1. As you will recall, this experiment involved asking children to imagine another person's view of model mountains of varying heights and shapes (see Figure 13.1). His younger subjects tended to fail at this task, claiming that the other person's view of the mountains was the same as theirs. Piaget concluded that these children were incapable of perceiving the viewpoints or feelings of others (Piaget & Inhelder, 1956). A large body of more recent research, however, shows that when the task is a familiar one, children as young as three can imagine another's viewpoint very well (Borke, 1983; Hughes & Donaldson, 1983). It may be that Piaget's mountains were just too unfamiliar for his young subjects to handle.

**FIGURE 13.1    Piaget's Three-Mountain Experiment.**
In the three-mountain experiment, the child is asked to describe how the mountains appear to the doll. The preoperational child is unable to see the doll's point of view, thereby demonstrating egocentrism.

In one modern experiment, children aged three to five were asked to decide whether a toy police officer could see a doll placed in different locations on a board divided by walls. The children were able to respond correctly most of the time, showing that they could easily perceive the police officer's point of view (Hughes & Donaldson, 1983). In another experiment, researchers discovered that four-year-olds adapt their speech to their listeners, speaking in short, simple sentences to two-year-olds but speaking normally to adults and to their peers. This experiment shows that preoperational children are aware of the limited communication ability of younger children and are willing to modify their speech to communicate effectively. The researchers concluded that children would not make such an effort to adjust their speech if they were truly egocentric (Shatz & Gelman, 1973).

Piaget may have underestimated the cognitive ability of preschool-age children in regard to his concept of conservation as well. One researcher found that three- and four-year-old children can understand conservation in certain very limited contexts (Gelman, 1972). Thus, children may develop the concept of conservation earlier than Piaget believed.

## The Social Construction of Knowledge

Humans have always passed on knowledge and skills from one generation to another. Among primitive peoples without a written language, knowledge was conveyed through demonstration and oral tradition. Parents shared essential knowledge about the environment with their children and taught them many basic skills, such as building shelters and making clay pots. According to Russian psychologist Lev Vygotsky, children acquire cognitive skills in much the same way. He theorized that children construct new knowledge through social interactions with adults or more advanced children. His theory, called the *social construction of knowledge*, characterizes development as an "apprenticeship in thinking" (Rogoff, 1990). Just as craftspeople help apprentices learn special skills, such as printing or carpentry, adults help children develop intellectual skills, such as memory or an understanding of numbers, by guiding them through activities slightly beyond their competence.

Vygotsky believed that as children grow intellectually, they develop a sensitivity or readiness to proceed to the next level of mental skill or ability. He called this concept the *zone of proximal development*. It is a state of readiness in which children learn cognitive skills that are not yet fully developed but are in the process of developing. It is as though the skills are "buds" ready to blossom rather than fully mature flowers or fruits. According to Vygotsky, language is the means by which adults guide children through each zone of proximal development. As a child learns a new cognitive skill, the external language of the adult teacher becomes transformed into a form of internal speech in the child. That is, young children often talk to themselves when carrying out a task in order to coordinate their thinking and their actions (Vygotsky, 1978).

Vygotsky's theory of the social construction of knowledge sounds very similar to formal educa-

*Vygotsky believed that children benefit intellectually from both formal and informal social exchanges with adults.*

tion. However, he believed that intellectual development is fostered in any social exchange between children and adults, whether formal or informal. A mother teaching her son how to bake a cake and a father helping his daughter count pennies are both guiding their children in developing intellectual skills. Vygotsky, like Piaget, also believed that children are not simply passive receivers of information. Rather, they actively seek out social interactions with adults, thus helping to create their own zone of proximal development.

## Early Childhood Memory

Another approach to cognitive development is the information processing theory. As noted in Chapter 2, this is not really a unified theory but rather a general description of the development of memory and

FOCUS ON **Decision Making in Child Care**

## Kids Who Swear

Amanda is responsible for the four-year-old class at Oak Grove Child Development Center. This year she has a bad case of "potty mouth" in her class. James, an outgoing, energetic redhead, is the main offender. He regularly calls other children poopy head and butt face.

Last year Amanda had a child who used four-letter words casually in conversation. She eliminated this habit by repeatedly telling the child her language was unacceptable and having her use other words to rephrase what she had said.

Much to Amanda's surprise, when she talked to James about his name-calling, his language became worse. He giggled and defiantly repeated the offensive words. Imposing time out didn't work either. Soon other children in the class were imitating James's language.

Amanda had to rethink her strategy. She had watched James often enough to know that he knew his language was unacceptable. While the girl in last year's class had used four-letter words unthinkingly, James was using bad words to get attention. Amanda noticed that he often looked at her and raised his voice when he used unacceptable language.

Amanda decided to ignore James's bad language. She got the class to help her by discussing name-calling at circle time. She told the children that in their class people were called by their right names. No one that she knew was called poopy, butt, or stupid, so no one in the class would answer to those names.

The children wanted to cooperate. At first when James called them a bad name, they would say, "That's not my name." Gradually, they began ignoring his name-calling. It took several weeks, but when James's unacceptable language no longer brought him attention, he stopped using it.

*What are some reasons why children use unacceptable language? How do you let a child know his language is unacceptable? Are there other, faster ways Amanda could have gotten rid of this problem in her class? What would you have done?*

---

problem solving. This approach likens the human brain to a computer. Just as a computer takes in data, stores and processes it, and outputs it on a disk or printed page, so too does the human brain take in, process, and output information. The processing function of computers is similar to problem solving in human thinking, and the information storage component of a computer is comparable to memory capacity in the human brain. Information processing researchers are especially interested in describing the process by which memory develops.

Psychologists define memory as the ability to recognize and recall information. *Recognition* is the simplest form of memory. It is the ability to identify an object as something that has been seen in the past. *Recall* is the ability to retrieve information from memory when no example of that information is present. When a child is asked to recite the alphabet or numbers from memory without using an alphabet or number book, she is using recall. Recognition develops before recall memory, which is a more active skill.

Preschoolers are able to form images of objects in their mind and recall information. However, their ability to recall is poor because they have less general knowledge and know fewer words than older children do to describe what they remember. Moreover, preschoolers have not yet developed the mechanisms or strategies that would enable them to perform memory functions such as recall effectively. These strategies include *rehearsal*, repeating material to be memorized, and *clustering*, or chunking, which means grouping information according to some common trait or element. As children get older, their ability to recall information improves; they acquire more knowledge and learn to use strategies such as clustering to remember information more efficiently. Of course, psychologists and caregivers recognize that preschool-age children are quite capable of remembering things if they are sufficiently interested in them. Preschoolers have no trouble remembering advertising jingles, songs from "Sesame Street" programs, or the names of toys they would like to have.

Some proponents of information processing theory believe that people, including young children, process information at different levels. Information that is stored at a shallow perceptual level is quickly forgotten, but information that is stored at deeper levels is retained and can be recalled. This approach is known as the *levels of processing* theory. According to this theory, preschool-age children can remember better when they are interested in the subject, when they have some previous knowledge about it, and when the information about it is provided in an age-appropriate manner. Psychologists theorize that under these conditions, preschoolers become more efficient at storing and retrieving information and don't have to devote so much of their mental resources to those functions. This enables them to devote more mental energy to processing or problem-solving functions, such as consolidating old ideas and generating new ones.

## Recent Research on Cognitive Abilities

In recent years, a considerable body of research has accumulated to explain how certain cognitive skills develop in young children. Among these skills are representation, number skills, and knowledge of events. Although children begin to develop these skills as infants and toddlers, some of the most important strides occur during the preschool years.

### Representational Skills

Between the ages of three and four, children undergo a significant transition in their ability to form mental representations. At age three, most children are able to hold only one idea of an object in mind, but by age five, they can hold two different ideas about the same object. They are thus able to tell the difference between the appearance and the reality of an object when the two do not match. John H. Flavell and his associates have conducted experiments to try to determine when children develop the ability to distinguish between appearance and reality. In one experiment, a sponge was shown to children between the ages of three and seven. Then the sponge was painted to look like a rock, and children were again asked about its appearance. The younger children reported that what they were seeing looked like a sponge. The older children could distinguish the fact that the sponge looked like a rock from the fact that it was really a painted sponge. In this and other experiments, Flavell found that children begin making the distinction between appearance and reality at around age four or five (Flavell, Green, & Flavell, 1986).

A related development is children's ability to understand that other people have separate, different mental states from themselves. Researchers call this "a theory of mind." One indication that a child has a theory of mind is his or her ability to understand false beliefs. This ability also develops at around age four or five, and it represents an important milestone in cognitive development. One group of researchers tested children's ability to understand false beliefs by having a group of them watch as a story character, Maxi, put some chocolate into a cupboard. Maxi then left and another character moved the chocolate to a second cupboard. The children were asked to decide which cupboard Maxi would go to in order to get the chocolate. The children were being asked to make a distinction between what they knew was true (the chocolate was in the second cupboard) and what Maxi believed to be true but was actually false (the chocolate was in the first cupboard). The four- and five-year-olds picked the wrong cupboard (the second one) more than half the time, but children six years old and above nearly always gave the correct answer (the first cupboard). A similar, but more simplified, group of experiments by other researchers confirmed that the ability to understand false beliefs seems to develop between ages three and five (Gopnik & Astington, 1988; Wimmer & Perner, 1983).

Another representational development that occurs during the preschool years is a substantial increase in

The ability of preschoolers to engage in lengthy periods of pretend play reflects an improvement in memory, attention span, and representational skills.

sociodramatic play and cooperative play (Fein, 1981). One of the distinguishing features of toddlers is their ability to engage in pretend play and deferred imitation. Preschoolers take these skills one step farther. They engage in *sociodramatic play*, lengthy and elaborate episodes of pretend play involving interaction with others (Lillard, 1993). The ability to stage complicated scenarios, as Molly and Jason did in playing house, reflects a significant improvement in memory, attention span, and representational skills. Preschool-age children can now imagine and imitate an entire day of adult activities in correct order, and they can recall many scraps of conversation they have heard spoken by adults. Moreover, they can remain focused on the scene they are acting out for an extended period of time because their attention span has greatly increased. In addition, the vastly improved language skills of preschoolers enable them to carry on meaningful conversations with one another and to give and receive directions.

## Number Skills

Parents and caregivers usually begin teaching children to count when they are toddlers. By the time children are three and a half years old, they already understand the basic process of counting. Psychologist Rochel Gelman, a pioneer in exploring how children learn to count, has concluded that preschoolers have a good grasp of three basic counting principles: (1) They know that there is a standard set of counting words in a certain order—one, two, three, and so on—even though some young children mix up the order. (2) They understand that each object in a group is counted only once. And (3) they understand *cardinality*, the concept that when a person counts a group of objects, the number of objects is represented by the number word assigned to the last object counted (Gelman & Gallistel, 1978).

Psychologist Karen Wynn has recently carried out a group of experiments that provides clear evidence that preschoolers understand the principle of cardinality. For example, a preschooler counting five pennies understands that the last word used, *five*, indicates how many pennies there are in total. According to Wynn's findings, cardinality develops by about age three and a half (Wynn, 1990). Once children understand this concept and the other basic principles of counting, the major change in counting skills is the acquisition of the standard set of counting words, which allows children to count larger and larger numbers of items. The development of counting skills is an important step in cognitive thinking because it demonstrates the child's increasing ability to think about abstract concepts as well as concrete ones.

### Knowledge of Events

What do young children know about the events in their lives, and how do they make sense of new experiences? In Chapter 10, you learned about Katherine Nelson's theory of scripts. Nelson theorizes that young children construct basic scripts, or representations of routine events, as they learn about their environment (Nelson, 1986). Eating dinner, getting dressed, going to a movie, going shopping, and going to preschool are all examples of common scripts held by preschoolers. According to Nelson, script making begins when children are very young and continues throughout life. Two-year-olds can describe scripts for eating, playing, or getting dressed, and adults use scripts to imagine novel events such as walking on the moon.

Scripts play an important role in preschoolers' conceptual development because they help children think about and understand events in their environment. Nelson theorizes that children learn about new experiences by building on general scripts for similar, familiar events. For example, if a child is going to the circus for the first time, he can make use of the script for going to the zoo to understand the new event. Nelson believes that children do this

*The acquisition of counting skills is an important milestone in cognitive development. It shows that a child is able to think about abstract concepts as well as concrete ones.*

by filling new information in appropriate slots in the general script. By using scripts in this way, young children are able to make sense of new experiences very quickly.

Nelson also concludes that scripts provide the appropriate background of social information and cultural knowledge that is necessary for social interaction. When Molly and Jason were playing, for example, Molly clearly had a detailed script in her mind of a typical day in her parents' life. Included in this script were gender role stereotypes—the daddy goes to work and the mommy stays home and cooks—that reflect societal and cultural values.

## Evaluating Intellectual Development: Measuring Intelligence

When children are about age four, it is possible to evaluate their cognitive development by using more sophisticated standardized tests than those used for younger children. Standardized intelligence tests are designed to measure a person's cognitive ability relative to that of a large group of similar people. Four-year-old children are able to sit at a desk, pay attention to various tasks, and respond to questions. They have also mastered the fundamentals of language and have developed counting, classification, and memory skills. Intelligence test scores become fairly stable at this age so they can be helpful in predicting performance, at least in the short term.

In the United States, psychologists usually use either the Stanford-Binet Intelligence Scale or the Wechsler Preschool and Primary Scale of Intelligence (WPPSI) to measure the intelligence of preschoolers. Both tests are commonly referred to as IQ tests because they are said to produce an *intelligence quotient*, a measurement of the subject's intelligence compared to the average performance of other children at the same chronological age. On the Stanford-Binet, for example, a score of 100 means that a child is performing at the same level as the average of all other children that age who have taken the test. A score of 120 means that a child is performing above the level of the average child in the particular age group, and a score of 80 means that the subject is performing below the average level.

---

### Cultural Stereotypes

To stereotype someone means to judge that person on the basis of his or her race, ethnic background, language, religion, gender, or age without knowing the person as an individual.

There are several different kinds of cultural stereotypes. Historical stereotypes characterize a group of people as they were at an earlier time in history, not as they are today. An advertisement showing a Native American family, dressed in buffalo skins, standing before a tepee is an example of historical stereotype.

Ethnic stereotypes come from the misguided belief that all people in an ethnic group share certain traits. The belief that all Asian children excel at math and science is an example of an ethnic stereotype.

Linguistic stereotypes develop when a person's native language is different from the language of the dominant culture. The most common linguistic stereotypes assume that those who are not native speakers of the dominant language are ignorant or stupid.

To counteract stereotyping behavior, caregivers should take an active role in presenting accurate information about the stereotyped person or group. Pointing out stereotypes in toys or advertising and intervening when a child is excluded or rejected on the basis of a stereotypical assumption sensitizes young children to the value of seeing each person as an individual.

Experts can use standardized intelligence tests to evaluate the cognitive development of a four-year-old.

The first IQ test was devised by the French psychologist Alfred Binet more than 100 years ago. That test was revised for English speakers at Stanford University in 1916 and became known in the United States as the Stanford-Binet. Critics of the Stanford-Binet charged that the test was too heavily weighted toward verbal abilities. In 1985, the test was revised to give added weight to nonverbal, quantitative, and memory skills. It was also changed to better account for differences within the American population in terms of geographical distribution, ethnic background, and gender.

Another criticism of the Stanford-Binet has been that it produces only one overall score of intellectual ability. On the other hand, the WPPSI—along with the other two tests that make up the Wechsler Scales—provides IQ scores for two subcategories of intelligence—verbal and performance—in addition to a full-scale IQ. The test consists of 11 subsections that check a variety of skills, including vocabulary, arithmetic, comprehension, the ability to see similarities in different items, and the ability to complete pictures, follow mazes, and copy geometric designs. Moreover, while the Stanford-Binet is used to test everyone over the age of three, the Wechsler Scales consist of three separate tests: one for children ages 4 to 6, one for children ages 6 to 16, and one for adults.

Anyone considering the value and significance of these IQ tests must face a difficult question: What exactly is intelligence? It is important to acknowledge that defining intelligence is the focus of one of the great unresolved debates in psychology and child development. Any individual's mental abilities are made up of a great many separate skills, such as quantitative skills, analytical reasoning, imagination, creativity, and so on. Individuals can vary greatly in their proficiency in any one of these or other intellectual skills. There are two other important questions to consider about IQ tests: Should we be measuring intelligence in young children? How will the test scores be used? Psychologists use standardized IQ tests primarily to predict a child's future success in academic achievement. The Stanford-Binet Intelligence Scale and Wechsler Scales are good predictors of academic achievement. Although IQ tests also provide a fairly good indication of the future success of an individual, many other variables besides mental ability may affect the outcome.

## Language Development

In Chapter 10, you learned how toddlers begin to acquire vocabulary and the structure of language. The chapter discussed Ellen Markman's theory of vocabulary acquisition. Chapter 10 also describes how toddlers begin to learn the structure of language even before talking themselves. For this reason, when they do begin to speak, they arrange words in the correct order and try to adhere to grammatical rules. For example, when children learn that words become plural by adding an *s*, they often add an *s* to all words to make plurals, even to those with irregular plurals. Thus, they may speak of sheeps and mouses instead of sheep and mice. These mistakes disappear as children grow older, but the fact that young children make them illustrates that they are aware that language follows certain general rules.

### Language Development in Preschoolers

Preschoolers continue to learn the meanings and structure of language in the same way as toddlers. However, some quantitative and qualitative differences develop as children become more proficient communicators. At age two, the average child understands about 300 words. From this age on, children acquire vocabulary at such a rapid rate that psychologists frequently refer to a "naming explosion." Preschoolers learn new words at the rate of 6 to 10 a day until, by the time they are six years old, they may know the meanings of 8,000 to 14,000 words.

Researcher Katherine Nelson (1988) describes the acquisition of vocabulary as taking place in three different stages. In stage one, which occurs in infancy and toddlerhood, children learn the meanings of their very first words. These first words are generally object labels, action words, and social phrases, such as *baby*, *go*, and *hi*. New words are learned at a relatively slow rate. During this stage, children understand more words than they speak and, according to Nelson, are "learning what words do." A common characteristic of this stage is overextension—applying the name of one object to others (for example, calling all four-legged animals dogs). Children begin moving from stage one to stage two when they are between 18 and 24 months old. This is when the "naming explosion" starts. Stage two encompasses the preschool period and can last several years. During this stage, children acquire the meanings of thousands of new words. Children also come to understand that words name categories of objects and actions. Stage three, which begins at age three or four and continues into the school years, is the period during which children revise, reorganize, and consolidate their understanding of meanings. Children in this stage are already proficient in language use, and they begin to use words more broadly to describe more than one function, just as adults do. They can distinguish, for example, between *play* as a verb ("Go play with your friend") and *play* as a noun ("We're going to see a play"). They also mentally organize words into groups, such as a group containing *father*, *mother*, *son*, and *daughter*, because they understand how the words are related.

### The Development of Complex Speech

During the preschool years, children's speech becomes much more complex than that of toddlers. For one thing, preschoolers speak in longer sentences. For example, while two-year-old children typically speak in two-word sentences, five-year-olds use sentences that are five, six, or more words long. The work of psychologist Roger Brown shows that just as preschoolers acquire vocabulary in stages, they also acquire the elements of grammar in a regular order or sequence. They learn, for example, to add an *s* to form plurals before they learn to use the articles *a* or *the* (Brown, 1973).

By age four or five, preschoolers have acquired most of the elements of grammar. They can form the past, present, and future tenses of verbs; they can use possessive pronouns correctly; and they

## FOCUS ON ◆ Communicating with Parents

### Explaining Policy on Toy Guns

Richard is the assistant director of a child care center that serves a small ranching community. Each September he holds a parents' meeting to welcome new families and explain the center's policies and goals for the year.

After dealing with administrative matters such as late-payment policies and sign-out procedures, he turns to the philosophy and goals of the center. One issue he feels strongly about is teaching peace.

RICHARD: During the year, children will have the opportunity to bring special toys from home to share with the class. However, we ask that you not allow your child to bring toy guns, knives, or other weapons. We believe in teaching that disagreements should be settled with words.

PARENT: I don't really understand what you have against toy guns. The children love to play with them. They know the difference between real guns and toy guns.

RICHARD: We believe that if we allow children to bring toy weapons to school, we are in a sense approving their use. In play, children don't make clear distinctions between fantasy and reality.

PARENT: What do you do when a kid picks up a stick and yells, "Bang! Bang!"?

RICHARD: We tell the child to drop the stick. We also say that playing with sticks can accidentally hurt other people's eyes.

SECOND PARENT: A lot of us in this community hunt and have guns in our homes. Are you teaching our children that this is wrong?

RICHARD: No. We teach that guns are not toys. Because hunting is popular around here, we stress that children should never play with guns. We know that many parents with guns are responsible and teach gun safety at home. We try to reinforce this teaching at the center.

THIRD PARENT: I think that's a good policy.

SECOND PARENT: I don't. If guns are an accepted part of this community, what right do you have to forbid children to play with them?

RICHARD: We have the right to make rules for behavior at our center, just as you have the right to make rules for behavior at home. Children understand that different places have different rules. We tell children that our school rule is no guns. They accept that. With all the incidents of shootings in high schools around the country, we believe it's important to make a statement at a very early age that no guns, toy or real, belong at school.

*Do you think Richard handled the parents' questions well? How would you have answered them?*

---

have added prepositions, interrogatives, and pronouns to their repertoire of spoken words. They can also use conjunctions to join together words and sentences ("Me and Bobby want to go outside"), construct indirect object–direct object sentences ("I gave Bobby my ice cream"), and form tag questions ("My shoes are dirty, aren't they, Mommy?") (Bowerman, 1979).

Preschoolers do, however, have trouble with concepts of size and distance, such as *big* and *little* and *far* and *near*, and with conditionals, such as *if* and *unless*. Although children at this age still tend to

The preschooler's improved language abilities and expanded vocabulary make it possible for him to effectively communicate his ideas to others.

overapply grammatical rules—for example, saying *comed* instead of *came*—by age five, they are also beginning to use irregular forms correctly.

Such greatly increased language competence does not mean that preschoolers have mastered all the elements of language. Many children, for example, continue to have difficulty with the pronunciation of certain consonants or combinations of consonants (such as *j*, *r*, *s*, *th*, and *sp*) until they are five or six years old. Misuse of these sounds is not an indication that a child needs a speech therapist. Most adults are familiar with the common mistake that young children make in pronouncing the word *spaghetti* so that it comes out *pesghetti*. These kinds of errors are common and usually disappear in time.

An amusing aspect of children's language understanding at this age is that they tend to take everything literally. For example, if an adult says, "I'd give an arm and a leg for that car," a preschooler may well imagine the adult detaching an arm and a leg at the auto dealership. Children also tend to use *creative vocabulary*, making up new words if they don't know a word for something. Among the most common errors are adding *-er* to a noun to mean someone who does something (*cooker* for one who cooks), adding *un-* to a word to show its opposite (*unhot* instead of cold), and using words to describe what an object does (*food cooker* for stove, *cutter* for knife).

### Language and Communication

It was noted in Chapter 7 that language and communication are not interchangeable. Communication occurs when someone transmits a message to another person, who understands it; language is just one way, although certainly the most complex way, of sending a message. Children learn language primarily to communicate with adults and other children. By the time they have reached preschool age, they have become very proficient in their ability to communicate, despite their language limitations. Molly and Jason could discuss the planning and preparation of their imaginary meals even though their cooking vocabulary was much smaller than an adult's. Researcher Katherine Nelson believes that children's ability to relate a script describing what they did the day before is a more accurate measure of their ability to communicate meaningfully than whether they use a large vocabulary or perfect grammar in their speech (Nelson & Gruendel, 1981).

Preschoolers also use speech for other purposes than to communicate with others. For example, they talk to themselves a great deal. This gives them an opportunity to practice language and behavior. Lev Vygotsky (1978) described this type of speech as *private speech,* and he theorized that children use private speech to order their thoughts and control their actions. Molly, for example, crooned, "Cook, cook, cook," to herself as she pretended to carry out that action. This type of speech is different from *social speech,* which is speech intended to communicate with others. Private speech later becomes inner speech, which is not vocalized.

Psychologists believe that private speech serves a variety of important purposes. Children use private speech simply to enjoy wordplay and the production of sounds. It may also give them practice in pronouncing certain sounds, just as the babble of infants helps prepare them for speaking words. Preschoolers frequently use private speech in pretend or fantasy play, and it is thus a way to rehearse behavior they have seen and heard. They may, for example, talk to their dolls, stuffed animals, and other toys. "Now you sit there and be quiet," a preschooler might tell her dolls, sternly shaking her finger at them. Children also use private speech to release emotions. "You darn table!" a preschooler may yell upon running into a coffee table and hurting himself. Private speech is also related to *social monologue,* in which two children are talking to each other but neither seems to be listening and neither responds to what the other is saying. In effect, the two children are carrying on two separate conversations. It doesn't seem to bother either one that the other is not participating in his or her conversation.

## Literacy

The preparations for reading and writing that began in toddlerhood continue to develop during the preschool period. Four- and five-year-olds still love to have adults read to them, and they especially love books that feature rhyming words and word repetition. Preschoolers already understand a good deal about books. They know where books begin and end, and they know that one reads through a book from one page to the next. They know that the pictures in the book follow the story, but they realize that the printed symbols—the words—are what really tell the story. They are also aware that readers progress through these symbols from top to bottom and left to right on the page.

Language development plays a crucial role in the development of literacy and the readiness to read. Psychologist I. Y. Liberman believes that children acquire an awareness of the structure of words around age five or six and that this awareness is an important step in reading readiness. Children of five or six realize that words can be broken down into individual sounds. They are able to pronounce a word without a specific sound part—for example, saying the word *tone* instead of *stone* (Liberman, Shankweiler, Fisher, & Carter, 1974).

The development of motor skills also plays a role in the development of literacy. By preschool age, children are more proficient in drawing. The scribbles of toddlerhood have now become sketches that somewhat resemble their subjects. Human figures have heads, facial features, and arms and legs, and houses have doors and windows. Many preschoolers also begin trying to imitate the handwriting of adults. They like to learn how to print their own name and other letters of the alphabet, although their printed letters vary greatly in size, spacing, and uniformity. Preschoolers' knowledge of books and written language and their growing mastery of the fine motor skills used in drawing and printing are all essential preparation for learning to read and write in elementary school.

## Socioeconomic, Familial, and Cultural Differences

By the time preschoolers start school, they may exhibit noticeable differences in language and literacy

Preschoolers' growing command of fine motor skills will help them learn to write in elementary school.

proficiency. Various studies have found that girls tend to be more proficient in language skills than boys and that firstborns and only children are more proficient than later children and twins (Rebelsky, Star, & Luria, 1967). A possible explanation for these differences may be found in other studies that show that parents talk more to girls, firstborns, and only children than to boys and later children (Goldberg & Lewis, 1969; Jacobs & Moss, 1976).

It should be noted that children not only learn their native language from their parents and other adults around them, but they also learn *dialects*, versions of a language that are characteristic of distinct ethnic groups or geographical regions. In addition, they may learn *accents*, minor speech differences common to particular groups or regions. It is im-portant to realize that accents and dialects do not indicate inferior social class, education, or upbringing.

Many children grow up in bilingual homes in which one or both parents speak a language other than English. Bilingual parents usually want to pass on their native language to their children. As a result, these children may learn more than one language. Young children are very capable of learning a second language; in fact, learning another language may improve such cognitive skills as verbal skills, categorization, and analytic reasoning (Diaz, 1985).

## Implications and Applications

For the most part, preschoolers are still learning from their environment through self-directed problem solving and experimentation. They are motivated to learn by their own curiosity and by the pleasure they receive from being able to accomplish new tasks. In addition, preschoolers are boisterous, active, and energetic. They are not yet ready to sit quietly and work at mental tasks for long periods of time. Nor are they ready for lectures, highly structured lessons, workbooks, flash cards, and many of the other teacher-directed learning activities that they will have to become accustomed to during their school years.

Of course, caregivers must always keep in mind that each preschooler learns at his or her own pace. They should also be aware that children from different social, economic, and cultural backgrounds have different individual needs and different learning styles.

### The Role of Adults in Cognitive Development

Although preschoolers are not yet ready for formal instruction in a classroom setting, this does not mean that they cannot benefit from the guidance and assistance of adults. Both parents and caregivers can, and should, influence the intellectual growth of children during the preschool years. In a position statement on developmentally appropriate practice in preschool programs, the National Association for the Education of Young Children (NAEYC) recommends that adults act as guides or

**TABLE 13.1**
**Milestones of Intellectual Development, Ages Three to Five**

| Age | Milestones |
| --- | --- |
| 3 years | *Cognitive Development*<br><br>Recognizes and remembers objects seen before and engages in deferred imitation<br>Mentally works out steps involved in solving a simple problem<br>Begins to develop representational skills, recognizing symbols and words and forming mental images<br>Begins categorizing by forming concepts and sorting and labeling objects and events by group<br>Begins to develop a sense of right and wrong<br>Tests reality through pretend play but cannot distinguish between reality and personal desires<br><br>*Language Development*<br><br>Begins speaking in short, simple sentences<br>Identifies and explains use of household objects<br>Understands more vocabulary words than he or she can say<br>Recognizes that language has a specific structure and rules |
| 4 to 5 years | *Cognitive Development*<br><br>Begins to develop the ability to deal with abstraction<br>Begins to distinguish between appearance and reality<br>Begins to understand false beliefs<br>Perceives another person's point of view<br>Develops increased memory and attention span and can recall objects and events<br>Develops counting, math, and problem-solving skills<br>Uses scripts, categorization, and other cognitive skills to combine ideas into more complex relationships<br><br>*Language Development*<br><br>Acquires vocabulary rapidly<br>Begins to use complex sentences, indicating increased understanding of grammar and structure of language<br>Uses private speech more<br>Understands and shows interest in printed and handwritten words; tries to read and write |

facilitators of learning rather than as lecturers or instructors (NAEYC, 1992). To do this, parents and caregivers should provide a stimulating environment that offers a wide variety of learning opportunities. They should also work with children during activities to help them solve problems and stretch their mind.

The NAEYC recommends that caregivers allow children to select their own activities from a variety of materials, including puzzles, toys, blocks, games, art and music materials, dress-up clothes, and books. Activities and materials should be relevant to the children's lives and experiences, as well as appropriate for their age and level of physical coordination. For example, preschoolers can work with blunt scissors and large crayons but not with sharp tools or small objects that are difficult to hold or manipulate. Caregivers should work with children individually or in small groups in an enjoyable, informal setting, assisting and advising them when they need help.

The NAEYC proposes that children should have many opportunities every day to play, to express themselves artistically and creatively, to learn about

## Multi-Age or Homogenous Age Grouping

Carmen and Roberta are preschool teachers who have been asked to investigate the educational implications of switching from homogenous age classes to multi-age classes. The school administration is interested in exploring this change because the number of children enrolled at each age varies from year to year. With multi-age grouping, class size can be kept smaller and more consistent. Before making a change, the school wants to understand the benefits and drawbacks of each approach. After conducting a study, Carmen and Roberta share their findings with the other teachers, the administration, and interested parents. As a result of the study, however, the two teachers have come to opposite conclusions.

Roberta:

"Multi-age grouping refers to intentionally creating a class in which the participants' age span is greater than 12 months. In most cases, the age span is 24 or more months.

"We all know that children learn from their peers as well as from their teachers. In a multi-age class, children learn from being with other children whose experiences, abilities, and maturity are different from their own.

"Older children develop patience and tolerance in dealing with younger children whose skills and attention span are not as great as their own. They have the opportunity to nurture the younger children. Younger children see older children as role models. The classroom becomes more like a family.

"Academically, there are benefits too. When rigid ideas about what a child should learn at a certain age are put aside, the teacher treats each child as an individual learner and teaches to his or her strengths and weaknesses. Moreover, older children instruct younger ones, both by direct instruction and by example, creating a richer classroom environment.

"A younger child who is ready for more challenging learning can work with older children. A late-blooming or immature older child who is slower than his age peers does not stand out. He maintains his self-esteem because the classroom gives him the opportunity to grow at his own rate.

"With the necessary teacher training, multi-age classrooms can give us an exciting opportunity to let our children develop at their own pace while sharing learning experiences and building self-esteem."

Carmen:

"Our school now has homogenous age grouping. Everyone whose birthday falls between certain dates is admitted to one class. Teachers prepare to teach children with a maximum age difference of 12 months.

"We have years of experience teaching homogenous groups, and our teachers have a good idea of the capabilities of each age group. Their lesson plans are built around working with a group that has limited diversity in maturity and life experience.

"These single-age classes have been successful in meeting the needs of our students. If we change to a multi-age classroom, we'll need to spend considerable time and money on retraining our teachers and revising our curricula, and we can't be sure of the results.

"Homogenous groups allow the teacher to present information to the class as a whole. There's little need to break into small groups for instruction. Classrooms are more controlled and less chaotic. Because one lesson is taught to all students, the teacher can prepare more thoroughly. When children are at the same level, information learned in one lesson can be carried over easily into another activity, creating integrated learning units.

"In a homogenous group, younger students do not become a burden to older, more advanced students. The behavior of the younger, less mature children does not distract older children or monopolize the teacher's time.

"Multi-age grouping is a step backward to the one-room schoolhouse and should not be implemented to solve an administrative problem."

*Would you like to teach in a multi-age classroom? What do you think would be the main advantages? The main drawbacks? Why do you think most schools use homogenous grouping?*

counting and letters of the alphabet, to be exposed to reading and writing, and to engage in activities that help prepare them for literacy. Such activities may include listening to stories, dictating and illustrating stories, playing games, doing pegboard puzzles, solving mazes, talking to others, participating in sociodramatic play, drawing, learning to print letters and write their own name, and working with books, classroom charts, and so on.

Parents play a special role in their children's intellectual development. They can play their part by being warm, loving, and supportive; by encouraging their children to explore their environment; and by fostering curiosity, speech, self-expression, and creativity. It is important for parents to play games with their children, to read to them, and to teach them to perform simple tasks. Parents should also encourage independence in their children, helping them learn to do things for themselves. Children who feel capable and competent are better able to develop the self-confidence and self-esteem they will need for further development.

### The Role of Adults in the Development of Language Skills

Probably the most important thing that adults can do to facilitate the language development of preschoolers is to provide a safe, supportive atmosphere where children feel comfortable speaking to others and expressing their feelings. Caregivers should offer many opportunities throughout the day for children to hold conversations, to sing, to ask questions, to use creative vocabulary and nonsense language, and to make up stories.

To reinforce and expand language skills, the NAEYC advises adults to speak clearly to children in short, grammatically correct sentences. It is important not to correct a child's incorrect grammar but simply to restate his comments correctly. Adults should never make fun of a child for asking silly questions or misusing language. Rather, they should give children every opportunity to ask questions, describe events, and express their feelings as best they can. It is equally important to listen attentively to children and always answer their questions, no matter how silly they may seem. Adults should also play games that amuse children and facilitate their language skills. Rhyming games such as farmer in the dell, tisket-a-tasket, and London Bridge are especially enjoyable to preschoolers.

### The Role of Play in Cognitive Development

Play is one of the most important activities in a preschooler's life. Like toddlers, preschoolers learn a great deal about their environment through play. When two or more preschoolers play together, they have many opportunities to learn and practice social skills, such as sharing, taking turns, and cooperating. Play also helps children develop the large and fine motor skills they will need and use as they grow older. Pretend play or sociodramatic play gives children an opportunity to rehearse speech, communicate with one another, and practice social skills. Sociodramatic play also reveals a great deal about the language competence of preschoolers. When Molly and Jason played house, they slipped easily back and forth from pretend speech, in which they spoke in the role of a character, to normal,

Caregivers can foster language development by encouraging children to ask questions and express their feelings and by listening attentively whenever children speak.

Day-care and preschool facilities offer a wide variety of programs designed to facilitate cognitive development. One program that has become very popular is the Montessori system. Today, thousands of Montessori schools are in operation throughout the United States, and many non-Montessori preschools make use of similar curriculum elements.

Maria Montessori was a physician in Italy at the turn of the century who developed a set of principles for educating children. The basis of all education, she believed, is to respect children as individuals. Children should always be treated with kindness and dignity, and they should be allowed to learn at their own pace according to individual needs and levels of development. Montessori believed that children pass through a series of sensitive periods during which they are more capable of learning certain cognitive skills. The role of the teacher is to observe when these periods occur and then provide the appropriate environment for learning.

Montessori incorporated a number of Piaget's ideas in her program, particularly the idea that children are participants in constructing their own knowledge. Since it was also her belief that children learn primarily through their senses, the Montessori program consists of a rich sensory environment in which children can learn on their own by manipulating specially designed sensory materials. Montessori materials include cloth swatches to develop the sense of touch; various rods, towers, stairs, blocks, and sticks to develop the visual senses; smelling jars to teach children to distinguish odors; and bells and sound boxes to develop the sense of hearing. Although the Montessori system has gained many followers, it has also been criticized for relying heavily on impersonal objects rather than social interaction to educate. The system has also been faulted for emphasizing intellectual development at the expense of emotional and physical development.

everyday speech, in which they planned and directed the action. Studies have shown that this ability to shift between fantasy and reality helps children develop cognitive, language, and social skills (Garvey, 1977; Rubin, 1980).

## The Impact of Preschool Education

Psychologists find it difficult to measure the effects of preschool education on intellectual development because so many other factors, such as culture, socioeconomic status, and the absence of a parent, also influence development. Nevertheless, researchers generally agree that high-quality preschool programs that involve parents do enhance cognitive and language development. High-quality programs should include a wide variety of age-appropriate activities and suitable caregiver to child ratios.

## The Impact of Early Intervention

Preschool programs can improve the cognitive development not only of children from normal backgrounds but also of children who are considered disadvantaged because of poverty, stimulus deprivation, or other factors. As a result, preschool edu-

Montessori preschools provide children with a rich sensory environment in which they can develop cognitive skills on their own.

cation is seen as a means of intervening early in a child's development to ensure that normal cognitive development takes place.

The federally funded Head Start program, which was introduced in the 1960s, is the largest and best known of the early intervention programs. The purpose of Head Start is to provide children with early *compensatory education* to make up for the disadvantages of their home life. Head Start is really a number of locally run programs. Some of these programs are part-time or full-time preschools. Others are in-home teaching programs that concentrate on training parents to provide appropriate educational experiences at home. Various studies have been made of the Head Start program over the years. Some research seems to show that the gains in IQ and academic accomplishment achieved by Head Start appear to fade away by the third or fourth grade. However, longitudinal studies that follow Head Start graduates all through school find that students continue to benefit from early intervention into adulthood. Head Start graduates tend to score higher on achievement tests and to get higher grades than children from the same background who did not participate in Head Start. They are also less likely to be placed in special education programs, less likely to be held back a grade, and more likely to stay in school than non-Head Start students (Lazar & Darlington, 1982). One study that followed Head Start graduates through age 19 found that they were more likely to have enrolled in college or vocational school or to have a job than similar students who had not been enrolled in preschool. The Head Start students were also more likely to earn more money during their working lives and less likely to require welfare assistance or to commit crimes. Head Start and other early intervention programs thus appear to be of great value in enhancing academic achievement, as well as in helping to mold productive citizens (Clement, Schweinhart, Barnett, Epstein, & Weikart, 1984).

## SUMMARY

- Although preschoolers have greatly improved their language abilities and cognitive skills, they are still incapable of adult thought processes.
- According to Piaget, children are active participants in their own learning.
- Piaget believed that preschool-age children are limited in their thinking. They do not understand conservation, the idea that quantities do not change despite changes in appearance. He also believed that preschoolers are limited by centration, meaning that they cannot focus on more than one aspect of a problem.
- Educators apply Piaget's concepts by providing a rich environment with a variety of materials that children can use to make discoveries on their own.
- Modern research indicates that Piaget underestimated the ability of preschoolers to perceive other people's viewpoints and to understand conservation.
- Lev Vygotsky's social construction of knowledge theory proposes that adults pass on knowledge and cognitive skills to children through language.
- The information processing theory likens the development of memory and problem solving to the input, processing, and output of a computer.
- Although preschoolers have not yet developed strategies for remembering information, they remember information that is relevant and interesting to them.
- The sociodramatic play of preschoolers is an indication of their growing ability to form mental representations, to remember, and to communicate with others.
- Children use mental scripts to understand the events in their lives. Scripts also help children learn cultural information and facilitate communication.
- The intellectual development of children can be measured by standardized IQ tests, such as the Stanford-Binet and the Wechsler Scales, starting at age three or four.
- During the preschool period, children learn the meanings of thousands of new words. They also learn to speak in longer, more grammatical, and more complex sentences.
- Children use private speech for a variety of noncommunication purposes, including wordplay, self-regulation, and the expression of emotions.
- The role of parents and other caregivers is to provide a warm, supportive atmosphere for preschoolers and to act as guides and facilitators of learning.
- Adults enhance language development when they speak simply and clearly, answer children's questions, read to them and play games with them, and make them feel comfortable about expressing themselves verbally.
- Play is one of the most important activities of preschoolers. It fosters imagination, creativity, social skills, and cognitive skills.

- High-quality preschool education programs promote cognitive and language skills. One popular program, the Montessori system, is based on learning through the senses.
- Early intervention can improve the cognitive skills of disadvantaged children. The best-known early intervention program is Head Start.

## BUILDING VOCABULARY

Write a definition for each vocabulary term listed below.

accent
cardinality
centration
clustering
compensatory education
conservation
creative vocabulary
dialect
intelligence quotient
levels of processing

private speech
recall
recognition
rehearsal
social construction of knowledge
social monologue
social speech
sociodramatic play
zone of proximal development

## ACQUIRING KNOWLEDGE

1. Name three cognitive skills that improve dramatically by the time a child reaches preschool age.
2. According to Piaget's constructivist approach, how do children learn?
3. How does Piaget's theory differ from both rationalism and empiricism?
4. Define centration.
5. Piaget said that preschool, or preoperational, children don't understand conservation. What did he mean by that?
6. According to Piaget, how should parents and caregivers help children learn?
7. According to Vygotsky, how do children acquire cognitive skills?
8. What does the term *zone of proximal development* mean?
9. According to Vygotsky, by what means do adults guide children through each zone of proximal development?
10. What is the difference between recognition and recall?
11. Name one strategy that children use to recall information as they get older.
12. According to the levels of processing theory, when are preschoolers better able to remember something?
13. How do periods of pretend play change as children move from toddlerhood to preschool age?
14. List two basic counting principles that children usually understand by the time they reach preschool age.

15. What are scripts? Give an example of a preschooler's script.
16. Name one difference between the Stanford-Binet Intelligence Scale and the Wechsler Scales.
17. What is the "naming explosion" period and when does it usually begin?
18. Contrast the speech of toddlers with the speech of preschoolers.
19. Give an example of a grammatical mistake that is common among preschoolers.
20. Why do children use private speech?
21. Name two factors that contribute to literacy.
22. Summarize the NAEYC recommendations on how adults should facilitate learning in a preschool environment.
23. What can adults do to foster the language development of preschoolers?
24. Describe the Montessori principles for educating children.
25. What is the purpose of early intervention programs such as Head Start?

## THINKING CRITICALLY

1. Recent studies have shown that preschoolers have certain mental abilities that Piaget claimed were lacking in preoperational children. What do these studies say about the validity of Piaget's theory as a whole? Should this recent information be used to reject his theory or to correct it?
2. The ideas of Jean Piaget and Maria Montessori have had a great influence on preschool education. How are their attitudes toward children similar? How are their perspectives different?
3. Standardized IQ tests can be used to assess a child's intelligence beginning at age three. Do you think these tests provide an accurate view of a child's intellectual capacity? What skills or abilities make up intelligence?
4. Vygotsky observed that children use private speech to practice adult behaviors. How does this observation reflect his social learning theory?
5. Early intervention programs provide disadvantaged preschoolers with a stimulating environment in which to learn. What impact do you think such programs have on a child's school performance and adult life?

## OBSERVATIONS AND APPLICATIONS

1. Observe two pairs of preschool children engaged in symbolic play in a home or child care setting. Observe each pair for 10 to 15 minutes. What situations do the children set up? How much do they speak to each other, and how much of their speech is directed toward themselves? How long do they stay with one imaginative situation before changing it? What similarities and differences do you observe in the type of situations imagined by boys and girls? What objects do the children use while engaged in play, and to what use do they put the objects?
2. Observe a preschool class of four-year-olds. Observe how literacy skills are presented to the children. How much time is spent on reading aloud to the children? Do the children look at books by themselves? Are they expected to recognize letter names? Letter sounds? Describe what else you observe that relates to the development of literacy skills.

3. Try Piaget's classic conservation experiment. Select four different children, ranging in age from three to five, for the experiment and do it separately with each child. First, fill two identical glasses with an equal amount of water. Ask the child if the two glasses have the same amount of water in them. (If a child does not agree that the two glasses contain the same amount of water, do not continue the experiment with that child.) Then pour the liquid from one of the glasses into a shorter, wider glass. Again, ask the child if the two glasses contain the same amount of water. If the child says no, ask which glass has more water in it. Record each child's responses and see if your results agree with Piaget's.

4. Mr. Patel asks you about his four-year-old daughter Shristie. While the family has not actively tried to teach her to read, she already recognizes a few words, including *stop*. The preschool where you work does not have a formal reading program. Mr. Patel wonders whether he should start teaching Shristie to read at home or whether the school can do more to encourage her reading development. What advice would you give Mr. Patel?

## SUGGESTIONS FOR FURTHER READING

Ausberger, C. et al. (1982). *Learning to talk is child's play*. Tucson, AZ: Communication Skill Builders.

Cazden, C. B. (Ed.). (1981). *Language in early childhood education*. Washington, DC: National Association for the Education of Young Children.

Donaldson, M. (1978). *Children's minds*. New York: Norton.

Elkind, D. (1987). *Miseducation: Preschoolers at risk*. New York: Knopf.

Forman, G. E., & Kuschner, D. S. *The child's construction of knowledge: Piaget for teaching children*. Washington, DC: National Association for the Education of Young Children.

Goldman, J., Stein, C. E., & Guerry, S. (1983). *Psychological methods of child assessment*. New York: Bruner/Mazel.

Iwamura, S. G. (1980). *The verbal games of pre-school children*. New York: St. Martin's.

Kamii, C. (1982). *Number in preschool and kindergarten*. Washington, DC: National Association for the Education of Young Children.

Meisels, S. J. (1989). *Developmental screening in early childhood: A guide*. Washington, DC: National Association for the Education of Young Children.

Montessori, M. (1965). *The Montessori method*. Cambridge, MA: Bentley.

National Association for the Education of Young Children. (1992). *Developmentally appropriate practice in early childhood programs serving younger preschoolers*. Washington, DC: Author.

Pressley, M., & Brainerd, C. J. (Eds.). (1985). *Cognitive learning and memory in children*. New York: Springer-Verlag.

Saunders, R., & Bingham-Newman, A. M. (1984). *Piagetian perspectives for preschools: A thinking book for teachers*. Englewood Cliffs, NJ: Prentice-Hall.

Schickedanz, J. (1986). *More than abc's: The early stages of reading and writing*. Washington, DC: National Association for the Education of Young Children.

# 14 | Emotional and Social Development

## OBJECTIVES
Studying this chapter will enable
you to

- Describe the development of self-
  concept and sexual identity in
  preschoolers.
- Describe how children develop
  emotionally.
- Identify the causes of childhood
  fears and anxiety.
- Explain how interacting with
  playmates and siblings promotes
  social development in preschool
  children.
- Discuss the evolution of moral
  development in preschoolers.
- Explain how adults can help
  children develop emotionally and
  socially during the preschool
  years.

FOUR-YEAR-OLD JOSH was playing on the floor with a dozen toy cars when his two-year-old brother, Adam, came over to him and snatched a car away.

"No! That's mine!" Josh shouted angrily, and he wrenched the car out of Adam's hands, causing the two-year-old to burst into tears.

Surprised by Adam's reaction, Josh patted his brother gently on the back crooning, "Don't cry, Adam; don't cry."

The boys' mother, who had observed the incident, came over and asked Josh, "Can't Adam have just one of your cars? You have so many and he doesn't have any."

"But, Mommy, he always wants my toys," Josh complained.

"That's because you're his big brother and he wants to do the things you do," she replied. "Maybe if you give him one car, he'll leave you alone so you can play with the rest."

"Okay, he can have this one," Josh said, selecting a car from his collection. "But that's all!"

Josh went back to playing with his cars, pushing them across the room and making engine noises with his mouth. Adam watched intently for a few minutes. Then he too began pushing his car across the room and making engine noises. Soon both boys were playing peacefully, although they did not play together or even seem to notice each other's activities.

Josh is a typical preschooler, and his reaction to his brother's interference was perfectly normal. At first he was angry and aggressive toward Adam. Then he clearly felt empathy toward the younger boy and tried to comfort him when he cried. Josh's emotional responses are already well developed, and his language skills enable him to express his feelings and desires very clearly. Josh is also developing a sense of morality and is beginning to learn right from wrong.

Josh's social skills are also developing normally. He attends a preschool where he has made friends with another boy. They insist on playing together whenever they can, even though their play sessions often end in conflict. Josh's experience with other children is helping him learn many new abilities such as sharing, cooperating, and compromising. At age four, he may be more willing to share his cars with Adam than he would have been a year earlier. As an older brother, Josh is an important role model to Adam. Through Josh, Adam will learn many cognitive and social skills, and the younger boy will imitate his brother in countless ways as they grow up. This chapter examines how preschoolers like Josh develop socially, morally, and emotionally. It also explores the ways in which children form their self-concept and sexual identity during the preschool years.

## Formation of Self-Concept in Preschool Children

As infants interact with other people, they start to form ideas about their existence as separate individuals. In toddlerhood, this idea of individuality develops into feelings of independence, as children realize that they are capable of influencing objects, events, and people. Once toddlers learn to talk, they soon start using the words I and me to identify themselves and express their wants and needs.

By the preschool years, children have acquired a definite set of perceptions and feelings that helps them define who they are and how they are different from others. Usually, this self-concept centers around physical attributes (I'm this tall), possessions (I have new skates), age (I'll be four next week), and abilities (I can button my coat). To adults, many of the statements preschoolers make seem to smack of bragging or possessiveness. However, child psychologists feel that such statements are simply the way children use their limited experiences and understanding of the world to identify themselves as separate individuals. At this age, children still think mostly of themselves and have difficulty seeing things from another's perspective.

When children become preschoolers, they grow more independent and less attached to their parents. As their self-concept develops, they tend to form very positive impressions of themselves and to overestimate their own physical and mental abilities. The rallying cry of the normal preschooler is "I can do it myself." Preschool children want to accomplish every task themselves, from getting dressed to performing household chores, and if they have a healthy self-image, they firmly believe they can successfully complete anything they attempt. Most children do not form a more accurate idea of their abilities and limitations until the early school years. The fact that preschool children want to do things for themselves but are not always able to do so leads to a conflict between expectations and reality.

### Initiative Versus Guilt

As you learned in earlier chapters, Erik Erikson believes that children go through a series of psychosocial stages in which opposite feelings contend with each other. In the first stage, children learn about trust and mistrust. The second stage involves the conflict between a desire for autonomy and a sense of shame.

According to Erikson, children arrive at the third stage of the psychosocial hierarchy, initiative versus guilt, during the preschool years. By age four, children have developed a strong sense of self and an internalized conscience. As a result, they often experience a conflict between the desire to take on new tasks and their moral reservations about carrying them out. For example, when a preschooler wants to pour a glass of milk, the desire to pour it herself is the initiative. However, if the child miscalculates and overfills the glass, her failure arouses feelings of guilt. Erikson has suggested that the conflict between initiative and guilt creates a split between the childlike part of personality—which wants to try new things—and the growing adult part—which weighs motives and actions. He believes that as children learn to balance these conflicting goals, they develop a sense of purpose and the courage to imagine and pursue goals without guilt or fear of punishment.

During this period, praise and blame become strong motivators. Praising children for performing specific tasks helps reinforce desirable behaviors, while blaming or criticizing them arouses strong feelings of guilt. According to Erikson, praise and blame act as motivators for children of this age because they are learning to see things from another person's perspective. They also have a greater understanding of social rules and roles. In other words, they have reached a stage of development in which they want others to think well of them.

## The Development of Sexual Identity

How do young children know what sex they are and what behaviors and roles are expected of them because of their gender? Researchers have found that children have some idea of *sexual identity*, the understanding that they are girls or boys, by age two. However, not until they are four or five do most children understand that gender is based on biology. For example, a three-year-old may believe that his baby sister's gender is determined by her pink dresses or long hair rather than by the fact that she has a vagina instead of a penis. Moreover, children do not develop an understanding of *gender constancy*, the concept that one's gender never changes, until they are about five or six years old. Thus a four-year-old girl may believe that she can grow up to be a daddy. It is normal for preschoolers to explore their body while they are learning about gender differences.

Preschoolers tend to describe themselves according to their physical attributes, age, possessions, and abilities.

In addition to learning about gender, preschoolers learn about *gender roles*, the outward behaviors and attitudes that society regards as appropriate for men and women in each culture. At around age three, children begin playing with gender-typed toys—cars and guns for boys, dolls and household equipment for girls. At about this same age, children also begin to form gender role stereotypes, which are oversimplified, fixed ideas about the behaviors and characteristics of each sex. One study found that preschool children from families in which the mother stayed home showed strong stereotypical behavior. In families where both parents worked outside the home, the children displayed less stereotyping, and girls appeared to be less prone to forming sexual stereotypes than boys (Huston, 1983).

Gender role stereotypes are often reflected in the fantasy play of preschoolers. Preschool girls usually insist on playing homemakers, teachers, nurses, and other stereotypically female roles, while

Preschool-age children often insist on playing with gender-typed toys.

preschool boys assume male stereotypes such as soldier, police officer, or family breadwinner. In these same-sex roles, preschoolers also tend to follow a stereotypical script about their characters' behavior. Daddies don't take care of babies or cook meals, and mommies don't go off to work or to war.

## The Freudian Theory of Sexual Identity

Sigmund Freud was a pioneer in the field of sexual development theory. Today, however, many researchers consider his ideas to be sexist and outdated. As you learned in Chapter 2, Freud believed that children go through what he called the phallic stage between ages three and seven. According to Freud, at about age three children become more aware of their genital areas, and they begin to feel a strong attachment toward their opposite-sex parent. Freud theorized that these attachments create psychological conflicts that must be resolved in order for children to form their own sexual identity.

Freud called the attachment of a boy to his mother the *Oedipus complex*, after a Greek myth in which the hero unknowingly slays his father and marries his mother. Freud believed that this attachment has sexual overtones and thus puts the little boy in competition with his father. Jealous of his father's relationship with his mother, the boy wants to take his father's place. As a result, the child experiences conflict between his real affection for his father and his rivalry, hostility, and fear of his father's power. Freud called the attachment of a girl to her father the *Electra complex*, after another Greek myth involving a daughter who kills her mother. He believed that a girl feels desire for her father and wants to exclude her mother, a situation that causes anxiety for the girl.

According to Freud, children resolve these sexual conflicts and cope with the feelings of guilt that arise by means of *identification*, a defense mechanism through which they adopt the behavior, values, and attitudes of a stronger, more admirable individual. Thus, to relieve feelings of jealousy and aggression toward their same-sex parents, boys adopt the masculine characteristics of their father and girls take on the feminine characteristics of their mother. Freud believed that this process of identification with the same-sex parent establishes each child's sexual identity as male or female.

## Alternative Theories

It is generally acknowledged that Freud's theories are virtually impossible to corroborate through testing. The theories themselves are criticized for failing to take various important factors such as biological traits and learning into account. The idea that biological factors can influence sexual identity has been demonstrated in laboratory experiments. For example, administering the male hormone testosterone to female animals can cause them to become very aggressive, while the female hormone prolactin can cause male animals to behave maternally (Rose, Gordon, & Bernstein, 1972).

Humans, of course, are also greatly influenced by their environment. Learning theorists contend that children learn about sexual identity and sex roles by observing and imitating their parents and other adults. Moreover, adults reinforce these learned behaviors by rewarding children when they imitate desirable sex roles and punishing them when they imitate undesirable behavior.

Cognitive development may also play an important role in the development of sexual identity. According to cognitive development theory, children develop sexual identity and gender constancy as a natural consequence of their cognitive development. As children's cognitive skills develop, they become able to form schemes or concepts about what it means to be a boy or a girl and then to integrate new information into those schemes. They also formulate certain scripts that help them form ideas about sex roles. For instance, when children see their mother fix breakfast every morning and dinner every evening, they incorporate into their existing scripts about male and female behavior the idea that mothers (women) cook meals.

## Adult Influences on Gender Identification

Adults, particularly parents, strongly affect children's gender identification. One way they do this is by treating boys and girls differently. Parents generally encourage boys to be more independent, and they often pay more attention to them. Boys are expected to roughhouse, to be loud, and to roam and explore. Girls, on the other hand, are expected to play quietly, help out around the house, and be more dependent. Parents also tend to put more pressure on boys to adopt gender-appropriate behavior. A little girl can be a tomboy without much censure, but a little boy who wants to play with dolls may be pressured to change this play behavior (Fagot, 1978).

Another way that children learn about gender roles is by observing how adults act. Men, for example, often engage in more physical activities than women and in many cases make more of the decisions in the family. Boys are likely to observe this behavior and adopt it as part of their gender role.

As children grow older, gender roles become more pronounced; by the preschool years, they have become quite rigid. At this age, fantasy play involves exaggerated stereotypes of male and female behavior. Once gender constancy is well established, however, generally by age eight, children become more flexible and relaxed about sex roles. They become

*Children learn about sex roles by observing and imitating the behavior of their parents and other adults.*

more willing to accept the idea that men can perform activities that are stereotypically female and that women can engage in the same activities as men (Ulian, 1976).

## Cultural Influences on Sexual Identity

Sex roles vary from culture to culture. Even so, in most societies, men tend to be more aggressive, more competitive, more powerful, and more highly valued than women. When Eleanor Maccoby and Carol Jacklin (1980) reviewed studies of gender differences in various cultures, they found that aggression was the only trait in which males and females consistently differed. In every culture studied, males were more aggressive from toddlerhood through adulthood. Moreover, most societies assign the most prestigious roles to males. Men traditionally have done the hunting and herding, while women have had the responsibility for farming and child care. In some societies, giving birth to girls is actually seen as a hardship, even a calamity, because girls represent a burden rather than a source of income. In India, for example, the strong desire for male children and the burden of providing expensive dowries for women lead some parents to abort female fetuses or kill female children at birth.

In many societies gender roles are in the midst of transformation. In the United States, for example, women have proved that they are capable of performing most traditionally male roles, such as police officer, fire fighter, soldier, and politician. In addition, American men have begun to share some of the more traditional female tasks, such as performing household chores and taking care of children. Many parents also are attempting to raise their children with a minimum of sex role stereotypes, encouraging their daughters to be more independent and their sons to be more nurturing. Today, most schools encourage girls to engage in sports, and many colleges offer sports scholarships to girls—an unheard of practice 30 years ago. Psychologists call this a trend toward *androgyny*, the concept that men and women can possess the characteristics of both masculinity and femininity. Androgyny means that men and women can be assertive, empathetic, sensitive, or logical, depend-

ing on the situation (Bem, 1976). In other words, people can be flexible in their gender roles. Despite such changes, it is unlikely that men and women will ever completely abandon their gender roles, but these roles may be less restricting than they were in the past.

## Emotional Development in Preschool Children

By the time children reach the age of three or four, they have already developed a full range of emotional responses. In the course of an average day, they may feel and express affection, happiness, sadness, fear, anxiety, pride, love, and anger. A little boy left at the child care center in the morning feels fearful and anxious about separating from his mother, but when she returns in the afternoon, he is joyful about the reunion. A little girl feels angry and frustrated when she cannot insert a shoelace into an eyelet, but she is happy and proud when she is finally able to accomplish the task.

As children grow and develop, the way that they express their emotions changes. This change is brought about in large part by their ability to talk. Instead of having a temper tantrum or crying to express anger and unhappiness, children of preschool age begin to learn to simply say that they are angry or unhappy and explain why. Similarly, the ways that they express love and affection also change. Toddlers typically cling to their parents and willingly exchange hugs, kisses, and other signs of affection with adults. Preschoolers, on the other hand, are more independent. They are more likely to greet adults verbally, smile, or exchange a quick hug to show their affection. Preschoolers also use language to seek reassurance that they are still loved. Parents of preschoolers are besieged daily with countless demands to "look at me." Demanding that their parents constantly pay attention and watch and admire every new action or ability is one way that children gain reassurance from their parents that they are loved.

### Fears and Anxieties in Preschoolers

During the preschool years, children seem to experience a sharp increase in the number and variety of fears and anxieties they feel. In fact, some young

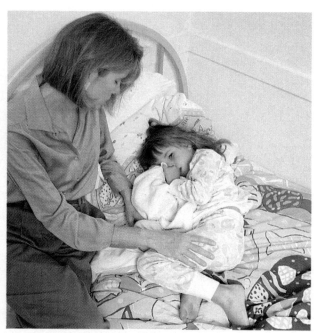

Children experience increased anxieties during the preschool years. This may be because preschoolers have a vivid imagination and are aware of their own weakness.

## FOCUS ON    Decision Making in Child Care

### Helping a Child Who Is Teased

Nancy, a short, overweight five-year-old, is constantly teased about her size by her classmates at St. Timothy's Preschool. When the children call her piggy or hippo, she runs crying to her teacher, Cheryl, for comfort. Nancy's mother is angry about the teasing. She has met with Cheryl several times to insist that the hurtful behavior stop.

First, Cheryl held a class meeting in which she talked about name-calling and reminded the children that she would not allow words that hurt to be used in her class. For a few days, the name-calling stopped; then it reappeared in a new form. Children would run up to Nancy and make snorting or oinking noises, and once again Nancy would go crying to Cheryl.

Privately, Cheryl thought that Nancy was overreacting to the other children's behavior as a way to get attention. She decided to concentrate on working with Nancy while continuing to discourage name-calling.

Cheryl had a private talk with Nancy. She told her that she understood that Nancy did not like being teased about her looks. She emphasized that the other children had no right to say hurtful things to her. But she also pointed out that some of the children enjoyed teasing Nancy because it gave them a sense of power to upset her.

Cheryl suggested that when Nancy was called a name, she should simply walk away and stick close to Cheryl for a few minutes. Together they invented a code word, *Rots-a-Ratsa*, that Nancy could yell instead of crying when she was frustrated and upset.

During center time, Cheryl made a point of assigning Nancy to centers with only a few children, where they were less likely to gang up on her. Cheryl also avoided placing Nancy in groups with the most aggressive name callers.

Finally, during story time, Cheryl used puppets to tell a series of stories about children and animal characters who were excluded because of their looks. She involved the class in finding solutions to the puppets' problems.

*Do you think Cheryl handled the situation effectively? Are there other steps she could have taken to keep the children from teasing Nancy? What would you do if this happened in your class?*

---

children seem to be afraid of practically everything, both real and imagined, from dogs to strangers to monsters under the bed. Psychologists theorize that these fears arise for several different reasons. One reason preschoolers experience so many fears is that they have developed a vivid imagination but are still at the stage of cognitive development in which they have difficulty distinguishing fantasy from reality.

Some television shows, movies, and cartoons may greatly increase their fears and anxieties. For example, a five-year-old boy may refuse to go into a swimming pool after watching a TV program about sharks. Even when his mother explains that sharks live only in the ocean, he still imagines that a shad-ow on the bottom of the pool is a shark and that he can see a shark's fin cutting through the water. Movies and television shows can stimulate children's imagination, and children's inability to separate fantasy from reality causes them to believe that the source of their fears exists despite all evidence and assurances to the contrary.

Children also develop fears through their own experience or by observing the experiences of others. For example, a child who observes her mother's fear of bees is likely to be afraid of bees herself. A child who has been bitten by a dog will understandably be afraid of dogs. As children of preschool age become more fearful, they also become more aware of their helplessness and weakness in many situations. As a result, they become more fearful for their own safety. Their imagination conjures up all kinds of real and imagined threats, such as robbers, bullies, and dragons in the closet, that they know they cannot defeat by themselves.

A continuing fear of both toddlers and preschoolers is separation anxiety, the fear of being separated from their parents for long periods of time. Many toddlers and preschoolers cling to *items of attachment*, such as a security blanket or a favorite toy, to soothe their fears and provide a measure of familiarity, especially in a strange environment or when separated from their parents. Children experience great anxiety when these objects of attachment are lost or temporarily removed, but they will eventually give up the objects when they feel they no longer need them (Brazelton, 1984).

Typically, as children develop cognitively, their experience and understanding increase and their fear of tangible situations decreases. Children who are afraid of mice, for example, may overcome their fear just by observing a pet mouse at preschool. They can see that their teacher is not afraid and that the mouse does not harm her when she handles it. Eventually, with her encouragement, they may muster the courage to touch and handle the mouse themselves. This kind of gradual, systematic exposure to a feared object is called *desensitization*.

### Dealing with Stress

Because preschoolers are still primarily egocentric thinkers, they tend to blame themselves for events beyond their control, such as a divorce or death in the family. Young children do not fully understand such situations, so they misinterpret them. For instance, a preschooler may think that she caused her father to leave home because she drew on the walls. The stress brought on by such situations and the misinterpretation of them often cause young children to regress temporarily in their behavior. Bedwetting, thumb sucking, temper tantrums, and clinging are common reactions to stressful situations such as divorce, the birth of a sibling, a parent's remarriage, or a move to a new area. Adults can help preschoolers overcome stressful situations by involving them in relaxing activities and reading books about children with similar problems.

Death is not generally as stressful a situation for preschoolers as it is for older children and adults. That is because most preschool children do not understand the concept of death. They view it as a temporary and reversible condition. In 1948, shortly after World War II, Maria Nagy studied hundreds of children in Budapest, Hungary, to determine their understanding of death. She found that preschool children between ages three and five thought of death as a temporary, reversible separation, much like a long trip or a period of sleep. The children she studied did not begin to think of death as permanent until age five or older (Nagy, 1948). Stories, such as "Snow White," that portray death as reversible may further confuse preschoolers. Other studies have also concluded that children do not comprehend death as the irreversible and universal end of life until they reach school age.

## Social Development in Preschoolers

During infancy and toddlerhood, most children spend the greater part of their time with their parents and siblings. As they get older, the opportunity to meet others—especially other children—increases. Many three- to five-year-old children attend preschool or some type of child care program. Others may join play groups or simply play with other children in the neighborhood. These opportunities to interact help preschoolers form friendships and develop *social competence*, the ability to make and maintain relationships and solve interpersonal conflicts. Mastering these social skills contributes greatly to the formation of a positive self-concept.

Children form their first true friendships between the ages of three and six. For preschoolers, a friend is someone who likes to do the same things as they do. For this reason, they tend to form friendships with children of the same sex and of about the same age as themselves. But even at age three or four, some children are more adept at social interactions and thus are more popular than others. Children who tend to be popular are generally skillful at using language to communicate, and they usually initiate conversations with other children and suggest or direct play activities more effectively than less popular children (Asher, Renshaw, & Hymel, 1982).

Conflicts provide caregivers with an opportunity to teach children about sharing, cooperation, and compromise.

A powerful factor in the development of social competence during the preschool years is reinforcement from peers. Those peers who are more adept socially generally act as role models for younger or less skilled children. Peers also reinforce desirable social behavior and discourage unacceptable behavior. For instance, children who are overly domineering, aggressive, or disruptive or who are excessively shy and withdrawn are usually excluded from a peer play group. However, such children can be taught strategies that will help them make and keep friends more easily (Roopnarine & Honig, 1985).

Conflicts are a very common feature of the interactions of preschool children. Children of this age don't have the social or language skills to avoid interpersonal conflicts. When a three-year-old snatches another child's shovel in the sandbox, the conflict that follows is predictable. In fact, such conflicts offer opportunities for adults and older children to teach younger children strategies for avoiding and resolving conflict. In this case, the squabbling children could be encouraged to take turns with the shovel or to play together cooperatively, helping each other dig and build sand castles.

Children need frequent opportunities to interact with other children in order to learn social skills such as sharing, cooperating, taking turns, working as a team, and resolving conflicts fairly. Frequent interactions enable children to practice such social skills and learn which behaviors and responses are most successful. For example, children need to learn when and how to join a game in progress so that they will create the least amount of disruption and will be most readily included in the action. Such a skill can be developed only with practice and experience. Sensitive and supportive adult role models can show children how to behave and assist them in learning various social skills. Adults should also remember that children's social skills vary at any given age and each child develops these skills at an individual pace.

### Developing Social Skills Through Play

Young children develop social skills and learn social and gender roles by playing with other children. As they grow older, the nature and style of their play changes. Infants engage primarily in solitary sensorimotor play, interacting with objects.

### Getting Dirty

Luanne provides family day care in her home. Cindy, one of the children who comes every day, is a lively four-year-old who never settles down to one toy or activity for very long. Luanne has discussed this with Cindy's mother, Mrs. DiAngelo. This evening when Mrs. DiAngelo comes by, Luanne wants to tell her that Cindy has become very involved in finger painting. But she also has to report that Cindy has smeared paint down the front of the fancy dress she is wearing for a visit to her grandmother.

LUANNE:  Cindy is really into finger painting now. She just loves to get her hands into the colors and has made some really great pictures. Unfortunately, she sort of messed up her dress today. She was wearing a smock, but she is so enthusiastic that she seems to get paint all over the place. Of course, the paint is washable.

MRS. DIANGELO [*angrily*]:  You know we're going to see her grandmother tonight, and now she's going to think I don't keep Cindy clean.

LUANNE:  I know and I'm sorry. Do you have time to go home first so Cindy can change?

MRS. DIANGELO [*still angry*]:  I don't know why she has to play with such messy stuff, especially when she's all dressed up. She wouldn't get so messed up with crayons. We'll be late if we go home first.

LUANNE:  I know Cindy wouldn't get as messy with crayons, but it's really not the same. She can't get into the colors in the same way. Maybe you could leave a pair of old overalls here for her to put on when she's likely to get dirty. Tomorrow when you have more time, I'll show you her paintings. I know you'll be very proud of her.

MRS. DIANGELO [*softening*]:  Oh yes? Hmmm. Well, maybe I could get here a little earlier tomorrow. And I'll see if I can find some clothes for her to paint in. Her grandmother's sure to be mad if we're late, but I guess it's either that or a dirty kid.

*How well do you think Luanne handled the situation with Cindy's mother? What would you have done differently? What made the problem easier for Luanne to talk about?*

Toddlers enjoy symbolic play and pretend play, in which they imitate others and begin to role-play. Preschoolers typically engage in fantasy or socio-dramatic play, in which they interact with other children, playing elaborate, sustained roles drawn from their everyday experiences.

In Chapter 11, you learned about different levels of play among toddlers. The classifications are based on a pioneering study by Mildred Parten in which she described six types of social play, each one characterized by a different degree of social interaction (Parten, 1932). At the lowest level of Parten's hierarchy, which she termed unoccupied behavior, a child does not really play but looks around at whatever is happening. The second level

in Parten's hierarchy, solitary play, involves a child playing independently and making no effort to interact with anyone else. The next level, onlooker play, occurs when a child watches other children play. At the fourth level, parallel play, a child plays in similar ways as another child and with similar toys but does not interact with the other child. When Adam and Josh played with their cars separately but near each other, they were engaging in parallel play.

In Parten's fifth category, associative play, children are involved in a common activity, but they do not attempt to organize the action to arrive at a common goal. For instance, several children may be sharing a pile of building blocks, but each works on an individual project rather than working together on one project. The sixth and highest level of play in Parten's hierarchy is cooperative play. This involves children playing together in an organized fashion with a goal or purpose in mind. Some children in a cooperative play group may direct the others, and all may share responsibilities and take on different roles to achieve the goal. When children work together to build a snow fort or act out a favorite movie with each player assuming a different role, they are engaging in cooperative play.

Researchers used to believe that as children grew older and more socially adept, they engaged in progressively higher levels of play involving more social interaction. However, studies have shown that while this is generally true, children at various ages frequently engage in several levels of play. For example, even the most socially competent children engage in solitary play at times, especially when they are performing problem-solving activities. Moreover, although solitary play decreases with age, it still makes up 11 to 19 percent of all play among five- and six-year-olds (Hetherington, Cox, & Cox, 1979). Although Parten's levels of play are not really an indicator of social maturity, they are useful in evaluating different types of play and the settings that promote them.

Early childhood experts view sociodramatic play, a form of cooperative play, as an important element in development. With its elaborate, sustained role-playing, sociodramatic play helps children express their fears and fantasies, try out social roles, learn social skills, and practice behaviors and skills they will use as adults. To begin the activity and keep it going, the players must cooperate, make compromises, and arrive at joint decisions. They have to decide which props to use and what each prop represents. They must also determine who will do what during the course of the game. For example, if two children are playing husband and wife, they have to decide which objects represent the home, the job, the children, the family car, and so on. They must also decide how they are going to act in their roles.

Children who have developed a positive self-concept are generally more skilled at social interaction and engage in more cooperative play. In one study, for example, researchers found that children

*Sociodramatic play helps children express fears and fantasies, try out social roles, and learn social skills.*

who regularly interacted with other children in play groups or preschools displayed more social competence than peers who had had fewer opportunities to play with other children (Harper & Huie, 1985). The researchers also found that the older, more experienced children tended to engage in higher levels of interactive play than younger, less experienced children. In general, socially competent children are better able to initiate play, to plan and organize games and activities, to understand and incorporate the ideas of other children into play situations, and to direct the sequence of actions over a period of time.

## Social Development and Sibling Relationships

Sibling relationships provide an important means for young children to learn social skills. Although the nature of the sibling relationship in each family is different, depending on the age, sex, and number of siblings, some basic patterns remain the same. For instance, older siblings tend to be more dominant, and younger siblings tend to be more submissive. Older siblings initiate more activities, while younger siblings are more likely to imitate them. The situation at the beginning of the chapter involving Josh and Adam represents a typical sibling interaction. Josh was aggressive, taking the car away

### Child-Centered or Teacher-Directed Preschools

As part of their early childhood education studies at Mesa Community College, students spend several weeks observing and assisting at area preschools and child care centers. The facilities they visit have different goals and philosophies, yet all provide quality child care. At the end of the semester, Michi and Larry report their experiences.

Michi:
"I went to the Claremont Child Development Center. The class I assisted in was a mixed-age class of three- and four-year-olds. There were 20 children and two teachers.

"The day begins at Claremont at 8:30. Before the children arrive, the teachers spend time organizing the room. The materials and organization of the room are important at Claremont because the school believes that children learn through play and through watching each other. The quality of the play and the learning depends on having developmentally appropriate toys and materials available.

"There are six centers in the room. Every week one of the centers changes so that there is always some new material for the children. When children arrive, they may go to any center they wish and stay as long as they want. The number of children at any one center is limited to four, but teachers make no effort to guide children to any particular activity. There is a brief circle time each morning during which the children sing songs and share experiences, but no one is pressured to participate.

"A large part of each teacher's job is to prepare materials that teach through self-discovery. For example, at the science center the teachers put out dishpans of water and a lot of small items, some of which sank and some of which floated. While playing with these in the water, the children made their own discoveries.

"The teachers are always available to the children. They circulate through the class and occasionally ask open-ended questions. Sometimes they suggest that an older child show a younger child what he or she is doing.

"There are only a few class rules, and these deal mostly with hurtful behavior. When conflicts arise, the teachers act as moderators. They involve the children in resolving the conflict by asking questions and encouraging the children to think out solutions. Just about the only times the teachers give a direct order are when everyone has to go outside to the playground and when it's time to clean up to go home.

"At first, I thought this classroom seemed very chaotic, but after several weeks of watching the teachers prepare for class and observing the children, I realized that the children were learning by following their own interests at their own pace."

Larry:
"I was at the Melville Road Preschool with a class of 15 four-year-olds and one teacher. School begins at 9:00. Children play for about 15 minutes, then the teacher calls them to the circle. Everyone sits down, and the teacher begins by asking one child to help with the calendar and the weather.

"Usually, the teacher shows the children something special that's tied to her lesson. She has a lesson plan for each day. When I was there, the class was doing a unit on the five senses. Each week, the class activities were centered around a different sense.

"Children are expected to sit quietly. When the teacher asks a question, they raise their hand to answer. If children are disruptive, they are asked to leave the circle. During free play if a conflict arises, the teacher settles it by assigning time-outs.

"After circle time, the class breaks into groups to do a project related to the day's topic. Half the children have free play, while the other half work with the teacher. The teacher usually gives step-by-step instructions and has a finished example of the project so the children know how their project should look. Throughout the day, children have specific helper jobs such as door holder, snack passer, and paintbrush washer that are assigned to them for the week.

"After playground time and a snack, there is another lesson. It usually involves reading readiness or number concepts. Sometimes the teacher reads a story and asks questions.

Occasionally, a number or letter work sheet is involved. Then there is free play until the day ends at noon.

"I was impressed with how orderly these children are. The teacher never loses control of the class. She is very organized and knows exactly what information she wants the children to learn. The only thing that bothers me is that the children don't get much of a chance to share their own ideas and experiences with the class."

*What do you think are the strengths of each preschool? The weaknesses? At which school would you feel more comfortable teaching? Why?*

from his younger brother and making him cry. Yet Josh also showed empathy and concern, and ultimately he agreed to share a car with Adam. The incident helped Josh learn how to share and helped Adam learn how to play with a toy car. After their exchange, Adam and Josh then engaged in parallel play.

Sibling rivalry is a predominant but not pervasive feature of sibling relationships. Positive interactions between siblings are also common. Studies have shown, for example, that siblings are as likely, or more likely, to display empathy, affection, interest, cooperation, and concern for each other as to engage in sibling rivalry (Abramovitch, Corter, Pepler, & Stanhope, 1986). Indeed, siblings provide companionship for each other, they learn family rules from each other, and they share the family's resources. Siblings also practice their social skills on one another, learning how to cooperate and resolve conflicts among themselves long before they engage in the same behaviors with other children.

Parents have great influence on sibling interactions. Parents who pay more attention to one sibling than another or compare one child unfavorably to another are promoting sibling rivalry. In some cases, parents foster such rivalry by insisting on stereotypical sex role behavior within the family. For example, if the older sister must always do the

dishes or babysit because she's a girl, her little brother is very likely to end up bearing the brunt of her resentment. The very presence or absence of a parent can affect how siblings react to each other. In one study, researchers found that when the mother was present, siblings were more likely to fight; when she was absent, they were more likely to play together peacefully (Lamb, 1978). Conversely, parents can foster affection and cooperation among siblings by enforcing rules consistently, treating all their children impartially, and avoiding comparisons among siblings.

## Moral Development in Preschool Children

The development of moral thought and behavior evolves gradually over the course of a person's childhood and adolescence. *Morality* refers to the system of rules and principles that people and societies adopt to govern their behavior toward others. These rules are usually based on a culture's ideas about fairness, justice, and compassion. They are handed down from one generation to the next by parents, religious leaders, and educators.

Sigmund Freud believed that morality is governed by the superego, or conscience, a part of the mind that internalizes social rules and values to make them part of the self. Jean Piaget thought that moral development in children depends on their level of cognitive development. Using a system similar to Piaget's stages of cognitive development, psychologist Lawrence Kohlberg (1976) developed a hierarchy of six stages of moral judgment (see Chapter 17). Kohlberg's system is widely cited as the definitive standard for measuring moral development in children.

All three researchers—Freud, Piaget, and Kohlberg—place preschoolers at an early stage of moral development. Freud said that the superego does not develop until about age six, when children resolve their Oedipus or Electra conflict by identifying with their same-sex parent.

Piaget suggested that preschoolers are only beginning to develop a concept of morality. They typically have a rigid, inflexible sense of right and wrong and believe that rules are dictated by an all-knowing higher authority. According to Piaget, children of this age view rules as unchangeable and automatically expect to be punished for breaking a rule. They are more likely to judge actions according to their consequences rather than in accordance with a person's intentions or values. Thus, they might see a child who drops a bottle of milk while trying to pour a glass for a younger sibling as more at fault than one who knocks over a glass of milk while trying to snatch another child's cookies.

Kohlberg placed preschoolers at the lowest level of moral development, which he called the *premoral level*. This level has two stages of moral reasoning. In the first stage, children behave morally because they want to avoid punishment and gain rewards, not because they have an internalized sense of right and wrong. The four-year-old who puts his toys away each day is doing so to avoid a scolding, not because it is "the right thing to do." In the second stage, children are most concerned with satisfying their own desires. They conform to moral standards out of self-interest and value the actions of others when those actions meet their needs.

Some studies indicate that Kohlberg may have underestimated the moral development of preschoolers. Children seem to begin internalizing moral concepts at around four and five years of age. Researchers have found, for example, that some young children have a fairly deep understanding of moral principles such as fairness and justice but do not yet have the vocabulary to express these ideas

## FOCUS ON  Cultural Diversity

### Unspoken Communication

Looking someone in the eye is a sign of trustworthiness, right? Not necessarily. It could be a sign of disrespect.

All communication has spoken and unspoken components. But different cultures place different meanings on body language such as eye contact, smiling, personal space, and touching. When talking with people from different cultures, you cannot assume that their staring past you is a sign of inattentiveness, that they pushy because they stand close to you while talking, or that a smiling face reflects a happy, cooperative outlook.

It is important to be aware of cultural differences in body language. Some Asians, for example, may avoid eye contact; many Native Americans consider prolonged eye contact to be rude. Some cultures believe that staring can hurt or hex the person being stared at. In a similar way, people have different attitudes about personal space. Anglo-Americans tend to want more space between them and the next person than people with a Hispanic background.

If you feel uncomfortable conversing with someone from a different culture, it may be that you are misinterpreting that person's body signals and do not understand the meaning of the unspoken part of your conversation.

(Schweder, Turiel, & Much, 1981). When parents ask a preschooler, "How would you like it if . . . ?" or "How do you think that makes (someone else) feel . . . ?" they are appealing to the child's concepts of fairness and empathy for others and helping the child express feelings about these concepts. Most researchers believe that children first experience guilt at the age of four or five. *Guilt* is the feeling of self-reproach that people experience when they do something that results in disapproval or punishment from others. A sense of guilt signals the development of a conscience, the internal moral code by which individuals learn to direct their own behavior through internalized thoughts and feelings rather than external rewards and punishments.

### Altruism and Aggression in Preschoolers

Although children of preschool age are still largely egocentric, they are capable of demonstrating prosocial behavior. Prosocial behavior encompasses a wide range of actions that are intended to benefit someone else, including cooperation, generosity, and comforting or helping others. As you read in Chapter 11, some researchers distinguish between altruism and other forms of prosocial behavior. They define altruism as action performed out of an unselfish concern for others that does not involve a benefit to the helper. When Josh tried to comfort Adam, he may have been acting altruistically out of concern for his brother's distress.

Researchers have studied the influence of various factors—such as age, gender, and socioeconomic status—on prosocial behavior. Some experiments have shown that older children are more willing than younger children to share (Radke-Yarrow, Zahn-Waxler, & Chapman, 1983). Studies have also suggested that girls are more apt to show empathy than boys are, although this may be due to the influence of societal expectations about feminine behavior (Berman & Goodman, 1984).

Prosocial behavior develops as children acquire the ability to put themselves in another's place and to perceive a situation from another's point of view. This type of behavior can be encouraged by adults. Parents and caregivers can play an important role in equipping children with the necessary skills to develop moral behavior and thought.

During the preschool years, children begin to experience feelings of guilt when they think their actions will result in disapproval or punishment.

Aggression is another type of behavior that is very common in preschool children. Aggressive behavior can take the form of hitting, kicking, shoving, biting, throwing objects, and forcibly taking objects away from others. In preschoolers, such behavior usually erupts during conflicts over objects or control of a space. Some psychologists divide aggression into two types: *instrumental aggression* is behavior that has a goal, and *hostile aggression* is behavior that is simply intended to hurt someone else (Caldwell, 1977). When Josh wrenched the car out of Adam's hands, he was engaging in instrumental aggression. His goal was to reclaim the car, not to hurt his brother.

Normally, aggression does not appear until around age three, and it is far more common in boys than in girls. It has been suggested that biological factors, such as the presence of the male hormone testosterone, may account in part for greater aggressive behavior in boys. Many psychologists

Supportive, tolerant, and nurturing caregivers give children the self-confidence to do things on their own.

also believe that such behavior is encouraged and rewarded in male children in most cultures. As children grow older, aggressive behavior tends to diminish in both boys and girls, perhaps because they have become more adept at using social and verbal skills to defuse conflicts.

## Implications and Applications

During the preschool years, children are developing emotionally and socially in a number of ways. They are establishing a self-concept and sexual identity, learning new social skills, and beginning to develop a rudimentary sense of morality. At the same time, new fears and anxieties can cause them distress. Child care professionals play an important role in helping children meet the challenges they encounter and cope with problems that may arise.

### Developing a Self-Concept and Sexual Identity

The preschool years are a crucial period in the formation of a self-concept. Children need opportunities to try things on their own, and they should be allowed to do as many things for themselves as possible. Caregivers should be aware of the power of praise and blame as motivators of behavior. Adults should make sure to praise children for their efforts but not to overuse praise so that it becomes

meaningless. Positive reinforcement helps build self-esteem and gives children the confidence to try new things, while blame and punishment may have a detrimental effect. Caregivers should not expect perfection, and they should use blame and punishment sparingly. Erikson believes that in dealing with children in the initiative versus guilt stage, the primary role of caregivers is to be supportive, tolerant, and nurturing. He concludes that if adults push children too hard to accomplish tasks beyond their abilities or punish them for failing, there is a risk of overwhelming children with feelings of guilt.

Adult role models are very important for the development of sexual identity at the preschool age. Children learn a great deal about sex roles from adults, particularly their mother and father. Adults can help children develop sexual identity by exemplifying positive characteristics in their own behavior. There is some evidence that when adult role models change their behavior, they also change the behavior of their children. Children typically form sex role stereotypes by observing the everyday behavior of their parents and other role models.

### Helping Children Develop Emotionally

Like adults, children are subject to a variety of stressors, and they need the support and guidance of caring adults to help them cope with emotional upheaval. Caregivers should be advised of situations such as divorce, new siblings, or death in a family so that they can understand the child's behavior and can help the child deal with the stress. They should also be on the lookout for behaviors that may signal other problems. Children who are sexually, physically, or emotionally abused or who grow up in homes where spouse abuse is present, often demonstrate behaviors that reflect that abuse. A physically abused child may be excessively aggressive with playmates or extremely withdrawn, and a sexually abused child may be unusually knowledgeable about sexual behavior and sex organs.

Child care professionals can help children overcome fears in a variety of ways. Among these are encouraging children to express their fears, taking their fears seriously, being supportive and reassuring, and helping children find ways to deal with their fears. Caregivers can also serve as role models in helping children learn to cope with fears and anxieties. For example, if a child is afraid of a dog or a monster under the bed, showing the child that you are not afraid can be helpful. In addition, caregivers can help children overcome their fears by desensitizing them, by exposing them gently and gradually to the objects that they fear. It is important for children to know that their parents and their caregivers will take care of them. It is also wise to steer young children away from scary and excessively violent movies, television programs, and cartoons that can overstimulate their imagination.

Caregivers should never ridicule children or make fun of their fears; such behavior destroys the bond of trust between children and caregivers and arouses feelings of shame and guilt. Using logic and reason with fearful preschoolers usually doesn't work either because they are still at a stage of cognitive development where they confuse fantasy and reality.

### Helping Children Develop Social Skills

Social competence is an important skill. Preschoolers who are socially competent tend to be more successful in school and to have a more positive attitude about school than children who are not yet socially competent. Child care providers can help children who have difficulty making friends by encouraging them to play in small groups, reading them books about shy children who make friends, and using role-playing games to teach them social skills. Providing opportunities to engage in fantasy play or sociodramatic play is also very important. These types of play help children develop skills that will serve them throughout their lives, such as sharing, taking turns, and resolving conflicts. Fantasy play also promotes imagination and creativity by allowing children to devise plots, plan scenarios, and adapt each other's ideas.

### Helping Children Develop Morally

Play that involves interaction with other children can help a child develop morally as well. Such play assists children in understanding the point of view and feelings of other children and provides opportunities for prosocial behaviors, such as helping and cooperating.

Caregivers play an important role in helping children develop the social skills they need to interact successfully with their peers.

Of course, interactions among children can also result in displays of aggressive or other disruptive behavior. Caregivers should take every opportunity to control such behavior among preschoolers and to foster prosocial behavior. Assertive behavior should not be permitted to become aggressive. Aggressive children are usually unpopular with their peers and tend to have a poor attitude toward school. Even more disturbing, at least one study has shown that aggressive and disruptive behavior during the preschool and early school years may be a precursor of later aggressive behavior, delinquency, and crime (Rutter & Garmezy, 1983).

Unfortunately, aggressive behavior is often learned. Children learn to be aggressive by imitating role models and by observing violence in the home and in the media. Caregivers can help curb aggressive behavior by intervening and teaching alternative behaviors. When breaking up a fight over a toy, for example, adults should teach the children to take turns and to solve their conflict through talking. Adults also serve as powerful role models, whether engaging in violence against each other or resolving conflicts peacefully.

Fortunately, prosocial behavior can also be learned. And child care professionals can play an important role in helping children develop such behavior.

## SUMMARY

- Preschoolers form self-concepts about themselves on the basis of such things as physical attributes, possessions, and abilities. They often form exaggerated estimates of their abilities and think they can accomplish anything they try.

- Erik Erikson believes that preschoolers experience a conflict between initiative, the desire to take on new tasks, and guilt, moral reservations about carrying them out.

- Children have some idea of their sexual identity when they are toddlers, but they learn about gender roles and adopt gender role stereotypes during the preschool years.

- Freud believed that sexual identity develops as a result of a psychological conflict between children and their same-sex parent. He said that children resolve the conflict by identifying with the same-sex parent.

- Other theorists believe that biological factors, learning, and cognitive development influence the development of sexual identity.

- Adults influence sexual identification both by acting as role models and by encouraging and punishing various behaviors.

- Culture also affects sexual identity. In many societies, men are more aggressive, more powerful, and more highly valued than women.

- Gender roles are changing in the United States as women take on more traditionally male roles and men feel free to be more nurturing.

- By preschool age, children have already developed a full range of emotions. Their method of expressing emotion changes, however, as they become more independent and more verbal.

- Preschoolers tend to develop a great many fears and anxieties because they have a vivid imagination and cannot yet distinguish fantasy from reality.

- Young children are subject to stress just as adults are. Children can be helped to overcome their fears and anxieties and to cope with stress.

- Children need to interact with other children in order to develop social competence.

- Play helps children learn social skills as well as social and gender roles.

- Older siblings help younger children develop social skills. Siblings are more likely to have positive interactions with each other than negative interactions, such as sibling rivalry.

- Preschoolers are at a low level of moral development. They act out of self-interest, and they defer to authority. They are also more likely to act out of a fear of punishment or desire for a reward than because they believe their actions are morally correct.

- Preschoolers are capable of both altruistic and aggressive behavior. Prosocial behavior, such as altruism, demonstrates children's ability to perceive other people's points of view.

- Preschoolers need caring, supportive adults, and positive adult role models to develop a positive self-concept and strong sexual identity.
- Caregivers need to be aware of any stressors that are affecting preschoolers so that they can help them confront and relieve their fears and anxieties.
- When children have difficulty making friends, adults can help them by providing opportunities to develop social skills.
- Adults should encourage altruistic behavior and try to curb aggressive behavior in preschoolers.

## BUILDING VOCABULARY

Write a definition for each vocabulary term listed below.

androgyny
desensitization
Electra complex
gender constancy
gender roles
guilt
hostile aggression
identification

instrumental aggression
item of attachment
morality
Oedipus complex
premoral level
sexual identity
social competence

## ACQUIRING KNOWLEDGE

1. What attributes do preschoolers usually refer to when they identify themselves?
2. How does the relationship between children and parents change during the preschool years?
3. Which stage of Erik Erikson's theory of psychosocial development do children reach during the preschool years?
4. According to Erikson, what qualities do children develop when they successfully negotiate the third stage of psychosocial development?
5. How do praise and blame affect preschool children?
6. Explain the difference between sexual identity and sex roles.
7. In Freud's theory of development, how are the Oedipus complex and the Electra complex similar? How are they different?
8. How does identification affect the sexual development of children, according to Freud?
9. How do adults influence the sexual identity of children?
10. How does language acquisition affect the way children express their emotions?
11. Why do preschoolers often demand that their parents pay attention to them and admire their abilities?
12. Why do children experience an increase in fears during the preschool years?

13. How do items of attachment help children cope with separation anxiety?
14. How does desensitization help children overcome fears?
15. Why do preschoolers often regress temporarily in their behavior in response to situations such as divorce, the birth of a sibling, or a move to a new area?
16. How do children's understanding of the concept of death change between the preschool years and middle childhood?
17. What skills are involved in social competence?
18. Why do preschoolers tend to form friendships with children of the same sex and similar age as themselves?
19. Give an example of the effect of peers on a child's social development.
20. Why is conflict a common part of preschoolers' interactions?
21. Explain the difference between associative play and cooperative play in Mildred Parten's hierarchy of types of play.
22. Describe the two stages of moral reasoning that make up the premoral level identified by Lawrence Kohlberg.
23. Give an example of a type of behavior that would be considered prosocial behavior.
24. Explain the difference between instrumental and hostile aggression.
25. List two ways in which adults can help children learn to make friends.

## THINKING CRITICALLY

1. Use Erik Erikson's theory to describe and explain the feelings a four-year-old might have about a new experience, such as attending preschool for the first time.
2. Children's thinking about social behavior is often evident in their sociodramatic play. In your opinion, what are the advantages or disadvantages to children in acting out various roles in play? Do you think adults should intervene? If so, to what extent?
3. When preschool children develop fears, the cause is not always apparent. What might a caregiver do to help a child overcome fear of a new activity, such as going on a playground slide?
4. According to Mildred Parten's hierarchy of types of play, cooperative play involves the most social interaction among children. What social skills do children learn through onlooker play, parallel play, and associative play?
5. How should caregivers explain and enforce rules controlling aggressive behavior among preschool children? What type of explanation would be most meaningful to children of this age? How should caregivers react when aggressive behavior occurs?

## OBSERVATIONS AND APPLICATIONS

1. Observe a preschool class of three-year-olds. Make note of the way teachers use praise and blame and how the children react to the teacher's comments. Do your observations tend to support Erikson's conclusion that praise and blame are strong motivators of behavior?

2. Observe four-year-old children in a child care setting. Describe any conflicts you observe among the children. What caused or precipitated these conflicts, and how are they resolved? Do most of the children attempt to work out conflicts verbally? Do some verbal conflicts end up in physical fights? Do the children generally attempt to work things out themselves, or do they call for a caregiver? When and in what ways do caregivers intervene?

3. Mr. and Mrs. Lewin ask to speak to you about their four-year-old son, Sam, who attends the preschool where you work. Sam enjoys playing with blocks and trucks, but he also likes to play with his sister's dolls. The Lewins ask you whether they should let Sam play as he wishes or discourage him from playing with what they consider to be girl's toys. What would you say to the Lewins?

4. Alisha, a four-and-a-half-year-old in your preschool class, comes to get you. She is afraid to get paper from the supply closet because she thinks there is a big, ugly monster in it. You open the supply closet and show her there is no monster in it. Later, she comes to you and says she thinks the monster is now in the toy box. You ask Alisha's mother whether this is going on at home as well. She tells you that it is. Alisha has been sleeping with the light on and the closet door securely shut. Her mother must also check under the bed before leaving the room. What can you and Alisha's parents do to help Alisha?

## SUGGESTIONS FOR FURTHER READING

Brazelton, T. B. (1984). *To listen to a child: Understanding the normal problems of growing up*. Reading, MA: Addison-Wesley.

Essa, E. (1983). *Practical guide to solving preschool behavior problems*. Albany, NY: Delmar.

Krogh, S. L., & Lamme, L. L. (1983). Learning to share: How literature can help. *Childhood Education, 59*, 188–192.

Liss, M. B. (Ed.). (1983). *Social and cognitive skills: Sex roles and children's play*. New York: Academic Press.

McCraken, J. B. (Ed.). (1986). *Reducing stress in young children's lives*. Washington, DC: National Association for the Education of Young Children.

Paley, V. G. (1984). *Boys and girls: Superheros in the doll corner*. Chicago: University of Chicago Press.

Piers, M. W., & Landau, G. M. (1980). *The gift of play and why young children cannot thrive without it*. New York: Walker.

Saarni, C., & Harris, P. L. (Eds.). (1989). *Children's understanding of emotion*. New York: Cambridge University Press.

Sammuels, S. C. (1977). *Enhancing self-concept in early childhood: Theory and practice*. New York: Human Sciences Press.

Sarafino, E. P. (1985). *The fears of childhood: A guide to recognizing and reducing fearful states in children*. New York: Human Sciences Press.

# PART 6

# The School Years

### CHAPTER 15
### Physical Development
Chapter 15 describes the physical changes experienced by children between the ages of six and eight. The chapter also discusses physical growth and development in late childhood and adolescence.

### CHAPTER 16
### Intellectual Development
Chapter 16 explains how the thinking of children changes as they advance to Piaget's last two stages of cognitive development, improve their memory skills, and master language.

### CHAPTER 17
### Emotional and Social Development
Chapter 17 describes how children's self-concept and social skills develop during the school years and adolescence. The chapter also discusses the influence of parents, teachers, and peers on emotional and social development.

# Physical Development

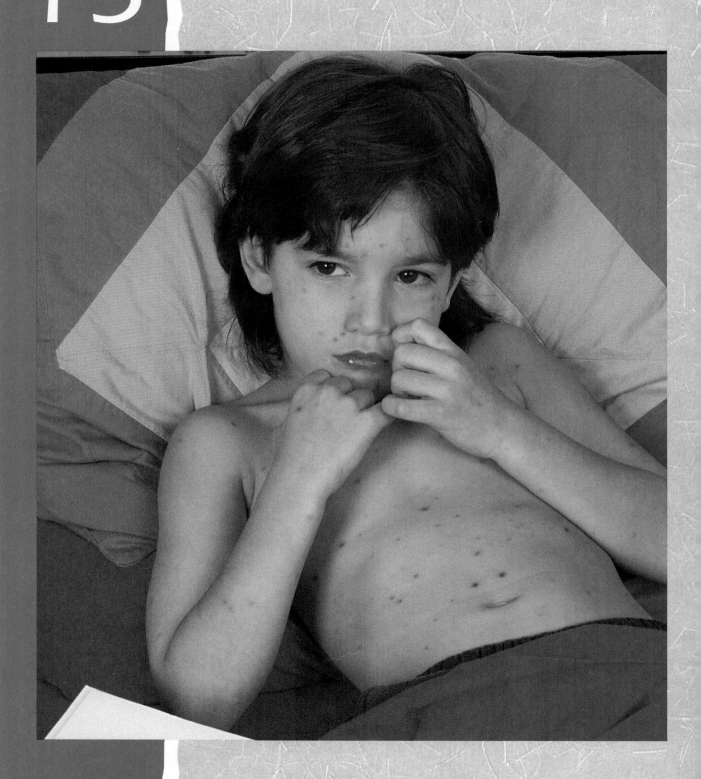

## OBJECTIVES

Studying this chapter will enable
you to

- Describe the physical changes
  experienced by children between
  the ages of six and eight, and
  identify the gross and fine motor
  skills acquired during this period.
- Explain why good nutrition and
  health care are so important to the
  growth and development of
  school-age children.
- Discuss ways of dealing with some
  of the common disabilities of
  school-age children.
- List steps that caregivers can take
  to provide a safe environment and
  reduce the risk of injury.
- Describe the physical changes that
  older school-age children and
  adolescents experience, and
  explain what caregivers can do to
  help children cope with these
  changes.

S IX-YEAR-OLD LUKE arrived at the Y's after-
school program very excited about a
project he was working on in first grade.
As Sandrine listened to him, she noticed a little
red mark on his forehead, right between his
eyebrows. She asked Luke if he knew what it
was. Luke said he thought he might have
bumped his head during gym.

Sandrine was called away by a minor scuffle,
but later in the afternoon, she took a closer look
at Luke's spot and noticed another one on his
forehead. Sandrine knew that chicken pox had
been reported in Luke's elementary school. She
asked Luke to lift his shirt, and sure enough, his
back and chest were covered with small red
spots.

Recognizing and dealing with illness is one part of working with children. This chapter focuses on the growth and development of school-age children, those between the ages of six and eight. This period is also known as middle childhood, and it differs from the periods that precede it. During middle childhood, physical growth continues but at a slower pace, and motor skills continue to improve. Middle childhood is generally a period of good health, but as the world of the child widens, so does his exposure to people and to more communicable diseases. These are passed along fairly easily from child to child. In many respects, however, middle childhood is a period of calm before the physical storm of the preteen years and adolescence.

## Growth and Development of School-Age Children

Growth slows during middle childhood, but the process continues. The distinctive characteristic of the growth pattern during this period is that it proceeds at a fairly steady rate rather than in spurts.

### Height, Weight, and Body Proportions

School-age children grow an average of 2 to 3 inches each year and gain approximately 5 to 7 pounds per year. The average six-year-old is 45 inches tall and weighs 44 pounds. Two years later, the average eight-year-old has reached 50 inches and weighs 55 pounds. Girls continue to weigh slightly less and to be slightly shorter than boys of the same age. However, the difference in size between boys and girls decreases each year during this period of development.

School-age children look different from preschoolers. Their arms and legs grow more quickly than other parts of their body, giving most school-age children a lanky, thin appearance. Their hands and feet are growing, too, but at a slower pace than arms and legs. Their shoulders become squarer, their posture more erect, and their abdomen flatter. As a result, school-age children look less top-heavy than they did when they were younger. Even their face is changing, as the forehead deepens and the nose grows larger. While girls and boys of this age continue to look more alike than different, girls retain more fatty tissue than boys.

Finding a school-age child of "average" height and weight is difficult because of individual differences. For example, two eight-year-old boys might have up to an 8-inch difference in height. Differences among cultures are even greater. School-age children tend to be taller in Europe, the United States, and eastern Australia, while children from Southeast Asia, South America, and islands in the Pacific tend to be shorter. Developmental experts believe that this disparity is due in large part to diet and access to medical care. Children grow tallest in those parts of the world where nutritious food is plentiful and infectious diseases are under control (Meredith, 1969).

As school-age children grow, they experience other physical changes. Their muscles grow in size and strength, and their lung capacity increases. Their digestive system matures further, retaining food for longer periods of time and becoming less sensitive than it was earlier.

### Teeth

Middle childhood is the time when children begin to shed their *deciduous teeth*, also known as primary, milk, or "baby" teeth. In their place, a set of permanent teeth erupts, beginning at about age 6. Deciduous teeth fall out at a rate of about four per year. Children continue to lose their teeth until the age of 11 or 12. The first molars also appear during middle childhood. They erupt at the back of the mouth behind existing deciduous teeth and do not replace any teeth.

The condition of the teeth affects a child's appearance, her ability to eat food, and her health. Thus, it is important that school-age children learn proper dental hygiene and visit a dentist regularly. Children in the United States have fewer cavities today than they did in the past. One survey reported that half of the children studied had no cavities or other tooth decay (Herrmann & Roberts, 1987). The use of fluoride and better dental care are responsible for much of this improvement.

### Vision

Vision improves noticeably during the school-age years as the eyes mature and change shape. Prior to

Individual patterns of physical growth become more pronounced during middle childhood, often resulting in considerable variations in height and weight among children of the same age.

the age of six, most children are *farsighted*, a condition in which vision is better for distant objects than for near objects. As children enter the school-age years, their vision becomes more acute and their ability to focus improves.

All school-age children should have their eyes examined. Both farsightedness and nearsightedness affect this age group. Children who are *nearsighted* are able to see near things more clearly than distant ones. The number of children who are nearsighted increases during the school-age years. It is important for children to have their eyes examined during this time when they are learning to read.

A small percentage of children begin to show poor color vision during middle childhood. Most color vision deficiencies are hereditary, and the defect is usually gender linked. More boys suffer from color vision deficiencies than girls. Among whites of European origin, about 8 percent of males and less than 1 percent of females have either green or

red deficiency (*American Medical Association Encyclopedia of Medicine*, 1989). These deficiencies are much less common among Asians, Native Americans, and African Americans. Color vision deficiencies can be detected through testing. While the deficiencies cannot be corrected, it is important that the affected children and those who care for them are aware of the problem.

## Motor Development

*Steady* is the word that describes the physical growth of school-age children; it can also be applied to the improvement in their motor skills. Children of this age continue to improve their skills, speed, and endurance. With each passing year, they get stronger and their coordination improves.

During middle childhood, children become more skilled at running, jumping, throwing, catching, climbing, sequencing their foot movements, and

As their motor skills improve, children between the ages of six and eight are able to handle scissors with precision, use household tools, and dress themselves.

balancing. Much of this improvement is the result of what seems to be a natural desire of children to test their body and acquire new skills. These basic skills are combined in various ways in the games and sports that school-age children enjoy. Young children who devote time and energy to mastering specific motor skills such as swimming or playing baseball can become skillful athletes by the time they are 10 or 11 years old. Opportunity and encouragement play an important role in the level of skill that children acquire at this age.

During middle childhood, fine motor skills also continue to improve. Between the ages of six and eight, children are able to hold pencils or other writing implements. They can also pick up the small pieces of a jigsaw puzzle, squeeze glue from a plastic bottle, and use scissors. School-age children begin to make more precise movements with their hands. They can perform such fine motor tasks as assembling models containing small pieces, shuffling cards, and using household tools. In terms of personal care, children of this age can handle eating utensils, dress themselves, and tie their shoes without assistance. They can also learn skills such as playing the piano that combine various fine motor abilities.

As children pass through this stage of development, their hand preference becomes more established, and more children begin to show a preference for the right hand. The tendency to use one side of the body over the other is known as *laterality*. Children also learn to distinguish left from right during the early school years.

### Disabilities

Some school-age children are not able to develop their motor skills to the levels just described because of specific physical disabilities. These children may not be able to participate on an equal basis in all physical activities. However, they should be given ample opportunity to practice and master skills at their own pace, and they should be encouraged to join the rest of the children whenever activities are appropriate to their level of skill. Child care professionals need to be aware of what differently abled children can and cannot do. They also need to know what, if anything, they can do to help these children improve their motor skills.

**Stuttering.** Stuttering affects about one out of ten schoolchildren. It is a speech disorder in which a person involuntarily repeats or prolongs sounds and syllables. Stuttering tends to run in families and is more common among boys than girls.

The cause or causes of stuttering have not been clearly identified. Some researchers believe that the cause is physical, arising from a problem in the brain or in breathing and articulation. Others believe stuttering is a psychological problem that develops as a result of stress or emotional conflicts. Speech therapy, in which new response patterns are learned, helps many children with stuttering problems.

**Learning Disabilities.** Certain disabilities do not become evident until children enter school and begin to have difficulty mastering one or more school-related skills. Children are said to have a specific learning disability when they are of average or above average intelligence but are about two years behind in a particular achievement area. It is estimated that about 10 percent of school-age children have a learning disability. Two of the most common learning disabilities are dyslexia and hyperactivity.

*Dyslexia*, a disability in reading, affects boys far more often than girls. Children with dyslexia seem to have trouble connecting written symbols with the sounds of language. They may read words backward or have trouble identifying the sound of a word with its written form. They may also have difficulty distinguishing letters that have similar shapes. Because dyslexia can take so many forms, it is difficult to treat. However, the earlier the problem is diagnosed and the sooner the child gets help in dealing with the specific condition, the greater the chance that the child will learn to read.

Children with *attention deficit disorder* (ADD) have difficulty paying attention for more than a few minutes. The disorder is often associated with a behavior pattern called *hyperactivity*. Hyperactive children are overly active, restless, and easily distracted. Their inability to sit quietly makes it difficult for them to concentrate on schoolwork and to learn school-related skills. The cause of hyperactivity is not known. It has been variously proposed that the disorder may be the result of heredity, parenting style, severe vitamin deficiency, food or environmental allergies, or lead poisoning. Hyperactivity is also more common among boys than girls.

Hyperactive children are often treated with stimulant drugs, such as amphetamine or methylphenidate (Ritalin). The drugs seem to have a calming effect, and the children are able to sit still and concentrate. Most professionals recommend that drug therapy be accompanied by behavior therapy to help these children learn self-control and develop social skills. But the use of drug therapy to treat hyperactivity is controversial. Critics question its value and its long-term effects (Barkley & Cunningham, 1978; Divorky, 1989). They also charge that the drugs are prescribed too freely and that they are sometimes used to subdue normally active, restless children.

Hyperactive children have difficulty sitting still and concentrating, which often results in poor performance at school.

Caregivers can help children with attention deficit disorder by making sure the care environment does not exacerbate their problems. For example, hyperactivity tends to increase in settings where there is either too much structure or none at all or too much stimulation. It appears to decrease in environments where teachers are tolerant of minor disruptions but where activities are planned around a structure and a consistent schedule.

## Health of School-Age Children

The school-age years are generally a healthy time of life. Children between the ages of six and eight have fewer upper respiratory illnesses than preschoolers, but they still get six or seven colds a year. Ear infections are less frequent at this age, as are gastrointestinal illnesses.

### Nutrition

Good nutrition is vitally important during this period of life for healthy growth and for intellectual and social development. School-age children need

**TABLE 15.1**
**Recommended Daily Food Intake, Ages Six to Ten**

| Food Group | Suggested Daily Servings | Serving Size |
|---|---|---|
| *Vegetables*<br><br>Dark-green leafy and deep-yellow vegetables<br><br>Starchy vegetables, such as potatoes and corn | 3–5 | 1 cup raw leafy greens<br><br>½ cup other kinds |
| *Fruits*<br><br>Citrus fruits, melons, berries<br><br>Fruit juices | 2–4 | 1 medium apple, orange, banana<br><br>½ cup small or diced fruit<br><br>¾ cup juice |
| *Breads, Cereals, Rice, and Pasta*<br><br>Whole-grain and multigrain breads and cereals | 4–8 | 1 slice bread, ½ bun, bagel, muffin<br><br>1 oz. dry cereal<br><br>½ cup cooked grain product |
| *Milk, Yogurt, and Cheese*<br><br>Milk products (mostly low-fat) | 2–3 | 1 cup milk or yogurt<br><br>1½ oz. cheese |
| *Meats, Poultry, Fish, Dry Beans and Peas, Eggs, Nuts*<br><br>Meat (trimmed fat) and poultry (without skin)<br><br>Dry beans and peas (instead of meat) | 2–3 | 3 oz. cooked meat<br><br>½ cup dry beans and peas<br><br>1 oz. nuts |

*Source:* Adapted from U.S. Department of Agriculture, Food and Nutrition Service. (1992). *Nutrition Guidance for the Child Nutrition Programs.* Washington, D.C.: Author.

approximately 1,800 to 2,000 calories per day, depending on their age, size, and activity level. Their diet should stress protein and complex carbohydrates and avoid the simple carbohydrates found in sweets. Table 15.1 lists the recommended daily food intake for children ages six to ten.

School-age children not only have a bigger appetite than preschoolers, but they are also less picky eaters. They will continue to snack between meals to fuel their energy needs. It is especially important to provide children of this age with snack foods that are high in complex carbohydrates, not fats. Recommended snacks include fresh fruit, breads and crackers, and low-fat yogurt.

## Obesity

Children in this age group can develop nutrition-related problems. One of the most serious and most common of these problems is obesity. *Obesity* is a condition in which there is too much body fat. Amount of body fat can be determined by pinching the skin from the upper arm between two fingers and measuring its thickness. If a child's skin-fold measurement is thicker than that of 85 percent of children who are the same age and sex, then the child is considered to be obese. Obesity affects approximately 30 percent of boys and 25 percent of girls between the ages of six and ten (Dietz, 1986).

Obesity affects children's self-esteem as well as their health. By middle childhood, children have already developed attitudes about "fat" and "thin." They may have absorbed the view that being thin is desirable and attractive (Feldman, Feldman, & Goodman, 1988). Children who are obese are often teased and rejected. They are likely to have negative feelings about themselves and to have fewer friends than other children (Grinker, 1981).

Obesity can have any of a number of causes. One of them is heredity. Body type, which includes the distribution of fat, height, and bone structure, is an inherited trait. One study compared the weight of adopted adults with the weight of their biological parents and their adoptive parents. The only strong correlation that emerged was between the adopted adults and their biological parents (Stunkard, Foch, & Hrubec, 1986).

Environment may also play a role in obesity. Children's eating habits are influenced by the habits of their family. If parents eat too much and consume a lot of fattening foods, children will tend to do the same. Children's activity level is also strongly influenced by the family environment. If parents are sedentary, it is likely that their children will be the same way. Children who are inactive or do not get adequate physical exercise are more likely than others to be obese.

Other factors that may contribute to obesity include television viewing, excessive playing of video games, and using computers. Children who watch a great deal of television or who spend all their free time in front of a computer tend to exercise less and to snack more than other children.

Stress can also cause children to overeat. Children's lives are probably more stressful today than ever before. Young children are in school and after-school care for longer hours, with little time for individual relaxation. Many also have less interaction with their parents. Children who feel they have no one to talk to may deal with their problems by turning to food. School also places new stresses on them as they learn to do homework and take tests.

It is important for obese children to get help. If left to their own devices, obese children tend to become obese adults and put themselves at risk for high blood pressure, cardiovascular disease, diabetes, and orthopedic problems. Many profession-

Environmental factors, such as excessive television watching and snacking, may play a role in childhood obesity.

als argue against placing a young child on a rigorous diet because it could negatively affect growth. Instead, they recommend stabilizing the child's weight through increased exercise and behavior modification.

While physical activity is a good way to lose or stabilize weight, obese children often find exercising difficult. Other children may not want to play with them, and obese children find themselves left out. Caregivers and parents should encourage obese children to engage in more individually oriented physical activities, such as walking, cycling, or swimming. It also helps if parents exercise with their children. In doing so, they provide companionship, role models, and emotional support.

## Communicable Diseases

Although immunizations have made many childhood diseases a thing of the past, certain communicable diseases are still common. Some occur because effective vaccines have not been developed to combat them. The chicken pox that Luke contracted, for example, is one of the most common communicable diseases of middle childhood. Other communicable diseases are contracted because parents have failed to have their children immunized. It is estimated that only 80 percent of preschool children are immunized against all of the preventable

## FOCUS ON   Child Care Issues

### Teacher Burnout

Lori has been teaching second grade at the Highland Avenue School for four years. She is bright and committed—a good teacher. But more and more often, Lori feels the effects of stress and is discouraged by her job. After school, she and Marianne, a veteran teacher with 18 years of experience, talk about the problem of teacher burnout.

Lori:

"I'm seriously thinking about leaving teaching. It isn't that Highland is a bad place to teach, but no matter what I do, it doesn't seem to be enough.

"Yesterday we were doing an introduction to our science unit on plants. A parent observer was in the room, and afterward she came up to me and said, 'Couldn't you do something a little more creative? No wonder these kids say they don't like science. You have to get them excited.'

"It was all I could do not to scream, 'Look lady. I don't tell you how to do your job. I work hard at being a good teacher. What do you know about handling a class of 27 kids? If you think you can do such a great, creative job with this class, then let's see you do it.' Instead, I told her that today's class was an overview of the unit and that we would be doing more hands-on things later.

"This parent obviously didn't appreciate the fact that we had just finished a unit on Native Americans in social studies. It was all new material because I wanted to work up some bias-free projects for the kids—no more beads and headdresses. That unit took a lot of time and a big chunk of my tiny classroom project budget. This year I don't have the time or the money to do much super science stuff.

"A lot of people see teaching as an easy job because we deal with children rather than adults. What a joke. We're supposed to be perfectly understanding and offer constructive solutions to social problems for 27 kids. At the same time, we're supposed to keep them physically safe and emotionally healthy and teach them in ways that make them want to learn—and all for a lot less pay than my friends from college are making now.

"I really love it when the kids light up and connect with an idea. There are days when you just know that you've gotten through to them, and it's exciting. But more and more that isn't enough. I need respect, better pay, more freedom to select my own classroom materials, and the money to buy them."

Marianne:

"You sound like you're burned out, and that's a shame because you are the kind of caring, dedicated teacher we need in this profession. When I was younger, I thought about leaving, too, but the kids always brought me back.

"There are lots of hassles in teaching. Parents can never walk in your shoes, so they'll never understand the responsibilities and stresses of the job. That's why you need to find a support group and network with other teaching professionals.

"One thing that helped me was becoming active in several professional groups. Until I did, I thought I was the only one facing a lot of classroom problems. Not only did these other teachers understand what I was up against, but they offered suggestions that worked.

"Try to go to as many professional workshops as possible. Sometimes you have to push the administration to give you the time off and the funds to go, but if you offer to run a seminar for other teachers about what you've learned, the administration often sees your going as a good investment.

"Parents can be frustrating. They're overworked and under stress, too, and some of them have problems that affect their children's

## FOCUS ON  Child Care Issues (continued)

performance in school. Getting parents involved in your classroom helps. It builds the children's self-esteem, and it gives the class access to a broad range of experiences. Besides, parents are less likely to criticize something they've invested in and understand.

"One thing that works for me is to get parents involved with a wish list of things for the classroom that the school doesn't have the money to provide. You can ask the parents to help make those things or to find businesses that will donate them.

"Last year a group of parents made window shelves for us so that we had enough space for each child to grow several plants for a science experiment. Other parents will help if you ask a small group of them to come in after school and prepare for a specific project. You'll be surprised at how positive an hour spent working with

parents can be, and it takes some of the responsibility for the project off you.

"Another thing. You have to take care of your health. Especially during the first few years of teaching, you catch a lot of the children's illnesses. You need to eat right and pace yourself so that you stay well. You won't do anyone any good if you're exhausted.

"Sometimes it seems as if no one appreciates what you're doing, but believe me, you are making a difference in these children's lives. For every person who tells you that you're doing a great job, there are dozens of others who think it but aren't comfortable telling you."

*Were Marianne's suggestions realistic? What other steps could Lori take to reduce her feeling of burnout? What other problems might lead to teacher burnout?*

childhood diseases (Hinman, 1986). The American Academy of Pediatrics recommends that children between the ages of four and six receive diphtheria, pertussis, and tetanus (DTP) and trivalent oral polio vaccine (TOPV) immunizations.

One of the most rapidly growing communicable diseases in the United States today is acquired immunodeficiency syndrome (AIDS). AIDS is the sixth leading cause of premature death in the United States. While most of the people with AIDS are adults, there are about 10,000 children in the United States with HIV, the virus that causes AIDS ("Growing Up in the Shadows," 1993).

The AIDS virus is transmitted through sexual contact with an infected partner or through blood contaminated with the virus. Most children who have HIV get it from their mother—during gestation or the birth process—or from a blood transfusion. The likelihood that children with HIV will pass the virus to other children or caregivers is extremely small. There are no documented cases of AIDS being transmitted among children in child care settings. In fact, the Centers for Disease Con-

trol (CDC) recommend that most HIV-infected children be allowed in group child care programs. The exception is children who are at high risk of exposing others to blood-contaminated body fluids, such as those with uncontrollable nosebleeds or open sores. All caregivers should wear disposable latex gloves when administering first aid to children and should wash their hands thoroughly afterward. (See Chapter 5 for a discussion of universal precautions to take in dealing with communicable diseases.)

## Implications and Applications

During middle childhood, wide variations exist in the physical size, motor development, and maturation of similarly aged children. Some school-age children may have the muscle maturity and coordination of preschoolers, while others may be as mature and coordinated as eight- to ten-year-olds. Caregivers and teachers must take these differences into account and provide school-age children with a variety of activities keyed to different competencies and abilities. Varying rates of development mean that caregivers and teachers must be flexible in their expectations for children in this age group.

Early childhood professionals should recognize that children of this age still fidget quite a bit and that they need to be able to move around in relative freedom. Opportunities for exercise and outdoor play provide an outlet for this extra energy and contribute to motor development. The children work better in an environment that has furniture suited to their size.

School-age children are much more aware than preschoolers of physical differences among themselves. They compare their size and skills with those of their classmates. Some children will inevitably feel deficient or inferior. Childhood friendships are formed in part on the basis of appearance and competence (Hartup, 1983). As a result, children who look very different from their classmates or who lack certain skills may find this period of life a lonely one. It is important for teachers and caregivers to be able to recognize possible developmental problems. If a child has a weight problem, for example, the sooner the problem is identified, the better the child's chances of successfully coping with it. Caregivers can help restore the confidence of children who lack certain skills by enlisting them in activities at which they can excel. Child care pro-

---

**FOCUS ON** **Communicating with Children**

### Talking About Drugs

The chance to talk about drugs, sex, racism, and other social issues often arises spontaneously from children's actions or comments. Anne, a caregiver in an after-school program for kindergartners and first graders, uses a spontaneous opportunity to talk about drugs.

Raoul is a cheerful first grader who suffers from allergies in the spring. Last week his father brought his allergy medicine, along with the physician's instructions, to the after-school program and asked that Anne give Raoul the medicine every afternoon.

ANNE:  Raoul, it's time to take your medicine.

RAOUL:  Yum! It tastes like bubblegum.

ERIC:  My medicine never tastes like bubblegum. It's yucky.

RAOUL:  Maybe you should ask your mom if you can have some of mine.

ANNE:  Boys, we should never take someone else's medicine. Do you know why?

*[The class doesn't answer but looks interested.]*

ANNE:  Medicine is a drug. Drugs are something that we put in our body to cause a change inside us. When you're sick and take medicine, the medicine causes changes in your body that help you get better.

JENNIFER:  What if you aren't sick?

ANNE:  If you aren't sick, the medicine might cause changes that would be bad for your body. *[Anne pauses, then continues.]* There are other kinds of drugs that are *never* good for your body. They always cause changes that are bad. We have to take care of our body so that it will grow strong and healthy. That's why you should never take someone else's medicine or take medicine when you aren't sick. And you should never take any drugs that aren't given to you by your doctor or your parents.

*Did Anne give too much, too little, or just enough information about drugs for kindergartners and first graders? Was the information clear or confusing? Can you think of a different way she might have given information on the subject?*

School plays and pageants give children the opportunity to express themselves both aesthetically and physically.

fessionals should also let the class know that comments that are critical of another person's appearance or skills will not be permitted.

During the school-age years, children also become aware of the changes that are occurring in their body. Caregivers and teachers should help children understand the normal physiological changes that all children experience. They should also be prepared to provide age-appropriate sex education should sex-related questions arise.

### Motor Development

Planned physical activities for school-age children should involve skills that the majority of the children possess. Most six- to eight-year-olds lack the advanced coordination and reaction time that are necessary to master sports such as softball and football, but they have the requisite skills for group games such as dodgeball, kickball, and relay races. Having the children engage in activities such as

these helps them feel competent and prevents them from feeling undue pressure to perform. According to the National Association for the Education of Young Children, "[W]hen expectations exceed children's capabilities and children are pressured to acquire skills too far beyond their ability, their motivation to learn as well as their self-esteem may be impaired" (Bredekamp, 1987, p. 65).

Children between the ages of six and eight need ample opportunities to practice their motor skills. Caregivers and teachers can assist children in practicing these skills by creating games and activities that involve jumping, hopping, throwing, and balancing. Skill practice opportunities should be both unstructured—such as playtime on well-designed, well-built outdoor play equipment—and structured—such as guided activities that involve rhythm and movement. Many experts recommend that movement, drama, and dance be integrated into the daily curriculum of school-age children because these activities are vehicles for children to express themselves both aesthetically and physically. Activities that are directed at individual motor development, such as yoga exercises and dance, also help children perform with greater confidence during group games. Providing children with a stimulating play environment helps make physical activity fun.

Physical exercise has many other benefits in addition to building motor skills. It establishes healthy living patterns and supports growth. Children who exercise regularly and enjoy physical activity tend to carry such habits and attitudes into adulthood. Moreover, research has shown that exercise increases bone width and mineralization, while inactivity causes bones to decalcify, making them weaker and more brittle. Exercise also reduces the risk of cardiovascular disease and obesity (Bailey, 1977).

During the school-age years, children's hand preference will play an important role in their ability to master several fine motor skills, most importantly handwriting. Left-handed individuals are at a disadvantage in learning to write because English is written from left to right. As left-handed people write, their hand covers the words, and it is difficult to write without smudging what has just been put down on the page. Forming letters is also harder for left-handed people because children are taught to form letters in a counterclockwise direction and from left to right. Left-handed people find it more natural to form letters in a clockwise direction and from right to left.

For teachers, this means that left-handed children may require more patience and encouragement when it comes to learning how to write. Left-handed children should be provided with ample desk space so that they do not bump elbows with right-handed children as they write. For other activities, it is important to have equipment and tools, such as baseball mitts and scissors, that are designed for left-handed children.

## Health

Keeping the care environment healthy is one of the most important jobs of a child care professional. A key component of maintaining a healthy environment is recognizing the symptoms of illnesses.

Caregivers who are familiar with the signs of common childhood illnesses (like Sandrine in the story at the beginning of this chapter) can help children get the medical attention they need as quickly as possible and curb the spread of illness. Some illnesses are contagious even before any symptoms appear, and there is little that a caregiver can do to stop them from being passed from child to child. However, caregivers can reduce the incidence of illness in the care setting by observing children closely for signs of illness. Table 15.2 lists the symptoms of common childhood illnesses.

Children who are coming down with an illness generally look different and act differently. Common signs of illness include sore throat, vomiting, rash, fever or achiness, and loss of appetite. Children who are ill should be taken to a separate room or otherwise isolated from the other children to rest quietly until their parents come for them.

The illnesses that caregivers are most likely to see include colds and flu. A child with an oral temperature higher than 100°F (37.8°C) or an axillary temperature higher than 99°F (37.2°C) should be sent home. Less common than colds and fever are complaints of headaches. Headaches are usually a symptom of some other problem, such as infection, nasal congestion, or eyestrain.

School-age children still need a good deal of rest. In fact, some school-age children need more sleep at this age than they did when they were five years old. Because the longer school day and the increase in academic activities are tiring, the daytime schedule should include a short rest period.

Caregivers can help children become aware of good health practices by making health education a part of the daily routine. Talking with children about good hygiene, good nutrition, and how diseases are spread helps them establish good health practices at an early age. Showing children proper handwashing techniques, for example, promotes good hygiene and prevents the spread of illness among children and caregivers. Instruction in the area of nutrition is important because school-age children are just beginning to prepare some food for themselves. Discussing what makes a healthy breakfast and which kinds of foods make nutritious snacks will help children make wiser choices. Children also learn by example. It is helpful for care-

**TABLE 15.2**
**Symptoms of Common Childhood Illnesses**

| Illness | Signs and Symptoms |
|---|---|
| Chicken pox* | Slight fever and coldlike symptoms; red, itchy, blisterlike rash most common on chest, back, and neck |
| Cold sores (Herpes Simplex) | Clear blisters on or near mouth |
| Common cold and flu* | Fever, chills, muscle aches; runny nose or congestion; fatigue |
| Head lice | Itchy scalp; white nits (eggs) may be visible on hair shaft |
| Impetigo | Crusty, moist lesions, usually on the face |
| Infectious conjunctivitis (pink eye) | Redness of white part of the eye, swelling of eyelid, yellow discharge from eye |
| Measles (Rubeola) | Fever, red blotchy rash, greater sensitivity of the eyes to light |
| Otitis media (middle ear infection) | Earache, headache, hearing impairment; may be accompanied by diarrhea, nasal discharge, or conjunctivitis |
| Pinworms | Itching of rectal area, irritability |
| Streptococcal sore throat | Sore throat, swollen tonsils, nasal congestion, fever |
| Viral gastroenteritis | Vomiting, diarrhea; may be accompanied by stomach cramps and headache |

*Caregivers should not give aspirin to children with chicken pox or flulike symptoms. Aspirin has been linked to the development of Reye's syndrome in children and adolescents.

givers to show a positive attitude toward eating a variety of nutritious foods.

**Safety**

School-age children are more likely than preschoolers to be injured in an accident. Between the ages of six and eight, children become involved in more activities and their activities take them beyond the borders of their home, classroom, and care setting. They may be free to explore their neighborhood with their friends or to take their bicycle to a nearby park. They are at an age when they are willing to take risks because of their friends. Traffic, swimming pools, playground equipment, tools, home appliances, firearms, and poisons pose some of the greatest hazards for this age group. While most accidents happen in the home or in the car, between 10 and 20 percent occur in or near school (Sheps & Evans, 1987).

Caregivers can help reduce the risk of injury by providing a safe environment. Toys and play equipment should be developmentally appropriate and well constructed. Playgrounds should have soft surfaces for the children to play on. Caregivers should know which equipment requires adult assistance. Above all else, supervision is critical in making the environment safe. Children who are left unsupervised will take chances, and the consequences could prove to be harmful. (For a more detailed discussion, see Chapter 5.)

It is also vitally important to teach children safe practices. On the playground, children need to learn the proper use of the equipment, such as going down a slide feet first. They also need to learn to use the appropriate protective clothing or headgear for various sports. When crossing streets, children must learn to cross only at a corner and to look both ways before crossing. Similarly, children must get into the habit of fastening their seat belts when riding in a car or truck.

Teaching children about safety includes talking about ways to prevent sexual abuse. According to the National Committee for Prevention of Child Abuse, more than 400,000 cases of sexual abuse were reported to child protection agencies in 1991 alone (Children's Defense Fund, 1992). In most cases, the abuser is someone the child knows.

Teaching children about safe practices, such as wearing protective equipment for various sports and looking both ways before crossing the street, can help prevent accidents and injuries.

Children should be reminded that they can say no to anyone who tries to touch them against their will, whether that person is a parent, relative, or friend. If someone does try to abuse them, children should be encouraged to talk about the incident with someone they trust. They must be reassured that they will not be punished or blamed for what has happened. In discussing sexual abuse, it is important to tell children that most adults do not want to hurt children. Reading books written for young children about sexual abuse will bring out many of these points. In addition, organizations such as Women Against Rape (WAR) provide sensitive and knowledgeable classroom counselors to teach children about sexual abuse prevention in a nonthreatening way. The focus of a curriculum on sexual abuse should be to alert and advise children, not frighten them.

If a child turns to caregivers to talk about abuse or if caregivers suspect a child has been sexually abused, they can help the child by providing her or him with opportunities to express feelings about it, whether through words or drawings. It is important that caregivers let the child know that they can help stop the abuse. Caregivers should report what they have found out to a supervisor so that appropriate action can be taken.

## Looking Ahead to Adolescence

Between the ages of 8 and 18, humans go through enormous changes that transform them from children into adolescents and from adolescents into adults. These years can be difficult ones because older children and adolescents are particularly sensitive about the way they look and constantly compare their own development and maturation with that of their peers.

### The Older School-Age Child

The changes that transform a child into an adolescent do not begin all at once. Between the ages of about eight and ten, older school-age children follow the same pattern of growth as six- to eight-year-olds. Each year they grow about 2 or 3 inches and gain about 5 to 7 pounds. Boys and girls still have very similar shapes.

Then, usually between the ages of 10 and 12, girls begin a growth spurt. This involves a rapid weight gain followed by an increase in height (an average of 3 inches per year). By the age of 12, most girls are taller and heavier than boys of the same age. Boys do not begin their growth spurt until sometime between the ages of 12 and 14.

Between the ages of eight and ten, children continue to refine and improve their motor skills. The average ten-year-old can throw a ball twice as far as the average six-year-old. At this age, the abilities of boys and girls are still quite similar, and most child development experts believe that separating boys and girls during physical activities is unnecessary.

The growth spurt between ages 10 and 12 is part of the body's preparation for puberty. *Puberty* is the period when the sex organs mature and secondary sex characteristics develop, making reproduction possible. Although puberty can start any time between the ages of 9 and 14, the average age for girls

## FOCUS ON ▸ Decision Making in Child Care

### Getting Children Motivated About Nutrition and Fitness

Carrie teaches kindergarten at the Vista Sierra School for Exceptional Children. After attending a professional workshop on the importance of establishing healthy life-style attitudes at an early age, Carrie decides to increase the emphasis she puts on fitness and nutrition in her class.

Carrie realizes that she is not going to change attitudes about food and fitness overnight. She decides to use the theme Food and Fitness Are Fun to tie together a yearlong series of activities highlighting the value of good nutrition and exercise. The activities will be enhanced by speakers, art projects, and stories that relate to the theme. Among the special activities she plans are the following:

- A classroom visit from a dental hygienist who will talk about steps to healthy teeth and why eating right is good for your teeth. The children will keep track of how many cavity-free baby teeth the students have lost.
- A visit from a high-school football player who will talk about getting in shape for the

football season. He will show the class some of the exercises he does and talk about how eating well and not smoking help keep his body strong.
- A special unit on occupations that require people to be in especially good physical condition. These jobs might include construction workers, fire fighters, dancers, and park rangers.
- A unit on fruits and vegetables during which the class will plant a small vegetable garden.
- A class recipe book of healthy snacks based on suggestions from the children and their families. The book will be duplicated and sent home with each child.
- A field day for parents and children, with group and individual sports.

*Which of these activities do you think would be likely to motivate children to eat well and exercise? Can you think of other activities that would fit the theme Food and Fitness Are Fun?*

---

is 12 or 13. Boys typically experience puberty two years later than girls. This period of rapid body change usually lasts about four years.

The changes that take place during puberty are caused by increases in hormone production. A part of the brain called the hypothalamus signals the pituitary gland to release hormones. These hormones in turn prompt other glands to release hormones. When the concentrations of these hormones reach a certain level, physical growth is stimulated and sex characteristics develop.

### Adolescence

During puberty, adolescents reach adult size, shape, and sexual maturity. Adolescents experience many striking changes. Although the whole body is growing, some parts grow more rapidly than others, particularly the legs, hands, and feet. These changes may make adolescents feel out of proportion until the body completes its growth process.

During adolescence, skeletal growth patterns take different paths in boys and girls. Boys develop broader shoulders, narrower hips, and longer legs in relation to their torso; girls develop narrower shoulders, broader hips, and shorter legs in relation to their torso. Skeletal growth ends when increased amounts of sex hormones cause all of the body's cartilage to calcify.

Muscles also grow during puberty, though at different rates for boys and girls. By the end of puberty, boys' muscles are bigger and stronger than girls'

Adolescents tend to be sensitive about their physical appearance and often compare themselves to their peers.

While adolescents reach sexual maturity at varying ages, the sequence of the events that leads to full sexual maturity are the same for all. For girls, the first signs of puberty are the development of breasts and the appearance of pubic hair. These events are followed by *menarche*, or the first menstruation, which signals that the uterus is mature. For boys, puberty is first marked by more rapid growth of the testes and scrotum. Soon afterward, pubic hair appears, and about a year later the penis begins to grow. It takes another year before boys are capable of ejaculation. The last change that boys experience is the lowering of their voice.

Because physical growth is so rapid during adolescence, it is especially important that adolescents eat a nutritious diet. Unfortunately, by the time they are teenagers, some adolescents have developed poor eating habits, such as snacking on high-fat and high-sugar foods. Other adolescents are so self-conscious about their appearance that they stay away from foods they need, such as milk, because they mistakenly believe that these foods are high in calories. Poor nutrition not only affects growth, but it can also contribute to fatigue and depression.

Nutrition plays an important role in puberty. A girl's body must contain a certain amount of stored fat for menstruation to begin or continue. Ballet dancers, some athletes, and girls with the eating disorder anorexia nervosa often do not reach this minimum level of fat and fail to menstruate until their eating habits and exercise routines change.

About 25 percent of adolescents' calories come from snack foods. It is extremely important to make sure that their snack food choices are healthy ones, such as low-fat yogurt, rice cakes, bread sticks, and raw vegetables. Adolescents who want to lose weight should increase their level of physical activity rather than diet.

Adolescents need extra calcium, iron, vitamin D, and protein. Calcium is essential to the development of bones and teeth and also plays a role in blood clotting, muscle contraction, and nerve transmission. Vitamin D and protein help the body absorb calcium. Iron enables the body to produce healthy red blood cells. If the body fails to get adequate iron, a condition known as iron deficiency anemia can develop. People with this condition usually experience weakness, shortness of breath,

muscles. In addition, boys develop a larger heart and lungs than girls, as well as a lower heart rate at rest and a greater capacity to carry oxygen in the blood.

Changes also take place in the skin and sweat glands during adolescence. The skin becomes rougher in texture and more oily. This oiliness causes many adolescents to develop acne. Sweat glands become more active, leading to the production of new body odors. These odors are particularly noticeable in the underarm and genital areas. Acne and body odors affect more boys than girls. Other changes that occur during puberty include the growth of hair on certain parts of the body and a lowering of the pitch of the voice.

paleness, and poor appetite and are more susceptible to infection. Menstruating girls have increased iron needs because of the blood they lose each month.

Crash diets and food fads can be particularly harmful during growth spurts. At these times, the body needs more food, not less. Food intake should also be well balanced. Preteen food preferences are greatly influenced by peers rather than by parents. This is why it is important to continue to teach older school-age children and adolescents about good nutrition.

### Implications and Applications

The timing of older school-age children's growth spurt affects the way these children feel about themselves. Between the ages of 11 and 13, girls tend to be taller than boys. Activities that highlight physical differences, such as dancing together, may make some children uncomfortable.

Boys and girls who mature particularly early or late may feel awkward in comparison to their peers. Planned activities should take developmental differences into account to lessen the feelings of awkwardness. The best activities for this age group are those that are noncompetitive and inclusive.

Both boys and girls tend to identify with older teenagers and young adults. Introducing 8- to 12-year-old children to adolescents who can be positive role models for them will help the younger children develop healthy interests and attitudes. Negative role models can lead preteens to engage in problem behaviors, such as shoplifting, sexual experimentation, and substance abuse. Some children may become involved with negative role models because they are bored and lonely. It is valuable to have young teacher aides or group leaders available for the children to talk to and do things with, especially for children who come from one-parent families or do not have older siblings.

Caregivers and teachers can help adolescents deal with the changes they are experiencing by educating them about the stages of puberty and reassuring them that these changes are normal. According to some experts, adolescents' reactions to puberty depend largely on what adolescents have learned to expect (Peterson & Taylor, 1980). If

Adolescents will be better equipped to deal with puberty if they understand the physical changes they are experiencing.

an adolescent girl has not been told about menstruation, for example, she can be quite frightened and ashamed when this change of life begins.

Adolescents are always comparing themselves with their peers. If they come up short because they are slow to develop breasts, for example, or are weaker than all the other boys, they can become quite anxious and unhappy. Their level of physical maturity can affect their participation in athletic and social activities. Boys who mature early tend to be viewed by their classmates as competent and tend to be treated more like adults by their parents and teachers. On the other hand, late-maturing boys often show more immature, attention-seeking behaviors and tend to have lower self-esteem than boys who mature early (Mussen & Jones, 1957).

The feelings that young people develop about themselves during adolescence are often carried into adulthood. Caregivers and teachers can help by being sensitive to the anxieties adolescents may be feeling. Activities that build upon their feelings of competence and their unique skills will help them feel better about themselves.

## SUMMARY

- School-age children continue to grow but at a slower, steadier pace than they did during earlier stages of development. Individual differences in height and weight are common and wide ranging.

- During middle childhood, children lose their deciduous teeth and get their permanent teeth. Proper dental hygiene is important because the condition of the teeth affects appearance, the ability to eat, and health.

- While vision becomes more acute and the ability to focus improves, many school-age children develop vision problems and should have their vision checked regularly.

- Gross motor skills improve steadily during the school-age years. Fine motor skills progress to the point where children can hold writing implements and perform fairly precise movements.

- Certain disabilities, such as dyslexia and attention deficit disorder, become evident when children enter school and begin to have difficulty with school-related skills.

- Good nutrition is important for healthy growth and for intellectual and social development. During middle childhood, many children develop the nutrition-related problem of obesity. Many factors can contribute to making a child obese including heredity, family eating and exercise habits, stress, and sedentary activities such as television viewing. Rigorous dieting is not recommended for growing children. Regular exercise can help obese children grow out of their fat.

- Some communicable diseases pose risks to the child care setting. Appropriate measures should be taken to prevent these diseases from spreading.

- Activities and equipment for school-age children should be varied enough to suit children with wide variations in physical development and motor skills. Caregivers should be flexible in their expectations for children and help them become confident by introducing activities at which they can excel.

- School-age children need opportunities to practice their motor skills. Physical exercise helps build these skills and also promotes growth, good health, independence, and academic performance.

- Caregivers should be familiar with the symptoms of common childhood illnesses as part of their effort to keep the care environment healthy. Health education that includes dental hygiene and nutrition information will help children establish good health habits.

- Supervision of children is critical to avoid accidents. It is also important to teach children the safe use of playground equipment, how to cross streets safely, car safety, and how to prevent sexual abuse.

- Older school-age children follow a slow but steady pattern of growth until just before they reach puberty. Then they experience a growth spurt.

The physical changes that occur during puberty are the result of increases in hormone production in the body.

- During puberty, adolescents reach adult size, shape, and sexual maturity. For the first time, the skeletal growth patterns of boys and girls differ.
- Good nutrition is important during this rapid period of development. Adolescents need extra calcium, iron, vitamin D, and protein.
- The timing of the growth spurt and puberty affects the way preteens and teenagers feel about themselves.

## BUILDING VOCABULARY

Write a definition for each vocabulary term listed below.

attention deficit disorder
deciduous teeth
dyslexia
farsighted
hyperactivity

laterality
menarche
nearsighted
obesity
puberty

## ACQUIRING KNOWLEDGE

1. Do seven-year-olds grow faster or more slowly than preschoolers?
2. How do differences in nutrition and medical care affect the average height of children in different parts of the world?
3. Why do deciduous teeth fall out?
4. If a child has difficulty seeing objects that are far away, is she nearsighted or farsighted?
5. Give an example of a motor ability that school-age children acquire and a game, skill, or task in which they could use the new ability.
6. What is laterality?
7. What symptoms might suggest that a child has dyslexia?
8. What are some of the problems associated with hyperactivity?
9. Which are more nutritious: simple carbohydrates or complex carbohydrates?
10. Describe two effects of obesity on school-age children.
11. List two causes of obesity among school-age children.
12. Why is it important for children to receive the recommended childhood immunizations?
13. How can caregivers help school-age children who look different from their peers or who lack certain skills?
14. Give an example of an unstructured physical activity and a structured physical activity.
15. List two benefits of physical exercise for school-age children.
16. Describe the difficulties left-handed children face in learning to write.

17. List three physical symptoms that might indicate that a child is becoming ill.
18. Which childhood illnesses are caregivers most likely to see?
19. Give an example of a safety precaution that caregivers need to help school-age children remember.
20. At about what age do girls begin the growth spurt that prepares them for puberty? When does the growth spurt begin for boys?
21. What happens to the body's hormones when puberty begins?
22. How does an adolescent's skin change during puberty?
23. Give one reason why it is particularly important for adolescents to get adequate nutrition.
24. Do the physical changes of puberty occur in the same order for all adolescents, or does the sequence vary for some individuals?
25. How can caregivers and teachers help adolescents deal with the changes they are experiencing during puberty?

## THINKING CRITICALLY

1. Children sometimes become ill while they are at school or in a child care setting. What do you think are the most important steps for caregivers to take when this occurs? Is there anything that caregivers should not do?
2. Suppose a seven-year-old child with attention deficit disorder is enrolled in an after-school program along with other children who do not have the disorder. What should the caregiver expect in this child's behavior? How will the rest of the group be affected? What might the caregivers do to help the child in this situation?
3. It is not unusual for school-age children to claim that they are always hungry and to request frequent snacks. In your opinion, what role should snacks play in a child's diet? How should caregivers determine when and what kinds of snacks to offer?
4. Describe a physical activity for school-age children that would minimize competitive physical comparisons between children and help to make children of all sizes and levels of ability comfortable.
5. Some people feel that watching television has an effect on the physical well-being of children and adolescents. Do you think there is a correlation between television viewing and physical fitness in young people? Does the type of programming and/or advertising make any difference? What policy should parents and caregivers follow regarding children's television viewing?

## OBSERVATIONS AND APPLICATIONS

1. Observe a class of seven-year-olds playing outside during school recess. Describe the activities you observe. What types of activities are favored? What motor skills are being used? Do any children sit quietly on the sidelines reading a book or talking to a friend? Do some groups include both girls and boys? Observe the same group of children during gym class. What activities do the children participate in during the class? What

motor skills are used? What similarities and differences do you observe in the activities that take place during recess and during gym class?

2. During lunch period at school, observe six- to eight-year-old children eating in the cafeteria. What is the menu offered by the school? What, if any, choices can students make in selecting their lunch? Make note of popular choices of food and drink. Make note, as well, of what and how much is thrown away. What food is brought in bag lunches? In both bag and school lunches, do nutritious foods or foods high in fat and sugar predominate?

3. Sheryl is an eight-year-old girl in the after-school program where you work. Her mother, Mrs. Barnes, tells you that she is concerned about Sheryl's weight. The pediatrician has told her that Sheryl should lose about 15 pounds. At the moment, although she is occasionally teased about her weight, Sheryl has many friends and participates in all school activities. Mrs. Barnes is afraid that if Sheryl does not lose weight, she will have problems when she reaches adolescence. Both Mrs. Barnes and her husband are overweight and have never succeeded in keeping off weight lost by dieting. Mrs. Barnes doesn't know how best to help Sheryl. What advice could you give her?

4. Matt is a 12-year-old boy. One day he tells you that he is unhappy about his appearance. He is much shorter than most of the girls he knows and this bothers him. The girls seem more mature than he is in every way. He feels awkward and uncoordinated not only around girls but around boys as well. He has begun to have acne, and none of the products advertised on television have helped much in controlling it. What could you tell Matt that might help him feel better about his appearance?

## SUGGESTIONS FOR FURTHER READING

Barkley, R. A. (1990). *Attention deficit hyperactivity disorder* (2nd ed.). New York: Guilford.

Bell, R., et al. (1988). *Changing bodies, changing lives*. New York: Vintage.

Bredekamp, S. (Ed.). (1987). *Developmentally appropriate practice in early childhood programs serving children from birth through age 8*. Washington, DC: National Association for the Education of Young Children.

Brown, E. W., & Branta, C. F. (Eds.). (1988). *Competitive sports for children and youth: An overview of research and issues*. Champaign, IL: Human Kinetics.

*Creating environments for school-age child care* (1980). Washington, DC: U.S. Government Printing Office.

Musson, S., & Gibbons, M. (1988). *The new youth challenge: A model for working with older children in school-age child care*. Vancouver, British Columbia: Challenge Education Associates.

Rothlein, L. (1989). Nutrition tips revisited: On a daily basis, do we implement what we know? *Young children, 44*(6), 30–36.

*3:00 to 6:00 P.M.: Programs for Young Adolescence* (1986). Carrboro, NC: Center for Early Adolescents.

Wang, M. C., Reynolds, M. C., & Walberg, H. J. (Eds.). (1990). *Special education: Research and practice*. Elmsford, NY: Pergamon.

## OBJECTIVES

Studying this chapter will enable
you to

- Explain how children progress
  from Piaget's preoperational stage
  to the operational stage.
- Describe how children develop
  strategies to improve memory
  skills.
- Discuss how children's mastery of
  language enables them to
  communicate better and to learn
  to read and write.
- Explain how formal education
  affects cognitive development,
  and describe what teachers can
  do to influence achievement.
- Describe the onset of adolescence
  and the attainment of the highest
  stage of cognitive development,
  the stage of formal operations.

MANUEL was working in art class with a lump of clay, rolling it beneath his fingers to form a snakelike roll. After making a long roll, he coiled it in a circle, one layer on top of another, to form a bowl.

"Look, Mrs. Peters, I'm making a bowl," the eight-year-old exclaimed to his art teacher as she walked by.

"That's excellent, Manuel," she said, sitting down next to him.

"Since you're working with clay, I want to try something and I need your help. Okay?"

"Okay," Manuel replied.

As Manuel watched, Mrs. Peters picked up another lump of clay, divided it evenly into two pieces, and then formed two balls.

"Now, Manuel, do you think these two balls have the same amount of clay, or does one have more than the other?" she asked him.

"Gee, I think they're both the same," Manuel replied.

Mrs. Peters then flattened one ball into a pancakelike shape and asked Manuel, "How about now? Does one have more clay than the other?"

"That's silly," Manuel laughed. "They're still both the same," he said.

Manuel then picked up the pancake-shaped clay, rerolled it into a ball, and showed his teacher that both balls were still the same.

"Yes, of course you're right," Mrs. Peters agreed.

"There's something else I'd like you to do now," she said. Mrs. Peters took eight pieces of clay and rolled them into balls of varying sizes. She then asked Manuel to place the balls in a row from the smallest to the largest.

Manuel arranged the balls in the correct order.

"Perfect!" she said. "All right, now I'd like you to do one more thing."

She selected three balls of clay and rolled them into three sausage-shaped pieces—a short one, a medium-length one, and a long one.

"Look at these two pieces. This is A," she said pointing to the shortest piece, "And this one is B," she said pointing to the one of medium length.

Mrs. Peters then removed piece A and replaced it with the longest one. "This is C," she said.

"What can you tell me about A and C?" she asked Manuel.

"That's easy," he replied; "C is longer than A."

"That's right," Mrs. Peters said, "But how did you know that?"

"I saw that B is longer than A, and then I saw that C is longer than B, so C has to be longer than A, right?" he asked.

"Exactly!" Mrs. Peters laughed. "I can see that I can't trick you!"

The early school years are a period of dramatic cognitive growth and development for children. At eight years old, Manuel has demonstrated the ability to perform some rather complicated intellectual operations. He can detect the difference between the appearance and reality of an object. He can arrange objects in a logical order. And he can compare two objects when one is absent. These skills are all indicators of Manuel's increasing cognitive abilities. Early school-age children (children between the ages of six and eight) can categorize objects according to multiple attributes, and they understand such abstract concepts as time and distance. They are able to remember more information for longer periods of time than preschoolers, and their attention span is greater—abilities that enable them to benefit from the formal instruction they begin receiving in school. The early elementary years are also a time during which children continue to expand and refine their knowledge of language, as well as a critical period in literacy development. Most children of this age learn the fundamentals of reading and writing, establishing the foundation for the remainder of their formal education.

Psychologists traditionally divide childhood into four periods. Early childhood lasts from birth to about 5 years of age. Middle childhood encompasses ages 6 through 8. Late childhood is the period between ages 9 and 12. And adolescence is the period from puberty to adulthood. During middle childhood, children consolidate their cognitive skills, mastering the symbols necessary for reading and mathematics and developing reasoning skills that enable them to solve increasingly complex problems. By the end of this period, most children are ready to enter Piaget's final and highest stage of cognitive development—the stage of formal operational thought.

In this chapter you will learn about the important cognitive changes that take place during the school years, especially the formative early school years. As children go through these years, several factors affect their academic achievement and mastery of literacy. These include the mastery of various cognitive skills, the desire to fulfill expectations and excel, the influence of parents and teachers, and emotional development. Emotional factors are especially important during early adolescence, when puberty causes enormous changes in physical development, hormonal activity, and a great preoccupation with sexuality. The school years are also a time in which children's individual intellectual abilities, levels of cognitive development, and inborn artistic or creative talents become more significant factors. Children with special needs, such as the gifted, the mentally deficient, and children with learning disorders, all require special attention in order to achieve their maximum intellectual potential.

## Piaget's Stage of Concrete Operations, Ages 7 to 12

By the time children reach age seven, they have already undergone considerable cognitive development. You may recall that Jean Piaget characterized the first two years of life as the sensorimotor stage of development, a period in which children learn about their world through their senses.

According to Piaget, the next stage of cognitive development is the *preoperational period*, which occurs between ages two and six. During this phase, children apply their cognitive skills to solve concrete problems involving objects they can see and manipulate and events they experience. Children also begin to form mental representations and use symbols to think. In the *period of concrete operations*, from age 7 to age 11, children still apply problem-solving skills to concrete situations, but their cognitive skills are more developed and they think more logically. In fact, the hallmark of the operational period is the ability to understand and utilize certain logical principles when they are applied to specific, concrete situations.

### "The 5–7 Shift"

Between the ages of five and seven, children's thought processes undergo a major transition from the preoperational to the operational stage. Many psychologists refer to this transition as "the 5–7 shift." During this phase, children are in the process of advancing from one stage to the next. For example, when children of this age are tested on problems involving logical thought, they are often able to provide the right answer to a problem. However, they do not yet understand the reasoning behind the answer.

Piaget noted several important indicators for knowing when the 5–7 shift has taken place and a child has become an operational thinker. One of the most important indicators is the child's understanding of the principle of conservation, the idea that the amount or quantity of something remains the same even if it is rearranged. Remember the perceptually limited preschooler in Piaget's experiment (described in Chapter 13) who thought that when a quantity of water was poured from a tall thin container to a short wide one, there was less

Children in the concrete stage of cognitive development are able to solve problems by using objects they can see and manipulate.

water in the short container. Children who have reached the stage of operational thinking understand that the properties of objects, such as weight, length, mass, and volume, remain the same despite appearances. They therefore understand that the quantity of water poured from one container to another remains the same.

Another of Piaget's standard tests of conservation was to line up a number of objects, such as checkers, into two adjacent rows. Each row would contain the same number of objects, and both rows would be about the same length. He would then stretch out one of the rows to make it longer. Preoperational children would say there were more objects in the longer row, but operational children are not misled by this rearrangement. Piaget believed that children are able to understand the principle of conservation behind this experiment because they are no longer limited in their thinking by centration (the ability to focus on only one aspect of a problem at a time). The preoperational thinker centers on the fact that one line is longer than the other and thinks that this line has more objects. Operational thinkers notice the longer line, but they also see that the objects in that line are farther apart than those in the other one. Because they grasp both aspects of the situation, they are able to arrive at the correct conclusion.

Countless experiments have been performed to test different types of conservation among children at various ages. Researchers generally find that children understand some kinds of conservation earlier than others. Children as young as three or four, for example, can be trained to grasp the conservation of numbers involving three or four objects (Gelman, 1982). Piaget concluded that seven-year-olds understand conservation of mass, but they do not comprehend conservation of weight until about age 9 or 10 or conservation of volume until about age 12 (Piaget & Inhelder, 1974).

According to Piaget, the principle of conservation is a major milestone in cognitive development because when children understand this principle, they are no longer fooled by differences between appearance and reality. For example, when Mrs. Peters asked Manuel whether he thought the quantity of clay had changed after she flattened one of the two balls, he was not tricked by the change in the clay's shape. In fact, he thought it was silly that Mrs. Peters would even think that he might be fooled. When Manuel was five years old, however, he would have told Mrs. Peters that there was less clay in the flattened ball.

### Other Milestones of Operational Thought

In order to understand the principle of conservation, children must also understand the concepts of *identity*, the idea that objects remain the same even though their appearance changes, and *reversibility*, the idea that changes in appearance can be reversed. Reversibility also refers to the ability to work backward and retrace the steps in solving a problem. When Manuel took the flattened ball of clay from Mrs. Peters and rerolled it into a ball, he showed that he understood both concepts.

Operational thinkers also understand the concepts of more than and less than. This enables them to perform *seriation*, the arrangement of a number of objects according to ascending or descending order. Manuel, for example, easily arranged the balls of clay into a row from smallest to largest. When children understand seriation, they can grasp the more complex concept of *transitivity*, the ability to compare objects mentally and make logical inferences. When Manuel was asked to compare the three different-length pieces of clay, he remembered that piece B was longer than piece A. Thus, he was able to reason that since piece C was longer than piece B, it must be longer than piece A.

Another milestone in operational thought during the school years is the ability to classify objects according to multiple attributes and order these objects into hierarchal classes. For example, if eight-year-old children are shown five mice and eight rabbits, they generally understand that the mice and rabbits are different from each other and that both belong to the overall category of animals. If you ask eight-year-olds whether there are more rabbits or more animals, most will answer "animals." Preoperational thinkers, on the other hand, are more likely to answer "rabbits." According to Piaget, this is yet another example of the shift away from centered thinking. While preschoolers center on smaller subclasses of objects, school-age children pay attention to both small subclasses and larger classes of objects. He called this ability to comprehend a subclass and its place within a larger class *class inclusion*.

### Time and Distance

One other notable development in operational thinking during the school years is the acquisition of an understanding of the passage of time. Preschoolers do not have a clear concept of time as duration. Instead, they tend to confuse the passage of time with speed and distance. Imagine, for example, two toy cars being pushed along a sidewalk. Both are started and stopped at the same time, but one stops at a shorter distance than the other. Preoperational thinkers insist that the car that went the shorter distance stopped first, while operational thinkers understand that one car was simply pushed along faster than the other (Piaget, 1970).

Piaget concluded that children cannot understand the passage of time until they have mastered the concepts of seriation and class inclusion and the idea that time can be measured in units. Once children grasp these concepts, they are able to understand that events can be arranged according to their occurrence over time—for example, breakfast is followed by school, and school is followed by supper. They can also understand that the intervals between these events represent the passage of time. Piaget believed that this comprehension of time does not occur until children are about eight years old.

### Piaget's Critics

Many psychologists have expressed reservations about Piaget's ideas of cognitive development in the concrete stage, just as they do for earlier stages. They have found, for example, that children do not move abruptly from one stage to another and that cognitive development occurs with a great deal of individual variation. Psychologist John H. Flavell, who has done extensive research on Piaget's theories, asserts that many of the cognitive changes that Piaget claimed occur at different stages may actually occur all at once. Flavell compared the process to "a three-ring circus," suggesting that there is less order and more chaos in the process of intellectual development than Piaget believed (Flavell, 1977).

Flavell believes that heredity and environment are responsible for the individual differences in cognitive development among children of the same age. Children are born with different degrees of intelligence and different talents and abilities. For example, one child may have a 140 IQ but no musical talent, while another child of average intelligence may be a musical genius. Each child thus starts out with inborn advantages and disadvantages that will influence future learning. Environment has an effect on cognitive development because each child's environment provides specific opportunities for intellectual growth. A ten-year-old African child, for example, may be fully capable of surviving alone on the African plains but unable to multiply or divide numbers because he has never been

School-age children begin to understand that daily events, such as recess and snack time, occur in a sequence and that the intervals between events represent the passage of time.

to school. A ten-year-old city dweller, on the other hand, may be able to navigate a subway system but would get lost in the woods. In the psychology laboratory, researchers have studied the effects of environment. They have found that it is possible to train children to perform many of Piaget's experiments at a much younger age than would normally be possible without training.

### The Development of Memory

The memory of young children is very unreliable. Toddlers and preschoolers often confuse actual events that have taken place in the past with events that they have only imagined or wished had taken place. Children at these ages may have

Improvements in working memory during the early school years allow children to synthesize new information at a rapid pace.

more trouble remembering information because they are not as familiar with the information they are asked to remember as older children are. They also have not yet learned strategies for helping them remember. As children enter middle childhood, however, their memory improves substantially, along with other aspects of cognitive development. In Mrs. Peters' experiment, for example, Manuel was able to compare the three different-length pieces of clay because he remembered the relationship between pieces A and B after piece A was removed from his sight.

One explanation for memory improvement in school-age children can be found in information processing theory. As you will recall, information processing theory states that the brain, like a computer, takes in, stores, processes, and outputs information. According to this theory, the brain stores information in three ways: by means of *sensory memory*, which is a brief awareness of sensory infor-

mation lasting only a few seconds; short-term or *working memory*, which is the active, yet temporary, storage of new information that a person is currently using; and *long-term memory*, a more permanent storage of information that lasts for days, months, and years. Information processing theorists believe that the increase in memory in the early school years is the result of an improvement in working memory. When working memory capacity increases, children are able to spend more time comparing and synthesizing new information with other information that is already stored in their long-term memory.

## Memory Strategies

Another explanation for the increase in memory capacity in school-age children is that they gradually learn various memory-aiding strategies, or *mnemonic devices*, to help them remember more efficiently.

These devices include rehearsal, which involves the repetition of information to be remembered; chunking or clustering, which is the grouping of information into meaningful categories; association, which is the linking of items in some way; and counting, which involves assigning numbers to units of information. Another common strategy for remembering is the use of external aids, such as writing information down or setting a timer to go off when you want to do something.

Preschool-age children may want to remember things, but they lack such strategies for helping them remember. For example, a preschooler may want to take a special book or toy to nursery school

## FOCUS ON  Communicating with Children

### Talking About Stranger Danger

Elise Martini, a third-grade teacher, decided to bring up the subject of stranger danger at the beginning of the school year. She knew that many of the children in her class walked to the bus stop or to school alone.

Ms. MARTINI:  Today we are going to talk about strangers. I know your families have already talked to you about not talking with strangers, but now that you are older, you are able to go more places without an adult. Many of you walk to school or to friends' houses by yourself, so we're going to review the rules about strangers. First, what is a stranger?

SUSAN:  A stranger is someone you don't know.

Ms. MARTINI:  That's right. But sometimes it's hard to decide whether someone is a stranger. What about people you see in town often, like the mail carriers or the checkout person at the supermarket? Are they strangers?

[*The children looked confused. They knew the rule about not talking to strangers but were not sure how to apply the rule.*]

Ms. MARTINI:  What did Susan say a stranger is?

WILLIAM:  Someone you don't know.

Ms. MARTINI:  That's right. And although you see some people around town regularly, these people are still strangers. You don't truly know them. So the second rule is "If you aren't sure someone is a stranger, treat them like a stranger." Now, pretend that you are walking to school and a women stops her car at the curb and asks for directions to the community center. What should you do?

NINA:  Ignore her.

Ms. MARTINI:  There's something else you should do.

LATEEF:  My mom says you should run away.

Ms. MARTINI:  That's right. Run away, even if the person is asking you for help. You do not have to be polite or helpful and answer a stranger. Let that person ask an adult for help. There's something else you should do. Do you know what it is?

[*The children did not volunteer an answer.*]

Ms. MARTINI: You should tell a grown-up you trust as soon as you can that a stranger was trying to talk to you.

Ms. Martini followed this discussion by reading the students a story that illustrated her points about not talking to strangers.

*Was the information Ms. Martini gave appropriate for third graders? What other things might she have said about stranger danger? Is there another way she could have presented the information more effectively?*

the next day, but he forgets about it the next morning. A third grader, on the other hand, might put the book on the chair next to her bed the night before so that she will see it in the morning and remember to take it with her.

Once children learn memory strategies, their ability to remember becomes much more efficient. For example, when eight-year-old Mara moved with her family to a new community, she employed several strategies to help remember her new address, 7110 Maple Avenue. First, she used rehearsal by repeating the address to herself several times. Then she associated the number 7110 with the name of the 7-Eleven store on the corner near her house. She also used clustering by thinking that maple is a kind of a tree and that the word *maple* begins with the same two letters as her first name.

Children's memory also improves as their attention span lengthens and their ability to concentrate increases. School-age children often use the strategy of *selective attention*, the ability to pay attention only to information they want to remember and to screen out or ignore other information. For example, if you asked a group of 11-year-olds to remember the names of colors listed with other randomly selected words, they would probably remember them very accurately. However, if they were then asked to recall other words from the list, they would probably do poorly because they would not have paid attention to those words. Research indicates that this ability to use selective attention improves significantly during the early school years. (Pick, Franket, & Hess, 1975).

### Metamemory and Metacognition

One of the reasons that school-age children are able to learn memory strategies is that they have developed an understanding of the process of remembering. In other words, they are aware that they are trying to remember and are conscious of the steps required to do so. This knowledge of the memory process is called *metamemory*. When Mara wanted to memorize her new address, she understood what it was she wanted to do (remember the street name and number), and she was therefore able to construct strategies for doing that. By third grade, most children have a good understanding of the memory process. They know what it means to remember and forget. They also know that some things are more difficult to remember than others and that small amounts of information are easier to remember than large amounts.

Metamemory is one kind of *metacognition*, the awareness or knowledge of the process of thinking. As children mature, they gradually become aware of their own cognitive functioning. Older children, for example, are able to decide consciously how to approach a problem, what problem-solving strategies to try, and how to test those strategies. Children who can do these things have developed metacognition, and their ability to manage or control their thought processes is called *executive control*. Consider, for example, a student who is trying to determine how to pronounce the word *grate*. He may think, "I already know several words, like *date* and *mate*, that are pronounced with a long *a* and end in a silent *e*. I think this word is pronounced the same way." He may then think, "I'll ask the teacher if I am right." This student has not only planned, monitored, and tested a solution to the problem, but he is also aware of having done so.

Researcher John Flavell has concluded that metacognition enables children to think more efficiently because it allows them to formulate solutions systematically, eliminate strategies that don't work, and keep their attention focused on the problem to be solved. He also recognizes several other metacognitive functions or executive control processes, including a faith in the power of thought to produce a correct solution, an ability to control the distractions and anxieties that interfere with problem solving, and a desire to arrive at the best or most elegant solutions to problems (Flavell, 1977).

### Language and Literacy

When 5- and 6-year-olds enter elementary school, they have already made enormous strides in learning their native language. But they still have a great deal more to learn. The early elementary school years are a critical period for language development, a time when many important advances take place. For example, if you compared the speech of a 6-year-old to that of a 12-year-old, you would notice great differences in their use of vocabulary and grammatical structure. While the 6-year-old's speech patterns are rather limited in variety and sophistication, the 12-year-old uses speech with nearly the same ease and mastery as adults.

Many of the improvements in language that occur during the early school years are gradual and subtle. They are not as noticeable to adults as earlier linguistic advances, such as when a child speaks his or her first word or first sentence. By age seven, children make far greater use of pronouns than they did when they were preschoolers. Sometime between ages five and eight, they learn the correct use of plurals, past tense verb forms, and possessives. By the end of the elementary school years, children can understand passive constructions (The tree was hit by the truck) and subjunctives (If I were grown up, I would . . .). Comprehending subjunctives, in particular, represents an important step in cognitive development because it requires an understanding of the difference between fantasy and reality and an awareness that a person can wish that things were different from what they are.

During the elementary school years, children also expand their vocabulary, adding about 5,000 words a year. They acquire a knowledge of abstract terms connoting relationships and comparisons, such as *uncle* and *aunt* and *large* and *small*. School-age children also add many new classification words to their vocabulary, enabling them to refine and revise their concepts and categories. For example, cars are no longer just cars; they are Fords and Hondas, station wagons and convertibles, and Mom's car and taxicabs.

With the growth of vocabulary and the ability to use more complex sentences, school-age children become very proficient at conversation. They can vary the length and makeup of their sentences and draw on their increased vocabulary to say what they mean more precisely. As they are exposed to new experiences and environments, they learn to adapt their speech to each situation. For example, children typically use very different speech patterns when talking to a teacher and to a friend, when participating in a sports event and attending religious services. Changing speech patterns in different social situations is called *code switching*. Using grammatically correct speech in the classroom but slang and profanity on the playground is an example of

School-age children learn to vary their speech patterns according to the social situation and the person with whom they are speaking.

code switching. Code switching reflects the child's ability to use language in a more sophisticated manner.

### Metacommunication

One of the most important changes in language development that takes place in the early elementary years is *metacommunication*, the knowledge or awareness of the processes of language and communication. It is the ability to think about language as language and to analyze verbal messages in order to solve problems. In one famous experiment, Flavell demonstrated metacommunication by asking children in kindergarten and second grade to construct a building out of blocks so that it was exactly like one built by another child. The children were supposed to do this from audiotaped instructions rather than from observation. The instructions were so contradictory and incomplete that it was impossible to duplicate the building exactly. The younger children went ahead and tried to build the building anyway, seemingly unaware that the instructions were inadequate. The older children, on the other hand, were aware that they could not duplicate the building on the basis of the instructions. They realized that they did not have adequate information. In his studies, Flavell concluded that metacommunication requires careful listening, an ability to shape messages clearly in order to communicate; and the ability to analyze, evaluate, and reshape messages to correct inadequacies in com-

---

**FOCUS ON** **Decision Making in Child Care**

### Dealing with Professional Jealousy

Betty Chou became a first-grade teacher because she loves working with children and finds it easy to communicate with them. But she is a quiet, private person; talking to parents or even a group of teachers is difficult for her. Last year Ms. Chou developed an innovative program for teaching measurement concepts by using various body parts—hands, arms, legs, and noses—to measure familiar objects. Her approach gives children an intuitive understanding of how the size of the measuring tool is related to the number of units it takes to measure an object.

The other first-grade teacher, Sabina Ladd, was so impressed with the program that she began using it too. Ms. Ladd is bubbly and outgoing. She is very sure of herself at public gatherings. At back-to-school night, it was Ms. Ladd who explained the new math program to the first graders' parents. Later she described the program in the school district newsletter and invited other teachers to visit her class and observe how the program worked. Meanwhile, Ms. Chou continues to teach her class, making revisions in the program and developing additional materials.

Toward the end of the school year, the principal asks Ms. Ladd to attend an out-of-state conference on innovative math methods for primary teachers. When Ms. Chou expresses an interest in going to the conference as well, the principal tells her there is only enough money to send one teacher.

Ms. Chou is angry and resentful because she feels her original work on body math is being ignored. The principal admits that Ms. Chou is the originator of the program but tells her that perhaps she should have made more of an effort to share her ideas and to demonstrate them. "Now everyone associates body math with Ms. Ladd because she introduced it to the other teachers and parents."

Ms. Chou is jealous of her colleague's success. But after thinking the matter over, she realizes that nothing constructive can come from her resentment. She resolves in the future to make more of an effort to speak up and explain her own ideas, to write an article about her program for the state teachers' association journal, and to make her interest in attending professional development conferences clear to the administration.

*What else might Ms. Chou do in the future to see that her achievements are recognized? Where do you draw the line between being pushy and taking professional pride in your own work? Should Ms. Chou tell Ms. Ladd how she feels?*

Children need more than just a sense of humor to understand a joke. By the time they reach school age, most have the language and cognitive abilities to enjoy wordplay, riddles, and puns.

munication. These abilities all develop fairly late in childhood (Flavell, 1977; Flavell, Speer, Green, & August, 1981).

Such findings about metacommunication have important implications. Parents and teachers have observed that young children frequently indicate that they understand instructions when they really don't. Typically, they try to follow directions without asking questions or seeking clarification. In some instances, this insensibility to miscommunication on the part of young children can cause problems or may even be dangerous.

### Humor and Wordplay

Another result of the cognitive and language development of school-age children is their ability to engage in humor, wordplay, riddles, and puns. Children of this age are now aware of the many ambiguities to be found in language, and they can begin to have fun with words. Much of their humor

depends on an understanding that words can have more than one meaning or that words that sound similar have different meanings. A typical children's joke might be, "Why is tennis such a noisy game?" "Because the players are always raising a racket." This joke depends upon understanding that a racket (racquet) is both a piece of equipment and a synonym for noise.

Humor also depends on the joke teller's ability to take the listener's perspective into account or to surprise the listener. Many children's jokes, for example, are based on absurdities that the listener must be willing to accept in order to enjoy the humor. Consider this children's joke: "How did the elephant get in the tree? He sat on an acorn and waited." The joke teller is depending on the listener to accept the absurdity that an elephant could get into a tree and the further absurdity that it would sit still and wait several years for the tree to grow under it. School-age children also begin to appreciate metaphors and sarcasm. Twelve-year-olds begin

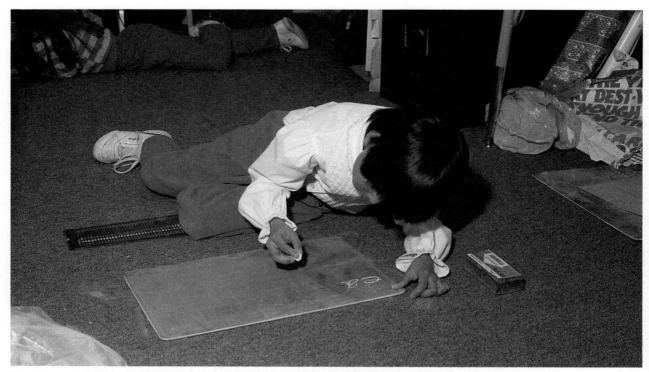

Reading and writing are complementary skills; learning and practicing one skill reinforces the other.

to understand that such sayings as "warm as toast" or "light as a feather" are not meant literally. They also recognize that if someone says, "Oh yeah, I'll bet you're sorry!" the speaker may really mean the opposite.

### Reading and Writing

Beginning in elementary school, children learn the fundamentals of reading and writing through formal classroom teaching methods. This formal educational approach is quite different from the casual, informal exposure to reading and writing skills that children experience in their preschool years. In school, children are expected to carry out certain assigned tasks in order to learn to read and write. These tasks may include doing workbook exercises, participating in reading groups, planning and dictating stories, working on a computer, and identifying words on flash cards. While many early reading

and writing exercises are designed to be relevant and fun, they are more structured than the types of activities used during the preschool years.

Learning to read is a cognitive activity that takes place on several different levels simultaneously. While learning to read, children must learn how to associate symbols with their sounds (phonics), how to separate words into letters and syllables, how to recognize specific words on sight, and how to determine the meanings of words from their context in a sentence. Increasingly, educators are recognizing that reading is not only a cognitive activity but a social activity as well. In many early elementary classrooms, when children are doing reading assignments, they confer with one another, ask each other for help, and work together in pairs or small groups.

Children learn reading and writing at the same time, and the two skills reinforce each other. As children learn to read, for example, they are also encouraged to write stories, poems, fairy tales, and letters, which reinforces their writing skills. As they write, they practice using grammar and vocabulary in ways that will enhance their reading skills. Research suggests, in fact, that children learn reading and writing best when thinking, speaking, and writing are interrelated (Goodman, 1986).

### Schools and Teaching

Schools and teachers fill many of the same roles that parents and caregivers filled in the preschool years; they provide children with rich environments and many opportunities to develop cognitively and to learn social skills. School, however, approaches learning more systematically and in a more formal manner than preschool. In school, children must learn to sit still and pay attention for increasingly longer periods of time. They learn and use various memory techniques to master a large amount of information. Classroom learning is more teacher directed than self-directed, and teaching is conducted increasingly through both written and spoken language.

School curricula are designed to train and improve children's cognitive functions in a logical, progressive sequence. As children's cognitive abilities improve, students are expected to listen to or read and carry out increasingly more complex directions and tasks and to use more difficult classroom materials. As children advance through school, both classroom pedagogy and materials change. More advanced materials such as microscopes and encyclopedias are gradually added to the games, puzzles, and children's books used in the first-grade classroom.

### Motivation

Most children entering first grade already possess both the physical and cognitive maturity to learn to read, write, add, subtract, and so on. As they progress through school, however, they may vary widely in how well they perform academically. Although overall intelligence and individual talents are important factors in academic achievement, *motivation*, the need or incentive to learn and the desire to do well, also plays a critical role. Many bright

Intelligence and ability alone cannot ensure success. On the playing field or in the classroom, the key to a child's success is often motivation.

children coast through school with average or poor grades, while some students of average intelligence excel. The difference is often the result of perseverance, effort, and hard work.

Most children start school with an internal motivation to perform well, and they are usually very confident of their ability to succeed. One of the teacher's most important roles is to build on that motivation and to help children develop self-esteem and a positive attitude toward learning. Highly motivated students work hard at mastering a subject and persist at difficult tasks. Some students have a

## FOCUS ON    Child Care Issues

### Technology in the Classroom

The Benjamin Franklin School District has asked its kindergarten teachers whether they think the district should allocate money for computers for kindergarten classrooms. Some of the teachers do not feel strongly one way or the other; two veteran teachers, however, have decided views on the subject. This is what each teacher has to say.

Isabel Assad:
"Working with computers in kindergarten will give students a great start toward computer literacy. Computers are a part of modern society, and children need to become comfortable with them as soon as possible.

"Many children don't have computers at home, so being able to use them at school is very important. Young children approach computers with confidence and curiosity. We need to build on this interest in preschool and kindergarten.

"Most young children prefer to use computers cooperatively. They work together in small groups, involved in positive social interaction. And as they help each other, make suggestions, and explore what they can do on the computer, they are practicing their language skills. In addition, using the computer gives children a sense of achievement, which increases their self-esteem.

"Computers don't push children and force their development in inappropriate ways. If they did, children would not stay interested for very long. While it's true that computers can be used in developmentally inappropriate ways, the same is true of pencils and workbooks. Good open-ended software allows children to experiment with problem solving in ways that are not possible with traditional materials. Also, computers can be used for remedial drills in prereading skills, giving the child who is behind a chance to catch up. I think we should invest in our children's future by investing in computers for our kindergartens."

Francis Browne:
"Computers have a place in schools but not in kindergarten. Exposing children to computers at such a young age is not developmentally appropriate. Computers stifle creativity by forcing children to respond with one "correct" answer. Too many programs are "graphic flash cards." We want to move away from academic repetition—drill and practice, flash cards, and worksheets—in kindergarten.

"Kids need a chance to be kids. They need materials they can touch, feel, and manipulate. They need concrete materials to stimulate their imagination, not abstract representations on a screen. Already my kindergarten children are hooked on television. I think a computer in the classroom would captivate children, but like television viewing, it would take away from creative play and give little in return.

"Also, a child tends to work alone at a computer. He wants the keyboard to himself. So there's a danger that, with computers in the kindergarten, the children's social development will be compromised.

"Computers are an expensive, trendy toy for kindergarten. I would rather see money spent on traditional and creative materials for the classroom."

*Which teacher's point of view seems more sensible to you? Do you think the way computers are used affects their appropriateness in the classroom? Can you suggest some good uses and some poor uses of computers at the kindergarten level?*

strong desire to do well in all academic areas, while others strive for success only in certain areas, such as music, sports, or mathematics. Students who attach a high value to succeeding, who set high standards for themselves, and who expect to do well have the highest motivation to succeed in school.

Children's motivation is affected by several factors. Among the most important are the attitudes of their parents, teachers, and peers. Parents and teachers who have high expectations and set high standards can greatly increase a child's motivation. Children believe adults who tell them, "You can do it." Unfortunately, they also believe adults who tell them, "You are stupid." Peers can affect motivation by rewarding or punishing certain attitudes and behaviors. A child whose friends tell him he's a sissy or a teacher's pet may not try as hard to earn good grades. On the other hand, capable children who are grouped with highly competitive peers often work harder to excel.

## Children with Special Needs

Some children need additional help in order to fulfill their intellectual potential. Among these children with special needs are gifted children—those with an IQ or special talent well above the norm—and children who are mentally deficient—those whose IQ falls significantly below the norm. About 85 percent of mentally deficient children are only mildly slow. With help, these children can acquire an elementary school education, hold a job, and live on their own. The other 15 percent are more severely retarded and require highly specialized schooling, sheltered living arrangements, or institutionalization.

Another group of children with special needs are children with learning disabilities. These are generally children with normal or above average intelligence who have difficulty learning because of specific problems with listening, speaking, or writing. For example, dyslexics are people who have difficulty learning to read. Dyslexics often confuse up and down and left and right or reverse the order of some letters or numbers. Children who have attention deficit disorder (ADD) have great difficulty concentrating or focusing on a task because they tend to be impulsive, disruptive, easily frustrated, and overly active.

Some children with special needs may have difficulty learning because of physical disabilities, such as impaired vision or hearing or confinement in a wheelchair because of an inability to control motor functions. Still others have emotional or psychological disorders that can interfere with normal cognitive development.

### Educating Children with Special Needs

As you learned in Chapter 5, the Education for All Handicapped Children Act requires public school districts to provide education to children with special needs. According to this law, an individualized education plan (IEP) must be designed for each child with special needs. Teachers, school administrators, and parents participate in planning this program. In some cases, children with mental and physical disabilities are taught in special education classrooms, where class size is small and teachers provide individual instruction. However, the law requires that children with special needs be educated in the least restrictive environment possible.

This attempt to mainstream children with disabilities is intended to help them learn to cope in the everyday world and to allow other children to interact with them and learn something about their special abilities and needs. Nevertheless, studies have shown that mainstreaming does not seem to affect the academic achievement of children with mental handicaps either positively or negatively; nor does it help them gain social acceptance among their classmates (Taylor, Asher, & Williams, 1987). In most cases, schools use a combination of special classes and mainstreaming to provide both kinds of educational experiences to children with special needs. For example, a child who must use a wheelchair might attend regular academic classes but might then go to a physical therapist when classmates go to gym. Similarly, children with learning disorders may be taken out of the classroom for one or more periods a day for small group or one-on-one instruction.

### Educating the Gifted

Schools often pay too little attention to gifted children, assuming that they do not need special help because they have superior intellectual abilities. It is true that many gifted children are highly successful academically and socially and need little extra attention in school. Others, however, have problems because their school does not provide enough intellectual stimulation to make them feel challenged instead of bored. In addition, some gifted underachievers suffer from emotional or social problems because they believe that they do not fit in with their classmates.

Schools generally take one of two different approaches to helping gifted children. One approach is simply to allow the gifted child to skip to a higher grade. Children who are socially well adjusted and possess high self-esteem can do well when advanced to a higher grade. For some gifted children, however, the social and psychological pressures of separating from friends and competing academically with older students may be overwhelming. Studies have shown that the best time to accelerate gifted children is when they are just starting school and have not yet formed close friendships that would be disrupted by a change in grade (Ziv, 1977).

The other approach is to provide *enrichment*, or additional activities that challenge the gifted child's mental abilities. Some enrichment programs consist of giving children special projects in addition to their regular class work. Other programs group gifted children in their own classes so that they can be taught at a higher level and compete with equals. Enrichment can be a very effective approach so long as the classes or special projects are truly challenging and not simply make-work.

## Implications and Applications

Parents are the most influential adults in a child's life during the early years. Once the child enters school, however, teachers play an almost equally important role. Teachers convey information and knowledge to children, as well as values, attitudes, and feelings. They also have an important impact on children's self-esteem. If a teacher treats a child as a capable learner and respects the student's individual and cultural differences, that child can blossom intellectually and socially. However, if a teacher seems not to respect and value a child, that

child's self-esteem and sense of competence can be damaged.

A teacher's expectations of her students' abilities can influence those students for the rest of their lives. In one study, researchers discovered just how important a teacher's influence can be. While exploring the relationship between elementary school performance and success in later life at one urban school, researchers stumbled on a startling fact. Students who had had a certain teacher in first grade scored higher on every measure of success—IQ score, employment status, housing, educational attainment—than students who had not had that teacher. When the researchers interviewed the teacher, she told them that she simply tried to treat children with kindness, caring, and respect; to show confidence in their ability and encourage them to work hard; and to maintain high expectations for their success (Pedersen, Faucher, & Eaton, 1978).

### Piaget's Legacy

The work of Piaget and of many researchers who came after him support the idea that as children grow and mature, their intellectual abilities develop in a relatively stable sequence. Psychologist David Elkind (1987) has concluded that educators do children a disservice when they try to educate them before they are developmentally ready. Trying to teach infants to read before they can think symbolically or to teach preschoolers algebra before they comprehend number conservation is an exercise in futility and may even be harmful. On the other hand, Elkind also notes that children can be taught many things if materials and methods of instruction are carefully adapted to their level of ability.

Several years ago, it was considered beneficial to enroll children in kindergarten a year or more early. Parents did this on the theory that the earlier children began their schooling, the more they would learn and the smarter they would become. Elkind found that this practice placed inappropriate pressures on children to perform cognitive skills before they were ready. In some instances, this resulted in serious short- and long-term effects, such as a higher incidence of drug abuse and suicide in adolescence. Today, parents are more inclined to wait until their children achieve an appropriate level of cogni-

Gifted children need an environment that stimulates their intellect without making them feel isolated or different from their peers.

tive and social development before enrolling them in school.

Piaget's beliefs that children actively construct their own knowledge, that they learn by exploring their environment, and that they think differently from adults are leading to changes in teaching methods and curricula in many schools. Increasingly, educators are designing learning materials and teaching styles that allow for individual differences. Learning materials have also become more relevant to children's lives, and teachers are making greater use of hands-on activities. For example, second graders may begin learning about fractions by following the measurements in a cookie recipe or by cutting up apples instead of by completing abstract workbook exercises. In addition, classrooms are becoming less regimented. Children are allowed to help one another and work in small groups instead of being made to sit quietly in orderly rows listening to the teacher lecture all day. Nor are curricula as rigidly divided into separate subjects as they used to be. Many schools today try to incorporate reading and writing in a number of different class-

room subjects and activities. This provides children with a variety of opportunities to use and expand their language skills. Teachers might also use experiences such as science field trips, a visit to a history museum, or a class project in raising gerbils to generate reading and writing activities.

### Fostering Creativity and Serving Children with Special Needs

*Creativity* is the ability to come up with new and unusual solutions to problems and to view things from a different perspective. Creative people are said to be divergent thinkers, that is, thinkers who can see more than one "correct" solution to a problem. Schools and teachers can foster children's creativity by recognizing and nurturing high achievers, by giving children opportunities to use their talents and stretch their imagination, and by being open to unusual questions, viewpoints, and ideas. Other ways to encourage creativity include exposing children to a variety of cultural and creative experiences and giving them the freedom and support to express themselves. Creative children are usually very successful in mastering a chosen endeavor when the adults around them support and encourage them over a long period of time. Unfortunately, the structure of school systems often limits opportunities for long-term support and encouragement of creative students.

Children with learning disabilities also need special attention throughout their schooling. Educators and other specialists once believed that children with dyslexia and other learning disorders eventually outgrew their disabilities in adolescence or adulthood. However, most researchers now believe that people simply learn to cope with learning disorders rather than outgrow them. Some children with dyslexia, for example, learn how to compensate for the visual reversals they experience. When reading, they learn to search the context for clues to enable them to translate what they are seeing into intelligible sentences. With special attention from teachers and other adults, many children with learning disabilities are able to master skills to help them use their strengths, compensate for their weaknesses, and live productive, satisfying lives.

## Looking Ahead to Adolescence

By the time most children reach the age of 12, they are very different from the youngsters who walked apprehensively into a classroom for the first time at age 5 or 6. They have had considerable experience with formal education, and most of them are comfortable and self-confident in a classroom setting. They have developed efficient strategies for reasoning and remembering, and they are conscious of the process of thinking and memory and aware of when those processes are taking place. Most 12-year-olds can read and write with ease and use these skills continually, both at home and in school. Their language skills have become so refined that

Field trips and class projects enhance the primary-school curriculum by exposing children to new environments and providing opportunities for hands-on learning.

FOCUS ON **Cultural Diversity**

### Celebrating Holidays

Celebrating holidays is a major, often overused, part of early childhood education curricula. When celebrated indiscriminately and insensitively, holidays reinforce cultural stereotypes. When used thoughtfully, however, they can enhance a curriculum on cultural diversity. To make positive use of your holiday celebrations, keep the following suggestions in mind.

- Set the holiday in the context of people's daily life and beliefs.
- Make a distinction for children between learning about someone else's holiday and celebrating their own holiday. Children who do not celebrate a particular day can participate as guests of those who do. But do not treat some holidays as exotic and others as familiar.

- Use holidays as an opportunity to talk about broader events. Thanksgiving can be a starting point for talking about stereotyping Native Americans. Martin Luther King Day can be used to talk about the struggle for justice for all people. Celebrate holidays from which something can be learned.
- When appropriate, focus on holidays that can be naturally grouped together. For example, Christmas, Kwanzaa, and Chanukah can be treated as December holidays.
- Work with parents whose beliefs do not permit participation in certain holiday celebrations to develop a plan for their children.

Based on Louise Derman-Sparks (1989). *Anti-Bias Curriculum: Tools for Empowering Young Children.* Washington, DC: National Association for the Education of Young Children.

they are capable of inventing jokes and puns and using wordplay for their own amusement.

### Formal Operational Thought

Between the ages of 11 and 15, most children enter Piaget's last and highest stage of cognitive development, the period of formal operational thought. *Formal operational thought* is marked by the ability to think logically about abstract problems and to understand the general principles behind solutions to problems. Formal operational thinkers can also imagine possibilities that lie outside the immediate environment of the problem. In one study, a researcher told children of various ages a story about a brave fighter pilot who while flying over the Alps, collided with an aerial cableway, severing the main cable and causing several people to fall to their death. The researcher then asked the children whether the pilot was a careful pilot. Younger chil-

dren were apt to say no. Adolescents, however, were able to realize that they did not have enough information to draw a conclusion, and they were able to imagine other possible reasons for the accident, such as bad weather or equipment failure (Peel, 1967).

As logical thinkers, formal operational thinkers are able to classify information and arrange it in sensible patterns according to several different attributes. They can also use scientific reasoning to arrive at the solution to a problem. In doing so, they imagine all the possibilities, formulate a hypothesis, and devise a systematic plan to test the hypothesis. One of the ways in which Piaget tested this ability was to ask children of various ages to balance weights on a balance scale. Only at age 14 were children able to formulate and test the hypothesis that there is an inverse relationship between the force a weight exerts and its proximity to the fulcrum of the scale. Thus, the scale could be balanced by a 1-pound

At about the age of 13, many children go through a period of extreme self-criticism and self-consciousness known as adolescent egocentrism.

weight at the end of one arm and a 3-pound weight that was two-thirds closer to the fulcrum on the other arm (Inhelder & Piaget, 1958).

Some people never reach the stage of formal operational thought, even in adulthood. When researchers conducted Piaget's balance scale experiment with children ranging in age from 5 to 18, they found that none of the 5-year-olds, about one-fourth of 7- and 10- year-olds, and about half of 13-year-olds could successfully complete the test. Although 90 percent of the 18-year-olds solved the problem, 10 percent of them did not, indicating that they had not yet become formal operational thinkers (Surber & Gzesh, 1984).

Piaget and other researchers believe that reaching this final stage of cognitive development depends on a combination of factors, including the physical maturity of the brain and social and environmental experiences. Educational opportunity is a crucial environmental factor in developing logical

thought, as is each individual's intellectual strengths and weaknesses. Some people may be better at applying logical thought to scientific and mathematical problems, while others excel in thinking logically about social and creative subjects, such as history, art, and literature.

### Adolescent Egocentrism

One aspect of formal operational thought is the ability to understand the perspectives and viewpoints of others. Because formal operational thinkers can imagine abstractions and other perspectives, they can speculate, fantasize, and plan for the future, and they can construct imaginary or ideal situations and compare them to the real world. The emotional turmoil of adolescence and puberty has a strong effect on this aspect of cognitive development. Teenagers, for example, often view others in a critical manner and thus are likely to see parents and other adults as failing to live up to their ideals. When 14-year-olds blame their parents for failing to provide a safe, peaceful, environmentally sound, crime-free world, they are merely exercising these newfound insights.

David Elkind has found that adolescents go through a period of extreme self-centeredness and self-consciousness. This adolescent egocentrism, which reaches its peak at about age 13, affects a teenager's ability to think rationally about his experiences. For example, a boy who has developed an acne blemish is likely to believe that everyone is staring at it and laughing at him behind his back. He does not realize that his friends are experiencing the same thoughts and anxieties about their own minor blemishes and imperfections. Elkind believes that adolescent self-centeredness contributes to self-destructive behavior among teens. Many young teenagers take up cigarette smoking, for example, because they believe that lung cancer and the other unhealthy effects of smoking only happen to others, not to themselves (Elkind, 1984).

Adults need to be tolerant of criticisms from teenagers. They should take them in stride and realize that such criticisms are normal and common at the adolescent stage of cognitive development. At the same time, adults should also be mindful of the acute self-consciousness of teenagers. The worst thing a person can do for a teen's self-esteem is to criticize or chastise her in front of others. On the other hand, adults also need to help teenagers recognize their self-destructive behavior and to understand that they, like other people, cannot escape the normal consequences of their behavior.

## CHAPTER 16 REVIEW

### SUMMARY

- According to Piaget, children's thought processes undergo a major transition from the preoperational to the operational stage sometime between the ages of five and seven.
- Operational thinkers understand the principles of conservation, identity, reversibility, and class inclusion. They also understand the concepts of distance and time.
- Piaget's critics believe that cognitive development does not take place in such orderly stages as Piaget theorized, and they believe that heredity and environment are largely responsible for individual differences in cognitive development.
- Memory increases significantly in the early school years because working memory capacity increases and because children learn strategies to remember more efficiently.
- Metamemory, the awareness of the memory process, is one kind of metacognition, which is a knowledge of the process of thinking.
- Children continue to develop language mastery in the early elementary school years. Their ability to hold a conversation improves along with their ability to use vocabulary, grammar, and syntax.
- Metacommunication is an awareness of the processes of language and communication. The development of metacommunication results in the ability to use humor, sarcasm, and metaphors.

- Beginning in elementary school, children learn the fundamentals of literacy through formal classroom teaching methods.

- Schools provide opportunities for children to develop cognitively in a more systematic and formal manner than was possible during the preschool years. Most classroom learning is teacher directed and imparted through both written and spoken language.

- Parents, teachers, and peers can have an important effect on a child's motivation or desire to learn.

- Children with special needs include children who are mentally deficient, who are gifted, and who have learning disorders or physical disabilities. Schools are mandated by law to help these children reach their fullest potential.

- Teachers have a great influence on cognitive development, and they need to encourage children to strive and excel. Piaget's work has resulted in a greater effort by schools to match teaching methods and materials to children's levels of ability.

- Teachers can foster creativity by nurturing and encouraging creative thinkers. They can help children with special needs learn to compensate for their disabilities.

- In adolescence, most children enter Piaget's last and highest stage of cognitive development—formal operational thought. Formal operational thinkers can think logically and use scientific reasoning to solve problems. They can also see beyond the immediate environment and understand the general principles behind the solutions to abstract problems.

- As adolescents become formal operational thinkers, they also undergo emotional turmoil that can interfere with their cognitive development. At this time, most adolescents become very egocentric and self-conscious.

## BUILDING VOCABULARY

Write a definition for each vocabulary term listed below.

| | |
|---|---|
| class inclusion | metamemory |
| code switching | mnemonic device |
| creativity | motivation |
| enrichment | period of concrete operations |
| executive control | reversibility |
| formal operational thought | selective attention |
| identity | sensory memory |
| long-term memory | seriation |
| metacognition | transitivity |
| metacommunication | working memory |

## ACQUIRING KNOWLEDGE

1. Describe the cognitive skills that children have acquired by the time they reach their school years.

2. What are the ages of early childhood? Middle childhood?
3. According to Piaget, at what stage are children able to understand and use logical principles in their thinking? When do most children enter this stage?
4. What is "the 5–7 shift"?
5. What cognitive ability did Piaget believe to be the most important indicator that a child has entered the operational stage?
6. What is seriation?
7. Define and give an example of transitivity.
8. Explain how the understanding of class inclusion marks a shift away from centered thinking for the school-age child.
9. Name two of the concepts that Piaget claimed children must understand before they can understand the passage of time.
10. How does Flavell explain individual differences in cognitive development among children of the same age?
11. What is the difference between sensory memory and working memory?
12. How does an increase in working memory help school-age children develop their cognitive abilities?
13. What is the strategy of selective attention?
14. What is metacognition? How does it help children think more effectively?
15. List two grammatical constructions that school-age children understand and use correctly.
16. Define and give an example of code switching.
17. How does the development of metacommunication help a child understand directions?
18. What are the most important factors that affect a child's motivation?
19. Give an example of a learning disability.
20. Why is it important that a learning disability be identified early in a child's education?
21. Describe the approaches that schools generally take to help gifted children.
22. What attitudes should teachers adopt to enhance the self-esteem and success of their students?
23. How can teachers foster creativity in their students?
24. Name two abilities that mark the development of formal operational thought.
25. According to Piaget, what factors have an important impact upon the ability of children to reach the stage of formal operational thought?
26. What is adolescent egocentrism?

## THINKING CRITICALLY

1. Some early childhood education programs encourage parents to begin teaching their children reading, math, and foreign languages in infancy. What would Piaget say about such programs? In what ways might these programs be helpful or harmful to young children?
2. Public schools are required to integrate children with disabilities, provide gifted children with a stimulating environment, and give average children a good education. How successful do you think public schools are in

meeting the needs of all children? How would you account for variation in performance among public schools across the country?

3. Some parents choose to educate their children at home rather than send them to school. What, if anything, are these children missing by not going to school? Why do you think parents might wish to educate their children at home?

4. Many teachers believe in the importance of fostering creativity during the school years. However, school is also a place where children learn to conform to specific sets of rules and social behaviors. Do you think teachers should emphasize creativity or conformity in school? Why?

5. Motivation has an important influence on a child's success in school. Do you think a child's desire to learn is the result of heredity or environment? Explain your answer.

## OBSERVATIONS AND APPLICATIONS

1. Observe the approach used to teach reading in a first-grade classroom. Do the children use a basal reading textbook or individual books? In what way, if any, are children grouped? Does the teacher focus on skills with small groups or with the whole class, or are skills incorporated into instruction in some other way? Is writing part of reading instruction? Do children write or dictate stories? Do they keep journals? Describe what else you observe during the class time devoted to reading instruction.

2. Observe a child between the ages of six and eight who is mainstreamed for part of the day and attends a special education class for part of the day. Explain why the child needs to attend special classes. List the subjects he or she studies in the regular classroom and the subjects studied in the special education classroom. Describe differences in the setup of the two places. How many students are in the regular classroom? How many are in the special education class? Observe the child's behavior in both classes. Note similarities and differences in the way he or she behaves in the two classes.

3. Try the conservation experiment outlined at the beginning of the chapter. Work first with a four-year-old and then with a seven-year-old. Take a lump of clay. Divide it evenly into two pieces and then form two balls. Ask each student whether the two balls have the same amount of clay or whether one has more than the other. Then flatten one ball into the shape of a pancake and ask the same question. Compare your findings with what you expected on the basis of Piaget's stages of cognitive development.

4. Every day Justine, a 14-year-old girl, comes to pick up her younger brother at the after-school program where you work. She is a bright and ambitious adolescent, and over the year the two of you have become friends. One day you notice a pack of cigarettes in her schoolbag. You know that Justine's grandmother died from lung cancer last year and are surprised Justine would risk smoking. You tell her about your concerns. She answers that she thinks adults exaggerate the link between smoking and lung cancer. Perhaps her grandmother got lung cancer some other way. Anyway, she thinks she can stop smoking whenever she wants. Right

now all her friends are trying it, and it is more important to her to fit in than to worry about dying from lung cancer 30 or 40 years from now. What aspect of adolescent development does Justine's attitude exemplify? What could you tell Justine in an attempt to persuade her to stop smoking?

## SUGGESTIONS FOR FURTHER READING

Baden, R., Genser, A., Levine, J. A., & Seligson, M. (1982). *School-age child care: An action manual.* Boston: Auburn House.

Bloom, B. S. (1985). *Developing talent in young people.* New York: Ballantine.

Bredekamp, S., & Shepard, L. (1989). How best to protect children from inappropriate school expectations, practices, and policies. *Young Children, 44*(3), 14–24.

*Caring for school-age children.* (1980). Washington, DC: U.S. Government Printing Office.

Elkind, D. (1984). *All grown up and no place to go: Teenagers in crisis.* Reading, MA: Addison-Wesley.

Eysencle, H. J., & Kamin, L. (1981). *The intelligence controversy.* New York: Wiley.

Horowitz, I. D., & O'Brien, M. (Eds.). (1985). *The gifted and talented: Developmental perspectives.* Washington, DC: American Psychological Association.

Katz, L. G., & Chard, S. C. (1989). *Engaging children's minds: The project approach.* Norwood, NJ: Ablex.

Lefstein, L. M., & Lipsitz, J. (1983). *3:00 to 6:00 P.M.: Programs for young adolescents.* Carboro, NC: Center for Early Adolescence, University of North Carolina at Chapel Hill.

Lipsitz, J. (1984). *Successful schools for young adolescents.* New Brunswick, NJ: Transaction.

Sternberg, R. J. (Ed.). (1988). *The nature of creativity.* New York: Cambridge University Press.

# Emotional and Social Development

## OBJECTIVES
Studying this chapter will enable you to

- Describe the development of self-concept, self-esteem, and sexual identity in the years of middle childhood.
- Discuss the importance of peer relationships and friendships in the development of self-concept and social competence during the school years.
- Explain the changes in moral and emotional development that occur in school-age children.
- Identify common problems that can occur in social and emotional development during the school years.
- Describe how adolescence and the onset of puberty affect the social and emotional development of children.

LEROY was working on a multiplication problem in class when he suddenly became frustrated and upset.

"I'll never learn how to do this," he cried, throwing his pencil down.

Leroy's teacher, Mr. Parker, came over to him and asked what the problem was.

"I can't do this stuff," Leroy replied. "I'm just a dummy when it comes to math."

"No, you're not," Mr. Parker responded. "It's just new to you. Anything is hard at first when you aren't used to it. Let me go over it with you again, and I'm sure you'll get it."

A week later, Leroy scored 96 out of a possible 100 on a mathematics test.

"Leroy, this was excellent work," Mr. Parker said as he handed him his test paper. "I see that you really know how to multiply now. Congratulations!"

"Thanks, Mr. Parker," Leroy said glowing with pride.

Later on the playground, some of Leroy's friends teased him.

"Teacher's pet," they jeered.

"Leroy really knows how to multiply," one said, mimicking Mr. Parker.

Leroy's face flushed in embarrassment and anger, and he fled from the group.

For the rest of the school year, Leroy continued to get good but not excellent grades in math. He kept his grades to himself, not sharing them with his friends, and he avoided giving Mr. Parker any opportunities to praise him in class.

When children reach school age, their world expands to include school, teachers, and friends. They develop new interests and engage in a wide variety of activities, such as sports, scouting, and music and dance lessons. Their self-image also changes as they begin to measure themselves against the expectations of others. Children of this age often become very critical of themselves, just as Leroy did, and they need the praise and reassurance of adults.

The years of middle childhood mark several milestones in social development. School-age children are more adept than younger children at getting along with others and resolving conflicts. The friendship of other children becomes very important to them, and they begin to conform to the norms of their peer group. Leroy's peer group rejected academic achievement as a group value, and they jeered him when he earned top grades. Leroy responded by hiding his achievement and avoiding praise from his teacher in order to conform. Despite such experiences, the early school years are usually a period of emotional calm for children. Nevertheless, some children may need help in becoming socially competent. This chapter examines more closely how school-age children develop socially, emotionally, and morally. It also describes the development of children's self-concept, self-esteem, and sexual identity during this period.

## Self-Concept in School-Age Children

One of the most important changes that occurs in children when they enter school is that they become less dependent on their parents and more responsi-
ble for their own behavior. Instead of constantly being reminded to do things by their parents, they now have to remember to catch the bus after school, take their schoolbags and lunch boxes to and from school, and do their homework on time. Typically, school-age children are required to assume more responsibilities at home as well, such as doing additional chores and helping care for younger siblings.

During the preschool years, children spend most of their time in the company of their family, from whom they generally receive a great deal of personal attention. At the same time, they have become accustomed to the family's rules and timetables. When a child enters school, however, she or he becomes just one of dozens of children in a classroom and one of hundreds in the school. All day long, school-age children are surrounded by strangers—teachers, coaches, principals, scout leaders—who expect them to work and learn and to conform to unfamiliar rules. These new experiences and demands have an enormous impact on the social and emotional development of children and on their image of themselves.

## Developing Competence and Self-Esteem

As you may recall from Chapter 14, the self-concept of preschoolers is based primarily on concrete attributes, such as physical characteristics ("I'm this tall"), specific abilities ("I can ride a tricycle"), or possessions ("I have new roller skates"). Their opinions of themselves are formed by what they think about themselves. During the school years, however, self-concept changes. The major influence in this period is children's perceptions of how other people regard them and of how well they think they are meeting society's expectations.

In Chapter 2, you learned about Erik Erikson's system of psychosocial development. According to Erikson, the early school years mark the fourth stage of development, the *industry versus inferiority stage* (Erikson, 1963). During this stage, according to Erikson, children strive to master the skills that their society values. In American society, these skills include reading, writing, and mathematics. In other societies, they might include hunting, farming, herding, and survival skills. Erikson suggests that when children succeed at mastering these

Children entering elementary school face the pressure of conforming to new rules and expectations.

skills, they see themselves as competent and industrious and develop high self-esteem. *Self-esteem* is the value an individual places on himself or herself. Leroy's self-esteem soared when he earned a high grade on his math test and won the approval of his teacher. The opposite of industry is inferiority. When children experience repeated failures in school or in other areas involving valued skills, they see themselves as incompetent and worthless and their self-esteem declines.

Erikson's theory is of enormous importance to those working in elementary education. If self-esteem is linked to achievement during this period, it is crucial that school-age children experience many successes and few failures in the early school years. When children have high self-esteem and feel competent, they are more willing to try new things, better able to accept criticism, and more likely to persevere with difficult tasks. Children with low self-esteem, on

the other hand, are more afraid to try new things, less able to accept criticism, and more likely to give up quickly when faced with an obstacle. Most importantly, once these patterns of success or failure are established, they can persist throughout a person's entire life.

## Other Theories About Self-Concept

In addition to Erikson, groups of other experts have developed their own theories about the development of *self-concept*, the way an individual views himself or herself. Learning theorists believe that children tend to imitate the behaviors, attitudes, and values of people they admire and respect. During the preschool years, these people are generally parents or perhaps older siblings. After children start school, they are exposed to many more people, including teachers, coaches, and other children, on whom they can model their behavior. Learning theorists also believe that children are very sensitive to praise and attention from the people they like and admire. Moreover, these theorists feel that such praise, attention, or expression of pride can be a much more powerful reinforcement for desirable behavior than tangible rewards such as toys, candy, or money. Mr. Parker's praise of Leroy's mathematical abilities, for example, probably meant more to Leroy than a toy or game would have. Such reinforcement helps children develop self-esteem and a positive self-concept. Learning theorists caution, however, that children should be praised for real accomplishments, not for everything they do.

Cognitive development theorists have a similar hypothesis concerning the development of self-concept in school-age children. These theorists believe that older children are less egocentric and better able to perceive the viewpoints of others. As a result, they become more aware of other people's opinions about them, and they develop their self-concept and self-esteem on the basis of what they believe others think of them. Cognitive development theorists also believe that school-age children are better able to consider the needs of others, which makes them more likely to use reason rather than aggression in trying to resolve conflicts.

All of these theories suggest that school-age children base their self-concept on how others see

*Praise, especially from people children admire and respect, plays an important role in the development of self-confidence and self-esteem.*

them; they use the opinions of others as a yardstick to judge their own performance. As a result, the early school years are a period of intense self-criticism. Children of this age form very definite views about their own talents and abilities in a great many areas. For example, a child may consider himself to be good at skateboarding but terrible at baseball or good in math but poor in English. Such self-criticism helps children form a more accurate self-concept because they become aware of their individual talents and shortcomings. On the other hand, several studies have shown that school-age children tend to focus more on their faults than on their accomplishments. They often adopt a distorted view of themselves, and as a result, their self-esteem declines throughout middle childhood before beginning to rise

again in adolescence (Wallace, Cunningham, & Del Monte, 1984).

### Self-Concept and Sexual Identity

You may recall from Chapter 14 that the preschool years are a time in which children begin to establish their sexual identity and learn sex roles, the typical behaviors that society assigns to each gender. The development of sexual identity and the learning of sex roles continue well into the school years. Psychologists believe that children establish gender constancy, the understanding that they are and always will be male or female, between the ages of five and seven.

When psychologist Lawrence Kohlberg studied sex role concepts and attitudes among children, he concluded that after children develop gender constancy, they identify strongly with people of the same sex and engage in behavior they feel is typical of that sex (Kohlberg, 1966). For example, a six-year-old girl may want to play exclusively with dolls, perform household chores, and try on make-up, while a five-year-old boy may want to learn to shave, use his father's tools, and wash the car. Children also choose same-sex friends and demand gender-appropriate toys and clothing.

Cognitive development theorists believe that when children establish their sexual identity, they are forming and building upon *gender schemas*, basic scripts about how males and females behave. Children pattern their own behavior on the schema for their own sex; when they encounter a new situation, they evaluate it on the basis of their schema. In this way, they learn about sex roles from exposures to males and females in school, at home, at the shopping mall, in the movies, and on television. They may learn, for example, that it is acceptable for women to wear pants but unacceptable for men to wear dresses because they see women in slacks but never see men in skirts. Cognitive development theorists believe that gender schemas help children learn many gender-related attitudes and attributes as well. They may learn that boys are competitive, girls are affectionate, boys shouldn't cry, girls should be submissive, boys are strong, girls are soft, and so on. Although many people now regard most of these attitudes as sexist and unfair, they are nevertheless based on the kinds of subtle messages that children are continuously exposed to in American society.

Between the ages of six and eight, children can be very rigid about adhering to gender-appropriate behavior, and they will tease or criticize playmates who try to play nontraditional roles. For example, if a girl wants to play soldier and a boy wants to play with dolls, they are likely to be admonished or rejected by their playmates. As children get older, however, they tend to be more flexible about sex roles, especially when girls want to play traditional male roles. Psychologists believe that this greater flexibility occurs because older children become more secure in their gender constancy, and they become more tolerant of exceptional behavior as a result (Ulian, 1976). Moreover, it has long been more acceptable for girls to be "tomboys" than for boys to be "sissies." Also, American society has come to ac-

cept women in many traditional male roles, such as construction worker, police officer, or athlete, thus blurring the lines of acceptable feminine sex roles.

### Self-Concept, Ethnic Groups, and Race

One of the major aspects of the development of self-concept in children is their awareness of their race or ethnic origin. Once children leave their own home and immediate neighborhood to go to school, they begin to notice that they, their families, and their friends may be different in some ways from others. Children of minority groups, in particular, realize that they are different from the dominant, white culture of the country. African American and Asian American children, for example, soon realize that their skin, hair, and facial features are different from those of white children. Hispanic children are aware that they speak a different language and eat

*As children establish their sexual identity during middle childhood, they often turn to same-sex friends for camaraderie and support.*

different foods from their "Anglo" classmates. White children, on the other hand, may be less aware of their own ethnic or racial identity because so many of the children and adults they come in contact with are similar to themselves. Nonetheless, they, too, are aware from an early age that some children are different.

The parents of children of minority groups face the challenge of instilling in their children a sense of appreciation, belonging, and pride for their own ethnic group. Adults convey these values to their children by teaching them about the culture, customs, history, language, and contributions of their ethnic group. This is important because it helps children develop a positive self-concept and high self-esteem in the face of a dominant culture to which they may not feel they belong. In some cases, this dominant culture may make them feel inferior or unworthy. Teachers, child care providers, and other adults working with children should be especially sensitive to the fact that exposing children of minority groups to prejudicial remarks, stereotypes, and lowered expectations can seriously damage their self-esteem. All children should be taught to understand and appreciate other cultures as well as their own.

Teaching children of minority groups to be proud of their heritage helps them develop a positive self-concept.

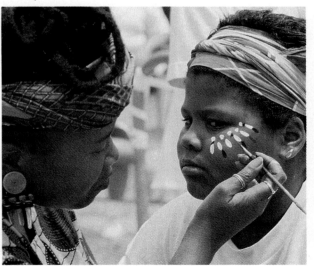

## Emotional Development in School-Age Children

School-age children are normally subject to many new stresses, such as the pressure to do well in school, to excel in sports, and to become socially competent. Most children handle these stresses well, especially if they are supported by loving, accepting parents and other adults and if they have developed a positive self-concept and high self-esteem. Others, however, may be less successful at handling stress, and this may lead to a number of problems.

### Dealing with Stress

In addition to the ordinary pressures of schooling and social interactions, children are often exposed to major life *stressors*, events or situations that produce a high level of stress. These might include the divorce or remarriage of parents, the death of a parent or other loved one, the birth of a sibling, or a move to a new home. Each of these events can cause enormous emotional upheaval. One study, for example, found that children of divorced parents experience deep feelings of helplessness, anxiety, depression, anger, and fear of abandonment (Wallerstein, 1987). School-age children also feel intense guilt because they are still egocentric enough to blame themselves for their parents' divorce.

Children respond to stress in different ways. School-age children tend to keep their feelings hidden because they are afraid of losing the love of their parents. Thus, many children of this age suffer emotional turmoil in silence. They feel lonely and isolated, and they believe that nobody understands their problems. While some children suffer in silence, others may react to emotional stress by *acting out*, that is, performing attention-getting antisocial acts such as petty theft, lying, vandalism, and rule breaking. Still others may regress to an earlier period of development, becoming uncharacteristically whiny, demanding, or clinging.

How children handle stress depends on a number of factors. Personality can play a significant role. Some children have a more resilient personality and are better able to bounce back from traumatic experiences than other children. Another factor is the support and understanding children receive from others. Children under stress can benefit greatly

## FOCUS ON Decision Making in Child Care

### Stopping Fights

Suzanne teaches second grade in a suburban school. She comes from a large family and has always believed that a certain amount of squabbling among children is natural. In the past, her solution has been to remain in the background and let children work out their own conflicts as much as possible.

This year Alex and Will, two children in her class, have had more than their share of pushing, shoving, and name-calling. The boys are friends, but they are highly competitive. Their friendship is one reason Suzanne has not yet involved herself in their conflicts.

On the playground the competition between Will and Alex, mock battles patterned after the behavior of cartoon characters, has escalated into shoving, pushing, and wrestling. As the squabbling becomes more physical, Suzanne realizes she will have to modify her strategy of letting the boys solve their own conflicts. The other children are beginning to imitate Alex and Will's behavior, and the potential for physical harm is too great. On the other hand, Suzanne does not want fighting to become a way of getting attention.

Suzanne decides to take the following steps when the boys start fighting:

- Intervene before the argument becomes too heated
- Physically separate the boys with time-outs if necessary
- Set clear limits on the amount of aggression, even pretend-play aggression, that is acceptable
- Arrange some classroom projects in which Alex and Will must work cooperatively rather than competitively

Although Suzanne puts this plan into action, she is not completely satisfied with the outcome and feels that too much of her time is spent policing the boys' behavior.

*What issues should a caregiver consider when deciding whether to intervene in children's disagreements? What if the squabbling is psychological (name-calling) rather than physical? What could Suzanne do to draw Alex and Will into the process of finding a solution to their conflicts?*

from having a nonjudgmental adult with whom they can share their feelings. Teachers, school counselors, and older siblings often fulfill this role. Some children may need more professional help, such as family counseling or psychotherapy.

### The Fears of School-Age Children

During middle childhood, children's fears begin to change, and this can contribute to the emotional stress they experience. Preschoolers are usually afraid of monsters, witches, ghosts, and other magical or supernatural beings. School-age children, on the other hand, develop more realistic fears about such things as the loss of a parent, a scary movie,

terrorism, homelessness, failure in school, and embarrassing themselves in front of others. In addition, children of this age are often afraid of not being accepted by their peers and not having friends. In recent years, the prevalence of violence in American life has added new fears to this list. Some school-age children now fear being killed by drug gangs or robbers, being sexually assaulted, or being kidnapped by carjackers.

Fears are a normal part of growing up, and children need to feel safe to express their fears without being belittled or ridiculed. Adults can help by treating children's fears seriously, by providing children with accurate information, and by helping them find ways to deal with their fears. For example, if a child is fearful of failing in school, an adult might tutor the child or arrange for extra academic help. If a child is anxious about violence, an adult might walk the child to and from school and always lock the house and car doors. If a child is afraid of contracting AIDS, an adult might help dispel this fear by providing a clear, factual explanation of how AIDS is spread. Helping children cope with or overcome their fears helps, in turn, to alleviate the stresses associated with them.

### Emotional Problems

While serious emotional problems are less common in middle childhood than in adolescence, children of this age can suffer from a number of emotional disturbances. Separation anxiety, for example, is a common emotional problem in the early elementary school years. One type of separation anxiety is *school phobia*, an irrational fear of school. Some children experience school phobia when report cards come out because they fear being punished for bad grades. A separation anxiety such as school phobia can manifest itself in physical symptoms such as nausea, stomachache, headache, and vomiting.

Another emotional problem that affects some school-age children is depression. Children who have not developed social competence or who are failing in school often become depressed. As a result, they may be tired and moody, experience overwhelming feelings of guilt, lose their appetite, have difficulty sleeping, and be unable to concentrate in school. Childhood depression can be a life-threatening illness because, in extreme cases, children sometimes attempt suicide to escape their problems. Psychiatrists and psychologists can treat both separation anxiety and childhood depression with psychotherapy and/or drugs once these conditions have been identified.

### Social Development in School-Age Children

As children grow, their social circle widens constantly. As infants, they interact primarily with parents and siblings and to a lesser extent with extended family members. As toddlers and preschoolers, their social interactions may include grandparents, aunts and uncles, caregivers or preschool teachers, and children they meet in play groups and child

*Emotional problems during childhood can be treated with psychotherapy and, in some cases, medication.*

care. When children start school, their social contacts expand dramatically to include school teachers, athletic coaches, counselors, and dozens of other children. School-age children learn how to interact with all these new people in a variety of ways, such as working together in the classroom, playing on a Little League team, or just hanging out in the backyard.

As the social world of the school-age child expands, people outside the family begin to exert a greater influence on the child's development. Of course, parents, siblings, and grandparents remain extremely important to children of this age. Parents, especially, continue to play the most important role in their children's lives, providing love, support, structure, values, assistance, and companionship. In the early school years, however, friends and peers become increasingly important because they offer other viewpoints against which children can measure their own abilities and ideas.

## Developing Social Skills

The process of developing social competence that began in the preschool years continues throughout middle childhood. As children sharpen their social skills, they become more acute observers of other people. They are more aware of other people's personality characteristics, and they begin to judge other people according to their own beliefs, motives, and other abstract traits. A second grader, for example, can perceive that his teacher seems to favor the girls in the class, and he therefore realizes that many of the teacher's actions toward him have less to do with who he is than with the fact that he is a boy.

A number of factors help facilitate social interaction among school-age children. To begin with, children of this age are less aggressive and better able to resolve conflicts than younger children. They are also less egocentric and more aware of the point of view of others, as well as more concerned about how others perceive them. In addition, school-age children are more adept at anticipating how others will react in a social situation, and they can tailor their actions to achieve what they want. A seven-year-old who wants a new bicycle may promise to keep her room clean in exchange for the bike be-

cause she knows that is what her parents want. Finally, school-age children are much more skilled at expressing themselves verbally than younger children. A six-year-old does not have to snatch a coveted toy away from a playmate; he can simply ask for it or even negotiate a fair means of sharing or borrowing it.

## Peer Group Relations

A *peer group* is a loosely knit group of people who are usually about the same age, live in the same area, attend the same school, and often are of the same race and socioeconomic class. In elementary school, peer groups are virtually always made up of children of the same sex as well. Members of school-age peer groups may adopt and adhere very closely to a special vocabulary of slang words, specific dress codes, and certain rules of behavior. If the dress code for a particular group is jeans, sneakers, and oversized T-shirts with rock group logos, peer group members will flatly refuse to wear anything else.

As children become more independent of their parents, they grow more dependent on their peer group. Such groups can fulfill a variety of positive functions. The children in a peer group help each other develop values, opinions, and self-esteem by measuring themselves against each other. For example, it is often not enough for a girl's parents to tell her that she is pretty or smart; she needs confirmation from her friends as well. Peer groups foster emotional stability because members share feelings and experiences with each other that they would not be willing to share with parents or other adults. Being in a peer group also facilitates a child's social development in a number of ways. The members of a group learn to compromise, negotiate, set and follow rules, and defer to others. In addition, they learn values such as loyalty and leadership and attitudes such as racial tolerance, fairness, and equality.

While peer groups fulfill many positive functions, they have some negative aspects as well. These groups exert a great deal of *peer pressure*, a demand for a high degree of conformity to the group's values, attitudes, and behavior. When Leroy's friends teased him on the playground because he

Peer groups can help foster social values and a sense of community among school-age children.

received a high grade on a math test and got praised by his teacher, they were exerting peer pressure. In this case, they were reinforcing a common attitude among boys that it is not socially acceptable to appear to be too smart and that smart boys are unpopular nerds. In a similar way, children may adopt undesirable attitudes and values, such as racial prejudice and disrespect for adults, as a result of peer pressure.

Peer groups and peer pressure may also encourage antisocial behaviors among members, such as shoplifting, smoking, and taking drugs. Children who wouldn't dream of spray painting the wall of a building on their own will often do so willingly in the presence of their peers. Children with low self-esteem are the most susceptible to negative peer pressure because of their need to be accepted within the group. Yet all children are susceptible to peer pressure to some extent. Studies have shown that susceptibility to peer pressure tends to increase throughout the middle childhood years but falls off after puberty (Costanzo & Shaw, 1966).

### The Need for Friendships

Friendships are as important as peer groups in middle childhood, and they serve many of the same purposes, including fostering social skills and emotional stability. Children generally make friends with other children who are similar to them. Best friends, for example, are usually of the same sex, race, age, and social class; they like to do the same things and hold many of the same attitudes and values. As children grow older, their friendships become more intense and intimate. Children tell secrets and share feelings with close friends, and they comfort each other when they are troubled or sad.

The basis of friendship changes as children grow older. In the preschool years, a child may consider someone a friend because he or she will do what

## Talking About Death

Wendy supervises a group of six- to eight-year-olds in an after-school program. Yesterday Joel, a boy in her group, was hit by a car and killed while riding his bicycle. Wendy realizes that some of the children will have already heard about Joel's death; others will be hearing the news for the first time at the after-school program this afternoon. She decides that her first priority today is talking to her group about the accident.

WENDY: We have something important and very sad to talk about today. Yesterday afternoon our friend and classmate Joel was hit by a car while he was riding his bike. Although the rescue squad and the doctors at the hospital worked very hard to save his life, Joel died.

*[Some of the children look stunned; a few begin to cry.]*

WENDY: Sometimes when something goes wrong, we try to pretend that it never happened. But Joel's accident did happen. Joel was special to us. It makes us feel very sad that he is dead. When I heard about the accident, I cried. It's all right to cry.

Joel was our friend. Sometimes we argued with him or said mean things to him. Sometimes we were angry with him. Sometimes we laughed with him. But nothing any of you did made him die. Joel died because a driver lost control of his car and smashed into Joel's bicycle.

I would like everyone to take a moment to think about some of the things Joel did that made us happy, some of the times we had fun with him in our class. Then we can share these memories and remember Joel together.

WENDY *[after pausing for a moment]*: I remember how Joel loved to take the attendance sheet to the office. He was always the first to volunteer.

ROBERT: I remember when Joel brought in his guinea pig and how it got out of its cage. We were chasing it all over the room before we caught it.

SARAH: I remember how Joel liked to draw monster faces on the back of his homework papers.

JAMAL: I remember how Joel used to share his food at snacktime.

HENRY: Joel loved to play baseball. He always wanted to be the pitcher. He was a good player.

*[A few other children mention special things they remember about Joel. Some children remain silent, and Wendy doesn't press them to speak.]*

WENDY: On Thursday there is going to be a funeral for Joel. Joel's parents have said that if you would like to go to the funeral, you may go with your parents. Mrs. Newcomb, the director, will be meeting with some of your parents tomorrow to talk about Joel's death. She will explain where the funeral will be.

You'll probably think about Joel and feel sad for a long time. That's all right. It's all right to feel upset. It's all right to talk about Joel, too. Over the next few weeks a special person called a counselor will be visiting the center to help us talk about our feelings about Joel. Later we'll have a ceremony and plant a tree to help us remember Joel.

*Do you think Wendy gave too much, not enough, or just the right amount of information about Joel's death? How would you have presented the information? What kind of follow-up activities could Wendy plan to help the children through the grieving process?*

the child wants. In middle childhood, friendship comes to involve cooperation, compromise, and mutual pleasure. As children grow older, they also become more selective about their friends. They may change friends several times, and their circle of friends becomes smaller. Most children tend to designate certain other children as "best friends," and they can be very possessive about these best friends. Children are often jealous, for instance, when their best friends make other friends. When friendships end, children can be very hurt and upset.

Having friends helps children develop self-esteem because it shows that they are liked and respected by others. Being unable to make or keep friends, on the other hand, can be very damaging to self-esteem. Some children are naturally more popular than others. These children tend to be more socially competent and more mature than unpopular children. They are also self-confident, cooperative, imaginative, and good-humored. Unpopular children may act aggressively, display immature behavior, or appear nervous and anxious. Adult caregivers can help unpopular children learn social skills and provide opportunities for them to practice these skills.

## Moral Development in School-Age Children

As children progress through the elementary school years, their moral reasoning and moral behavior become more mature. Psychologist Lawrence Kohlberg theorizes that children pass through six stages of moral development as they grow to adulthood (Kohlberg, 1976). Preschoolers are in the first stage, the "what will happen to me" stage. Children in this stage believe that authority figures are all powerful beings whose rules cannot be changed. Their primary motivation for obeying rules is to avoid punishment. They ignore motives and focus instead on the physical form of an act (the size of a lie) and its consequences. Beginning at about age five, children enter Kohlberg's second stage, the "look out for number one" or "what's in it for me" stage. During this phase, children become very interested in the issue of fairness and the principle of equality, the concept that everyone should be treated equally, particularly as it applies to themselves. Children at this stage will complain, "You

gave him more than me" and will negotiate chores and treats: "If I take out the trash, what will you give me?"

Gradually during the elementary school years, by about age ten, children progress to stage 3 of Kohlberg's hierarchy. At this point, children care about what others think, and they want to please and help others. Kohlberg calls this phase the "golden rule stage" because children want to be thought of as "good" and able to live up to the expectations of their parents, teachers, and peers. Thus, the same concern about what others think of them, which influences the development of self-concept and self-esteem, influences the moral thinking and behavior of school-age children.

Between the ages of five and ten, children become more flexible in their moral thinking. They no longer regard rules as rigid and unchangeable, and they understand that rules can be altered. According to psychologist Elliot Turiel, children begin differentiating between social conventions and ethical principles in middle childhood. His research has shown that children understand that social conventions can be easily changed, whereas ethical principles are more permanent (Turiel, 1983). For example, rules governing a sandlot baseball game can be changed as the players wish, but the principle against killing another human being must not be violated except in times of war.

Teachers and caregivers should keep in mind that individual children develop moral thought at different rates. Some children enter Kohlberg's third stage in middle childhood, while many others do not enter it until adolescence. Moreover, the same child can exhibit stage 1, stage 2, or stage 3 thinking and behavior at different times. For example, a seven-year-old who is tired or overly excited may cry and whine and make demands like an egocentric preschooler (stage 1), while that same child as a kindergartner a year or two earlier may have tried to be well behaved because he had a strong desire to make a good impression on a new teacher (stage 3).

## The Emergence of Conscience

Kohlberg's stage 3 is the period when children begin to develop *conscience*, the inner voice that tells a person the difference between right and wrong. Although a conscience may not always prevent children from immoral behavior, such as shoplifting, it does trigger feelings of guilt when they perform the behavior. In effect, conscience takes the place of parental training. Instead of listening to their parents' instructions, children learn to follow the dictates of their own conscience in order to avoid the guilt that arises when they disregard it.

### Prosocial Behavior

In Chapter 14 you learned that children begin to develop prosocial behavior in the preschool years. Prosocial behavior is defined as any action performed to benefit others, such as cooperating, helping, sharing, and comforting. Researchers have found that as children get older, they become more selective about the objects of their prosocial behavior. A school-age child, for example, is more likely to help a friend or someone she admires than to help a stranger or an acquaintance.

Children learn prosocial behavior from observing adult role models and from being rewarded for altruistic acts. If children are praised for sharing toys or cooperating with other children, they learn that adults value that behavior. Similarly, if children see adults give money to a panhandler or volunteer their time to a community project, they learn that society values generosity.

The development of prosocial behavior is also influenced by the child's culture. For example, the Japanese culture places great value on cooperation and group effort. Children are usually assigned important family responsibilities at an early age, and they are taught to share, to work together, and to be considerate of others. American culture, on the other hand, tends to stress competitiveness and individual achievement instead of cooperation and group effort. As a result, American children are

Prosocial behavior is influenced by culture. Many Asian cultures, for example, stress cooperation, sharing, and working together to reach a goal.

### Sex in the Media

Recently, the parents of a second-grade boy complained to his teacher, Todd Davis, that their son, Rob, was acquiring inappropriate sexual information at school. After talking to Rob's parents, Todd realized that another boy in the class, Jonathan, was repeating graphic descriptions of sexual behavior that he had seen at home on cable television pay movie channels and videos.

Todd explained to Rob's parents that the school could not control children's conversations on the playground, but that he would talk to Jonathan and his parents because he felt exposure to such material was harmful to young children.

At the conference with Jonathan's parents, Todd explains why he is concerned about Jonathan's precocious sexual education. Then Jonathan's father, Alan Hershey, explains his view of the situation.

Todd Davis:
"Jonathan has been sharing some very explicit sexual information with his classmates. I'm concerned that Jonathan is regularly seeing movies on television that are not appropriate for his age.

"Television has a very powerful and persuasive influence on children. Studies repeatedly indicate that children who see repetitive violence on television resort more frequently to violence as a way of solving their problems than do children who watch less violent programs. I'm concerned that exposing Jonathan to sexually explicit information at such a young age will give him a similar unrealistic and inappropriate outlook on sexuality.

"Young children are quick to imitate what they see as adult behavior. Second graders don't have the maturity and experience to discriminate between the fantasy world of television and the real world. Exposing them to adult movies does a great deal of harm. Children are rushed into adult behaviors rather than being allowed to mature at a natural pace.

"I think you should also be aware that when Jonathan shares this adult information with his classmates, it's disturbing to other parents who wish to introduce adult subjects at a later time. I urge you to restrict Jonathan's television viewing to more age-appropriate shows because of the potential for psychological harm."

Alan Hershey:
"My wife and I feel that there's no way we can protect Jonathan from sexual imagery and information in the media; nor do we want to. The things that Jonathan sees when he watches R-rated movies with us are no worse than the advertisements he sees on regular network television. Today's reality is that sex is used to sell products and to entertain. There's no way to avoid it or protect our children from its influence.

"We're realists. We believe that by exposing Jonathan to the real world at a young age, we're giving him the information and toughness he needs to survive in today's world. Besides, we don't really believe that he understands a lot of what he sees. He just imitates some of the conversations he hears in the movies because he thinks it makes him sound grown up. So what? That's just a form of showing off, and all kids show off occasionally.

"We think it's better to let Jonathan watch these movies with us rather than make a big mystery of what we like to watch. We like to watch TV as a family. And my wife and I don't think we should have to wait until Jonathan is in bed before we watch the movies we want to see.

"What Jonathan sees and hears at home is none of the school's or other parents' business. It isn't as if he's bringing dirty pictures to school; it's just conversation. Boys always talk about likely to be less cooperative than children of certain other cultures (Knight & Kagan, 1977).

## Implications and Applications

For the school-age child, the development of a positive self-concept and high self-esteem and the growth of social competence are of crucial importance. Each of these developments depends upon a child's feeling of achievement or failure, which is summarized in Erikson's stage of industry (competence) versus inferiority. Parents remain the main facilitators of social and emotional development in school-age children. But other adults, particularly teachers, also play important roles in helping children develop competence and self-esteem.

Because parents are still the most important adults in a child's life, they have great power to foster or damage self-esteem. As in every other stage of development, children need parents who are warm, nurturing, and supportive. Once children begin school, parents cannot be as protective as they once were. Even so, home and family still provide safety and comfort for children. During the school years, children often need their parents to act as go-betweens in resolving conflicts in school, especially conflicts involving adults.

One of the most significant factors in the self-concept of school-age children is academic achievement. Most children start school with great enthusiasm and confidence in their own abilities. Within a few years, however, many children begin to think of themselves as academic failures. One reason this happens is that children become more self-critical and adopt an exaggerated view of their shortcomings. This may result, in turn, in what is

known as *learned helplessness*; that is, the past failures of children lead them to believe they are unable to improve their performance or situation. Such feelings of incompetence and low self-esteem can affect a child's entire life unless recognized and remedied at an early stage.

American children are especially vulnerable to learned helplessness because our society puts such emphasis on competition in the classroom, in sports, and even in social interactions. Children quickly come to identify the smartest students, the best athletes, and the most popular classmates by the way that adults treat them and their peers react to them. When average children compare themselves to the best and the brightest, they may feel that they are stupid, clumsy, or unpopular.

Although school-age children are very susceptible to learned helplessness, the condition can be avoided. Parents, teachers, and school administrators should insist on developmentally appropriate programs and curricula that instruct children on a level they can understand. Caregivers need to be very supportive of children and to develop relationships with them based on acceptance and understanding. They should also praise children for real accomplishments and help them recognize their abilities and achievements. In addition, children should be exposed to school curricula and games based on cooperation, teamwork, and mutual goals to help lessen the negative effects of competition.

In dealing with school-age children, caregivers need to be extremely sensitive about their own attitudes toward gender, racial, and cultural differences. Social attitudes about these classifications play a significant role in the establishment of an individual's self-concept and self-esteem. Studies

Acceptance by one's peers is crucial to social development and emotional well-being during middle childhood.

have shown, for example, that many teachers unconsciously treat girls differently from boys in the elementary school classroom. They talk to boys more, praise them more, and give them more directions than they do girls. This differential treatment reinforces independence in boys and submissiveness in girls (Serbin, O'Leary, Kent, & Tonick, 1973). Similarly, some teachers may have a preconceived idea that children of minority groups are poor achievers and may have lower expectations for them than for middle-class white students. Minority children may thus receive the message that they are not as bright as other children and may incorporate that message into their self-concept.

### Social Acceptance and Self-Esteem

In middle childhood, high self-esteem is closely related to acceptance by one's peers. Children who are rejected by their peers are usually socially immature; they may be overly talkative, overly aggressive, and insensitive to social nuances. Rejected children often have difficulty sharing possessions and cooperating in group projects, and they tend to misunderstand the overtures of others.

Children who are rejected by their peers often feel self-hatred and helplessness. They know that they are not making or keeping friends, but they don't know what to do about it. Social isolation or rejection by peers in middle childhood can have serious consequences. Rejected children tend to develop serious emotional problems, such as childhood depression, or they may become juvenile delinquents in adolescence. Moreover, as these children grow older, they may have difficulties with their academic performance, family relationships, and emotional and social development.

The main remedy for social rejection is simply to practice social skills. Children need many opportunities to learn social skills during the preschool and early school years. Teachers and caregivers can help by making sure that rejected children are included in pairs or small groups while working on projects or playing games. In some cases, adults can help by teaching children specific social skills, such as how to start a conversation, how to share toys, and so on. Adults can also reinforce desirable behaviors and ignore undesirable ones in rejected children.

Sometimes children can improve their social acceptance just by improving their academic skills.

One research study revealed that when a group of youngsters were tutored, the children became more readily accepted by their peers. The researchers concluded that the increased attention from teachers and greater classroom participation led to higher self-esteem in these children. As a result, they were also viewed in a more positive light by their classmates (Coie & Krehbiel, 1984).

## After-School Care

During the early elementary years, many children are enrolled in before- and after-school programs because their parents work. Caregivers in these programs should be sensitive to the social and emotional needs of these children, who are spending long periods of time away from home. The children are expected to conform to different sets of rules in different environments, and they have to deal with different authority figures and different classmates.

At the end of the school day, most young children are tired, hungry, and cranky. Child care programs must deal with this and provide a variety of activities and environments to capture the children's interest and accommodate their needs. Some children may need quiet and solitude; others will want the opportunity to run, play, and make noise. After-school programs are not simple extensions of the school day. They should give children a break from academic activities and offer them the possibility of choosing their own pursuits.

Child care providers must be attentive to the individual needs of each child and help the child find activities to fulfill those needs. Often, caregivers can best help children by building trusting, nurturing relationships with them, relationships based on mutual liking and respect. Such close relationships enable children to talk about their feelings and express their fears so that they can learn to cope with the normal emotional turmoil of growing up.

After-school child care should provide a variety of activities to interest and engage children after a long day in the classroom.

## Looking Ahead to Adolescence

Adolescence is the last period of childhood before an individual becomes an adult. It is defined by the onset of puberty, the physical changes that bring about sexual maturation. Puberty is marked by increased hormonal activity, growth spurts, enlargement of the genitals and breasts, and the growth of body hair. Naturally, these drastic physical changes greatly affect the self-concept of adolescents and also trigger major psychological, social, and emotional changes.

### Adolescent Self-Concept

According to developmental psychologists, adolescence is the period in which the individual establishes his or her own identity as a budding adult and as a newly sexual being. In a very real sense, it is a time in which one "finds oneself." Erikson views adolescence as a period in which the individual must resolve the conflict between *identity versus identity confusion* (Erikson, 1963). He believes that the search for identity leads adolescents to organize their self-concept, personality, talents, and abilities in order to conform to the needs and demands of their society. When this process progresses smoothly, the individual develops a well-integrated personality with established moral, sexual, political, and religious values and beliefs. The individual also has an idea of the type of career or work he or she wants to pursue. The completion of this process, Erikson maintains, enables the individual to take his or her place in adult society.

The other side of this search for identity is identity (or role) confusion. Erikson believes that role confusion can lead to an inability to establish a clear identity, which is expressed in taking an overly long time to "grow up" or reach adulthood. According to Erikson, teenagers naturally experience a certain amount of identity confusion before establishing an adult identity. This may account for much of the conflict, emotional upheaval, and antisocial behavior of adolescents.

Erikson also believes that there is a relationship between identity and intimacy—the capacity to love, to have close friendships, and to have emotionally satisfying sexual relationships with others. The development of the capacity for intimacy enables ado-

According to Erikson, adolescents must develop a strong sense of identity before they are able to have emotionally satisfying sexual relationships with others.

lescents to feel a strong sense of loyalty or belonging to peer groups and to feel love for romantic partners. Erikson has suggested that intimacy cannot occur until the adolescent has established a strong sense of identity. However, research has shown that while boys tend to achieve identity before intimacy, most girls achieve intimacy first or achieve identity and intimacy at the same time (Schiedel & Marcia, 1985). In other words, girls define themselves as much by their relationships with others as by their own aspirations, beliefs, and personality traits. This difference may reflect the fact that, in most cultures, girls are socialized to care for others and transmit social values to later generations.

### Adolescent Sexuality

Adolescents must also struggle with a changing self-concept. They must adapt their self-concept to include the image of themselves as sexual beings. The vast majority of teenagers identify themselves as heterosexual. For the small minority of teenagers who consider themselves homosexual, their emerging sexuality is usually the source of considerable pain, isolation, and confusion.

Sexual feelings and behavior are different for boys and girls. Girls achieve intimacy sooner, and their concept of sexuality is often intertwined with ideas of romance and feelings of love and tenderness. A girl is most likely to have her first sexual experience with a longtime boyfriend, someone with whom she believes she is in love and to whom she has made an emotional commitment. Boys, on the other hand, tend to be more interested in sexuality as a physical experience, a sign of maturity, and a means to satisfy their curiosity. They are not as likely to feel an intimate bond with their sexual partners as girls are, and they tend to change sexual partners more often.

Societal attitudes have a significant effect on sexual attitudes and behavior. The sexual revolution of the 1960s and 1970s brought about enormous changes in attitudes toward premarital and teenage sex in American society. As a result, parents today are more accepting of the idea that their children may become sexually active before marriage; and society is generally more accepting of children born out of wedlock than it was 20 or 30 years ago. Moreover, today's movies, television, music, and other media all push adolescents toward sexual activity. These factors have combined to encourage teenagers to engage in sexual activity at an earlier age than was the case in previous generations. One result of this early sexual activity is the increase in teenage

Contrary to popular belief, most adolescents get along fairly well with their parents and often turn to them for guidance and support.

pregnancy and of children born to single teenage mothers.

## Parents and Peers

Traditionally, adolescence has been viewed as a period of great conflict between parents and children. In reality, however, most teenagers get along reasonably well with their parents. When conflicts do develop, they are usually resolved rather quickly. Adolescence, of course, is a time in which children break away from parental control and become more independent. This usually leads to disagreements over how much freedom children should be granted. Most disagreements between parents and teenagers revolve around such issues as curfews, dating, appearance, clothing, and the like. Typically, conflicts between parents and teens reach a high point at around age 13 or 14 and then decrease in the later teens. During this time, despite their increased desire for independence, adolescents still look to their parents as a source of attitudes and values, as well as for support and acceptance. Peer groups help adolescents define their identity and smooth the transition from the protected, safe world of childhood to the sometimes frightening, independent world of adulthood. Friends and peers also act as a support group for teenagers who are struggling with the task of breaking away from parents and from adult authority. They offer sympathy, understanding, and support for teens who are going through a difficult period in their lives and cannot talk to adults about their problems.

Like school-age children, adolescents frequently define themselves and their individuality through the distinctive clothing, hairstyles, activities, and preferences of their peer group. Peer group support gives adolescents the opportunity to try out different things, keeping those aspects of style and personality that work for them and discarding others.

## Moral Development in Adolescence

As you learned earlier, adolescence is the period in which children move up to Kohlberg's third stage of moral development (if they have not already done so in middle childhood). Many but not all adolescents will move on to Kohlberg's next three stages as they progress through adolescence and into adulthood (see Table 17.1).

In stage 4 of Kohlberg's hierarchy, individuals behave morally because they believe that laws and rules are necessary to maintain a stable, orderly society. Thus, they obey traffic laws so that traffic can flow in a safe and orderly fashion, and they pay income taxes because they believe that taxes are necessary for a functioning government. Individuals at this stage are concerned with fulfilling their duty to their family, country, and society in general.

---

**TABLE 17.1**
**Kohlberg's Stages of Moral Development**

**Preconventional Morality (The Preschool Years)**

| | |
|---|---|
| Stage 1: | *Avoid Punishment* <br> Authority figures are all-powerful. Rules cannot be changed and should be followed to avoid punishment. |
| Stage 2: | *Gain Rewards* <br> Principles of fairness and equality should be used to protect a person's self-interest. Favors for other people are done to gain rewards in return. |

**Conventional Morality (The School Years)**

| | |
|---|---|
| Stage 3: | *Follow the Golden Rule* <br> Acting morally will gain the approval of others. Being thought of as good by others is important. |
| Stage 4: | *Obey the Law* <br> Correct behavior involves obeying the law and doing one's duty to family and country. |

**Postconventional Morality (Adolescence and Adulthood)**

| | |
|---|---|
| Stage 5: | *Act According to the Social Contract* <br> The laws and principles by which society is governed protect everyone's welfare and should be followed. |
| Stage 6: | *Determine Personal Ethical Principles* <br> Moral principles are determined through individual reflection and may be held even if they contradict social laws. |

Individuals achieve stages 5 and 6, which make up the highest level in Kohlberg's hierarchy of moral development, only in late adolescence or adulthood. At this level, which Kohlberg calls the postconventional or principled morality stage, individuals are able to look beyond conventional morality to discern the underlying moral principles that define right and wrong.

Moral development gives adolescents a greater awareness of the rules and principles of the society in which they live. They begin to develop more fixed ideas about who they are and what they believe in. During this period, as in all stages of development, adolescents can benefit greatly from the support and concern of others. Loving parents, supportive friends, and understanding teachers and other adults all play an important part in easing the emotional turmoil of these years and helping adolescents make the often difficult transition to adulthood.

Loving and supportive parents can ease the emotional turmoil of adolescence.

# CHAPTER 17 REVIEW

## SUMMARY

- School-age children strive to learn the skills that society values, and they develop self-esteem from mastering those skills.

- Children tend to model their behavior on people they admire and respect; this helps them develop their self-concept.

- School-age children become better able to perceive the viewpoints of others, and they develop a self-concept and self-esteem according to what others think of them. The school years are a period in which children are highly self-critical.

- Children develop gender constancy in the early school years, and they identify strongly with people of the same sex.

- Gender schemas, or scripts about how males and females act, help children learn gender-appropriate behaviors, attitudes, and attributes.

- An important aspect of the self-concept of school-age children is their understanding that they belong to certain races and ethnic groups that are different from others.

- Children respond to stress in different ways, depending on their personality and the amount of support they receive from those around them.

- The early school years are a period of relative emotional calm, although certain fears and problems can develop, such as school phobia and childhood depression.

- The process of learning social competence continues throughout the school years. Peer groups and friends provide emotional stability and help children learn social skills and build self-esteem.

- Peer pressure may exert a negative as well as a positive influence on children. It can, for example, encourage antisocial behavior. All children are susceptible to peer pressure.

- Friendships serve many of the same purposes as peer groups. The basis of friendship changes as children grow older.

- School-age children progress through stage 2 and sometimes stage 3 of Kohlberg's moral development hierarchy. In stage 2, fairness and equality are major concerns, while in stage 3, children are concerned with pleasing and helping others.

- Conscience, the internal regulator of right and wrong, begins to emerge in children during Kohlberg's stage 3.

- Children learn prosocial behavior from observing adult role models, from being praised for their altruistic acts, and from the values of their culture.

- Children who are overly critical of themselves and have an exaggerated view of their shortcomings sometimes develop learned helplessness, a feeling of incompetence and low self-esteem that prevents them from trying new things.

- Children who are rejected by their peers can develop serious emotional problems.

- Adults can help children overcome learned helplessness and social rejection by teaching social skills and by reinforcing desirable behaviors.

- After-school day-care programs for children should be tailored to individual children's emotional and social needs. They should not simply be an extension of the school day.

- Adolescence is marked not only by drastic physical changes but also by significant emotional and social changes.

- Adolescence is a period in which children integrate their identity and develop the capacity for intimacy. They also adjust their self-concept to accept themselves as sexual beings.

- Adolescence is a time in which children break away from parental control and move toward becoming independent adults. However, this process does not cause as much conflict between parents and children as is generally believed.

- Peers help adolescents find their identity and achieve independent adulthood.

- Adolescents move into stage 3 of Kohlberg's moral development hierarchy; many eventually move into stages 4, 5, and 6 in late adolescence and early adulthood.

## BUILDING VOCABULARY

Write a definition for each vocabulary term listed below.

acting out
conscience
gender schema
identity versus identity confusion
   stage
industry versus inferiority stage
learned helplessness

peer group
peer pressure
self-concept
self-esteem
school phobia
stressor

## ACQUIRING KNOWLEDGE

1. How does a child's self-concept change from the preschool years to the school years?
2. Describe Erikson's fourth stage of psychosocial development.
3. How can adults use Erikson's ideas when working with school-age children?
4. According to learning theorists, how do children develop a self-concept?
5. Why are the early school years a period of intense self-criticism?
6. What are gender schemas?
7. According to psychologists, why are older children more tolerant than school-age children of behavior that is not gender appropriate?
8. How can caregivers and other adults enhance the self-esteem of children of minority groups?
9. Give two examples of a major life stressor that a school-age child might experience.
10. Describe the different ways that a school-age child might respond to stress.
11. What factors influence the way a child deals with stress?
12. How do the fears of school-age children differ from the fears of preschoolers?
13. How can adults help alleviate children's fears?
14. What is school phobia? What are the physical symptoms that may be associated with this problem?
15. Name three developing social skills or qualities that help facilitate social interaction among school-age children.
16. What positive functions do peer groups serve?
17. Define peer pressure.
18. Describe the moral thinking of children in stage 3 of Kohlberg's hierarchy of moral development.
19. How do children learn prosocial behavior?
20. What is learned helplessness?
21. How can adults help children avoid learned helplessness?
22. Describe the main remedy for social rejection.
23. According to Erikson, how are identity and intimacy related during adolescence?
24. How does the sexual behavior of adolescent boys and girls differ?

**25.** Why is adolescence a period characterized by disagreements between children and parents?

**26.** Describe the moral thinking of individuals in stage 4 of Kohlberg's hierarchy.

## THINKING CRITICALLY

**1.** Children tend to adhere strictly to gender stereotypes during the school years and then become more flexible in how they view sex roles as they get older. Do you think caregivers should work actively to counteract sex stereotyping during the school years, or should they view attitudes about gender as something children will outgrow?

**2.** Some people contend that children of minority groups have low self-esteem because society makes them feel inferior or unworthy. Others think that a child's personality and family support system are the decisive factors. Which view do you think is a better explanation for low self-esteem? Why?

**3.** How would you compare the stress that children experience today with the stress that children experienced 20 years ago? What reasons can you think of for any differences?

**4.** The fears of school-age children reflect realistic concerns: violence, AIDS, homelessness. Should adults try to protect children from exposure to these issues, or should they let children learn about the world as it is?

**5.** How would a child in stage 1 of Kohlberg's hierarchy view shoplifting? How might the thinking of this child change during stage 3?

## OBSERVATIONS AND APPLICATIONS

**1.** Observe the way children in a fifth-grade class dress. Describe typical outfits. Do you see a wide variety of styles of dress, or are the majority of boys dressed in similar shirts and pants and the girls dressed in similar outfits as well? What brand names, if any, are predominant? Note the styles and brands of footwear the children are wearing. What about hairstyles?

**2.** Observe school-age children in an after-school program for an hour for two or three days. Make note of peer relationships. Does the grouping of children vary, depending on the activity, or do the groups stay pretty much the same? During homework time, do the children tend to work in groups or by themselves? Do some children work and play by themselves most of the time? Are any children excluded by others? If so, what seems to be the reason for the exclusion?

**3.** Michelle Joseph, an eight-year-old girl in an after-school program where you work, has moved to town recently. One afternoon, her mother asks to speak to you privately. She says that Michelle has been complaining that she has no friends. Ms. Joseph knows this is true at home but was hoping that Michelle had made a few friends at school. Ms. Joseph asks whether you have any suggestions for helping Michelle make friends. You have to admit that Michelle generally works and plays alone in your program. In group activities, she often has arguments with other children. She also seems immature compared to the other children, bursting into tears at the slightest provocation. What advice can you give Ms. Joseph, and how can you help Michelle?

4. Allen is a student in the third-grade class where you work as an aide. Lately, he seems preoccupied with fears. One day he asks you what you would do if a man holding a machine gun suddenly appeared at the door of the room. The next day he asks you if you can tell by looking at people whether or not they're murderers. Then he tells you that he doesn't feel safe in his own house because it has no burglar alarm system. How can you help Allen cope with his fears?

## SUGGESTIONS FOR FURTHER READING

Barret, M., & Trevitt, J. (1991). *Attachment behavior and the schoolchild*. New York: Routledge.

Blakely, B., Blau, R., Brady, E. H., Streibert, C., Zavitkovsky, A., & Zavitkovsky, D. (1989). *Activities for school-age child care*. Washington, DC: National Association for the Education of Young Children.

Bredekamp, S. (Ed.). (1987). *Developmentally appropriate practice in early childhood programs serving children from birth through age 8*. Washington, DC: National Association for the Education of Young Children.

Curry, N., & Johnson, C. (1990). *Beyond self-esteem: Developing a genuine sense of human value*. Washington, DC: National Association for the Education of Young Children.

Durkin, K. (1985). *Television, sex roles, and children*. Philadelphia: Open University Press.

Elkind, D. (1984). *All grown up and no place to go*. Reading, MA: Addison-Wesley.

Erikson, E. (1963). *Identity: Youth in crisis*. New York: Norton.

Foster, S. (1981). *The one girl in ten: A self-portrait of the teen-age mother*. Claremont, CA: Arbor.

Humphrey, J. H. (Ed.). (1984). *Stress in childhood*. New York: AMS Press.

Schwartzberg, N. (1988). The popularity factor. *Parents, 63*(11), 144–148.

Wallach, L. B. (1993). Helping children cope with violence. *Young Children, 48*(4), 4–11.

# PART 7

# Careers in Early Childhood Education

**CHAPTER 18**
**Planning for a Career with Young Children**
Chapter 18 discusses different career opportunities in early childhood education and offers guidelines on conducting a job search and succeeding as a child care professional.

## CHAPTER OUTLINE

## OBJECTIVES

Studying this chapter will enable
you to

- Identify the personal, educational, and experiential qualifications necessary to become a child care professional.
- Describe different types of early childhood programs, and discuss job opportunities in the child care profession.
- Explain how to prepare for a job search and how to succeed on the job once you are hired.
- Discuss the advantages, disadvantages, and requirements of working independently as a family day-care provider.
- Discuss the challenges and rewards of working in the early childhood field.

JANINE was headed for her first job interview. She had seen a help-wanted ad in the newspaper for a teacher assistant at the Westside Preschool. She had called the school, sent in a cover letter and a copy of her résumé, and had been asked to come in for an interview. Janine was nervous. To calm herself, she again went over her answers to the questions she thought she might be asked: "Why do you want to work with children? What previous experience have you had? How has your education helped prepare you for this job? What special skills and abilities do you have? How do you feel about working with children with disabilities? How would you describe your philosophy of teaching?" She pulled into the parking lot of the school, checked her hair and makeup in the mirror, and took a deep breath. "Here goes!" she said as she got out of the car and headed for the main entrance.

## Qualifications of Child Care Professionals

At this point in your study of child development, it should be clear that people who want to work with young children need more than a love of children. While warmth and caring are very important, so are knowledge and experience. The more you know about young children and the more time you spend teaching them and caring for them, the more likely you are to make their early years fulfilling ones.

### Personality

People who are interested in careers with young children should have a personality suited to the needs of their "clients." Caregivers will spend most of their time working with young children, of course, but they also need to be able to develop good working relationships with the families of the children and with their coworkers and volunteers in the child care setting.

Young children have many needs. These range from a diaper change to a hug after a fall, from a snack to words of understanding that help settle a dispute. They may need someone to help them learn a new song or practice a new skill. These varied needs mean that caregivers must possess many qualities. They should be observant so that they can respond to infants and young toddlers who are not yet talking. They must be flexible so that they can react quickly to constantly changing situations and to all the minor crises that arise in a child care setting. They must be warm and nurturing so that children feel loved and cared for while they are away from their families. Caregivers must also be even tempered and patient so that they can help children gain and develop self-confidence. Finally, they must be energetic and enthusiastic so that learning can be a joyful experience for children.

Dependability and consistency are other critical qualities for caregivers. Children need to know that the person caring for them and the kind of care they

Caregivers must have energy and enthusiasm to communicate to children that learning is exciting and fun.

receive will be the same from one day to the next. This gives them a sense of security and predictability about their world. Interaction with child care providers is often the first experience that children have with people outside their family. Because this experience will influence later interpersonal encounters, it is important for the caregiver-child relationship to be a positive and consistent one.

Caregivers must be self-assured enough to be able to accept children's challenges to their authority. As children grow, their abilities expand and so does their need to exercise independence and control over their lives. Caregivers must be able to channel these challenges in positive directions by sharing leadership and day-to-day tasks with the children as they grow.

Caregivers also need to be accepting and respectful of others. In the course of a career, caregivers will meet children of different cultures and backgrounds, children of differing ability levels, children at various stages of development, and children with disabilities. Caregivers should be able to use their understanding of a child's background and abilities to enhance the child's day-care experience.

Many of these same qualities are useful in developing a good relationship with the families of children. For example, caregivers need to be sensitive to the conflicting emotions many parents feel about placing their child in child care. This turmoil can manifest itself in expressions of jealousy or resentment toward a caregiver. Caregivers who show understanding have a much better chance of developing a positive and productive relationship with the families of the children in their care.

Child care professionals must also be team players. In most child care settings, they work closely with other teachers and child care providers and with aides and volunteers. It is important that your colleagues know that you value what they are doing and that you want to work with them. After reasonable expectations and responsibilities are defined, open communication will help establish a professional, successful team.

### Education and Training

To create a developmentally appropriate environment for young children, child care professionals need to learn as much as they can about child development. This kind of knowledge goes beyond the hands-on experience caregivers get in a child care setting. Caregivers also need to learn about different aspects of the growth and development of young children and to be informed about their nutritional needs. In addition, they should have an understanding of the basic guidelines for safety in the child care setting. This kind of knowledge can be acquired through various education and training programs.

Anyone who is considering working in the field of child care needs to make some decisions about career goals before choosing a program of study. The courses and credits you need will be determined by the direction you want to take and the type of position you would like in the early childhood field. There are two basic college degrees: the two-year Associate degree and the four-year Bachelor of Arts or Bachelor of Science degree. Child care professionals interested in greater specialization can pursue postgraduate degree programs leading to a master's or doctoral degree.

In addition, many community colleges and training programs offer a credential called the Child Development Associate (CDA). This certificate is designed for people who are already working in the field of early childhood education. The candidates can use their work experience and current job situations to fulfill many of the requirements of the credential. Each candidate for a CDA must meet specific personal, setting, education, and experience requirements. For example, infant/toddler caregivers must be working at a state-approved child development center where they can be observed; they must have a total of three "formal or informal educational experiences," which can be courses, training sessions, workshops, or other in-service programs that focus on infant/toddler education or development; and they must have at least 640 hours of experience working with children under age three in a group setting.

Most college degree and certificate programs require a combination of course work and supervised experience in a child care setting. The latter allows those in training to receive feedback on their performance as well as to observe experienced child care professionals in action.

Teamwork is an important part of a child care professional's job. In most preschool settings, teachers, aides, and volunteers work closely together.

In many areas, graduates of degree programs must obtain a state certificate or license before they can work with young children. Often, successful completion of the degree program is all that is required for certification. However, requirements vary considerably from state to state.

To deal with this lack of standardization, the Association of Teacher Educators (ATE) and the National Association for the Education of Young Children (NAEYC) have developed guidelines for national certification standards for teachers of young children. These guidelines, published in 1991, do not mandate a specific program. Instead they call for "*all* teachers of young children from birth through age eight to be adequately prepared with the knowledge, skills, and understandings specific to their teaching specialization, regardless of where they are employed" (Association of Teacher Educators and National Association for the Education of Young Children, 1991, p. 18). To date, no national standards have been adopted; however, as the demand for early childhood programs continues to grow, so will demands for higher and more uniform standards for the training and education of teachers of young children.

### Experience

Experience can provide excellent preparation for working with young children. Many child care professionals embark on their chosen career path after caring for younger siblings or babysitting, spending the summer as a camp counselor or playground director, or being parents themselves. Most communities offer many opportunities for working with young children. Church groups are frequently looking for helpers in Sunday school classes. Youth groups such as the Brownies and Boy Scouts welcome adult volunteers. Your college placement office may be able to help you locate organizations and families with young children who are looking for help. These positions can provide you with valuable experience as well as help you determine the area of child care in which you would like to specialize.

## Learning About the Field

The child care field is growing rapidly as the number of young children whose parents work outside the home increases. Jobs for child care workers are expected to increase by 50 percent by the year 2005 (Bureau of Labor Statistics, 1990). With this expanding employment outlook, it is worthwhile to examine the types of child care and the job opportunities that are available to professionals in child care and early childhood education.

### Early Childhood Education and Care

There are many different types of settings where child care professionals can work. There are half- and full-day educational programs, child care centers, family day-care operations, and home-based care. The approach and content of the programs vary widely, and the programs are sponsored by many different types of organizations.

**Half-Day Educational Programs.** One of the most popular types of child care in the United States today is the half-day educational program for preschoolers, also known as preschool or nursery school. These programs place great emphasis on the educational importance of the early childhood years, and they attempt to provide a variety of educational experiences through an organized daily schedule. Full-day educational programs are similar but, obviously, involve a longer period of time. Various public and private organizations operate programs of this type, which vary according to the location, clients, and program goals.

Many educational programs reflect a specific philosophy, curriculum, or orientation. For example, Montessori programs emphasize the learning and teaching concepts that Maria Montessori developed in the early part of this century. Montessori believed that children learn through their senses, and she developed a set of materials designed to stimulate the senses and help children learn. She also believed that all children have the capacity to educate themselves if given an appropriately prepared environment. Teachers in certified Montessori programs must go through special training to become familiar with the materials, the methods, and the Montessori philosophy before entering the classroom. Other programs may incorporate concepts and materials from the Montessori approach, without adopting the Montessori philosophy entirely.

A different educational emphasis is found in the Bank Street early childhood program. The Bank Street program is based on a *developmental-interactionist* philosophy that emphasizes the children and their interests rather than the subject matter. The goals, objectives, and teaching practices of this child-centered approach are focused on what the child needs, not on what adults or society needs. In the Bank Street program, the teacher is a facilitator and has no predetermined curriculum. The goal is to provide an environment in which children can pursue their interests and learn from them. Most of the children's interests are discovered and developed through play.

Another popular early childhood educational program follows the High/Scope curriculum. This curriculum is based on the Piagetian principle of constructivism: children build knowledge internally rather than acquire it externally. Children and teachers work together to develop a three-stage plan-do-review process in which a particular activity is undertaken. From each activity, children will derive "key experiences" in the area of active learning. Key experiences might involve active exploration using all the senses, discovering relationships through direct experience, and manipulating, transforming, and combining materials.

Most educational programs actually follow an *eclectic* approach, one based on a sampling of several philosophies. A quality educational program, for example, may well incorporate elements of hands-on learning, the "child-centered" approach, and cooperative social skill development.

**Child Care Centers.** Many families rely on full-day programs to meet their child care needs. Historically, child care centers were seen as places that provided for the physical care and nurturing of children from infancy to school age. In other words,

Working with young children, whether as a babysitter, camp counselor, or troop leader, is a way for aspiring child care professionals to gain experience as well as a basic understanding of the field.

they served as an extended babysitting service and play group. In recent years, however, the increasing number of single parents and of families in which both parents work has created a great demand for full-day child care. It has also led to a change in emphasis. Today most centers have adopted programs devoted to the cognitive, social, and emotional development of children as well as to their physical care. Many centers also offer early morning and afternoon programs for school-age children whose parents work full-time.

**Family Day Care.**    Family day care consists of a single caregiver taking care of a small group of infants, toddlers, and preschoolers in a private home. Many family day-care operations also provide after-school care for school-age children. Families who prefer this kind of setting often choose it because it is the most homelike.

Family day care is a more informal, less uniform service than child care at a center. Most homes in

this country are not licensed or certified, so conditions, equipment, and the level of training of the caregiver can vary considerably. While a license does not guarantee quality care, it does tell families that the caregiver has met state and local standards for space, equipment, and safety; that the home has been inspected; and that the child care professional has received some kind of training. Daily activities also differ from provider to provider. In some family day-care programs, providers may do little more than supervise the children; in others, caregivers will have a daily schedule of activities. In quality family day care, caregivers plan a full range of developmentally appropriate activities to address each child's individual growth and development.

**Private, Home-Based Care.**    Some families want to keep their children at home and hire private, home-based caregivers. Nannies are child care providers who work full-time for a family and often live in the family's home. Many have had some preparation in a one- or two-year college training program or at a nanny training school. Their course of study is likely to include classes in child development, nutrition, and family management. Families who hire a nanny usually do so because they are looking for consistency, reliability, and quality in caregiving.

The nature of a nanny's work can vary widely, depending on family needs. It is important to define expectations and responsibilities through an initial agreement. Families generally expect their nanny to provide for the care and early education of the children and to take on certain child-related responsibilities. They may also expect their nanny to prepare meals and do laundry and light housekeeping. Working hours for nannies can range from eight hours a day to round-the-clock responsibility during the week.

Other types of private home-based care include au pairs and mother's helpers. An au pair is usually someone from another country who provides child care for a certain period of time (usually one year) in exchange for room, board, and other benefits. A mother's helper takes care of the children in the home, but a parent is often present. Many mother's helpers have little or no formal training in child development or early childhood education.

Job opportunities for home-based caregivers are plentiful. Although there are no standards or certification, those with education and training are likely to get the best salaries and benefits.

### Specialized Child Care Programs

Some types of child care do not fit easily into the categories described above. For example, there are

## FOCUS ON **Cultural Diversity**

### Child Care in Other Countries

Most industrialized countries have developed some kind of child care system to meet the needs of parents and children. In the United States, child care is provided primarily by the private sector. Parents choose and pay for the services of child care centers, family day care, or in-home care. However, the Head Start program in the United States, which serves children from low-income families and children with disabilities, is funded by the federal government. Great Britain has a similar system and also relies primarily on the private sector to provide child care.

Some countries have a more centralized approach. In China, for example, the state runs and subsidizes both day and boarding schools for preprimary children. About half the children of kindergarten age attend public boarding schools six days a week—a necessity when both parents work long hours. Many formerly Communist countries have well-established networks of state-run centers that provide child

care at minimal cost to parents. The quality of care at these centers varies from excellent to marginal.

France and Denmark also have government-supported child care centers that serve parents regardless of income level. In Denmark 70 percent of children ages three to six attend some form of public child care. In France, most children start public preprimary school when they are three years old.

Germany has a liberal maternity leave policy that encourages mothers to stay home with young children. In addition, the German government wants to be able to guarantee every three-year-old a space in a public kindergarten by the year 1996.

Japan has a lower percentage of working mothers than many other industrialized countries. However, nonworking parents often send their children to private preschools because of the high value they place on early group experiences.

various types of special-purpose care. These include after-school, drop-in, and sick-child care as well as programs for children with special needs. In addition, there are schools or programs for young children that are sponsored or operated by various groups.

**Cooperative Programs.**    Some parents want to have an active role in their child's preschool or care program and join a parent cooperative. Parent cooperatives are generally play-based programs that emphasize social and emotional development. However, the activities and approach may differ significantly from one cooperative to the next because the parents determine the approach and curriculum. Most cooperatives also require parent participation in the program; parents are expected to volunteer a certain number of hours each month and to assist with work projects or fund-raising activities. Most cooperatives are half-day programs or preschools for children between the ages of two and five.

**Corporate Child Care.**    Some employers, corporations, and industries offer day care for employees' children. The settings and services vary according to the size of the work force and the particular child care needs. Most provide care for young children from the ages of six weeks to five years. Employers often help establish such a program on or near the work site. They may also help by donating space or services for the center and by subsidizing employee families who use the center.

**Religious Organizations.**    Many churches and synagogues operate child care programs. Some are open only to the congregation; others are open to the community at large. Some make religious activities or education a part of the daily schedule; others take a more secular approach. In general, church-supported or church-affiliated schools provide for the whole child, with an emphasis on spiritual or moral development. For the most part, they take a play-oriented approach to academic and religious education.

**Head Start.**    The federal government sponsors early childhood education through programs such as Head Start. Head Start was developed to help prepare children from low-income families for school. It is designed to help these children begin school on an equal footing with children who have had more economic and cultural advantages. Head Start offers the children and their families a comprehensive program that is developmentally and educationally appropriate. It provides broad social, health, and career development services to staff members and parents. The caregivers encourage parents to get involved in the program. Head Start emphasizes activities that encourage children's growth and development, particularly in the areas of cognitive, language, and social skills. The programs serve children between the ages of two and five.

**Laboratory Schools.**    A number of colleges, universities, and hospitals operate model preschool educational programs that provide student teachers and researchers with a "laboratory" for practice and learning. Laboratory schools study how children learn best and how teachers teach most effectively. They may offer a half-day traditional preschool program or a full-day educational program.

At first, most laboratory schools served the children of faculty members. Today, most of these schools serve student-parents and have opened to the public in an effort to attract a population that is culturally and socioeconomically diverse. Some laboratory schools have programs for infants and toddlers as well as preschoolers.

**Public Preschools.**    The public school systems in several cities and states operate preschools for four-year-olds. In some states, such as Texas and Florida, these programs are only offered to children who are economically disadvantaged. Their purpose is to help the children prepare for school by developing basic skills. Some public schools also operate after-school programs for children who would otherwise be left on their own after school.

## Types of Jobs

In the past, a person who wanted to work in the field of early childhood education became a nursery school teacher. Today, that person might work as an aide in a child care center, a teacher in a preschool, or a nanny in a private home. And there are many jobs in other professions—from school nurse to speech therapist to retailer—that also involve working with children.

**Jobs in Early Childhood Education.** What are the qualifications for jobs in early childhood education, and what do the jobs entail? The National Association for the Education of Young Children (NAEYC) describes the qualifications and responsibilities of various positions in early childhood education. A teacher aide is a preprofessional who implements program activities under direct supervision. No specialized training or experience beyond a high school education is usually required. An associate teacher is a professional who independently implements program activities and who may be responsible for the care and education of a group of children. Associate teachers must usually have a CDA credential or an associate's degree in early

childhood education or child development. Early childhood teachers are responsible for the care and education of a group of children. In most cases, a bachelor's degree in early childhood education or child development is required for this position. The director of a preschool or day-care center will need an associate's or bachelor's degree, depending on the size and nature of the program and on licensing requirements.

Professionals who supervise and train staff, design curricula, and/or administer programs may be called early childhood specialists or early childhood educators. In most cases, they need a graduate degree in early childhood education or child development and/or three years of experience as an early childhood teacher.

The qualifications for the jobs described above are only recommendations. Education requirements vary from state to state, although most require a certificate or license for teachers of young children.

*Head Start encourages parents to get involved in fostering their children's cognitive, language, and social development.*

Kindergarten and elementary school teachers help young children learn the basic skills they will need throughout their education, including communication, reading, writing, arithmetic, and science concepts. Some early childhood professionals are trained to work with children who have special needs, such as children with disabilities or chronic illness and gifted children.

Kindergarten and elementary school teachers must have a bachelor's degree that includes courses in the liberal arts and education as well as student-teaching experience. Teachers who are trained in special education need similar course work and possibly a specialty. A teaching certificate or license issued by the state is required to teach in that state's public schools. Many states require a master's degree for permanent certification and/or specialization.

Salaries and hours vary widely for teachers. Public school teachers generally earn more than teachers in other programs. They also work fewer hours.

For example, a teacher assistant in a public school preschool might work six to seven hours a day; the same job in a child care center might require a teacher assistant to work eight hours a day. Public school educators and many Head Start and preschool educators work nine to ten months each year. Professionals at child care centers usually work year-round.

**Other Jobs That Involve Working with Children.** There are many professions related to the care and education of young children. Jobs that serve children directly include school nurse, pediatrician, physical therapist, speech therapist, occupational therapist, and counselor. Social workers serve families, while children's librarians organize services for children and families. Other jobs provide information to the professionals who work with children and families, such as in-service trainers and school psychologists.

Pediatric nursing is one of many professions that someone interested in working with children might consider.

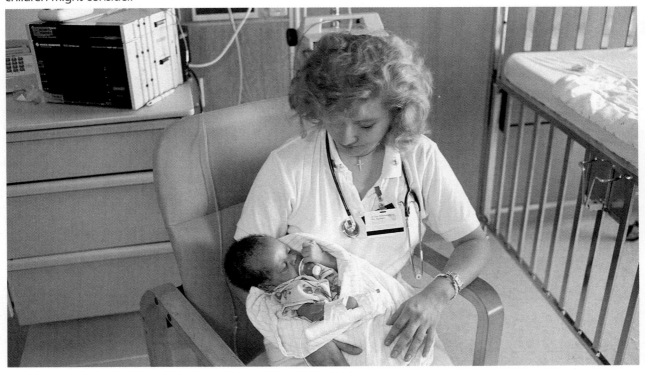

## FOCUS ON  Decision Making in Child Care

### Establishing a Family Day Care

Claudia has two children who are now in elementary school. As a result, she has free time during the school day and an empty house. For several years, she has been working as a part-time babysitter, and she knows she is a good caregiver. Now she would like to have steady employment with more control over her hours and an opportunity to develop a creative program for preschool children. Claudia decides to put her child care services on a professional footing by opening a full-day family day-care business.

Claudia's first step is to write to the National Association for Family Day Care to find out whether a local or state support organization can provide information and guidance on operating a family day-care program. With the help of the association, she draws up a list of the steps she must take to get started. Claudia's list includes the following items:

- Check on state regulations concerning the legal requirements of operating a family day-care facility.
- Find out whether local zoning regulations permit family day care in my home, or whether a variance is needed.
- Meet with insurance agents to discuss insurance coverage.

- Study the indoor and outdoor areas that will be used for child care to see what modifications need to be made to create a safe, accessible environment for young children.
- Develop a written policy statement and fee structure for interested parents.
- Develop contacts with child care resource and referral agencies.
- Meet with an accountant to discuss the tax implications of offering day care in my home.
- Find out about family day-care accreditation.

Claudia discovers that providing family day care requires a strong commitment, a keen sense of responsibility, and a willingness to conform to regulations. However, she believes that operating a family day-care facility will bring her more job satisfaction and more income than casual babysitting. She will also be able to create a better environment for the children in her care.

*What other issues should Claudia consider before she opens her family day-care program? Why do you think parents might prefer sending a child to a structured family day-care program rather than a babysitter? What are some disadvantages of providing day care in one's home?*

---

The duties and educational requirements of these jobs vary. School nurses have a good deal of contact with young children. They treat children who are sick or hurt, instruct students on health care and nutrition, and may also help administer vision and hearing tests. A school nurse must be a graduate of a nursing program. Pediatricians usually see children when they are sick or when they need a physical examination. These doctors play an important role in preventing and treating illnesses and helping children acquire a positive attitude toward health care. A pediatrician must attend college and medical school and then do a residency in pediatric medicine.

Physical therapists help children with a disability adapt to limitations imposed by their physical handicap. Their goal is to help the children become more self-reliant through individual programs designed to improve gross motor skills and coordination. Speech therapists work with children who are

## FOCUS ON   Communicating with Parents

### Guiding Parent Volunteers

Ms. Rose is a second-grade teacher. Normally she avoids asking parents to help in the classroom. She finds that they are not really helpful because they don't know the children and are unfamiliar with the classroom routine. She also finds the presence of parents disruptive. However, two parents have volunteered to help with a messy mask-making project, and she has accepted their offer.

MS. ROSE [to the class]: Mrs. Watson and Mrs. Rivera are going to help us with our mask making today. I'm going to divide the class into three groups and assign you to different work areas.

[To the parents]: I want each of you to take a group. Here are the directions for making the masks and a sample of a finished one. All the supplies are on those tables. Take your group to a table and help them get started.

MRS. WATSON: I don't think I know all the children in my group. Do you have some paper so they could make name tags?

MS. ROSE: We don't really have time for that. Just ask them their names.

MRS. RIVERA: How long should this project take?

MS. ROSE: An hour.

[The class divides. The noise level is high.]

MS. ROSE: Will the children at Mrs. Watson's table please quiet down.

[The children become slightly quieter and begin cutting and pasting.]

MS. ROSE: Edward, where are you going?

EDWARD: To wash my hands. They're all full of paste. Mrs. Rivera said I could.

MS. ROSE: You know we always wash our hands at the end of project time. I can't have everyone running in and out of the classroom.

[Edward sits down, and the class continues to work. Ms. Rose moves over to Mrs. Rivera's table.]

MS. ROSE: Children, you'll have to work faster. We only have ten minutes left.

MRS. RIVERA: I'm having a little trouble explaining to my group how they should make the eye holes.

MS. ROSE: It doesn't matter. Just tell them to cut holes.

[Ms. Rose moves to Mrs. Watson's group.]

MS. ROSE: This table is a disaster. I want all of you to stop what you're doing and pick up the paper around your chairs.

MRS. WATSON: I thought the children would have time to clean up the floor while their paste was drying.

[Finally the project is finished. Ms. Rose thanks the parents for their help. The parents leave.]

MRS. WATSON [to Mrs. Rivera, outside the door]: What an experience! That's the last time I'll ever volunteer to help in this class.

*The parent volunteers did not have a good experience in this class. Suggest three or more things Ms. Rose could have done differently to put the parents at ease and help them be more useful in her classroom. Why do you think some teachers do not like having parent volunteers in their classroom? What guidelines can you suggest for making parents an effective part of your classroom?*

having difficulty communicating. They use a variety of learning activities to help children improve their speaking, listening, and comprehension skills. Occupational therapists work with children who have difficulties in the areas of fine motor skills and hand-eye coordination. Counselors work with children who are having behavioral, emotional, or educational problems to help them function better at school and at home. Each of these professions requires at least a bachelor's degree in the field. Counselors must have teaching and counseling certificates and most have a master's degree.

Social workers help families provide for their children by getting to know the families, assessing their needs, and organizing the services they need. These services might include helping an unemployed parent get job training or work, then arranging after-school care for the children. Children's librarians make the library an attractive place for children, order new materials, catalog and classify new books, and organize activities for children such as story time. Children's librarians work in some elementary schools and in many public libraries. Both social workers and children's librarians need specialized training and education beyond a bachelor's degree.

Many publications focus on careers. Some include information about the advantages and disadvantages of various professions as well as the prospects for employment in each and the salary ranges. These books can help you sort out the reasons for wanting to work with young children, identify your skills, interests, and abilities, and determine what degree of involvement with children is best for you.

## Getting a Job

Deciding what you would like to do in the field of child care and early childhood education is the first step in embarking on your career with young children. Getting actual experience in the field can be extremely valuable in helping you make your decision. The next step involves getting the necessary education and training. The last step is finding a job. Looking for work takes as much preparation and as much effort as the career planning steps that precede it.

## Looking for a Job

Finding a job as a child care professional or early childhood teacher can take time. Competition is keen for the best jobs, and it is not unusual to have to apply for a number of positions before you are hired. Knowing where to look for work and how to follow up on job leads will make your search easier.

**Where to Look.**  The first place to look for job openings is your school or college placement office. Employers who have hired graduates from your school in the past and have been pleased with their training and performance will come to your school first to look for new employees. New job listings will probably be posted, so it is a good idea to check in at the placement office on a regular basis.

Another important source of information about job openings is the help-wanted ads in newspapers and professional journals. Help-wanted ads usually include a description of the job, the qualifications required, and how to contact the employer. Some ads will also provide salary information.

To fit all of this information in a small space, employers may abbreviate some of the words in an ad. The ad that Janine responded to in the story at the beginning of this chapter read "CHILD CARE Teacher Asst. Dntn location. Full day program for low income families. Enthusiastic. ECE degree or 1 yr work exper. Bnfts. Appt. 627-1313." Most abbreviations, such as Asst (assistant), Dntn (downtown), and ECE (early childhood education) are understandable.

You can also find employers by looking through the Yellow Pages of the telephone directory. Under headings such as "Child Care," "Education," "Preschools," and "Schools," you will find the names, addresses, and telephone numbers of businesses that may have job openings in your field. You can write to these organizations to inquire about openings, enclosing a copy of your résumé.

Referral agencies and placement agencies can also help with the job search. Most agencies are paid by employers after they hire someone referred by the agency. This means that agencies will try to find a job for applicants who register with them. Some agencies specialize in nanny placement. To find agencies that handle child care professionals, check the Yellow Pages of the telephone book or your school placement office.

Placement opportunities are often described in the newsletters and journals of professional organizations. This source of job information is particularly useful for those who wish to relocate.

**Networking.**    Networking is an effective way of getting the word out that you are looking for work. *Networking* involves letting your friends and acquaintances know what kind of job you are seeking and asking for their help in your search. Acquaintances in this case include teachers, former employers, and anyone else you know who might be aware of openings in your field. You can also network by attending classes or seminars in your field and by joining professional organizations that will enable you to make contacts with other people in your field.

### Applying for a Job

Most prospective employers will ask to see your résumé before arranging an interview. A résumé is a one- or two-page summary of your educational background, work experience, and special skills and abilities. Because many others may be applying for the same position you are, it is important that your résumé present you in the best possible light.

**Preparing a Résumé.**    Begin your résumé with your name, address, and telephone number. Then write a brief job objective, such as "full-time position working with young children." It is best to make your objective fairly general so that you can use the same résumé to apply for a number of different positions.

The main part of your résumé should consist of descriptions of your education and work experience; this is the information that employers consider most important. List your employment history first if you have had extensive work experience in the early childhood field. If your work experience is limited, describe your education first.

Whether you begin with your work experience or education, list the jobs you have held and the schools you have attended in reverse chronological order. That is, start with the most recent job or most recent training first. For each job you have held, list your job title, the name and location of the employer, the dates of your employment, and a brief description of your responsibilities. For your education, include the name and location of the school(s), the years attended, and the degree or certificate earned. Highlight any special courses you took or honors you received if they are related to the career you are pursuing. (See the sample résumé shown in Figure 18.1.)

If there are certain facts about your skills or qualifications that are not directly related to your education and experience but that you want to include in your résumé, you may create an additional section. The last item in your résumé should deal with references. Let the employer know that your references are available upon request. Make sure you have contacted three or four former employers, teachers, or character references who are willing to speak or write positively to employers about your abilities, personality, and work habits.

Your résumé needs to create a good impression because it may be the first thing a prospective employer sees about you. If your résumé is not neat and professional looking and the information is not clearly presented, your job application may not receive serious consideration. Take time to prepare your résumé well, check it carefully for any errors (especially in spelling, grammar, and contact information), and have someone review it for you. Then, if possible, have the résumé reproduced professionally.

**Letter of Application.**    When you send a résumé to a prospective employer, you should send a cover letter, or letter of application, with it. A cover letter briefly explains why you are writing, what your qualifications are, and why you are well suited to the particular job you are seeking. Limit your cover letter to three or four short paragraphs. (See the sample letter shown in Figure 18.2.)

Some employers may want you to send additional supporting documents, such as a school transcript, letters of reference, or samples of your work. It is important to have copies of these documents available in case you need them to complete your application. Some employers may also request a copy of your driving record, your health records, your

College placement offices and help-wanted ads in newspapers and professional journals are good places to begin a job search in early childhood education.

diploma or license, and your First Aid and CPR certificates.

**Interview.** If employers like what they see in your résumé and supporting documents, they will ask you to come in for an interview. Prepare for the interview by reviewing your résumé, asking yourself what questions are likely to be asked and how you will answer them, and making a list of what you would like to know about the job and the work environment. Dress appropriately for the interview, and make sure that you are on time. Take extra copies of your résumé with you in case the interviewer asks for one. Also take other relevant material, such as work samples, letters of reference, and credentials.

Try to relax and be yourself during the interview. Answer questions briefly, and be prepared to ask questions of your own. However, save questions about salary until the end of the interview. Don't expect to be offered a job on the spot. Most employers want to interview several people before they reach a decision.

**Follow-Up.** It is important to make sure prospective employers know that you are seriously interested in a position. Follow up by writing a note to the employer after the interview. Thank the person you saw for taking the time to speak with you and for considering your application. If you have not heard from the employer within a week or two, write again or call to ask when a decision will be reached. This will remind the employer of you and show that you are interested in the job.

### Succeeding on the Job

Once you are hired, you will be able to put your education and training into practice. You will also have the opportunity to increase your competence and expand your expertise on the job, learning from your experiences with children and their families and learning from other child care professionals. Many employers consider the first three or six months to be a period of orientation and probation for new employees. Use this time to learn all you can about the program.

Lydia A. Jeffries
39 Samson Way
Town, State 12345
(000) 123-4567

| | |
|---|---|
| **Objective** | Position as early childhood associate teacher in preschool or child care center. |

**Experience**

| | |
|---|---|
| **1992 to 1993** | *Early Childhood Teacher Assistant*, Sunshine Valley Preschool, Town, State |
| | Assisted preschool teachers in the daily care of three- to five-year-olds. Responsible for organizing circle time, leading music and movement experiences, and planning age-appropriate outdoor activities. Helped evaluate children annually and conducted parent conferences with head teacher. |
| **Summer, 1991 and 1992** | *Camp Counselor*, Camp Winatooga, Town, State |
| | Co-supervised group of 20 eight-year-old girls. Organized outdoor activities, including nature walks, relay races, and swimming lessons. Led drama class and directed play put on by campers. |
| **Part-Time, 1988 to 1990** | *Teacher's Aide*, Little People Child Care, Town, State |
| | Helped early childhood teachers care for infants and toddlers. |

**Education**

| | |
|---|---|
| **1992** | *Associate Degree*, Early Childhood Education, Thomas County Community College, Town, State |
| **1990** | *Diploma*, Black Rock High School, Town, State |

**Additional Qualifications**
First Aid and CPR certification

| | |
|---|---|
| **References** | Available upon request. |

FIGURE 18.1   Sample Résumé.

39 Samson Way
Town, State 12345
June 1, 1993

Ms. Joanne Caldwell
Director
Georgetown Preschool
26 Georgetown Avenue
Town, State 12345

Dear Ms. Caldwell:

As I mentioned during our telephone conversation this afternoon, I am interested in applying for an associate teacher position at the Georgetown Preschool.

I have experience working with young children and an Associate degree in Early Childhood Education. Most recently, I have been employed as an early childhood teacher assistant at the Sunshine Valley Preschool. I am familiar with developmentally appropriate practices, and I have experience in planning and organizing all types of activities. Considering my education, training, and experience, I feel that I am qualified and prepared to assume the responsibility of group leader in the preschool classroom.

My résumé is enclosed, as you requested. I would be happy to discuss my qualifications with you in further detail.

Thank you.

Very truly yours,


Lydia Jeffries

Enclosure

**FIGURE 18.2**   Sample Letter of Application.

Independent day-care providers usually have a good deal of freedom in determining the hours they will work, the number of children they will care for, and the activities they will offer.

A successful early childhood professional works well with others. Showing respect for coworkers is one of the best ways of creating a positive work environment. By sharing your ideas with others and asking others for help, you can make the workplace a source of professional support and growth.

After several years on the job, you may feel that you are ready for a different or more challenging position. Discuss your interest and goals with your supervisor. It may be that you need additional education or training to advance in the profession. Many programs plan for and encourage the continuing development of their staff.

Career development should be ongoing. It can take the form of advanced training and additional schooling, as well as joining professional groups and keeping up with the professional literature in the field. Job evaluations also offer opportunities for professional growth and change. Succeeding in your field means continually trying to improve the quality of your work and expand the depth of your knowledge.

## Working as an Independent Provider

Some early childhood professionals decide to establish day-care operations in their own home. In some ways, family day-care providers have more freedom in their work than caregivers in child care centers. They can determine the hours they will work, the number of children they will care for, and the curriculum and activities they will offer the children. Running a business out of their home also allows them to stay at home with their own children. In addition, family day-care providers have the potential of earning much more money than caregivers in child care centers.

However, like any business, starting a family day care operation requires capital, equipment, and planning. Money is needed to buy furniture, toys,

## FOCUS ON     Child Care Issues

### Dealing with Violence

For many children, the world is a violent place. In some neighborhoods gunfire is routine. In one study of 1,000 children in Chicago, 74 percent of them had witnessed a murder, shooting, stabbing, or robbery. Almost half of these acts of violence involved friends, relatives, or neighbors. Not all children witness violence firsthand, but if they watch television regularly, they are likely, between the ages of 5 and 15, to see more than 13,000 on-screen killings.

Karina, an inner-city preschool teacher, is not surprised to find five-year-olds in her class playing violent games such as "mugging" and "knife fight." She knows these children are imitating events that they have seen or heard about. Looking for a constructive way to help the children deal with the violence in their lives, Karina turns to two more experienced teachers for advice.

Anita Calabrese:
"My rule is that we don't play violent games in the classroom. There is enough violence in these children's lives without allowing it to creep into school, even as play. I allow no toy guns or knives and no 'bang-bang' finger-pointing in my classroom.

"I strive to provide a caring, consistent environment at school. I set definite limits to behavior. When conflict occurs, we work on finding nonviolent solutions. This involves getting children to talk about their feelings. I've found that asking children to draw pictures of conflict situations is a good way to get them started talking about what they feel.

"I also spend a lot of time using story puppets. Some of the puppets experience violence and conflict. Through them, I suggest ways to resolve the conflict.

"As a preschool teacher, all I can do is build up children's self-esteem and help them cope with their day-to-day life. I realize that some of these children live in neighborhoods where street violence is common. I can give them a violence-free school environment, but I can't change their neighborhoods. I provide as many positive activities as possible in the hope that these will give them the resilience they need to cope with their lives outside of school."

Janice Lee:
"I allow the children in my class to play what some teachers consider to be 'violent' games. I believe play helps children make sense of the complexities of their world. The events these children are playing out—muggings, robberies, and so on—are real parts of their lives. Play allows them to express their feelings about these events. Children are not permitted to hurt each other, but I do not stop them if they take out their anger on dolls or stuffed animals.

"Many people think children should put unpleasant experiences out of their mind and not talk about them. I've found, however, that some children need to repeat unpleasant experiences in play. This repetition allows them to come to grips with the reality of the unpleasantness and then move on. I try to permit all sorts of play situations so long as no one is hurt.

"Besides allowing children to express themselves through play, I encourage them to tell me pretend stories. Often children will talk about their feelings more easily in a story or 'let's pretend' situation. I don't think children find my classroom any less safe and secure simply because we talk about the dangers that exist in their world."

*Which teacher's approach do you think is a better one for dealing with violence? Why?*

materials, and outdoor equipment and to make any alterations (such as extra toilets) needed to turn a private home into a child care setting. In addition, family day-care providers must pay for their own health insurance and for day-care liability insurance.

Running a family day-care operation involves a great deal of responsibility. Once the hours of service are established, it may be difficult for the provider to close early or take time off for personal or professional reasons. Family day-care providers who work on their own at home may also feel isolated. Some providers offer group family day care; they hire an assistant and provide care for more children.

The requirements for operating a family day-care program vary from state to state. Some states require family day-care homes to meet certain safety and health standards in order to obtain an operating license. Some states regulate family day care through a process called registration. This usually requires an application and written plans but not inspection. It is up to the parents to monitor the conditions in the home and to report any serious violations. To find out about licensing or registration requirements in your state, contact your state's Department of Human Services. At the community level, a family day-care home must comply with local zoning regulations.

Many states also have requirements for family day-care providers. Most states require a provider to be at least 18 years old. Many require a physical exam and/or tuberculosis test and also a criminal record check; some also require screening for reports of child abuse or maltreatment. In some states, family day-care providers must be certified, either through a CDA credential or a degree in early childhood education; first-aid or CPR training is often required. In recent years, many child development experts and early childhood organizations have mounted a campaign to establish national standards for day-care providers.

Numerous organizations are available to help child care professionals establish and maintain a family day-care business. Many states have family day-care associations made up primarily of providers. These associations offer peer and mentor support, provide training, and represent the interests of

Child care professionals have the opportunity to act as advocates for children. This may involve lobbying government at the local, state, or national level to fund more programs for young children.

providers in working with the government on family day-care issues. At the national level, the National Association for Family Day Care (NAFDC) has an accreditation program for family day-care providers. By preparing a self-evaluation and having it validated by a parent and a professional appointed by the NAFDC, providers can become accredited.

Financial assistance is available from the federal Child Care Food Program. This program reimburses nonresidential child care institutions, including licensed or approved family day-care homes, for furnishing nutritious meals to children enrolled in the program.

Child care resource and referral agencies are another source of help. In addition to referring families to approved or accredited family day-care providers, they also provide training and a help line. In some states, corporations are involved in sponsoring programs that help recruit new family day-care providers, train them, and provide them with incentives and support. While much remains to be done to make family day care a better child care and career option nationwide, it is finally being recognized as an important service and profession.

## The Early Childhood Profession

Being an early childhood professional involves more than caring for and educating children. It requires a commitment to improving your skills and knowledge through study, training programs, and courses such as child development, health and nutrition, preschool curriculum, and special education. It involves keeping up with the literature in the field so as to be aware of major developments and current issues in the profession. Joining professional organizations such as the NAEYC or the

NAFDC will demonstrate your support for the profession and keep you abreast of current issues.

### Ethical Issues

An important matter in any profession is a code of ethics governing conduct. In the field of early childhood education, ethical behavior is responsible behavior. Early childhood educators must demand it from themselves, and they must be willing to monitor it in others. To help early childhood professionals, the NAEYC has drafted a code of ethical conduct (see Figure 18.3). This code addresses the early childhood professional's ethical responsibilities to children, their families, the community, and society. It asks early childhood educators not to engage in practices that could psychologically or physically hurt children. It encourages professionals to help family members improve their understanding of their children and to base early childhood programs on developmentally appropriate practice.

The NAEYC Code of Ethical Conduct also calls on early childhood professionals to become advocates on behalf of young children. An *advocate* is a person who actively promotes the cause of another,

**FIGURE 18.3**    **Excerpt from the NAEYC Code of Ethics.**

Standards of ethical behavior in early childhood education are based on commitment to core values that are deeply rooted in the history of our field.

We have committed ourselves to

- Appreciating childhood as a unique and valuable stage of the human life cycle
- Basing our work with children on knowledge of child development
- Recognizing that children are best understood in the context of family, culture, and society
- Respecting the dignity, worth, and uniqueness of each individual (child, family member, and colleague)
- Helping children and adults achieve their full potential in the context of relationships that are based on trust, respect, and positive regard

*Source:* Feeney, S., and Kipnis, K. (1992). *Code of ethical conduct and statement of commitment.* Washington, D.C.: National Association for the Education of Young Children.

Caring for young children can be highly rewarding. Child care professionals are able to share in the wonder, joy, and excitement of children as they discover and explore their world.

in this case the quality of life for young children. It is critical for early childhood professionals to be advocates because children cannot promote their own cause. They cannot vote, write laws, or campaign for change. The adults who work with children and care for them must do these things for them.

Early childhood professionals must be willing to act as advocates for children at the local level, the regional level, and the national level. At each level, the goal is the same: to work for policies that promote the growth and development of children. At the community level, this might involve organizing a resource and referral agency to provide parents with up-to-date information about child care options in the area. At the state level, this could mean lobbying legislators to fund more programs for young children. At the national level, it could mean writing to members of Congress, expressing support for such policies as national standards in early childhood programs. Dedicated professionals focus

on more than the here and now, on more than the children and families they are serving today. They care about the future and the children who will live in it.

## Challenges and Rewards

One characteristic of employment in the early childhood field is the high turnover—up to 40 percent. Why do so many child care professionals leave their jobs? One reason is that they often work long hours for low pay. The National Child Care Staffing Study found that salaries for child care professionals decreased by 25 percent between 1977 and 1988, even though the education levels of child care providers increased (Children's Defense Fund, 1992). In addition to poor pay, early childhood professionals receive little proper recognition of their professional expertise. Many of these professionals become frustrated because the opportunities for advancement

Chapter 18 • Planning for a Career with Young Children **439**

in the field are so few. A study of child care centers revealed that only about one in ten had a policy on professional advancement (Jorde-Bloom, 1989).

Despite this bleak picture, there is cause for hope. The rapid growth of the early childhood field and the increasing demand for the services of qualified personnel make it more likely that working conditions and salaries will improve in the future. In addition, federal and state governments are beginning to initiate policies that address these issues. For example, a federal pilot program that increased caregiver salaries at military child care centers led to a major drop in staff turnover. This pilot project was part of the Military Child Care Act of 1989, which was designed to make child care salaries more competitive. At the state level, several states have established planning commissions to develop a model regarding staffing and compensation. Advocacy groups are also working to focus public attention on these issues. According to the Child Care Employee Project (1992, p. 42), "the prospects have never been brighter for making child care a well-recognized and well-rewarded profession at last."

The rewards of working with young children are many. The work is varied, and there is ample opportunity for creativity. Helping others provides a deep sense of satisfaction. Early childhood professionals also have many opportunities to interact with fellow professionals who share their values and commitment to the well-being of children and their families. Most important of all, working with children can be a source of great pleasure and fulfillment. It will give you the opportunity to help children grow and learn and to share in their joy of discovery.

Society is becoming more aware of the critical role of the early years of life in an individual's growth and development. With increasing education, training, and advocacy, early childhood professionals may at last receive the recognition and remuneration they deserve for performing one of the most important jobs in our society.

## CHAPTER 18 ▸ REVIEW

### SUMMARY

- Child care professionals need to be warm, nurturing, flexible, observant, even tempered, patient, energetic, and enthusiastic. They need to be dependable, consistent, self-assured, and respectful of others as well. Because most child care professionals do not work in isolation, they also need to be able to work well with others.

- After determining what their career goals are, future child care professionals should determine the courses, credits, and degrees they will need to achieve their goals. Many states also require child care professionals to obtain a state certificate or license.

- Experience provides good preparation for working with young children and will help you determine the area of child care in which you would like to specialize.

- The types of child care programs that are available today include infant/toddler/preschooler half- and full-day educational programs at preschools and child care centers; family day care; home-based care; and a variety of other programs.

- Some of the job opportunities that are available in the early childhood profession include early childhood teacher assistant, early childhood associate teacher, early childhood teacher, early childhood specialist, kindergarten and elementary school teachers, school nurse, pediatrician, physical therapist, speech therapist, occupational therapist, counselor, social worker, and children's librarian.

- Job openings can be located through your school or college placement office, help-wanted ads in newspapers and professional journals, networking, and referral and placement agencies.

- Preparing a résumé is a significant part of good job-finding strategies. The résumé should be neat and carefully prepared. It should include brief descriptions of your educational background and work experience listed in reverse chronological order. When a prospective employer asks you to send a résumé, be sure to include a letter of application with it.

- Dress appropriately for interviews and be on time. Prepare yourself by reviewing your résumé and questions you are likely to be asked. Follow up your interview with a thank-you note.

- Succeeding on the job requires getting along well with supervisors and coworkers. It also involves planning to improve the quality of your work through advanced training or additional schooling.

- Independent family day-care providers have more control over their work and many earn a higher income than caregivers in child care centers. However, they need adequate funding to start up and maintain their business. The requirements for operating a family day-care program vary from state to state. Many organizations are available to help family day-care providers with financial, business, and professional support.

- Being an early childhood professional means being committed to improving your skills and knowledge continually, keeping informed of the latest developments and issues in the profession, practicing ethical behavior, and being an advocate for children at the local, state, and national levels.

- Although pay, working conditions, and opportunities for advancement in the early childhood profession have been poor in the past, the rapid growth of the field and the increasing demand for the services of well-qualified child care providers make it likely that the situation will improve in the future. Caring for young children is truly a rewarding and important profession.

## BUILDING VOCABULARY

Write a definition for each vocabulary term listed below.

advocate                                    eclectic
developmental-interactionist                networking

## ACQUIRING KNOWLEDGE

1. Name three groups of people with whom caregivers work in a child care setting.
2. List three personality characteristics of a good child care professional.

3. Why is it important for caregivers to be accepting and respectful of others?
4. In many child care settings, child care professionals are part of a team. Give an example of the other individuals who might make up the team.
5. How does the Child Development Associate credential (CDA) differ from other educational credentials in the field?
6. How does supervised experience help prepare individuals to work as child care professionals?
7. In some places, child care workers need a license or certificate to work in the profession. Who determines the requirements for certification?
8. Name two forms of experience that provide preparation for a career in child care.
9. Why is the need for child care professionals increasing?
10. Many educational child care programs follow an eclectic approach. What does this mean?
11. How is family day care different from child care at a center?
12. What distinguishes cooperative child care programs from other programs?
13. What is the goal of Head Start?
14. What type of research is done in laboratory schools?
15. Describe the difference in training and responsibilities between an early childhood teacher aide and an early childhood teacher.
16. What are the job requirements for kindergarten and elementary school teachers?
17. Name two kinds of health care professionals who work with children.
18. Where are ads for child care job openings found and what type of information do they contain?
19. Name two sources of job information that can be used for networking.
20. What type of experience should be listed on a résumé?
21. Why is it important that a résumé and cover letter be neat and professional looking?
22. List two ways in which job applicants can prepare for interviews.
23. What steps can child care professionals take to advance in the profession?
24. Describe how family day-care associations can assist people interested in becoming independent child care providers.
25. What is an advocate? Why do young children need advocates?

## CRITICAL THINKING

1. For many jobs in early childhood education, hands-on experience is either recommended or required. What are the benefits of hands-on experience? What skills or abilities can be developed by working with children in a child care setting?
2. Some jobs in child care involve caring for children as young as six weeks of age, others focus on the preschool years, and still others involve school-age children. In your opinion, how does the age group of the children change the nature of the caregiver's job?
3. There are various state and local licensing and certification requirements for many jobs in early childhood education. What are the benefits of such requirements for children, their families, and caregivers?

4. Prepare a list of questions that an employment interviewer might ask a candidate for a job as an early childhood teacher assistant. What questions might the applicant ask the interviewer?

5. Discuss the advantages and disadvantages of working as an early childhood teacher, as a family day-care provider, and as a nanny. For what type of person would each position be a good career choice?

## OBSERVATIONS AND APPLICATIONS

1. Observe a family child care provider at work. How many children does the provider care for? What ages are the children? Are any of the children related to the provider? Are formal educational or directed play activities included in the daily schedule? Is a regular routine followed? If so, describe it. How are meals and naps handled? Describe the facilities and materials provided for the children. Is the home licensed?

2. Observe a local Head Start program. What are the hours of operation? Where is the school located? Note the ages of the children, and describe the daily routine. In what ways are the special needs of the children addressed? Describe the enrichment activities that are part of the curriculum. What special programs are offered for parents? Do you note any ways in which the facility or the program differs from other child care programs you have observed? Note similarities as well.

3. You are looking for a part-time job in the field of early childhood education and see a job notice in the college placement office for a part-time aide in an after-school program at a local primary school. The hours are convenient for you and the pay is acceptable. Write a cover letter, no more than one page in length, explaining your interest in the job and highlighting your qualifications for it.

4. You are asked by the after-school program director to come in for an interview. To prepare for some of the questions you think you will be asked, write down brief answers to the following questions: What previous experience have you had working with children? What were the ages of the children? Why do you want to pursue a career in early childhood education? What are three activities you think would be appropriate and enjoyable to plan for six- to eight-year-old children? Explain how you would handle a disruptive child. How has your education helped prepare you for this job?

## SUGGESTIONS FOR FURTHER READING

Benham, N., Miller, T., & Kontos, S. (1988). Pinpointing staff training needs in child care centers. *Young children, 43*(4), 9–16.

*Career information center.* (1993). (Vols. 5, 11). New York: Macmillan.

Council for Early Childhood Professional Recognition. (1989). *The national directory of early childhood training programs.* Washington, DC: Author.

Dresden, J., & Myers, B. K. (1989). Early childhood professionals: Toward self-definition. *Young Children, 44*(2), 62–66.

Feeney, S., Christensen, D., & Moravcik, E. (1991). *Who Am I in the lives of young children?* New York: Macmillan.

Fennimore, B. S. (1989). *Child advocacy for early childhood educators.* New York: Teachers College Press.

Godwin, A., & Schrag, L. (Eds.). (1988). *Setting up for infant care: Guidelines for centers and family day care homes.* Washington, DC: National Association for the Education of Young Children.

Goffin, S. G., & Lombardi, J. (1988). *Speaking out: Early childhood advocacy.* Washington, DC: National Association for the Education of Young Children.

Hendrick, J. (1987). *Why teach?* Washington, DC: National Association for the Education of Young Children.

*Homework.* International Nanny Association Newsletter. Austin, TX.

Jensen, M. A., & Chevalier, L. W. (1990). *Issues and advocacy in early childhood education.* Boston: Allyn & Bacon.

Kontos, T. (1992). *Family day care: Out of the shadows and into the limelight.* Washington, DC: National Association for the Education of Young Children.

National Association for the Education of Young Children (1990). *Early childhood teacher education guidelines: Basic and advanced.* Washington, DC: Author.

Seaver, J. W., Cartwright, C. A., Ward, C. B., & Heasley, C. A. (1979). *Careers with young children: Making your decision.* Washington, DC: National Association for the Education of Young Children.

Squibb, B. (1986). *Family day care: How to provide it in your home.* Cambridge, MA: Harvard Common Press.

# Appendices

# Appendix A

## Height Charts for Boys and Girls, 6 Months to 12 Years of Age

**Table 1** Recumbent Length in Centimeters of Males 6 Months to 1 Year of Age

| Age | Number of examined persons* | Mean | Standard deviation | Percentile | | | | | | | | |
|---|---|---|---|---|---|---|---|---|---|---|---|---|
| | | | | 5th | 10th | 15th | 25th | 50th | 75th | 85th | 90th | 95th |
| 6–11 months | 176 | 72.9 | 3.8 | 66.8 | 68.4 | 69.5 | 70.5 | 73.3 | 75.5 | 76.1 | 77.1 | 78.8 |
| 1 year | 366 | 82.4 | 5.0 | 75.7 | 76.7 | 77.8 | 79.3 | 82.1 | 85.5 | 87.2 | 88.1 | 89.9 |

**Table 2** Standing Height in Centimeters of Males 2 to 12 Years of Age**

| Age | Number of examined persons* | Mean | Standard deviation | Percentile | | | | | | | | |
|---|---|---|---|---|---|---|---|---|---|---|---|---|
| | | | | 5th | 10th | 15th | 25th | 50th | 75th | 85th | 90th | 95th |
| 2 years | 375 | 91.2 | 4.3 | 84.5 | 85.8 | 86.5 | 88.2 | 91.3 | 94.2 | 95.8 | 96.6 | 97.6 |
| 3 years | 418 | 99.2 | 4.5 | 92.0 | 94.3 | 94.9 | 96.5 | 98.8 | 102.0 | 103.9 | 105.0 | 107.0 |
| 4 years | 404 | 106.0 | 5.2 | 97.8 | 99.5 | 100.5 | 102.5 | 106.4 | 109.2 | 111.0 | 112.4 | 115.0 |
| 5 years | 397 | 112.6 | 5.4 | 104.0 | 105.8 | 107.2 | 109.4 | 112.6 | 115.6 | 118.1 | 119.6 | 121.2 |
| 6 years | 133 | 119.5 | 5.1 | 111.2 | 112.6 | 114.5 | 115.9 | 120.1 | 122.6 | 124.7 | 125.5 | 126.8 |
| 7 years | 148 | 125.1 | 5.9 | 115.4 | 117.6 | 119.1 | 121.8 | 125.9 | 128.1 | 130.2 | 131.5 | 133.6 |
| 8 years | 147 | 129.9 | 7.0 | 118.6 | 122.0 | 123.5 | 125.3 | 130.6 | 134.1 | 136.5 | 138.0 | 142.0 |
| 9 years | 145 | 135.5 | 5.8 | 125.9 | 128.4 | 129.4 | 131.2 | 136.1 | 139.6 | 141.2 | 143.1 | 144.7 |
| 10 years | 157 | 141.6 | 7.3 | 130.3 | 132.8 | 134.0 | 137.0 | 141.5 | 146.4 | 149.6 | 150.6 | 153.0 |
| 11 years | 155 | 146.0 | 7.8 | 133.1 | 135.9 | 138.0 | 141.1 | 145.6 | 151.2 | 153.9 | 155.2 | 160.2 |
| 12 years | 145 | 152.6 | 7.9 | 139.0 | 142.6 | 144.9 | 147.5 | 152.0 | 158.0 | 160.5 | 162.0 | 164.4 |

**Table 3  Recumbent Length in Centimeters of Females 6 Months to 1 Year of Age**

| Age | Number of examined persons[*] | Mean | Standard deviation | Percentile | | | | | | | | |
|---|---|---|---|---|---|---|---|---|---|---|---|---|
| | | | | 5th | 10th | 15th | 25th | 50th | 75th | 85th | 90th | 95th |
| 6–11 months | 176 | 71.2 | 4.5 | 64.5 | 66.2 | 66.8 | 68.4 | 71.3 | 74.2 | 75.5 | 76.5 | 77.5 |
| 1 year | 333 | 80.3 | 4.5 | 73.1 | 74.7 | 76.0 | 77.0 | 80.1 | 83.2 | 85.3 | 86.5 | 87.8 |

**Table 4  Standing Height in Centimeters of Females 2 to 12 Years of Age[**]**

| Age | Number of examined persons[*] | Mean | Standard deviation | Percentile | | | | | | | | |
|---|---|---|---|---|---|---|---|---|---|---|---|---|
| | | | | 5th | 10th | 15th | 25th | 50th | 75th | 85th | 90th | 95th |
| 2 years | 336 | 89.7 | 4.2 | 83.1 | 84.4 | 85.5 | 86.7 | 89.8 | 92.2 | 93.6 | 94.9 | 97.2 |
| 3 years | 366 | 97.5 | 4.8 | 89.6 | 91.1 | 92.5 | 94.5 | 97.6 | 100.8 | 102.5 | 103.4 | 104.5 |
| 4 years | 396 | 104.6 | 5.0 | 96.1 | 98.2 | 99.5 | 101.5 | 104.5 | 108.2 | 109.8 | 110.7 | 112.4 |
| 5 years | 364 | 111.6 | 5.3 | 103.0 | 105.1 | 106.4 | 108.1 | 111.6 | 115.2 | 116.5 | 118.8 | 120.3 |
| 6 years | 135 | 118.4 | 6.1 | 109.9 | 111.1 | 111.5 | 113.3 | 118.5 | 122.2 | 124.5 | 126.5 | 128.7 |
| 7 years | 157 | 123.7 | 6.7 | 113.3 | 116.6 | 117.4 | 119.6 | 124.1 | 128.1 | 130.1 | 132.2 | 134.7 |
| 8 years | 123 | 130.2 | 5.7 | 120.8 | 123.4 | 124.4 | 125.8 | 130.6 | 133.2 | 135.4 | 137.5 | 140.5 |
| 9 years | 149 | 134.4 | 7.6 | 124.0 | 126.4 | 127.8 | 129.0 | 134.8 | 139.0 | 140.7 | 142.6 | 147.1 |
| 10 years | 136 | 141.9 | 6.5 | 131.6 | 133.6 | 135.1 | 137.6 | 141.6 | 146.3 | 148.1 | 150.4 | 153.8 |
| 11 years | 140 | 147.9 | 7.8 | 134.7 | 139.3 | 140.6 | 142.2 | 147.9 | 152.2 | 154.7 | 156.9 | 162.7 |
| 12 years | 147 | 154.4 | 7.2 | 143.9 | 145.7 | 146.7 | 149.2 | 154.8 | 158.6 | 161.9 | 164.7 | 165.9 |

*Note:* To convert centimeters to inches, multiply by 0.39.

[*]Number examined, United States, 1976–1980.

[**]Height without shoes.

*Source:* National Center for Health Statistics, M. F. Najjar and M. Rowland; Anthropometric Reference Data and Prevalence of Overweight, United States, 1978–80. *Vital and Health Statistics.* Series 11, No. 238. DHHS Pub. No. (PHS) 87–1688. Public Health Service. Washington. U.S. Government Printing Office, Oct. 1987.

# Appendix B

## Weight Charts for Boys and Girls, 6 Months to 12 Years of Age

**Table 1** Weight in Kilograms of Males 6 Months to 12 Years of Age*

| Age | Number of examined persons** | Mean | Standard deviation | Percentile | | | | | | | | |
|---|---|---|---|---|---|---|---|---|---|---|---|---|
| | | | | 5th | 10th | 15th | 25th | 50th | 75th | 85th | 90th | 95th |
| 6–11 months | 179 | 9.4 | 1.3 | 7.5 | 7.6 | 8.2 | 8.6 | 9.4 | 10.1 | 10.7 | 10.9 | 11.4 |
| 1 year | 370 | 11.8 | 1.9 | 9.6 | 10.0 | 10.3 | 10.8 | 11.7 | 12.6 | 13.1 | 13.6 | 14.4 |
| 2 years | 375 | 13.6 | 1.7 | 11.1 | 11.6 | 11.8 | 12.6 | 13.5 | 14.5 | 15.2 | 15.8 | 16.5 |
| 3 years | 418 | 15.7 | 2.0 | 12.9 | 13.5 | 13.9 | 14.4 | 15.4 | 16.8 | 17.4 | 17.9 | 19.1 |
| 4 years | 404 | 17.8 | 2.5 | 14.1 | 15.0 | 15.3 | 16.0 | 17.6 | 19.0 | 19.9 | 20.9 | 22.2 |
| 5 years | 397 | 19.8 | 3.0 | 16.0 | 16.8 | 17.1 | 17.7 | 19.4 | 21.3 | 22.9 | 23.7 | 25.4 |
| 6 years | 133 | 23.0 | 4.0 | 18.6 | 19.2 | 19.8 | 20.3 | 22.0 | 24.1 | 26.4 | 28.3 | 30.1 |
| 7 years | 148 | 25.1 | 3.9 | 19.7 | 20.8 | 21.2 | 22.2 | 24.8 | 26.9 | 28.2 | 29.6 | 33.9 |
| 8 years | 147 | 28.2 | 6.2 | 20.4 | 22.7 | 23.6 | 24.6 | 27.5 | 29.9 | 33.0 | 35.5 | 39.1 |
| 9 years | 145 | 31.1 | 6.3 | 24.0 | 25.6 | 26.0 | 27.1 | 30.2 | 33.0 | 35.4 | 38.6 | 43.1 |
| 10 years | 157 | 36.4 | 7.7 | 27.2 | 28.2 | 29.6 | 31.4 | 34.8 | 39.2 | 43.5 | 46.3 | 53.4 |
| 11 years | 155 | 40.3 | 10.1 | 26.8 | 28.8 | 31.8 | 33.5 | 37.3 | 46.4 | 52.0 | 57.0 | 61.0 |
| 12 years | 145 | 44.2 | 10.1 | 30.7 | 32.5 | 35.4 | 37.8 | 42.5 | 48.8 | 52.6 | 58.9 | 67.5 |

# Table 2  Weight in Kilograms of Females 6 Months to 12 Years of Age[*]

| Age | Number of examined persons[**] | Mean | Standard deviation | Percentile | | | | | | | | | | | |
|---|---|---|---|---|---|---|---|---|---|---|---|---|---|---|---|
| | | | | 5th | 10th | 15th | 25th | 50th | 75th | 85th | 90th | 95th |
| 6–11 months | 177 | 8.8 | 1.2 | 6.6 | 7.3 | 7.5 | 7.9 | 8.9 | 9.4 | 10.1 | 10.4 | 10.9 |
| 1 year | 336 | 10.8 | 1.4 | 8.8 | 9.1 | 9.4 | 9.9 | 10.7 | 11.7 | 12.4 | 12.7 | 13.4 |
| 2 years | 336 | 13.0 | 1.5 | 10.8 | 11.2 | 11.6 | 12.0 | 12.7 | 13.8 | 14.5 | 14.9 | 15.9 |
| 3 years | 366 | 14.9 | 2.1 | 11.7 | 12.3 | 12.9 | 13.4 | 14.7 | 16.1 | 17.0 | 17.4 | 18.4 |
| 4 years | 396 | 17.0 | 2.4 | 13.7 | 14.3 | 14.5 | 15.2 | 16.7 | 18.4 | 19.3 | 20.2 | 21.1 |
| 5 years | 364 | 19.6 | 3.3 | 15.3 | 16.1 | 16.7 | 17.2 | 19.0 | 21.2 | 22.8 | 24.7 | 26.6 |
| 6 years | 135 | 22.1 | 4.0 | 17.0 | 17.8 | 18.6 | 19.3 | 21.3 | 23.8 | 26.6 | 28.9 | 29.6 |
| 7 years | 157 | 24.7 | 5.0 | 19.2 | 19.5 | 19.6 | 21.4 | 23.8 | 27.1 | 28.7 | 30.3 | 34.0 |
| 8 years | 123 | 27.9 | 5.7 | 21.4 | 22.3 | 23.3 | 24.4 | 27.5 | 30.2 | 31.3 | 33.2 | 36.5 |
| 9 years | 149 | 31.9 | 8.4 | 22.9 | 25.0 | 25.8 | 27.0 | 29.7 | 33.6 | 39.3 | 43.3 | 48.4 |
| 10 years | 136 | 36.1 | 8.0 | 25.7 | 27.5 | 29.0 | 31.0 | 34.5 | 39.5 | 44.2 | 45.8 | 49.6 |
| 11 years | 140 | 41.8 | 10.9 | 29.8 | 30.3 | 31.3 | 33.9 | 40.3 | 45.8 | 51.0 | 56.6 | 60.0 |
| 12 years | 147 | 46.4 | 10.1 | 32.3 | 35.0 | 36.7 | 39.1 | 45.4 | 52.6 | 58.0 | 60.5 | 64.3 |

*Note:* To convert kilograms to pounds, multiply by 2.2.

[*]Includes clothing weight, estimated as ranging from 0.09 to 0.28 kilogram (3.18 to 9.88 ounces).

[**]Number examined, United States, 1976–1980.

*Source:* National Center for Health Statistics, M. F. Najjar and M. Rowland; Anthropometric Reference Data and Prevalence of Overweight, United States, 1978–80. *Vital and Health Statistics.* Series 11, No. 238. DHHS Pub. No. (PHS) 87–1688. Public Health Service. Washington. U.S. Government Printing Office, Oct. 1987.

# Appendix C

## National Association for the Education of Young Children: Recommended Child-Staff Ratios and Group Sizes

| Age of child | Group Size* | | | | | | | | | | |
|---|---|---|---|---|---|---|---|---|---|---|---|
| | 6 | 8 | 10 | 12 | 14 | 16 | 18 | 20 | 22 | 24 | 28 |
| Birth to 12 mos. | 3:1 | 4:1 | | | | | | | | | |
| 12 to 24 mos. | 3:1 | 4:1 | 5:1 | 4:1 | | | | | | | |
| 24 to 30 mos. | | 4:1 | 5:1 | 6:1 | | | | | | | |
| 30 to 36 mos. | | | 5:1 | 6:1 | 7:1 | | | | | | |
| Three-year-olds | | | | | 7:1 | 8:1 | 9:1 | 10:1 | | | |
| Four-year-olds | | | | | | 8:1 | 9:1 | 10:1 | | | |
| Five-year-olds | | | | | | 8:1 | 9:1 | 10:1 | | | |
| Six- to eight-year-olds | | | | | | | | 10:1 | 11:1 | 12:1 | |
| Nine- to 12-year-olds | | | | | | | | | | 12:1 | 14:1 |

*Smaller group sizes and fewer children per staff have been found to be strong predictors of compliance with indicators of quality.

*Source:* "Research Into Action. The Effects of Group Size, Ratios, and Staff Training on Child Care Quality," *Young Children, 48*(2), 65.
© Copyright 1993 by the National Association for the Education of Young Children. Used by permission.

| Children Aged 0–35 Months | | | |
|---|---|---|---|
| **Title/Role Responsibility** | **Age** | **Education** | **Skills/Experience** |
| Director | 21 | Undergraduate degree in early childhood education, child development, social work, nursing, or other child-related field, OR a combination of college coursework and experience and 2 or more years' experience as a teacher of infants and toddlers. Coursework in business administration or business-related experience. Preservice training in child development, early childhood education, and health management in child care. Directors of large centers meet more stringent qualifications. | · Knowledge of, and competence in dealing with, infant/toddler skills and behavior.<br>· Administrative and management skills in facility operations.<br>· Capability in curriculum design.<br>· Knowledge of community resources.<br>· Verbal and written communication skills.<br>· Ability to communicate with parents.<br>· Pediatric first aid, including rescue breathing and first aid for choking. |
| Lead teacher | 21 | Undergraduate or master's degree in early childhood education, child development, social work, nursing, or other child-related field. Licensed as lead teacher, teacher, or associate teacher. Education and experience related to infant and toddler development and caregiving. One or more years' experience in child care under qualified supervision. | · Knowledge of, and competence in dealing with, infant/toddler skills and behavior.<br>· Ability to respond appropriately to these children's needs.<br>· Verbal and written communication skills.<br>· Recognition of signs of illness and safety hazards.<br>· Pediatric first aid, including rescue breathing and first aid for choking.<br>· Ability to communicate with parents. |
| Early childhood teacher | 21 | Undergraduate degree in early childhood education, child development, social work, nursing, or other child-related field, OR a combination of college coursework and experience. Also, 1 year's experience, OR one semester practicum, OR associate degree and 1 year's experience, OR CDA credential, 2 years' experience, and one additional course in early childhood education, OR four courses in child development. | · Competence in the care and education of young children. |
| Early childhood associate teacher | 18 | CDA credential or associate degree in early childhood education or child development. Six or more months' experience in child care. | · Competence in the care and education of young children. |
| Early childhood teacher assistant | 18 | High school diploma or GED. Participation in ongoing training. | · Competence in assigned tasks.<br>· Ability to respond appropriately to young children's needs. |

# Appendix D: continued

| Children Aged 0–35 Months | | | |
|---|---|---|---|
| **Title/Role Responsibility** | **Age** | **Education** | **Skills/Experience** |
| Aide | 18 | On-the-job training. | • Ability to nurture children, as attested to by a qualified educator who has observed the caregiver caring for children.<br>• Sound judgment.<br>• Ability to follow instructions.<br>• Ability to carry out assigned tasks under supervision of another staff member. |
| Health advocate | 18 | Health training related to infant and toddler development and caregiving. Licensed as lead teacher, teacher, or associate teacher, or shall be a health professional or social worker employed by and at the facility. | • Knowledge of, and competence in dealing with, infant/toddler skills and behavior.<br>• Ability to respond appropriately to these children's needs.<br>• Verbal and written communication skills.<br>• Recognition of signs of illness and safety hazards.<br>• Pediatric first aid, including rescue breathing and first aid for choking. |
| Large family home caregiver | 21 | High school diploma or GED. CDA credential, associate or undergraduate degree in early childhood education or child development, OR coursework in child growth and development plus 1 year's experience in a facility or as a licensed small family home caregiver. Preservice training in health management in child care. | • Knowledge of, and competence in dealing with, infant/toddler skills and behavior.<br>• Ability to respond appropriately to these children's needs.<br>• Verbal and written communication skills.<br>• Recognition of signs of illness and safety hazards.<br>• Pediatric first aid, including rescue breathing and first aid for choking.<br>• Ability to communicate with parents. |
| Small family home caregiver | 21 | Preservice training in health management in child care. Ongoing training courses related to care specific to this age group. | • Knowledge of, and competence in dealing with, infant/toddler skills and behavior.<br>• Ability to respond appropriately to these children's needs.<br>• Verbal communication skills.<br>• Recognition of signs of illness and safety hazards.<br>• Ability to communicate with parents.<br>• Pediatric first aid, including rescue breathing and first aid for choking. |

| Children Aged 3–5 Years | | | |
|---|---|---|---|
| **Title/Role Responsibility** | **Age** | **Education** | **Skills/Experience** |
| Director | 21 | Undergraduate degree in early childhood education, child development, social work, nursing, or other child-related field, OR a combination of college coursework and experience and 2 or more years' experience as a teacher of preschoolers. Coursework in business administration or business-related experience. Preservice training in child development, early childhood education, and health management in child care. Directors of large centers meet more stringent qualifications. | • Knowledge and understanding of child development. <br>• Administrative and management skills in facility operations. <br>• Capability in curriculum design. <br>• Verbal and written communication skills. <br>• Knowledge of community resources. <br>• Ability to communicate with parents. <br>• Pediatric first aid, including rescue breathing and first aid for choking. |
| Lead teacher | 21 | Undergraduate or master's degree in early childhood education, child development, social work, nursing, or other child-related field. Licensed as lead teacher, teacher, or associate teacher. Education in child development and early childhood education and supervised experience with preschoolers. One or more years' experience working in child care under qualified supervision. | • Knowledge and understanding of developmental characteristics of 3- to 5-year-olds. <br>• Independence and competence in assigned tasks. <br>• Ability to respond appropriately to preschoolers' needs. <br>• Verbal and written communication skills. <br>• Recognition of signs of illness and safety hazards. <br>• Pediatric first aid, including rescue breathing and first aid for choking. <br>• Ability to communicate with parents. |
| Early childhood teacher | 21 | Undergraduate degree in early childhood education, child development, social work, nursing, or other child-related field, OR a combination of college coursework and experience under qualified supervision. Also, 1 year's experience, OR one semester practicum, OR associate degree and 1 year's experience, OR CDA credential, 2 years' experience, and one additional course in early childhood education, OR four courses in child development. | • Competence in the care and education of young children. |
| Early childhood associate teacher | 18 | CDA credential or associate degree in early childhood education or child development. Six or more months' experience in child care. | • Competence in the care and education of young children. |

| Children Aged 3–5 Years | | | |
|---|---|---|---|
| **Title/Role Responsibility** | **Age** | **Education** | **Skills/Experience** |
| Early childhood teacher assistant | 18 | High school diploma or GED. Participation in ongoing training. | • Competence in assigned tasks.<br>• Ability to respond appropriately to young children's needs. |
| Aide | 18 | On-the-job training. | • Ability to nurture children.<br>• Sound judgment.<br>• Ability to follow instructions.<br>• Ability to carry out assigned tasks under supervision of another staff member. |
| Health advocate | 18 | Health training related to development and care for 3- to 5-year olds. Licensed as lead teacher, teacher, or associate teacher, or shall be a health professional or social worker employed by and at the facility. | • Knowledge and understanding of developmental characteristics of 3- to 5-year-olds.<br>• Ability to respond appropriately to these children's needs.<br>• Verbal and written communication skills.<br>• Recognition of signs of illness and safety hazards.<br>• Pediatric first aid, including rescue breathing and first aid for choking. |
| Large family home caregiver | 21 | High school diploma or GED. CDA credential, associate or undergraduate degree in early childhood education or child development, OR coursework in child growth and development plus 1 year's experience in a facility or as a licensed small family home caregiver. Preservice training in health management in child care. | • Knowledge and understanding of child development.<br>• Ability to respond appropriately to the needs of 3- to 5-year olds.<br>• Verbal and written communication skills.<br>• Recognition of signs of illness and safety hazards.<br>• Ability to communicate with parents.<br>• Pediatric first aid, including rescue breathing and first aid for choking. |
| Small family home caregiver | 21 | Preservice training in health management in child care. Ongoing training courses related to care specific to this age group. | • Knowledge and understanding of child development.<br>• Ability to respond appropriately to the needs of 3- to 5-year-olds.<br>• Verbal communication skills.<br>• Recognition of signs of illness and safety hazards.<br>• Pediatric first aid, including rescue breathing and first aid for choking.<br>• Ability to communicate with parents. |

| School-Age Children | | | |
|---|---|---|---|
| **Title/Role Responsibility** | **Age** | **Education** | **Skills/Experience** |
| Director | 21 | Undergraduate degree in early childhood education, elementary education, child development, recreation or other child-related field, OR a combination of college coursework and experience under qualified supervision and 2 years' experience working with school-age children. Coursework in business administration or business-related experience. Preservice training in child development, early childhood education, and health management in child care. Directors of large centers meet more stringent qualifications. | • Knowledge and understanding of child development.<br>• Administrative and management skills.<br>• Verbal and written communication skills.<br>• Capability in curriculum design.<br>• Knowledge of community resources.<br>• Pediatric first aid, including rescue breathing and first aid for choking. |
| Group leader | 21 | Undergraduate or master's degree in early childhood education or child development (covering ages 0 to 8 or 3 to 8), elementary education, recreation, or a related field. Licensed as lead teacher, teacher, or associate teacher. Education in child development and programming specific to school-age children and supervised experience specific to this age group. Training in child development and education appropriate for school-age children. One or more years' experience in child care under qualified supervision. | • Knowledge and understanding of developmental characteristics of 5- to 12-year-olds.<br>• Independence and competence in assigned tasks.<br>• Verbal and written communication skills.<br>• Recognition of signs of illness and safety hazards.<br>• Pediatric first aid, including rescue breathing and first aid for choking. |
| Aide | 18 | On-the-job training. | • Ability to nurture children.<br>• Sound judgment.<br>• Ability to follow instructions.<br>• Ability to carry out assigned tasks under supervision of another staff member. |
| Health advocate | 18 | Health training related to development and care of school-age children. Licensed as lead teacher, teacher, or associate teacher, or shall be a health professional or social worker employed by and at the facility. | • Knowledge of the social and emotional needs and developmental tasks of 5- to 12-year-olds.<br>• Verbal and written communication skills.<br>• Recognition of signs of illness and safety hazards.<br>• Pediatric first aid, including rescue breathing and first aid for choking. |

# Appendix D: continued

| School-Age Children | | | |
|---|---|---|---|
| **Title/Role Responsibility** | **Age** | **Education** | **Skills/Experience** |
| Large family home caregiver | 21 | High school diploma or GED. CDA credential, associate or undergraduate degree in early childhood education or child development, OR coursework in child growth and development plus 1 year's experience in a facility. Preservice training in health management in child care. | • Knowledge of, and competence in dealing with, school-age children's skills and behavior.<br>• Ability to respond appropriately to these children's needs.<br>• Verbal and written communication skills.<br>• Recognition of signs of illness and safety hazards.<br>• Ability to communicate with parents.<br>• Pediatric first aid, including rescue breathing and first aid for choking. |
| Small family home caregiver | 21 | Preservice training in health management in child care. Ongoing training courses related to care specific to this age group. | • Knowledge of, and competence in dealing with, school-age children's skills and behavior.<br>• Ability to respond appropriately to the needs of 5- to 12-year-olds.<br>• Verbal communication skills.<br>• Recognition of signs of illness and safety hazards.<br>• Ability to communicate with parents.<br>• Pediatric first aid skills, including rescue breathing and first aid for choking. |
| **All Children (for very large centers, chains, or systems)** | | | |
| Child care nutrition specialist | 21 | Registered Dietitian designation. Undergraduate and master's degrees in nutrition. Supplemental courses in child growth and development. Two or more years' related experience. | • Expertise in nutrition consultation and training.<br>• Experience in food budgeting. |
| Child care food service manager | 18 | High school diploma or GED. Food-handler class certification; relevant nutrition coursework; 2 years' food service experience. | • Supervisory skills in food service. |
| Child care food service worker (Cook) | 18 | High school diploma or GED. Food-handler class certification; basic menu planning coursework; 1 or more years' experience in food service. | • Experience in menu planning.<br>• Experience in food preparation and service. |
| Child care food service aide | 18 | High school diploma or GED. Food-handler class certification within 1 to 2 months of employment. | |
| Transportation staff: Drivers/other attendants | 18 | Training in child passenger safety precautions. | • Pediatric first aid, including rescue breathing and first aid for choking. |
| Maintenance staff | 18 | | |

# Appendix E
## Food Components for Infants

| | 0–3 Months | 4–7 Months | 8–11 Months |
|---|---|---|---|
| **Morning** | 4–6 fluid oz. breast milk or iron-fortified formula | 4–8 fluid oz. breast milk or iron-fortified formula | 6–8 fluid oz. breast milk, iron-fortified formula, or whole cow's milk |
| | | 0–3 tablespoons dry, iron-fortified infant cereal (optional before 6 months, but introduce by 6 months) | 1–4 tablespoons fruit of appropriate consistency |
| | | | 2–4 tablespoons dry, iron-fortified infant cereal |
| **Mid-day** | 4–6 fluid oz. breast milk or iron-fortified formula | 4–8 fluid oz. breast milk or iron-fortified formula | 6–8 fluid oz. breast milk, iron-fortified formula, or whole cow's milk |
| | | 0–3 tablespoons dry, iron-fortified infant cereal (optional—see above) | 1–4 tablespoons fruit *and/or* vegetable of appropriate consistency |
| | | 0–3 tablespoons strained fruit and/or vegetable (optional, but if introduced, introduce as close to 6 months as possible) | 2–4 tablespoons dry, iron-fortified infant cereal *and/or* 1–4 tablespoons fish, lean meat,* poultry, or cooked dry beans or peas (all of appropriate consistency), *or* ½ to 1½ oz. cheese *or* 1–3 oz. cottage cheese *or* 1 egg yolk (introduce at 11 months of age) |
| **Supplement snack** | 4–6 fluid oz. breast milk or iron-fortified formula | 4–6 fluid oz. breast milk or iron-fortified formula | 2–4 fluid oz. breast milk, iron-fortified formula, or whole cow's milk, *or* 2 oz. full-strength fruit juice |
| | | | 0–½ slice hard toast or 0–2 crackers or teething biscuits (optional) suitable for infants, made from whole-grain or enriched flour |

*Note:* On the infant's arrival at the facility, the caregiver must ascertain what foods and/or formula the infant was fed at home in order to determine the infant's nutritional needs.

*Lean meat is beef, pork, or veal without visible fat. Luncheon meats and frankfurters are high in fat and are *not* considered lean meat.

*Source*: From *Caring for Our Children, National Health and Safety Performance Standards: Guidelines for Out-of-Home Child Care Programs*, a Collaborative Project. Copyright 1992 by the American Public Health Association and the American Academy of Pediatrics. Reprinted with permission.

# Appendix F
## Food Components for Toddlers, Preschoolers, and School-Age Children

### Breakfast

|  | 1–2 years | 3–5 years | 6–12 years |
|---|---|---|---|
| Milk, fluid | ½ cup | ¾ cup | 1 cup |
| Juice (full-strength) *or* fruit *or* vegetable | ¼ cup | ½ cup | ½ cup |
| Bread *and/or* cereal (whole-grain or enriched) | | | |
| Bread | ½ slice | ½ slice | 1 slice |
| Cereal | | | |
| Cold/dry *or* | ¼ cup | ⅓ cup | ¾ cup |
| Hot/cooked | ¼ cup | ¼ cup | ½ cup |

### Lunch or Supper

|  | 1–2 years | 3–5 years | 6–12 years |
|---|---|---|---|
| Milk, fluid | ½ cup | ¾ cup | 1 cup |
| Lean meat* *or* meat alternate | | | |
| Lean meat, fish, *or* poultry, cooked (lean meat without bone) | 1 ounce | 1½ ounces | 2 ounces |
| *or* Cheese | 1 ounce | 1½ ounces | 2 ounces |
| *or* Egg | 1 | 1 | 1 |
| *or* Cooked dry beans *or* peas | ¼ cup | ⅜ cup | ½ cup |
| *or* Peanut butter (smooth) | 2 tablespoons | 3 tablespoons | 4 tablespoons |
| *or* Nuts *and/or* seeds** | ½ ounce** | ¾ ounce** | 1 ounce** |
| Fruit *and/or* vegetable (two or more total) | ¼ cup | ½ cup | ¾ cup |
| Bread *or* bread alternate (whole-grain or enriched) | ½ slice | ½ slice | 1 slice |

| **Supplement (Snack)**—Select two of the four components (midmorning or midafternoon supplement) | | | |
|---|---|---|---|
| | **1–2 years** | **3–5 years** | **6–12 years** |
| Milk, fluid | ½ cup | ½ cup | 1 cup |
| Lean meat* *or* meat alternate | ½ ounce | ½ ounce | 1 ounce |
| (see page 458) *or* yogurt | ¼ cup | ¼ cup | ½ cup |
| Juice (full strength) *or* fruit *or* vegetable | ½ cup | ½ cup | ¾ cup |
| Bread *and/or* cereal (whole-grain or enriched) | | | |
|   Bread | ½ slice | ½ slice | 1 slice |
|   Cereal | | | |
|     Cold/dry *or* | ¼ cup | ⅓ cup | ¾ cup |
|     Hot/cooked | ¼ cup | ¼ cup | ½ cup |

*Note:* On the child's arrival at the facility, the caregiver must ascertain what food was fed at home in order to determine the child's nutritional needs.

*Lean meat is beef, pork, or veal without visible fat. Luncheon meats and frankfurters are high in fat and are *not* considered lean meat.

**This portion can meet only one-half of the total serving of the meat/meat alternate requirement for lunch or supper. Nuts or seeds must be combined with another meat/meat alternate to fulfill the requirement. For determining combinations, 1 ounce of nuts or seeds is equal to 1 ounce of cooked lean meat, poultry, or fish. *CAUTION:* Children under 5 are at the highest risk of choking. Any nuts and/or seeds must be served to them in a prepared food and be ground or finely chopped.

*Source:* From *Caring for Our Children, National Health and Safety Performance Standards: Guidelines for Out-of-Home Child Care Programs*, a Collaborative Project. Copyright 1992 by the American Public Health Association and the American Academy of Pediatrics. Reprinted with permission.

# Appendix G
## Get Medical Help Immediately

For some conditions, you need to get medical help immediately. When this is necessary, and you can reach the parent without delay, tell the parent to come right away. You may also have to have the parent tell the doctor that you will be calling because you are with the child. If the parent or the child's doctor is not immediately available, contact the facility's health consultant or EMS for immediate medical help.

**Tell the parent to come right away and get medical help immediately when any of the following things happen:**

- An infant under 4 months of age has an axillary temperature of 100 degrees Fahrenheit or higher or a rectal temperature of 101 degrees Fahrenheit or higher.
- A child over 4 months of age has a temperature of 105 degrees Fahrenheit or higher.
- An infant under 4 months of age has forceful vomiting (more than once) after eating.
- Any child looks or acts very ill or seems to be getting worse quickly.
- Any child has neck pain when the head is moved or touched.
- Any child has a stiff neck or severe headache.
- Any child has a seizure for the first time.
- Any child acts unusually confused.
- Any child has uneven pupils (black centers of the eyes).
- Any child has a blood-red or purple rash made up of pinhead-sized spots or bruises that are not associated with injury.
- Any child has a rash of hives or welts that appears quickly.
- Any child breathes so fast or hard that he or she cannot play, talk, cry, or drink.
- Any child has a severe stomachache that causes the child to double up and scream.
- Any child has a stomachache without vomiting or diarrhea after a recent injury, blow to the abdomen, or hard fall.
- Any child has stools that are black or have blood mixed through them.
- Any child has not urinated in more than 8 hours; the mouth and tongue look dry.
- Any child has continuous clear drainage from the nose after a hard blow to the head.

*Note for programs that provide care for sick children:* If any of the conditions listed above appear after the child's care has been planned, medical advice must be obtained before continuing child care can be provided.

Courtesy of the American Red Cross.

# Appendix H
## Injury Report Form

**Name of injured** _____

**Sex** _____

**Age** _____

**Date when injury occurred** _____

**Time when injury occurred** _____

**Location where injury occurred** _____

_____

**Description of how injury occurred** _____

_____

_____

_____

**Description of part of body involved** _____

**Name of consumer product involved (if any)** _____

**Action taken on behalf of the injured** _____

_____

_____

_____

**Was parent/legal guardian specifically advised of injury?** _____

**Was parent/legal guardian specifically advised to obtain medical attention?** _____

**Name of individual(s) involved in supervision at time of injury** _____

_____

**Name of person completing this report form** _____

**Date of completion of form** _____

*Source:* From *Caring for Our Children, National Health and Safety Performance Standards: Guidelines for Out-of-Home Child Care Programs*, a Collaborative Project. Copyright 1992 by the American Public Health Association and the American Academy of Pediatrics. Reprinted with permission.

# Appendix I
## About Poisonous Plants

### Tips about Poisonous Plants

- Keep **all** plants away from small children. Teach children never to eat unknown plants.
- Different parts of plants are poisonous. Phone the Poison Control Center before treating a child who has eaten a plant. Follow their directions. Keep an unexpired bottle of syrup of ipecac in a locked place if your policy allows. Use it only if the Poison Control Center tells you to make a child vomit.

### Poisonous Plants (not a complete list)

#### Trees and Shrubs
Black Locust
Boxwood
Elderberry
English Yew
Holly
Horse Chestnut
Mistletoe
Oak Tree
Rhododendron

#### Vegetable Garden Plants
Sprouts and green parts of potato
Rhubarb leaves
Green parts of tomato

#### Wild Plants
Bittersweet
Buttercups
Jack-in-the-pulpit
Jimson weed
Mushroom (certain ones)
Nightshade
Poison hemlock
Poison ivy, oak, sumac
Skunk cabbage

#### Flower Garden Plants
Autumn crocus
Bleeding heart
Chrysanthemum
Daffodil
Foxglove
Hyacinth
Iris
Jonquil
Lily of the valley
Morning glory
Narcissus

#### House Plants
Bird of paradise
Castor bean
Dumbcane (Dieffenbachia)
English ivy
Jequirty bean (rosary pea)
Jerusalem cherry
Mother-in-law
Oleander
Philodendron

Courtesy of the American Red Cross.

# Appendix J
## Recommended Schedule for Immunization

| Age at vaccination | Hepatitis B[*~] | DTP[*] | Polio[*] | Hib[*†] | Measles mumps rubella | Tetanus-diphtheria (Td) |
|---|:---:|:---:|:---:|:---:|:---:|:---:|
| Birth | ✔ | | | | | |
| 1–2 months | ✔ | | | | | |
| 2 months | | ✔ | ✔ | ✔ | | |
| 4 months | | ✔ | ✔ | ✔ | | |
| 6 months | | ✔ | | ✔[††] | [**] | |
| 6–18 months | ✔ | | | | | |
| 12–15 months | | | | ✔[†††] | | |
| 15 months | | | | | ✔ | |
| 15–18 months | | ✔ | ✔ | | | |
| 4–6 years | | ✔ | ✔ | | [**] | |
| 11–12 years | | | | | ✔[**] | |
| 14–16 years | | | | | | ✔ |

Adapted from recommendations of the American Academy of Pediatrics, 1992.

[*]DTP = Diphtheria, tetanus, and pertussis vaccine; Polio = poliovirus vaccine; Hib = Haemophilus b conjugate vaccine; Hepatitis B = Hepatitis B vaccine.

[**]Except where public health authorities require otherwise. Measles only vaccine may be suggested for infants at 6 months of age. Some experts recommend the second dose of M-M-R®II at 4–6 years instead of at 11–12 years.

[†]As of March, 1991, two vaccines for Haemophilus influenzae infections have been approved for use in children younger than 15 months of age. See individual manufacturers' prescribing information for details on dosing and administration.

[††]Indicated only if HIBTITER® (Lederle) is used for the primary regimen.

[†††]12–15 months for PedvaxHIB® (Merck). 15 months for HIBTITER® or PROHIBIT® (Connaught).

[~]As of March, 1992, both the AAP and the CDC recommend universal immunization of infants against Hepatitis B virus with a 3-dose series, beginning at birth or at 1–2 months of age. The AAP also recommends immunization of all adolescents whenever resources permit. Compliance with these recommendations will require a phase-in period.

The Immunization Dose Counter is a device to check immunization dates that was developed by Susan S. Aronson, M.D., F.A.A.P. It is distributed by the PA Chapter of the American Academy of Pediatrics which is solely responsible for its content. Grant support was provided by Merck Vaccine Division.

REMINDER: The content of the Immunization Dose Counter was reviewed by the Centers for Disease Control and the American Academy of Pediatrics in 1992. Check for updates annually with a pediatrician or your local Department of Health.

Copyright © 1992 by PA AAP.

Reprinted with permission of the PA Chapter of the American Academy of Pediatrics.

# Appendix K

## Recommendations for Preventive Pediatric Health Care

| | Infancy | | | | | | Early Childhood | | | | | Late Childhood | | | | | Adolescence[1] | | | |
|---|---|---|---|---|---|---|---|---|---|---|---|---|---|---|---|---|---|---|---|---|
| **Age**[2] | By 1 mo. | 2 mos. | 4 mos. | 6 mos. | 9 mos. | 12 mos. | 15 mos. | 18 mos. | 24 mos. | 3 yrs. | 4 yrs. | 5 yrs. | 6 yrs. | 8 yrs. | 10 yrs. | 12 yrs. | 14 yrs. | 16 yrs. | 18 yrs. | 20+ yrs. |
| **History** Initial/Interval | • | • | • | • | • | • | • | • | • | • | • | • | • | • | • | • | • | • | • | • |
| **Measurements** Height and Weight | • | • | • | • | • | • | • | • | • | • | • | • | • | • | • | • | • | • | • | • |
| Head Circumference | • | • | • | • | • | • | | | | | | | | | | | | | | |
| Blood Pressure | | | | | | • | • | • | • | • | • | • | • | • | • | • | • | • | • | • |
| **Sensory Screening** Vision | S | S | S | S | S | S | S | S | S | S | O | O | O | O | S | O | O | S | O | S |
| Hearing | S | S | S | S | S | S | S | S | S | S | O | O | S³ | S³ | S³ | O | S | S | O | S |
| **Devel./Behav.** Assessment[4] | • | • | • | • | • | • | • | • | • | • | • | • | • | • | • | • | • | • | • | • |
| **Physical Examination**[5] | • | • | • | • | • | • | • | • | • | • | • | • | • | • | • | • | • | • | • | • |
| **Procedures**[6] Hered./Metabolic Screening[7] | • | | | | | | | | | | | | | | | | | | | |
| Immunization[8] | | • | • | • | | • | • | • | | | • | • | | | | | • | | | |
| Tuberculin Test[9] | | | | | | • | | | • | | | | | | | | | | • | |
| Hematocrit or Hemoglobin[10] | | | | • | | | | | • | | | | | • | | | | | • | |
| Urinalysis[11] | | | | | | | | | • | | | • | | | | | | | • | |
| **Anticipatory**[12] **Guidance** | • | • | • | • | • | • | • | • | • | • | • | • | • | • | • | • | • | • | • | • |
| **Initial Dental**[13] **Referral** | | | | | | | | | | • | | | | | | | | | | |

## American Academy of Pediatrics
### Practice and Ambulatory Care
### Recommendations for Preventive Pediatric Health Care
### Committee on Practice and Ambulatory Medicine
### (September 1987)

Each child and family is unique; therefore these **Recommendations for Preventive Pediatric Health Care** are designed for the care of children who are receiving competent parenting, have no manifestations of any important health problems, and are growing and developing in satisfactory fashion. **Additional visits may become necessary** if circumstances suggest variations from normal. These guidelines represent a consensus by the Committee on Practice and Ambulatory Medicine in consultation with the membership of the American Academy of Pediatrics through the Chapter Presidents. The Committee emphasizes the great importance of **continuity of care** in comprehensive health supervision and the need to avoid **fragmentation of care.**

**A prenatal visit** by the parents for anticipatory guidance and pertinent medical history is strongly recommended.

**Health supervision** should begin with medical care of the newborn in the hospital.

**Key:** ▪ = to be performed; S = subjective, by history; O = objective, by a standard testing method.

1. Adolescent related issues (e.g. psychosocial, emotional, substance usage, and reproductive health) may necessitate more frequent health supervision.
2. If a child comes under care for the first time at any point on the schedule, or if any items are not accomplished at the suggested age, the schedule should be brought up to date at the earliest possible time.
3. At these points, history may suffice: if problem suggested, a standard testing method should be employed.
4. By history and appropriate physical examination: if suspicious, by specific objective developmental testing.
5. At each visit, a complete physical examination is essential, with infant totally unclothed, older child undressed and suitably draped.
6. These may be modified, depending upon entry point into schedule and individual need.
7. Metabolic screening (e.g., thyroid, PKU, galactosemia) should be done according to state law.
8. Schedule(s) per Report of Committee on Infectious Disease, *1986 Red Book.*
9. For low risk groups, the Committee on Infectious Diseases recommends the following options: (1) no routine testing or (2) testing at three times—infancy, preschool, and adolescence. For high risk groups, annual TB skin testing is recommended.
10. Present medical evidence suggests the need for reevaluation of the frequency and timing of hemoglobin or hematocrit tests. One determination is therefore suggested during each time period. Performance of additional tests is left to the individual practice experience.
11. Present medical evidence suggests the need for reevaluation of the frequency and timing of urinalyses. One determination is therefore suggested during each time period. Performance of additional tests is left to the individual practice experience.
12. Appropriate discussion and counselling should be an integral part of each visit for care.
13. Subsequent examinations as prescribed by dentist.

N.B.: Special chemical, immunologic, and endocrine testing are usually carried out upon specific indications. Testing other than newborn (e.g., inborn errors of metabolism, sickle disease, lead) are discretionary with the physician.

*Source: AAP News,* July 1991. Used with permission of the American Academy of Pediatrics.

# Glossary

## A

**accent**  A speech pronunciation or pattern that is characteristic of a particular group or region. [Ch. 13]

**accommodation**  According to Piaget, the process of learning about a new object or experience by creating a new mental structure. [Ch. 2]

**acting out**  Reacting to emotional stress by performing attention-getting and antisocial acts. [Ch. 17]

**activity level**  According to Thomas and Chess, a characteristic of infant temperament that refers to the tendency to be either more or less active. [Ch. 8]

**adaptability**  According to Thomas and Chess, a characteristic of infant temperament that refers to the ability to adjust to changes. [Ch. 8]

**advocate**  A person who actively promotes the cause of another. [Ch. 18]

**ages and stages approach**  An approach to studying child development that focuses on the physical, intellectual, and emotional changes that occur during various ages. [Ch. 1]

**altruism**  Behavior that is aimed at helping others and does not involve a benefit to the helper. [Ch. 11]

**amniocentesis**  A prenatal test in which amniotic fluid is removed from the mother's abdomen and analyzed to assess the health of the fetus. [Ch. 3]

**anal stage**  According to Freud, the stage between the ages of one and three during which children find pleasure in sensing and controlling their bowel movements. [Ch. 2]

**androgyny**  The idea that men and women can possess characteristics of both masculinity and femininity. [Ch. 14]

**anthropometry**  The study of human body measurement. [Ch. 12]

**Apgar scale**  A method used to assess the health of infants immediately after birth. Infants are evaluated according to appearance, pulse, grimace, activity, and respiration. [Ch. 3]

**approach/withdrawal**  According to Thomas and Chess, a characteristic of infant temperament that refers to the tendency to approach rather than withdraw in response to new stimuli. [Ch. 8]

**assimilation**  According to Piaget, the process of learning about a new object or experience by fitting it into an existing mental structure. [Ch. 2]

**attachment**  The emotional tie between one person and another. [Ch. 4]

**attention deficit disorder (ADD)**  A condition characterized by inattention, impulsivity, and hyperactivity. [Ch. 15]

**attention span**  According to Thomas and Chess, a characteristic of infant temperament that refers to the length of time an infant pursues a particular activity. [Ch. 8]

**authoritarian**  According to Baumrind, a parenting style that emphasizes obedience, respect for authority, and proper behavior. [Ch. 4]

**authoritative**  According to Baumrind, a parenting style in which parents establish rules but are willing to listen to the child's point of view and to make compromises. [Ch. 4]

**autonomy**  The ability to fend for oneself. [Ch. 9]

**avoidant attachment**  According to Ainsworth, a pattern in infant-mother relationships in which the infant does not show distress when the mother is absent and shows indifference or active aversion when the mother returns. [Ch. 8]

## B

**behaviorist**  A view of human behavior that focuses on observable and verifiable responses to stimulation. [Ch. 2]

**behavior modification** A technique that involves gradually changing a pattern of responses by rewarding or punishing certain actions. [Ch. 2]

**bias** An attitude or belief that results in unfair treatment of an individual because of his or her identity. [Ch. 5]

**birthrate** The ratio between births per year and the total population. [Ch. 4]

**bonding** The loving and accepting attitude a mother takes toward her baby. [Ch. 8]

# C

**calcification** The process by which bones harden through the deposit of calcium salts in body tissues. [Ch. 6]

**cardinality** The concept that when a person counts a group of objects, the number of objects is represented by the number word assigned to the last object counted. [Ch. 13]

**carrier** A person who has a recessive gene for a disease or abnormality. [Ch. 3]

**centration** According to Piaget, the tendency of children in the preoperational stage (ages two to seven) to focus on only one aspect of a problem. [Ch. 13]

**cephalocaudal** Referring to a pattern of physical growth in which the upper body of an organism develops before the lower body. [Ch. 6]

**child abuse** A nonaccidental injury or pattern of injuries to a child for which there is no "reasonable" explanation (National Committee for Prevention of Child Abuse). [Ch. 5]

**child development** The study of how children change over time from infancy to adolescence. [Ch. 1]

**chorionic villi sampling** A prenatal test that involves analysis of a sample of the placenta for indications of genetic or developmental defects. [Ch. 3]

**chromosome** A threadlike body found in all cells that contains groups of genes. [Ch. 3]

**chunking** Grouping small bits of related information to make them easier to remember. [Ch. 2]

**classical conditioning** A process of learning that involves associating a particular response with a neutral stimulus. [Ch. 2]

**class inclusion** According to Piaget, the ability to comprehend a subclass of objects and its place within a larger class of objects. [Ch. 16]

**clinical method** Observational research that focuses on individual subjects. [Ch. 1]

**code switching** Changing speech patterns in different social situations. [Ch. 16]

**cognition** Processes performed by the mind and brain, such as perceiving, remembering, and thinking. [Ch. 2]

**cognitive development theory** Piaget's explanation of the mental development of children in terms of the physical development of the brain and interaction with the environment. [Ch. 2]

**communication** The act of conveying a message to another through speaking, writing, or body language. [Ch. 7]

**compensatory education** Educational programs that try to make up for disadvantages experienced by children early in life. [Ch. 13]

**complementary and reciprocal rituals** Play activities that require the participation of two or more people. [Ch. 11]

**concept** A mental representation for a group of related objects or events. [Ch. 10]

**conditioning** According to behaviorist theory, the process by which learning occurs. [Ch. 2]

**conscience** The inner voice that tells a person the difference between right and wrong. [Ch. 17]

**conservation** According to Piaget, the idea that the same quantity can look different under different circumstances. [Ch. 13]

**control group** The group of subjects in an experiment that does not receive any special treatment or training. See also *experimental group*. [Ch. 1]

**convergence** The coordination of the movement of both eyes so that they focus on a nearby object. [Ch. 6]

**cooperative play** According to Parten, a type of play in which children work together toward a joint goal. [Ch. 11]

**coordination of secondary schemes stage** The fourth substage in Piaget's sensorimotor period, when infants learn to combine and coordinate previously learned behaviors to reach a goal and develop a sense of purpose about their actions. [Ch. 7]

**correlational study** An observational study that examines the relationship between two variables. [Ch. 1]

**cortex** The outer layer of the brain, in which the areas responsible for thinking and problem solving are located. [Ch. 6]

**cortical association areas** The parts of the cortex that form mental connections between the sensory and motor sections of the brain. [Ch. 9]

**creative vocabulary** New words that children make up if they do not know the actual word for something. [Ch. 13]

**creativity** The ability to think of new and unusual solutions to problems and to view things from a different perspective. [Ch. 16]

**critical period** A period of sensitivity during which children are most responsive to developmental change. [Ch. 1]

**cross-cultural study** A study that compares children of different cultural backgrounds to determine how they are alike and different. [Ch. 1]

**cross-sectional study** A study that examines a single developmental change in a large group of children of varying ages. [Ch. 1]

**D**

**deciduous teeth** The first set of teeth, also known as primary, milk, or "baby" teeth. [Ch. 15]

**defense mechanism** According to Freud, a process the mind uses to protect itself when the ego is faced with a conflict that it cannot handle rationally. [Ch. 2]

**deferred imitation** The duplication of an action hours or days after it was observed. [Ch. 10]

**Denver Developmental Screening Test** A test that assesses motor, social, and language development in children under age three. [Ch. 6]

**desensitization** The gradual, systematic exposure to a feared object with the goal of reducing or eliminating the fear. [Ch. 14]

**developmental-interactionist** An approach to early childhood education that emphasizes children and their interests rather than subject matter. [Ch. 18]

**developmentally appropriate** Referring to programs and practices that are designed to meet the needs of children of specific ages and levels of development. [Ch. 1]

**dialect** A version of a language characteristic of a distinct ethnic group or geographical region. [Ch. 13]

**differentiation** The progression of physical development from the general to the specific. [Ch. 6]

**disability** "A physical or mental impairment that substantially limits one or more major life activities" (Americans with Disabilities Act of 1990). [Ch. 5]

**discontinuity** The degree to which the atmosphere of a child care program and the atmosphere of a family do not match. [Ch. 4]

**discrimination** In behaviorist theory, the ability to differentiate among stimuli that are similar. [Ch. 2]

**disorganized attachment** According to Ainsworth, a pattern in infant-mother relationships in which the infant appears depressed when the mother is absent and displays disturbed behavior when the mother returns. [Ch. 8]

**distractibility** According to Thomas and Chess, a characteristic of infant temperament that refers to the tendency for other stimuli to alter the direction of ongoing behavior. [Ch. 8]

**diversity** Differences in racial, religious, and ethnic background. [Ch. 5]

**DNA (deoxyribonucleic acid)** The chemical of which genes are made that carries instructions telling cells how to grow and function. [Ch. 3]

**dominant gene** A gene that suppresses the action of another, weaker gene. [Ch. 3]

**dysfunctional family**   A family in which the parents are overwhelmed by various problems, such as drug or alcohol abuse, and do not care for and nurture the children. [Ch. 4]

**dyslexia**   A disability in reading. [Ch. 15]

### E

**eclectic**   Based on several different philosophies or approaches. [Ch. 18]

**ecological approach**   A view of child development that focuses on the interactions between children and all the people, places, and processes that make up their environment. [Ch. 1]

**ego**   According to Freud, the rational part of the mind that enables a person to work out effective ways to satisfy the id while obeying the orders of the superego. [Ch. 2]

**egocentric thinker**   According to Piaget, a child in the preoperational stage (ages two to seven), who does not yet have the ability to understand another person's point of view. [Ch. 10]

**Electra complex**   According to Freud, the conflict that girls experience when they feel sexually attracted to their father and jealous of their mother. [Ch. 14]

**embryo**   A developing human organism in the uterus between the third and eighth week of pregnancy. [Ch. 3]

**emotional abuse**   The use of words or actions that make an individual feel rejected, ignored, or terrorized. [Ch. 5]

**emotional development**   The evolution of emotions, personality, identity, moral judgment, and social skills. [Ch. 1]

**engrossment**   A father's feelings of extreme happiness, excitement, and interest in his baby immediately following the baby's birth. [Ch. 8]

**enrichment**   Additional educational activities that are provided to gifted children in order to challenge their mental abilities. [Ch. 16]

**equilibration**   According to Piaget, the process by which children achieve a balance by revising their system of thinking to handle new situations. [Ch. 2]

**ethology**   The study of how behavior patterns promote survival in a natural environment. [Ch. 2]

**executive control**   The ability to manage one's own thought process. [Ch. 16]

**experimental group**   The group of subjects in an experiment that receives special treatment or training. [Ch. 1]

**experimental method**   A method of conducting research by systematically controlling conditions to investigate one variable. [Ch. 1]

**extended family**   A type of family arrangement in which the parents and children live with other relatives, such as grandparents, uncles, aunts, and cousins. [Ch. 4]

### F

**family day care**   A child care arrangement in which an individual cares for a small number of children in her own home. [Ch. 4]

**farsighted**   Able to see distant objects better than near objects. [Ch. 15]

**fetal alcohol syndrome**   A condition characterized by slow growth, mental retardation, and physical abnormalities in infants. It is caused by the mother's consumption of alcohol during pregnancy. [Ch. 3]

**fetus**   A developing human organism between the ninth week of pregnancy and birth. [Ch. 3]

**fine motor skills**   Abilities that involve the use of the small muscles of the body. [Ch. 9]

**first acquired adaptations stage**   The second substage in Piaget's sensorimotor period, when infants move beyond reflexive behavior to take action on their own. [Ch. 7]

**fontanelle**   Commonly referred to as a soft spot, the area on an infant's head where the bones of the skull have not yet fused together. [Ch. 6]

**formal operational thought**   The ability found in the highest of Piaget's stages of cognitive development to classify and think logically about abstract concepts. [Ch. 16]

## G

**gender constancy**    The concept that one's gender never changes. [Ch. 14]

**gender roles**    The outward behaviors and attitudes that society regards as appropriate for men and women in each culture. [Ch. 14]

**gender schema**    A basic script about how males and females behave. [Ch. 17]

**gene**    A minuscule structure found in every living cell that contains the characteristics a child receives from his or her parents. [Ch. 3]

**generalization**    In behaviorist theory, the process by which an unconditioned stimulus that is similar to a conditioned stimulus evokes a conditioned response. [Ch. 2]

**genotype**    An individual's underlying genetic makeup. [Ch. 3]

**gestation**    The period in which an organism develops in the mother's uterus. [Ch. 3]

**gifted children**    Children who show the potential for outstanding achievement in intellectual, artistic, or other creative areas. [Ch. 5]

**global concept**    According to Mandler, the most basic category that children establish to organize and classify information. [Ch. 10]

**grammar**    The rules for forming words and sentences. [Ch. 10]

**gross motor skills**    Abilities that involve the use of the large muscles of the body. [Ch. 9]

**guilt**    The feeling of self-reproach that people experience when they do something that results in disapproval or punishment from others. [Ch. 14]

## H

**habituation**    The process in which infants lose interest in an object once it becomes familiar. [Ch. 7]

**hand-eye coordination**    The ability of the brain to organize hand movement according to visual perception. [Ch. 7]

**heredity**    The characteristics a child receives from his or her parents and earlier ancestors. [Ch. 3]

**holophrase**    A sentence made up of a single word. [Ch. 10]

**hostile aggression**    Belligerent behavior intended to hurt someone else. [Ch. 14]

**hyperactivity**    A behavior pattern often associated with attention deficit disorder in which children are overly active, restless, and easily distracted. [Ch. 15]

**hypothesis**    A reasonable prediction of an answer to a problem or question. [Ch. 1]

## I

**id**    According to Freud, the part of the mind that contains the basic instincts that drive human behavior. [Ch. 2]

**identification**    According to Freud, a defense mechanism in which children adopt the behavior, values, and attitudes of a person they admire. [Ch. 14]

**identity**    According to Piaget, the idea that objects remain the same even though their appearance changes. [Ch. 16]

**identity versus identity confusion**    The fifth stage of Erikson's theory of psychosocial development, when adolescents organize their self-concept to conform to societal demands. [Ch. 17]

**immunization**    The administration of a substance that prevents an individual from contracting a specific disease. [Ch. 6]

**individualized educational plan (IEP)**    An educational program designed specifically to meet the individual needs of a child with a disability (Education for All Handicapped Children Act of 1975). [Ch. 5]

**induction**    The technique of telling children about the consequences that their behavior has for others. [Ch. 11]

**industry versus inferiority stage**    The fourth stage of Erikson's theory of psychosocial development, in which children strive to master the skills that society values. [Ch. 17]

**information processing theory** An approach to learning in which memory and other mental processes are explained with reference to computer functions. [Ch. 2]

**insecure attachment** According to Ainsworth, a pattern of behavior shown by children with a weak emotional tie to their mother. [Ch. 4]

**instrumental aggression** Belligerent behavior that has a goal. [Ch. 14]

**intellectual development** The development of mental processes, such as perception, memory, learning, and imagination. Also called cognitive development. [Ch. 1]

**intelligence quotient** A measurement of a subject's intelligence compared to the average performance of other people of the same age. [Ch. 13]

**intensity of reactions** According to Thomas and Chess, a characteristic of infant temperament that refers to the energy level of both positive and negative responses. [Ch. 8]

**item of attachment** A familiar object that children cling to when they are anxious or afraid. [Ch. 14]

# L

**language** A system of symbols organized by grammatical rules that is used to convey messages to others. [Ch. 7]

**laterality** The tendency to use one side of the body over the other. [Ch. 15]

**learned helplessness** A phenomenon in which past failures lead a person to believe that his or her performance or situation cannot be improved. [Ch.17]

**learning disability** A disorder in the basic process of understanding or the use of language or numerical concepts. [Ch. 5]

**least restrictive environment** The least specialized classroom in which children with disabilities will be able to learn. [Ch. 5]

**levels of processing theory** The idea that people tend to forget information stored at shallow percep-

tual levels and retain information stored at deeper levels. [Ch. 13]

**libido** According to Freud, the force that seeks the satisfaction of basic biological urges. [Ch. 2]

**locomotion** The ability to change position and move from place to place. [Ch. 6]

**longitudinal study** A study that examines developmental change in individuals over a long period of time. [Ch. 1]

**long-term memory** According to information processing theory, the storage of information in the brain over a period of days, months, and years. [Ch. 16]

**looking-glass self** A metaphor used by Cooley that refers to the importance of interactions with other people in an individual's development of a sense of self. [Ch. 11]

# M

**mainstreaming** Integrating children with special needs into regular classrooms. [Ch. 5]

**mapping** In language development, the process of matching a word to its meaning. [Ch. 10]

**maturation** The appearance of a genetically determined physical trait or pattern of behavior over time. [Ch. 1]

**menarche** The first menstruation, which signals that the uterus is mature. [Ch. 15]

**mental combination** According to Piaget, a child's ability to keep in mind two or more representations of an object at the same time. [Ch. 10]

**metacognition** Knowledge or awareness of the thinking process. [Ch. 16]

**metacommunication** Knowledge or awareness of the language and communication process. [Ch. 16]

**metamemory** Knowledge or awareness of the memory process. [Ch. 16]

**mnemonic device** A strategy that is used to remember information more efficiently. [Ch. 16]

**model** In social learning theory, a person whom another person observes and learns from. [Ch. 2]

**morality** The system of rules and principles that people and societies adopt to govern their behavior toward others. [Ch. 14]

**motherese** A slow, high-pitched, repetitive form of speech that adults often use when speaking to infants. [Ch. 7]

**motivation** The need or incentive to learn and the desire to succeed. [Ch. 16]

**multifactorial characteristic** A trait determined by the interaction of genetic predisposition and environmental conditions. [Ch. 3]

**myelin** The fatty, insulating substance in the brain that helps nerve cells transmit messages faster and more efficiently. [Ch. 6]

## N

**nativist theory** The view that language acquisition is such a complex and difficult task that children must be born with a biological mechanism for learning language. [Ch. 10]

**naturalistic observation** The observation of a group of children in a natural, uncontrolled setting. [Ch. 1]

**nature versus nurture** The debate over the relative influence of heredity and environment. [Ch. 1]

**nearsighted** Able to see near objects better than distant objects. [Ch. 15]

**negative reinforcement** The process of rewarding an action by removing an unpleasant stimulus. [Ch. 2]

**neonate** A newborn infant. [Ch. 3]

**networking** Building contacts with other people to advance business or career interests. [Ch. 18]

**normal** Referring to behavior or characteristics that a majority of children exhibit at any given age. [Ch. 1]

## O

**obesity** A condition characterized by an excess of body fat. [Ch. 15]

**object constancy** The ability to maintain the image of a person or object in one's mind. [Ch. 11]

**object permanence** The understanding that objects continue to exist when they are out of sight. [Ch. 7]

**observational method** A method of conducting research in which children are studied by means of direct observation techniques in a nonexperimental environment. [Ch. 1]

**Oedipus complex** According to Freud, the conflict that boys experience when they feel sexually attracted to their mother and jealous of their father. [Ch. 14]

**onlooker behavior** According to Parten, an activity in which children watch others play. [Ch. 11]

**operant conditioning** A type of learning that occurs when a certain action is rewarded or punished. [Ch. 2]

**oral stage** According to Freud, the stage in personality development that occurs in the first year of life when an individual is focused on pleasurable sensations from the mouth. [Ch. 2]

**orienting response** The reaction of newborns to sound by turning their head toward it. [Ch. 7]

**ossification** The growth of bones through the conversion of the cartilage or membrane at bone ends into bone. [Ch. 6]

**overextension** The application of a word to an object outside the group of objects to which it usually refers. [Ch. 10]

**overregularization** The tendency to overapply a grammatical rule. [Ch. 10]

## P

**parallel play** According to Parten, a type of play in which children engage in the same activity as other children without interacting. [Ch. 11]

**parenting style** The methods each parent uses to control, educate, and discipline his or her child. [Ch. 4]

**peer group** A loosely knit group of people who are usually about the same age, live in the same area, and have similar socioeconomic backgrounds. [Ch. 17]

**peer pressure** The demand for a high degree of conformity to a group's values, attitudes, and behavior. [Ch. 17]

**period of concrete operations** The third stage in Piaget's theory of cognitive development, which is characterized by the ability to classify and think logically about concrete objects. [Ch. 16]

**permissive** According to Baumrind, a parenting style in which parents set few rules, tolerate a wide range of destructive behavior, and avoid intervening in their children's activities. [Ch. 4]

**personality** The individual traits and temperament of a person. [Ch. 2]

**phallic stage** According to Freud, the stage between ages three and five when children discover pleasure in the sensations of their sex organs. [Ch. 2]

**phenotype** The observable traits or characteristics of an individual. [Ch. 3]

**phobia** According to Freud, an irrational fear of a particular object or situation. [Ch. 2]

**physical development** The changes that take place in the body, including growth and the development of the senses, muscles, and motor skills. [Ch. 1]

**plasticity** The capacity of the brain to be shaped by experience. [Ch. 6]

**play** According to Garvey, a spontaneous, pleasurable, and voluntary activity that has no practical objective or goal. [Ch. 10]

**positive interaction** The actions that a mother takes to nurture, stimulate, and encourage her child and the child's response to those actions. [Ch. 4]

**prelinguistic speech** A period of language development when infants use sounds to communicate. [Ch. 7]

**premoral level** According to Kohlberg, the lowest level of moral development, in which children behave morally to avoid punishment and gain rewards. [Ch. 14]

**preoperational period** The second stage in Piaget's theory of cognitive development (lasting from two to seven or eight years of age), during which children begin to use objects to represent other objects and to use mental images. [Ch. 2]

**primary circular reaction** According to Piaget, a sequence of behavior in which an infant repeats an action because it is pleasurable. [Ch. 7]

**primitive reflex** A reflex controlled by the subcortex that gradually disappears during the first year of life. [Ch. 6]

**private speech** According to Vygotsky, the speech of children talking to themselves to practice language and behavior. [Ch. 13]

**prosocial behavior** Actions that are aimed at helping others. [Ch. 11]

**protective reflex** A reflex, such as breathing or coughing, that is essential to basic survival and that grows stronger during childhood. [Ch. 6]

**proximodistal** Referring to a pattern of physical growth that starts from the center and continues outward. [Ch. 6]

**psychoanalysis** A type of therapy developed by Freud that is designed to make people aware of their unconscious motivation. [Ch. 2]

**psychosocial** Referring to the key role an individual's social relationships play in Erikson's stages of development. [Ch. 2]

**puberty** The period when the sex organs mature and secondary sex characteristics develop, making reproduction possible. [Ch. 15]

**punishment** An unpleasant action intended to stop a behavior or prevent it from reoccurring. [Ch. 2]

**qualitative** Involving changes in kind. [Ch. 1]

**quality of mood** According to Thomas and Chess, a characteristic of infant temperament that refers to the relative frequency of positive versus negative behavior. [Ch. 8]

**quantitative**   Involving changes in amount. [Ch. 1]

### R

**random selection**   A method of selection based solely on chance. [Ch. 1]

**rapid eye movement (REM)**   Referring to a stage of sleep during which dreaming occurs. [Ch. 8]

**recall**   The ability to retrieve information from memory when no example of that information is present. [Ch. 13]

**recessive gene**   A weak gene that is unable to produce a trait by itself. [Ch. 3]

**recognition**   The ability to identify an object as something that has been seen in the past. [Ch. 13]

**reflex**   An automatic, involuntary response to external stimulation. [Ch. 6]

**reflexive stage**   The first substage in Piaget's sensorimotor period, when infants can only make simple movements based on reflexes. [Ch. 7]

**regression**   According to Freud, a defense mechanism by which a person temporarily reverts back to an earlier stage of development. [Ch. 2]

**rehearsal**   The repeating of information to be memorized in order to remember it more effectively. [Ch. 13]

**reinforcement**   The process of rewarding an action to increase the likelihood that it will be repeated. [Ch. 2]

**repression**   According to Freud, a defense mechanism by which a person blocks a memory or urge from consciousness. [Ch. 2]

**resistant or ambivalent attachment**   According to Ainsworth, a pattern in infant-mother relationships in which the infant becomes distressed when the mother leaves and resists the mother when she returns. [Ch. 8]

**response**   A person's reaction to a stimulus. [Ch. 2]

**reversibility**   The idea that changes in appearance can be reversed. [Ch. 16]

**rhythmicity**   According to Thomas and Chess, a characteristic of infant temperament that refers to the predictability or unpredictability of functions such as sleeping, eating, and defecating. [Ch. 8]

**rough-and-tumble play**   Active play that involves running, chasing, and make-believe fighting. [Ch. 12]

### S

**scaffolding**   According to Vygotsky, the process of building on experience to provide new information. [Ch. 10]

**scheme**   According to Piaget, a mental structure that children develop to gain knowledge and act upon their environment. [Ch. 2]

**school phobia**   An irrational fear of school. [Ch. 17]

**scientific method**   A method of conducting research that involves formulating a question to be answered, developing a hypothesis, designing and carrying out ways to test the hypothesis, gathering data, and finally drawing conclusions from the data. [Ch. 1]

**script**   According to Nelson, a mental representation of a routine event that children use to learn about new situations. [Ch. 10]

**secondary circular reaction**   According to Piaget, a sequence of behavior in which infants repeat an action because it gets a response. [Ch. 7]

**secure attachment**   According to Ainsworth, a pattern of behavior shown by children with a strong emotional tie to their mother. [Ch. 4]

**selective attention**   The ability to pay attention to information that must be remembered and to ignore other information. [Ch. 16]

**self-concept**   The way that an individual sees himself or herself. [Ch. 17]

**self-esteem**   The value an individual places on himself or herself. [Ch. 17]

**self-fulfilling prophecy**   A phenomenon characterized by an individual responding to the expectations of another by acting in ways that confirm those expectations. [Ch. 5]

**self-recognition** The ability to recognize oneself. [Ch. 11]

**self-regulation** The ability to control one's behavior. [Ch. 11]

**semantics** The meaning of words. [Ch. 10]

**sensorimotor period** The first stage in Piaget's theory of cognitive development, during which children develop action schemes based on inborn reflexes and interactions with the environment. [Ch. 2]

**sensory memory** According to information processing theory, an awareness of information taken in by the senses that lasts only a few seconds. [Ch. 16]

**separation-individuation** According to Mahler, the sense of self as separate from others that children develop between the ages of five months and three years. [Ch. 11]

**seriation** The arrangement of a number of objects in ascending or descending order. [Ch. 16]

**sexual identity** The understanding of children that they are male or female. [Ch. 14]

**shaping** A procedure in which behavior to be learned is divided into stages. [Ch. 2]

**sibling rivalry** A pattern of behavior in which siblings vie for parental attention and act aggressively toward each other. [Ch. 4]

**skeletal age** The degree of ossification of the bones. [Ch. 12]

**social competence** The ability to form and maintain relationships and solve interpersonal conflicts. [Ch. 13]

**social construction of knowledge** According to Vygotsky, the acquisition of cognitive skills and new information through social interaction. [Ch. 13]

**social learning** Learning by observing how others behave and interact in a social environment. [Ch. 2]

**social monologue** A situation in which two children are talking to each other but neither seems to be listening or responding to what the other is saying. [Ch. 13]

**social referencing** The practice of using the reactions of another person to guide one's own behavior. [Ch. 11]

**social speech** Speech intended to communicate with others. [Ch. 13]

**sociodramatic play** Elaborate episodes of pretend play involving interaction with others. [Ch. 13]

**solitary play** According to Parten, play involving individual children not interacting with anyone else. [Ch. 11]

**standards of behavior** Principles of proper and improper conduct. [Ch. 11]

**stimulus** An object or action that provokes a response. [Ch. 2]

**stressor** An event or situation that produces a high level of stress. [Ch. 17]

**subcortex** The brain stem and midbrain, which regulate basic biological functions such as breathing. [Ch. 6]

**superego** According to Freud, the part of the mind that contains ideas about morality and acceptable behavior. [Ch. 2]

**support system** A group of people, composed of family members, friends, and health and child care professionals, that help a family function effectively. [Ch. 4]

**symbolic play** Play involving the ability to pretend that an object or person is something or someone else. [Ch. 10]

# T

**telegraphic speech** Two-word sentence combinations. [Ch. 10]

**temperament** An individual's emotions, moods, and ways of interacting with the environment. [Ch. 8]

**teratogen** Any environmental factor that can harm fetal development. [Ch. 3]

**tertiary circular reaction stage** Substage 5 of Piaget's sensorimotor period, when infants begin to manipulate the same objects in several different ways or different objects in the same ways to observe the results. [Ch. 7]

**theory**   A logical set of ideas designed to explain a group of observations in a particular field. [Ch. 2]

**threshold of responsiveness**   According to Thomas and Chess, a characteristic of infant temperament that refers to the amount of stimulation needed to make an infant react. [Ch. 8]

**toilet training**   The process through which children learn to control their bladder and bowel movements and to use the toilet successfully. [Ch. 8]

**topical approach**   An approach that examines major areas of child development separately over a long period of time. [Ch. 1]

**tracking**   Following a slowly moving object with the eyes. [Ch. 6]

**transitivity**   The ability to compare objects mentally and make logical inferences. [Ch. 16]

## U

**ultrasound**   A prenatal test that uses high-frequency sound waves to detect structural abnormalities in a fetus. [Ch. 3]

**unconscious**   According to Freud, the part of the mind that is outside of awareness. [Ch. 2]

**underextension**   The application of a word to an object in some circumstances but not in others. [Ch. 10]

**universal precautions**   Procedures for handling blood and body fluids to prevent infection with a communicable disease. [Ch. 5]

## V

**visual acuity**   The ability to see in fine detail. [Ch. 6]

**visual fixation**   The ability to look at an object with sustained attention. [Ch. 6]

## W

**well-baby check**   A periodic visit to a pediatrician during the first two years of life to monitor a child's growth, development, and behavior. [Ch. 6]

**working memory**   According to information processing theory, the active yet temporary storage of information that a person is currently using. [Ch. 16]

## Z

**zone of proximal development**   According to Vygotsky, a state of readiness to proceed to the next level of mental skill or ability. [Ch. 13]

**zygote**   A cell produced when male and female sex cells unite. [Ch. 3]

# References

ABEL, E. L. (1980). Fetal alcohol syndrome: Behavioral teratology. *Psychology Bulletin, 87*, 28–50.

ABRAMOVITCH, R., CORTER, C., PEPLER, D. J., & STANHOPE, L. (1986). Sibling and peer interaction: A final follow-up and comparison. *Child Development, 57*, 217–229.

ABRAMOVITCH, R., PEPLER, D., & CORTER, C. (1982). Patterns in sibling interaction among preschool-aged children. In M. E. Lamb & B. Sutton-Smith (Eds.), *Sibling relationships: Their nature and significance across the life span*. Hillsdale, NJ: Erlbaum.

AINSWORTH, M. (1973). The development of infant-mother attachment. In B. Caldwell & H. Ricciuti (Eds.), *Review of child development research* (Vol. 3). Chicago: University of Illinois Press.

AINSWORTH, M. D. S., & WITTIG, B. A. (1969). Attachment and the exploratory behavior of one-year-olds in a strange situation. In B. M. Foss (Ed.), *Determinants of infant behavior* (Vol. 4, pp. 113–136). London: Methuen.

ALFORD, B. B., & BOGLE, M. L. (1982). *Nutrition during the life cycle*. Englewood Cliffs, NJ: Prentice-Hall.

ALLEN, K. E. (1992). *The exceptional child: Mainstreaming in early childhood education* (2nd ed.). Albany, NY: Delmar.

AMERICAN ACADEMY OF PEDIATRICS. (1973). The ten-state nutrition survey: A pediatric perspective. *Pediatrics, 51*(6), 1095–1099.

AMERICAN ACADEMY OF PEDIATRICS. (1992). *Immunization dose counter*. Chicago: Author.

AMERICAN ACADEMY OF PEDIATRICS TASK FORCE ON INFANT POSITIONING AND SIDS. (1992). Positioning and SIDS. *Pediatrics, 89*(6).

*American Medical Association Encyclopedia of Medicine*. (1989). New York: Random House.

ANAND, K. J., & HICKEY, P. R. (1987). Pain and its effect in the human neonate and fetus. *New England Journal of Medicine, 317*(21), 1321–1329.

ANNIS, L. (1978). *The child before birth*. Ithaca, NY: Cornell University Press.

AREND, R., GOVE, F., & SROUFE, L. A. (1979). Continuity of individual adaptation from infancy to kindergarten: A predictive study of ego-resiliency and curiosity in preschoolers. *Child Development, 50*, 950–959.

ASHER, S. R., RENSHAW, P. D., & HYMEL, S. (1982). Peer relations and the development of social skills. In S. G. Moore & C. R. Cooper (Eds.), *The young child: Reviews of research* (Vol. 3). Washington, DC: National Association for the Education of Young Children.

ASLIN, R. N., PISONI, D. B., & JUSCZYK, P. W. (1983). Auditory development and speech in infancy. In P. H. Mussen et al. (Eds.), *Handbook of child psychology* (4th ed.): *Vol. 2. Infancy and developmental psychobiology*. New York: Wiley.

ASSOCIATION OF TEACHER EDUCATORS & NATIONAL ASSOCIATION FOR THE EDUCATION OF YOUNG CHILDREN. (1991). Early childhood certification. *Young Children, 47*(1), 16–21.

BAILEY, D. A. (1977). The growing child and the need for physical activity. In R. C. Smart & M. S. Smart (Eds.), *Readings in child development and relationships*. New York: Macmillan.

BAILLARGEON, R., & DE VOS, J. (1991). Object permanence in young infants: Further evidence. *Child Development, 62*, 1227–1246.

BALDWIN, J. M. (1987). *Social and ethical interpretations in mental development*. New York: Macmillan.

BANDURA, A. (1977). *Social learning theory*. Englewood Cliffs, NJ: Prentice-Hall.

BANKS, M. S., & SALAPATEK, P. (1983). Infant visual perception. In P. H. Mussen et al. (Eds.), *Handbook of child psychology* (4th ed.): *Vol 2. Infancy and developmental psychobiology*. New York: Wiley.

BARBERO, G. J., & SHAHEEN, E. (1967). Environmental failure to thrive: A clinical view. *Journal of Pediatrics, 71,* 639–644.

BARKLEY, R., & CUNNINGHAM, C. (1978). Do stimulant drugs improve the academic performance of hyperkinetic children? A review of outcome research. *Clinical Pediatrics, 17,* 85–93.

BARRETT, K. C. (1993, March). Origins of social emotions and self-regulation: Appreciation of "right" and "wrong." In S. Lamb (Chair), *The beginnings of morality.* Symposium conducted at the meeting of the Society for Research in Child Development, New Orleans.

BARRETT, K. C., & CAMPOS, J. J. (1987). Perspectives on emotional development: II. A functionalist approach to emotions. In J. D. Osofsky (Ed.), *Handbook of infant development* (2nd ed., pp. 555–578). New York: Wiley.

BARRETT, K. C., MACPHEE, D., & SULLIVAN, S. (1992, May). *Development of social emotions and self-regulation.* Paper presented at the meeting of the International Society for Infant Studies, Miami.

BARRETT, K. C., MORGAN, G. A., & MASLIN-COLE, C. (1993). Three studies of the development of mastery motivation during infancy and toddlerhood. In D. Messer (Ed.), *Mastery motivation: Children's investigation, persistence, and development.* London: Routledge.

BARRETT, K. C., ZAHN-WEXLER, C., & COLE, P. M. (1993). Avoiders versus amenders: Implications for the investigation of guilt and shame during toddlerhood? *Cognition and Emotion.*

BASSUK, E. L., & ROSENBERG, L. (1988). Why does family homelessness occur? A case-control study. *American Journal Of Public Health, 78*(7).

BATES, J., MASLIN, C., & FRANKEL, K. (1985). Attachment security, mother-child interaction, and temperament as predictors of behavior problem ratings at age three years. In I. Bretherton & E. Waters (Eds.), *Growing points in attachment theory and research. Monographs of the Society for Research in Child Development, 50*(Whole No. 209), 167–193.

BAUMRIND, D. (1967). Child-care practices anteceding three patterns of preschool behavior. *Genetic Psychology Monographs, 75,* 43–88.

BELSKY, J. (1988). The "effects" of infant day care reconsidered. *Early Childhood Research Quarterly, 3,* 235–272.

BEM, S. L. (1976). Probing the promise of androgyny. In A. G. Kaplan & J. P. Bean (Eds.), *Beyond sex-role stereotypes: Reading toward a psychology of androgyny.* Boston: Little, Brown.

BERMAN, P. W., & GOODMAN, V. (1984). Age and sex differences in children's responses to babies: Effects of adult caretaking requests and instructions. *Child Development, 55,* 1071–1077.

BILLER, H. D. (1981). Father absence, divorce, and personality development. In M. E. Lamb (Ed.), *The role of the father in child development* (2nd ed.). New York: Wiley Interscience.

BLAU, Z. S. (1972). Maternal aspirations, socialization and achievement of boys and girls in the working class. *Journal of Youth and Adolescence, 1,* 35–37.

BLOCK, J. H., BLOCK, J., & GJERDE, P. (1986). The personality of children prior to divorce: A prospective study. *Child Development, 57,* 827–840.

BORKE, H. (1983). Piaget's mountains revisited: Changes in the egocentric landscape. In M. Donalson, R. Grieve, & C. Pratt (Eds.), *Early childhood development and education: Readings in psychology.* New York: Guilford Press.

BORNSTEIN, M. H. (1984). A descriptive taxonomy of psychological categories used by infants. In C. Sophian (Ed.), *Origins of cognitive skills. Proceedings of the 18th Annual Carnegie Symposium on Cognition* (pp. 313–338). Hillsdale, NJ: Erlbaum.

BORNSTEIN, M. H. (1985). Human infant color vision and color perception. *Infant Behavior and Development, 8,* 109–113.

BOUCHARD, R. (1981, August). *The Minnesota study of twins reared apart: Description and preliminary findings.* Paper presented at the annual meeting of the American Psychological Association, Los Angeles.

BOWER, T. G. R., & WISHART, J. G. (1979). Towards a unity theory of development. In E. B. Thomas (Ed.), *Origins of the infant's social responsiveness.* Hillsdale, NJ: Erlbaum.

BOWERMAN, M. (1979). The acquisition of complex sentences. In P. Fletcher & M. Garman (Eds.),

*Language acquisition.* Cambridge, England: Cambridge University Press.

BOWLBY, J. (1969). *Attachment and loss: Vol. 1. Attachment.* New York: Basic Books.

BRAZELTON, T. B. (1984). *To listen to a child: Understanding the normal problems of growing up.* Reading, MA: Addison-Wesley.

BREDEKAMP, S. (1987). *Developmentally appropriate practice in early childhood programs serving children from birth through age eight.* Washington, DC: National Association for the Education of Young Children.

BRETHERTON, I., FRITZ, J., ZAHN-WEXLER, C., & RIDGEWAY, D. (1986). Learning to talk about emotions: A functionalist perspective. *Child Development, 57,* 529–548.

BRIDGES, K. M. (1930). A genetic theory of the emotions. *Journal of Genetic Psychology, 37,* 514–527.

BRONFENBRENNER, U. (1979). *The ecology of human development.* Cambridge, MA: Harvard University Press.

BRONFENBRENNER, U., & CROUTER, A. (1982). Work and family through time and space. In S. B. Kamerman and C. D. Hayes (Eds.), *Families that work: Children in a changing world.* Washington, DC: National Academy Press.

BROWN, R. (1973). *A first language: The early stages.* Cambridge, MA: Harvard University Press.

BRYANT, B. K. (1982). Sibling relationships in middle childhood. In M. E. Lamb & B. Sutton-Smith (Eds.), *Sibling relationships: Their nature and significance across the life span.* Hillsdale, NJ: Erlbaum.

BUHLER, C. (1930). *The first year of life* (P. Greenberg & R. Ribin, trans.). New York: John Day.

BUSS, A. (1980). *Self-consciousness and social anxiety.* San Francisco: Freeman.

BUSS, A. H., & PLOMIN, R. (1975). *A temperament theory of personality development.* New York: Wiley.

CALDWELL, B. M. (1977). Aggression and hostility in young children. *Young Children, 32*(2), 4–13.

CAMPOS, J. J., BERTENTHAL, B., & KERMOIAN, R. (1992). Early experience and emotional development: The emergence of wariness of heights. *Psychological Science, 3,* 61–64.

CAMPOS, J. J., HIATT, S., RAMSAY, D., HENDERSON, C., & SVEDJA, M. (1978). The emergence of fear on the visual cliff. In M. Lewis & L. Rosenblum (Eds.), *The origins of affect.* New York: Plenum Press.

CAMRAS, L., MALATESTA, C., & IZARD, C. (1991). The development of facial expressions in infancy. In R. Feldman & B. Rime (Eds.), *Fundamentals of nonverbal behavior* (pp. 73–105). New York: Cambridge University Press.

CANTWELL, D. P., & BAKER, L. (1984). Research concerning families of children with autism. In E. Schopler & G. B. Mesibov (Eds.), *The effects of autism on the family.* New York: Plenum Press.

CARON, A. J., CARON, R. F., & CARLSON, V. R. (1978). Do infants see objects or retinal images? Shape constancy revisited. *Infant Behavior and Development, 1,* 229–243.

CASE, R., HAYWARD, S., LEWIS, M., & HURST, P. (1988). Toward a neo-Piagetian theory of cognitive and emotional development. *Developmental Review, 8,* 1–51.

CAUDILL, W., & FROST, L. (1974). A comparison of maternal care and infant behavior in Japanese-American, American, and Japanese families. In W. P. Lebra (Ed.), *Youth, socialization, and mental health: Vol. 3., Mental health research in Asia and the Pacific.* Honolulu: University Press of Hawaii.

CENTER FOR THE STUDY OF SOCIAL POLICY. (1993). *Kids count data book: State profiles of child well-being.* Washington, DC: Author.

CERNOCH, J. M., & PORTER, R. H. (1985). Recognition of maternal axillary odors by infants. *Child Development, 56,* 1593–1598.

CHILD CARE EMPLOYEE PROJECT. (1992). On the horizon: New policy initiatives to enhance child care staff compensation. *Young Children, 47*(5), 39–42.

CHILDREN'S DEFENSE FUND. (1991). *The state of America's children.* Washington, DC: Author.

CHILDREN'S DEFENSE FUND. (1992). *The state of America's children.* Washington, DC: Author.

CHOMSKY, N. (1968). *Language and mind.* New York: Harcourt, Brace & World.

CHURCH, M. (1979). Nutrition: A vital part of the curriculum. *Young Children, 35*(1), 61–65.

CLARKE-STEWART, K. A. (1980). The father's contribution to child development. In F. A. Pedersen (Ed.), *The father-infant relationship: Observational studies in a family context.* New York: Praeger.

CLARKE-STEWART, K. A. (1988). "The 'effects' of infant day care reconsidered" reconsidered. *Early Childhood Research Quarterly, 3,* 293–318.

CLEMENT, J., SCHWEINHART, L. J., BARNETT, W. S., EPSTEIN, A. S., & WEIKART, D. P. (1984). *Changed lives: The effects of the Perry Preschool Program on youths through age 19.* Ypsilanti, MI: High/Scope Press.

COHEN, E., PERLMUTTER, M., & MYERS, N. A. (1977). *Memory for location of multiple stimuli by 2- to 4-year-olds.* Unpublished manuscript, University of Minnesota, Minneapolis.

COIE, J. D., & KREHBIEL, G. (1984). Effects of academic tutoring on the social status of low-achieving, socially rejected children. *Child Development, 55,* 1465–1478.

COMER, D. (1987). *Developing safety skills with the young child.* Albany, NY: Delmar.

COOK, J. T., & BROWN, J. L. (1992). *Estimating the number of hungry Americans.* Unpublished working paper, Tufts University, Center on Hunger, Poverty, and Nutrition, Medford, MA.

COOLEY, C. H. (1902). *Human nature and the social order.* New York: Scribner's.

COSTANZO, P. R., & SHAW, M. E. (1966). Conformity as a function of age level. *Child Development, 37,* 967–975.

COURCHESNE, E., YEUNG-COURCHESNE, R., PRESS, G. A., HESSELINK, J. R., & JERNIGAN, T. L. (1988). Hypoplasia of cerebellar vermae lobules VI and VII in autism. *New England Journal of Medicine, 318,* 1349–1354.

CRATTY, B. (1979). *Perceptual and motor development in infants and children.* Englewood Cliffs, NJ: Prentice-Hall.

CROCKENBERG, S., & LITMAN, C. (1990). Autonomy as competence in 2-year-olds: Maternal correlates of child defiance, compliance, and self-assertion. *Developmental Psychology, 26,* 961–971.

CURTISS, S. (1977). *Genie: A psycholinguistic study of a modern-day "wild child."* New York: Academic Press.

DECASPER, A., & FIFER, W. (1980). Of human bonding: Newborns prefer their mothers' voices. *Science, 208,* 1174–1176.

DENNEY, N. W. (1972). Free classification in preschool children. *Child Development, 43,* 1161–1170.

DENNIS, W. (1973). *Children of the crèche.* New York: Appleton-Century-Crofts.

DERMAN-SPARKS, L. (1989). *Anti-bias curriculum: Tools for empowering young children.* Washington, DC: National Association for the Education of Young Children.

DIAZ, R. M. (1985). Bilingual cognitive development: Addressing three gaps in current research. *Child Development, 54,* 1376–1378.

DIETZ, W. H. (1986). *Prevention of childhood obesity.* Philadelphia: Pediatric Clinics of North America /Saunders.

DIVORKY, D. (1989). Ritalin: Education's fix-it drug. *Phi Delta Kappan, 70,* 599–605.

DUFFY, F. H., ALS, H., & MCANULTY, G. B. (1990). Behavioral and electrophysiological evidence for gestational age effects in healthy preterm and fullterm infants studied two weeks after expected due date. *Child Development, 61,* 1271–1286.

EATON, W. D. (1983). *Motor activity from fetus to adult.* Unpublished manuscript.

EDWARDS, C. P., & WHITING, B. B. (1980). Differential socialization of girls and boys in the light of cross-cultural research. In C. M. Super & S. Harkness (Eds.), *Anthropological perspectives on child development.* San Francisco: Jossey-Bass.

EGER, D. (1993). *Mother-infant bonding: A scientific fiction.* New Haven, CT: Yale University Press.

EICHORN, D. (1979). *Physical development: Current foci of research.* In J. D. Osofsky (Ed.), *Handbook of infant development.* New York: Wiley.

EIMAS, P. D., SIQUELAND, E. R., & JUSCZYK, P. W. (1971). Speech perception in infants. *Science, 171,* 303–306.

EISENBERG, N., & FABES, R. (1991). Prosocial behavior and empathy: A multimethod developmental perspective. In M. Clark (Ed.), *Prosocial behavior* (pp. 34–61). Newbury Park, CA: Sage.

EKMAN, P. (1973). Cross-cultural studies of emotion. In P. Ekman (Ed.), *Darwin and facial expression: A century of research in review* (pp. 169–222). New York: Academic Press.

ELDER, G. H. (1962). Structural variations in the child-rearing relationship. *Sociometry, 25,* 241–262.

ELKIND, D. (1984). *All grown up and no place to go: Teenagers in crisis.* Reading, MA: Addison-Wesley.

ELKIND, D. (1987). *Miseducation: Preschoolers at risk.* New York: Knopf.

EMDE, R., GAENSBAUER, T., & HARMON, R. (1976). Emotional expression in infancy: A biobehavioral study. *Psychological Issues Monograph Series, 10*(Serial No. 37).

ERIKSON, E. (1963). *Childhood and society* (2nd ed.). New York: Norton.

ERLENMEYER-KIMLING, L., & JARVIK, L. F. (1963). Genetics and intelligence: A review. *Science, 142,* 1477–1479.

EVELETH, P., & TANNER, J. M. (1976). *World wide variations in human growth.* Cambridge, England: Cambridge University Press.

FAGAN, J. F., III. (1979). The origins of facial pattern recognition. In M. H. Bornstein & W. Kessen (Eds.), *Psychological development from infancy: Image to intention.* Hillsdale, NJ: Erlbaum.

FAGOT, B. L. (1978). The influence of sex of child on parental reaction to their children. *Child Development, 49,* 459–465.

FALBO, T. (1984). *The single child family.* New York: Guilford Press.

FALBO, T., & POLIT, D. F. (1986). Quantitative review of the only child literature: Research evidence and theory development. *Psychological Bulletin, 100*(2), 176–189.

FANTZ, R. L. (1963). Pattern vision in newborn infants. *Science, 140,* 296–297.

FANTZ, R. L. (1964). Visual experience in infants: Decreased attention to familiar objects relative to novel ones. *Science, 146,* 668–670.

FANTZ, R. L. (1965). Visual perception from birth as shown by pattern selectivity. In H. H. Whipple (Ed.), *New issues in infant development. Annals of the New York Academy of Science, 118,* 793–814.

FEIN, D., HUMES, M., KAPLAN, E., LUCCI, D., & WATERHOUSE, L. (1984). The question of left hemisphere dysfunction in infantile autism. *Psychological Bulletin, 95,* 259–281.

FEIN, G. G. (1981). Pretend play in childhood: An integrative view. *Child Development, 52,* 1095–1118.

FELDMAN, W., FELDMAN, E., & GOODMAN, J. T. (1988). Culture versus biology: Children's attitudes toward thinness and fatness. *Pediatrics, 81,* 190–194.

FERGUSSON, D. M., HORWOOD, L. J., & SHANNON, E. T. (1986). Factors related to the age of attainment of nocturnal bladder control: An 8-year longitudinal study. *Pediatrics, 78*(5), 884–890.

FIELD, T., MASI, W., GOLDSTEIN, S., PERRY, S., & PARL, S. (1988). Infant day care facilitates preschool social behavior. *Early Childhood Research Quarterly, 3,* 341–359.

FISHER, K. W., & PIPP, S. L. (1984). Processes of cognitive development: Optimal level and skill acquisition. In R. J. Steinberg (Ed.), *Mechanisms of cognitive development.* San Francisco: Freeman.

FLAVELL, J. H. (1977). *Cognitive development.* Englewood Cliffs, NJ: Prentice-Hall.

FLAVELL, J. H., GREEN, F. L., & FLAVELL, E. R. (1986). Development of knowledge about the appearance-reality distinction. *Monographs of the Society for Research in Child Development, 51*(1, Serial No. 212).

FLAVELL, J. H., SPEER, J. R., GREEN, F. L., & AUGUST, D. L. (1981). The development of comprehension monitoring and knowledge about communication. *Monographs of the Society for Research in Child Development, 46.*

FRAIBERG, S. (1977). *Insights from the blind.* New York: Basic Books.

FREUD, S. (1970). *An outline of psychoanalysis.* New York: Norton.

FROSCHL, M., & SPRUNG, B. (1983). Providing an anti-handicappist early childhood environment. *Interracial Books for Children Bulletin, 14*(7–8), 21–23.

GALLER, J. R., RAMSEY, F., & SOLIMANO, G. (1984). The influence of early malnutrition on subsequent development: 3. Learning disabilities as a sequel to malnutrition. *Pediatric Research, 18,* 309.

GALLER, J. R., RAMSEY, F., & SOLIMANO, G. (1985). A follow-up study of the effects of early malnutrition on subsequent development: 2. Fine motor skills in adolescence. *Pediatric Research, 19,* 524.

GARDNER, H. (1980). *Artful scribbles: The significance of children's drawings.* New York: Basic Books.

GARVEY, C. (1977). *Play.* Cambridge, MA: Harvard University Press.

GELMAN, R. (1972). The nature and development of early number concepts. In H. W. Reese & L. P. Lipsitt (Eds.), *Advances in child development and behavior.* New York: Academic Press.

GELMAN, R. (1982). Accessing one-to-one correspondence: Still another paper on conservation. *British Journal of Psychology, 73,* 209–220.

GELMAN, R., & GALLISTER, C. R. (1978). *The child's understanding of numbers.* Cambridge, MA: Harvard University Press.

GEPPERT, U., & KUSTER, U. (1983). The emergence of "wanting to do it oneself": A precursor of achievement motivation. *International Journal of Behavioral Development, 6,* 355–369.

GIBSON, E. J. (1982). The concept of affordances in development: The renascence of functionalism. In W. W. Collins (Ed.), *The concept of development: The Minnesota symposia on child psychology* (Vol. 15). Hillsdale, NJ: Erlbaum.

GIBSON, E. J. & WALK, R. D. (1960, April 10). The "visual cliff." *Scientific American,* pp. 64–71.

GIBSON, J. J. (1979). *The ecological approach to visual perception.* Boston: Houghton Mifflin.

GOLD, D., & ANDRES, D. (1978). Developmental comparisons between ten-year-old children with employed and nonemployed mothers. *Child Development, 49,* 75–84.

GOLDBERG, S., & LEWIS, M. (1969). Play behavior in the year-old infant: Early sex differences. *Child Development, 40,* 21–31.

GOMBY, D., & SHIORNO, P. (1991). Estimating the number of substance exposed infants. *The Future of Children, 1*(1).

GONZALEZ-MENA, J. (1992, January). Taking a culturally sensitive approach in infant-toddler programs. *Young Children.*

GONZALEZ-MENA, J. (1993). *Multicultural issues in child care.* Mountain View, CA: Mayfield.

GOODMAN, K. (1986). *What's whole in whole language?* Portsmouth, NH: Heinemann.

GOODMAN, Y. (1980). The roots of literacy. In M. P. Douglas (Ed.), *Claremont Reading Conference Forty-fourth Yearbook.* Claremont, CA: Claremont Graduate School.

GOPNIK, A., & ASTINGTON, J. W. (1988). Children's understanding of representational change and its relation to the understanding of false beliefs and the appearance-reality distinction. *Child Development, 59,* 26–37.

GOPNIK, A., & MELTZOFF, A. N. (1987). The development of categorization in the second year and its relation to other cognitive and linguistic developments. *Child Development, 58,* 1523–1531.

GRINKER, J. A. (1981). Behavioral and metabolic factors in childhood obesity. In M. Lewis and L. A. Rosenblum (Eds.), *The uncommon child.* New York: Plenum Press.

Growing up in the shadows of the AIDS virus. (1993, March 21). *The New York Times,* p. L33.

GRUBER, H., & VONECHE, J. (1977). *The essential Piaget.* New York: Basic Books.

GUNNAR, M., FISCH, R., KORSVIK, S., & DONHOWE, J. (1981). The effects of circumcision on serum cortisol and behavior. *Psychoneuronendocrinology, 6,* 269–276.

HALE-BENSON, J. (1986). *Black children: Their roots, cultures, and learning styles.* Baltimore: Johns Hopkins University Press.

HAMILL, P. V., JOHNSTON, F. E., & LEMESHOW, S. (1972). *Height and weight of children: Socioeconomic status: United States.* Rockville, MD: U.S. Department of Health, Education, and Welfare.

HARPER, L. V., & HUIE, K. S. (1985). The effects of prior group experience, age, and familiarity on the quality and organization of preschoolers' social relationships. *Child Development, 56,* 704–717.

HARRIS, P. L. (1983). Infant cognition. In P. H. Mussen et al. (Eds.), *Handbook of child psychology* (4th ed.): *Vol. 2. Infancy and developmental psychobiology.* New York: Wiley.

HARTUP, W. W. (1983). Peer relations. In P. H. Mussen et al. (Eds.), *Handbook of child psychology* (4th ed.): *Vol. 4. Socialization, personality, and social development* (pp. 103–196). New York: Wiley.

HERRMANN, H. J., & ROBERTS, M. W. (1987). Preventive dental care: The role of the pediatrician. *Pediatrics, 80*(1), 107–110.

HESS, R. D. (1970). Social class and ethnic influences on socialization. In P. H. Mussen (Ed.), *Carmichael's manual of child psychology* (3rd ed., Vol. 2, pp. 457–557). New York: Wiley.

HETHERINGTON, E. M. (1979). Divorce: A child's perspective. *American Psychologist, 34,* 851–858.

HETHERINGTON, E. M., COX, M., & COX, R. (1979). Play and social interaction in children following divorce. *Journal of Social Issues, 35,* 26–49.

HETHERINGTON, E. M., COX, M., & COX, R. (1982). Effects of divorce on parents and children. In M. E. Lamb (Ed.), *Nontraditional families: Parenting and child development.* Hillsdale, NJ: Erlbaum.

HETHERINGTON, E. M., & PARKE, R. (1979). *Child psychology: A contemporary viewpoint* (2nd ed.). New York: McGraw-Hill.

HINDE, R. (1983). Ethology and child development. In P. H. Mussen et al. (Eds.), *Handbook of child psychology* (4th ed.): *Vol. 2. Infancy and developmental psychobiology.* New York: Wiley.

HINMAN, A. (1986). Vaccine preventable diseases and day care. *Reviews of Infectious Diseases, 8*(4), 622–625.

HIRSCH, H. V., & SPINELLI, D. N. (1970). Visual experience modifies distribution of horizontally and vertically oriented receptive fields in cats. *Science, 168,* 869–871.

HOFFMAN, L. W. (1989). Effects of maternal employment in the two-parent family: A review of recent research. *American Psychologist 44*(2).

HOLDEN, G. W., & WEST, M. J. (1989). Proximate regulation by mothers: A demonstration of how differing styles affect young children's behavior. *Child Development, 60,* 64–90.

HOOKER, D. (1952). *The prenatal origin of behavior.* Lawrence: University of Kansas Press.

HORNER, T. (1980). Two methods of studying stranger reactivity in infants: A review. *Journal of Child Psychology and Psychiatry, 21,* 203–219.

HOROWITZ, F. D., & O'BRIEN, M. (1986). Gifted and talented children. *American Psychologist, 41*(10).

HUGHES, M., & DONALDSON, M. (1983). The use of hiding games for studying coordination of points. In M. Donaldson, R. Grieve, & C. Pratt (Eds.), *Early childhood development and education: Readings in psychology.* New York: Guilford Press.

HUSTON, A. C. (1983). Sex-typing. In P. H. Mussen et al. (Eds.), *Handbook of child psychology* (4th ed.): *Vol 4. Socialization, personality, and social development* (pp. 387–468). New York: Wiley.

HYMES, J. L., JR. (1990). *The year in review: A look at 1989.* Washington, DC: National Association for the Education of Young Children.

INHELDER, B., & PIAGET, J. (1958). *The growth of logical thinking from childhood to adolescence.* New York: Basic Books.

IZARD, C. (1971). *The face of emotion.* New York: Appleton-Century-Crofts.

IZARD, C., HEMBREE, E., & HUEBNER, R. (1987). Infants' emotional expressions to acute pain: Developmental changes and stability of individual differences. *Developmental Psychology, 23,* 105–113.

IZARD, C., & MALATESTA, C. (1987). Perspectives on emotional development: 1. Differential emotions theory of early emotional development. In J. D. Osofsky (Ed.), *Handbook of infant development* (2nd ed., pp. 494–554). New York: Wiley.

JACOBS, B., & MOSS, H. (1976). Birth order and sex of sibling as determinants of mother-infant interaction. *Child Development, 47,* 315–322.

JOHNSON, J. S., & NEWPORT, E. L. (1989). Critical period effects in second language learning: The influence of maturational state on the acquisition of English as a second language. *Cognitive Psychology, 21,* 60–99.

JORDE-BLOOM, P. (1989). Professional orientation: Individual and organizational perspectives. *Child and Youth Care Quarterly, 18*(4), 227–240.

KAGAN, J. (1978). *The growth of the child.* New York: Norton.

KAGAN, J. (1981). *The second year: The emergence of self-awareness.* Cambridge, MA: Harvard University Press.

KAGAN, J., REZNICK, J. S., CLARKE, C., SNIDMAN, N., & GARCIA-COLL, C. (1984). Behavioral inhibition to the unfamiliar. *Child Development, 55,* 2212–2225.

KELLOGG, R. (1970). Understanding children's art. In P. Cramer (Ed.), *Readings in developmental psychology today.* Delmar, CA: CRM.

KENDALL, E. D., & MOUKADDEM, V. E. (1992). Who's vulnerable in infant child care centers? *Young Children, 47*(5), 72–78.

KENDRICK, A. S., KAUFMANN, R., & MESSENGER, K. P. (Eds.). (1991). *Healthy young children: A manual for programs.* Washington, DC: National Association for the Education of Young Children.

KLINNERT, M., CAMPOS, J., SORCE, J., EMDE, R., & SVEJDA, M. (1983). Emotions as behavior regulators: Social referencing in infancy. In R. Plutchik & H. Kellerman (Eds.), *Emotion: Theory, research, and experience* (Vol. 2, pp. 57–86). New York: Academic Press.

KNIGHT, G. P., & KAGAN, S. (1977). Development of prosocial and competitive behaviors in Anglo-American and Mexican-American children. *Child Development, 48,* 1385–1394.

KOEPPEL, J. (1992). The sister schools program: A way for children to learn about cultural diversity—when there isn't any in their school. *Young Children, 48*(1), 44–47.

KOHLBERG, L. (1966). A cognitive-developmental analysis of children's sex-role concepts and attitudes. In E. E. Maccoby (Ed.), *The development of sex differences.* Stanford, CA: Stanford University Press.

KOHLBERG, L. (1976). Moral stages and moralization: The cognitive-developmental approach. In T. Lickona (Ed.), *Moral development and behavior.* New York: Holt, Rinehart & Winston.

KOPP, C. B. (1982). Antecedents of self-regulation: A developmental perspective. *Developmental Psychology, 18,* 199–214.

LABOV, W. (1970). The logic of nonstandard English. In F. Williams (Ed.), *Language and poverty: Perspectives on a theme.* Chicago: Markham.

LAMB, M. (1978). Interactions between 18-month-olds and their preschool-aged siblings. *Child Development, 49,* 51–59.

LAMB, M. E. (1981). The development of father-infant relationships. In M. E. Lamb (Ed.), *The role of the father in child development* (rev. ed.). New York: Wiley.

LAMB, M. E. (1982). Maternal employment and child development: A review. In M. E. Lamb (Ed.), *Nontraditional families: Parenting and child development* (pp. 45–70). Hillsdale, NJ: Erlbaum.

LAZAR, I., & DARLINGTON, R. (1982). Lasting effects of early education: A report from the Consortium for Longitudinal Studies. *Monographs of the*

*Society for Research in Child Development, 47*(2–3, Serial No. 195), 1–63.

LEACH, P. (1989). *Your baby and child: From birth to age five.* New York: Knopf.

LEBOYER, F. (1975). *Birth without violence.* New York: Random House.

LENNEBERG, E. H. (1967). *Biological foundations of language.* New York: Wiley.

LEVY-SHIFF, R. (1982). The effects of father absence on young children in mother-headed families. *Child Development, 53,* 1400–1405.

LEWIN, T. (1992, October 5). Rise in single parenthood is reshaping U.S. *The New York Times,* pp. B2, B6.

LEWIS, M., & BROOKS, J. (1974). Self, other, and fear: Infants' reactions to people. In M. Lewis & L. Rosenblum (Eds.), *Origins of fear* (pp. 195–227). New York: Wiley.

LEWIS, M., & BROOKS-GUNN, J. (1979). *Social cognition and the acquisition of self.* New York: Plenum Press.

LEWIS, M., SULLIVAN, M., STANGER, C., & WEISS, M. (1989). Self-development and self-conscious emotions. *Child Development, 60,* 146–156.

LIBERMAN, I. Y., SHANKWEILER, D., FISHER, F. W., & CARTER, B. (1974). Reading and the awareness of linguistic segments. *Journal of Experimental Child Psychology, 18,* 201–212.

LILLARD, A. S. (1993). Pretend play skills and the child's theory of mind. *Child Development, 64,* 348–371.

LIPSITT, L. P. (1986). Learning in infancy: Cognitive development in babies. *Journal of Pediatrics, 109*(1), 172–182.

LITTLE SOLDIER, L. (1992). Working with Native American children. *Young Children, 47*(6), 15–21.

LOWREY, G. H. (1978). *Growth and development of children.* Chicago: Year Book Medical Publishers.

LYTTON, H. (1980). *Parent-child interaction.* New York: Plenum Press.

MACCOBY, E. E., & JACKLIN, C. N. (1980). Sex differences in aggression: A rejoinder and reprise. *Child development, 51,* 964–980.

MACCOBY, E. E., & MARTIN, J. A. (1983). Socialization in the context of the family: Parent-child interaction. In P. H. Mussen et al. (Eds.), *Handbook of child psychology* (4th ed.): *Vol. 4. Socialization, personality, and social development* (pp. 1–102). New York: Wiley.

MACFARLANE, A. (1977). *The psychology of childbirth.* Cambridge, MA: Harvard University Press.

MAHLER, M. (1968). *On human symbiosis and the vicissitudes of individuation.* New York: International Universities Press.

MANDLER, J. (1988). How to build a baby: On the development of an accessible representational system. *Cognitive Development, 2,* 113–136.

MANDLER, J., BAUER, P. J., & MCDONOUGH, L. (1991). Separating the sheep from the goats: Differentiating global categories. *Cognitive Psychology, 23,* 263–298.

MANGELSDORF, S. C. (1992). Developmental changes in infant-stranger interaction. *Infant Behavior and Development, 15,* 191–208.

MARCUS, G. S., PINKER, S., ULLMAN, M., HOLLANDER, M., ROSEN, T. J., XU, F. (1992). Overregularization in language acquisition. *Monographs of the Society for Research in Child Development, 57* (Serial No. 228).

MARKMAN, E., & HUTCHINSON, J. (1984). Children's sensitivity to constraints on word meaning: Taxonomic vs. thematic relations. *Cognitive Psychology, 16,* 1–27.

MAROTZ, L. R., RUSH, J. M., & CROSS, M. Z. (1989). *Health, safety, and nutrition for the young child.* Albany, NY: Delmar.

MAURER, D., & BARRERA, M. (1981). Infants' perception of natural and distorted arrangements of schematic face. *Child Development, 47,* 523–527.

MCCALL, R. B., EICHORN, D. H., & HOGARTY, P. S. (1977). Transitions in early mental development. *Monographs of the Society for Research in Child Development, 42*(Serial No. 171).

MCCORMICK, L., & HOLDEN, R. (1992). Homeless children: A special challenge. *Young Children, 47*(6), 61–67.

MCDANIEL, K. D. (1986). Pharmacological treatment of psychiatric and neuro-developmental disorders in children and adolescents (Pts. 1–3). *Clinical Pediatrics, 25*(2,3,4).

McRoy, R. G., & Zurcher, L. A. (1983). *Transracial and interracial adoptees: The adolescent years.* Springfield, IL: Thomas.

Mead, G. H. (1925). The genesis of the self and social control. *International Journal of Ethics, 35,* 251–273.

Meltzoff, A. N., & Moore, M. K. (1983). Newborn infants imitate adult facial gestures. *Child Development, 44,* 709.

Meredith, H. V. (1969). Body size of contemporary groups of eight-year-old children studies in different parts of the world. *Monographs of the Society for Research in Child Development, 34*(1).

Meredith, H. V. (1978). Research between 1960 and 1970 on the standing height of young children in different parts of the world. In H. W. Reese & L. P. Lipsitt (Eds.), *Advances in child development and behavior* (Vol. 12, pp. 2–59). New York: Academic Press.

Miller, L. B., & Bizzell, R. P. (1983). Long-term effects of four preschool programs: Sixth, seventh, and eighth grades. *Child Development, 54,* 727–741.

Morgan, H. (1976). Neonatal precocity and the black experience. *Negro Educational Review, 27,* 129–134.

Mussen, P. H., & Jones, M. C. (1957). Self-conceptions, motivations, and interpersonal attitudes of late- and early-maturing boys. *Child Development, 28,* 243–256.

Nadi, N. S., Nurnberger, J. I., & Gershon, E. S. (1984). Muscarinic cholinergic receptors on skin fibroblasts in familial affective disorder. *New England Journal of Medicine, 311,* 225–230.

Nagy, M. (1948). The child's theories concerning death. *Journal of Genetic Psychology, 73,* 3–27.

National Association for the Education of Young Children. (1985). *Guidelines for early childhood education programs in associate degree granting institutions.* Washington, DC: Author.

National Association for the Education of Young Children. (1989). *Developmentally appropriate practice in early childhood programs serving infants.* Washington, DC: Author.

National Association for the Education of Young Children. (1990). *Early childhood teacher education guidelines: Basic and advanced.* Washington, DC: Author.

National Association for the Education of Young Children. (1992). *Developmentally appropriate practice in early childhood programs serving younger preschoolers.* Washington, DC: Author.

National Center for Health Statistics. (1990). *Advanced report of final natality statistics.* Washington, DC: U.S. Public Health Service.

Nelson, K. (1986). *Event knowledge: Structure and function in development.* Hillsdale, NJ: Erlbaum.

Nelson, K. (1988). Constraints on word learning. *Cognitive Development, 3,* 221–246.

Nelson, K., & Gruendel, J. M. (1981). Generalized event representations: Basic building blocks of cognitive development. In A. Brown and M. Lamb, (Eds.), *Advances in developmental psychology.* Hillsdale, NJ: Erlbaum.

Nowlis, G. H., & Kessen, W. (1976). Human newborns differentiate differing concentrations of sucrose and glucose. *Science, 191,* 865–866.

Olson, G. M., & Sherman, T. (1983) Attention, learning, and memory in infants. In P. H. Mussen et al. (Eds.), *Handbook of child psychology* (4th ed.): *Vol. 2. Infancy and developmental psychobiology.* New York: Wiley.

Park, K., & Waters, E. (1989). Security of attachment and preschool friendships. *Child Development, 60,* 1076–1081.

Parke, R. D., & O'Leary, S. (1976). Family interaction in the newborn period: Some findings, some observations, and some unresolved issues. In K. F. Riegel & J. Meacham (Eds.), *The developing indi-*

*vidual in a changing world: Vol. 2. Social and environmental issues.* The Hague: Mouton.

PARTEN, M. B. (1932). Social participation among preschool children. *Journal of Abnormal and Social Psychology, 27,* 243–269.

PEDERSEN, E., FAUCHER, T. A., & EATON, W. W. (1978). A new perspective of the effects of first-grade teachers on children's subsequent adult status. *Harvard Educational Review, 48,* 1–31.

PEEL, E. A. (1967). *The psychological basis of education* (2nd ed.). Edinburgh: Oliver & Boyd.

PELLEGRINI, A. D., & PERLMUTTER, J. C. (1988). Rough-and-tumble play on the elementary school playground. *Young Children, 43*(2), 14–17.

PETERSEN, A. C., & TAYLOR, B. (1980). The biological approach to adolescence. In J. Adelson (Ed.), *Handbook of adolescent psychology.* New York: Wiley.

PIAGET, J. (1952). *The origins of intelligence in children.* New York: International Universities Press.

PIAGET, J. (1954). *The construction of reality in the child.* New York: Ballantine.

PIAGET, J. (1970). *Genetic epistemology.* New York: Columbia University Press.

PIAGET, J., & INHELDER, B. (1956). *The child's conception of space.* London: Routledge & Kegan Paul.

PIAGET, J., & INHELDER, B. (1969). *The psychology of the child.* New York: Basic Books.

PICK, A. D., FRANKET, D. G., & HESS, V. (1975). Children's attention: The development of selectivity. In E. M. Hetherington (Ed.), *Review of child development research* (Vol. 5.). Chicago: University of Chicago Press.

PIPES, P. L. (1989). *Nutrition in infancy and childhood.* St. Louis: Times Mirror/Mosby.

PIPP, S., FISCHER, K. W., & JENNINGS, S. (1987). Acquisition of self and mother knowledge in infancy. *Developmental Psychology, 23,* 86–96.

PLOMIN, R. (1983). Developmental behavioral genetics. *Child Development, 54,* 253–259.

PLOMIN, R., DEFRIES, J. C., & FULKER, D. W. (1988). *Nature and nurture during infancy and early childhood.* New York: Cambridge University Press.

PORTER, F. L., PORGES, S. W., & MARSHALL, R. E. (1988). Newborn pain cries and vagal tone: Parallel changes in response to circumcision. *Child Development, 59,* 495–505.

POWER, T., & CHAPIESKI, M. L. (1986). Childrearing and impulse control in toddlers: A naturalistic investigation. *Developmental Psychology, 22,* 271–275.

PREEMIES' IQ. (1990). *Stanford Observer, 23*(6), 23.

PULASKI, M. (1971). *Understanding Piaget.* New York: Harper & Row.

RADIN, N. (1981). The role of the father in cognitive, academic, and intellectual development. In M. E. Lamb (Ed.), *The role of the father in child development* (2nd ed., pp. 379–428). New York: Wiley.

RADIN, N. (1982). Primary caregiving and role-sharing fathers. In M. E. Lamb (Ed.), *Nontraditional families: Parenting and child development.* Hillsdale, NJ: Erlbaum.

RADKE-YARROW, M., ZAHN-WAXLER, C., & CHAPMAN, M. (1983). Children's prosocial behaviors and dispositions. In P. H. Mussen et al. (Eds.), *Handbook of child psychology* (4th ed.). New York: Wiley.

RAGOZIN, A. S., BASHAM, R. B., CRNIC, K. A., GREENBERG, M. T., & ROBINSON, N. M. (1982). Effects of maternal age on parenting role. *Developmental Psychology, 18,* 627–634.

RAMEY, C. T., & CAMPBELL, F. A. (1979). Compensatory education for disadvantaged children. *School Review, 87,* 171–289.

RAMEY, C. T., MACPHEE, D., & YEATES, K. O. (1982). Preventing developmental retardation: A general systems model. In L. A. Bond & J. M. Joffe (Eds.), *Facilitating infant and early childhood development.* Hanover, NH: University Press of New England.

RAMSEY, P., & DERMAN-SPARKS, L. (1992). Multicultural education reaffirmed. *Young Children, 47*(2), 10–11.

RAPOPORT, J. L. (1986). Diet and hyperactivity. *Nutrition Review, 44* (Suppl.), 158.

REBELSKY, F. G., STARR, R. H., & LURIA, Z. (1967). Language development: The first four years. In Y. Brackbill (Ed.), *Infancy and early childhood.* New York: Free Press.

RITVO, E. R., FREEMAN, B. J., MASON-BROTHERS, A., Mo, A., & RITVO, A. M. (1985). Concordance for the syndrome of autism in 40 pairs of afflicted twins. *American Journal of Psychiatry, 142,* 74–77.

ROGOFF, B. (1990). *Apprenticeship in thinking: Cognitive development in social context.* New York: Oxford University Press.

ROOPNARINE, J., & HONIG, A. S. (1985, September). The unpopular child. *Young Children,* pp. 59–64.

ROSCH, E. M., MERVIS, C. B., GRAY, W. D., JOHNSON, D. M., & BOYES-BRAEM, P. (1976). Basic objects in natural categories. *Cognitive Psychology, 8,* 382–439.

ROSE, R. M., GORDON, T. P., & BERNSTEIN, I. S. (1972). Plasma testosterone levels in the male rhesus: Influences of sexual and social stimuli. *Science, 178,* 643–645.

ROSE, S. A., FELDMAN, J. F., & WALLACE, I. F. (1992). Infant information processing in relation to six-year cognitive outcomes. *Child Development, 63,* 1126–1141.

ROSENBLITH, J., & SIMS-KNIGHT, J. (1985). *In the beginning: Development in the first two years.* Belmont, CA: Brooks/Cole.

ROSENZWEIG, M. R. (1984). Experience, memory, and the brain. *American Psychologist, 39*(4), 365–376.

ROVEE-COLLIER, C. K. (1987). Learning and memory in infancy. In J. D. Osofsky (Ed.), *Handbook of infant development* (2nd ed.). New York: Wiley.

ROVEE-COLLIER, C. K., & GEKOSKI, M. J. (1979). *Reactivation of infant memory.* Paper presented at the biennial meeting of the Society for Research in Child Development, San Francisco.

RUBENSTEIN, J. L., HOWES, C., & BOYLE, P. (1981). A two-year follow-up of infants in community based day care. *Journal of Child Psychology and Psychiatry, 22,* 209–218.

RUBIN, Z. (1980). *Children's friendships.* Cambridge, MA: Harvard University Press.

RUFF, H. (1984). Infants manipulative exploration of objects: Effects of age and object characteristics. *Developmental Psychology, 20,* 9–20.

RUTTER, M. (1981). *Maternal deprivation reassessed.* Harmondsworth, England: Penguin.

RUTTER, M. (1983). Stress, coping, and development. In N. Garmezy and M. Rutter (Eds.), *Stress, coping, and development in children.* New York: McGraw-Hill.

RUTTER, M., & GARMEZY, N. (1983). Developmental psychopathology. In P. H. Mussen et al. (Eds.), *Handbook of child psychology* (4th ed.): *Vol. 4. Socialization, personality, and social development.* New York: Wiley.

SACKET, G. P. (1968). Abnormal behavior in laboratory research monkeys. In M. Fox (Ed.), *Abnormal behavior in animals.* Philadelphia: Saunders.

SAGI, A. (1982). Antecedents and consequences of various degrees of paternal involvement in child rearing: The Israeli Project. In M. E. Lamb (Ed.), *Nontraditional families: Parenting and child development.* Hillsdale, NJ: Erlbaum.

SANTROCK, J. W., WARSHAK, R. A., & ELLIOTT, G. L. (1982). Social development and parent-child interaction in father-custody and stepmother families. In M. E. Lamb (Ed.), *Nontraditional families: Parenting and child development.* Hillsdale, NJ: Erlbaum.

SCARR, S. (1984, May). What's a parent to do? [Interview with E. Hall]. *Psychology Today,* pp. 58–63.

SCARR, S., & KIDD, K. K. (1983). Developmental behavior genetics. In P. H. Mussen et al. (Eds.), *Handbook of child psychology* (4th ed.): *Vol. 2. Infancy and developmental psychobiology.* New York: Wiley.

SCARR, S., & MCCARTNEY, K. (1983). How people make their own environments: A theory of genotype-environment effects. *Child Development, 54,* 425–435.

SCHNIEDEL, D. G., & MARCIA, J. E. (1985). Ego identity, intimacy, sex role orientation, and gender. *Developmental Psychology, 21,* 149–160.

SCHOENDORF, K. (1992). Relationship of sudden infant death syndrome to maternal smoking during and after pregnancy. *Pediatrics, 90,* 905–908.

SCHULMAN-GALAMBOS, C., & GALAMBOS, R. (1979). Brain-stem-evoked response audiometry in newborns hearing screening. *Archives of Otolaryngology, 105,* 86–90.

SCHWEDER, R., TURIEL, E., & MUCH, N. (1981). The moral intuitions of the child. In J. H. Flavell & L. Ross (Eds.), *Social cognitive development: Frontiers and possible futures.* New York: Cambridge University Press.

SCHWEINHART, L., & WEIKART, D. (Eds.). (1993). *Significant benefits: The High/Scope Perry Preschool study through age 27.* Ypsilanti, MI: High/Scope Press.

SEGAL, P. (1990). What you should know about preschool testing. *Parents, 65,* 116.

SEPKOWSKI, C. (1985). Maternal obstetric medication and newborn behavior. In J. W. Scanlon (Ed.), *Prenatal anesthesia.* London: Blackwell.

SERBIN, L. A., O'LEARY, K. D., KENT, R. N., & TONICK, I. J. (1973). A comparison of teacher response to the pre-academic and problem behavior of boys and girls. *Child Development, 33,* 796–804.

SEXTON, M., & HEBEL, R. (1984). A clinical trial of change in maternal smoking and its effect on birth weight. *Journal of the American Medical Association, 251*(7), 911–915.

SHATZ, M., & GELMAN, R. (1973). The development of communications skills: Modifications in the speech of young children as a function of listening. *Monographs of the Society for Research in Child Development, 38.*

SHEPS, S., & EVANS, G. D. (1987). Epidemiology of school injuries: A 2-year experience in a municipal health department. *Pediatrics, 79*(1), 69–75.

SKEELS, H. M. (1942). A study of the effects of differential stimulation on mentally retarded children: A follow-up report. *American Journal of Mental Deficiency, 46,* 340–350.

SKEELS, H. M. (1966). Adult status of children with contrasting early life experiences: A follow-up study. *Monographs of the Society for Research in Child Development, 31*(3, Serial No. 105).

SKINNER, B. F. (1976). *About behaviorism.* New York: Random House.

SLATTER, A., MORRISON, V., & ROSE, D. (1984). Habituation in the newborn. *Infant Behavior and Development, 7,* 183–200.

SLOBIN, D. I. (1971). *Psycholinguistics.* Glenview, IL: Scott, Foresman.

SNOW, C. E. (1972). Mother's speech to children learning language. *Child Development, 43,* 549–565.

SOLOMONS, H. (1978). The malleability of infant motor development. *Clinical Pediatrics, 17*(11), 836–839.

SOLOMONS, H., Larkin, J., SNIDER, B., & PAREDES-ROJAS, R. (1982). Is day care safe for children? *Children's Health Care, 10*(3), 90.

SORCE, J., EMDE, R., CAMPOS, J., & KLINNERT, M. (1985). Maternal emotional signaling: Its effect on the visual cliff behavior of 1-year-olds. *Developmental Psychology, 21,* 195–200.

SPITZ, R. A. (1965). *The first year of life.* New York: International Universities Press.

SPOCK, B. (1985). *Dr. Spock's baby and child care.* New York: Pocket Books.

SROUFE, L. A. (1977). Wariness of strangers and the study of infant development. *Child Development, 48,* 731–746.

SROUFE, L. A. (1984). The organization of emotional development. In K. R. Scherer & P. Ekman (Eds.), *Approaches to emotion* (pp. 109–128). Hillsdale, NJ: Erlbaum.

STEINER, J. E. (1979). Facial expressions in response to taste and smell stimulation. In H. W. Reese & L. P. Lipsitt (Eds.), *Advances in childhood development and behavior* (Vol. 13). New York: Academic Press.

STENBERG, C., & CAMPOS, J. J. (1990). The development of anger expressions in infancy. In N. Stein, B. Leventhal, & T. Trabasso (Eds.), *Psychological and biological approaches to emotion* (pp. 247–282). Hillsdale, NJ: Erlbaum.

STIPEK, D., RECCHIA, S., & McCLINTIC, S. (1992). Self-evaluation in young children. *Monographs of the Society for Research in Child Development, 57*(1, Serial No. 226).

STRAUS, M. A., GELLES, R. J., & STEINMETZ, S. K. (1980). *Behind closed doors: Violence in the American family*. Garden City, NY: Doubleday.

STUNKARD, A. J., FOCH, T. T., & HRUBEC, Z. (1986). A twin study of human obesity. *Journal of the American Medical Association, 256,* 51–54.

SURBER, C. F., & GZESH, S. M. (1984). Reversible operations in the balance scale task. *Journal of Experimental Child Psychology, 38,* 254–274.

TAFFEL, S. M., TLACEK, P. J., & KOSARY, R. C. L. (1992). U.S. cesarean-section rates, 1990: An update. *Birth, 19*(1).

TANNER, J. M. (1970). Physical growth. In P. H. Mussen (Ed.), *Carmichael's manual of child psychology.* New York: Wiley.

TANNER, J. M. (1973). The regulation of human growth. In F. Rebelsky & L. Borman (Eds.), *Child development and behavior.* New York: Knopf.

TANNER, J. M. (1978). *Fetus into man: Physical growth from conception to maturity.* Cambridge, MA: Harvard University Press.

TAYLOR, A. R., ASHER, S. R., & WILLIAMS, G. A. (1987). The social adaptation of mainstreamed mildly retarded children. *Child Development, 58,* 1321–1334.

THOMAS, A., & CHESS, S. (1977). *Temperament and development.* New York: Brunner/Mazel.

THOMAS, A., CHESS, S., & BIRCH, H. G. (1968). *Temperament and behavior disorders in children.* New York: New York University Press.

TURIEL, E. (1983). *The development of social knowledge: Morality and convention.* Cambridge, England: Cambridge University Press.

ULIAN, D. Z. (1976). The development of conceptions of masculinity and femininity. In B. Lloyd & J. Ascher (Eds.), *Exploring sex differences.* London: Academic Press.

U.S. BUREAU OF LABOR STATISTICS. (1990). Washington, DC: U.S. Department of Labor.

U.S. DEPARTMENT OF AGRICULTURE. (1992, April). *Nutrition guidance for the child nutrition programs.* Washington, DC: U.S. Government Printing Office.

VAUGHAN, V. C., III. (1983). Developmental pediatrics. In R. E. Behrman & V. C. Vaughan III (Eds.), *Pediatrics.* Philadelphia: Saunders.

VYGOTSKY, L. S. (1962). *Thought and language.* Cambridge, MA: MIT Press.

VYGOTSKY, L. S. (1978). *Mind in society: The development of higher mental processes.* Cambridge, MA: Harvard University Press.

WALLACE, J. R., CUNNINGHAM, T. F., & DEL MONTE, V. (1984). Change and stability in self-esteem between late childhood and early adolescence. *Journal of Early Adolescence, 4,* 253–257.

WALLERSTEIN, J. S. (1987). Children of divorce: Report of a ten-year follow-up of early latency-age children. *American Journal of Orthopsychiatry, 57*(2), 199–211.

WERNER, E. E. (1979). *Cross-cultural child development: A view from planet earth.* Monterey, CA: Brooks/Cole.

WEST, B. E. (1983). The new arrivals from Southeast Asia: Getting to know them. *Childhood Education, 60,* 84–89.

WHALEY, L. F., & WONG, D. L. (1991). *Nursing care of infants and children* (4th ed.). St. Louis: Mosby.

WHITE, B. L. (1985). *The first three years of life.* Englewood Cliffs, NJ: Prentice-Hall.

WHITE, B. L. (1990). *The first three years of life* (rev. ed.). New York: Prentice-Hall.

WHITING, B., & WHITING, J. (1975). *Children of six cultures: A psycho-cultural analysis.* Cambridge, MA: Harvard University Press.

WILSON, R. S. (1983). The Louisville twin study: Developmental synchronies in behavior. *Child Development, 54,* 298–316.

WILSON, R. S., & HARPRING, E. B. (1972). Mental and motor development in infant twins. *Developmental Psychology, 7,* 277–297.

WIMMER, H., & PERNER, J. (1983). Beliefs about beliefs: Representation and constraining function of wrong beliefs in young children's understanding of deception. *Cognition, 13,* 103–128.

WOLFF, PETER (1973). The classification of states. In L. J. Stene (Ed.), *The competent infant.* New York: Basic Books.

WYNN, K. (1990). Children's understanding of counting. *Cognition, 36,* 155–193.

YAKOVLEV, P. I., & LECOURS, A. R. (1967). The mylogenetic cycles of regional maturation of the brain. In A. Minkowski (Ed.), *Regional development of the brain in early life.* Oxford, England: Blackwell.

YANDO, R., SEITZ, V., & ZIGLER, E. (1978). *Imitation in developmental perspective.* Hillsdale, NJ: Erlbaum.

ZAHN-WEXLER, C., RADKE-YARROW, M., & KING, R. (1979). Child rearing and children's prosocial initiations toward victims of distress. *Child Development, 50,* 319–330.

ZAHN-WEXLER, C., RADKE-YARROW, M., WAGNER, E., & CHAPMAN, M. (1992). Development of concern for others. *Developmental Psychology, 28,* 126–136.

ZIV, A. (1977). *Counselling the gifted child.* Toronto: University of Toronto Press.

# Index

**Note:** Page references to features, tables, and charts are indicated by *italic* type.